Forms of Speeches

Speaking beyond the Speech Classroom

Sample Speeches

Reference and Research Appendices

Quick Access Menu
Using *A Speaker's Guidebook*

The menu to the left briefly displays the book's content. Each menu box corresponds to a tabbed divider in the text. The dividers contain more detailed menus for each section and are followed by "Speaker's Reference" pages that offer executive-like summaries of the subsequent chapters.

At the back of the book, you will find other reference aids:

• the index
• a list of feature boxes
• a list of checklists

To learn more about how to use the book's reference aids, turn to "How to Use This Book" (p. v), which includes tutorials that show you how to get quick answers to your questions.

For in-depth help with the research process, see Chapters 8–10 and the "From Source to Speech" sections on pages 142, 144, 150, and 162.

Online Speech Center at bedford stmartins.com/speakersguide

The Speech Study Center includes content quizzes, sample speeches, and video quizzing for key concepts. The Speech Toolkit offers tools for speech building including choosing a topic, outlining and creating a bibliography, using PowerPoint, and other resources for students and instructors.

Video Theater 3.0

This companion CD-ROM is available packaged *free* with this text. The software reinforces and extends the main text's pedagogy by offering full student speeches with extensive author commentary plus professional speech clips, a powerful visual presentation tutorial, and interactive vocabulary flashcards.

W9-AYZ-355

A Speaker's Guidebook

Text and Reference

THIRD EDITION

A Speaker's Guidebook

Text and Reference

Dan O'Hair
University of Oklahoma

Rob Stewart
Texas Tech University

Hannah Rubenstein

Bedford / St. Martin's

Boston ◆ New York

For Bedford/St. Martin's

Senior Editor: Simon Glick
Editorial Assistants: Michaela Garibaldi and Matt Burgess
Production Editor: Bernard Onken
Senior Production Supervisor: Nancy Myers
Senior Marketing Manager: Rachel Falk
Art Director: Lucy Krikorian
Text Design: Claire Seng-Niemoeller
Copy Editor: Wendy Annibell
Indexer: Riofrancos & Co. Indexes
Cover Design: Donna Dennison
Composition: Stratford Publishing Services, Inc.
Printing and Binding: Quebecor World Taunton Press

President: Joan E. Feinberg
Editorial Director: Denise B. Wydra
Executive Editor for Communication: Erika Gutierrez
Director of Marketing: Karen Melton Soeltz
Director of Editing, Design, and Production: Marcia Cohen
Managing Editor: Erica T. Appel

Library of Congress Control Number: 2005934864

Manufactured in the United States of America.
1   0   9   8   7   6
f   e   d   c   b   a

For information, write: Bedford/St. Martin's, 75 Arlington Street, Boston, MA 02116   (617-399-4000)

ISBN-10: 0-312-44318-8

ISBN-13: 978-0-312-44318-4

Acknowledgments
Acknowledgments and copyrights appear at the back of the book on pages 537–538, which constitute an extension of the copyright page.

How to Use This Book

A Speaker's Guidebook: Text and Reference has been carefully designed to help you easily and quickly access the information you need to prepare speeches and presentations not only in a public speaking course but also in other college courses, in your working life after college, and in whatever role you may eventually play in your community.

The Main Menu and Table of Contents

The twelve tab dividers (discussed in more detail below) allow the book to flip open easily, and the book's binding lets it lie flat. In the beginning of the book, you will find tools that give you an overview and are designed to make *A Speaker's Guidebook* even easier to use. On the inside front cover you will find the **Main Menu** that offers a listing of the thirty chapters in the text and a visual link to help you find each one. For even more information or to find a specific topic, simply turn to the full **table of contents** on page xxiii.

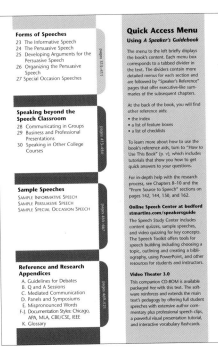

The Tabs

A Speaker's Guidebook is divided into twelve tabbed sections. Each section opens with a tab divider. These tabs are arranged into three colorful banks—red, green, and blue—and each tab is labeled to identify that section's coverage. To find specific information you want, look for the appropriate tab and open the book to it. On the front of the tab, you will find the tab name and the numbers of the chapters contained in that section. On the back of the tab, you will find even more detailed information, including the chapter titles and the major topics in each chapter.

The back of each tab divider offers a table of contents for the chapters within that tabbed section. The **Speaker's Reference** pages for the chapters within the section follow each tab divider.

Speaker's Reference Sections

You may well find one of the most useful features of *A Speaker's Guidebook* to be its **Speaker's Reference** pages that immediately follow each tab divider. These pages provide executive-like summaries of the material covered within the subsequent chapters. A listing of key terms in the chapters appears at the end of the **Speaker's Reference** pages, just before the opening of the first chapter within that tabbed section.

Speaker's Reference pages offer a quick review of the most important information in subsequent chapters through summaries and key terms.

To refer to the full in-text coverage of a topic, simply flip to the page indicated in parentheses.

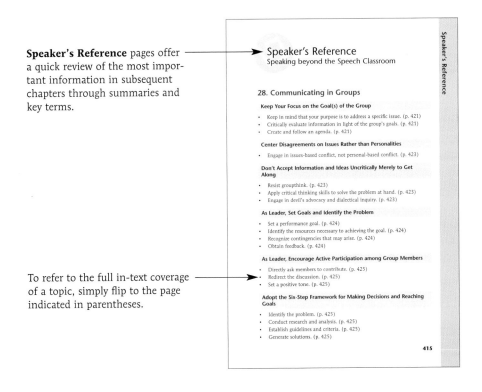

Speaker's Reference
Speaking beyond the Speech Classroom

28. Communicating in Groups

Keep Your Focus on the Goal(s) of the Group

- Keep in mind that your purpose is to address a specific issue. (p. 421)
- Critically evaluate information in light of the group's goals. (p. 421)
- Create and follow an agenda. (p. 421)

Center Disagreements on Issues Rather than Personalities

- Engage in issues-based conflict, not personal-based conflict. (p. 423)

Don't Accept Information and Ideas Uncritically Merely to Get Along

- Resist groupthink. (p. 423)
- Apply critical thinking skills to solve the problem at hand. (p. 423)
- Engage in devil's advocacy and dialectical inquiry. (p. 423)

As Leader, Set Goals and Identify the Problem

- Set a performance goal. (p. 424)
- Identify the resources necessary to achieving the goal. (p. 424)
- Recognize contingencies that may arise. (p. 424)
- Obtain feedback. (p. 424)

As Leader, Encourage Active Participation among Group Members

- Directly ask members to contribute. (p. 425)
- Redirect the discussion. (p. 425)
- Set a positive tone. (p. 425)

Adopt the Six-Step Framework for Making Decisions and Reaching Goals

- Identify the problem. (p. 425)
- Conduct research and analysis. (p. 425)
- Establish guidelines and criteria. (p. 425)
- Generate solutions. (p. 425)

415

The Checklists

Useful checklists located throughout the text are another hallmark of *A Speaker's Guidebook*. These offer step-by-step directions, assessment checks, and content review checks. Consult one of the 101 checklists to review key concepts and to get tips on applying those concepts to your own presentations. For a full list of checklists, see the inside back cover.

Checklists appear throughout the text, highlighting key concepts and offering useful tips and guidelines.

> **✓ CHECKLIST**
>
> **Minimizing Distractions**
>
> ✓ If you have trouble seeing or hearing at a distance, arrive early and sit in the front.
>
> ✓ If you are going to a group meeting and you have trouble hearing when others are talking at the same time, sit next to the leader so that most of the messages will be communicated toward your side of the room.
>
> ✓ Monitor yourself for lapses in attention and consciously redouble your efforts to concentrate on listening.
>
> ✓ Monitor yourself for signs of defensive listening.
>
> ✓ Don't assume ahead of time that you know what the speaker will say.

The Glossary

When you wish to verify the meaning of a key term (e.g., one that is boldfaced in the text), refer to the glossary that begins on page 501. There you will find explanations of the many terms associated with the fields of rhetoric and communication. These important terms are vital to your understanding of the book's content and are likely to appear on tests.

List of Boxes

A Speaker's Guidebook offers special boxed features highlighting useful topics for students and trends in the study of public speaking. For a complete list of boxes, including "ESL Speaker's Notes," "Public Speaking in Cultural Perspective," and "Ethically Speaking," refer to the very last page of the book.

Preface

A Speaker's Guidebook: Text and Reference is a new kind of public speaking text that offers better solutions to the wide range of challenges that students face. Adopted at more than four hundred schools since the first edition was published in 2001, the book grew out of the realization that public speaking courses are not ends in themselves. The principles and skills taught in this book are meant to be of lasting use to students, to help them beyond merely meeting the requirements of the course — in their other college courses, in their working lives after college, and in whatever roles they play in their communities. The book functions not only as a brief yet comprehensive classroom text but also as a unique and useful post-classroom reference — one that will prove an invaluable resource in any public speaking situation.

The Story of the New Edition

In preparing the third edition of *A Speaker's Guidebook*, we talked to over 250 speech instructors across the U.S. to find the answer to a single question: **What are the most pressing challenges of the public speaking course?** Based on the responses we received, we built on the proven features of the text to create a book that offers even better solutions by giving you:

- A book that students will want to use
- A book that reinforces basic skills
- A book that helps students apply what they learn to their own speeches

A BOOK THAT STUDENTS WILL WANT TO USE

Easy-to-use format.   *A Speaker's Guidebook* has been carefully designed to help students quickly access and retrieve the information they need to prepare speeches and presentations. Twelve tabbed dividers allow the book to flip open easily, a comb binding allows it to lie flat, and a quick access menu directs students to the section they need. The format enhances students' ability to learn and retain information. For more, see the inside front and back covers and the "How to Use This Book" section on pages v–viii.

A new, full-color design pulls students into the text and gets them excited about their reading. The user-friendly look brings the concepts of public speaking to life, highlighting key ideas and making *A Speaker's Guidebook* more accessible than ever.

A book that's useful for a lifetime of public speaking.   *A Speaker's Guidebook* is a text that students will want to keep and refer to for years to come. Along with the useful format, it includes unparalleled treatment of speaking beyond the speech classroom (in other courses and on the job) and a host of useful research and reference appendices, such as advice for handling question-and-answer sessions and tips on preparing for mediated communication.

A BOOK THAT REINFORCES BASIC SKILLS

More on supporting the speech.   Because students struggle with the research process, we have added new coverage that gives them help at every stage and offers concrete guidelines for building strong support for their claims.

- **New sections on creating a balanced research strategy** emphasize the importance of going beyond Internet research and incorporating a greater variety of credible print, electronic, and other sources into the research process.

- **A new section on using statistics** offers in-depth coverage and a host of relevant examples to help students better use quantitative information as support material. A hands-on tutorial shows students how to distinguish among three types of averages and describes steps students can take to present statistics accurately and ethically.

- **New models demonstrating how to orally credit sources** help students build credibility and provide accurate source information for the various examples, testimony, narratives, and facts and statistics that they plan to use in speeches.

- **Completely updated Chapter 10, "Using the Internet to Support Your Speech,"** includes reviews and critiques of the latest Internet search tools, a detailed discussion of the many commercial factors affecting search results, and guidance on using advanced ("field") searches.

- **Updated coverage of citing sources in speech bibliographies.** Thoroughly revised for this edition are five appendices showing students how to use the Chicago, APA, MLA, CBE/CSE, and IEEE documentation styles.

New "From Source to Speech" walkthroughs in Chapters 9 and 10 guide students through the process of incorporating materials from books, periodicals, and online sources into their own presentations. Unique to *A Speaker's Guidebook*, these powerful visual explanations address some of students' biggest challenges — evaluating source credibility, identifying key citation elements, creating notes from a given source, and orally incorporating those notes into speeches.

Expanded coverage of organizing and outlining.   New step-by-step models for each stage of the organizing and outlining process help students understand the value of organizational skills.

- **Expanded Chapter 11, "Organizing the Speech,"** offers a new, in-depth discussion of the ways that organizational skills are prized by employers and includes expanded discussions of coordination and subordination, supporting points, and transitions.
- **Revised Chapter 12, "Types of Organizational Arrangements,"** contains new examples of the various patterns and offers a detailed explanation, with examples, of the narrative pattern.
- **Completely revised Chapter 13, "Outlining the Speech,"** takes students step by step from working to speaking outlines. A new student informative speech on the dangers of spyware demonstrates each stage of the outlining process and includes an annotated full-text version of the speech. Other new sections cover delivery cues, creating titles, and listing sources.

More on listening in Chapter 3 emphasizes the central role of listening in everyday communication and includes updated research references and a new self-assessment checklist.

A BOOK THAT HELPS STUDENTS APPLY WHAT THEY LEARN TO THEIR OWN SPEECHES

New and unique visually annotated model speeches in Chapters 23, 26, and 27 *show* students proper delivery in a useful and innovative fashion unique to *A Speaker's Guidebook.* Each model speech includes the full text and traditional annotations as well as photographs of speakers demonstrating delivery techniques in action.

Expanded coverage of audience analysis in Chapter 6 reinforces the connection between an audience-centered approach and effective public speaking. A new discussion of identification offers specific strategies on creating common ground and connecting with target audiences. Additional new coverage includes sections on avoiding stereotypes and conducting audience analysis through oral and written questionnaires.

A deep revision of Chapter 23 on informative speaking contains new speech excerpts throughout and now demonstrates concrete ways to communicate a variety of informative topics. New coverage helps students learn *why* audience members might have difficulty understanding information and offers concrete strategies to overcome these difficulties, such as building on prior knowledge and checking for understanding.

New guidelines on plagiarism, copyright, and fair use in Chapters 4 and 9 help students follow accepted citation guidelines and use source material ethically. Students are introduced to the concepts of copyright, public domain, intellectual property, and fair use and learn from legal experts how to apply these concepts to speeches in and outside of the classroom.

Completely revised Chapter 22, "Using Presentation Software," includes updated screenshots for PowerPoint 2005 and offers more help with the basic design principles students need to create powerful presentations.

Enduring Features

The following features have made *A Speaker's Guidebook: Text and Reference* extremely successful in its first two editions:

A COMPREHENSIVE CLASSROOM TEXT

A Speaker's Guidebook covers all the topics included in standard public speaking texts — and much more. Although we designed the coverage to be accessible, we didn't lose sight of the need for comprehensiveness. *A Speaker's Guidebook* covers all the traditional topics, including listening, speaking ethically, managing speech anxiety, analyzing the audience, selecting a topic and purpose, locating and using supporting material, organizing and outlining ideas, using language, creating presentation aids, delivering the speech, and constructing various speech types. But *A Speaker's Guidebook* offers much more than traditional texts, including chapters on using the Internet to support the speech, using presentation software, preparing business and professional presentations, and speaking in other courses.

This text has been built on the assumption that students will incorporate the Internet and other technological tools into every step of the speechmaking process; thus we offer a special chapter on using the Internet as well as technology coverage integrated throughout. Widely praised by reviewers and expanded in this new edition, Chapter 10, "Using the Internet to Support Your Speech," teaches students how to research effectively on the Internet. Chapter 22, "Using Presentation Software," shows students how to use the latest hardware and software to produce powerful presentation aids and includes a tutorial on using Microsoft's PowerPoint.

To give students advice that is grounded in the theory of speech communication, we have included references to current communication research and classical rhetorical theory throughout the book and used these references as the basis for concrete suggestions in real-world speaking situations. Examples range from coverage of individual contemporary theorists and their work to discussions of rhetorical proofs and the classical canons of rhetoric.

Because persuasive speaking is a major aspect of most speech courses, the text offers three full chapters on persuasion, more than any other text. The unique Chapter 26, "Organizing the Persuasive Speech," demonstrates how to organize persuasive speeches using Monroe's motivated sequence, cause-effect, comparative-advantage, and refutative patterns.

A *Speaker's Guidebook* also offers students a wealth of resources to help them adapt their speeches to the cultural requirements of the speech situation. Along with extensive coverage within chapters, **Public Speaking in Cultural Perspective** boxes feature such topics as comparing cultural values, vocal delivery and culture, and variations in nonverbal communication.

Special consideration has also been given to the non-native speaker. **ESL Speaker's Notes** focus on critical areas of concern to speakers whose first language is not English and offer practical ways to address those concerns. Sample features include "Avoiding the Pitfalls of Manuscript Delivery" and "Vocal Variety and the Non-Native Speaker." Another characteristic that defines *A Speaker's Guidebook* is its strong focus on ethics. Chapter 4, "Ethical Public Speaking," is devoted to this topic and includes an in-depth consideration of the role that values play in the ethical quality of speeches. **Ethically Speaking** boxes appear throughout the text, continually reminding students that ethical conduct should apply to all aspects of the speechmaking process.

Finally, *A Speaker's Guidebook* recognizes the importance of solid sample speeches, and it provides ten total. Speeches include one speech of introduction, one speech of demonstration, three informative speeches, three persuasive speeches, and two special occasion speeches. All of the sample speeches are excellent models for student study and analysis, and three of them include new, innovative visual annotations.

AN INVALUABLE REFERENCE BEYOND THE SPEECH CLASSROOM

A Speaker's Guidebook features a unique, user-friendly design, convenient and accessible reference features throughout, and extensive reference and research appendices.

The information in *A Speaker's Guidebook* is designed for quick and easy retrieval. Twelve tabbed dividers allow the book to flip open easily, and a spiral binding lets it lie flat. A **Main Menu** on the inside front cover listing all tabs and chapters, paired with a full table of contents beginning on p. xxiii, quickly directs students to the sections they need.

Speaker's Reference pages at the beginning of each tabbed section allow students to quickly access and review the most important information in each chapter; convenient cross-references enable readers to flip quickly to a full discussion of the material, should they so choose.

Every chapter in *A Speaker's Guidebook* contains **checklists**, offering step-by-step directions, self-assessments, and content review checks. Widely praised by reviewers for their precision and conciseness, these checklists help students and professionals both plan their speeches and assess their efforts.

A wealth of reference appendices—including "Commonly Mispronounced Words," "Sample Speeches," and a useful glossary of key terms—allows students to easily access practical information.

A SUPERIOR RESOURCE IN ANY PUBLIC SPEAKING SITUATION

Along with providing students with an accessible, up-to-date classroom guide, *A Speaker's Guidebook* contains many features that will make it an invaluable resource in other college courses and *after* the public speaking course.

"Speaking in Other College Courses."   Chapter 30 provides guidance for creating the kinds of oral presentations students are likely to deliver in other college courses, from the social sciences and humanities to science and engineering. Separate sections describe sample presentations in technical, scientific and mathematical, arts and humanities, social science, and education courses, along with a new section on speaking in nursing and allied health courses.

More about Public Speaking on the Job.   *A Speaker's Guidebook* gives students more in-depth preparation than any other text for the kinds of speaking situations they are likely to encounter on the job. Chapters 28 and 29 cover business and professional speeches, sales presentations, status reports, and staff reports.

Extensive Help with the Research Process.   In addition to three full chapters dedicated to finding and developing supporting material (Chapters 8–10), *A Speaker's Guidebook* includes unique appendices showing students how to use the Chicago, APA, MLA, CBE/CSE, and IEEE documentation styles.

Microsoft PowerPoint Tutorial.   Generating presentation aids in a presentation software program has become one of the key challenges for the contemporary public speaker and presenter. Chapter 22, "Using Presentation Software," includes a tutorial on using Microsoft's PowerPoint (updated for PowerPoint 2005) that teaches readers how to enter and edit text, insert objects into slides, and use PowerPoint's text animation and transition effects.

Resources for Students and Instructors

RESOURCES FOR STUDENTS

Powerful *Video Theater 3.0* Interactive CD-ROM Available *Free*.   We designed the student CD-ROM, available free with each copy of the book, to provide examples and tools that a text alone cannot. An innovative *Video Theater 3.0* offers full student speeches — informative, persuasive, special occasion, and demonstration — along with professional speech clips. These video examples work not just as models but as powerful teaching tools. For each full speech we offer a speech outline and text, and also much more. We analyze each speech in five areas — audience analysis; content and supporting ideas; introduction, transitions, and conclusion; delivery; and visual aids — and offer "hot-links" so that while reading about a specific example, students or instructors can click and see the point exemplified. The CD-ROM also offers a tutorial to help students use visual aids effectively. To order the book/CD-ROM package, use ISBN 0-312-45196-2.

Online Speech Center available at <bedfordstmartins.com/speakersguide>. This Web site provides quick access to our extensive student aids for *A Speaker's Guidebook,* Third Edition. The Online Speech Center is organized into two distinct sections, a Speech Toolkit and a Speech Study Center.

- The Speech Toolkit offers tools that help students as they build their own speeches. It offers speech topics lists and topic research links, research tools including tutorials on evaluating sources and avoiding plagiarism, new **outlining** and **bibliography tools** that make the process easier, and guidelines for creating effective visual presentations.
- The Speech Study Center helps students review and internalize key concepts. It includes self-assessment quizzes for each chapter, sample speeches, an online version of the video theater, and brand new **video quizzes** that pair video clips with content questions, allowing students to see key concepts in action and testing their ability to identify these concepts.

Outlining and Organizing Your Speech (0-312-45202-0) by Merry Buchanan, University of Central Oklahoma. This student workbook provides step-by-step guidance for preparing informative, persuasive, and professional presentations and gives students the opportunity to practice the critical skills of conducting audience analysis, dealing with communication apprehension, selecting a speech topic and purpose, researching support materials, organizing and outlining, developing introductions and conclusions, enhancing language and delivery, and preparing and using presentation aids.

Using Presentation Software in Public Speaking: A Guide for Students (0-312-45204-7) by Rob Patterson, James Madison University. This guide shows students how presentation software can be used to support, not overtake, their speeches. Sample screens and practical advice make this an indispensable resource for students preparing electronic visual aids.

Media Career Guide: Preparing for Jobs in the 21st Century, **Fifth Edition** (0-312-44336-6), by James Seguin, Robert Morris College. Practical and student-friendly, this revised guide includes a comprehensive directory of media jobs, practical tips, and career guidance for students considering a major in communication studies and mass media.

Research and Documentation in the Electronic Age, **Fourth Edition** (0-312-44339-0), by Diana Hacker, Prince George's Community College, and Barbara Fister, Gustavus Adolphus College. This handy booklet covers everything students need for college research assignments at the library and on the Internet, including advice for finding and evaluating Internet sources.

RESOURCES FOR INSTRUCTORS

Instructor's Resource Manual (0-312-45201-2) by Jennifer Emerling Bone, University of Colorado at Boulder, and Elaine Wittenberg-Lyles and Melinda Villagran, University of Texas at San Antonio. This comprehensive manual is a valuable resource for new and experienced instructors alike. It offers extensive advice on topics such as setting and achieving student learning goals; managing the classroom; facilitating group discussion; understanding culture and gender considerations; dealing with ESL students; evaluating speeches (for both instructors and students); and evaluating Internet resources. In addition, each chapter of the main text is broken down into chapter challenges, detailed outlines, suggestions for facilitating class discussion from topics covered in feature boxes, additional activities and exercises, and recommended supplementary resources. The new edition includes more guidelines for first-time instructors, advice for integrating technology into the speech class, and expanded suggestions for videos and other classroom resources.

ESL Students in the Public Speaking Classroom: A Guide for Teachers (0-312-45197-0) by Robbin Crabtree and Robert Weissberg, New Mexico State University. As the United States increasingly becomes a nation of non-native speakers, instructors must find new pedagogical tools to aid students for whom English is a second language. This guide specifically addresses the needs of ESL students in the public speaking course and offers instructors valuable advice for helping students deal successfully with the challenges they face.

Print and Electronic *Test Bank* (Print: 0-312-45203-9; Electronic: 0-312-45196-2) by Tom Howard, University of Oklahoma, and Merry Buchanan, University of Central Oklahoma. *A Speaker's Guidebook* offers a complete testing program, available both in print and for Windows and Macintosh environments. Each chapter includes multiple-choice, true-false, and fill-in-the-blank exercises, as well as essay questions. Sample midterm and final examinations are also included in the testing program.

Instructor's Materials at <bedfordstmartins.com/speakersguide>.   The companion Web site to *A Speaker's Guidebook,* Third Edition, offers rich teaching resources for new and experienced instructors, including a downloadable version of the *Instructor's Resource Manual,* PowerPoint slides for each chapter in the text, speech assignment suggestions, discussion questions for sample speeches, an electronic gradebook for online quizzing, and links to course management software including WebCT, Blackboard, and Angel.

Microsoft PowerPoint Slides.   These slides provide visual support for the key concepts covered in each chapter and are available to be downloaded from the instructor's section of the book's companion Web site at <bedfordstmartins .com/speakersguide>.

VIDEO RESOURCES

Professional Speeches (0-312-19222-3). Available in DVD and VHS formats, Volume 19 of the esteemed *Great Speeches* series offers dynamic contemporary speeches for today's classroom. The most recent in the series, this video features compelling speeches including President Clinton's 1998 State of the Union Address, Madeleine Albright's first speech as secretary of state, Christopher Reeve's address to the 1996 Democratic National Convention, and a speech on spirituality by the Dalai Lama. Additional videos are available from the Bedford/St. Martin's Video Library.

Student Speeches (0-312-39300-8). Three videotapes of student speeches provide students with attainable models for study, analysis, and inspiration. Included are a variety of speeches that fulfill the most common assignments in public speaking — informative and persuasive speeches — by students of varying ability from Texas Tech and the University of Oklahoma.

Acknowledgments

We are especially thankful for the contributions of several experts whose advice allowed us to make *A Speaker's Guidebook: Text and Reference,* Third Edition, better: Robbin Crabtree and Bob Weissberg of New Mexico State University, for their expertise in ESL issues; Deanna Dannels of North Carolina State for her help in creating Chapter 30, "Speaking in Other College Courses," and Robert Weiss of DePauw University, Michael Daly of Southwest Missouri State, and Susan King of Florida State University School of Nursing, who kindly gave their thoughts on the chapter; Jennifer Keohane of the Simsbury Public Library for her expert guidance on reference materials; Stephen E. Gillen of Greenbaum Doll & McDonald PLLC for his insights on copyright law; Melinda Morris Villagran of the University of Texas at San Antonio for the Microsoft Power-Point presentation material and Ryan Burns for contributing material on using presentation software; Dr. Lauren Sewall Coulter of the University of Tennessee for preparing the citation guidelines appendices and Barbara Flanagan for updating them; Jennifer Emerling Bone of the University of Colorado for her excellent work revising the *Instructor's Resource Manual* (originally created by Elaine Wittenberg-Lyles and Melinda Villagran of the University of Texas at San Antonio); and Tom Howard of the University of Oklahoma and Merry Buchanan of the University of Central Oklahoma for the Testing Program.

For the third edition, we sent reviews and surveys to over 250 speech instructors across the United States. Their feedback was essential in creating the book you see before you. Please see the following pages that list each of these reviewers.

Reviewers who helped us on the second edition include Cameron Basquiat, Community College of Southern Nevada; Carolyn Clark, Salt Lake Community

College; Letitia Dace, University of Massachusetts–Dartmouth; Francis Dance, University of Denver; Layne Dearden, Brigham Young University–Idaho; Rebecca Faery, Massachusetts Institute of Technology; Joyce Fernandes, Bristol Community College; John Giertz, Bakersfield College; Heather Grace, University of Pittsburgh–Bradford; Marc Martin, San Francisco State University; Charles McMahan, Vincennes University; Deborah Meltsner, Old Dominion University; Andrea Morgan, Georgia Perimeter College; Dann Pierce, University of Portland; Patricia Rockwell, University of Louisiana–Lafayette; Robert Sadowski, University of Michigan–Flint; Michael Searcy, University of Iowa, Scott Community College; Lisa Stefani, Grossmont College; Elena Strauman, Auburn University; Jeremy Teitelbaum, California Polytechnic State University; Gregory Thomas, Morgan Community College; and Robert Witkowski, Midlands Technical College.

Reviewers who helped us on the first edition include Linda Brown, El Paso Community College; Tamara Burk, Columbia College; Lawrence J. Chase, California State University–Sacramento; Helen Chester, Milwaukee Area Technical College; Jeanine Congalton, Fullerton College; Lauren Sewell Coulter, University of Tennessee–Chattanooga; Karen D. Covey, New River Community College; Michal Dale, Southwest Missouri State; William F. Ferreira, Houston Community College, Southwest; Eric Fife, College of Charleston; William Fustield, University of Pittsburgh; Kathleen M. Galvin, Northwestern University; Kelby Halone, Clemson University; William J. Jordan, North Carolina State University; Ruth Ann Kinzey, University of North Carolina–Charlotte; Lt. Col. George Luker, USAF Academy; Joseph Martinez, El Paso Community College; Virgil Moberg, Flagler College; Carlos Perez, Maple Woods Community College; Jean Perry, Glendale Community College; Tina Pieraccini, State University of New York–Oswego; Lora Sager, Greenville Technical College; Dr. Roy Schwartzmann, Northwest Missouri State University; John Kares Smith, State University of New York–Oswego; Kimberly Terrill, Francis Marion University; and Glenda Treadaway, Appalachian State University.

It has been a privilege to work with the pioneering editors and publishers of Bedford/St. Martin's, whose innovative ideas led to the format of this text. President Joan Feinberg, Editorial Director Denise Wydra, and Executive Editor Erika Gutierrez understand how to deliver information to readers in ways that are most useful, and also most compelling, and we are grateful to them for sharing their expertise with us. Development Editor Simon Glick was the maestro of the orchestra, directing the coauthors with great skill. He has been an effective and patient encourager, manager, and coach as well as a skillful editor and writer. Bernie Onken expertly guided the text through a complicated production process, while Nancy Myers helped turn the book from a manuscript into a beautiful publication. We thank Editorial Assistants Michaela Garibaldi and Matthew Burgess for their swift and efficient help, hard work, and good instincts, along with Jamie Weiss, who worked diligently and effectively on a host of supplements. Finally, for their work in developing the Web site and other technology products, we are grateful to Nick Carbone, Rae Guimond, Midge Goldberg and everyone at A/T Media Services, John Philp, and Nathan Ryan.

Reviewers and Survey Respondents

Helen Acosta, *Bakersfield College*

Nedra Adams-Soller, *College of Lake County*

Sue Aiello, *New York Institute of Technology-Main Campus*

Robert Alexander, *Bucks County Community College*

Jason Ames, *Chabot College*

James Anderson, *Johnson & Wales University*

Robert Arend, *San Diego Miramar College*

Mike Armstrong, *Tallahassee Community College*

Jay Baglia, *San Jose State University*

Kaylene Barbe, *Oklahoma Baptist University*

Cameron Basquiat, *Community College of Southern Nevada*

Kimberly Batty-Herbert, *Broward Community College North*

Elizabeth Bell, *University of South Florida*

Ray Bell, *John C. Calhoun State Community College*

Christina Benac, *Ball State University*

Mary Jane Berger, *College of Saint Benedict*

Kathy Berggren, *Cornell University*

Mark Bergmooser, *Monroe County Community College*

Sandra Berkowitz, *University of Maine*

Constance Berman, *Berkshire Community College*

Bob Betts, *Rock Valley College*

Pete Bicak, *Rockhurst University*

Rochelle Bird, *Utah Valley State College*

T. Black, *Shepherd College*

Marian Blue, *Skagit Valley Community College-Oak Harbor*

Jennifer Emerling Bone, *University of Colorado-Boulder*

Robert Bookwalter, *Marshall University*

Jennifer Boyenga, *Indian Hills Community College*

Chris Braden, *Alverno College*

Linda Brigance, *SUNY College at Fredonia*

Joel Brouwer, *Montcalm Community College*

Nate Brown, *Santa Monica College*

Jin Brown, *University of Alaska-Fairbanks*

Ferald Bryan, *Northern Illinois University*

Glenn Byrne, *Stonehill College*

Lisa Callihan, *Florence Darlington Technical College*

Diana Cameron, *North Iowa Area Community College*

Amy Capwell-Burns, *University of Toledo*

Harry Carrell, *Missouri Valley College*

Karishma Chatterjee, *Ohio State University-Main Campus*

Susan Childress, *Santa Rosa Junior College*

Sally Cissna, *Milwaukee School of Engineering*

Carolyn Clark, *Salt Lake Community College*

Annie Clement, *Winona State University*

Robert Cohen, *Ohio State University-Mansfield*

Jennifer Cohen-Rosenberg, *Los Angeles Pierce College*

Linda Combs, *Daytona Beach Community College*

Melanie Conrad, *Midwestern State University*

John Cook, *University of Texas at Brownsville*

Diana Cooley, *North Harris College*

Kimberly Corey, *McIntosh College*

Ed Coursey, *Palm Beach Community College Glades Center*

Ken Cox, *Florence Darlington Technical College*

Sandra Coyner, *Southern Oregon University*

Christine Cranford, *East Carolina University*

Rita Crockett, *Howard College*

Billye Currie, *Samford University*

Daniel Dahlquist, *University of Wisconsin at Platteville*

Phillip Dalton, *Stetson Univerity*

William Davidson, *University of Wisconsin-Stevens Point*

Dale Davis, *University of Texas at San Antonio*

Thomas DelVecchio, *Iona College*
Andrew Denhart, *Stetson University*
Ron Dluger, *North Park University*
Paul Duax, *American River College*
Betty Dvorsen, *City College of San Francisco*
Jarvis Elena, *Daytona Beach Community College*
Dennis Elkins, *Savannah College of Art Design*
Scott Ellis, *San Jacinto College-Central Campus*
Valerie Endress, *Rhode Island College*
Carolyn Engdahl, *Fitchburg State University*
David Engel, *Marshalltown Community College*
Kathleen M. Farrell, *St. Louis University*
Judy Ferrand, *Wor-Wic Community College*
William Ferreira, *Houston Community College Southwest*
Nilo Figur, *Concordia University*
Sondra Fishinger, *Union County College*
Peter Fjeld, *Berkeley College*
Charles Fleischman, *Hofstra University*
James J. Floyd, *Central Missouri State University*
Marjorie Ford, *Stanford University*
Christine Foster, *Ramapo College of New Jersey*
James Friauf, *Milwaukee School of Engineering*
William Furnell, *Santa Monica College*
James Gallagher, *New Mexico State University at Alamogordo*
Pat Gehrke, *University of South Carolina*
John Gillette, *Lake City Community College*
Susan Gilpin, *Marshall University*
Valerie Giroux, *University of Miami*
Curt Gilstrap, *Drury University*
Louis Giuliana, *Holy Family College*
Susan Giusto, *Francis Marion University*
Eric Gnezda, *Ohio Wesleyan University*
Robert Gobetz, *University of Indianapolis*
William "Bubba" Godsey, *John C. Calhoun State Community College*
Janna Goodwin, *Regis University*
Luke Gordon, *Portland State University*

Michelle Gorthy, *City College of San Francisco*
Frank Gray, *Ball State University*
Neil Gregersen, *University of Wisconsin at Waukesha*
Laura Gregg, *Saginaw Chippewa Tribal College*
Jean Groshek, *Alverno College*
Diane Gruber, *Arizona State University-West*
Phil Hamilton, *San Bernardino Valley College*
Greg Hammond, *New Mexico Junior College*
Reeze Hanson, *Haskell Indian Nations University*
Eric Harlan, *Mississippi University for Women*
John Hatch, *University of Dubuque*
Linda Heil, *Harford Community College*
Mark Henderson, *Jackson State University*
Andrew Herman, *State University of New York at Genesee*
Dan Higgins, *Heidelberg College*
Rick Hogrefe, *Crafton Hills College*
Angela Holland, *Community College of Southern Nevada*
Emily Holler, *Kennesaw State University*
Victoria Howitt, *Grossmont College*
Kevin Howley, *DePauw University*
Karen Huck, *Central Oregon Community College*
W. A. Kelly Huff, *Truett-McConnell-Watkinsville*
Lynette Jachowicz, *Maple Woods Community College*
Dale Jenkins, *Virginia Technical College*
Ronald C. Jones, *Norfolk State University*
Linda Karch, *Norwich University*
Susan Katz, *University of Bridgeport*
Bill Keith, *University of Wisconsin-Milwaukee*
Tim Kelley, *Northwest-Shoals Community College*
Helen Kingkade, *Midlands Technical College-Airport*
David Kosloski, *Clark College*
Jeffrey Kotz, *University of Connecticut*
Mary Lahman, *Manchester College*

Jon Larson, *Inver Hills Community College*

Betty Jane Lawrence, *Bradley University*

Peter Lee, *Golden West College*

Diana Leonard, *University of Arizona*

Victoria Leonard, *College of the Canyons*

Douglas Lepter, *Trevecca Nazarene University*

Wendy Leslie, *Missouri Valley College*

Jason Lind, *Skagit Valley College*

Linda Linn, *Western Wyoming College*

Steven Long, *Wayland Baptist University*

Bob Loss, *Barton County Community College*

Louis Lucca, *La Guardia Community College, CUNY*

Thomas Marshall, *Robert Morris University*

Ben Martin, *Santa Monica College*

Michael McFarland, *Stetson University*

Lee McGavin, *University of Texas–Permian Basin*

Libby McGlone, *Columbus State Community College*

Annie McKinlay, *North Idaho College*

Gordon McLean, *Arizona Western College*

Scott McLean, *Arizona Western College*

Miriam McMullen-Pastrick, *Pennsylvania State University at Erie, Behrend*

Rebecca Meisnebach, *Concord College*

Deborah Meltsner, *Old Dominion University*

Andrew Merolla, *Ohio State University*

John Morrison, *Rollins College*

Alfred Mueller, *Pennsylvania State University at Mont Alto*

Lisa Mueller, *Northeast Iowa Community College*

Donna Munde, *Mercer County Community College*

Diana Karol Nagy, *University of Florida*

Helen Nelson, *Spalding University*

Linda Norris, *Indiana University of Pennsylvania*

Kathleen Norris, *Loyola Marymount University*

Karen O'Donnell, *Finger Lakes Community College*

Jennifer O'Dorisio, *Pomona High School*

Richard Olsen, *University of North Carolina at Wilmington*

Susan Ondercin, *Carroll Community College*

Elenie Opffer, *Regis University*

Donald Painter, Jr., *University of South Florida*

Teresa Palmitessa, *Pennsylvania State University at Erie, Behrend*

Emily Paramonova, *Cogswell Polytechnical College*

Daniel Paulnock, *Saint Paul College*

Holly Payne, *Western Kentucky University*

Karl Payton, *Le Tourneau University*

Kimberly Pearce, *De Anza College*

Sheila Peebles, *Baldwin-Wallace College*

Ray Penn, *Lincoln Memorial University*

Pamela Perkins, *San Diego City College*

Jean Perry, *Glendale Community College*

William Petkanas, *Western Connecticut State University*

Chuck Pierce, *Central Carolina Technical College*

Dann Pierce, *University of Portland*

Michael Pitts, *Los Angeles Southwest College*

Dwight Podgurski, *Colorado Christian University*

Linda Powers, *Wofford College*

Joyce Puls, *Baker College*

Kathleen Quimby, *Messiah University*

Susan Rabideau, *University of Wisconsin-Fox Valley*

Alan Ragains, *Windward Community College*

Pamela Reid, *Copiah-Lincoln Community College*

Gail Reid, *State University of West Georgia*

Paula Reif, *Carl Albert State College*

Larry Reynolds, *Johnson City Community College*

William Richter, *Lenoir-Rhyne College*

Lisa Riede, *Lockhaven University of Pennsylvania*

Nita Ritzke, *University of Mary*

Rick Roberts, *University of San Francisco*

Patricia Rockwell, *University of Louisiana at Lafayette*

Rita Rosenthal, *Boston College and Stonehill College*

Susan Sanders, *Northern Essex Community College*

Carol Saunders, *Chipola Junior College*

Kimberly Schwartz, *University of Dubuque*

Steve Schwarze, *University of Montana*

Marlene Sebeck, *Wheeling Jesuit University*

Lois Self, *Northern Illinois University*

Susan Selk, *El Paso Community College*

Colleen Shaughnessy-Zeena, *Salem State College*

Charla Markham Shaw, *University of Texas at Arlington*

Alisa Shubb, *American River College*

Elizabeth Simas, *California State University at Northridge*

Jacqueline Simon, *Palomar College*

John Kares Smith, *SUNY Oswego State University*

Andrew Snyder, *Saint Gregory's University*

Jay Soldner, *Western Wisconsin Technical College*

Rick Soller, *College of Lake County*

Pam Speights, *Wharton County Junior College*

Ebba Stedillie, *Casper College*

Susan Stehlik, *Rutgers University-Newark Campus*

Lesa Stern, *Southern Illinois University-Edwardsville*

James Stewart, *Tennessee Technical University*

Pamela Stovall, *University of New Mexico-Gallup*

Anthony Stubbs, *Iowa Lakes Community College South*

Pat Sutherland, *Tennessee Wesleyan College*

Michael Swinford, *Shorter College*

Sarah Symonds, *Costal Carolina Community College*

Kelly Tait, *University of Nevada-Reno*

Georgia Talsma, *Mount Marty College*

April Dupree Taylor, *University of South Alabama*

Katherine Taylor, *University of Louisville*

Donna Thomsen, *Johnson & Wales University*

Ray Tipton, *Walters State Community College*

Hank Tkachuk, *Concordia College-Moorehead*

Candice Todd, *Lynchburg College*

Michael Tomaschyk, *Cuyahoga Community College-Western*

Amy Trombley, *Western Michigan University*

Anita Turpin, *Roanoke College*

Clint Uhrich, *Luther College*

Joseph Valcourt, *Central Carolina Technical College*

Marilyn Valentino, *Lorain County Community College*

Jay VerLinden, *Humboldt State University*

Valerie Vlahakis, *John Wood Community College*

Steve Vrooman, *Texas Lutheran University*

Chris Wagner, *Cosumnes River College*

Anthony Wainwright, *Onondaga Community College*

Lisa Waite, *Kent State University-Stark Campus*

Bill Wallace, *Northeastern State University*

Dennis Waller, *Northwest Nazarene University*

David Weinandy, *Aquinas College*

Nancy Wendt, *Oregon State University*

Estelle Wenson, *Stonehill College*

Beverly West-Dorny, *San Joaquin Delta College*

Steven Wiegenstein, *Culver-Stockton College*

Thomas Wilkinson, *Rowan University*

David Williams, *Texas Technical University*

Frances Winsor, *Pennsylvania State University at Altoona*

Marianne Worthington, *Cumberland College*

Miriam Zimmerman, *Notre Dame de Namur University*

Joe Zubrick, *University of Maine-Fort Kent*

CONTENTS

Supporting the Speech

Organizing and Outlining

Vocal and Nonverbal Delivery

Presentation Aids

Forms of Speeches

Speaking beyond the Speech Classroom

Sample Speeches

Reference and Research Appendices

A Speaker's Guidebook

Text and Reference

Getting Started with Confidence

Getting Started with Confidence

Speaker's Reference
Getting Started with Confidence

1. Becoming a Public Speaker

Recognize the Many Benefits of Public Speaking

- Enhance your professional and personal goals. (p. 6)
- Aid your work as a student. (p. 7)
- Learn to share your values and explore the values of others. (p. 8)
- Hone your critical thinking and listening skills. (p. 8)

Recognize the Similarities between Public Speaking and Other Forms of Communication

- As in *conversation,* you attempt to make yourself understood, involve and respond to your conversational partner, and take responsibility for what you say. (p. 9)
- As in *small group communication,* you address a group of people who are focused on you and expect you to clearly discuss issues that are relevant to the topic and to the occasion. (p. 9)
- As in *mass communication,* you must understand and appeal to audience members' interests, attitudes, and values. (p. 9)

Recognize the Differences between Public Speaking and Other Forms of Communication

- Opportunities for feedback are fewer than in conversation or in small group communication, and greater than in mass communication. (p. 9)
- The level of preparation required is greater than in other forms of communication. (p. 10)
- The degree of formality tends to be greater than in other forms of communication. (p. 10)

As You Prepare Your Speeches, Consider the Speech Context

- The speech context — the rhetorical situation — includes anything that influences the speaker, the audience, the speech, the occasion, or the situation. (p. 12)

3

Set Clearly Defined Goals for Your Speeches

- Establish a set of goals early in the speechmaking process. (p. 13)
- Keep a clear focus in mind. (p. 13)

Don't View Your Speech as Complete Until You've Assessed the Outcome

- Ask yourself whether you accomplished what you set out to do. (p. 13)
- Use constructive feedback for self-evaluation and improvement. (p. 13)

Draw on the Familiar Skills of Conversation and Writing

- Consider that in both conversation and writing, you try to uncover the audience's interests and needs before speaking. (p. 14)
- Consider that in both conversation and writing, you check to make certain that you are understood, and adjust your speech to the listeners and to the occasion. (p. 14)
- Much of what you've learned about organizing written papers can be applied to organizing your speeches. (p. 14)

Foster a Sense of Inclusion in All of Your Speeches

- Try to identify and respectfully address the diversity of values and viewpoints held by audience members. (p. 15)
- Work toward making every member of the audience feel recognized and included in your message. (p. 15)

Recognize the Enduring Nature of the Study of Public Speaking

- The *canons of rhetoric,* a five-part speechmaking process developed in ancient Greece, remains relevant for today's public speaker. (p. 16)

2. Giving It a Try: Preparing Your First Speech

To Gain Confidence, Deliver a Brief First Speech

Use This Overview to Construct and Deliver the First Speech

- Select a topic. (p. 18)
- Analyze the audience. (p. 18)
- Determine the speech purpose. (p. 19)
- Compose a thesis statement. (p. 20)
- Develop the main points. (p. 20)
- Gather supporting materials. (p. 21)

- Separate the speech into its major parts: introduction, body, and conclusion. (p. 21)
- Outline the speech using coordinate and subordinate points. (p. 22)
- Consider presentation aids. (p. 24)
- Practice delivering the speech. (p. 24)

KEY TERMS

Chapter 1

dyadic communication	audience perspective	cultural intelligence
small group communication	message	rhetoric
mass communication	channel	canons of rhetoric
public speaking	noise	invention
source	shared meaning	arrangement
encoding	rhetorical situation	style
receiver	rhetorical proofs	memory
feedback	culturally sensitive speaker	delivery
decoding	ethnocentrism	

Chapter 2

topic	main points	coordinate points
audience analysis	supporting material	subordinate points
general speech purpose	introduction	presentation aids
specific speech purpose	body	vocal delivery
thesis statement	conclusion	nonverbal delivery

1 Becoming a Public Speaker

As a student of public speaking, you are joining a very large and venerable club. People have studied public speaking in one form or another for well over two thousand years. Indeed, public speaking may be the single most studied skill in history. Since before the time of the great Greek thinker Aristotle (384–322 B.C.E.) and the brilliant Roman statesman and orator Cicero (106–43 B.C.E.), practitioners of this ancient art have penned countless volumes bearing advice on how to address an audience. Our own frenzied era of electronic communication has not diminished the need for this singularly effective form of communication, and public speaking remains an indispensable vehicle for the expression of ideas. Whatever people care deeply about, public speaking offers a way to communicate their concerns with others. Indeed, few other activities offer quite the same opportunity to make one's voice heard.

This guidebook contains the tools you need to create and deliver effective speeches, from brief presentations made to fellow students, co-workers, or fellow citizens to major addresses given to large audiences. Here you will discover the basic building blocks of any good speech, as well as the requirements for delivering presentations in a variety of specialized contexts ranging from the college psychology class to the business and professional arena. You'll also find proven techniques to build your confidence by overcoming the anxiety associated with public speaking.

The Power to Make Yourself Heard

The ability to speak confidently and convincingly in public is an asset to anyone who wants to take an active role in his or her classroom, workplace, or community. As you master the skills of public speaking, you'll find that it is a powerful vehicle for professional and personal growth.

ADVANCE YOUR PROFESSIONAL GOALS

Whatever your career, chances are that public speaking will be a valuable, even crucial, skill to master. As a report entitled "What Students Must Know to Succeed in the Twenty-first Century" states:

> Clear communication is critical to success. In the marketplace of ideas, the person who communicates clearly is also the person who is seen as thinking

clearly. Oral and written communication are not only job-securing, but job-holding skills.[1]

Skill in public speaking tops the list of skills that are sought after by many organizations. Dozens of surveys of corporate managers and executives reveal that oral communication is the most important skill they look for in a college graduate. In a recent survey of employers, for example, oral communication skills ranked first in such critical areas as interpersonal, analytical, teamwork, and computer skills (see Table 1.1).

TABLE 1.1 • Top Personal Qualities/Skills Rated by Employers

1. Communication skills (written and verbal)
2. Honesty/integrity
3. Interpersonal skills (relates well to others)
4. Strong work ethic
5. Teamwork skills (works well with others)
6. Analytical skills
7. Motivation/initiative
8. Flexibility/adaptability
9. Computer skills
10. Detail-oriented
11. Leadership skills
12. Organizational skills

Source: "Communication Skills, Honesty/Integrity Top Employers' 'Wish List' for Job Candidates." *Job Outlook 2005 Survey,* Jan. 20, 2005. National Association of Colleges and Employers. www.naceweb.org/products/jo2005report.htm. Accessed June 12, 2005.

ACCOMPLISH PERSONAL GOALS

Perhaps more than any other course of study, public speaking offers both extraordinarily useful practical knowledge and skills that will set you firmly on the path of satisfying personal development. Whether you're concerned about the environment or lower taxes, public speaking offers a way to communicate your concerns with others. As an effective speaker, you will be better able to inform others about important issues and perhaps even persuade them to adopt your viewpoints.

ENHANCE YOUR CAREER AS A STUDENT

Preparing speeches involves numerous skills that you can use in other courses. Many forms of writing or composition, for example, also require that you research topics, analyze audiences, support and prove claims, and select patterns for organizing ideas. In addition, courses as diverse as engineering and art history include an oral-presentation component. Students in technical disciplines and the sciences are often called upon to explain complex information clearly and accessibly. Charts, graphs, and other presentation aids are often an important part of such presentations (Chapters 20–22 and 30), as are effective introductions and conclusions (Chapters 14 and 15). Identifying target audiences and selecting appropriate modes of delivery are critical skills for everyone, and no less so for the business major who must communicate with multiple audiences, including co-workers, managers, clients, and customers (Chapters 6 and 28). Other applications of public speaking skills across the curriculum are the focus of Chapter 30, "Speaking in Other College Courses."

EXPLORE AND SHARE VALUES

A speech is an occasion for speaker and audience to focus on ideas and events about which they feel strongly, even passionately. Thus public speaking offers a unique opportunity to explore values, deep-seated feelings, and ideas about what is important in life. Public speaking enables you to express your values and explore those of others in a civil dialogue, regardless of whether the audience shares your viewpoint. Speaking to an audience whose knowledge or opinions differ from your own can be an equally and sometimes even more satisfying experience than addressing a like-minded audience, especially when speaker and listeners end up gaining a fuller appreciation of each other.

HONE CRITICAL THINKING AND LISTENING SKILLS

Public speaking training will sharpen your ability to reason and think critically. As you study public speaking, you will learn to construct claims and then present evidence and reasoning that logically support them. As you practice organizing and outlining speeches, you will become skilled at structuring ideas so that they flow logically from one to another. You will be able to identify the weak links in your thinking and work to strengthen them.

Public speaking training also hones the highly valued skill of listening. As you learn what goes into a good speech, you will become a more critical receiver of speeches. In a world in which misleading information is often disguised as logic for purposes of selling, deception, or exploitation, the ability to listen critically enables you to separate fact from falsehood.

Public Speaking as a Form of Communication

Communication scholars generally identify four categories of human communication: dyadic, small group, mass, and public speaking. **Dyadic communication** is a form of communication between two people, as in a conversation. **Small group communication** involves a small number of people who can see and speak directly with one another. A business meeting is an example of small group communication. **Mass communication** occurs between a speaker and a large audience of unknown people. In mass communication the receivers of the message are not present with the speaker, or they are part of such an immense crowd that there can be little or no interaction between speaker and listener. Television, radio news broadcasts, and mass rallies are examples of mass communication.

In **public speaking** a speaker delivers a message with a specific purpose to an audience of people who are present during the delivery of the speech. Public speaking always includes a speaker who has a reason for speaking, an audience that gives the speaker its attention, and a message that is meant to accomplish a specific purpose.[2] Public speakers address audiences largely without interruption and take responsibility for the words and ideas being expressed. Public speaking shares many similarities with dyadic, small group, and mass communication, but there are notable differences as well.

SIMILARITIES BETWEEN PUBLIC SPEAKING AND OTHER FORMS OF COMMUNICATION

Like small group communication, public speaking requires that you address a group of people who are focused on you and expect you to clearly discuss issues that are relevant to the topic and to the occasion. As in mass communication, public speaking requires that you understand and appeal to the audience members' interests, attitudes, and values. And like dyadic communication, or conversation, public speaking requires that you attempt to make yourself understood, involve and respond to your conversational partners, and take responsibility for what you say.

A key feature of any type of communication is sensitivity to the listeners. Whether you are talking to one person in a coffee shop or giving a speech to a hundred people, your listeners want to feel that you care about their interests, desires, and goals. Skilled conversationalists do this, and so do successful public speakers. Similarly, skilled conversationalists are in command of their material and present it in a way that is organized and easy to follow, believable, relevant, and interesting. Public speaking is no different. Moreover, the audience will expect you to be knowledgeable and unbiased about your topic and to express your ideas clearly.

DIFFERENCES BETWEEN PUBLIC SPEAKING AND OTHER FORMS OF COMMUNICATION

Although public speaking shares many characteristics of other types of communication, several factors distinguish public speaking from these other forms. These include (1) opportunities for feedback, (2) level of preparation, and (3) degree of formality.

Public speaking presents different opportunities for *feedback,* or listener response to a message, than does dyadic, small group, or mass communication. Opportunities for feedback are high both in conversation and in small group interactions. Partners in conversation continually respond to one another in back-and-forth fashion; in small groups, participants expect interruptions for purposes of clarification or redirection. However, because the receiver of the message in mass communication is physically removed from the messenger, feedback is delayed until after the event, as in TV ratings.

Public speaking offers a middle ground between low and high levels of feedback. Public speaking does not permit the constant exchange of information between listener and speaker that happens in conversation, but audiences can and do provide ample verbal and nonverbal cues to what they are thinking and feeling. Facial expressions, vocalizations (including laughter or disapproving noises), gestures, applause, and a range of body movements all signal the audience's response to the speaker. The perceptive speaker reads these cues and tries to adjust his or her remarks accordingly. Because feedback is more restricted in public speaking situations than in dyadic and small group communication, *preparation* must be more careful and extensive. Because you have fewer opportunities to know how your listeners feel about what you are saying, you must anticipate how they will react to your remarks. With each audience member focused on you, it is important to be in command of your material. In dyadic and small group communication, you can always shift the burden to your conversational partner or to other group members. Public speaking offers no such shelter, and lack of preparation stands out starkly.

Public speaking also differs from other forms of communication in terms of its *degree of formality*. In general, speeches tend to occur in more formal settings than do other forms of communication. Formal gatherings such as graduations, weddings, religious services, and the like naturally lend themselves to speeches; they provide a focus and give form — a "voice" — to the event. In contrast, with the exception of formal interviews, dyadic communication (or conversations) is largely informal. Small group communication also tends to be less formal than public speaking, even in business meetings.

Thus public speaking shares many features of everyday conversation, but because the speaker is the focal point of attention in what is usually a formal setting, listeners expect a more systematic presentation than they do in conversation or small group communication. As such, public speaking requires more preparation and practice than the other forms of communication.

Public Speaking and the Communication Process

Communication, whether between two people or between one person and an audience of a thousand listeners, is an interactive process in which people exchange and interpret messages with one another.

ELEMENTS OF COMMUNICATION

In any communication event, including public speaking, several elements are present. These include the source, the receiver, the message, the channel, and shared meaning, as well as context, goals, and outcome (see Figure 1.1).[3]

The Source

The **source**, or sender, is the person who creates a message. The speaker transforms ideas and thoughts into messages and sends them to a receiver, or an au-

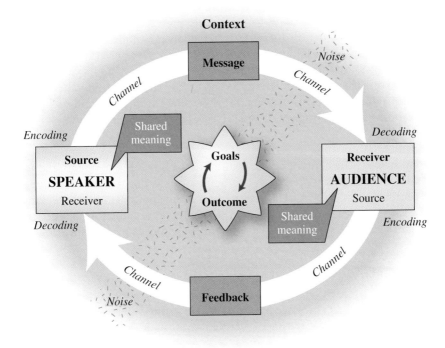

Figure 1.1 The Communication Process

dience. The speaker decides what messages are to be sent and how they will be sent. The process of organizing the message, choosing words and sentence structure, and verbalizing the message is called **encoding**. Encoding is this cumulative process of the source transforming thoughts into messages and delivering them to the audience.

The Receiver

The recipient of the source's message is the **receiver**, or audience. Although the speaker provides meaning for the message, the receiver interprets the message in ways that are unique to himself or herself. The process of interpreting the message is called **decoding**. Although a speaker may intend a message to carry a specific interpretation, audience members decode the meaning of the message selectively, based on their own experiences and attitudes. The audience's response to a message is called **feedback**, which can be conveyed both verbally and nonverbally. For example, an audience member may blurt out, "I don't think so," or may smile and nod. Feedback from the audience often indicates whether a speaker's message has been understood. Note that feedback is a message sent by the receiver to the speaker. In this way, the original receiver is now in the role of source (an audience member is encoding a message) and the original source is in the role of receiver (the speaker is decoding a message). This change in roles between speaker and audience represents the interactive nature of public speaking.

Often, speakers deliver ineffective or inappropriate messages because they do not know or do not understand their audience (the receivers). Whether you are speaking to an audience of one or a hundred, always adopt an **audience perspective**—that is, try to determine the needs, attitudes, and values of your audience before you begin speaking. Let their relevant interests and background guide you in constructing your speech (see Chapter 6).

The Message

The **message** is the content of the communication process: thoughts and ideas put into meaningful expressions. Content can be expressed verbally (through the sentences and points of a speech) and nonverbally (through eye contact and gestures). Miscommunication can happen when audience members misinterpret the speaker's intended message, or when the speaker misreads audience feedback.

The Channel

The medium through which the speaker sends a message is the **channel**. If a speaker is delivering a message in front of a live audience, the channel is the air; sound waves deliver the message by traveling through the air. Other channels include telephones, televisions, computers, and written correspondence. If interference, or noise, occurs, the message may not be understood. **Noise** is any interference with the message. Although noise includes physical sounds such as a slamming door or ringing cell phone, it can also include psychological distractions such as heated emotions, and environmental interference such as a frigid room or the presence of unexpected people.

Shared Meaning

Shared meaning is the mutual understanding of a message between speaker and audience. Shared meaning occurs in varying degrees. The lowest level of shared meaning exists when the speaker has merely caught the audience's attention. As the message develops, depending on the method of encoding selected by the source, a higher degree of shared meaning is possible. Thus it is listener and speaker together who truly make a speech a speech—who co-create its meaning.

Context (Rhetorical Situation)

Context, or the rhetorical situation, influences all aspects of public speaking. Considering the context involves more than just audience analysis. The **rhetorical situation** includes anything that influences the speaker, the audience, or the occasion—and thus, ultimately, the speech itself. In the case of classroom speeches, context would include (among other things) the physical setting (e.g., a small classroom or large auditorium), the order and timing of speeches, recent events on campus or in the outside world, and the cultural orientations of audience members. Considering the rhetorical situation allows the speaker to address audience concerns with sensitivity.

Immediately after the terrorist attacks on September 11, 2001, speakers around the world adapted their already-prepared speeches to address the event; not doing so would have given audiences the impression that they were out of touch with an event with which everyone was preoccupied. Context is a way of examining each of the public speaking components in a holistic manner.

Goals

Goal setting is one of the primary tenets of most communication models. A clearly defined goal is a prerequisite for an effective speech. What is it that you want the audience to learn or do or believe as a result of your speech? How much ground do you want to cover? What do you personally want to achieve by delivering the speech? Establishing a set of goals early in the speechmaking process and writing them down in the form of concise sentences will help you proceed through speech preparation and delivery with a clear focus in mind. All the steps you take will be in concert with the clearly articulated goals that you have set. (See Chapter 7 for more on formulating the specific speech purpose.)

Outcome

A speech is not truly complete until its effects have been assessed and you decide whether you have accomplished what you set out to do. Usually this assessment is informal, as in listening to audience reactions. Sometimes it is more formal, as in receiving an evaluation from an instructor or from the audience itself. Constructive feedback is an invaluable tool for self-evaluation and improvement. (See Chapter 3 for further discussion and tips on giving and receiving constructive criticism.)

Learning to Speak in Public

Some people are so afraid of speaking in public that they refuse any opportunities that come their way. The result is often stalled careers and stilled personal voices. As described in Chapter 5, fear of public speaking is a widespread feeling — perhaps *the* number-one fear. Equally true, however, is the exhilaration people experience when they cope with the inevitable nervousness and go on to deliver successful speeches.

None of us is born knowing how to speak in public. Even seemingly effortless communicators such as Los Angeles Mayor Antonio Villaraigosa and former U.S. President Ronald Reagan have worked hard — perhaps hardest of all — to achieve good results. Similarly, the employee who convincingly presents a new business strategy to his bosses, the lab worker who clearly describes her latest experiment to her colleagues, and the PTA parent who builds a groundswell of opposition to lengthening the school year all succeed because they have devoted time and effort to preparing their speeches.

DRAW ON FAMILIAR SKILLS

Learning any new skill — whether it's parachuting off mountain cliffs or speaking in public — involves mastering a set of techniques and then practicing them until you gain proficiency. For many activities, the process can be made less daunting by drawing on related skills that you already have. For example, you may think baking is difficult until you realize that, if you can read, use measurement tools, and follow directions carefully, you can indeed prepare many delicious recipes.

In a similar vein, consider the many "ingredients" public speaking shares with other things you've done for much of your life, such as conversation and writing.

Conversation and Public Speaking

Planning and executing the delivery of a speech, according to contemporary scholars, is much the same as engaging in a particularly important conversation. Although it requires more thinking and effort than ordinary conversation, delivering a speech rests on the same basic principles. Intuitively, you are already familiar with many of the basic principles of public speaking. For example, when speaking with a friend, you automatically check to make certain that you are understood and then adjust your meaning accordingly. You also tend to discuss issues that are appropriate to the circumstances. If you're speaking to someone you know quite well, you're likely to address any number of topics with ease. When a relative stranger is involved, however, you try to get to know his or her interests and attitudes before revealing any strong opinions.

These instinctive adjustments to your audience, topic, and occasion represent critical steps in putting a speech together. Although the means of discovery are of necessity more involved, both the conversationalist and the public speaker try to uncover the audience's interests and needs before speaking.

Speaking and Writing

As with conversation, preparing a speech has much in common with writing. For example, both effective speaking and effective writing depend on having a focused sense of who the audience is.[4] Both often require that you research a topic and document your sources, use effective transitions to signal the logical flow of ideas, and use **rhetorical proofs**, or various types of persuasive appeals, to appeal to an audience (see Chapter 25). Furthermore, familiarity with the organizing principles in one discipline prepares you to work effectively in the other. As Robert Perrin notes in "The Speaking-Writing Connection,"

> The principles that guide the organizing of a speech are the same as those that help organize papers. Interesting introductions draw listeners and readers into the topic; clear thesis statements or controlling ideas direct the audience's attention; a series of supporting topics describe, illustrate, elaborate, substantiate, and ultimately articulate the premise that is laid out in the thesis; thoughtful conclusions draw ideas together and create a sense of closure.[5]

RECOGNIZE PUBLIC SPEAKING'S UNIQUE REQUIREMENTS

As you can see, many of the skills required for public speaking are skills that you may already use elsewhere. You can also apply what you learn as a public speaker to your repertoire of conversational and writing skills.

Although public speaking has much in common with everyday conversation and with writing, it is, obviously, "its own thing." More so than writers, for example, successful speakers generally use familiar words, easy-to-follow sentences, straightforward syntax (subject-verb-object agreement), and transitional words and phrases. Speakers also routinely repeat key words and phrases to emphasize ideas and help listeners follow along, and even the briefest speeches make frequent use of repetition (see Chapter 16).

Oral language is often more interactive and inclusive of the audience than written language. The personal pronouns *we, I,* and *you* occur more frequently in spoken than in written text. Audience members want to know what the speaker thinks and feels, and that he or she recognizes them and relates them to the message. Speakers accomplish this by making specific references to themselves and to the audience.

In general, spoken language is more conversational than written language. Yet because public speaking usually occurs in more formal settings than does everyday conversation, listeners expect a somewhat more formal style of communication from the speaker. When you hold the floor of communication for an extended period of time, as in a speech, listeners expect you to speak in a clear, recognizable, and organized fashion. Thus, in contrast to conversation, in order to develop an effective oral style you must practice the words you will say and the way you will say them.

AIM TO BECOME A CULTURALLY SENSITIVE SPEAKER

Every audience member wants to feel that the speaker has his or her particular needs and interests at heart, and to feel recognized and included in the speaker's message. To create this sense of inclusion, the public speaker must attempt to understand the audience's beliefs and norms and to be culturally sensitive. The **culturally sensitive speaker** assumes differences and addresses them with interest and respect. The flip side of cultural sensitivity is **ethnocentrism**, the belief that the ways of one's own culture are superior to those of other cultures. Ethnocentric speakers don't bother to consider other perspectives or ways of behaving. No matter how passionately they believe in an issue, our most admired public speakers strive to acknowledge and respectfully consider alternative viewpoints.

More than ever, public speakers must demonstrate not only cultural sensitivity but also **cultural intelligence**.[6] As David C. Thomas and Kerr Inkson explain, cultural intelligence means

> being skilled and flexible about understanding a culture, learning more about it from your ongoing interactions with it, and gradually reshaping

your thinking to be more sympathetic to the culture and to be more skilled and appropriate when interacting with others from the culture.[7]

As a public speaker, you will continually confront values that are different from your own. In this guidebook you will find numerous suggestions for increasing your cultural intelligence so that you can become a more culturally sensitive speaker. These discussions range from assessing audience members' cultural values (see Chapter 6), avoiding stereotypes, and refraining from hate speech (see Chapter 4) to the crucial role that language plays in creating a culturally sensitive speech (see Chapter 16).

The Classical Roots of Public Speaking

The practice of oratory, or **rhetoric,** emerged full force in Greece in the fifth century B.C.E. It flourished primarily as a means of persuasive speaking and became an essential tool in settling civil disputes, determining public policy, and establishing laws. Classical scholars, notably Aristotle and Cicero, divided the process of preparing a speech into five parts—*invention, arrangement, style, memory,* and *delivery*—called the **canons of rhetoric. Invention** refers to adapting speech information to the audience in order to make your case. **Arrangement** is organizing the speech in ways that are best suited to the topic and the audience. **Style** is the way the speaker uses language to express the speech ideas. **Memory** is the practice of the speech until it can be artfully delivered. Finally, **delivery** is the vocal and nonverbal behavior you use when speaking (see Table 1.2).

Although scholars such as Aristotle and Cicero surely didn't anticipate the omnipresent PowerPoint slide show that accompanies so many contemporary speeches, the speechmaking structure they bequeathed to us as the canons of rhetoric remains remarkably intact. Although these canons are often identified by terms other than the original ones, they continue to be taught in current books on public speaking, including this one. For example, Chapters 6–10 and 24–25 (analyzing the audience; selecting and researching a topic; composing arguments) correspond to the *invention process.* Chapters 11–13 and 26 (on outlining and organizing the speech) represent *arrangement.* Chapter 16 (on language) focuses on *style.* Finally, Chapters 17–19 describe the process of *practice (memory)* and *delivery* (see Table 1.2).

It certainly isn't necessary for today's public speaker to be familiar with the classical canons of rhetoric. Yet it never hurts to be aware of a heritage as rich as that of public speaking. As Patricia Bizzell and Bruce Herzberg, writers on rhetoric, note:

> The fundamental concerns of rhetoric in all ages appear to be those defined in the classical period: purpose, audience, composition, argumentation, organization, and style. Not only do the classical categories persist, but so do many of the particulars.[8]

TABLE 1.2 • The Classic Canons of Rhetoric and Speechmaking Today	
The Canons of Rhetoric	**Addressed in *A Speaker's Guidebook***
1. Invention (Selecting and adapting speech material to the audience; constructing arguments)	Chapter 6: Analyzing the Audience Chapter 7: Selecting a Topic and Purpose Chapter 8: Developing Supporting Material Chapter 9: Locating Supporting Material Chapter 10: Using the Internet to Support Your Speech Chapter 24: The Persuasive Speech Chapter 25: Developing Arguments for the Persuasive Speech
2. Arrangement (Ordering the speech)	Chapter 11: Main Points, Supporting Points, and Transitions Chapter 12: Types of Organizational Arrangements Chapter 13: Types of Outline Formats Chapter 26: Organizing the Persuasive Speech
3. Style (Use of language, including figures of speech)	Chapter 16: Using Language to Style the Speech
4. Memory (Practice of the speech)	Chapter 17: Methods of Delivery Chapter 18: The Voice in Delivery
5. Delivery (Vocal and nonverbal delivery)	Chapter 19: The Body in Delivery

2 Giving It a Try: Preparing Your First Speech

Novice speakers in any circumstances—at school, at work, or in the community—will benefit from preparing and delivering a first short speech of between two and five minutes. An audience of as few as two other people will suffice to test the waters and help you gain confidence in your ability to "stand up and deliver." Experts will tell you that the best way to overcome nervousness about speaking in public is to get up and deliver a speech. After all, you can't learn how to swim if you don't get wet. It is for this reason that instructors often assign a brief first speech within days of the start of class.

A Brief Overview of the Speechmaking Process

As a beginning speaker preparing your first classroom speech, you will not be required to know all the conventions of speechmaking as described in subsequent chapters. However, it is helpful to have a sense of the various steps involved in putting together and delivering a speech or a presentation (see Figure 2.1). In this chapter you will find a brief overview of the entire speechmaking process, from choosing a topic to rehearsing the speech for actual delivery.

SELECT A TOPIC

The first step in creating a speech involves finding a **topic**, or something to speak about. Unless the topic is assigned, let your interests—your passions—be your guide. What deeply engages you? What are your areas of expertise? Your hobbies? Are there controversies brewing on campus or at your workplace that you might wish to address? Beware, however, that personal interest should not be the only criterion for selection. It's equally important that you feel confident that your topic will be of interest to the audience. For example, if you are a college student your classmates might not be terribly excited about yet another talk on safe sex, but a brief speech on little-known facts related to the history of the college or some of its famous alumni might capture their attention. Whatever you settle on, make sure to consider your audience members and their interests.

ANALYZE THE AUDIENCE

Audiences have personalities, interests, and ambitions all their own. These factors affect how receptive an audience will be toward a given topic. Thus it is imperative that you learn as much as you can about the similarities and differ-

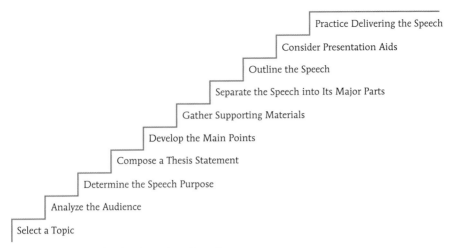

Practice Delivering the Speech
Consider Presentation Aids
Outline the Speech
Separate the Speech into Its Major Parts
Gather Supporting Materials
Develop the Main Points
Compose a Thesis Statement
Determine the Speech Purpose
Analyze the Audience
Select a Topic

Figure 2.1 Steps in the Speechmaking Process

ences among the members of your audience. Begin with some fairly easily iden-tifiable *demographic characteristics:* ratio of males to females, racial and ethnic differences represented in the group, noticeable age variations, and proportion of the group that is from out of state or out of the country. Next, consider how different people (e.g., older and younger, men and women, international and native-born) might think or feel differently about your topic. For example, if you decide to speak on the controversy of a proposed increase in resident stu-dent tuition, your talk will be less interesting to out-of-state and international students than to resident students.

Yet how can you know what the audience thinks? **Audience analysis** is ac-tually a highly systematic process of getting to know your listeners relative to the topic and the speech occasion. The process involves studying the audience through techniques such as interviews and questionnaires (see Chapter 6). However, for this first speech assignment it should be sufficient to ask three or four people who will be part of your audience a few questions about your topic. For example, what do they already know about it? Does it interest them? What else would they like to know about it? A few answers to these questions will be helpful in narrowing your topic and relating it to the audience.

DETERMINE THE SPEECH PURPOSE

Once you settle on a topic, the next step is to decide what you wish to convey about it—and why. As you will learn in Chapter 7, there are three **general speech purposes** toward which you should direct your speeches: *to inform, to persuade,* or *to mark a special occasion.* Regarding the campus controversy topic, for example, you need to decide whether to simply inform your audi-ence about the issue and the positions each side takes, or to persuade the audi-ence to accept one position to the exclusion of other positions, or perhaps even to entertain your listeners by making light of the issue in a creative but judicious way.

Your speech should also have a **specific purpose**. This is a declarative sentence stating what you expect the speech to accomplish. For example, if the general purpose of your campus controversy speech is to inform, its specific purpose could be "to identify the three key points on which students and administrators disagree about increasing resident tuition." If the general purpose is to persuade, its specific purpose might be "to convince my listeners that the administration does not need to increase resident tuition."

Write your specific purpose on a sheet of paper or on a Post-it note placed on the edge of your computer monitor. It will be an important guide in developing the rest of the speech.

COMPOSE A THESIS STATEMENT

Once you've identified the general and specific speech purposes, you need to compose a **thesis statement** that clearly expresses the central idea of your speech. While the specific purpose describes what *you* want to achieve with the speech, the thesis statement concisely identifies for your audience, in a single sentence, what the speech is about:

GENERAL PURPOSE: To inform

SPECIFIC PURPOSE: To inform my audience about the evolution of the MTV network.

THESIS STATEMENT: MTV has evolved from a single music video cable station to a multichannel, multientertainment network.

As with the specific speech purpose, you will use the thesis statement as a guidepost to construct your speech. Wherever you are in the planning stage, always refer to the thesis statement to make sure that you are on track to illustrate or prove your thesis.

DEVELOP THE MAIN POINTS

Organize your speech around two or three **main points**. These are the primary pieces of knowledge (in an informative speech) or the key arguments in favor of your position (in a persuasive speech) (see Chapter 11). If you create a clear, specific purpose statement for your speech, the main points will be easily identifiable (if not explicit). For example, the statement "to convince my listeners that the university's administration does not need to increase resident tuition" points to ideas that should be developed into main points — compelling reasons that tuition should not be increased. In this hypothetical case, let's say the primary reason given by administrators for the higher tuition is to offset the costs of increased enrollment. The following is an example of a specific purpose and three main points supporting it:

SPECIFIC PURPOSE: To convince my listeners that the university's administration does not need to increase resident tuition.

    I. Monies from the state surplus should be used to offset the costs of increased enrollment.

    II. Three other states have diverted funds from their budget surpluses for precisely this purpose.

    III. Yet another tuition hike will put the state's institutions of higher education out of reach for too many of the state's residents.

GATHER SUPPORTING MATERIALS

Supporting material illustrates the main points by clarifying, elaborating, and verifying the speaker's ideas. Supporting material includes the entire world of information available to you — from personal experiences to statistics from outside sources. Supporting material is crucial because it lends credibility to your message by signifying that your ideas are consistent with other people's ideas and with actual events.

Unless your speech is about yourself (or focuses on an extraordinarily compelling personal experience), plan to research your topic for supporting material. For short classroom speeches, your research might be as minimal as a few comments that other people have made about the topic, editorials in the campus newspaper, or statistics gathered from a reputable Internet site. As your assignments become more involved, so too will your research. Chapters 8–10 describe developing, locating, and using many kinds of supporting material.

SEPARATE THE SPEECH INTO ITS MAJOR PARTS

There are three major parts to every speech: introduction, body, and conclusion (see Table 2.1). As you begin the process of outlining (as described below), separate these parts so that you can give each section the attention it requires. Use transition statements (see Chapters 11 and 13) to bring together the different parts.

Introduction

The **introduction** serves to introduce the topic and the speaker and to alert audience members to your specific speech purpose. This sets them on the journey that is your speech, like the airplane heading from the gate to the runway. Introductions often set the tone for the entire speech. A good introduction should catch the audience's attention and interest. Some of the many ways in which speakers do this include making a startling statement, telling a story, or using humor (see Chapter 14).

Speech Body

Just like the body of a written essay, the speech **body** contains the speech's main points and subpoints, all of which support the speech's thesis. It is here that you

TABLE 2.1 • Major Speech Parts		
Introduction	**Body**	**Conclusion**
• Welcome your audience. • Introduce yourself, your topic, and your speech purpose. • Catch the audience's attention and interest with the use of a quote, a short story, an example, or another kind of supporting material. • Provide a clear transition statement to the body of the speech.	• Introduce the main ideas of the speech and illustrate them with a variety of supporting materials. • Organize your ideas and evidence in a structure that suits your topic, audience, and speech occasion. • Use transition statements and phrases to move between main points and to the conclusion.	• Restate the specific speech purpose and reiterate how the main points confirm it. • Leave your audience with something to think about. • Answer questions.

should illustrate or argue each of your main ideas, using the supporting material you have gathered to clarify, elaborate, or substantiate your points.

Conclusion

The **conclusion** restates the speech purpose and reiterates how the main points confirm it. Because the conclusion represents your last opportunity to motivate your listeners and to state your theme in a memorable manner, make sure to end on a strong note (see Chapter 15).

OUTLINE THE SPEECH

An outline provides the framework upon which to arrange main points in support of your thesis and subordinate points in support of your main points. Outlines are based on the principle of *coordination* and *subordination* — the logical placement of ideas relative to their importance to one another. **Coordinate points** are of equal importance and are indicated by their parallel alignment (see below). **Subordinate points** are given less weight than the main points they support and are identified in outlines by their placement to the right of the points they support. A smooth flow of thought among and within coordinate points requires using clear transition statements, ideally written into the outline. (For a full discussion of outlining, see Chapter 13.)

Coordinate Points

I.   Main Point 1

II. Main Point 2

Subordinate Points

I.   Main Point 1

    A.   First level of subordination

        1.   Second level of subordination

  2. Second level of subordination

      a. Third level of subordination

      b. Third level of subordination

Transition statement

  B. Next point at first level of subordination

      1. Second level of subordination

      2. Second level of subordination

And so on . . .

As your speeches become more involved, you will need to select an appropriate **organizational pattern** (see Chapters 12 and 26). You will also need to familiarize yourself with developing both *working* and *speaking* outlines (see Chapter 13). To allow for the full development of your ideas, *working outlines* generally contain points stated in complete sentences, including the transition statements. As a rule, *speaking outlines* (also called presentation outlines) are far briefer than working outlines and are usually prepared using either short phrases or key words. The content of the speaking outline is placed on 4 × 6 index cards for use during the speech.

Following is a working full-sentence outline created by a beginning public speaking student for a speech of introduction (see speech below):

TOPIC:	Speech of Introduction for Lisa Tran
SPEECH PURPOSE:	To inform
SPECIFIC SPEECH PURPOSE:	To inform my audience about my odyssey as a refugee from war-torn Vietnam to a person fulfilling her potential and realizing her dreams in America

Introduction

(Captures audience attention — in this case, with a startling statement and select dramatic details of her story.) My story begins in Saigon, where my father was imprisoned. We fled the country without taking any belongings. The boat ride was horrific, and we arrived to harsh media attention. We first settled in Kansas, where we were finally reunited with Dad.

(States thesis statement and previews main points. In a brief speech, the preview can act as a transition.) We set forth on American soil some years ago, but my journey has just begun. Little did I dream then of what was in store for me. Little do I know of what my future will bring.

Body

I. We become American citizens, and I achieve things I never dreamed of.

      A. I become the first Asian pom captain at the University of Oklahoma.

      B. I become a member of Kappa Kappa Gamma and the 1999 Miss Greek OU.

II. My achievements could not have occurred if I did not have some knowledge of the difficulties and hardships of life.

    A. Though I could not afford lessons in Vietnam, as a child I trained myself to dance.

        1. Nine years later, I earned honors as a dancer and today I teach dance.

        2. In 1999, I was crowned the first Asian Miss Greek OU.

    B. Thanks to the love and support of my sorority, my friends, and my family, I have come far.

    C. The journey is not over.

Conclusion

(Restates the thesis in a memorable way.) As an anonymous poet once wrote, "Dream what you want to dream, go where you want to go, be what you want to be, because you have only one life and one chance to do all the things you want to do." Rather than proving my self-worth, my accomplishments merely symbolize the true passion and drive we have for living and succeeding.

(Leaves the audience with a motivating message.) We are what we learn and take with us during this journey we call life. I am the past because I have appreciation; I am the present because I have learned humbleness; I am the future because I have so much more to learn.

CONSIDER PRESENTATION AIDS

As you prepare your speech, consider whether using visual or audio aids, a combination of the two, or other **presentation aids** will help your audience understand your points. A presentation aid can be as simple as writing the definition of a word on a blackboard or as involved as a multimedia slide show. Presentation aids that summarize and highlight information, such as charts and graphs, can often help the audience to retain ideas and understand difficult concepts. They can also provide dramatic emphasis that listeners will find memorable (see Chapter 20).

PRACTICE DELIVERING THE SPEECH

The success of even your first speech in class depends on how well prepared and practiced you are. So practice your speech — often. It has been suggested that a good speech is practiced at least six times. For a four- to six-minute speech, that's only thirty to forty minutes (figuring in re-starts and pauses) of actual practice time. Like an actor in a play, a public speaker must deliver his or her "lines" to the audience. You will want to feel and appear "natural" to your listeners, an effect best achieved by rehearsing both the verbal and the nonverbal elements of your speech.

✔ **CHECKLIST**

Using the Audio Recorder to Bolster Confidence

Many public speaking experts agree that of the vast array of high-tech audio-visual gizmos available, along with the video camera (see Chapter 20), the tape recorder, or the digital audio recorder, are among the few truly indispensable aids to building confidence in public speaking. Listening to your speech helps to make it real and, therefore, less scary.

✓   Record yourself at least one of the six times that you rehearse your speech.

✓   As you play back the recording, listen for clarity. Is your pronunciation clear?

✓   Watch for the tempo of your sentences. Are they too long? Too choppy? Have you included any tongue twisters that cause you to stumble as you speak?

✓   Time your speech as you record it. This will help you decide how to edit it and where to add or cut.

✓   Use positive self-imagery. Close your eyes and visualize yourself standing in front of the audience and being well received. Let the sound of your voice relax you as you sit back and appreciate all the good work you've done.[1]

1. Ron Hoff, *I Can See You Naked,* rev. ed. (Kansas City, Mo.: Andrews McMeel, 1992), 66.

Vocal Delivery

Vocal delivery includes speech volume, rate, pitch, variety, pronunciation, and articulation. As you rehearse, pay attention to how loudly or softly you are speaking. If you rehearse with a friend, ask him or her to sit at the far end of the room; if your friend cannot hear you from that distance, practice adjusting your volume. Pay attention to the *rate* at which you speak and aim to speak neither too fast nor too slowly. Beware of speaking in a *monotone;* audiences will quickly become turned off by a speaker who uses an unvarying, flat tone. Decide how you want to phrase your statements, and then practice saying them. Finally, check that you are pronouncing words correctly and clearly. (See Chapter 18 and Appendix D, "Commonly Mispronounced Words.")

Nonverbal Delivery

Beyond the words of a speech, audiences are also highly attuned to a speaker's **nonverbal delivery** or nonverbal speech behavior — facial expressions, gestures, general body movements, and overall physical appearance.

Facial Expression and Eye Contact.   Practice smiling and otherwise animating your face in ways that feel natural to you. Audiences want to feel that you care about what you are saying, so avoid a deadpan, or blank, expression. Practice making eye contact with your listeners. Doing so will make audience members feel that you recognize and respect them. As you speak, practice scanning with your eyes around the room. Imagine that people are looking at you, and pause to gaze at different audience members.

Gestures, Body Movement, and Posture.   As you practice, consider your hand and arm *gestures,* or movements that express meaning during the speech. Practice gestures that feel natural to you, steering clear of exaggerated movements. A rule of thumb for the making of gestures in speeches is to begin a speech with your hands in a relaxed and free position, possibly at your sides or with one at your side and the other (with your forearm) crossing your abdomen. From this relaxed position, raise your hands and arms into the gesture you wish to make. Once you've completed the movement, return your hands to the original position (see Chapter 19).

Another area to consider as you practice is *body movement.* Consider the physical layout of your speech setting (e.g., the classroom) and how you will

ESL Speaker's Notes
Identifying Linguistic Issues as You Practice Your Speech

As noted in the preceding checklist, most experts recommend that you prepare for delivering your first speech (as well as for subsequent speeches) by practicing with an audio recorder. Non-native speakers may wish to pay added attention to pronunciation and articulation as they listen. *Pronunciation* is the correct formation of word sounds. *Articulation* is the clarity or forcefulness with which the sounds are made, regardless of whether they are pronounced correctly. It is important to pay attention to and work on both areas. If possible, try to arrange an appointment with an instructor to help you identify key linguistic issues in your speech practice tape. If instructors are unavailable, try asking a fellow student.

Because languages vary tremendously in the specific sounds they use and the way in which these sounds are produced by the vocal chords, each of us will speak a non-native language a bit differently than do native speakers. That is, we will have some sort of accent. This should not concern you in and of itself. What is important is identifying which specific features of your pronunciation, if any, seriously interfere with your ability to make yourself understandable. Listening to your speech with an audio recorder or a videotape, perhaps in the presence of a native speaker, will allow you to identify trouble spots. Once you have identified which words you tend to mispronounce, you can work to correct the problem.

As you listen to your recording, watch as well for your articulation of words. ESL students whose first languages don't differentiate between the /sh/ sound and its close cousin /ch/, for example, may say "share" when they mean "chair" or "shoes" when they mean "choose."[1] It is therefore important that you also check to make sure that you are using the correct meaning of the words you have selected for your speech.

1. Based on Robbin Crabtree and Robert Weissberg, *ESL Students in the Public Speaking Classroom* (Boston: Bedford/St. Martin's, 2000), 23.

position yourself. Rather than remaining fixed behind a podium, many speakers move around it in ways that bring them closer to the audience. Avoid nervously shifting from one foot to the other, and be sure to stand upright with good posture.

Finally, dress for the occasion. Your clothes and grooming are the first cues you give an audience, and they will create an important initial impression of you.

Anticipate Questions from the Audience

At the close of your speech, you are likely to face questions from the audience. As you review your speech before delivery, consider what questions the audience is likely to ask. See Appendix A for an in-depth discussion of how to handle the question-and-answer session.

Take the Plunge

The first speech is usually simple and fun, but it does require you to fulfill each of the steps in the speechmaking process described above. It is very important that you try to gauge your progress in preparing the speech, including your feelings of anxiety about the process—from the time the assignment is given to the few minutes immediately following the speech. Use the accompanying self-assessment checklist to evaluate your preparation for and presentation of this first assignment. Whenever you begin to feel anxious, try some of the strategies for alleviating speech anxiety described in Chapter 5. Begin by thinking positively!

✓ **CHECKLIST**

Self-Assessment of My First Speech

It is important to keep track of your progress throughout the speechmaking process. Consider each item in this checklist in two ways—as something to accomplish during preparation, and as something to consider after you have presented your speech. Use this self-assessment tool to improve future speeches by isolating areas where you need improvement.

Introduction

_____ 1. How will/did I capture attention?

_____ 2. What is/was my thesis statement?

_____ 3. What will/did I say to relate the topic to the audience?

_____ 4. What will/did I say to preview the main points of the speech?

_____ 5. What will/did I say to make the transition from my introduction to my first main point?

(Continued)

Body

_____ 1. Is/was the arrangement of my main points clear and logical?
_____ 2. What transition statements will/did I use between main points?
_____ 3. Do I have/did I use appropriate support material for each point?

Conclusion

_____ 1. How will/did I restate the thesis/purpose of my speech?
_____ 2. What will/did I say to summarize the main points?
_____ 3. What memorable thought will/did I end the speech with?

Delivery

_____ 1. What will/did I do to assure consistent eye contact?
_____ 2. What will/did I do to project appropriate vocal qualities (rate and volume, clear articulation)?
_____ 3. What will/did I do to ensure proper posture, gestures, and general movement?

My overall assessment of this speech is: _____

What I consider strengths in this speech: _____

Elements I need to improve on: _____

Goals for my next speech: _____

Sample Introductory Speech

LISA TRAN

Introduction

● Everybody has a history; some, perhaps, more interesting than others. Mine began nearly twenty-one years ago in Saigon, Vietnam. My father, who was an affluent businessman, was taken captive along with many other men by the Vietnamese communist government and imprisoned because of his Chinese descent. All of our money, property, and rights were stripped away from us. My mother, three sisters, brother, and I escaped with thousands of other Vietnamese and Chinese refugees in search of safety and freedom. For six long months, my

● The speaker captures the audience's attention with a short but dramatically phrased introductory statement.

family and I survived the most horrific boat ride to the United States. Hundreds of people died due to the grotesque conditions and diseases prevalent on the boat. Nevertheless, we landed on the coast of California only to find harsh media attention focused on us upon our arrival. A program was implemented by placing each refugee family with an American caretaker. •
For three years, my family and I resided in Caney, Kansas, with Father Mike. In 1981, my family and I were finally reunited with my father, who was released by the strict communist government. Due to the untimely death of Father Mike, we moved south to Tulsa, Oklahoma, where my family and I have lived for almost twenty years. • Although my journey seemed to begin in Vietnam, it has only just begun.

Even in a short speech like this, the speaker probably should offer a little information about Father Mike.

This preview—that the speaker's journey "has only just begun"— also acts as a transition statement.

Body

Through the trials and tribulations my family and I have undergone, we are lucky and fortunate to have become American citizens. • I never dreamed that I would be the first Asian pom captain at the University of Oklahoma, a member of Kappa Kappa Gamma, and the 1999 Miss Greek OU. I could not have accomplished these honors without knowing the difficulties and hardships of life. • As a young child, I would mimic the choreography performed by the dancers on the television show *Star Search*. However, because we were poor, I could not afford dance lessons each week. Through hard work and perseverance, I trained myself to dance. Nine years later, I have earned individual honors as a dancer and have been teaching dance for a national company. Because of my ability to dance, my sorority encouraged me to enter a pageant. I had never been in a pageant before, and was apprehensive from the moment my sorority voted me in. The house was confident in me, though, and offered support throughout the weeks I was training. On April 23, 1999, I was crowned Miss Greek OU. This title has allowed me to be a role model for young women in my community. •
Most important, I have also been given the opportunity to represent my culture as one of the first Asian women to be voted Miss Greek OU. I could not have achieved this honor without the love and support of my sorority, my friends, and my family. These three accomplishments have shown me how far my life

In just one sentence the speaker sets up three main, coordinate points—becoming pom captain, a sorority member, and a pageant winner.

A series of subordinate points shows how the speaker overcame several personal trials and attained several noteworthy accomplishments.

Rather than merely reciting a list of her accomplishments, the speaker frames them within the larger context of support from family, friends, and community.

has come. My story does not end here, because the journey is not over.

Conclusion

• "Dream what you want to dream, go where you want to go, be what you want to be, because you have only one life and one chance to do all the things you want to do." I do not let the achievements that I have accomplished prove my self-worth. They merely symbolize the true passion and drive we have for living and succeeding. • We are what we learn and take with us during this journey we call life. I am the past because I have appreciation; I am the present because I have learned humbleness; I am the future because I have so much more to learn.

• This quotation reinforces the inspirational nature of the speech. Using her own life as an example, the speaker exhorts others to use their time wisely.

• The speaker's strong conclusion leaves the audience with something to think about as we ponder the precise meaning of her near-poetic statement, "I am the past because. . . ."

Public Speaking Basics

Public Speaking Basics

Speaker's Reference
Public Speaking Basics

3. Listeners and Speakers

As You Prepare, Consider Factors That Influence Listening

- People pay attention to what they hold to be important. (p. 39)
- People pay attention to information that touches their experiences and backgrounds. (p. 39)
- People filter new information based on what they already know. (p. 39)

Incorporate the Factors That Influence Listening into Your Speech

- Try to uncover what is important to your listeners. (p. 39)
- When explaining unfamiliar concepts, consider using analogies, metaphors, and other figures of speech. (p. 39)
- When introducing new information, associate it with something with which your listeners are already familiar. (p. 39)
- Appeal to your listeners' experiences and backgrounds. (p. 39)

Anticipate and Cope with Common Obstacles to Listening

- Plan ahead in order to minimize the impact of external distractions such as noise, movement, light, darkness, heat or cold, and so forth. (p. 40)
- Internal distractions such as daydreaming, time pressures, emotional turmoil, or fatigue due to illness or lack of sleep can disrupt concentration. (p. 41)
- Channel your energy into truly listening. (p. 41)
- Beware of listening defensively: Wait for the speaker to finish before devising your own mental arguments. (p. 41)
- Don't assume that you already know what the speaker will say. (p. 41)
- As a speaker be sensitive to any distractions your audience may face. (p. 41)
- Don't judge the speaker on the basis of his or her accent, appearance, or demeanor. Focus instead on what is actually being said. (p. 42)
- Reveal your needs to the speaker, try to gain clarification, and ask questions. (p. 42)

Use Strategies to Become a More Active Listener

- Set listening goals that encourage action. (p. 43)
- Listen for main ideas, take notes, and focus on the organizational pattern. (p. 44)
- Watch for nonverbal cues: eye contact, body language, facial expressions, and gestures. (p. 45)

Listen Critically to the Speaker's Evidence and Arguments

- Evaluate the speaker's evidence for accuracy and credibility. (p. 45)
- Analyze the speaker's assumptions and biases. (p. 45)
- Assess the speaker's reasoning: Look for faulty logic or inappropriate causal relationships. (p. 46)
- Resist false assumptions, overgeneralizations, and either-or thinking. (p. 46)
- Consider multiple perspectives. (p. 46)
- Summarize and assess the relevant facts and evidence before deciding how you will act on the speaker's information or argument. (p. 46)

Offer Constructive Feedback When Evaluating Speeches and Presentations

- Be honest and fair in your evaluation. (p. 47)
- Do not judge the message's content on the basis of the speaker's communication style. (p. 47)
- Be compassionate in your criticism: Start with something positive; focus on the speech, not on the speaker; and be selective in your criticism. (p. 47)

4. Ethical Public Speaking

Take Responsibility for Your Power to Influence Others

- Be morally accountable for your message. (p. 49)
- Accept responsibility for the stands you take. (p. 49)

Earn the Audience's Trust

- Develop a solid grasp of your subject. (p. 50)
- Display sound reasoning skills. (p. 50)
- Present information honestly and without manipulation. (p. 50)
- Be genuinely interested in the welfare of your listeners. (p. 50)

Recognize That Legal Speech Is Not Always Ethical Speech

- The First Amendment provides protection both to truthful speakers and to speakers whose words are inflammatory and offensive. (p. 50)
- Codes of ethical speech are built on moral rather than legal principles: Though often legally protected, racist, sexist, homophobic, and pornographic speech are clearly unethical. (p. 50)

Be Aware That Certain Types of Speech Are Illegal

- Speech that provokes people to violence ("fighting words") (p. 50)
- Speech that can be proved to harm an individual's reputation (slander or defamatory statements) (p. 50)
- Words spoken with a reckless disregard for the truth (p. 51)

Recognize and Respect Audience Values

- Acknowledge alternative viewpoints. (p. 52)
- Consider your topic from a culturally sensitive perspective. (p. 52)
- Identify listeners' values using audience analysis tools such as interviews, surveys, and published materials. (p. 52)

Exhibit Trustworthiness, Respect, Responsibility, and Fairness

- Tell the truth, don't distort information, and acknowledge sources. (p. 54)
- Focus on issues, not on personalities. (p. 55)
- Make sure that your topic is socially constructive. (p. 57)
- Strive hard for accuracy. (p. 57)
- Acknowledge alternative and opposing views so that the audience can make informed decisions. (p. 57)

Avoid Plagiarism

- Orally acknowledge any source that requires credit in written form: other people's ideas, opinions, theories, evidence, and research; direct quotations; paraphrased information; facts and statistics. (p. 58)

Know the Copyright Law

- Copyright law protects *intellectual property* (original authorship or expression). (p. 61)
- The Fair Use Doctrine permits limited use of copyrighted materials without permission; such material must be orally credited in your speech. (p. 61)
- Facts and statistics that are common knowledge cannot be copyrighted but must be orally credited in your speech. (p. 61)

5. Managing Speech Anxiety

Recognize What Underlies the Fear of Public Speaking

- A lack of public speaking experience: It can be difficult to put the anxiety that often precedes new experiences into perspective. (p. 63)
- Feeling different: Everyone is different from everyone else and even seasoned speakers experience anxiety. (p. 64)
- Being the center of attention: The audience won't notice things about you that you don't want to reveal. (p. 64)

Pinpoint the Onset of Your Anxiety and Plan to Overcome It

- Some people become anxious upon hearing that they must give a speech (pre-preparation anxiety). (p. 65)
  Don't allow your anxiety to deter you from planning your speech.
- For some, the onset of anxiety occurs as they begin to prepare the speech (preparation anxiety). (p. 66)
  Beware of avoidance and procrastination.
- Some people don't feel anxious until it's time to rehearse the speech (pre-performance anxiety). (p. 66)
  Practice your speech to build confidence.
- Many people don't experience public speaking anxiety until they actually begin to deliver the speech (performance anxiety). (p. 66)
  Practice stress-control breathing and other relaxation techniques.

To Build Confidence, Prepare and Practice

- Manage your time wisely during the preparation phase. (p. 68)
- Pick topics that interest you and research them thoroughly. (p. 68)
- Rehearse until you know how you want to express yourself. (p. 68)
- Research your audience and speaking environment. (p. 68)

Try to View Giving a Speech as a Positive Opportunity

- Use positive thoughts prior to delivery to lessen anxiety. (p. 68)
- Picture the speech as an extension of an ordinary conversation. (p. 69)

Use Visualization and Relaxation Techniques to Gain a Sense of Control

- Learn about visualization. (p. 69)
- Learn how to use stress-control breathing, natural gestures, and movement as you speak. (p. 70)

Remember: Audience Members Are Evaluating Your Message, Not You

• Try to lessen your fear of being judged: Listeners tend to evaluate the content of a message rather than who the speaker is as a person. (p. 71)

Focus on the Enjoyable and Empowering Aspects of Speaking

• You have the chance to influence others. (p. 71)
• You can express your own views. (p. 71)
• You can inform, persuade, entertain, or even console others. (p. 71)

KEY TERMS

Chapter 3

feedback loop	external listening distraction	critical thinking
listening	internal listening distraction	valid generalization
selective perception		overgeneralization
active listening	defensive listening	
listening distraction		

Chapter 4

responsibility	values	wholesale plagiarism
ethics	dignity	patchwrite plagiarism
ethos	integrity	direct quotation
speaker credibility	trustworthiness	paraphrase
First Amendment	respect	common knowledge
free speech	jargon	copyright
fighting words	ethnocentrism	public domain
slander	stereotype	intellectual property
reckless disregard for the truth	hate speech	Fair Use Doctrine
	plagiarism	public performance

Chapter 5

public speaking anxiety (PSA)	preparation anxiety	performance anxiety
pre-preparation anxiety	pre-performance anxiety	visualization

3 Listeners and Speakers

As a student of public speaking, you wear two hats—those of speaker and listener. Listeners and speakers are interdependent: Listeners need someone to whom they will listen, and speakers need someone to whom they will address their remarks. Thus it is listener and speaker together who truly make a speech a speech—who "co-create" its meaning. Successful speakers adjust their message based on their listeners' reactions, and vice versa. Communication scholars call this continual flow, or *circular response* between speaker and listener, the **feedback loop**.

Listening is a communication activity that you do more than any other. Studies show that you listen 40 percent of the time, but speak only 35 percent. Executives listen even more, spending upwards of 50 percent of their day listening to others.[1] Because listening research reveals that most people retain only half of what they hear immediately and only 35 percent of what they heard after twenty-four hours, it is essential to hone your listening skills.[2] This course is the perfect place to do so.

The more skilled you are at listening to speeches, the more you will learn about what will and won't work for your speech. Focusing on the art of listening will also serve you well in many arenas other than public speaking. Numerous studies show that competent listeners—those who are conscious of the pitfalls of poor listening as well as the rewards of effective listening—tend to be efficient and successful in both their personal and professional lives.[3]

The Selective Nature of Listening

Most of us understand that giving a speech involves preparation and practice, but fewer recognize the hard work that listening requires. Rather than being a passive activity that simply "happens" to us, listening is a complex behavior. In contrast to hearing, which is the physiological process of perceiving sound, **listening** is the conscious act of recognizing, understanding, and accurately interpreting the messages communicated by others. While *hearing* is largely reflexive or automatic in nature, listening is a proactive and discriminating process.

Can you recall sharing reactions with a friend about a lecture, movie, or other event and noticing that even though you both attended the same affair, you formed quite different impressions? In any given situation, no two listeners will process information in exactly the same way. The reason lies in **selective perception**—people pay attention selectively to certain messages while ignoring others. Several factors influence what we listen to and what we ignore:

1. *We pay attention to what we hold to be important.* We are most motivated to listen to others if we think that what is being said will be of consequence to us. This is why audience analysis is so crucial to speechmaking (see Chapter 6). People look for information that reflects their interests, needs, values, attitudes, and beliefs.

2. *We pay attention to information that touches our experiences and backgrounds.* If we listen to something that is foreign to us, chances are we'll just zone out. To catch and sustain listeners' attention, a speaker must in some way touch upon audience members' experiences and backgrounds.

3. *We sort and filter new information on the basis of what we already know.* According to learning theory, all new concepts are understood as analogies to previous concepts.[4] As listeners, this means that we try to understand new information by comparing it with what we already know.

As a speaker, in line with these principles, try to uncover what is important to your audience. To capture listeners' attention, appeal to their experiences and backgrounds. When explaining unfamiliar concepts, consider using analogies, metaphors, and other figures of speech (see Chapters 16 and 23). When introducing new information, make it relevant by associating it with something with which your listeners are already familiar. Consider clarifying your meaning through descriptive language and helpful presentation aids (see Chapters 16 and 20–22).

ESL Speaker's Notes
Learning by Listening

As every student of a foreign language knows, listening is the key to learning a language. Using textbooks to study usage and grammar is important, but it is through the spoken language—hearing it and speaking it—that we gain fluency.

Listening to the speeches of colleagues or classmates, as well as those broadcast by television channels such as C-Span, can help you hone the skills you need to become a better speaker. Nearly all college libraries own many DVDs, videocassettes, and other recorded materials made specifically for ESL speakers such as yourself, and the reference librarian will be happy to locate them for you. The Internet also offers many helpful listening resources. Among the many sites you will find is the *Merriam-Webster Online Dictionary* (**www.webster.com**), which includes an audio feature that allows you to hear the correct pronunciation of words. You can also download and listen to speeches directly on the Internet.

As you listen to these resources, you can:

- Build your vocabulary.
- Improve pronunciation through guided repetition.
- Learn new idioms, or informal expressions, used by native speakers of English.
- Observe body posture, gestures, intonation, and other nonverbal aspects of delivery.

Barriers to Active Listening

Active listening is focused, purposeful listening. It is a multistep process of gathering and evaluating information. Before reviewing these steps, however, consider the following stumbling blocks to active listening. According to one study, the poor listening habits that rank highest among college students include inattentiveness and being prone to distraction, scriptwriting and defensive listening, and laziness and overconfidence.[5] Active listening isn't possible unless we recognize and overcome these habits.

LISTENING DISTRACTIONS

A **listening distraction** is anything that competes for attention that you are trying to give to something else. You may have every intention of listening to someone's presentation but instead find yourself thinking about an upcoming exam. Or perhaps you're hungry, tired, or angry about a recent incident. Distractions can originate outside of us, in the environment (external distractions), or within us, in our thoughts and feelings (internal distractions).

 CHECKLIST

Minimizing Distractions

✓ If you have trouble seeing or hearing at a distance, arrive early and sit in the front.

✓ If you are going to a group meeting and you have trouble hearing when others are talking at the same time, sit next to the leader so that most of the messages will be communicated toward your side of the room.

✓ Monitor yourself for lapses in attention and consciously redouble your efforts to concentrate on listening.

✓ Monitor yourself for signs of defensive listening.

✓ Don't assume ahead of time that you know what the speaker will say.

External Distractions

Virtually anything in the environment — noise, movement, light, darkness, heat, or cold — can be considered an **external listening distraction**. The din of jackhammers or competing conversations may make it impossible to listen well. The problem may be poor lighting or people walking into or out of a meeting. The room may be excessively warm or cold.

To minimize external distractions, try to anticipate and plan for them — even if you do so just minutes before a presentation begins. If you have trouble seeing or hearing at a distance, arrive early and sit in the front. If you have trouble hearing at group meetings, sit near the leader so that most messages will be communicated to your side of the room.

Ethically Speaking
The Responsibilities of Listening

As a speaker you have the power of the podium, but as a listener you also have considerable power that you can wield constructively or destructively. An example of the latter includes rude listening behaviors such as heckling, name-calling, interrupting out of turn, and other breaches in civility. Beyond short-circuiting communication, these acts can easily lead to explosive results—from menacing clashes among activists on opposite sides of a cause to eruptions at school board meetings and other civic venues.

Perhaps you have witnessed the fallout of such clashes on your college campus in the form of student demonstrations gone awry. In one such instance, at San Francisco State University, a heated exchange arose between pro-Palestinian student demonstrators and a group of Jewish students; the police were ultimately called to maintain order. In another instance, this one at a school board meeting in Connecticut, an audience member who took exception to a board member's proposal threw a pitcher of ice water in his face. Visibly shaken, the board member had to be escorted out of the room by the police. The meeting was adjourned abruptly, some on the board considered resigning, and many parents were fearful of attending other meetings.

The ability to dissent from prevailing opinion is one of the hallmarks of a free society. As listeners, we are ethically bound to refrain from disruptive and intimidating tactics that are meant to silence those with whom we disagree. If we find the arguments of others morally offensive, we are equally bound to speak up in refutation. Only in this manner can we preserve the freedom to express our ideas. Clearly, the power to listen can translate into being socially responsible or socially destructive.

Paying attention to external distractions is also critical for speakers. As a speaker, try to address promptly any distractions your audience may face. For example, you can close windows and doors against intruding noise or ask audience members to move closer to you.

Internal Distractions

Internal listening distractions are thoughts and feelings, both positive and negative, that intrude on our attention. Internal distractions can take the form of daydreaming, anxiety due to time pressures, distress over an argument, fatigue owing to lack of sleep or illness, or any kind of strong emotion. Optimally, distracting strong emotions are best dealt with before you enter the listening environment.

SCRIPTWRITING AND DEFENSIVE LISTENING

Instead of focusing on the speaker, people who are "scriptwriters" are thinking about what they, rather than the speaker, will say next.[6] Similarly, people who engage in **defensive listening** decide either that they won't like what the speaker is going to say or that they know better. This usually occurs when listeners sense that their attitudes or opinions are being challenged.

When you find yourself scriptwriting or listening with a defensive posture, try waiting for the speaker to finish before devising your own arguments in your mind. Hear the speaker out. That way, at least your arguments will be based on the facts as the speaker actually presented them. Try to focus on the speaker's motives for the remarks that offend you. You may still end up disagreeing with the speaker, but at least you'll do so from a position of actually having heard what he or she has said. Remind yourself that effective listening precedes effective rebuttal.[7]

LAZINESS AND OVERCONFIDENCE

Sometimes we think we already know, or perhaps don't need to know, the speaker's message. Close cousins to defensiveness, laziness and overconfidence can manifest themselves in several ways: We expect too little from speakers, ignore important information, or display an arrogant attitude. Later, we discover that we missed important information. Never assume that you already know what a speaker will say. You'll very seldom be right. And remember the value of modesty. Rarely do we know as much as we think we do.

 CHECKLIST

Listening to Speakers Who May Be Difficult to Understand

✓ Refrain from judging a speaker on the basis of his or her accent, appearance, or demeanor. Focus instead on what is actually being said.

✓ Put yourself in the speaker's shoes, and imagine what it would be like if you were addressing an audience in a new language.

✓ Instead of judging the speaker, reveal your needs to him or her whenever possible. Try to gain clarification. Ask questions. Turn confusion into curiosity and an opportunity to learn about other people's experiences.

CULTURAL BARRIERS

Differences in dialects or accents, nonverbal cues, word choice, and even physical appearance can serve as barriers to listening. Nonverbal cues such as gestures can also throw a listener off. Most gestures are culture-specific rather than universal. For example, a thumbs-up gesture in the United States usually means "good job" or "things are going fine." In Australia and Nigeria the same gesture is considered rude and insulting. In the United States, students of public speaking are counseled to maintain eye contact when they speak. In some Eastern cultures, however, direct eye contact is seen as disrespectful or even intolerable. And in Korea lowering the eyes signals rejection. (See Checklist: Listening to Speakers Who May Be Difficult to Understand for tips on becoming a better listener in situations where cultural differences make comprehension difficult.)

Public Speaking in Cultural Perspective
Helping Diverse Audiences Understand You

To help your audience listen effectively and truly get your message, consider reviewing your speech or presentation for the following cultural barriers to understanding:

1. Do you use *idioms,* or colloquial expressions such as "under the weather," "apple of his eye," and "bad mouth," that non-native speakers aren't likely to know? Watch for such expressions and either eliminate them or pause and define them for your audience. (See Chapter 16 for additional tips on using language in a culturally sensitive manner.)

2. Do you speak at an appropriate rate—one that is neither too fast nor too slow? By paying particular attention to speech rate, pronunciation, and articulation, you can help non-native speakers of English understand what you are saying (see Chapter 18).

3. Are you alert to nonverbal cues that suggest that your listeners may not comprehend you? Be alert to confused expressions, and ask your listeners if you can clarify points for them.

Becoming a More Active Listener

Active listeners use their eyes as well as their ears to decode a speaker's nonverbal and verbal cues. They listen for the speaker's main points and critically evaluate evidence used to support claims. Active listeners:

- Set listening goals.
- Listen for main ideas.
- Watch for the speaker's nonverbal cues.

SET LISTENING GOALS

Setting listening goals helps you prepare to get the most from a listening situation. What do you need and expect from the listening situation? Keep these goals in mind as you listen. Try to state your listening goals in a way that encourages action. Table 3.1 illustrates the steps in setting listening goals.

TABLE 3.1 • Steps in Setting Listening Goals

Identify Need: "I have to know Suzanne's speech thesis, purpose, main points, and type of organization in order to complete and hand in a written evaluation."

Indicate Performance Standard: "I will get a better grade on the evaluation if I am able to identify and evaluate the major components of Suzanne's speech."

Make Action Statement (Goal): "I will minimize distractions and practice the active listening steps during Suzanne's speech. I will take careful notes during her speech and ask questions about anything I do not understand."

Assess Goal Achievement: "Before I leave the classroom, I will review my notes carefully to make sure that I covered everything."

LISTEN FOR MAIN IDEAS

No one has perfect retention. To ensure that you hear and retain the speaker's most important points, try these strategies:

- *Listen for the speaker's organizational pattern* (see Chapters 12 and 26). Knowing the sequence and structure of a speech makes it easy for you to understand and remember the content.

- *Listen for introductions, transitions, and conclusions to alert you to the main points.* Most speakers will introduce their main points in their introductory remarks. This gives the listener the chance to identify these points and focus on their discussion later: "I have three points I want to make tonight. First, . . ."

  Transitions can also alert the listener to the fact that a main point is about to be discussed: "My next major point is. . . ." Speakers often use many of the following transitions to preview a main idea: "One, two, three, . . . ," "First, second, third, . . . ," "Most important, . . . ," "Another point (issue) I would raise. . . ."

  Conclusions are a valuable place to recheck your memory of the main points: "Let me recap those three rules for living overseas. One, . . ."

- *Watch for a more direct eye gaze.* Speakers are more likely to look at you when they are trying to make an important point. In addition, they are likely to shift their gaze to a different part of the audience when moving from one main point to another.

- *Take notes on the speaker's main points.* Several different methods of note taking are possible when listening to public speeches. The bullet, column, and outline methods can be helpful (see Table 3.2 on note-taking methods.)

TABLE 3.2 • Methods of Note Taking

Method	Description	Example	
Bullet	Notes list the main points and/or supporting material in bullet form.	• Bipolar disorder is actually a spectrum of disorders. • Adults suffer more classical patterns of mood swings.	
Column	Notes are taken in two columns. One column is used for verbatim notes, and the other is used for interpretations or notes to yourself.	"Make sure your hands are dry."	Grip the ball with the thumb and first two fingers.
Outline	Notes are taken according to the organizational format or outline that the speaker is using (see Chapters 12 and 26).		

> ✓ **CHECKLIST**
>
> ### Strategies for Active Listening
>
> 1. Set listening goals and state them in a way that encourages action: "In my colleague's presentation, I will learn why it took the team six months to complete the last phase."
> 2. Listen for the speaker's main ideas.
> 3. Take notes.
> 4. Try to detect the speaker's organizational pattern.
> 5. Seek out main ideas in the speaker's introduction, use of transitions, and conclusion.
> 6. Watch for the speaker's nonverbal cues.
> 7. Take note of body language, eye contact, facial expressions, and gestures.

WATCH FOR NONVERBAL CUES

Much of a message's meaning is communicated nonverbally, and you can use this information as you listen to speeches. *Body language* is an excellent source of information. Watch the speaker's stance and posture. Do they seem rigid and wooden? If so, the speaker may be nervous and may not feel comfortable with the material he or she is presenting. *Facial expressions* also provide cues to help you listen better. Speakers who are committed to their material are more likely to display facial expressions that are consistent with their commitment to the message. Smiling, frowning, raising eyebrows, and other expressions of emotion are useful cues in determining the speaker's sincerity and enthusiasm for the message. The same cues can betray the speaker's real feelings. If verbal and nonverbal messages do not correspond, the nonverbal cues are usually the more honest ones.

Active Listening and Critical Thinking

Active listening and critical thinking go hand in hand. The use of one skill builds the other. **Critical thinking** is the ability to evaluate claims on the basis of well-supported reasons. Critical thinkers are able to look for flaws in arguments and resist claims that have no supporting evidence.[8] They don't take things at face value.

As you listen to speeches, use your critical faculties to:

- *Evaluate the evidence.* Is the evidence accurate? What is the source of the evidence? Is the source credible?
- *Analyze assumptions and biases.* What lies behind the speaker's assertions? Does the evidence support or contradict these assertions? What standards

✓ CHECKLIST

Using the Thought/Speech Differential to Listen Critically

Did you know that we listen at a much faster rate than we speak? We speak at the rate of between ninety and two hundred words a minute; we listen at a rate of perhaps as much as five hundred to six hundred words per minute. This differential between "thought speed" and "speech speed" is one reason we are so easily distracted. But rather than using the thought-speech differential as an excuse to let your mind wander, you can turn it into an opportunity to apply your critical thinking skills. The next time you find yourself "thinking ahead" of the speaker—usually by thinking of something that's unrelated to the speech—use the time instead to listen with the following questions in mind:

✓ What's the speaker saying?
✓ What does it really mean?
✓ Is he or she leaving anything out?
✓ Is this an assumption? A generalization? A fact or an opinion?
✓ Are my biases intruding on my listening?
✓ How can I use what the speaker is telling me?[1]

1. Thomas E. Anastasi Jr., *Listen! Techniques for Improving Communication Skills* (Boston: CBI Publishing, 1982), 35.

and values lie behind your own interpretation or attitude toward the speaker's message? Are these interfering with an objective evaluation of the evidence? Are they creating biases?

- *Assess an argument's logic.* Does the speaker's reasoning betray faulty logic? (See Chapter 25.)

- *Resist false assumptions, overgeneralizations, either-or thinking, and other fallacies in reasoning.* A **valid generalization** is supported by different types of evidence from different sources, but it does not make claims beyond a reasonable point. **Overgeneralizations** are unsupported conclusions (e.g., "All welfare recipients are lazy"). Test the validity of a generalization by determining if the basis of support is biased in any way. *Either-or thinking* is dominated by just two choices and creates false dilemmas that do not in fact exist. (See Chapter 25.)

- *Consider multiple perspectives.* There is often more than one way to look at things. Similarly, there are often multiple solutions to problems. Consider different perspectives, and realize that both your own perspective and that of the speaker are subject to error.

- *Summarize and judge.* Summarize the speaker's facts and evidence for yourself. If the speaker asks for an action on the part of listeners (as is often the case in persuasive speeches; see Chapter 24), decide how you will act on the basis of the evidence.

Guidelines for Evaluating Speeches and Presentations

As public speakers, we want to know the results of our efforts. While audience members' reactions during the speech provide clues to their feelings about it, more specific feedback is needed if we are to gain insight into our strengths and weaknesses. By critically evaluating the speeches of others, you'll be better able to assess your own strengths and weaknesses as a speaker. Consider the following guidelines.

BE HONEST AND FAIR IN YOUR EVALUATION

Always keep in mind the need to be honest and fair in your evaluation. Sometimes we have a tendency to focus on certain aspects of a speech and, as a result, minimize some of the most important elements. Focusing on a topic that you really like or dislike, for example, may cause you to place undue importance on that speech element. It is also important to remain open to ideas and beliefs that differ from your own. You can always learn something from differing viewpoints.

ADJUST TO THE SPEAKER'S STYLE

Each of us has a unique communication style, a way of presenting ourselves through a mix of verbal and nonverbal signals. As listeners, we form impressions of speakers based on this communication style. Depending on our own preferences, we may find some speakers dull, others dynamic, still others off-putting, and so on. Adjusting to a speaker means not judging the content of that speaker's message based on his or her communication style. As listeners, it's up to us to identify which impressions create the most difficulty and then develop techniques for overcoming any listening problems. Accents, awkward grammatical phrases, and word choice are not good reasons to "tune out" a speaker. Maintaining respect for all types of speakers is a sign of good listening.

BE COMPASSIONATE IN YOUR CRITICISM

How can you critically evaluate a presentation in a way that's constructive rather than cruel? In keeping with the biblical injunction to "do unto others," consider the following approach:[9]

1. *Start by saying something positive.* No one's speech is all bad, so why not start off by saying something nice? The benefits of this are twofold: You'll boost the speaker's self-confidence, and he or she will probably be more receptive to the criticism you do offer.

2. *Focus on the speech, not on the speaker.* One of the most challenging aspects of giving a speech is the feeling of being exposed to others. Don't confirm the speaker's fears of being ripped apart. Address your remarks to the characteristics of the speech, not to the speaker.

3. *Target your criticism.* Global statements such as "I just couldn't get into your topic" or "That was a great speech" don't give the speaker any information that he or she can use. If something fell short, be as specific as possible in describing it: "I wanted to hear more about the importance of such and such as it related to. . . ."

Peer Evaluation Form

In the space below, offer your evaluation of the speaker. Make your evaluation honest but constructive, providing the sort of feedback that you would find helpful if you were the speaker.

Did the speaker seem confident?   Yes   Somewhat   No
Suggestions: _____

Did the speaker use appropriate volume?   Yes   Somewhat   No
Suggestions: _____

Did the speaker use good eye contact?   Yes   Somewhat   No
Suggestions: _____

Did the speaker use effective vocal expression? Yes   Somewhat   No
Suggestions: _____

Did the speaker use appropriate gestures
and facial expressions?   Yes   Somewhat   No
Suggestions: _____

Was the speaker's introduction effective?   Yes   Somewhat   No
Suggestions: _____

Was the speaker's conclusion effective?   Yes   Somewhat   No
Suggestions: _____

Could you easily identify and remember
the speaker's main points?   Yes   Somewhat   No
Suggestions: _____

Did the speaker's organizational patterns
make sense to you?   Yes   Somewhat   No
Suggestions: _____

Did the speaker use effective supporting
evidence?   Yes   Somewhat   No
Suggestions: _____

The best thing about the speaker was: _____

The best thing about the speech was:_____

Recommendations for improvement: _____

Ethical Public Speaking 4

One of the most consistent expectations that we as listeners bring to any speech situation is that the speaker will be honest and straightforward with us. Why else give our attention to someone unless we believe that he or she is sincere? Yet, while we assume an attitude of trust, we instinctively remain alert to hints that might signal dishonesty. As we listen to the actual words the speaker utters, for example, we are simultaneously evaluating his or her posture, tone of voice, gaze, and other potential markers of sincerity or lack thereof.

How can you ensure that your listeners will find you worthy of their trust? As ethicist Michael Josephson[1] has noted, there are both practical and moral reasons for maintaining an ethical stance in public speaking. At the practical level, you must establish credibility with listeners before they will accept your message. Credibility is based on trust, honesty, and believability. You also have a moral obligation to treat your listeners with respect—to behave ethically toward them. Central to ethical public speaking is responsibility to oneself and others.

Ethical Speaking and Responsibility

Public speakers are in a unique position not only to share their ideas but also to influence or persuade their listeners and, at times, move them to act—for better or for worse. With this unique power to affect the minds and hearts of others comes **responsibility**—the heart of ethics. One definition of *responsibility* is "a charge, trust, or duty for which one is accountable"[2] **Ethics** is the study of moral conduct—how people should act toward one another. In terms of public speaking, ethics refers to the responsibilities we have toward our audience and ourselves. It also encompasses the responsibilities listeners have toward speakers.

ETHICS, ETHOS, AND SPEAKER CREDIBILITY

Ethics is derived from the Greek word **ethos**, meaning "character." According to the ancient Greek rhetorician Aristotle, audiences listen to and trust speakers who demonstrate positive ethos (positive character). Positive ethos includes *competence* (as demonstrated by the speaker's grasp of the subject matter), *good moral character* (as reflected in the speaker's trustworthiness, straightforwardness, and honest presentation of the message), and *goodwill* (as demonstrated by the speaker's knowledge and attitude of respect toward the audience and the particular speech occasion).

For Aristotle, speakers were regarded positively only when they were well prepared, honest, and respectful toward their audience. Some 2,500 years after Aristotle, surprisingly little has changed. Modern research on **speaker credibility** reveals that people place their greatest trust in speakers who

- have a solid grasp of the subject,
- display sound reasoning skills,
- are honest and unmanipulative, and
- are genuinely interested in the welfare of their listeners.[3]

Listeners tend to distrust speakers who deviate even slightly from these qualities. However, merely being an expert is not enough to inspire listeners' trust. Studies reveal that we trust only those speakers who we believe have our best interests in mind.[4]

FREE SPEECH AND YOUR RESPONSIBILITY AS A SPEAKER

Perhaps no other nation in the world has as many built-in safeguards for its citizens' right to free expression as the United States. The **First Amendment** of the U.S. Constitution plays a pivotal role in enforcing these safeguards by guaranteeing freedom of speech ("Congress shall make no law . . . abridging the freedom of speech . . ."). However, it is often difficult for our state and federal judges (who are charged with interpreting the Constitution) to find a satisfactory balance between our right to express ourselves (our civil liberties) and our right to be protected from speech that harms us (our civil rights). Whose rights, for example, should be protected? Should the neo-Nazis' right to argue that certain groups are racially inferior be upheld over the objections of those groups?

As today's judges interpret the Constitution, it would appear that neo-Nazis are free to argue in favor of racial superiority. In the United States, **free speech**—defined as the right to be free from unreasonable constraints on expression[5]—is strongly protected, even when the targets of that speech claim that it infringes on their civil rights to be protected from discrimination.

Nevertheless, there remain important limits on our right to speak freely, and as a public speaker it is critical that you are aware of these limitations. For example, certain types of speech are actually illegal, including the following:

- Speech that provokes people to violence (incitement or "**fighting words**")
- Speech that can be proved to be defamatory (termed **slander**), or potentially harmful to an individual's reputation at work or in the community
- Certain kinds of speech that invade a person's privacy

The law makes a distinction between whether the issues or individuals you are talking about are public or private. If you are talking about a public figure or a matter of public concern, you have much more latitude to say what you think, and you will not be legally liable unless it can be shown that you spoke with a **reckless disregard for the truth**. That is, you can be legally liable if it can be shown that you knew that what you were saying was false but said it anyway. If, on the other hand, in your speech you talk about a private person or private matters involving that person, it will be easier for that person to successfully assert a claim for defamation. You will then have the burden of proving that what you said was true.[6]

While a limited range of speech is not legal, speakers who seek to distort the truth about events often can do so and not suffer any consequences. A speaker may, for example, express an opinion questioning the severity of the Holocaust or the suffering of African Americans under slavery in the United States. The fact that many kinds of offensive speech *are* legal, however, does not necessarily mean that they are ethical. In fact, in most instances the First Amendment ensures protection to both the speaker who treats the truth — and other people — with respect and those whose words are inflammatory and offensive. While there are various approaches to evaluating ethical behavior, common to all of them are the fundamental moral precepts of not harming others and telling the truth. Seen from this perspective, many kinds of legally protected speech — whether they are racist, sexist, homophobic, pornographic, antireligious, or just plain mean — are clearly unethical.

Values: The Foundation of Ethical Speaking

Our ethical conduct is a reflection of our **values** — our most enduring judgments or standards of what's good and bad in life, of what's important to us. Values shape our worldview, drive our behavior, and form the basis on which we judge the actions of others. Our ethical choices — including those we make in our speeches — are our values in action.

In large measure, values are culturally determined and transmitted through key social institutions such as the family, schools, and religious organizations. We learn many of our values fairly early in life and tend to hold on to them. In U.S. culture, researchers have identified such "core" values as achievement and success, equal opportunity, material comfort, hard work, practicality and efficiency, change and progress, science, democracy, and freedom.[7] A survey of several Asian societies reveals such core values as the spirit of harmony, humility toward one's superiors, awe of nature, and a desire for prosperity.[8] In addition to broad societal values, we hold values related to our professions, personal relationships, religion, and so forth.

VALUE CONFLICTS AND ETHICAL DILEMMAS

Like human behavior itself, values are not a tidy affair but can conflict or clash. The larger and more diverse the society, such as exists in the United States, the greater these clashes will tend to be. One has only to think back to the aftermath of the 2004 U.S. presidential contest, when much was made of the so-called "values divide" between "red states" (representing conservative values) and "blue states" (representing liberal values).

Conflicting values lie at the heart of ethical dilemmas. We value freedom of religion, but does prayer in the schools infringe on the rights of individuals? We value our right to privacy, but does the Patriot Act, which gives the government sweeping powers to conduct surveillance of American citizens, violate our civil liberties?

RECOGNIZING AND RESPECTING YOUR LISTENERS' VALUES

Whether in conversation or during a speech, clashes of values can lead quickly to anger and alienation. For this reason, it is especially important in public speaking to demonstrate respect for your audience's values. But simply knowing an audience's values doesn't necessarily lead to ethical speaking. Unscrupulous salespeople try to sell us things we neither need nor want by skillfully appealing to our values. Cynical politicians get our vote by convincing us that they have our best interests at heart when they don't. Ethical speaking requires not only recognition of but also respect for an audience's values regardless of whether they diverge from our own.

As a rule, anticipate that audience members will hold a range of values that may differ from your own values, and proceed with sensitivity. (See Chapter 6 for specific techniques you can use to uncover your listeners' values, attitudes, and beliefs.)

Bring Your Own Values into Focus

Usually, if you find that certain values are important to you and your own life, you will want others to hold the same values. This is a critical assumption in preparing for and presenting speeches. Imagine, for example, advocating for or against stem cell research (or simply laying out the opposing positions). Analyzing the underlying values that lead you to your position on this controversial issue can help you anticipate the potential sensitivities of audience members. How do you define the beginnings of life, for instance? How might your audience members?

To bring some of your personal values into focus, consider completing the self-assessment exercise in the accompanying checklist. Through extensive re-

Figure 4.1 Comparing Values

search, psychologist Milton Rokeach identified these thirty-six values important to a large cross section of people. He also distinguished between two kinds of values: terminal and instrumental. *Terminal values* are desirable ends in themselves; you can think of them as end states or states of being. *Instrumental values* are valued characteristics that people can possess. Ranking both terminal and instrumental values from least to most important will help you to identify which values mean the most to you. You can then compare what you value with what your audience analysis indicates that your listeners value (see Figure 4.1). When your values overlap those of your audience, you should be able to find some common ground from which to approach your topic and present your speech. (See Chapter 6 for an in-depth discussion of audience analysis.)

✔ **CHECKLIST**

Self-Assessment: Identifying Values

As a way of uncovering where your values lie, rank each item from *1* to *10* (from least to most important). From these, select your top five values and write them down in the circle labeled "Your Values" in Figure 4.1. Repeat the exercise, but this time rank each value in terms of how important you think it is to your audience. Select the top five of these values and place them in the circle labeled "Audience Values." Finally, draw arrows to the overlapping area to indicate where your highest values (of those listed) coincide with those you think are most important to your listeners.

Terminal Values (states of being you consider important)	*Instrumental Values (characteristics you value in yourself and others)*
A comfortable life	Ambitious
An exciting life	Broadminded
A sense of accomplishment	Capable
A world at peace	Cheerful
A world of beauty	Clean
Equality	Courageous
Family security	Forgiving
Freedom	Helpful
Happiness	Honest
Inner harmony	Imaginative
Mature love	Independent
National security	Intellectual
Pleasure	Logical
Salvation	Loving
Self-respect	Obedient
Social recognition	Polite
True friendship	Responsible
Wisdom	Self-controlled

Source: Milton Rokeach, *Value Survey* (Sunnydale, Calif.: Halgren Tests, 1967).

Ground Rules for Ethical Speaking

The qualities of dignity and integrity should infuse every aspect of a speech. Although there is no single agreed-upon code of ethical standards for communication, the qualities of dignity and integrity are universally seen as central to ethical behavior. **Dignity** refers to "feeling worthy, honored, or respected as a person."[9] Each of us wants to be accorded dignity. **Integrity** refers to incorruptibility—the ability to avoid compromise for the sake of personal expediency.[10] For example, slanting facts in your favor during a speech to persuade others to take your side demonstrates a lack of integrity. Speakers who demonstrate dignity and integrity care about themselves and their listeners. They exhibit a hallmark of ethical speaking: concern for the greater good.

Ethical speaking also requires that we adhere to certain ethical ground rules, or, in the words of ethicist Michael Josephson, "pillars of character."[11] These include being trustworthy, respectful, responsible, and fair in our presentations.

TRUSTWORTHINESS

We find speakers credible when we sense that they are honest about their intentions and about the information they present. **Trustworthiness** is a combination of honesty and dependability. At the broadest level, truth is essential to the democratic process because democracy depends on an informed citizenry. [12]

For the public speaker, trustworthiness includes (but isn't necessarily limited to) the following:

- *Revealing your true purpose to your audience*—and not sacrificing the truth to it. Truth telling can be an especially difficult issue in persuasive speeches (see Chapters 24–26). When the goal is to try to persuade others, the temptation is to fashion the information in a way that fits the goal, even if it means omitting a fact here or there that would convince the audience otherwise. But all kinds of speeches, not just persuasive ones, should be built on the truth. This means acknowledging rather than omitting relevant alternative viewpoints (see Chapter 25 for guidelines on addressing competing arguments).

- *Not using misleading, deceptive, or false information.* Manipulating information to achieve a particular purpose is unethical, as are any attempts to deceive an audience by misrepresentation, omission, or the manufacture of data (see Chapter 8 for more on the ethical use of statistics). Ethically, you are required to support your points truthfully and accurately.

- *Acknowledging sources.* Acknowledging sources is an essential aspect of ethical speechmaking. To do otherwise is to commit plagiarism (discussed later in this chapter).

RESPECT

A shorthand definition for **respect** is "treating people right." For the ethical speaker, respect means addressing audience members as unique human beings and refraining from rudeness and other forms of personal attack.

- *Focus on issues rather than on personalities.* Civil disagreement is quite appropriate in a speech. Personal attacks on the character of those with whom you disagree are not.

- *Allow the audience the power of rational choice.* Audiences deserve to hear information in a way that permits them to exercise the power of rational choice. Sensationalist or lurid appeals rob people of this power. In most cases, it's not necessary to use graphic pictures or upsetting verbal descriptions just to make a point.

- *Avoid in-group and out-group distinctions.* Each of us wants to feel included. One of the most unethical things a public speaker can do is make some members of the audience feel excluded or, worse, victimized. Promoting such distinctions violates the universal rule of avoiding harm to others.

On a practical level, one simple thing you can do to make audience members feel included is maintain eye contact. This assures people that they aren't seen as passive objects but as unique human beings. (Preferences for eye contact do vary by culture, so be certain to consider your audience.) In addition, try to use language that everyone can understand. Avoid using **jargon**, or specialized terminology, if the terms are unfamiliar to even a small segment of the audience.

A serious ethical breach is the expression of ethnocentrism, stereotypes, or outright prejudice in a speech. **Ethnocentrism** is the belief that the ways of your culture are superior to those of other cultures. Speakers who exhibit ethnocentrism act as though everyone shares their point of view and points of reference, whether or not this is the case. They may tell jokes that require a certain context or refer only to their own customs. Ethical speakers, by contrast, assume differences and address them respectfully. The mistake of generalizing about an apparent characteristic of a group and applying that generalization to all of its members is another serious affront to people's dignity. When such racial, ethnic, gender, or other **stereotypes** roll off the speaker's tongue, they pack a wallop of indignation and pain for the people to whom they refer.

Hate speech is the ultimate vehicle for promoting in-group and out-group distinctions. Hate speech is any offensive communication—verbal or nonverbal—that is directed against people's racial, ethnic, religious, gender, or other characteristics. Racist, sexist, or ageist slurs, gay bashing, and cross burnings are all forms of hate speech.

Ethically Speaking
Campus Life: Free Speech versus Hate Speech

U.S. colleges and universities have long been at the center of the debate over what constitutes free speech versus hate speech. On the one side are those who resist censorship of any kind, often in support of the constitutional rights of the First Amendment. On the other side are advocates of hate speech codes and policies that limit what students and faculty can and cannot say and do; these advocates argue that such codes are necessary to ensure a tolerant and safe environment.

In the 1980s and early 1990s, more than three hundred schools instituted hate speech codes prohibiting certain forms of offensive speech and acts that were deemed intimidating or hostile to individuals or groups.[1] Many of these codes were later found to be unconstitutional, but anti-harassment policies designed to do much the same thing remain in place today.[2] These, along with federal laws designed to protect students from a hostile learning environment, allow administrators to punish students and faculty for what they judge to be offensive speech. Some universities limit student protests and demonstrations to designated areas on campus called "free speech zones." In several instances students have sued university officials over this policy, arguing that such zones infringe on students' First Amendment rights.

Hate speech codes and policies raise important ethical questions. Supporters of such policies claim that they are necessary to protect students from intimidation. Detractors argue that limits on free speech prevent students with unpopular or politically incorrect views from freely expressing themselves. As Kermit L. Hall, president of Utah State University, has written:

> Free speech at public universities and colleges is at once the most obvious and the most paradoxical of constitutional principles. It is obvious because given the nature of academic inquiry, only an open, robust and critical environment for speech will support the quest for truth. At the same time, universities are at once communities that must balance the requirements of free speech with issues of civility, respect and human dignity. They are also part and parcel of the larger social order with its own, often competing set of values.[3]

What do you think?

1. Markkula Center for Applied Ethics Web site, "The Price of Free Speech: Campus Hate Speech Codes," from *Issues on Ethics* 5, no. 2 (Summer 1992), **http://www.scu.edu/SCU/Centers/Ethics/publications/iie/v5n2/codes.html** (accessed June 26, 2002).

2. David L. Hudson, "Hate Speech and Campus Speech Codes," First Amendment Center Web site, **http://www.firstamendmentcenter.org** (accessed February 8, 2005).

3. Kermit L. Hall, "Free Speech on Public College Campuses," First Amendment Center Web site, **http://www.firstamendmentcenter.org** (accessed February 8, 2005).

RESPONSIBILITY

Because communication is a strong tool for influencing people — even one message has the potential to change people's lives — it must be approached responsibly. When preparing a speech, consider the following:

- *Topic and purpose.* Will learning about your topic in some way benefit your listeners? Are your overall speech aims socially constructive? What effect will your speech have on your listeners? (See Chapter 7 for more on selecting an ethical topic and purpose.)

- *Evidence and reasoning.* Are your arguments sound? Have you examined them critically? Sloppy evidence and reasoning distort the truth.

- *Accuracy.* Is the content of your message accurate? Are the facts correct? Accuracy is a hallmark of ethical speaking.

- *Honest use of emotional appeals.* Using emotional appeals supported by facts is a legitimate way for a speaker to achieve his or her goal (see Chapter 24). However, using emotional appeals as a crutch when your argument is weak on evidence or facts is a breach of ethics.

Public Speaking in Cultural Perspective
Comparing Cultural Values

Do the criteria for an ethical speaker outlined in this chapter—that is, displaying the qualities of trustworthiness, respect, responsibility, and fairness—apply equally in different cultures? For example, does telling the truth always take precedence over other qualities, such as being eloquent or protecting the interests of your clan or group? Are ethical standards for speeches merely a product of a particular culture? What about the concept of plagiarism? In the United States, speakers who fail to acknowledge their sources meet with harsh criticism and often suffer severe consequences, even if, as in the case of a recent college president (see p. 58), the speaker is otherwise highly respected. Is this universally true? Can you think of examples in which ideas of ethical speech expressed in this chapter are not necessarily shared by other cultures? Do you personally hold values for ethical speech that are different from those cited here?

✓ CHECKLIST

Self-Assessment: An Ethical Inventory

_____ 1. Do I distort any information to make my point?

_____ 2. Do I acknowledge each of my sources?

_____ 3. Does my speech focus on issues rather than on personalities?

_____ 4. Do I try to foster a sense of inclusion?

_____ 5. Is my topic socially constructive?

_____ 6. Is the content of my message as accurate as I can make it?

_____ 7. Whenever appropriate, do I acknowledge alternative and opposing views so that my audience can make informed decisions?

FAIRNESS

Few subjects are black and white; rarely is there only one right or wrong way to view a topic. Fairness is ensured when you make a genuine effort to see all sides of an issue and to be open-minded. Using only information that helps your case is unfair to listeners because it prevents them from making informed decisions.[13] Speakers who do so also betray a lack of sensitivity to other people's values and moral stances.

Plagiarism

To their everlasting regret, more than one otherwise honorable speaker has succumbed to the pressure of creating a moving speech by appropriating someone else's ideas or words. For example, in the fall of 2002, Eugene Tobin, a historian and the president of Hamilton College, stepped down after admitting that he failed to credit his sources in his speeches. The plagiarism came to light after a faculty member pointed out similarities in Tobin's words and those of a book reviewer at Amazon.com. Tobin issued an apology for "the omissions that resulted from the way I develop and present my speeches."[14]

Crediting sources is a crucial aspect of any speech. **Plagiarism**—the passing off of another person's information as one's own—is unethical. To plagiarize is to use other people's ideas or words without acknowledging the source. **Wholesale plagiarism** occurs when you simply cut-and-paste material from print or online sources into your speech and represent it as your own. **Patchwrite plagiarism** is copying material into your speech draft from a source and then changing or rearranging words and sentence structures here and there to make the material appear as if it were your own.[15]

Whether it's done intentionally or not, plagiarism in any form is stealing and is a serious breach of ethics. Plagiarism is also an act of disrespect for the provenance of someone else's work. It violates the tenets of academic integrity. When you present plagiarized material as your own, you abuse the trust that an audience places in you. One of the consequences of plagiarism is a loss of the positive *ethos,* or credibility, that you must establish with audience members. More than any other single action, acknowledging sources lets listeners know that you are trustworthy and will represent both fact and opinion fairly and responsibly.

RULES FOR AVOIDING PLAGIARISM

The basic rule for avoiding plagiarism as a public speaker is straightforward: *Any source that requires credit in written form should be acknowledged in oral form.* These include direct quotations, paraphrased information, facts, statistics, and most other kinds of information that was gathered and reported by someone other than yourself. For each source, plan on alerting audience members to the following:

1. *Type of source* (e.g., magazine, book, personal interview, or Web site)
2. *Author or origin of the source* (e.g., "In a documentary on New York produced by Ken Burns . . ." or "On the National Science Foundation Web site . . .")
3. *Title or description of the source* (e.g., "In *Endangered Minds,* author Jane Healy . . ." or "In an article on sharks . . .")
4. *Publication date of the source* (e.g., "In an article on sharks published in the October 10, 2005, issue of *Oceanography* . . .")

Oral presentations need not include full bibliographic references (including full names, dates, titles, and volume and page numbers). However, you should include complete references in a bibliography or works cited list or at the end of the speech outline. (For detailed guidelines on creating a bibliography or list of works cited for a speech, see Chapters 8, 9, 10, and Appendices F–J.)

Orally Credit Direct Quotations

Direct quotations are statements quoted verbatim, or word for word, from a source. Direct quotes should always be acknowledged in a speech. Although it is not a requirement, you can call attention to a source's exact wording with phrases such as "And I quote" and "As [the source] put it." For example:

> As my esteemed colleague Dr. Vance Brown told an audience of AIDS researchers at the International AIDS Convention last year, *and I quote,* "The cure may be near or it may be far, but the human suffering is very much in the present."
>
> *As Shakespeare would say,* "A rose by any other name would smell as sweet."

CHECKLIST

Plagiarism Check

To avoid plagiarism, you must acknowledge:
- ✓ Other people's ideas, opinions, and theories
- ✓ Other people's evidence
- ✓ Other people's research
- ✓ Direct quotations
- ✓ Paraphrased information
- ✓ Facts and statistics gathered from any source other than your own research

Orally Credit Paraphrased Information

A **paraphrase** is a restatement of someone else's ideas, opinions, or theories in the speaker's own words.[16] Because paraphrases alter the form but not the substance of another person's ideas, the speaker must acknowledge the original source. After all, they are not the speaker's ideas. For example:

> *According to John Slater, a teacher at the Cranberry Middle School in New York,* students' increasing reliance on the Internet as a research tool will only result in more cases of plagiarism. *Slater sees* a trend in which students equate cyberspace with "free." Unless we address the issue at the grade-school level, *Slater says,* we risk raising a generation of plagiarizers.

 CHECKLIST

Steps to Avoid Plagiarism

1. Know how to quote, paraphrase, and summarize sources.
2. Keep track of your sources as you collect them.
3. Learn how to keep track of and cite Internet sources (see Chapter 10).
4. Create a system for tracking sources, such as using the footnote feature in Microsoft Word.

Orally Credit Facts and Statistics

The source for any data that was not gathered by you should be cited in your speech. You don't have to cite **common knowledge** — information that is likely to be known by many people, but such information must truly be widely disseminated. For example, it is common knowledge that terrorists flew two planes into the World Trade Center towers on September 11, 2001. It is not common knowledge that the towers were, respectively, 1,368 and 1,362 feet high. These facts require acknowledgment of a source, in this case the Port Authority of New York and New Jersey, the owners of the World Trade Center.[17] The following three examples illustrate how you can orally acknowledge and cite facts and statistics in a speech.

> *According to the public information office of the Port Authority of New York and New Jersey, which owned the World Trade Center towers,* the towers were, respectively, 1,368 and 1,362 feet high. The Center was actually a complex of seven buildings on sixteen acres.

> *In a lecture on academic honesty, Grinnell College Professor Judy Hunter described* how two-thirds of the cases of plagiarism at the university resulted not because students deliberately sought to deceive their professors but from, *and I quote,* "a mistaken notion of the importance of citation."[18]

> *According to Tiffini Theisen, a reporter for the Orlando Sentinel,* about 4,200 pregnancy-discrimination complaints are filed every year with the U.S. Equal Employment Opportunity Commission and other agencies.

FAIR USE, COPYRIGHT, AND ETHICAL SPEAKING

Whether as a speaker in the classroom or outside of it, many of your presentations will include the use of one or more *presentation aids* (see Chapter 20). For example, in a speech about union organizer César Chávez you might include an audio clip of one of his speeches and a photograph of him in a PowerPoint slide. For a speech on Social Security, you might prepare charts based on data you found in a print or online magazine. How do you determine when and if you must seek permission to use these and other materials in your speech?

Copyright is a legal protection afforded original creators of literary and artistic works, including musical, dramatic, choreographic, pictorial, graphic, sculptural, audiovisual, and architectural works.[19] For any work created since 1978, the copyright is good for the author's life plus fifty years. After that time the work is considered to be within the **public domain**, and anyone may reproduce it. Not subject to copyright are federal (but *not* state or local) government publications, common knowledge, and select other categories.

When a work is copyrighted, you may not reproduce, distribute, or display it without permission from the copyright holder or you will be liable for copyright infringement. As publishing attorney Steve Gillen explains:

> Copyright law concerns authorship or expression, i.e., words and images, not the underlying facts or ideas. . . . Facts, statistics, and concepts can be recited without permission [though failure to cite the source for them constitutes plagiarism unless they are common knowledge]. What you cannot do is copy or plagiarize the original or creative manner in which the original data was expressed.[20]

Copyright laws are designed to protect **intellectual property** — the ownership of an individual's creative expression. Exceptions to copyright restrictions exist, however, and these exceptions are particularly relevant to student speakers. The **Fair Use Doctrine** permits the limited use of copyrighted works without permission for the purposes of scholarship, criticism, comment, news reporting, teaching, and research.[21] In terms of preparing speeches for the classroom, this means that you have much more latitude to use other people's creative work (*with* credit in all cases) without seeking their permission. For example, as long as you acknowledged your source, you could use a song from 50 Cent's CD as part of an in-class presentation. However, if you were to include the same track when speaking in a public forum, and particularly if you were a paid professional speaker, your speech would be considered a **public performance**, and you would need to obtain a performance license from a performing rights society such as ASCAP (American Society of Composers, Authors and Publishers).

If you accompany your speech with tables and charts, the same principles of fair use apply. Bear in mind, however, that while the data within a table or chart may not be copyrighted, its particular visual arrangement usually is.[22] Thus, you must accurately credit both the *source of the data* as well as the *creator of its graphic display*. Suppose that for a speech on women in the sciences you locate a graph in *Time* magazine that visually illustrates the percentage of men versus women who receive Ph.D.s in the sciences and engineering. The source of the data is a federal government agency, which falls within the public domain. However, as the creator of the graph, *Time* magazine owns the copyright for this particular display of the data.

The long and short of it? If you are a professional public speaker who makes use of copyrighted materials in your speeches, you must obtain copyright clearance. For speeches created for onetime use in the classroom or for other nonprofit, educational purposes, accurately crediting your sources will often suffice. (For more on copyright, visit the U.S. Copyright Office online at www .copyright.gov.)

PLAGIARISM ON THE INTERNET

The rules for copyright and fair use apply equally to print and online sources; thus failure to accurately credit online sources is plagiarism. As with print sources, direct quotations, paraphrased information, facts, statistics, or other information that was gathered and reported by someone other than yourself must be accurately credited. This includes information obtained from Web sites, electronic publications, mailing lists, newsgroups, and online databases. (For specific guidelines on acknowledging Internet sources, see Chapter 10 and Appendices F–J. For additional direction on orally crediting sources of various types, see Chapter 8, "Developing Supporting Material.")

Managing Speech Anxiety 5

Nothing in life is to be feared. It is only to be understood.
                                        –Marie Curie

For many of us public speaking tops the list of things we fear. According to one study, at least 75 percent of students in public speaking courses approach the course with anxiety, while some other surveys show public speaking to be the number-one fear, mentioned more often than death at number two.[1] Even accomplished speakers often feel jittery before they give a speech. It turns out that feeling nervous is not only normal but desirable. "Of course I was nervous," baseball great Lou Gehrig replied when asked if he was anxious about coming to bat in the ninth inning. "If I wasn't, I couldn't have hit that double off the wall."[2]

Channeled properly, nervousness can boost performance. The difference between seasoned public speakers and the rest of us is not that the seasoned speakers don't feel nervous or anxious. It's just that they're more practiced at making it work *for* rather than against them. They've also mastered specific techniques that help them cope with and minimize their tension.

What Makes Speakers Anxious?

Researchers have identified several factors that underlie the fear of addressing an audience.[3] These include lack of public speaking experience (or having previously had a negative public speaking experience), feeling different from members of the audience, and uneasiness about being the center of attention. Each factor can lead to the onset of **public speaking anxiety (PSA)** — that is, fear or anxiety associated with either actual or anticipated communication to an audience as a speaker.[4]

LACK OF POSITIVE EXPERIENCE

Anxious anticipation is a natural reaction to new experiences, especially those that are challenging or complex. For those who have had no public speaking experience, anxiety about what to expect is only natural. And with no experience to fall back on, it's hard to put these anxieties in perspective. It's a bit of a vicious circle. Some people react by deciding to avoid making speeches altogether. Unfortunately, although they avoid the anxiety of speechmaking, they also lose out on the considerable rewards it brings. Lack of experience may be particularly hard on females. One study found that female executives experience markedly higher levels of speech anxiety (42 percent) than their male counterparts (15 percent) when they make only occasional speeches.[5]

Anxious anticipation also results from previous negative experiences with public speaking that led to unfavorable audience reactions. This can sometimes happen to inexperienced speakers when, for example, they lose track of their thoughts during a speech or misjudge audience expectations. Gaining more speaking experience provides opportunities to assess different kinds of audiences, to adapt to unexpected occurrences, and to self-evaluate each speech, thus providing more successful speech experiences and more confidence.

FEELING DIFFERENT

Novice speakers often feel alone — as if they were the only person ever to experience the dread of public speaking. Moreover, the prospect of getting up in front of an audience makes them extra-sensitive to their personal idiosyncrasies, such as a less-than-perfect haircut, a slight lisp, or thinking that no one could possibly be interested in anything they have to say.

As novice speakers, we become anxious because we assume that being different somehow means being inferior. Actually, everyone is different from everyone else in many ways. Just as true, nearly everyone experiences nervousness about giving a speech.

BEING THE CENTER OF ATTENTION

Speakers often comment about how audience members appear to behave toward them during a speech. Listeners might fail to make eye contact with the speaker, converse with one another during a speech, or point at the speaker. When this

---

✓ **CHECKLIST**

Recognizing and Overcoming Your Underlying Fears about Public Speaking

Problem	Solution
✓ Does a lack of public speaking experience intimidate you?	Prepare and practice rehearsing your speech at least several times. Do it in front of at least one other person. This way, you'll feel more confident that you have experience with your present speech.
✓ Do you worry about appearing different to others?	Remember that everyone is different from everyone else in many ways. Dress well, be well groomed, and trust that you will make a good impression.
✓ Do you dread being the center of attention?	Remind yourself that the audience won't notice anything about you that you don't want to reveal, especially if your speech is well planned and rehearsed. Put the focus on the speech instead of on yourself.

occurs, our tendency is to think that we must be doing something inappropriate; then we wonder what's wrong and whether the entire audience has noticed it.

This kind of thinking builds rapidly and, left unchecked, can distract us from the speech itself, with all our attention now focused on "me." As we focus on "me," we become all the more sensitive to things that might be wrong with what we're doing—and that makes us feel even more conspicuous, which increases our anxiety. In actuality (and ironically), an audience notices very little about us that we don't want to reveal, especially when the speech is well developed and effectively delivered. Consequently, there is no good reason to be anxious about being the center of attention. You see yourself more critically than the audience does, so relax and focus on delivering your message.

Pinpointing the Onset of Public Speaking Anxiety

Different people become anxious at different times during the speechmaking process. For some people PSA arises as soon as they learn that they will have to give a speech at some point in the future. For others it arises as they approach the podium. Research suggests that females may experience higher anxiety than males at all stages of the speechmaking process.[6] As such, it is particularly important that they experiment with the anxiety-reducing techniques described in this section. Figure 5.1 illustrates the different points during the speechmaking process at which PSA can occur.[7]

PRE-PREPARATION ANXIETY

Some people feel anxious the minute they know they will be giving a speech. **Pre-preparation anxiety** at this early stage can have several negative consequences. First, depending on its severity, the person may be reluctant to begin planning for the speech. Second, it can preoccupy the person to such an extent

Figure 5.1 Where Anxiety Can Occur in the Speechmaking Process

that he or she misses vital information that is required to fulfill the speech assignment.

PREPARATION ANXIETY

For a minority of people, anxiety arises only when they actually begin to prepare for the speech. At that point they might feel overwhelmed at the amount of time and planning required. They might hit a roadblock that puts them behind schedule, or they might be unable to locate adequate support for a critical point. These kinds of preparation pressures produce a vicious circle of more stress, avoidance of the process, and procrastination—all of which contributes to **preparation anxiety**. Research has shown, however, that for the great majority of people, anxiety is lowest during the preparation phase.[8]

PRE-PERFORMANCE ANXIETY

Some people experience anxiety when they rehearse their speech. At this point, the reality of the situation sets in: Soon they will face an audience of people who will be watching and listening only to them. As they rehearse, they may also realize that their ideas don't sound as focused or as interesting as they should. Knowing that time is short, they begin to get nervous. If this **pre-performance anxiety** is strong enough, and is interpreted negatively, they may even decide to stop rehearsing.

PERFORMANCE ANXIETY

For the majority of people, anxiety levels tend to be highest just before speaking begins.[9] This is true even of celebrities, who report that their worst stage fright occurs just as they walk onstage to begin their performances. **Performance anxiety** in speechmaking is probably most pronounced during the introduction phase of the speech. This is when the speaker utters the first words of the speech and is most cognizant of the audience's attention. In fact, the speaker's perceptions of the audience are important here—an audience perceived to be hostile or negative usually elicits higher anxiety in the speaker than either positive or neutral audiences.[10] However, experienced speakers agree that if they control their nervousness during the introduction, the rest of the speech comes relatively easily.

Strategies for Getting Started with Confidence

Depending on when it strikes, the consequences of public speaking anxiety can include everything from procrastination to poor speech performance. The important thing to remember is to manage your anxiety and not let it manage you—by harming your motivation or by causing you to avoid investing the time and energy required to prepare and deliver a successful speech. The first step in effective management of speech anxiety involves planning and practicing your speech.

ESL Speaker's Notes
Confidence and Culture: When English Isn't Your First Language

In addition to the normal fear of being at center stage, non-native speakers of English face the burden of worrying about delivering a speech in a non-native language. If English is your first language, remind yourself of how difficult it would be for you to deliver a speech in another language. As you listen to a non-native speaker, place yourself in his or her shoes. If necessary, politely ask questions for clarification.

If you are a non-native speaker of English, try to think about public speaking as an opportunity to learn more about the English language and how to use it. As you listen to your classmates' speeches, for example, you will gain exposure to spoken English. Practicing your speech will give you time to work on any accent features you want to improve.[1] In addition, by spending time writing and outlining your speech, you will gain confidence in your written language skills.

Throughout this text there are exercises that you may find useful. You can practice some of them while rehearsing your speeches. Some can be done alone, and others during conversations with friends. Here are a few to get you started. Native English speakers can also use the following tips:

1. Take your time and speak slowly as you introduce the purpose and the main points of your speech. This will give your listeners time to get used to your voice and to focus on your message.

2. You may already be aware of certain English words that you have trouble saying. Practice saying these words five times. Pause. Then say the words again, five times. Progress slowly until the word becomes clearer and easier to pronounce.

3. Avoid using words that you don't really have to use, such as some kinds of jargon (see Chapter 16 and the Glossary). Learn to use a thesaurus to find *synonyms,* or words that mean the same thing, that are simpler and easier to pronounce.

4. Offer words from your native language as a way of drawing attention to a point you're making. This helps the audience appreciate your native language and your accent. For example, the Spanish word *corazón* has a more lyrical quality than its English counterpart *heart.* Capitalize on the beauty of your native tongue.

Remember, practicing oral English is the surest way to master it.

1. J. E. Flege, J. M. Munro, and I. R. A. MacKay, "Factors Affecting Strength of Perceived Foreign Accent in a Second Language," *Journal of the Acoustical Society of America* 97 (1995), 3125ff.

PREPARE AND PRACTICE

There's nothing magical about gaining confidence in public speaking—except, of course, the glow of accomplishment that sets in after the hard work is done and the speech is over. Confidence comes with knowing what you're doing, and the surest route is through preparation and practice. If you are confident that you know your material and have adequately rehearsed your delivery, you're far more likely to feel confident at the podium than otherwise. Thus preparation

✓ CHECKLIST

Preparation and Practice Check

Note the date each item is started and completed. Place a check mark in the space at the front of each item to indicate its completion.

Activity	Date Started	Date Completed
When did I receive the assignment? When will I complete it?		
_____ In advance of preparing my speech, have I planned what I need to do and where I need to get it done?	_____	_____
_____ Have I selected an appropriate speech topic and purpose?	_____	_____
_____ When will I need to spend time in the library?	_____	_____
_____ When will I need to work on a computer?	_____	_____
_____ Have I tried to discover as much information as possible about the audience and the speaking environment? (See Chapter 6.)	_____	_____
_____ Have I allowed enough time to thoroughly research the material required to support my key points? (See Chapters 8–10.)	_____	_____
_____ Have I organized and outlined main and supporting points? (See Chapters 11–13.)	_____	_____
_____ Have I rehearsed delivering my speech, beginning two or three days prior to the speech date? (See Chapters 17–19.)	_____	_____
_____ Have I planned and constructed any necessary presentation aids? (See Chapters 20–22.)	_____	_____
_____ Am I confident that I know how I want to express myself?	_____	_____
_____ Have I checked out the site where I will be speaking?	_____	_____
_____ Have I made sure that any audiovisual equipment I plan to use is in good working order?	_____	_____

should begin as soon as possible after a speech is assigned. Once you have prepared the speech, you should rehearse it several times.

MODIFY THOUGHTS AND ATTITUDES

Negative thoughts increase speech anxiety.[11] Maintaining a positive attitude toward speechmaking, however, results in lowered heart rate and reduced anxiety during delivery of the speech.[12] Thus, as you prepare for and deliver your speech, it's important to regard it as a valuable, worthwhile, and challenging activity.

Remind yourself of all the reasons that public speaking is helpful personally, socially, and professionally. The point is to think positively about public speaking and to remind yourself that it is an opportunity, not a threat. One communication researcher has shown that altering one's thinking about public speaking from a "performance orientation" to a "communication orientation" can significantly increase confidence.[13] Rather than thinking of your speech as a formal performance or event in which you will be judged and evaluated, try thinking of it as an extension of an ordinary conversation. By doing so, you will feel less threatened and more relaxed about the process. And with each successive speech experience, your mind-set about public speaking will grow more positive.

VISUALIZE SUCCESS

Visualization is a highly successful way to reduce nervousness and help you prepare effectively for your speech.[14] Speech communication professors at Washington State University have been working for several years to develop visualization techniques for increasing positive expectations associated with speechmaking.[15] Below is their script for visualizing success on a public speaking occasion. The exercise requires you, the speaker, to close your eyes and visualize a series of positive feelings and reactions that will occur on the day of your speech.

> Practicing the mental exercise of seeing yourself give a successful speech will help you prepare with confidence and strengthen your positive attitudes and expectations for speechmaking.
>
> Close your eyes and allow your body to get comfortable in the chair in which you are sitting. Move around until you feel that you are in a position that will continue to be relaxing for you for the next ten to fifteen minutes. Take a deep, comfortable breath and hold it . . . now slowly release it through your nose. Now take another deep breath and make certain that you are breathing from the diaphragm . . . hold it . . . now slowly release it and note how you feel while doing this. Now one more deep breath . . . hold it . . . and release it slowly . . . and begin your normal breathing pattern. Shift around if you need to get comfortable again.
>
> Now begin to visualize the beginning of a day in which you are going to give an informative speech. See yourself getting up in the morning, full of energy, full of confidence, looking forward to the day's challenges. You are putting on just the right clothes for the task at hand that day. Dressing well makes you look and feel good about yourself, so you have on just what you want to wear, which clearly expresses your sense of inner well-being. As you are driving, riding, or walking to the speech setting, note how clear and confident you feel, and how others around you, as you arrive, comment positively regarding your fine appearance and general demeanor. You feel thoroughly prepared for the target issue you will be presenting today.
>
> Now you see yourself standing or sitting in the room where you will present your speech, talking very comfortably and confidently with others in the room. The people to whom you will be presenting your speech appear to be quite friendly, and are very cordial in their greetings and conversations prior to the presentation. You feel absolutely sure of your material and of your ability to present the information in a forceful, convincing, positive manner.

Now you see yourself approaching the area from which you will present. You are feeling very good about this presentation and see yourself move eagerly forward. All of your audiovisual materials are well organized, well planned, and clearly aid your presentation.[16]

USE RELAXATION TECHNIQUES

Relaxation techniques are to public speaking anxiety what warm-ups are to exercise. Just as you would warm up before taking a lengthy jog, you should practice relaxation techniques before — and even during — your speech. The goal is to feel a sense of control over the physiological reactions you're experiencing, keeping in mind that physiological changes are normal. According to public speaking experts Laurie Schloff and Marcia Yudkin,[17] the following techniques will lessen anxiety before and during a speech.

Stress-Control Breathing

When you feel stressed, the center of your breathing tends to move from the abdomen to the upper chest, leaving you with a reduced supply of air. The chest and shoulders rise, and you feel out of breath. With *stress-control breathing*, you will feel more movement in the stomach than in the chest. Try stress-control breathing in two stages.

Stage One. Inhale air and let your abdomen go out. Exhale air and let your abdomen go in. Do this for a while until you get into the rhythm of it.

Stage Two. As you inhale, use a soothing word such as *calm* or *relax*, or a personal mantra, as follows: "Inhale *calm*, abdomen out, exhale *calm*, abdomen in." Go slowly. Each inhalation and exhalation of stress-control breathing takes about three to five seconds.

Begin practicing stress-control breathing several days before you're scheduled to speak. Then, once the speaking event arrives, begin stress-control breathing while awaiting your turn at the podium. (You can even place your hand on your abdomen unobtrusively to check how you're doing.) After you've been called to the podium, you can focus on breathing once more while you're arranging your notes and getting ready to begin.

Natural Gestures

Practice some controlled, natural gestures that might be useful in enhancing your speech, such as holding up your index finger when stating your first main point. Think about what you want to say as you do this, instead of thinking about how you look or feel. (See Chapters 2 and 19 for tips on practicing natural gestures.)

Move as You Speak

You don't have to stand perfectly still behind the podium when you deliver a speech. Walk around as you make some of your points. Movement relieves tension and helps hold the audience's attention.

LEARN FROM THE SPEECH EVALUATION

Evaluation helps you identify needed improvements and problems to avoid in what you do. You can learn a lot by evaluating your own behavior, but relying on the objective evaluations of others often is even more helpful because self-evaluations tend to be distorted.[18] For instance, your physician evaluates your physical condition to identify your healthy living choices or your need to make adjustments for healthier living. Although no one likes to feel evaluated, it is a necessary part of a speech class; inevitably, your speech assignments will be evaluated by your instructors and probably by your classmates as well. Whether the evaluation is formal (i.e., written and graded) or informal, it's easy but not necessary to take it personally

First, your instructor and your classmates don't know everything about you; they know only how you've presented a speech. Second, if that speech is planned and delivered well, your listeners will be most aware of your message, not of you personally. That is the way it should be in any good speech. After all, the audience is there to evaluate the information you've presented. Audience members will be deciding whether the information is relevant and accurate and interesting. Your concern as a speaker should be with the audience's evaluation of your message, not of you as a person. Your classmates and instructor will provide practical feedback to help you do better in your next speech. Using their evaluations is part of learning to be an effective speaker.

 CHECKLIST

Steps in Gaining Confidence

- ✓ Prepare and practice often.
- ✓ Modify thoughts and attitudes—think positively.
- ✓ Accept your nervousness as normal—work with it rather than against it.
- ✓ Concentrate on your message, not on yourself.
- ✓ Visualize success.
- ✓ Use relaxation techniques.
- ✓ Anticipate learning from the speech evaluation.
- ✓ Enjoy the occasion.

ENJOY THE OCCASION

Although no one can be forced to enjoy something, most people ultimately find that giving speeches can indeed be fun. It's satisfying and empowering to influence people, and a good speech is a sure way to accomplish that goal. Preparation and practice, maintaining a positive attitude, managing the inevitable stress of public speaking by making it work for you, and visualizing success—all of this makes public speaking both challenging and exciting. Think of it in these terms, and chances are it will come out that way.

Audience Analysis and Topic Selection

Audience Analysis and Topic Selection

Speaker's Reference
Audience Analysis and Topic Selection

6. Analyzing the Audience

Learn about Your Audience and Adapt Your Message Accordingly

- Identify what your audience needs and wants to know. (p. 78)
- Show audience members why the topic should interest them. (p. 78)

Evaluate Audience Attitudes toward the Topic

- Adjust your approach depending on whether they have positive, negative, or neutral attitudes. (p. 79)
- Enhance a sense of identification between you and your listeners. (p. 81)
- Seek common ground. (p. 81)

Anticipate Audience Expectations of the Speech Occasion

- Adjust your speech to the occasion. (p. 81)
- Adjust your speech when addressing a captive audience. (p. 81)

Address the Age Range of Your Audience

- Offer examples they will recognize and find relevant. (p. 82)

Be Sensitive to the Ethnic and Cultural Composition of Your Audience

- Be alert to differences in values and try to address them sensitively. (p. 83)
- Beware of ethnocentrism. (p. 85)

Consider the Socioeconomic Status of Your Audience

- Know that personal attitudes, beliefs, and goals are closely tied to occupational status. (p. 85)
- Use examples that are appropriate to the audience's level of sophistication and education. (p. 86)

Consider Religious and Political Affiliations

- Identify potential religious sensitivities and tread sensitively. (p. 86)
- To the extent possible, gauge the audience's degree of political involvement and tread sensitively. (p. 86)

Consider How the Audience Breaks Down along Gender Lines

- Base any assumptions about gender differences on carefully considered evidence. (p. 87)
- Avoid judgments based on gender stereotypes and avoid sexist language. (p. 87)

Gather Information about Your Audience from a Variety of Sources

- Consider interviewing a representative of the audience. (p. 88)
- For classroom speeches, consider questionnaires or instant polls. (p. 88)
- Look for information about the audience in published sources, such as company Web sites, brochures, articles, and other related materials. (p. 91)

Investigate the Logistics of the Speech Setting

- Find out in advance what the physical setting will be like. (p. 92)
- Plan appropriately for the length of your speech, and be on time. (p. 92)
- Learn about the seating arrangement and where you will be placed. (p. 92)

7. Selecting a Topic and Purpose

Be Aware That Speech Topics May or May Not Be Assigned

Select from the Three General Speech Purposes

- Use an informative speech to increase audience understanding and awareness. (p. 95)
- Use a persuasive speech to effect change in audience attitudes, beliefs, values, or behavior. (p. 96)
- Use a special occasion speech when the specific event calls for entertainment, celebration, commemoration, inspiration, or setting a social agenda. (p. 97)

Consider Various Approaches to Selecting Your Topic

- Rely on your own interests. (p. 97)
- Survey current events. (p. 98)
- Consider controversial and community issues. (p. 99)
- Avoid overused topics and rely instead on your own expertise. (p. 99)

Try Brainstorming to Generate Ideas

- Use lists and word association. (p. 100)
- Diagram your ideas on paper using a topic map. (p. 100)
- Use subject indexes at Internet search sites. (p. 101)

Narrow Your Topic and Purpose

- Narrow your topic to align with time constraints, audience expectations, and the occasion. (p. 101)
- Use action terms to develop your specific purpose. (p. 102)

Formulate the Thesis Statement

- State the thesis as a single, declarative sentence that poses the central idea of your speech. (p. 103)
- Use the thesis to help you develop main points. (p. 105)
- Make the thesis statement relevant and motivating by adding key words or phrases and considering audience interests. (p. 106)

KEY TERMS

Chapter 6

audience analysis	generational identity	gender
audience-centered approach	co-culture	gender stereotypes
pandering	individualistic cultures	sexist language
attitudes	collectivist cultures	interview
beliefs	uncertainty avoidance	questionnaire
values	high-uncertainty avoidance cultures	closed-ended question
perspective-taking		
identification	low-uncertainty avoidance cultures	fixed alternative question
captive audience		
demographics	power distance	scale question
target audience	ethnocentrism	open-ended question

Chapter 7

rhetorical situation	special occasion speech	specific speech purpose
general speech purpose	brainstorming	
informative speech	word association	thesis statement
persuasive speech	topic map	

6 Analyzing the Audience

Have you ever seen an advertisement that was so convincing that you made a mental note to purchase the product it described? What was it about the ad that made such an impression? Perhaps it advertised a pair of athletic shoes or a particular brand of clothing. Did the ad suggest that it could fulfill a need you had? Did it suggest an image that you wanted to adopt?

Advertisers are astute analysts when it comes to reading people's needs and wants. The best of them can closely target both our desires and our fears. In at least one sense, to make a successful speech or presentation you must function like an advertiser. To capture an audience's attention and bring your listeners to your point of view, you too must present a topic in ways that are meaningful to them. **Audience analysis** is the process of gathering and analyzing information about audience members *with the explicit aim of adapting your message to the information you uncover.* What are your listeners' views with respect to your topic? What do they need or want to know? How much do audience members have in common with one another? How familiar are they with the speech topic? What most concerns them about it?

Adapt to Audience Psychology

One of the most important lessons you can learn as a speaker is that people tend to evaluate messages in terms of their own — rather than the speaker's — attitudes, beliefs, and values. As a result, you are far more likely to truly engage your listeners' attention if you let their relevant interests and background guide you in constructing your speech.

Maintaining an **audience-centered approach** to all phases of the speech preparation process — from selection and treatment of the speech topic to making decisions about organization, language, and even method of delivery — allows you to communicate a message that will be meaningful to your audience. Being audience-centered does not mean that you must abandon your own convictions or cater to the audience's whims. This practice, called **pandering**, will only undermine your credibility in the eyes of the audience. Think of audience analysis as an opportunity to get to know and establish common ground with audience members, just as you might do with a new acquaintance.

IDENTIFYING LISTENERS' ATTITUDES, BELIEFS, AND VALUES

Your listeners' attitudes, beliefs, and values provide crucial clues to how receptive they will be toward your topic and your position on it. While we tend to use these three terms interchangeably, each reflects a distinct mental state that reveals a great deal about us.

Attitudes are our general evaluations of people, ideas, objects, or events.[1] To evaluate something is to judge it as relatively good or bad, useful or useless, desirable or undesirable, pretty or ugly, tasteful or tasteless, and so on. People generally act in accordance with their attitudes (although the degree to which they do so depends on many factors).[2] If listeners have a positive attitude toward reading, for example, they're likely to read and they're likely to want to listen to a speaker discuss books. If they have a negative attitude toward religion, chances are they'll avoid attending religious services — as well as speeches praising the value of religion.

Attitudes are based on **beliefs** — the ways in which people perceive reality.[3] They are our feelings about what is true. Whereas attitudes deal with the felt quality of some activity or entity ("Reading is good" or "God is good"), beliefs refer to our level of confidence about the very existence or validity of something ("I believe God exists" or "I'm not so sure that God exists"). The less faith listeners have that something exists — UFOs, for instance — the less open they are to hearing about it.

Both attitudes and beliefs are shaped by **values** — our most enduring judgments about what's good and bad in life, as shaped by our culture and our unique experiences within it. For some of us, the sanctity of marriage between a man and woman is a core value. For others, the value of social justice supersedes that of material comfort. Whatever the nature of our core values, they are central to our sense of who we are. Values are more general than either attitudes or beliefs. We have fewer of them than of either of the former, but we hold on to them more dearly. Values are also more resistant to change.

If you can determine your listeners' relevant core values, often you can determine what their attitudes may be with respect to your message. For example, if preserving nature is their highest ideal, your listeners will likely display negative attitudes toward unrestrained development. Consider the case of Naomi, an outreach health worker who was invited to speak at a clinic in a small town in the southwestern United States.

> Naomi's audience was a group of Mexican Americans who had been hospitalized for lead poisoning caused by drinking out of cups and bowls made from a certain kind of pottery. The clinic health workers, frustrated at their inability to convince the group to stop using the pottery, turned to Naomi because of her long background in working with this population. Naomi interviewed several of the patients at length and also consulted local healers. She discovered that the patients believed that drinking from the pottery enhanced fertility, a deeply held value. In her speech she acknowledged the group's belief, discussed alternate ways to enhance fertility in keeping with their values, and then argued that using the pottery posed too high a risk to their health.

IDENTIFYING LISTENERS' DISPOSITION TO THE TOPIC, SPEAKER, AND OCCASION

With any speech, it's important to try to uncover the audience's feelings and expectations or, for brevity's sake, *disposition* toward (1) the topic of your speech, (2) you as the speaker, and (3) the speech occasion. Such **perspective-taking** is critical in seeing things from your listeners' point of view.

Disposition toward the Topic

As a general rule, people give more interest and attention to topics toward which they have positive attitudes and that are in keeping with their values and beliefs. The less we know about something, the more indifferent we tend to be. One way to gauge an audience's attitudes toward a topic is by asking: What do listeners know about the topic? What is their level of interest? How do they feel about it? Then you can adjust the speech accordingly. Table 6.1 contains some general guidelines for addressing different types of audiences.

Disposition toward the Speaker

How audience members feel about you will have considerable bearing on their attentiveness and responsiveness to the message. A speaker who is well liked can gain at least an initial hearing by an audience even if the listeners are unsure of

TABLE 6.1 • Guidelines for Appealing to Different Types of Audiences

Type of Audience	Strategy
If listeners know *relatively little* about the topic . . .	Stick to the basics, explain the topic's relevance, and include background information. Steer clear of jargon, and define any unclear terms.
If the topic is *new to listeners* . . .	Tell them why the topic should interest them. Make the topic relevant by relating it to issues, events, people, or activities about which listeners already have positive attitudes.
If listeners hold *negative attitudes* toward the topic . . .	Focus on establishing rapport and credibility. Don't directly challenge listeners' attitudes; look instead for areas of agreement and move from there. Offer evidence from sources they are likely to accept in order to demonstrate why a negative attitude is unfounded, and then give good reasons for developing a positive attitude toward the topic.[1] (See Chapters 24 and 25 on persuasion.)
If listeners hold *positive attitudes* toward the topic . . .	Focus on telling a story with vivid and colorful language that reinforces listeners' attitudes.[2]
If listeners are a *captive audience* . . .	Analyze captive audience members as you would any other type, but be sensitive to situational factors. Why are they there? Pay close attention to the length of your speech, especially if other speakers precede and follow you. Focus on motivating the audience to pay attention to your topic.

1. James C. McCroskey, Virginia P. Richmond, and Robert A. Stewart, *One-on-One: The Foundations of Interpersonal Communication* (Englewood Cliffs, N.J.: Prentice-Hall, 1986), 76.

2. Herbert Simon, *Persuasion in Society* (Thousand Oaks, Calif.: Sage, 2001), 385–87.

what to expect in terms of the substance and quality of the message. Conversely, an audience that holds negative attitudes toward the speaker will disregard even the most important or interesting message. We tend to put up barriers against people whom we hold in low regard.

To create positive audience attitudes toward you (positive ethos), try to display the characteristics of a credible speaker described in Chapter 4. Look for ways to enhance a sense of **identification** between you and the audience. Listeners have a natural need to identify with the speaker and to feel that he or she shares their perceptions.[4] Creating a common bond with audience members by focusing on areas of agreement fosters identification. When speaking to an audience of abortion rights activists, for example, Senator Hillary Clinton called on opposing sides in the debate to find "common ground" by focusing on education and abstinence:

> We should all be able to agree that we want every child born in this country and around the world to be wanted, cherished, and loved. The best way to get there is to do more to educate the public about reproductive health, about how to prevent unsafe and unwanted pregnancies.[5]

Clinton clearly was attempting to reach out beyond her core constituency and achieve some measure of identification in a traditionally hostile camp.

Sharing a relevant personal story, emphasizing a shared role, and otherwise stressing mutual bonds all help create identification. Even your physical presentation can foster identification. We're more apt to identify with the speaker who dresses like us (or in a manner we aspire to) than with someone whose style and grooming seems strange or displeasing.

Disposition toward the Occasion

Depending on the occasion, people bring different sets of expectations and emotions to a speech event. Imagine attending your college graduation ceremonies. Your general feelings of joy and goodwill are likely to spill over to the commencement speaker, and unless he or she does quite poorly, you will probably enjoy the speech. In contrast, imagine being a businessperson, your third night away from home, tired from long hours of meetings, who must now attend the closing session of a conference and listen to company officers explain routine production charges for the coming fiscal year. You may have a less-than-stellar attitude toward this speech occasion. In contrast to the graduation ceremony, your presence at the business meeting is *a requirement of your job* — you must be there. Obviously, a **captive audience** will tend to present greater challenges than one that is voluntary (see Table 6.1 for tips on appealing to a captive audience).

Adapt to Audience Demographics

The audience's underlying attitudes, beliefs, and values provide many important clues to its profile, but by no means do they tell the entire story. As a public speaker, you are far more likely to sustain your listeners' attention and interest if you develop your speech with an understanding of certain markers, or demographic characteristics, about them. **Demographics** are the statistical characteristics of a given population. Six such characteristics are typically considered in an analysis of speech audiences: age, ethnic or cultural background, socioeconomic status (including income, occupation, and education), religious and political affiliations, and gender. Bear in mind that any number of other traits — for example, physical disability, place of residence, and group membership — may be important to investigate. This also holds true with regard to different cultures. In the African nation of Kenya, for instance, students report that rural/urban origin and literacy level are key demographic variables to consider when addressing an audience of Kenyans.[6]

Knowing where audience members fall in relation to audience demographics will help you identify your **target audience** — those individuals within the broader audience whom you are most likely to influence in the direction you seek. Consider, for example, a student preparing his or her first speech for a public speaking class at a community college. According to the American Association of Community Colleges, the average age of community college students is twenty-nine years. Students as young as sixteen attend classes alongside 40-year-olds. Fifty-four percent work full-time, and many are female single parents.[7] Community college students also bring a mix of diverse racial and ethnic characteristics to the classroom. How does your own classroom compare, and what is your target audience? Are you just as likely to engage a 40-year-old single mother of two school-aged children about the need for an all-volunteer military as the 19-year-old single male classmate sitting nearby?

AGE

Age can be a very important factor in determining how listeners will react to a topic. Each age group brings with it its own concerns and, broadly speaking, psychological drives and motivations. The quest for identity in adolescence (around the ages of 12–20), for example, differs markedly from the need to establish stable careers and relationships in early adulthood (ages 20–40). Similarly, adults in their middle years (40–65) tend to grapple with a full plate of issues related to career, children, aging parents, and an increased awareness of mortality. And as we age (65 and older), physical changes and changes in lifestyle (from work to retirement) assume greater prominence.

In addition to sharing the concerns associated with a given life stage, people of the same generation often share a familiarity with significant personages, local and world events, noteworthy popular culture, and so forth. Thus, bearing in mind the **generational identity** of your audience can help you evaluate your topic from an audience-centered perspective. Americans born in the United States in the 1950s, for example, are likely to retain vivid memories of John F. Kennedy's assassination as well as television shows such as *The Mickey Mouse Club* and *Gunsmoke*. If you mention these TV programs to younger people, however, chances are you'll draw blank stares. By the same token, most older people take little notice of today's popular youth figures or the current stars of rap, hip-hop, and Top 40 music.

ETHNIC OR CULTURAL BACKGROUND

An understanding of and a sensitivity to the ethnic and cultural composition of your listeners are also a key factor in delivering a successful—and ethical—speech. As a speaker in a multicultural and multiethnic society, you are all but certain to encounter a variety of audience members. Some may have a great deal in common with you. Others may be fluent in a language other than yours and must struggle to understand you. Still other members of the audience may belong to a distinct **co-culture**, a social community whose perspectives and style of communicating may or may not mesh with your own.

How might you prepare to speak in front of an ethnically and culturally diverse audience, including that of your classroom? In any speaking situation, your foremost concern should be to treat your listeners with dignity and to act with integrity. You do this by infusing your speech with the pillars of character described in Chapter 4: trustworthiness, respect, responsibility, and fairness. Since values form the basis of people's attitudes and actions, identifying the values of your listeners can help you to communicate with sensitivity and appeal to their interests and needs in an appropriate manner.

ADAPTING TO CULTURAL DIFFERENCES

When analyzing a diverse audience, especially one composed of people of different national origins (or of first-generation Americans), it can be helpful to consider your listeners' underlying cultural orientations. Geert Hofstede has identified the following four major cultural patterns or "value dimensions" as being significant across all cultures in varying degrees;[8] he then ranks forty countries in terms of how they compare on these dimensions.[9]

Individualism versus Collectivism.   **Individualistic cultures** tend to emphasize the needs of the individual rather than those of the group, upholding such values as individual achievement and decision making. In **collectivist cultures**, by contrast, personal identity, needs, and desires are viewed as secondary to those of the larger group. In Hofstede's analysis, the United States, Australia, Great Britain, and Canada rank highest on individualism. Venezuela, Peru, Taiwan, and Pakistan rank highest in collectivist characteristics.

High Uncertainty versus Low Uncertainty.   **Uncertainty avoidance** refers to the extent to which people feel threatened by ambiguity. **High-uncertainty avoidance cultures** tend to structure life more rigidly and formally for their members, while **low-uncertainty avoidance cultures** are more accepting of uncertainty in life and therefore allow more variation in individual behavior. Among the nations Hofstede investigated, Portugal, Greece, Peru, Belgium, and Japan rank highest in uncertainty avoidance; the United States, Sweden, Denmark, Ireland, and Norway rank lowest.

High Power Distance versus Low Power Distance.   **Power distance** is the extent to which a culture values social equality versus tradition and authority.

Cultures with *high levels of power distance* tend to be organized along more rigidly hierarchical lines, with greater emphasis placed on honoring authority. Those with *low levels of power distance* place a higher value on social equality. High power distance countries include India, Brazil, Singapore, Greece, Venezuela, and Mexico. Austria, Finland, Denmark, Norway, New Zealand, and Israel rank lowest on this dimension. The United States ranks somewhat above the midpoint range among the nations in Hofstede's survey.

Masculine versus Feminine. The *masculinity and femininity dimension* refers to the degree to which a culture values traits that it associates with masculinity and with femininity. Traditional masculine traits include ambition, assertiveness, performance, and overt displays of manliness. Feminine traits stress nurturance and cooperation. In Hofstede's analysis, Ireland, the Philippines, Greece, and South Africa ranked highest in masculinity, while Sweden, Norway, Finland, and Denmark ranked highest in femininity. The dominant values in the United States were weighted toward masculinity.

Practical Implications for Addressing Cultural Variations

These broad cultural patterns offer insights into the ways in which people may differ in their basic approach to life. For example, some members of an audience may believe that the wishes of parents and the family group must come

Public Speaking in Cultural Perspective
Cross-National Comparisons of Attitudes, Values, and Beliefs

Cross-national surveys can be extremely useful in learning about how values vary across cultures. Globally, the largest-scale cross-national surveys are the World Values Survey and those conducted by the International Social Survey Program (ISSP). Using representative national samples of at least one thousand individuals, the World Values Survey offers a fascinating look at the values and beliefs of people in sixty-six countries. Through this resource, available on the Web at **www.gesis.org/en/data_service/issp/search/index.htm**, you can discover how people of other nations feel about work, family, religion, and even who should do the housework.

The International Social Survey Program (**www.issp.org**) surveys thirty-nine nations on the following broad topics: environment, family and changing gender roles, national identity, religion, role of government, social inequality, social networks, and work orientations. Researchers pose the same series of questions to a representative sample in each of the thirty-nine member nations. For example: "What percentage of people believe that the Bible is the actual word of God?" In Great Britain, only 5 percent believe that it is, whereas in the United States, 30 percent hold this belief. To investigate attitudes, values, and beliefs related to your topic, go to the ISSP Web site and click on "Search in Codebooks and Question." Then insert a phrase or a key term (e.g., "belief in God"). A list of surveys that focus on your terms may appear; you can then examine the individual surveys.

ESL Speaker's Notes
Comparing Cultural Values

As you consider your own values, think about the influence of culture. Can you identify values that you hold but that your listeners probably will not share? What role does culture play in these values? Are there certain values your listeners are likely to hold that you do not share? What are these? Have you experienced clashes of values between yourself and others regarding what you believe to be good and bad, important and unimportant? As you think about your own values, the role culture plays in them, and the values of those around you, consider how you can use this information to develop a speech that will best express what you want to say.

before their own (e.g., those linked to cultures marked by collectivism) or that authority figures should be given great deference (e.g., those linked to cultures marked by high power distance).

Bear in mind that these patterns reflect the values of the *dominant culture;* they do not necessarily reflect the values of all the groups living within a society. Although individualism characterizes the dominant culture of the United States, for example, various co-cultures, such as Mexican Americans and, to varying degrees, African Americans, have been described as collectivist in nature.[10] Being alert to differences in values can help you avoid **ethnocentrism** and deliver your message in a culturally sensitive manner. The accompanying Public Speaking in Cultural Perspective box, "Cross-National Comparisons of Attitudes, Values, and Beliefs," offers additional suggestions on investigating attitudes, beliefs, and values across cultures; see also "Published Sources" on p. 91.

SOCIOECONOMIC STATUS

Socioeconomic status (SES) includes income, occupation, and education. Knowing roughly where an audience falls in terms of these key variables can be critical in effectively targeting your message.

Income

Income determines people's experiences on many levels. It directly affects how they are housed, clothed, and fed and determines what they can afford. Beyond this, income has a ripple effect, influencing many other aspects of life. For example, depending on income, health insurance is either a taken-for-granted budget item or an out-of-reach dream. The same is true for travel and leisure activities. Given how pervasively income affects people's life experiences, insight into this aspect of an audience's makeup can be quite important.

Occupation

In most speech situations, the occupation of audience members is an important and easily identifiable demographic characteristic that the speaker should try to determine in advance. The nature of people's work has a lot to do with what interests them. Occupational interests are tied to several other areas of social concern, such as politics, the economy, education, and social reform. Personal attitudes, beliefs, and goals are also closely tied to occupational standing.

Education

Level of education strongly influences people's ideas, perspectives, and range of abilities. For example, studies show that people who have a college education work in higher-status occupations and generally earn higher pay than do non-college graduates. A higher level of education, moreover, appears to be associated with greater fluctuation in personal values, beliefs, and goals. In other words, people with higher levels of education may be more open to changing their minds.

If the audience is generally well educated, your speech may need to be quite sophisticated. When speaking to a less-educated audience, you may choose to clarify your points with more examples and illustrations.

RELIGION

The *Encyclopedia of American Religions* identifies more than 2,300 different religious groups in the United States,[11] from Adventists to Zen Buddhists, so don't assume that everyone in your audience shares a common religious heritage. Furthermore, don't assume that all members of the same religious tradition agree on all issues. For example, Catholics disagree on birth control and divorce, Jews disagree on whether to recognize same-sex unions, and so forth. Being aware of an audience's general religious orientation can be especially helpful when your speech topic is potentially controversial on religious grounds. Abortion rights, capital punishment, same-sex marriage, and teaching about the origins of humankind — all are rife with religious overtones and implications.

POLITICAL AFFILIATION

As with religion, beware of making unwarranted assumptions about an audience's political values and beliefs. Some people like nothing better than a lively debate about public-policy issues. Others avoid anything that smacks of politics. And many people are either very serious or very touchy about their views on political issues. Unless you have prior information about the audience's political values and beliefs, you won't know where your listeners stand.

GENDER

Gender can be another important factor to investigate when you analyze an audience, if only as a reminder to avoid the minefield of gender stereotyping. As distinct from biological sex, with its fixed physical characteristics, **gender** is our social and psychological sense of ourselves as males or females.[12] Thus someone whose biological sex is male may identify his gender as predominantly female, and someone whose sex is female may identify her gender as predominantly male. But gender identity is merely one manifestation of the ways gender may influence audience members' receptivity to your message. Consider the following case of the speaker, Kaitlin:

> Kaitlin felt confident that she was ready to deliver her speech to a local travel club for singles under age 30. About three-quarters of the audience [members] were female. Kaitlin had thoroughly researched her topic—holiday travel in the Caribbean—and offered lively descriptions of five destinations, including information about hotels, restaurants, and points of interest for each. Nevertheless, during her presentation she noticed that some of the women looked restless. Only when she opened up the presentation for discussion did she realize that a series of hotel-room break-ins, rapes, and muggings had caused the women considerable worry. Preoccupied with issues of safety, they were anxious to know if it was even safe enough for them to consider travel to these destinations.

Though Kaitlin had been aware of the crime wave, she did not address the issue of safety in her speech. Yet a good deal of research suggests that concerns for safety rank high among single women;[13] presumably, had she considered more closely how current events may have affected her audience members, this concern would have surfaced. Thus always consider the rhetorical situation when planning your speech (see "Analyzing the Speech Setting" on p. 91). In other respects, though, Kaitlin's presentation was sensitive to gender. She avoided

---

✓ CHECKLIST

Reviewing Your Speech in Light of Audience Demographics

_____ 1. Have you reviewed your topic in light of the age range and generational identity of your listeners? Do you use examples they will recognize and find relevant?

_____ 2. Have you avoided making judgments based on stereotypes?

_____ 3. Is your speech free of biased, insensitive language?

_____ 4. Does your speech acknowledge potential differences in values and beliefs and address them sensitively?

_____ 5. Have you evaluated your vocabulary for potentially confusing meanings?

_____ 6. Have you considered the appropriateness of your topic in relation to the demographic factors you have uncovered about your audience?

_____ 7. Are your explanations and examples at a level that is appropriate to the audience's sophistication and education?

_____ 8. Do you make any unwarranted assumptions about the audience's political or religious values and beliefs?

_____ 9. Does your topic carry religious or political overtones that are likely to stir your listeners' emotions in a negative way?

_____ 10. Do you address the concerns of both male and female listeners?

sexist language and other **gender stereotypes** — oversimplified and often se-verely distorted ideas about the innate nature of what it means to be male or fe-male. She did not automatically assume, for example, that the women in the audience would be interested in one type of recreation (such as golf) and the men in another. She also avoided the generic use of the pronouns *he* and *she* and other forms of **sexist language** when speaking to a mixed audience. Over-all, her language was inclusive of and respectful toward both sexes.

BEWARE OF OVERGENERALIZING

While no one can know everything about every group, gaining a sense of the audience's demographic profile can help you craft a well-targeted and respect-ful message. At the same time, beware of stereotyping your audience based on your demographic analysis. Just as a lack of knowledge about important traits can hinder effective communication, overgeneralizing about these same char-acteristics can lead to a poor speech outcome. The fact that a majority of the audience is of a certain age or ethnic or religious background, for example, does not automatically guarantee that they will share the same tastes in music or lit-erature, hold the same political views, or otherwise fall into neat categories.

Techniques for Learning about Your Audience

Now that you know the kind of information to look for when analyzing an au-dience, how do you actually uncover it? Unlike a professional pollster, you can-not survey thousands of people and apply sophisticated statistical techniques to analyze your results. On a smaller scale, however, you can use the same tech-niques. These include the interview, the survey, and published sources.

THE INTERVIEW

An **interview** is a face-to-face communication for the purpose of gathering in-formation. Interviews, even brief ones, can reveal a lot about the audience's in-terests and needs. You can conduct interviews one-on-one or in a group, in person, or by telephone or e-mail, depending on the time and the feasibility of making such arrangements. Rather than interviewing everyone in an audience, which often would be impractical, consider interviewing a smaller sampling or even just *one* knowledgeable representative of the group that you will address. As in questionnaires (see below), interviews usually consist of a mix of open- and closed-ended questions. (See Chapter 9 for more on conducting interviews.)

THE SURVEY

Written surveys, or **questionnaires**, are designed to gather information from a pool of respondents. Because you can distribute them simultaneously to large groups, questionnaires offer a more efficient means of gathering information from a pool of people than do interviews.

A questionnaire consists of a series of questions containing a mix of open- and closed-ended questions. **Closed-ended questions** are designed to elicit a small range of specific answers supplied by the interviewer:

"Do you or did you ever smoke cigarettes?"
Yes ＿＿＿＿   No ＿＿＿＿   Sometimes ＿＿＿＿

Answers will be "Yes," "No," or "I smoked for *x* number of years." Closed-ended questions are especially helpful in uncovering shared attitudes, experiences, and knowledge of audience members.

Closed-ended questions may be either fixed alternative or scale questions. **Fixed alternative questions** contain a limited choice of answers, such as "Yes," "No," or "Sometimes" (as in the preceding example). **Scale questions** — also called *attitude scales* — measure the respondent's level of agreement or disagreement with specific issues:

"Flag burning should be outlawed":
Strongly agree ＿＿＿＿   Agree ＿＿＿＿   Undecided ＿＿＿＿   Disagree ＿＿＿＿
Strongly disagree ＿＿＿＿

In addition to agreement, scale questions can be used to measure how important listeners judge something to be and how frequently they engage in a particular behavior:

"How important is religion in your life?"
Very important ＿＿＿＿   Important ＿＿＿＿   Moderately important ＿＿＿＿
Of minor importance ＿＿＿＿   Unimportant ＿＿＿＿

"How frequently do you attend religious services?"
Very frequently ＿＿＿＿   Frequently ＿＿＿＿   Occasionally ＿＿＿＿   Never ＿＿＿＿

Open-ended questions are designed to allow respondents to elaborate as much as they wish:

"How do you feel about using the results of DNA testing to prove innocence or guilt in criminal proceedings?"

Open-ended questions are particularly useful for probing beliefs and opinions. They elicit more individual or personal information about the audience members' thoughts and feelings. They are also more time-intensive than closed-ended questions.

Often, it takes just a few questions to get some idea of where audience members stand on each of the demographic factors. By using a mix of open- and closed-ended questions, you can draw a fairly clear picture of the backgrounds and attitudes of the members of your audience.

✓ **CHECKLIST**

Sample Audience Analysis Questionnaire

Part I: Demographic Analysis

1. What is your age?   _____ years
2. What is your sex?   _____ Male   _____ Female
3. Please indicate your primary heritage:
   _____ American Indian   _____ African American
   _____ Asian American   _____ European   _____ Latino
   _____ Middle Eastern   _____ Other
4. Please indicate your level of formal education:
   _____ High school   _____ Some college   _____ College degree
   _____ Other (please specify) _____
5. What is your approximate annual income range?
   _____ less than $10,000   _____ $10,000–$25,000
   _____ $25,000–$50,000   _____ $50,000–$75,000
   _____ $75,000–$100,000   _____ over $100,000
6. With which political party are your views most closely aligned?
   _____ Democratic   _____ Republican   _____ Neither (Independent)
7. Please check the box below that most closely matches your religious affiliation:
   _____ Buddhist   _____ Christian   _____ Hindu
   _____ Jewish   _____ Muslim   _____ Not religious
   _____ Other (please specify) _____
8. How would you characterize your religious involvement?
   _____ Very religious   _____ Somewhat religious
   _____ Not very religious
9. How would you characterize your political position?
   _____ Liberal   _____ Conservative   _____ Moderate

Part II: Analysis of Attitudes, Values, and Beliefs on a Specific Topic

Indicate your answers to the following questions about stem cell research by checking the appropriate blank.

10. It is unethical and immoral to permit any use of stem cells for medical research.
    _____ Strongly agree   _____ Agree   _____ Undecided
    _____ Disagree   _____ Strongly disagree
11. Do you think the government should or should not fund stem cell research?
    _____ Should   _____ Should not   _____ Neutral

(Continued)

12. Rather than destroy stem cells left over from *in vitro* fertilization, medical researchers should be allowed to use them to develop treatments for diseases.

    ___ Strongly agree   ___ Agree   ___ Undecided

    ___ Disagree   ___ Strongly disagree

13. What kind of cells come to mind when you think of stem cell therapy?

    _____

14. Which of the following has had the biggest influence on your thinking about stem cell research?

    ___ Media reports   ___ Opinions of friends and family

    ___ Your religious beliefs   ___ Personal experience

PUBLISHED SOURCES

Another avenue to explore when analyzing your audience is published sources. Organizations of all kinds publish information describing their missions, goals, operations, and achievements. Sources include Web sites and related online articles, print brochures, newspaper and magazine articles, annual reports, and industry guides. These materials often contain a wealth of information that you can use to identify salient information about your listeners.

You might also consider consulting published opinion polls, such as the following:

* National Opinion Research Center (NORC): www.norc.uchicago.edu
* Roper Center for Public Opinion Research: ropercenter.uconn.edu
* The Gallup Organization: www.gallup.com.

Although these polls won't specifically reflect your listeners' responses, they offer excellent insight into the range of attitudes that exist about a given issue as well as how representative state, national, or international samples responded to questions about your issue. You may also wish to use the published data as supporting material for your speeches (see Chapter 8).

Analyze the Speech Setting

As important as analyzing the audience is assessing (and then preparing for) the setting in which you will give your speech — size of audience; location, time, and length of speech; and rhetorical situation.

SIZE OF AUDIENCE AND PHYSICAL SETTING

The size of the audience and the physical setting in which a speech occurs can have a significant impact on the outcome of the speech. The atmosphere of a classroom is different from that of a banquet room, an outdoor amphitheater, or a large auditorium. The larger the group, the less you are likely to interact with the audience; you will also need to plan how to position yourself and adjust your voice, sometimes with the aid of acoustical equipment.

TIME AND LENGTH OF SPEECH

Both the time at which your speech is scheduled and its length will affect listeners' receptivity to it. People gathered at breakfast, lunch, or dinner meetings, for example, come to the speech occasion with more than one agenda. They may wish to hear you, but they will also want time to eat and converse with other people. Your boss or fellow employees may expect to receive information quickly so that they can proceed to other business.

In any speaking situation, always find out how long you are expected to speak. Bear in mind that few matters of speech etiquette are as annoying to an audience as a speaker's apparent disregard for time. Start on time and end well within the time allotted to you. Table 6.2 includes typical lengths for various presentations.

TABLE 6.2 • Typical Length of Presentations

Kind of Presentation	Length
In-depth speech	15–20 minutes
Presentation to boss	1–10 minutes
Toast	1–2 minutes
Award acceptance speech	3–5 minutes

THE SPEECH CONTEXT (RHETORICAL SITUATION)

Any speech or presentation you deliver will always occur in a particular context. You may be the third of six speakers on a panel, for instance. You might precede or follow a speaker who is more dynamic or well known than you are. Your listeners may be preoccupied with unusual circumstances — a local sports team just won a championship, extreme weather conditions have disrupted everyday life, the president of the company just resigned, and so forth. By being alert to any of these contingencies, you can address them in your speech.

✓ CHECKLIST

Analyzing the Speech Situation

_____ 1. Where will the speech take place?

_____ 2. How long am I expected to speak?

_____ 3. How many people will attend?

_____ 4. Will I need a microphone?

_____ 5. How will any projecting equipment I plan to use in my speech, such as an LCD projector, function in the space?

_____ 6. Where will I stand or sit in relation to the audience?

_____ 7. Will I be able to interact with listeners?

_____ 8. Who else will be speaking?

_____ 9. What special events or circumstances of concern to my audience should I acknowledge?

7 Selecting a Topic and Purpose

Whether speaking to two, ten, or a hundred people, the first task in preparing any speech or other type of presentation is to select a topic and purpose for speaking that are appropriate to the audience, the occasion, and the overall speech situation (i.e., the **rhetorical situation**). Choosing a topic and identifying the underlying purpose of your speech answers three key questions you should pose to yourself as you prepare your speech: "What is my goal in speaking to the audience?" "What specifically do I want my listeners to know or do?" and "What precisely is my speech about?"

Assigned versus Self-Selected Topics

In the speech classroom you will probably be assigned a variety of speeches, some of which will have a specified topic. Outside the classroom, you may or may not select your own speech topic. Your boss might ask you to prepare a talk explaining how your group developed its latest product. The local Chamber of Commerce might request that you address "businesses that grow a town's tax base." Often speakers are invited because of their expertise in a given area, so they cover the same general ground in every speech.

Even speakers who give frequent speeches on the same general topic never give the same speech twice. Similarly, even though you might be assigned a topic, or speak on the same topic over and over, you still must refine and adapt it to each speech situation. You must decide on a specific purpose or goal for the talk. Even when the choice of topic is your decision, you are usually given some direction as to how your talk should be presented. For example:

- You may be given a *purpose.* The adviser for the youth group you volunteer for asks you to speak at the next meeting to "boost morale." The topic you select for this is yours to decide.

- You are given *time constraints.* Your boss informs you that you are on the agenda to talk to a group of grade school visitors for three to five minutes next Monday. How you fill this time is up to you.

- You are given a *challenge.* The master of ceremonies for a roast to honor a retiring local newspaper writer asks you to "make the audience laugh."

Seldom does anyone mean it when they tell you, "Whatever you talk about is fine." Yes, the topic may be fine, but in most cases the person who invited you to speak has an outcome or end result in mind. In other words, when you select a topic for a speech, you are also held accountable for accomplishing a certain purpose.

Identifying the General Speech Purpose

Public speeches can be classified as addressing one of three general speech purposes: to *inform,* to *persuade,* or to *mark a special occasion.* The **general speech purpose** for any speech answers the question "Why am I speaking on this topic for this particular audience and occasion?"

The general speech purpose is sometimes defined or, at least, suggested by the occasion. Often, however, rather than specifically dictating a speech purpose, the occasion only suggests parameters of appropriateness. For example, one commencement speaker may decide to prepare a persuasive speech that exhorts the graduates to contribute time after graduation to public service, whereas another speaker might decide to entertain the audience with a light-hearted look at what the students' degrees will, or perhaps will not, do for them in the future. Although the two speakers select different general speech purposes (one to persuade and the other to entertain), both select and adapt their topics to ensure appropriateness to the occasion.

WHEN THE GENERAL SPEECH PURPOSE IS TO INFORM

When you deliver an informative speech, you share your knowledge or point of view about a subject with others. To do so, you define, describe, explain, or demonstrate this knowledge. Thus the general purpose of an **informative speech** is to increase the audience's understanding and awareness of a topic. You want the audience to learn something.

When selecting a topic for an informative speech, try to gauge how much the audience already knows about it. There's no surer way to lose audience members' attention than to speak over — or under — their heads. If the speech topic assumes a lot of background knowledge, make certain that the audience has it. Likewise, if the audience is familiar with the topic, it's important to present it in a way that is fresh and interesting. Everyone knows about taxes, for instance, but we're always eager to hear about new ways to avoid paying them. Just about any topic is appropriate for an informative speech (see Tables 7.1 and 7.2), as long as you present it with the goal of enlarging the audience's understanding and awareness.

TABLE 7.1 • Some General Categories of Informative Topics

Objects	People	Events	Concepts	Processes	Issues
Their construction, function, symbolic or concrete meaning	Their biographies, noteworthy achievements, anecdotes about them	Noteworthy or unusual occurrences, both past and present	Abstract and difficult ideas or theories	A series of steps leading to an end result	Problems or matters of dispute

---

TABLE 7.2 • Sample Informative Speech Topics

- The Importance of Sleep to General Well-Being
- Getting the Most from the Campus Recreation Center
- Trends in Religion in the Workplace
- Low-Carb Cooking
- Careers in Forensic Science
- Mentoring Teens
- Switching from a PC to a Mac
- Advances in Breast Cancer Treatment
- Understanding the Effects of the "Date Rape" Drug Rohypnol

WHEN THE GENERAL SPEECH PURPOSE IS TO PERSUADE

As with informative speeches, persuasive speeches also increase listeners' knowledge of a topic. But rather than primarily seeking to increase listeners' knowledge, the general purpose of a **persuasive speech** is to effect some degree of change in the audience's attitudes, beliefs, or even basic values (the latter being the hardest to change). Or the purpose may be to change specific behaviors (e.g., "Don't practice unsafe sex") or reinforce existing behaviors (e.g., "Keep practicing safe sex").

Topics or issues on which there are competing perspectives are particularly suitable for persuasive speeches. Controversial issues such as free speech, stem cell research, and binge drinking naturally lend themselves to a persuasive purpose because people hold strongly contrasting opinions about them. But other topics can be suitable as well. The only requirement is that the topic allow the speaker to fashion a message that is intended to effect some degree of change in the audience (see Table 7.3).

Consider the topic of binge drinking. A persuasive purpose (e.g., "To persuade my audience to avoid binge drinking") would be appropriate if:

- The audience feels considerably different about the topic than you do (e.g., members of the audience engage in binge drinking).
- The audience holds similar attitudes and beliefs about the topic as you do but needs direction in taking action (e.g., the audience consists of

---

TABLE 7.3 • Sample Persuasive Speech Topics

- Take College Courses Online
- Study Abroad for a Semester
- Avoid Cosmetic Surgery
- Take Nutritional Supplements for Better Health
- Plagiarism Will Ruin Your Career
- Switch to Hands-Free Cell Phones in Cars
- Let's Restructure the College Football Championships
- Adopt a Senior Citizen
- Learn Another Language

people who want to help friends avoid binge drinking and are seeking strategies to do so).

- The audience agrees with your position but is likely to encounter opposing information or circumstances in the near future (e.g., at an upcoming annual celebration of college students, beer will be readily available).

WHEN THE GENERAL SPEECH PURPOSE IS TO MARK A SPECIAL OCCASION

Some speeches are prepared for a purpose dictated by a special occasion. **Special occasion speeches** include speeches of introduction, speeches of acceptance, speeches of presentation, roasts and toasts, eulogies, and after-dinner speeches, among others. Depending on the specific event, the general purpose of a special occasion speech will be variously to entertain, celebrate, commemorate, inspire, or set a social agenda (see Chapter 27).

 CHECKLIST

Identifying Your General Speech Purpose

✓ Is your goal in speaking primarily to increase the audience's knowledge of a topic or to share your point of view? (Your general purpose is to inform.)

✓ Is it primarily to effect some degree of change in the way your listeners view things? (Your general purpose is to persuade.)

✓ Is it primarily to mark a special occasion? (Your general purpose will be variously to entertain, celebrate, commemorate, inspire, or set a social agenda.)

Choosing a Topic for the Classroom Speech

Many students assume that since they can't think of a topic instantly, they won't find one at all. Fortunately, a prod in the right direction is all it takes to open the floodgates. And once you settle on a topic, the real challenge becomes taming your enthusiasm to fit the available time and the audience's interests.

Selecting a topic for a classroom speech can be approached from a variety of angles. You can begin "at the top," so to speak, by focusing on broad social issues of national or even global consequence; or you can start closer to the ground, by considering your own interests and life experiences.

PERSONAL INTERESTS: LOOKING WITHIN

Selecting a topic you are familiar with — and, most important, enthusiastic about — offers many advantages. Because you are interested in the topic, researching it will be enjoyable. You'll look forward to learning more about it and will probably pay more attention to what you discover. You'll bring a sense of genuine enthusiasm to your presentation. Depending on the depth of your background knowledge, you may convey great competence and thereby encourage the audience to see you as a highly credible speaker. In the classroom, your instructor, as well as your classmates, may be much more interested in learning about topics based on your own experiences and expertise.

As seen in Table 7.4, personal interests run the gamut from favorite activities and hobbies to deeply held goals and values. Personal experiences provide powerful topics, especially, if by your sharing them, the audience in some way benefits from your experience. "What it's like" stories also yield interesting topics. For example, what is it like to ride horse trails across the southwestern United States or to be part of a medical mission's team working in Uganda?

CURRENT EVENTS AND CONTROVERSIAL ISSUES

People are constantly barraged with newsworthy topics, but few of us have the time to delve into them. What is actually behind the oil-for-food scandal involving the United Nations and Iraq? What can and cannot be done to better secure

TABLE 7.4 • Identifying Topics

Favorite Hobbies	Personal Experiences	Values	Goals
• Sports • Volunteering • Cars • Fashion • Reading • Video games • Music • Travel • Outdoor life	• Exotic travel destinations • Service in the armed forces • Volunteer work in a foreign country • Immigration • Life-threatening disease	• Building a greater sense of community • Spirituality • Philanthropy • Political activism	• Being a high-tech entrepreneur • Attending graduate or professional school • Starting a family • Being fit • Learning more about my religion
Specific Subject Interests	**Social Problems**	**Health and Nutrition**	**Current Events**
• Local history • Ancient history • Politics • Art • Religion • Science	• Road rage • Violence in the schools • Lack of affordable child care • Environmental issues	• Diets • Herbal and vitamin supplements • Exercise regimens • HMOs • Health insurance • Assisted living	• Pending legislation—crime bills, property taxes, land use • Political races • Race relations • National security
Grassroots Issues	**New or Unusual Angles**	**Issues of Controversy**	
• Land development versus conservation • Local organizations • School issues	• Unsolved crimes • Unexplained disappearances • Scandals	• Creationism versus evolution • Gun control • Stem cell research	

our nation's borders? Similarly, controversial issues of the day—patenting human genes, Bible study in the schools, and so on—usually earn their place in the limelight because they reflect our deepest concerns and profoundly affect us as individuals and as members of society. Many of us appreciate and even hunger for information that broadens our understanding of these topics.

GRASSROOTS ISSUES

Most people respond with interest to issues that affect them directly, and, barring war and federal tax hikes, these tend to be of a local nature. Parents want to know about quality day care in the area; town residents need information about upcoming referendums. People are also interested in what other people in their communities are doing. Are you involved in a club on campus, or do you volunteer for a local charity? Consider giving a speech about the organization's mission, membership, or upcoming event.

AVOID TOPICS THAT ARE OVERDONE: YOU BE THE EXPERT

Even though there an almost limitless number of speech topics, some seem to be repeated over and over again in student classroom speeches across the country. Imagine how many students give speeches on the following topics each year: abortion, gun control, women's rights, race inequality, steps for getting a job, how to change a flat tire, Oprah Winfrey, *Star Wars*, the Bush administration, and spring break vacations.

   Why do students choose these topics so often? Because they are controversial, they touch on deep-seated beliefs and values, and there is ample information available for researching the topics. Yet it is extremely difficult to give a strong speech on such overused topics. Because it's very hard to come up with any new claims or arguments, you are unlikely to change anyone's mind on the topic and may cause an in-class controversy. Perhaps most important, you are likely to bore your instructor who has probably heard dozens if not hundreds of speeches on this same topic.

   You stand a better chance of engaging the interests of your classmates and your instructor if you avoid very common topics and develop ones that are novel or unique. One way to do this is to consider your own expertise, ranging from an unusual hobby (collecting vintage cars on eBay; hiking city neighborhoods) or uncommon job for people your age (opening your own tea room; piloting a shrimp boat) to a particular skill your possess (constructing Web sites; managing small investments; refereeing youth sports). Fresh ideas based on firsthand knowledge and experience are more intriguing and provide an opportunity for others to get to know you better.

Using Brainstorming to Generate Ideas

Brainstorming is a problem-solving technique that involves the spontaneous generation of ideas through word association, topic mapping, or even Internet browsing of subject indexes.

WORD ASSOCIATION

To brainstorm by **word association**, write down *one* topic in which you are interested and that you think will appeal to your audience. If you have trouble getting started, simply write down a word related to anything — music, relationships, food — that currently interests you. Then jot down the first thing that comes to mind when you read the word or words you have just written. It doesn't have to be related to the first topic. As soon as your words remind you of something, write it down. Now read the second item on the list, and write down your next thought. If a word or words remind you of more than one thing, write down all of them. Try writing your thoughts as quickly as you can, without analyzing them as topics. Repeat the process until you have a list of fifteen to twenty items.

Once you have generated a list, review each item as a potential topic. Narrow the list to two or three, and then select a final topic. The following list is an example of the word-association brainstorming technique:

- health ⇒ alternative medicine ⇒ naturopathy ⇒ fraud
- children ⇒ parenting ⇒ working ⇒ day care ⇒ living expenses
- diving ⇒ snorkeling ⇒ Bahamas ⇒ conch shells ⇒ deep-sea fishing
- Internet ⇒ searching ⇒ search engines ⇒ wasting time
- exercise ⇒ StairMaster ⇒ weight lifting ⇒ swimming

TOPIC MAPPING

If you find it helpful to visualize ideas, try drawing a **topic map** (see Figure 7.1). Put a potential topic in the middle of a piece of paper and draw a circle around it. As related ideas come to you, write them down as shown in Figure 7.1. Keep going until you hit upon an idea that appeals most to you.

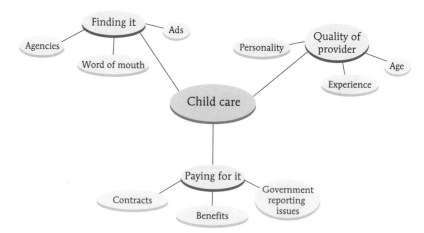

Figure 7.1 A Topic Map

INTERNET SEARCH INDEXES

Popular Internet portals offer alphabetized directories covering a wide range of topics; examples include Yahoo! Web Directory, Lycos Topics, and MSN Directory. To access these directories, consult the portal's home page for a link to an A–Z list of topics. Then click on any one of the categories ("Arts," e.g.) to access a page full of links to subtopics within that category, some of which lead to pages with even more subtopics. Essentially what you get is an electronic version of word-association brainstorming, except that Web servers provide the keywords; all you need to do is isolate the topic that interests you. (See Chapter 10 for more on using subject directories.)

✔ **CHECKLIST**

Criteria for Selecting a Topic

_____ 1. Is the topic appropriate to the occasion?
_____ 2. Will the topic appeal to my listeners' interests and needs?
_____ 3. Is the topic something I can speak about with enthusiasm and insight?
_____ 4. Can I research and report on the topic in the time allotted?
_____ 5. Will I be able to offer a fresh perspective on the topic?

Refining the Topic and Purpose

Once you have an idea of what you'd like to speak about and have established the general speech purpose, you need to narrow your focus so that it's in line with time constraints, audience expectations, and the nature of the occasion.

NARROWING THE TOPIC

When you narrow a topic, you focus on specific aspects of it to the exclusion of others. Naturally, you focus on those aspects of the topic that interest you the most. You also carefully evaluate them in light of audience interests, knowledge, and needs. If you already know the general speech purpose, you incorporate this knowledge into the process.

How long is the speech to be? How much time do you have to do research? How much information can you responsibly review so that you avoid distorting or falsifying the material? Imagine, for example, how your approach to the topic "Americans' Love of Cell Phones" may change as you consider the following factors:

- The time limit is five to seven minutes.
- The speech is for an informative speaking assignment.

- The library does not have a copy of a recent telecommunications industry report on cell phone use, and your computer is down.

Just as brainstorming can be used to discover a general topic, it can also be helpful in narrowing one. One way of doing this is to brainstorm by category. What sorts of categories can you break your general topic into? For the general topic of cell phones, some related categories are models, manufacturers, and calling plans. As you brainstorm by category, ask yourself, "What questions do I have about the topic? Am I more interested in how cell phones work or in how much they cost? What aspect of cell phones is my audience most likely to want to hear about?" You can also use topic mapping or browsing an Internet directory to narrow your topic. Here's how it's done:

- Write your topic in the middle of a blank piece of paper and circle it.
- Using the topic circle as the spoke of a wheel, surround it with as many categories as you can associate it with.
- Keep breaking down the categories until you settle on an aspect of the topic that you can research and report on with competence in the time allotted and that will interest your audience.

 CHECKLIST

Narrowing Your Topic

✓   What is my audience most likely to know about the subject?
✓   What are my listeners most likely to want to learn?
✓   What aspects of the topic are most relevant to the occasion?
✓   Can I develop the topic using just two or three main points?
✓   How much can I competently research and report on in the time I am given to speak?

FORMING A SPECIFIC SPEECH PURPOSE

The **specific speech purpose** zeroes in more closely than the general speech purpose on the goal of the speech. It expresses both the topic and the general speech purpose in action form and in terms of the specific objectives you hope to achieve with your speech. The specific purpose statement answers the question, "Precisely what is it about my topic that I want the audience to learn/do/reconsider/agree with?"

Consider the topic of cooking. You've narrowed the topic to "Alternative Cooking Methods" and further to "Solar Cooking," and selected an informative speech purpose. Now you would need to decide what you want to accomplish in your speech. Given that your speech goal is to inform, perhaps you want audience members to understand the process and benefits of solar cooking. Or perhaps you want to provide them with resources for obtaining equipment and recipes for solar cooking. Your primary objective becomes your specific speech purpose:

GENERAL TOPIC:	Alternative Cooking Methods
NARROWED TOPIC:	The Process and Benefits of Solar Cooking
GENERAL PURPOSE:	To inform
SPECIFIC PURPOSE:	To inform my audience about the benefits associated with the process of solar cooking

From Topic and Purpose to Thesis Statement

At this stage, you know your topic and have devised your general and specific purposes. The next step is to formulate a thesis statement. The **thesis statement** is the theme or central idea of the speech stated in the form of a single, declarative sentence. The thesis statement concisely expresses what the speech will attempt to support from the speaker's point of view. It is a single line that serves to connect all the parts of the speech, much like a backbone. The main points, the supporting material, and the conclusion all emanate from and relate to the thesis.

Ethically Speaking
Ethical Considerations in Selecting a Topic and Purpose

Respect for your audience members and adaptation to their needs and interests should always guide your topic choices. What makes a speech ethical or unethical depends on how it empowers the audience to think or act. In other words, ethical considerations begin with your goal or purpose. Speakers who select persuasive purposes should be particularly careful; under pressure to sway an audience, some speakers may be tempted to tamper with the truth. As you review your speech goal, consider the following:

- Have you deliberately distorted information to achieve a desired result?
- Is it your intent to deceive?
- Do you try to coerce the audience into thinking or acting in a certain way?
- Have you knowingly tried to appeal to harmful biases?

Although few hard-and-fast rules exist when it comes to ethical guidelines for selecting topics, some areas are clearly off-limits—at least in U.S. culture:

- The topic shows an audience how to perform actions prohibited by law.
- The topic provides audience members with information that may result in their physical or psychological harm.
- The topic humiliates or degrades the fundamental values of an audience's culture, religion, or political system.

The thesis statement and the specific purpose are closely linked. Both state the speech topic, but in different forms. *The specific purpose describes in action form what you want to achieve with the speech; the thesis statement concisely identifies, in a single idea, what the speech is about.* Note also that even though the specific speech purpose is seldom spoken by the speaker (whereas the thesis must be clearly stated because the entire speech rests on it), it is important to formulate the specific purpose for yourself (and to state it in writing for your instructor). By clearly stating the goal for your speech, you implant in your mind exactly what you want it to accomplish.

USE THE THESIS STATEMENT TO CONVEY THE CENTRAL IDEA

The thesis statement conveys the central idea or core assumption about the topic. Whether the speech is informative or persuasive, the thesis offers your comment on the topic. For instance, the thesis statement "Three major events caused the United States to go to war in 1941" expresses your view that three factors played a part in the U.S. entry into World War II. The speech is then developed from this thesis, presenting facts and evidence to support it.

The thesis statement aids you in developing a coherent, understandable speech. Without the thesis statement, the audience cannot easily follow the ideas that make up the body of the speech. Thus you should postpone the development of main points and supporting material until you have correctly formulated the speech purpose and thesis statement (see Chapter 11).

The nature of the thesis statement varies according to the speech purpose. In a persuasive speech, your comment on the speech as stated in the thesis represents what you are going to prove in the address. All the main points in the speech are arguments that develop this position. Consider the following examples (all with the general purpose of persuading the audience):

Example 1

GENERAL PURPOSE: To persuade

SPECIFIC PURPOSE: To persuade the audience to raise money on behalf of the Sierra Club

THESIS: A donation to the Sierra Club is an investment in nature.

Example 2

SPECIFIC PURPOSE: To persuade the audience to vote for a political candidate

THESIS: A vote for Senator Juarez is a vote for progress.

Example 3

SPECIFIC PURPOSE: To persuade the audience that abstinence is the way to avoid the harm alcohol can cause

THESIS: Abstinence is the best way to avoid the harm alcohol can cause.

Notice that in each case, after you read the thesis you find yourself asking "Why?" or saying "Prove it!" This will be accomplished by the evidence you give in the main points (see Chapter 11).

The thesis statement in an informative speech conveys the scope of the topic, the steps associated with the topic, or the underlying elements of the topic. It describes what the audience will learn. Consider the following examples:

Example 1

GENERAL PURPOSE: To inform

SPECIFIC PURPOSE: To educate the audience about how the U.S. government is structured

THESIS: The three branches of the U.S. government form our unique representative democracy.

Example 2

SPECIFIC PURPOSE: To enable audience members to invest their money properly

THESIS: There are six steps to investing in the stock market.

Example 3

SPECIFIC PURPOSE: To establish the chronology of the U.S. entry into World War II

THESIS: Three major events caused the United States to go to war in 1941.

USE THE THESIS STATEMENT TO GUIDE YOUR SPEECH PREPARATION

The point of creating a thesis statement is to help you identify precisely what your speech is about. As you develop the speech, use the thesis to keep yourself on track. As you research materials, for example, review them in the light of whether they contribute to the thesis or stray from it. When you actually draft your speech, work your thesis statement into it and restate it where appropriate. Doing so will encourage your audience to understand and accept your message.

Following are some examples of student speech topics and the corresponding general and specific speech purposes and thesis statements:

Example 1

SPEECH TOPIC: Web Logs (Blogs)

GENERAL SPEECH PURPOSE: To inform

SPECIFIC SPEECH PURPOSE: To inform my audience of three benefits of keeping a Web log

THESIS STATEMENT:	Maintaining a Web log provides the opportunity to practice writing, a means of networking with others who share similar interests, and the chance to develop basic Web site management skills.

Example 2

SPEECH TOPIC:	Student Internships
GENERAL SPEECH PURPOSE:	To persuade
SPECIFIC SPEECH PURPOSE:	To persuade my audience that internships are beneficial
THESIS STATEMENT:	To prepare for a difficult job market and enhance your résumé, you should get a student internship to help link your academic studies.

 CHECKLIST

Formulating the Thesis Statement

_____ 1. Does my thesis statement sum up in a single sentence what my speech is about?

_____ 2. Is it restricted to a single idea?

_____ 3. Is it in the form of a complete declarative sentence?

_____ 4. Is it stated in a way that is relevant to the audience?

Making the Thesis Statement Relevant and Motivating

As you refine the draft of your speech, try to express the thesis statement in a way that will motivate the audience to listen. In many cases, creating a relevant thesis can be accomplished quite easily by adding a few key words or phrases. You can preface an informative thesis statement with a phrase such as "Few of us know" or "Contrary to popular belief" or "Have you ever." A persuasive thesis statement can also be adapted to establish relevance for the audience. Phrases such as "As most of you know" or "As informed members of the community" or "As concerned adults" can attract listeners' attention and interest and help them see the topic's relevance.

The exact phrasing or rewording of your thesis statement depends on the type of audience to which you are speaking. Once you gain some information about your audience members, you won't have trouble making the topic relevant for them.

Supporting
the Speech

Supporting the Speech

Speaker's Reference
Supporting the Speech

8. Developing Supporting Materials

Alternate among Different Types of Supporting Materials

- Provide more than your own personal opinions or experiences. (p. 115)
- Illustrate each main point with several different types of supporting material. (p. 115)

Orally Cite Your Sources

- Reveal the source of your ideas in your speech. (p. 115)
- Provide enough context to establish the source's credibility. (p. 115)

Choose Accurate, Relevant, and Compelling Supporting Material

- Seek out compelling *examples* to illustrate or describe your ideas. (p. 116)
- Share *stories*, either real or hypothetical, to drive your point home. (p. 117)
- Use firsthand findings in the form of testimony. (p. 119)
- Hunt for relevant *facts*, or documented occurrences. (p. 121)
- Consider whether you need *statistics*, or quantified evidence, including frequencies, percentages, and averages. (p. 121)
  Draw your statistics from reliable sources and present them in context. Beware of cherry-picking and other unethical ways of presenting data.

9. Locating Supporting Material

Consider Using Both Primary and Secondary Sources

- *Primary research* includes interviews and surveys you conduct yourself. (p. 128)
- Sources for *secondary research* include all credible information gathered by others, such as a library's holdings. (p. 128)

Plan a Research Strategy

- Avoid wasting time in the wrong places. (p. 128)
- Keep in mind your goal of substantiating your thesis. (p. 128)

111

- Consult reference librarians. (p. 129)
- When searching databases, consult the Search Tips section. (p. 130)

Consider Various Secondary Sources

- Books (p. 130)
- Newspapers and periodicals (p. 130)
- Government publications (p. 132)
- Reference works (e.g., encyclopedias, almanacs, books of quotations, poetry collections, and atlases) (p. 132)

Consider Conducting Interviews to Uncover Information

- Plan your questions well in advance; beware of vague, leading, and loaded questions. (p. 135)
- Strive to make a positive first impression. (p. 136)
- Use active listening strategies such as paraphrasing. (p. 136)
- Close the interview effectively. (p. 137)

Consider Conducting Surveys to Learn about Audience Attitudes

Develop an Effective System for Documenting Your Sources

- Accurately record each of your references. (p. 138)
- Select a method to organize your sources, and follow it systematically. (p. 138)
- Record appropriate bibliographic information for each piece of evidence. (p. 138)

As You Gather Your Research, Evaluate Its Credibility

- How was the data gathered? (p. 144)
- What is the author's background in the field of study? (p. 144)
- How credible is the publication? Who is the publisher? What are the contributors' qualifications? (p. 144)
- How reliable is the data? (p. 144)
- How recent is the reference? (p. 144)

10. Using the Internet to Support Your Speech

Strive for a Mix of Print and Internet Sources

- Recognize that much information is available only in print. (p. 148)
- Some materials are more readily accessible online, however, including those collected by the U.S. government. (p. 148)

Begin Your Search with Library Holdings

- Sources drawn from library holdings, including electronic holdings, have been vetted for quality. (p. 148)
- Library holdings are organized systematically by professionals. (p. 148)

Critically Evaluate All Information Found Online

- Check the most authoritative Web sites first. (p. 149)
- Evaluate authorship and sponsorship. (p. 149)
- Check for currency. (p. 149)
- Check that the site credits its sources and that sources are credible. (p. 149)
- Distinguish information from misinformation, propaganda, and disinformation. (p. 152)

Make the Most of Internet Search Tools

- *Search engines* automatically index the contents of the Web. (p. 153)
- *Meta-search engines* search several search engines simultaneously. (p. 153)
- *Specialized search engines* focus on specific topics. (p. 154)
- *Subject directories* contain searchable databases of sites organized by subject and reviewed by human editors. (p. 154)

Know When to Use a Search Engine or Subject Directory

- To find very defined information, use a *search engine* first. (p. 155)
- To find sites on a given subject, use a *subject directory*. (p. 156)
- To narrow a topic, use a *subject directory* first. (p. 156)

Know That Commercial Influences Can Taint Search Results

- For a fee, some search tools guarantee a higher ranking ("paid placement"). (p. 156)
- For a fee, some search tools guarantee inclusion, without guaranteeing higher ranking ("paid inclusion"). (p. 156)

Use Library Gateways and Virtual Libraries

- *Gateways* include specialized search engines plus subject directories whose links have been evaluated by experts. (p. 157)
- Gateways and virtual libraries can help you access the invisible Web. (p. 157)

Use Search Commands to Enhance Results

- Use the basic search commands correctly. (p. 159)
- Refine your search with field searching. (p. 159)

Orally Credit Your Sources

- Include relevant information to establish the source's authority. (p. 161)
- Keep records of bibliographic information. (p. 161)
- Learn what to document for a written bibliography. (p. 161)

KEY TERMS

Chapter 8

supporting material	testimony	average
example	expert testimony	mean
brief example	lay testimony	median
extended example	facts	mode
hypothetical example	statistics	cherry-picking
narrative	frequency	
anecdote	percentage	

Chapter 9

invention	Dewey decimal number	fact book
primary research	periodical	atlas
secondary research	U.S. Government Printing	interview
database	Office (GPO)	neutral questions
full-text database	encyclopedia	active listening
reference librarian	general encyclopedia	fabrication
Library of Congress call number	specialized encyclopedia	
	almanac	

Chapter 10

World Wide Web	disinformation	gateway (information portal)
hyperlinks	search engine	virtual library
library gateway	individual search engine	invisible Web
domain	meta-search engine	Boolean operators
tilde (~)	specialized search engine	field searching
information	subject directory	
propaganda	paid placement	
misinformation	paid inclusion	

Developing Supporting Material ⑧

Often, the most important element in a good speech is not the topic itself but how it is developed and supported. You can easily see this in speeches on the same topic prepared by different speakers. Good speeches contain accurate, relevant, and interesting **supporting material** in the form of memorable examples, narratives, testimony, facts, and statistics. These "flesh out" the speech—they give substance to the speech's thesis or central idea.

Broadly speaking, supporting material performs three functions: (1) It creates interest and engages attention; (2) it illustrates, clarifies, and elaborates on the meaning of your ideas; and (3) it substantiates or proves that a statement is correct. As you gather supporting material, consider how you can use it to generate interest and to add solid evidence to your assertions.

Use a Variety of Supporting Materials

Virtually any speech you deliver will require a variety of supporting material other than your own personal opinion or experience. This holds true whether or not you possess expert knowledge on a topic. People want to know the truth about a given matter, and they will not merely accept your word for it. In general, listeners respond most favorably to a variety of supporting materials derived from multiple sources to illustrate each main point. Alternating among different types of supporting material—moving from a story to a statistic, for example—will make the presentation more interesting and credible while simultaneously appealing to your audience members' different learning styles.

Refer Orally to Your Sources

Equally important as the types of supporting material you select is mentioning the sources for them in your speech. Listeners place more value on conclusions drawn by multiple sources that they find credible.[1] Unlike a written bibliography, there is no set format for orally citing sources. As long as you clearly identify where your information came from and provide your listeners with enough context to accurately interpret it, you can vary your wording to suit your needs (see Chapter 4 and the following section on citing facts and statistics).

Offer Examples

"We learn by example" became a popular saying because it is indeed true. **Examples** illustrate, describe, or represent things. Their purpose is to aid understanding by making ideas, items, or events more concrete and to clarify and amplify meaning.

Study the text of any engaging speech and you will see that it is liberally sprinkled with good examples that clarify and enliven the speaker's message. Examples are particularly helpful when they are used to describe or explain things with which the audience may not be familiar. Examples can be brief or extended and may be either factual or hypothetical.

BRIEF EXAMPLES

Brief examples offer a single illustration of a point. Barrington D. Parker, in a speech about visa problems among foreign-born graduate students, uses the following brief example to illustrate that unlike students in many other countries, relatively few U.S. students pursue degrees in science and engineering:

> Your children and mine gravitate towards humanities and social science majors as opposed to the quantitative ones such as mathematics, natural science, or engineering. . . . This aspect of our culture is radically different from many other places in the world. For example, a member of the Yale Corporation originally from Bombay told us that if you were at a social gathering of professionals there, and a son or daughter was going to college, you would be positively embarrassed to admit that he or she was studying humanities or liberal arts. This meant you had somehow failed. The ablest, hardest-working students there are expected to become scientists, physicians, or engineers.[2]

EXTENDED EXAMPLES

Sometimes it takes more than a brief example to effectively illustrate a point. **Extended examples** offer multifaceted illustrations of the idea, item, or event being described, thereby getting the point across and reiterating it effectively. Risa Lavizzo-Mourey, M.D., uses an extended example to illustrate how the physicians in her audience could use their knowledge to shift the course of childhood obesity:

> In the questions you ask about childhood obesity, and in the answers you find, you will hold the power to alter the course of America's health history as it occurs. . . . For example, I can think of at least three moments in the past half century that dramatically shifted the course of America's medical and scientific history. The first time came exactly 51 years ago today — March 26, 1953 — when Jonas Salk called a press conference to announce the discovery of a polio vaccine. The second time, amazingly, came just four weeks later, when Watson and Crick published their discovery of the double helix structure of DNA. The third time was in 1964, when U.S. surgeon general Luther

Terry courageously reported that cigarette smoking does cause cancer and other deadly diseases. For many of you, that was the first day of what turned into a 40-year movement to alter a culture of harm that was anchored in centuries of acceptable behavior. Your science and determination helped America turn the tide against tobacco and smoking — saving the lives of millions.[3]

CHECKLIST

Possible Forms for Citing Examples

✓ "Let me give you two examples of outsourcing . . ."
✓ "Lance Armstrong's Livestrong Foundation is an example of a fiscally effective charity . . ."
✓ "For example, what if, in five years, the average temperature of the Pacific Ocean rises one half of one degree Fahrenheit?"

HYPOTHETICAL EXAMPLES

Real-life examples are fine when your topic is about something that has already occurred, but in some speeches you may need to make a point about something that could happen in the future if certain things occurred. For example, if you argue the thesis "We should eliminate summer vacations for all school-age children," you automatically raise the question of what will happen if this comes to pass. Since it hasn't happened yet, you'll need a **hypothetical example** of what you believe the outcome will be. Republican Representative Vernon Ehlers of Michigan offered the following hypothetical example when he spoke at a congressional hearing in support of a bill to ban human cloning. Representative Ehlers, who is also a research scientist, claimed that human cloning should be banned because it will create moral dilemmas that humanity is not prepared to handle:

> What if in the cloning process you produce someone with two heads and three arms? Are you simply going to euthanize and dispose of that person? The answer is no. We're talking about human life.[4]

Share Stories

Often, one of the most powerful means of conveying a message is through a story or **narrative**. Narratives tell tales, both real and imaginary, about practically anything under the sun. Scholars of narratives have commented that all human history consists of stories. "Most of our experience, our knowledge, and our thinking is organized as stories," notes language scholar Mark Turner. "One story helps us make sense of another."[5] A growing body of neuroscientific evidence even suggests that it is through stories that we organize our thinking.[6]

CHECKLIST

Selecting the Right Example or Story

_____ 1. Does the example or story truly illustrate or prove the point I need to make?

_____ 2. Is it credible?

_____ 3. Is it compelling enough?

_____ 4. Is it suitable for my audience's background and experiences, or would another illustration be more appropriate?

Stories come in many guises, from simple recitations of an event to fairy tales, legends, parables (short moral lessons), biblical narratives, and myths. They can be Horatio Alger-type success stories or Charles Dickens-type hard-luck tales. Many stories are passed down orally from one generation to the next. Common to all narratives are the essential storytelling elements of plot, characters, setting, and some sort of time line. Narratives can be brief and simple descriptions of short incidents worked into the body of the speech, or relatively drawn-out accounts that constitute most of the presentation. In either event, the key to a successful story is choosing one that will strike a responsive chord with the audience.

Personal experiences can be the basis for powerful narratives. In a keynote address delivered to the annual convention of the Asian American Journalists Association (AAJA), Helen Zia, a Chinese American writer and activist, revealed a personal experience that shed light on growing up as an Asian American in the 1950s and 1960s:

> I, like most of you, remember what it was like never to see people who looked like me in the world beyond my immediate circle. When I was growing up in the 1950s, Asians were nowhere to be found in the media, except occasionally in the movies. There at the Saturday matinee, my brothers and I would sit with all the other kids in town watching old World War II movies — you know, where the evil Zero pilots would be heading for their unsuspecting prey, only to be thwarted by the all-American heroes, who were, of course, always

CHECKLIST

Possible Forms for Citing Narratives

✓ "In J. R. R. Tolkien's classic trilogy *The Lord of the Rings,* a young Hobbit boy named Frodo . . ."

✓ "Some of you will recall when, in the animated movie *The Incredibles,* a family of superheroes — including Mr. Incredible, his wife Elastigirl, and their three kids — try to blend into the suburbs . . ."

✓ "I can never forget the day . . ."

✓ "At 9 A.M. on December 3, 2006, Shawn Bailey left her home for work . . ."

ESL Speaker's Notes
Broadening Your Listeners' Perspectives

As a non-native speaker of English, consider sharing a personal experience with the audience. Stories from other lands and other ways of life often fascinate listeners. Unique cultural traditions, eyewitness accounts of newsworthy events, or tales passed down orally from one generation to the next are just some of the possibilities. Depending on the goal of your speech, you can use your experiences as supporting material for a related topic or as the topic itself.

One adult public speaking student from Poland related what life for her was like after the fall of communism in 1989. She described how goods she had never seen before suddenly flooded the country. A wondrous array of fruit and meat left the most vivid impression on the then 11-year-old, as both had been nearly impossible to find under the old regime. The speaker's audience was fascinated with her firsthand account of historical events, and she found that sharing her unique experiences boosted her confidence in her speaking ability.

white. These movies would have their defining moment, that crescendo of emotion when the entire theater would rise up, screaming "Kill them!" "Kill them!" "Kill them!" ("Them" being the Japanese.) When the movie was over and the lights came on, I wanted to be invisible so that my neighbors wouldn't direct their red-*white*-and-blue fervor toward me.[7]

Many speakers, whether they're ministers at the Sunday morning pulpit or high-tech entrepreneurs rallying the troops, liberally sprinkle their speeches with **anecdotes** — brief stories of interesting, humorous, or real-life incidents. Obviously, the most effective anecdotes are those that the audience hasn't heard before and that link back to the speaker's theme. In a speech about the need to preserve our national parks, Brock Evans, the director of the Endangered Species Coalition, does this artfully:

One of the leaders of the fight was a fifth-generation rancher, Carroll Noble. . . . [H]e had a spread over near Pinedale. I'll never forget how he loved this Wyoming land, and how he expressed his feelings about it. One day, we were having dinner at his place. He had a big picture window there, framing that whole magnificent vista of the Wind River Range, its snow-capped jagged peaks, and the great tumbling mass of green forest spilling down its flank to the lake. At one point, he gestured out there, and turned to me with the greatest sadness: "You see that?" he said. "If they start cutting that, I'll never look out that window again."[8]

Draw on Testimony

When looking for supporting material, consider quoting or paraphrasing people who have an intimate knowledge of your topic. **Testimony** (from the Latin word for "witness") includes firsthand findings, eyewitness accounts, and opinions

CHECKLIST

Possible Forms for Citing Testimony

✓ "According to John Miller, one of the three founders of the community's rapid-transit committee . . ."

✓ "Teresa Allen, fund-raising chairperson from the Chicago Society of the Performing Arts, gave some insight into the proper way to obtain donations when she said . . ."

✓ "Dr. Mary Klein, a stem cell researcher from the Brown University School of Medicine, echoed this sentiment when she spoke Monday at the Public Health Committee meeting . . ."

by people, both lay (nonexpert) and expert. **Expert testimony** includes any findings, eyewitness accounts, or opinions by professionals who are trained to evaluate or report on a given topic. A medical doctor may provide cutting-edge information on the threat of cholesterol. A representative of an organization can appear before a government committee to testify for or against a proposed bill. **Lay testimony**, or testimony by nonexperts, can also serve as powerful supporting material. For example, eyewitnesses, such as survivors of the December 26, 2004, tsunami in Southeast Asia, can reveal compelling firsthand information that may be unavailable to others, often in a powerful way.

Credibility plays a key role in the effectiveness of testimony. It's up to you to establish the source's reputation, and to do so in as compelling and accurate a manner as possible. When citing testimony, make sure that you supply the name and qualifications of the person whose testimony you use and that you inform your listeners when and where the testimony was offered. It isn't necessary to cite the exact date (though do keep a written record of this); in an oral presentation, terms such as "recently," "last year," and so forth are fine:

CHECKLIST

Evaluating the Credibility of Testimony

✓ Are the experts I've cited proven in their fields?

✓ Is the lay testimony reliable?

✓ Do the sources have any obvious biases?

✓ Is their testimony timely? Is it relevant?

✓ Do their views effectively support my thesis?

✓ Do their views add power to my assertions or arguments?

✓ Are there reasons that the audience may not react favorably to the testimony?[9]

Testimony that does not meet these standards is likely to do more harm to your speech than good.

In testimony before the U.S. House Subcommittee on Human Rights and Wellness last week, Derek Ellerman, co-executive director of the Polaris Project said, "Many people have little understanding of the enormity and the brutality of the sex trafficking industry in the United States. When they think of sex slavery, they think of Thailand or Nepal — not a suburban house in the DC area, with $400,000 homes and manicured lawns. . . ."[10]

Provide Facts and Statistics

Chances are you'll need to present facts in your presentation. **Facts** represent documented occurrences, including actual events, dates, times, people involved, and places. Research has demonstrated that most people require some type of evidence, usually in the form of facts and statistics, before they will accept someone else's claims or position.[11]

Facts are truly facts only when they have been independently verified by people other than the source. For example, we accept as true that Abraham Lincoln was the sixteenth president of the United States because this fact has been independently verified by eyewitnesses, journalists, historians, and so forth. Listeners are not likely to accept your statements as factual unless you back them up with credible evidence.

A **statistic** is quantified evidence. We use statistics to quantitatively describe, compare, and predict a nearly infinite range of things, from batting averages to birthrates. Statistics can be an excellent form of supporting material because they summarize and clarify complex information; they also help make

TABLE 8.1 • Types and Functions of Supporting Material

Type of Supporting Material	Definition	Purpose
Example	Illustrates, describes, or represents things; it can be brief or extended, and real or hypothetical.	Aids understanding by making ideas, items, or events more concrete; creates interest.
Narrative	A story, either real or imaginary, short or drawn-out in length. Can constitute a small part of the presentation or serve as a basis for the speech itself.	Generates interest and identification.
Testimony	Firsthand findings, eyewitness accounts, and opinions by people, both lay (nonexpert) and expert.	Provides evidence and aids credibility.
Facts	Actual events, dates, times, and places that can be independently verified.	Provides evidence (including people involved) and demonstrates points.
Statistics	Data that demonstrate relationships.	Summarizes information, demonstrates proof, makes points memorable.

abstract concepts or ideas concrete for listeners. Claiming that "the university awarded more scholarship money last year than the year before," for example, is less informative and meaningful than stating that "the university awarded $100,000 in scholarships last year compared to $84,000 the year before."

USE STATISTICS ACCURATELY

Audience members often accept a speaker's statistics without question, believing that "numbers never lie" and that the speaker will be ethical in his or her use of them. Unfortunately, this may not always be the case. To be of value as supporting evidence, you should understand what the statistics actually mean and use terms that describe them correctly.

Use Frequencies to Indicate Counts

A common type of statistic used in speeches, a **frequency** is simply a count of the number of times something occurs or appears. When your instructor reports back to the class on how many students made each of the letter grades (A, B, C, etc.) on an exam, he or she is reporting frequencies: "On the midterm exam there were 8 As, 15 Bs, 7 Cs, 2 Ds, and 1 F."

Frequencies can help listeners easily see comparisons between two or more categories:

> According to *Census 2000*, the total population of the State of Colorado comprised 2,165,983 males and 2,135,278 females.[12]

Frequencies also help audience members understand the magnitude or capacity of something you are trying to describe:

> Inside the cabin, the Airbus A380 has room for at least 550 passengers — and as many as 1,000.[13]

You can also use frequencies to demonstrate trends, as when counts increase or decrease between two points in time:

> The birth rate among young adolescents aged 10 to 14 has fallen to the lowest level since 1946 according to a report released . . . by the Centers for Disease Control and Prevention (CDC). . . . This number has declined steadily from a peak of 12,901 in 1994, to the current low of 7,315.[14]

Use Percentages to Express Proportion

As informative as frequencies can be, the similarity or difference in magnitude between things may be more meaningfully indicated in percentages. A **percentage** is the quantified portion of a whole, or 100 percent. Describing the frequencies of males and females in the 2000 Colorado population (2,165,983 and 2,135,278, respectively) in percentages shows even more clearly how similar the two amounts are: 50.36 percent male and 49.64 percent female. Although numerically different (50.36 is not 49.64), common practice permits us to round off the figures, stating that, "As of the 2000 census, the population of Colorado is 'roughly' 50 percent female and 50 percent male."

Percentages are especially useful when comparing categories or classes of something. Consider this example comparing eight factors involved in on-time arrivals of domestic flights:

> In March 2005, 76.94% of domestic large carrier airline flights were on time. The leading factors among the 23.06% of flights that did not arrive as scheduled were late arriving aircraft (6.46%), air carrier delay (5.88%), and cancelled flights (1.65%). Weather delays, national aviation system delays, security delays, and diverted traffic occurred in less than 1% of March flights.[15]

As much as these percentages succeed in showing comparisons, listeners still need time to interpret them. But because audience members cannot take the time to pause and reflect on the figures as they would with written text, speakers must help listeners interpret the numbers:

> As you can see, the great majority of passenger flights were on time in March 2005. Where there were delays, they were due largely to late arriving single aircraft and to delays elsewhere within an air carrier (a single company's flight operations). Cancelled flights were rare, and other factors rarer still.

(See Chapter 16 for more on the differences between oral and written language.)

Use Averages to Describe Typical Characteristics

Frequencies and percentages are invaluable tools for quantitatively describing and comparing counts and proportions. But many times we need to describe information according to its typical or *average* characteristics. Usually we think of the **average** as the sum of the scores divided by the number of scores. This is referred to as the **mean**, the arithmetic (or computed) average. But there are two other kinds of averages — the median and the mode. It is important for you to distinguish among these three kinds of averages.

Suppose, for example, that your instructor wants to determine the average score he or she gave to nine students who delivered informative speeches on a given day. The frequency is nine. Here is how the instructor would determine the *mean* score: If the nine students scored 5, 19, 22, 23, 24, 26, 28, 28, and 30, the highest possible speech grade is 30 points. Along with the individual scores, the instructor wants to know how the group did as a whole. To do this, she finds the average of the nine scores. Here, the *mean* score is 22.5.

A second kind of average the instructor can consider is the **median** — the center-most score in a distribution, the point above and below which 50 percent of the scores fall. Arranging our sample set of scores from lowest to highest (5, 19, 22, 23, 24, 26, 28, 28, and 30), we see that the center-most score is 24. The *median* is 24. Thus, on the first day of informative speeches, half the students scored above 24 and half scored below 24.

A third kind of average is the **mode**, the most frequently occurring score in the distribution. In this case, the *mode* is 28, the only score appearing more than once. The mode tells the instructor the most frequently occurring score in a set of scores.

You can see from the outcomes of the three kinds of averages that simply reporting an average can be misleading, even if unintentionally so. It would be misleading to report that the average for these students is 28 (the *mode*) rather than 22.5 (the *mean*).

Confusing the different types of averages is an all-too-common error (inadvertent and otherwise) in speeches. Say, for instance, that you want to discuss the average income in an emerging nation. That nation may have a small minority of wealthy entrepreneurs and a vast majority of poor laborers. Merely citing the *mean* average may give an extremely distorted picture of reality. The *mode,* the most frequently occurring number, may depict things much more accurately. This can be seen clearly in the following example, in which a liberal policy advocate argues that a conservative think tank misinterprets the average tax rate paid by Americans:

> The Tax Foundation determines an *average* [*mean*] tax rate for American families simply by dividing all taxes paid by the total of everyone's income. It calls this the amount of tax that the "typical family" pays, even though the proportionately larger share of taxes that the wealthy pay inflates the average and makes the taxes paid by middle-class families appear higher than they really are. For example, if four middle-income families pay $3,000, $4,000, $5,000, and $6,000, respectively, in taxes, and one very wealthy family pays $82,000 in taxes, the *average* [*mean*] tax paid by these five families is $20,000 ($100,000 in total taxes divided by five families). But four of the five families have a tax bill equaling $6,000 or less.
>
> [Many] analysts would define a *median* income family—a family for whom half of all families have higher income and half have lower income—to be the "typical family" and describe the taxes paid by a such a median-income family as the taxes that typical middle-class families owe.[16]

PRESENT YOUR STATISTICS ETHICALLY

Whether done inadvertently or intentionally, offering listeners inaccurate statistics is unethical. Following are some steps you can take to reduce the likelihood of using false or misleading statistics in your speeches:

Choose Your Sources Carefully.   Be discerning about the sources for your statistics. This is particularly important given our tendency to place our faith in numbers. Are they taken from trustworthy and reputable sources? Are they drawn from a secondary or tertiary source such as a media outlet or personal Web site, or from a primary source such as a polling organization or a government statistical repository (e.g., FirstGov.gov)? Bear in mind that the more information that is available about the methods used to generate the data, including why it was collected and what researchers hoped to learn from it, the more authoritative the source of the information is likely to be.

Ethically Speaking
Assessing Statistics for Reliability and Validity

Researchers use many different statistical tools to analyze their data. Unfortunately, it's extremely easy to misuse any of these methods. If misuse does occur, whether intentionally to advance an agenda or accidentally, through error, the conclusion may misrepresent an important relationship or effect.[1] The flawed data that results from such misinterpretations often evolves into widespread misconceptions. One classic example is the oft-quoted statement that 95 percent of all dieters never lose weight, and 95 percent of those who do lose weight will not keep it off. In fact, this figure is based on a study done in the 1950s of one hundred patients in an obesity clinic.[2] Clearly, the study's results cannot be extrapolated with any degree of accuracy to today's general population.

Before using statistics in your speeches, be sure to take the time to assess their reliability and validity. Consider whether the data were collected scientifically and interpreted objectively. Ask yourself "What is the sample size? Are the results statistically relevant? Was the experiment well designed?"

If you are reporting on a poll, ask yourself "Who took the poll, and when was it conducted? Who paid for the poll, and why was it taken? How many people were interviewed for the survey, and how were they chosen? What area (nation, state, or region) or group (teachers, lawyers, Democratic voters, etc.) were these people chosen from? Are the results based on the answers of all the people interviewed? Who should have been interviewed and was not? What is the sampling error for the poll results? What other kinds of factors could have skewed the poll results?[3]

1. John S. Gardenier and David B. Resnik, "The Misuse of Statistics: Concepts, Tools, and a Research Agenda," proceedings of 2001 conference, "Investigating Research Integrity," of the U.S. Department of Health and Human Services, Office of Research Integrity, ori.dhhs.gov/multimedia/acrobat/papers/gardenier.pdf (accessed July 2, 2002).
2. Gary Taubes, *Bad Science: The Short Life and Weird Times of Cold Fusion* (New York: Random House, 1993).
3. Excerpted from Sheldon R. Gawiser and G. Evans Witt, "Twenty Questions a Journalist Should Ask about Poll Results." Earl Babbie, *The Practice of Social Research* (Belmont, CA: Wadsworth, 1998). National Council on Public Opinion Polls Web site www.ncpp.org/qajsa.htm (accessed July 2, 2002).

Although some audience members may accept your figures at face value, critical listeners will find them convincing only if they believe the source to be reliable. Consider, for example, the following two speakers. Which speaker would you find most convincing?

Speaker 1: People in this country are as fat as they've been ever. Countless news reports and magazine articles describe an epidemic of obesity. Yesterday on *Oprah*, a doctor said that about 30 percent of older adults are now obese.

Speaker 2: People in this country are as fat as they've been ever. Countless news reports and magazine articles describe an epidemic of obesity. A 2004 report by the Federal Interagency Forum on Aging-Related Statistics found that as of 2002, 73 percent of Americans ages 65–74 were overweight, and 36 percent were obese. The report documents a shocking rise since the 1960s, when just ten percent of men and 23 percent of women were obese.[17]

Although many people rank talk-show host Oprah Winfrey and her guests as trustworthy, most people would tend to assign greater credibility to the second speaker. While the first speaker's claim begs to be validated by a trustworthy source, the second speaker offers multiple statistics collected by a U.S. government agency. In addition, by noting the sharp rise in obesity over time, the second speaker drives home the point that an epidemic exists.

Present Statistics in Context.   Statistics are meaningful only within a proper context. To help audience members accurately interpret statistical information, indicate why the statistics were collected, who or what they are intended to represent, what methods were used to collect them, and what period of time they refer to. The best and maybe only sure way to answer these questions is to know the sources of your statistical information.

Note how this speaker describes when the data were collected (2003), the method used to collect the data (survey), and the scope of the research (national):

> According to a report posted on the Centers for Disease Control and Prevention Web site, 70.8 percent of all deaths among youth and young adults aged 10–24 years result from only four causes: motor-vehicle crashes (32.3 percent), other unintentional injuries (11.7 percent), homicide (15.1 percent), and suicide (11.7 percent). These figures represent data collected during 2003 from questionnaires distributed to all public and private schools in the U.S. with students in at least one of grades 9–12 in the 50 states and the District of Columbia.[18]

Avoid Confusing Statistics with "Absolute Truth."   Rather than the absolute or only truth, statistics represent a quantification of something at a given point in time. Thus, statistics are rarely definitive. Even the most recent data available on a subject will change the next time the data are collected. Nor are statistics necessarily any more perfect than the people who collect them.

 CHECKLIST

Using Statistics in Your Speech: An Ethical Inventory

✓   Do I include statistics from the most authoritative sources I can locate?

✓   Do I briefly tell listeners about the method(s) used to collect the statistics (such as a survey), the scope of the research (e.g., sample size), and where the data is drawn from)?

✓   Do I alert listeners to when the statistics were collected?

✓   Do I offer the data as they appropriately represent my point or claim, but refrain from declaring that these data are absolute?

✓   Do I refrain from using or ignoring statistics selectively to make my point (cherry-picking)?

✓ **CHECKLIST**

Possible Forms for Citing Facts and Statistics

✓   "As published in the October 2005 edition of *Nature* . . ."

✓   "According to the U.S. Department of Health and Human Services Web site, accessed on May 18, 2005 . . ."

✓   "According to a January 2005 report posted on the Centers for Disease Control and Prevention Web site, 70.8 percent of all deaths . . ."

✓   "In a May 2004 study published in *Morbidity and Mortality Weekly Report,* available online at the Centers for Disease Control and Prevention Web site . . ."

One way to avoid presenting statistics as definitive is to present them as tentative information. Offer the data as they appropriately represent your point or claim, but refrain from declaring that these data are absolute.

Avoid Cherry-Picking.   To **cherry-pick** is to selectively present only those statistics that buttress your point of view while ignoring competing data.[19] Cherry-picking is a popular tool of politicians and policymakers, who are often accused of selectively referring to only those statistics that boost their arguments and policies.

When you find yourself searching for statistics to confirm an opinion or belief you already hold, you are probably engaging in cherry-picking.[20] Choosing from among the mean, median, and mode of a distribution the one average that makes the best case for your point, when in fact one of the other averages is the better indicator of what your data represent, is an instance of cherry-picking. Researching statistical support material is not a trip through a buffet line to select what looks good and discard what doesn't. You must locate as much information as possible that is pertinent to your particular point, and then present it in context or not at all.

USE VISUAL AIDS WHENEVER POSSIBLE

When your speech relies heavily on statistical information, use appropriate tables, graphs, and charts to display the statistics (see Chapters 20–22).

9 Locating Supporting Material

The search for supporting material can be one of the most enjoyable parts of putting together a speech. It is at this stage that you can delve into your subject, sift through sources, and select material that best conveys and supports your message. Classical rhetoricians termed the process of selecting information to illustrate or prove your points **invention**. According to Aristotle, one of the speaker's most important tasks is to select from among the many different types of evidence available those materials that are most likely to lead listeners to accept the speaker's point of view.[1]

To find the right mix of examples, facts and statistics, opinions, stories, and testimony for your speech, you will want to conduct primary research, secondary research, or a combination of the two. **Primary research** is original or first-hand research, such as interviews and surveys conducted by you the speaker. **Secondary research** is the vast world of information gathered by others.

The main sources for primary research are interviews and surveys; secondary research resides in a nearly infinite number of library and Internet resources. As you gather these materials, consider how you can use them to generate interest, illustrate and clarify your meaning, and add solid evidence to your assertions.

Before You Begin: Plan A Research Strategy

A common pitfall of research is getting sidetracked. In reviewing secondary research particularly, the biggest pitfall is wasting time in the wrong places. By keeping the reason for your search — to substantiate your thesis with material that is most likely to be accepted by your audience — clearly in mind, you stand a better chance of avoiding this trap.

Before beginning your search, take a few moments to review your thesis statement. Consider what you need to support it. What do you need to elaborate upon, explain, demonstrate, or prove? What kinds of evidence will your audience most likely accept? (See Chapter 25.) Different topics suggest different research methods, so reflect on what might work best for your particular topic, purpose, and occasion. A topic such as drinking habits on campus clearly begs for primary research in the form of interviews, surveys, or personal observations. Other topics can be supported only through secondary research. Nearly all topics benefit from a mix of both.

✓ **CHECKLIST**

Making an Inventory of Your Research Needs

_____ 1. What do I personally know about my topic?

_____ 2. What does my thesis statement require me to explain, demonstrate, or prove?

_____ 3. What type of supporting material does my topic call for?

   _____ Primary research such as interviews or surveys?

   _____ Facts and statistics?

   _____ Examples that will clarify material?

   _____ Stories that will capture attention and make a point?

   _____ Testimony that will bolster my argument?

_____ 4. What type of supporting material will most influence my audience?

   _____ Primary research such as interviews or surveys?

   _____ Facts and statistics?

   _____ Examples that will clarify material?

   _____ Stories that will capture attention and make a point?

   _____ Testimony that will bolster my argument?

Secondary Resources: Print and Electronically Stored Sources

Secondary research includes all information recorded by individuals other than actual participants in an event or study. The most likely sources of secondary research include books, newspapers, periodicals, government publications, and reference works such as encyclopedias, almanacs, books of quotations, and atlases. In the past, these sources appeared only in print. Increasingly, however, the information they contain is being stored simultaneously on CD-ROMs, on DVDs, and in online databases. A **database** is a searchable place, or "base," in which information is stored and from which it can be retrieved. A **full-text database** is one in which at least some of the records in the database contain the full text of articles.

LIBRARY RESOURCES TO FACILITATE YOUR SEARCH

If you conduct your search in a library, you may wish to begin by consulting two essential resources: the reference librarian and the card or online catalog. (See Chapter 10 for information on using virtual libraries on the World Wide Web.)

The Reference Desk

Every library contains a unique mix of print works and database subscription services. At the reference desk you can find out what this mix is and, with the help of a reference librarian, learn how to use these resources to research your topic. **Reference librarians** are information specialists who are trained to help you in your search. Don't hesitate to ask for their assistance.

The Library Catalog

You can find out what the library owns by consulting the library catalog, which is searchable by author, title, and subject. Libraries organize books and other holdings according to the **Library of Congress call number** or the **Dewey decimal number**. Once you've located an entry in the catalog, jot down or print out this call number so that you can locate it on the shelves.

The Search Tips Section

Whatever it is you want to locate on a database—book, newspaper, magazine, journal article, or other media—smart search techniques will make your job less stressful and more productive. Every database has its own way of conducting searches, so it is vital that you consult the "Search Tips" section (see also Chapter 10, "Using the Internet to Support Your Speech").

BOOKS

Books explore topics in depth. A well-written book provides detail and perspective and can serve as an excellent source of supporting examples, stories, facts, and statistics. To locate a book in your library's holdings, refer to the library's catalog. To search the titles of all books currently in print in the United States, refer to *Books in Print* (in print form) or *Books in Print* Online (www .booksinprint.com). Alternatively, log on to the Library of Congress Online Catalog (www.catalog.loc.gov) or an online bookseller and key in your topic; because *Books in Print* is a subscription-based service (i.e., it charges a fee), many librarians search for books in this manner.[2]

NEWSPAPERS AND PERIODICALS

Newspapers are a rich source of support material. In addition to reports on the major issues and events of the day, many newspaper stories—especially feature articles—also include detailed background or historical information. Three comprehensive online sources for searching newspaper articles include *Lexis-Nexis Academic Universe News Service, InfoTrac Newspaper Collection,* and *ProQuest Newstand.* Several Web sites are also devoted to newspapers, in such categories as newspaper archives (e.g., www.newspaperarchive.com), U.S newspapers (www .newsvoyager.com), and online world newspapers (world-newspapers.com). Indexes to individual newspapers such as the *New York Times* and *Wall Street Journal* are also available on microfiche. News reported on television and radio may be accessed on sites such as NPR Online, CNN.com, and BBC.co.uk.

A **periodical** is a regularly published magazine or journal. Periodicals are an excellent source for speeches because they usually include the various types of supporting material discussed in Chapter 8 (examples, narratives, testimony, facts and statistics). Periodicals include general-interest magazines such as *Time* and *Newsweek,* as well as the thousands of specialized academic, business, and technical magazines, newsletters, and journals in circulation. Most popular magazines are indexed in *Wilson Periodical Abstracts.* Many libraries offer access to the online databases *InfoTrac Online, Expanded Academic ASAP,* and *EBSCO Academic Search Elite,* all of which cover both general periodicals and more specialized journals.

In addition, an ever-increasing number of periodical databases are devoted to special topics. For business-related topics, consider using *ABI/Inform* and *Lexis-Nexis Academic Universe, Business.* If you plan to talk about a health or medical topic, examine Health and Wellness Resource Center (www.galegroup .com/HealthRC) or PubMed (www.ncbi.nlm.nih.gov/entrez/query.fcgi). See Table 9.1 for a list of specialized databases available in many college libraries.

TABLE 9.1 • Specialized Databases Found in Many Libraries

Database	Description
WorldCat *(Accessed through Firstsearch)*	A unique resource that allows users to review and locate virtually everything that has been published about a topic in any form—from books to musical scores to video and sound recordings. Contains millions of online records built from the bibliographic and ownership information of more than 9,000 contributing libraries.
ABI/INFORM GLOBAL	Covers business, management, economics, and a wide range of related fields. Contains abstracts of material from 1971 onward and full text (various formats) from 1987.
¡Informe! (Revistas en Español)	Searches popular and scholarly Spanish-language articles from 1980. Also searches information on over 450,000 companies, health and wellness, and more.
ALT-HEALTH WATCH	Focuses on the many perspectives of complementary, holistic, and integrated approaches to health care and wellness; offers full-text articles from more than 170 international journals, periodicals, booklets, and book excerpts.
ERIC (Education Resources Information Center)	The world's largest digital library of educational information, with more than 1.1 million citations of education-related documents and journal articles; 1966–present. Also offers free access to more than 107,000 full-text nonjournal documents published between 1993 and 2004 (www.eric.ed.gov).
ProQuest Science Journals	A growing full-text science database offering journal articles in subjects ranging from acoustics to zoology.
PsycINFO	Includes indexes and summaries of journal articles, book chapters, books, and reports—all in the field of psychology, psychiatry, and related disciplines. Journal coverage, spanning 1887–present, includes international material selected from more than 1,700 publications.
PubMed	The National Library of Medicine's database of citations to more than 15 million articles in the biomedical fields; includes a growing list of full-text entries (www.ncbi.nlm.nih.gov/ entrez/query.fcgi).

GOVERNMENT PUBLICATIONS

Part of every tax dollar supports the constant production of publications by the **U.S. Government Printing Office (GPO)**, and the result is a resource that every citizen should enjoy. The GPO is responsible for publishing and distributing all information collected and produced by federal agencies, from the U.S. Census Bureau to the Department of Education and the Environmental Protection Agency. GPO publications also include all congressional reports and hearings. Most federal, state, and local government agencies provide statistics and other information freely and in a timely manner.

Finding and using government documents can be a daunting task, but, given that nearly all the information comes from primary sources, it's usually well worth the effort. Get started by logging on to www.access.gpo.gov, where you will find an "A to Z Resource List." Alternatively, go directly to FirstGov.gov, the official portal to all government information and services. FirstGov.gov contains links to millions of Web pages from federal, local, and tribal governments to foreign nations around the world. The site includes links to statistics of every kind. You may also wish to access FirstGov en Español, which offers resources in Spanish.

Online, the University of Michigan's Document Center (www.lib.umich.edu/govdocs) is another excellent starting point for government documents, whether local, state, federal, foreign, or international.

REFERENCE WORKS

Reference works include, but are not limited to, encyclopedias, almanacs, biographical reference works, books of quotations, poetry collections, and atlases.

Encyclopedias

Encyclopedias summarize knowledge that is found in original form elsewhere. Their usefulness lies in providing a broad overview of subjects and in helping you to generate a list of key terms for your search. **General encyclopedias** attempt to cover all important subject areas of knowledge; **specialized encyclopedias** delve deeply into one subject area. The most comprehensive of the general encyclopedias is the *Encyclopedia Britannica,* which is available in print form, on CD-ROM and DVD, and online at (www.britannica.com). Published continually since 1768, the *Britannica* is revered by scholars worldwide as the most authoritative compendium of information in encyclopedia form. Because almost one-third of the encyclopedia is devoted to biographies, it is an ideal reference for topics involving people.

For a more in-depth look at a topic, there are specialized encyclopedias of all types (stored on CD-ROM, on DVD, and online), ranging from the *McGraw-Hill Encyclopedia of Science and Technology* to the *Encyclopedia of Religion*

Public Speaking in Cultural Perspective
Multicultural Reference Works—Filling the Gap

Until fairly recently, standard reference works such as encyclopedias and almanacs claimed to be comprehensive but, in fact, generally paid little attention to the culture and accomplishments of the many groups that make up the United States. Today, publishers are addressing the long-standing need for detailed information on these groups' experiences. The *Gale Encyclopedia of Multicultural America,* for example, contains 152 original essays on specific minority and ethnic groups in the United States, from Arab Americans to the Yupiat.[3]

Among biographical resources, Gale Research publishes *African American Biography, Contemporary Black Biography, Hispanic American Biography, Asian American Biography, Arab American Biography,* and *Native American Biography.* All are multivolume sets that contain portraits, quotes, interviews, and articles about prominent men and women.

Among specialized almanacs, available now are the *Asian American Almanac, Muslim Almanac, St. James Press Gay and Lesbian Almanac, Native North American Almanac, African American Almanac,* and *Hispanic American Almanac* (all published by Gale Research), along with a host of similar publications. Each reference work contains essays that focus on all major aspects of group life and culture. One way to see what's available is to search a database such as WorldCat.

and the *Encyclopedia of Physical Education, Fitness, and Sports.* Your reference librarian will help you identify those in your school library's collection.

Almanacs

To find facts and statistics that support your topic, **almanacs** and **fact books** are a good choice. (See also U.S. government publications listed previously.) As with encyclopedias, there are both general and specialized almanacs. In the general category, one of the most comprehensive sources is the *World Almanac and Book of Facts.* This reference work's well-organized alphabetical index gives readers easy access to subjects. It contains facts and statistics in many categories, including those related to historical, social, political, and religious subjects, plus the top-ten news stories of the year, notable Supreme Court decisions, notable quotes of the year, and a complete listing of vital statistics for all nations of the world. Other helpful almanacs include the *Information Please Almanac; Famous First Facts: A Record of First Happenings, Discoveries, and Inventions in American History; People's Almanac;* and *Guinness Book of Records* (see also the Guinness World Records Web site at www.guinnessworldrecords.com, which provides facts on world records of all kinds). Information from almanacs can supplement other research for your speech. As with encyclopedias, however, don't rely on them as your only means of support.

Biographical Resources

For information about famous or noteworthy people, the *Biography Index* is an excellent starting point. Available in print, on CD-ROM, and online, this comprehensive resource indexes biographical material from periodicals, books, and even obituaries from the *New York Times*. Published quarterly, it is quite up to date. For analyses and criticism of the published works of individuals you may be speaking about, consider such biographical resources as *American National Biography, Dictionary of American Biography, Famous Hispanics in the World and in History* (access is free at coloquio.com/famosos/alpha.htm), *Current Biography,* and *The African American Biographical Database (AABD)*.

Books of Quotations

For public speakers, books of quotations are an indispensable tool. Quotations are often used in the introductions and conclusions of speeches; they are also liberally sprinkled throughout examples, narratives, and, of course, testimony. First published in 1855, *Bartlett's Familiar Quotations* contains a collection of passages, phrases, and proverbs traced to their sources in ancient and modern literature. Other collections are targeted specifically at public speakers, including *Quotations for Public Speakers: A Historical, Literary, and Political Anthology,* by Robert G. Torricelli,[4] and *Nelson's Complete Book of Stories, Illustrations, and Quotes: The Ultimate Contemporary Resource for Speakers,* by Robert J. Morgan.[5]

Poetry Collections

Lines of poetry, if not entire poems, are often used by speakers both to introduce and conclude speeches and to illustrate points in the speech body. Every library has a collection of poetry anthologies as well as the collected works of individual poets. Updated yearly, the *Columbia Granger's Index to Poetry* indexes poems by author, title, and first line. This index is available in print and on CD-ROM. Online, you can search for poetry and other classic works on Bartleby .com (www.bartleby.com/index.html).

Atlases

An **atlas** is a collection of maps, text, and accompanying charts and tables. As well as serving to locate a particular locale (and to learn about its terrain, demographic information, and proximity to other places), many atlases use the medium of maps to explore art history, human anatomy, and even dog breeds. Indeed, a search for atlases at Amazon.com will yield in excess of 26,000 hits. For straightforward geographic atlases, consult *National Geographic Atlas of the World* and *Rand McNally Commercial Atlas and Guide*. Both are in print form; online you can access maps at the National Geographic Web site (www .nationalgeographic.com/maps/index.html).

To learn about what atlases can offer beyond geography, consider conducting a search of atlases related to your topic. A subject search involving the keywords *art* AND *atlas,*" for example, would likely lead to the highly regarded *Atlas of World Art,* published by Oxford University Press (2004).

Primary Resources: Interviews and Surveys

Supporting material drawn from primary research can include any source developed directly by the participants involved. The Declaration of Independence is a primary document created by the founding fathers of the United States. Firsthand oral or written histories, diaries, letters, and recordings of meetings and other events are also primary sources. Two additional types of primary research commonly used to support speeches are interviews and surveys that you conduct yourself. Both methods can provide valuable kinds of information to support and enliven a speech.

INTERVIEWS

Even with all the printed and online information available today, oftentimes you can gain considerably more insight into a topic by speaking personally to someone who has expertise on the subject. An **interview** is a face-to-face communication for the purpose of gathering information. Productive interviews require advance planning.

Preparing for the Interview

In a series of interviews on the art of interviewing, well-known journalists Bob Schieffer and Jim Short, among others, point out that getting the information you need from a subject requires advance planning. Questions should be carefully prepared and written down; take care to avoid posing poorly phrased questions[6] that are vague, leading, or loaded.

- *Vague questions* don't give the person being interviewed enough to go on. He or she must either guess at what you mean or spend time asking you for clarification. Vague questions waste the interviewee's time and reflect the interviewer's lack of preparation.
- *Leading questions* encourage, if not force, a certain response and reflect the interviewer's bias: "Like most intelligent people, are you going to support candidate X?"
- *Loaded questions* are likewise phrased to reinforce the interviewer's agenda. They may also have a hostile intent: "Isn't it true that you've never supported school programs?"

As you draft your questions, aim to create **neutral questions**, or those that don't lead the interviewee to a desired response. Usually, neutral questions consist of a mix of open, closed, primary, and secondary questions (see Table 9.2).

Structuring the Interview

Think about an interview as having the same broad structure as a speech, with an introduction (the opening), a body, and a conclusion (the closing).

TABLE 9.2 • Forms of Interview Questions	
Question Form	Description/Purpose in the Interview
Open/closed	• **Open questions:** Allow the interviewee to elaborate as he or she desires.
	• **Closed questions:** Permit only "Yes," "No," or other limited responses (see Chapter 6; section on questionnaires).
Primary/secondary	• **Primary questions:** Introduce new topics or areas of questioning (e.g., "What made you want to become a veterinarian?").
	• **Secondary questions:** Expand upon topics introduced in primary questions (e.g., "Did you go to veterinary school right after college?" and "Was it difficult to get student loans?").
Types of Secondary Questions: Questions seeking clarification Questions seeking elaboration "Clearinghouse" questions	• **Questions seeking clarification:** Designed to clarify the interviewee's statements (e.g., "By 'older mothers,' do you mean over 30, over 40, or over 50?"). • **Questions seeking elaboration:** Designed to elicit additional information (e.g., "Were there other reasons that you chose your profession?"). • **"Clearinghouse" questions:** Designed to check that all important information has been discussed (e.g., "Have we covered all the important points?").[1]

1. James C. McCrosky, in *An Introduction to Rhetorical Communication,* 8th ed. (Boston: Allyn and Bacon, 2001), makes this point throughout his text, and particularly on pages 223–24.

The Opening: Getting off to a Good Start. A spirit of collaboration is crucial in the interview setting, so focus on creating a positive first impression. It is at this stage that your interviewee will decide whether you are credible and trustworthy:

• Acknowledge the interviewee and express respect for his or her expertise.

• Briefly summarize your topic and informational needs.

• State a (reasonable) goal — what you would like to accomplish in the interview — and reach agreement on it.

• Establish a time limit for the interview and stick to it.

The Body: Posing the Questions. It is in the body of the interview that you will pose your substantive questions.[7] Using your prepared questions as a guide, permit the interviewee to introduce new topics and elaborate as he or she sees fit. Don't be afraid to ask for clarification or to repeat your questions if they remain unanswered.

It is vital to listen well as your subject answers your questions. As journalist Jim Short counsels, "Listen to what the subject is saying, not just to what you want to hear."[8] In addition, strive to use the **active listening** strategies described in Chapter 3 (e.g., set goals, listen for main ideas, and watch for nonverbal cues). Don't break in when the subject is speaking or interject with leading comments. *Paraphrase* the interviewee's answers where appropriate in order to establish understanding. Ask for *clarification* and *elaboration* when necessary.

✓ **CHECKLIST**

Preparing for the Interview

_____ 1. Do I have a written set of questions?

_____ 2. Can each of the questions be answered within a reasonable time frame, or within the time agreed upon with the interviewee?

_____ 3. Are each of my questions relevant to the central idea and purpose of my speech?

_____ 4. Are my questions posed in a well-thought-out sequence in relation to my topic?

_____ 5. Are my questions free of bias or hostile intent?

_____ 6. Are controversial questions reserved until the end of the interview?

_____ 7. Have I obtained advance permission to record the interview?

_____ 8. Do I have a working writing implement and ample notepaper (or a working laptop)?

_____ 9. Am I thoroughly comfortable about operating any recording equipment I plan to use during the interview?

The Closing: Recheck and Confirm. Too often, people who conduct interviews end them in haste. Before ending the interview, recheck your notes and, if necessary, confirm them:

- Check to see that your notes have been properly recorded and are legible.
- Briefly offer a positive summary of important things you learned in the interview.
- Offer to send the interviewee the results of the interview, as in a printed speech.
- Send a written note of thanks.

Recording the Interview

More than one interview has gone splendidly — and entirely — unrecorded. As a result, the interviewer had to reconstruct from memory what was said, with the result usually being a slew of inaccuracies. You can avoid this pitfall by taking detailed notes, tape-recording the interview, or using a combination of note taking, recording, and videotaping. To establish an air of authenticity, you might even decide to replay short excerpts during your speech.

If you do wish to record the interview, always seek permission from the subject ahead of time. Check that the equipment works before the actual time of the interview. You should feel comfortable enough about operating the equipment that using it does not intrude on the interviewee's time or attention.

Conducting the Interview Professionally

The individuals you interview are helping you, and in return you should treat them in a professional manner. Allow them to set the pace, and always allow them to ask you questions or make comments that are not part of your questionnaire.

SURVEYS

Like interviews, a *survey* is useful both as a tool to investigate audience attitudes (see Chapter 6) and as supporting material. Surveys are an especially effective source of support for topics related to the attitudes, values, and beliefs of people in your immediate environment. Perhaps, for example, your central idea is, "School-age children who regularly attend religious services have a greater sense of well-being than those who don't." Although secondary research would be necessary to prove your claim, a survey of students at a local school could serve as an excellent source of additional support with direct relevance to your audience. (For information on creating surveys, refer to Chapter 6.)

Remember, however, that any informal survey you conduct is unlikely to be statistically sound enough to be taken as actual proof of your claims. Present your findings to the audience in a manner that acknowledges this, and be certain to shore up any informal survey research you conduct with other, more credible forms of support. (See Chapter 8 for a discussion of using statistics in speeches).

Documenting Your Resources

Doing research can be fascinating, but organizing it can be frustrating. Fortunately, a few simple steps can help you keep track of your sources and their origins. (For visual guidelines on citing print sources and incorporating source material into your speech, see "From Source to Speech" on citing books, p. 142, and on citing periodical articles, p. 144).

RECORD REFERENCES AS YOU GO

One of the biggest problems any researcher encounters is keeping track of bibliographic information. The easiest way to avoid this problem is to maintain a **working bibliography** as you review potential sources. Whether you are photocopying an article, downloading it from the Internet, or copying a passage by hand, for each source make sure to record the information outlined in the accompanying checklist. (See Chapter 10 for more on how to organize Internet sources.)

Of course, you won't cite all of this information in the speech itself. (See Chapter 4 for examples of how to acknowledge other people's ideas in your speeches.) You *will* need a complete record of your references, however, for an end-of-speech bibliography. For your written bibliography, the most commonly used documentation systems are the *Chicago Manual of Style,* the APA (American Psychological Association) method, the MLA (Modern Language Association) method, the CSE (Council of Science Editors, formerly Council of Biology

> ✓ **CHECKLIST**
>
> **Creating a Bibliography**
>
> For each relevant source, be sure to record the following elements:
>
> _____ 1. Names of author(s) or editor(s) as cited
>
> _____ 2. Title of publication
>
> _____ 3. Volume or edition number, if applicable
>
> _____ 4. Name of publisher
>
> _____ 5. Place of publication (city and state); if published only online, give Internet address
>
> _____ 6. Date and year of publication
>
> _____ 7. Page numbers on which the material appears
>
> _____ 8. All relevant information for any direct quotations, paraphrases, or specific ideas or theories put forth by others
>
> _____ 9. The source of the facts and statistics used in the speech
>
> _____ 10. All relevant bibliographic information for any examples and stories supplied by someone else
>
> _____ 11. The source of any testimony presented in the speech, including the name of the person who offered the testimony and the date and context of the testimony
>
> _____ 12. Any relevant information related to any presentation aids to be used, including charts and figures based on other people's data; photographs or videos produced by other people; music composed and performed by others; objects or models created by another

Editors) method, and the IEEE (Institute of Electrical and Electronic Engineers) method. (See Appendices F through J for a description of each of these documentation styles.)

CHOOSE HELPFUL TOOLS

Rather than jotting down your notes helter-skelter, develop a system for organizing your research. Use notecards, spiral notebooks, and hard-copy and computer file folders to store your research. Insert the reference for each source directly onto the applicable note. Consider software programs such as EndNote to organize your bibliography.

IDENTIFY QUOTED, PARAPHRASED, AND SUMMARIZED MATERIAL

To avoid plagiarism (see Chapter 4), insert quotation marks around directly quoted material. When paraphrasing someone else's words or summarizing passages in articles, books, or other sources, record the page number on which the original quotation or passage appears (see Figures 9.1, 9.2, and 9.3).

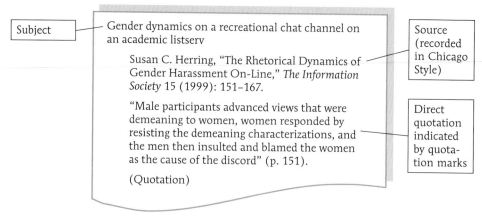

Figure 9.1 Sample Note for a Direct Quotation

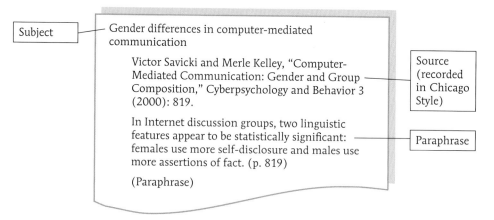

Figure 9.2 Sample Note for a Paraphrase

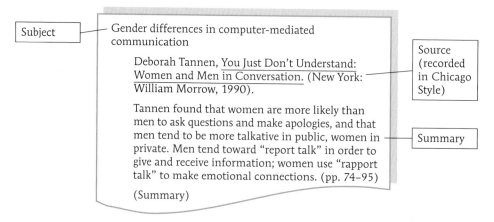

Figure 9.3 Sample Note for a Summary

Ethically Speaking
Researching Your Speech in an Ethical Manner

As you research your speech topic, it's helpful to remind yourself of your ethical responsibilities. As discussed in Chapter 4, central to conducting ethical research is properly citing sources. Using other people's ideas or words without acknowledging the source is **plagiarism** — a serious breach of ethics. In addition to plagiarism, unethical research conduct also includes fabricating information, deceiving research subjects about your real purposes, and breaching confidentiality. **Fabrication** is the making up of information, such as falsifying data or experiments or claiming a source when none exists. Perhaps the most widely publicized case of fabrication in recent times was that of former *New York Times* reporter Jayson Blair. According to an investigation by the *Times* in 2003, Blair

> filed dispatches that purported to be from Maryland, Texas and other states, when often he was in New York; fabricated comments; concocted scenes and lifted material from other newspapers and wire services; also he selected details from photographs to create impression he had been somewhere or seen someone, when he had not.[1]

Fabrication can also include altering quotes to "fit" a point; claiming credentials or expertise for yourself that you don't possess, in an effort to boost your credibility; inflating figures to promote your point; and so forth. Each of these examples represents an act of deception.

Conducting research ethically extends to any interviews or surveys that you undertake. In some cases, for example, people will not talk with you or provide information unless you agree to maintain their anonymity. Ethically, it is the speaker's responsibility to protect his or her source's confidentiality when requested. This is true whether the source is a respondent to a questionnaire to whom you have promised anonymity or an expert in a field who gives you an inside tip.

Ethical conduct in public speaking goes beyond doing no harm. The goal of any speech should be to in some way serve the audience well. For example, by investigating whether a certain food ingredient can harm the body, a speaker may help audience members live healthier and longer lives. By conducting research into the pros and cons of different savings options, a speaker may assist audience members in better preparing for retirement. Use your research to advance the knowledge of others or to show them a new way of viewing a problem or an issue.

1. Dan Barry, David Barstow, Jonathan D. Glater, Adam Liptak, and Jacques Steinberg, "Correcting the Record: *Times* Reporter Who Resigned Leaves Long Trail of Deception," *New York Times,* May 11, 2003.

CRITICALLY EVALUATE YOUR SOURCES

Respect for the written word is deeply ingrained in many of us, and for good reason. Yet not all words are created equal. Some are written by people who distort the facts, either knowingly or unknowingly. In an age of exploding information, it is now easier than ever for both the honest and the dishonest to get into print — or its electronic equivalent in cyberspace. (See Chapter 10 for more

From Source to Speech
Recording and Citing Books

When using a book as a source, record the following elements:

1 Title
2 Author
3 Publisher
4 City of Publication
5 Year of Publication
6 Page Number

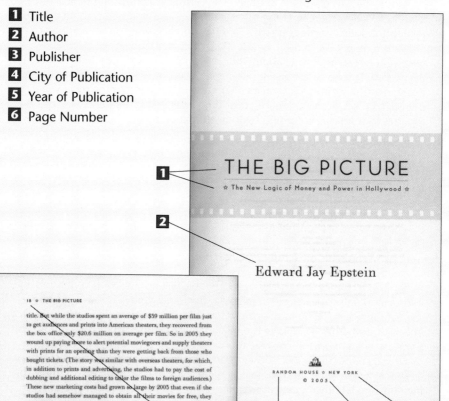

THE BIG PICTURE

☆ The New Logic of Money and Power in Hollywood ☆

Edward Jay Epstein

RANDOM HOUSE ☆ NEW YORK
© 2005

3 RANDOM HOUSE

4 NEW YORK

5 © 2005

6 18

18 ☆ THE BIG PICTURE

title. But while the studios spent an average of $59 million per film just to get audiences and prints into American theaters, they recovered from the box office only $20.6 million on average per film. So in 2003 they wound up paying more to alert potential moviegoers and supply theaters with prints for an opening than they were getting back from those who bought tickets. (The story was similar with overseas theaters, for which, in addition to prints and advertising, the studios had to pay the cost of dubbing and additional editing to tailor the films to foreign audiences.) These new marketing costs had grown so large by 2003 that even if the studios had somehow managed to obtain all their movies for free, they would still have lost money on their American releases.

But studios, of course, did *not* make these movies for free. And, to make matters far worse, the costs of producing a film have also risen astronomically. At the end of the studio-system era, in 1947, the cost of producing an average studio film, or negative cost, was $752,000. In 2005 it was $63.8 million. To be sure, the dollar had decreased in value sevenfold between 1947 and 2005, but even after correcting for inflation, the cost of producing films had increased more than sixteen times since the collapse of the studio system.

Part of the studios' cost problem is the result of stars being freed from their control. Instead of being tethered to studios by seven-year contracts, stars are now auctioned off—with the help of savvy agents—to the highest bidder for each film. Since there are fewer desirable stars than film projects, they can command eight-digit fees. By 20 getting not only between $20 and $50 million a fil tion and perks but a percentage of the film's total cash outlays.

For example, Arnold Schwarzenegger received tract, a $29.25 million fixed fee for his role in the 2 *Rise of the Machines*, as well as a $1.5 million perk private jets, a fully equipped gym trailer, three-bed locations, round-the-clock limousines, and persona tion, once the film reached its cash break-even po anteed him 20 percent of the gross receipts from (including video, DVD, theatrical box office, tele Under any scenario—whether the film failed, b profit—the star was assured of making more mo

At the end of the studio-system era, in 1947, the cost of producing an average studio film, or negative cost, was $752,000. In 2003 it was $63.8 million. To be sure, the dollar had decreased in value sevenfold between 1947 and 2005, but even after correcting for inflation, the cost of producing films had increased more than sixteen times since the collapse of the studio system.

Part of the studios' cost problem is the result of stars being freed from their control. Instead of being tethered to studios by seven-year contracts, stars are now auctioned off—with the help of savvy agents—to the highest bidder for each film.

Your Notes

When taking notes, create a separate heading for each idea and record the source. Insert quotation marks around any quoted material, label paraphrased material, and otherwise indicate the source of your ideas.

NOTE FOR A PARAPHRASE:

Subject

Source

Paraphrase

Increasing cost of producing movies
Edward Jay Epstein, The Big Picture: The New Logic of Money and Power in Hollywood (New York: Random House, 2005).

Between 1947—the end of the studio-system era—and 2003, the cost of producing a studio film skyrocketed from $732,000 to $63.8 million. (p. 18)
(Paraphrase)

NOTE FOR A SUMMARY:

Subject

Source

Summary

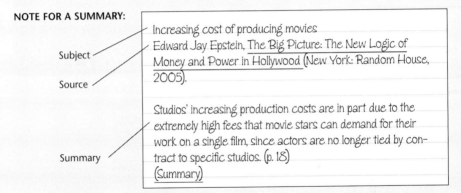

Increasing cost of producing movies
Edward Jay Epstein, The Big Picture: The New Logic of Money and Power in Hollywood (New York: Random House, 2005).

Studios' increasing production costs are in part due to the extremely high fees that movie stars can demand for their work on a single film, since actors are no longer tied by contract to specific studios. (p. 18)
(Summary)

Your Speech

When orally citing sources in your speech, identify direct quotations and indicate the source of paraphrased material and other ideas not your own:

SPEECH EXCERPT INDICATING A PARAPHRASE:

Hollywood studios now need deeper pockets than ever before. In addition to rising promotion, advertising, and distribution costs, studios face rapidly increasing production costs. In his book *The Big Picture: The New Logic of Money and Power in Hollywood*, Edward Jay Epstein notes that between 1947—the end of the studio-system era—and 2003, the cost of producing a studio film skyrocketed from $732,000 to $63.8 million.

SPEECH EXCERPT INDICATING A SUMMARY:

According to Edward Jay Epstein in *The Big Picture: The New Logic of Money and Power in Hollywood*, studios' increasing production costs are in part due to the extremely high fees that today's stars can demand. No longer tied by contracts to studios, stars' salaries are now settled by bidding wars.

From Source to Speech
Recording and Citing Articles from Periodicals

When using an article as a source, you must find the material you will use and locate the following citation elements:

1 Author

2 Article Title

3 Periodical Title

4 Date of Publication

5 Page Number

1 BY PEG TYRE AND SARAH STAVELEY-O'CARROLL

2

3 NEWSWEEK

4 AUGUST 8, 2005

5 50

How to Fix School Lunch

Celebrity chefs, politicians and concerned parents are joining forces to improve the meals kids eat every day.

BY PEG TYRE AND
SARAH STAVELEY-O'CARROLL

FOR JORGE COLLAZO, EXECUTIVE chef for the New York City public schools, coming up with the perfect jerk sauce is yet another step toward making the 1.1 million schoolkids he serves healthier. In a little more than a year, he's introduced salad bars and replaced whole milk with skim. Beef patties are now served on whole-wheat buns. Until recently, "every piece of chicken the manufacturers sent us was either breaded or covered in a glaze," says Collazo. Brandishing the might of his $125 million annual food budget, he switched to plain cutlets and asked suppliers to come up with something healthy—and appealing—to put on top. Collazo tastes the latest offering. The jerk sauce isn't overly processed and doesn't have trans fats. "Too salty," he says with a grimace. Within minutes, the supplier is hard at work on a lower-sodium version.

A cramped public-school test kitchen might seem an unlikely outpost for a food revolution. But Collazo and scores of others across the country—celebrity chefs and lunch ladies, district superintendents and politicians—say they're determined to improve what kids eat in school. Nearly everyone agrees something must be done. Most school cafeterias are staffed by poorly trained, badly equipped workers who churn out 4.8 billion hot lunches a year. Often the meals, produced for about $1 each, consist of breaded meat patties, french fries and overcooked vegetables. So the kids buy muffins, cookies and ice cream instead—or they feast on fast food from McDonald's, Pizza Hut and Taco Bell, which is available in more than half the schools in the nation.

Vending machines packed with sodas and candy line the hallways. "We're killing our kids" with the food we serve, says Texas Education Commissioner Susan Combs.

As rates of childhood obesity and diabetes skyrocket, public-health officials say schools need to change the way kids eat. It won't be easy. Some kids and their parents don't know better. Home cooking is becoming a forgotten art. And fast-food companies now spend $3 billion a year on television ads aimed at children. Along with reading and writing, schools need to teach kids what to eat to stay healthy, says culinary innovator Alice Waters, who is introducing gardening and fresh produce to 16 schools in California. It's a golden opportunity, she says, "to affect the way children eat for the rest of their lives." Last year star English chef Jamie Oliver took over a school cafeteria in a working-class suburb of London. A documentary about his work shamed the British government into spending $500 million to revamp the nation's school-food program. Oliver says it's the United States' turn now. "If you can put a man on the moon," he says, "you can give kids the food they need to make them lighter, fitter and live longer."

Changing school food takes time. More than a decade ago, when local restaurateur Lynn Walters lobbied school-board members in Santa Fe, N.M., to provide kids with

50 NEWSWEEK AUGUST 8, 2005

FOR JORGE COLLAZO, EXECUTIVE chef for the New York City public schools, coming up with the perfect jerk sauce is yet another step toward making the 1.1 million schoolkids he serves healthier. In a little more than a year, he's introduced salad bars and replaced whole milk with skim. Beef patties are now served on whole-wheat buns. Until recently, "every piece of chicken the manufacturers sent us was either breaded or covered in a glaze," says Collazo.

Last year star English chef Jamie Oliver took over a school cafeteria in a working-class suburb of London. A documentary about his work shamed the British government into spending $500 million to revamp the nation's school-food program. Oliver says it's the United States' turn now. "If you can put a man on the moon," he says, "you can give kids the food they need to make them lighter, fitter and live longer."

For guidelines on various citation styles including Chicago, APA, MLA, CBE/CSE, and IEEE see Appendices F–J.

Your Notes

When taking notes, create a separate heading for each idea and record
each of the citation elements from your source. Insert quotation marks
around any quoted material and label paraphrases or summaries.

NOTE FOR A DIRECT QUOTATION:

Subject

Source

Quotation

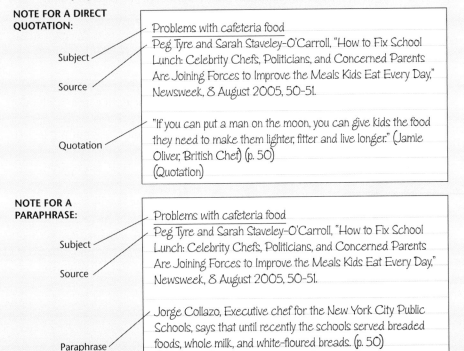

Problems with cafeteria food

Peg Tyre and Sarah Staveley-O'Carroll, "How to Fix School
Lunch: Celebrity Chefs, Politicians, and Concerned Parents
Are Joining Forces to Improve the Meals Kids Eat Every Day,"
Newsweek, 8 August 2005, 50-51.

"If you can put a man on the moon, you can give kids the food
they need to make them lighter, fitter and live longer." (Jamie
Oliver, British Chef) (p. 50)
(Quotation)

NOTE FOR A PARAPHRASE:

Subject

Source

Paraphrase

Problems with cafeteria food

Peg Tyre and Sarah Staveley-O'Carroll, "How to Fix School
Lunch: Celebrity Chefs, Politicians, and Concerned Parents
Are Joining Forces to Improve the Meals Kids Eat Every Day,"
Newsweek, 8 August 2005, 50-51.

Jorge Collazo, Executive chef for the New York City Public
Schools, says that until recently the schools served breaded
foods, whole milk, and white-floured breads. (p. 50)
(Paraphrase)

Your Speech

When orally citing sources in your speech, identify direct quotations and
indicate the source of paraphrased material and other ideas not your own:

SPEECH EXCERPT INDICATING A DIRECT QUOTATION:

The drive to improve nutrition in schools is not restricted to the
United States. **According to an article on fixing school lunches published in the August 8th, 2005 edition of** Newsweek, star chef Jamie
Oliver's success in transforming cafeteria food in England has led
him to claim that the U.S. should do the same. Newsweek **quoted
Oliver as saying,** "If you can put a man on the moon, you can give
kids the food they need to make them lighter, fitter and live longer."

SPEECH EXCERPT INDICATING A PARAPHRASE:

As reported in the August 8th, 2005 edition of Newsweek, Executive chef Jorge Callazo of the New York City public schools claimed
that until recently, virtually every piece of chicken that was served
was breaded or glazed; students drank whole rather than skim milk,
and ate white rather than whole-wheat bread.

on evaluating Internet sources.) Thus it is vital to critically evaluate sources before using them. Whether you are reviewing a book, a newspaper article, or any other source, consider the following:

- What is the author's background — for example, his or her experience, training, and reputation — in the field of study?

- How credible is the publication? Who is the publisher? Is the person or organization reputable? What other publications has the author or the organization published?

- How reliable is the data, especially the statistical information? Generally, statistics drawn from government documents and scientific and academic journals are more reliable than those reported in the popular press (e.g., general-interest magazines). This is because the former kinds of publications print primary data officially collected by the government or by researchers who are subject to peer review. (See also "Using Statistics Accurately" in Chapter 8.)

- How recent is the reference? As a rule, it is best to be familiar with the most recent source you can find, even when the topic is historical. Scholars are continually uncovering new information and offering new perspectives on past events. (See also "From Source to Speech: Evaluating Web Sources" [p. 150] and "Ethically Speaking: Learn to Distinguish among Information, Propaganda, Misinformation, and Disinformation" [p. 152] in Chapter 10.)

Using the Internet to Support Your Speech 10

The Internet represents a vast world of possibilities for discovering material for your speech. In this often unruly and unregulated electronic universe, you can consult daily newspapers from Asia to Africa — and translate them into any one of a dozen languages. You can study Supreme Court decisions, access government documents, browse museum holdings, and drill for information lying deep within the recesses of little-known databases. As with conducting research in a library, the key to a productive search in cyberspace lies in a well-thought-out research strategy, an understanding of the kinds of information that are available on the Internet, and a grasp of how to use Internet search tools.

The most frequently used portion of the Internet is the **World Wide Web**, a graphics-rich environment of electronic "pages" that contain text, images, sound, and video. The distinguishing feature of the Web is **hyperlinks** — connections that link individual pieces of information or entire sites to other pieces of information or sites. Other aspects of the Internet that you may be familiar with are e-mail, chat rooms, blogs, listservs, and newsgroups, all of which may serve as valuable resources as you search for supporting material for your speech (see Table 10.1).

Balance Print and Online Sources

Easy access to the Internet may lead you to rely heavily or even exclusively on online sources for your speeches. But just as our various branches of government rely on a system of checks and balances to guard against "excesses" in any one branch, a mix of print and online sources will help to correct any weaknesses that either online or print materials alone might contain.

This analogy can only be taken so far, however, for unlike the different institutions of government, print and online sources have not necessarily been created equally. For example, in considering what library holdings offer — including both print and electronic resources — that the Web does not, Reference Librarian Susan Gilroy notes the following:[1]

1. *Library holdings are built through careful and deliberate selection processes by trained professionals.* When you select a speech source from a library's holdings (including from its electronic or "e-resources"), you can be assured that an information specialist has vetted that source for quality. In most cases, this is not true of material on the Web.

2. *Libraries classify and order their resources according to well-defined standards.* No such standards exist for Internet sources, which can be posted in any

number of forms. Consequently, it is much easier to overlook important resources when you search exclusively online.

3. *Libraries allow you to trace previous versions of a given source.* In the print world, original and subsequent versions of books and other materials are clearly marked and often remain available. Quite the opposite is true for the Internet, which, as Gilroy notes, "is notorious for providing links to information that is here today and gone tomorrow."

4. *Although information is being digitized at a rapid rate, many books, journals, and historical documents remain available only in print.*

Despite the pitfalls of Internet research, the Web offers certain benefits that a library may not.[2]

1. *Online sources have the potential for currency.* Books, journals, and other print materials take time to publish. Documents can be posted to the Web as they are being created or shortly thereafter, and many organizations (including the U.S. government), now publish their statistics exclusively online. However, countless outdated Web sites remain out there, and unless you carefully check a site's currency, you are likely to find inaccurate information (see the accompanying checklist for more on evaluating the currency of Web documents).

2. *The Internet permits access to previously unavailable or hard-to-locate materials.* Although many sources remain available only in print, in some cases exciting collections of research are only available (or logistically accessible) to you online. An important case in point is the U.S. Library of Congress's remarkable American Memory project (memory.loc.gov/ammem/index .html), which offers more than nine million items documenting U.S. history and culture.

3. *Online forums provide access to computer-mediated communications.* When approached with an extremely critical mind-set, online forums such as

---

TABLE 10.1 • The Internet's Information Sources

Here's what you'll find when you use the following Internet sources:

- **World Wide Web**—texts, graphics, sounds, and videos on every topic imaginable
- **e-mail**—personal messages and attached files
- **Web discussion forums**—Web pages that contain articles, ideas, questions, and comments addressed to specific audiences and posted for public discussion
- **Web logs (also known as Blogs)**—Web pages that contain a log of a writer's (often personal) thoughts in chronological order
- **Listservs**—e-mail messages on specific topics, exchanged among subscribers
- **Newsgroups**—e-mail-like bulletin boards where messages addressed to specific communities of Internet users and posted for public discussion are stored
- **Real-time communication**—electronic forums or "rooms" for conversing with others and attending online classes and conferences
- **FTP, gopher, telnet**—files, texts, and connections to other computers

Source: Andrew Harnack and Eugene Kleppinger, *Online! A Reference Guide to Using Internet Sources* (Boston: Bedford/St. Martin's, 2002), 18.

> ✓ **CHECKLIST**
>
> **Evaluating the Credibility of a Web Site**
>
> ✓ Have I sought out the most authoritative sources for my topic? For example, have I searched for the official Web sites of the sponsoring organization related to my topic? Have I consulted government Web sites?
>
> ✓ Does the home page of each Web site offer information about its author or organization?
>
> ✓ Can I locate additional information about the credibility of the site's author or organization in other sources, such as newspaper articles?
>
> ✓ Is the "date last modified/updated" indicated at the top or bottom of each Web site or page? Does it seem that the author or organization routinely updates the site to ensure the information is accurate and current?

listservs, blogs, videoconferences, and the like offer a unique way to learn about the opinions and expertise of others.

To ensure that you make the best of both print and online resources, start your search at your college library. To use the Internet, begin by logging on to the library's home page (also called the **library gateway**) and find the "online resources" link (also labeled "e-resources" and "electronic resources"). The databases and other resources you will find there are as much a part of the library's holdings as are its shelved materials.[3] Table 10.2 lists the types of online resources available at most college libraries.

TABLE 10.2 • Typical Electronic Resources Found on Library Gateways

- Full-text databases (newspapers, periodicals, journals)
- Reference works (dictionaries, encyclopedias, quotation resources, fact books, directories)
- Statistical resources (e.g., FedStats.gov and *Statistical Abstract*)
- Electronic journals
- Digitized texts (primary documents; digitized books)
- Digitized image collections (e.g., ARTstor Digital Library and Internet Archive)

Be a Critical Consumer of Information

Apart from a library's electronic resources section, how can you distinguish between information on the Internet that is reputable and credible and information that is untrustworthy? As discussed in the nearby Ethically Speaking box, search engines cannot discern the quality of information; only a human editor can do this. Each time you examine a document, especially one that has not been evaluated and rated by credible editors, ask yourself, "Who put this information here? Why did they do it? Where is similar information found?"[4]

From Source to Speech
Evaluating Web Sources

Check the most authoritative Web sites first

Begin your search by looking for the most authoritative Web sites on your topic. If your speech explores the NBA draft, investigate the NBA's official Web site first. If you find related sites sponsored by the U.S. government (or the government of another country), go there first: Government-sponsored sites are free of commercial taint and contain highly credible primary materials.

Evaluate authorship and sponsorship

1 Examine the **domain** in the Web address—the suffix at the end of the address that tells you the nature of the site: educational (.edu), government (.gov), military (.mil), nonprofit organization (.org), business/commercial (.com), and network (.net). A **tilde** (~) in the address usually indicates that it is a personal page rather than part of an institutional Web site. You need to assess the credibility of each site, whether it is operated by an individual, a company, a government agency, or a nonprofit group.

2 For institutional or organizational sites, look for an "About" link that describes the organization or a link to a page that gives more information. These sections can tell a great deal about the nature of the site's content.

3 Who is the creator of the information? If an individual operates the site, does the document provide relevant biographical information, such as links to a résumé or a listing of the author's credentials? Look for contact information, including e-mail addresses, phone numbers, and physical mail addresses. A source that doesn't want to be found, at least by e-mail, is not a good source to cite.

Check for currency

4 Is there a date that indicates when the page was placed on the Web? When was the last time the site was updated? Web sites that do not have this information may contain outdated or inaccurate material.

Check that the site credits its sources and that sources are credible

5 Reputable Web sites document the sources they use. Check that the site gives citations for sources, and check for links to these sources. Follow these links and apply the same criteria to them that you did to the original source document. A good rule of thumb is to verify information you find with at least two other reputable and independent sources.

1 http://www.nasa.gov/home/hqnews/2005/jan/HQ_05004_chandra.html

2 + ABOUT NASA

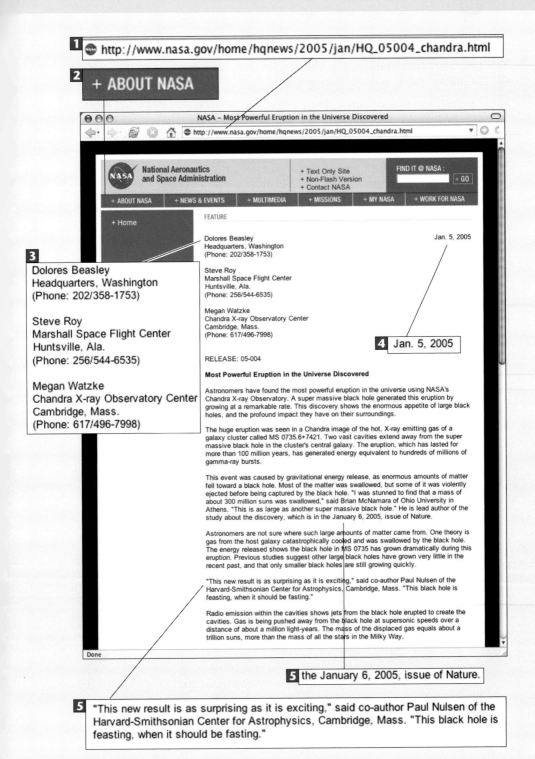

NASA – Most Powerful Eruption in the Universe Discovered

http://www.nasa.gov/home/hqnews/2005/jan/HQ_05004_chandra.html

National Aeronautics and Space Administration

+ Text Only Site
+ Non-Flash Version
+ Contact NASA

FIND IT @ NASA :
+ GO

+ ABOUT NASA   + NEWS & EVENTS   + MULTIMEDIA   + MISSIONS   + MY NASA   + WORK FOR NASA

+ Home

FEATURE

Dolores Beasley
Headquarters, Washington
(Phone: 202/358-1753)

Jan. 5, 2005

Steve Roy
Marshall Space Flight Center
Huntsville, Ala.
(Phone: 256/544-6535)

Megan Watzke
Chandra X-ray Observatory Center
Cambridge, Mass.
(Phone: 617/496-7998)

RELEASE: 05-004

Most Powerful Eruption in the Universe Discovered

Astronomers have found the most powerful eruption in the universe using NASA's Chandra X-ray Observatory. A super massive black hole generated this eruption by growing at a remarkable rate. This discovery shows the enormous appetite of large black holes, and the profound impact they have on their surroundings.

The huge eruption was seen in a Chandra image of the hot, X-ray emitting gas of a galaxy cluster called MS 0735.6+7421. Two vast cavities extend away from the super massive black hole in the cluster's central galaxy. The eruption, which has lasted for more than 100 million years, has generated energy equivalent to hundreds of millions of gamma-ray bursts.

This event was caused by gravitational energy release, as enormous amounts of matter fell toward a black hole. Most of the matter was swallowed, but some of it was violently ejected before being captured by the black hole. "I was stunned to find that a mass of about 300 million suns was swallowed," said Brian McNamara of Ohio University in Athens. "This is as large as another super massive black hole." He is lead author of the study about the discovery, which is in the January 6, 2005, issue of Nature.

Astronomers are not sure where such large amounts of matter came from. One theory is gas from the host galaxy catastrophically cooled and was swallowed by the black hole. The energy released shows the black hole in MS 0735 has grown dramatically during this eruption. Previous studies suggest other large black holes have grown very little in the recent past, and that only smaller black holes are still growing quickly.

"This new result is as surprising as it is exciting," said co-author Paul Nulsen of the Harvard-Smithsonian Center for Astrophysics, Cambridge, Mass. "This black hole is feasting, when it should be fasting."

Radio emission within the cavities shows jets from the black hole erupted to create the cavities. Gas is being pushed away from the black hole at supersonic speeds over a distance of about a million light-years. The mass of the displaced gas equals about a trillion suns, more than the mass of all the stars in the Milky Way.

Done

3

Dolores Beasley
Headquarters, Washington
(Phone: 202/358-1753)

Steve Roy
Marshall Space Flight Center
Huntsville, Ala.
(Phone: 256/544-6535)

Megan Watzke
Chandra X-ray Observatory Center
Cambridge, Mass.
(Phone: 617/496-7998)

4 Jan. 5, 2005

5 the January 6, 2005, issue of Nature.

5 "This new result is as surprising as it is exciting," said co-author Paul Nulsen of the Harvard-Smithsonian Center for Astrophysics, Cambridge, Mass. "This black hole is feasting, when it should be fasting."

Ethically Speaking
Learn to Distinguish among Information, Propaganda, Misinformation, and Disinformation

Elizabeth Kirk of the Johns Hopkins University's Sheridan Libraries offers important distinctions among information, propaganda, misinformation, and disinformation (see Figure 10.1). Bearing in mind these distinctions when evaluating both print and Internet sources can help you to critically assess their credibility.

- **Information** is data set in a context for relevance. Information tells us something that is understandable and has the potential to become knowledge when we view it critically and add it to what we already know. To illustrate the difference between data and information, Kirk offers this example:

    "Eight million" and "nine percent" are . . . bits of data. However, "The population of New York City in 2000 was reported to top 8,000,000 persons, a growth of 9% since 1990" is . . . information.

- **Propaganda.** Many people believe that propaganda is based on false information, but this is not necessarily so. Instead, propaganda may well be based in fact, but the facts are presented in a way intended to provoke a certain response. The purpose of propaganda is to instill a particular attitude: to encourage you to think in a particular way.

- **Misinformation.** While propaganda may include information that is in fact true, misinformation always refers to something that is not true. One common form of misinformation on the Internet is the *urban legend*—a fabricated story passed along by unsuspecting people.

- **Disinformation.** Propaganda emphasizes one point of view, and misinformation mistakenly represents something as true when it is in fact false. Disinformation is the deliberate falsification of information. For example, the Enron Corporation's falsified 2002 profit and loss statements are a good example of disinformation in action. Unfortunately, the Internet is widely used for disinformation.

Meaningful speeches are based on sound information rather than on misinformation, propaganda, or disinformation. Being alert to such distinctions is an important step in creating such speeches.

Source: Elizabeth E. Kirk, "Information and Its Counterfeits," Sheridan Libraries of Johns Hopkins University, 2001, www.library.jhu.edu/researchhelp/general/evaluating/counterfeit.html (accessed May 4, 2005).

Information———➤	Propaganda ———➤	Misinformation———➤	Disinformation
Data set in a context for relevance	Information represented in such a way as to provoke a desired response	Something that is not true	Deliberate falsification of information

Figure 10.1 Information, Propaganda, Misinformation, and Disinformation

Make the Most of Internet Search Tools

Just as you wouldn't look for a book in a library without first locating its placement in a card catalog (computerized or otherwise), neither should you simply log on to the Internet and expect to stumble upon the information you need. To locate information on the Internet efficiently, you must be familiar with the function of search engines, subject directories, and information gateways.

SEARCH ENGINES

Search engines index the contents of the Web. These engines use powerful software programs (called spiders, crawlers, or bots) that "crawl" the Web, automatically scanning millions and, in the case of the largest engines, billions of documents that contain the keywords and phrases you command them to search. Results are generally ranked from most to least relevant, though search engines use markedly different criteria to determine relevance. Some search engines search only the Web. Others also scan the files of public discussion groups (Usenet) and mailing lists (e.g., Google Groups at groups.google.com). Some engines index more Web pages than others or index pages more often than others.

Individual versus Meta-Search Engines

Search engines are distinguished by whether or not they compile their own databases. **Individual search engines** compile their own databases of Web pages. Three of the largest individual search engines are:

- Google (google.com)
- Yahoo! (search.yahoo.com)
- MSN Search (search.msn.com)

Of these, Google indexes the most Web pages (over eight billion at last count) and offers searches that focus on images, maps, newsgroups, and local sources, among other options.

Rather than compiling their own databases, **meta-search engines** scan a variety of individual search engines simultaneously. Since meta-search engines scan multiple search engines, why use an individual search engine? Meta-search engines run wide but not necessarily deep. Existing meta-search engines can produce disappointing results that include only the top listings from each search engine and far too many paid listings.[6] As a result, some librarians no longer recommend using them.[7] With that disclaimer, here are several of the most comprehensive meta-search engines:

- Ixquick (ixquick.com)
- Metacrawler (www.metacrawler.com)
- Dogpile (www.dogpile.com)

Specialized Search Engines

You should also consider using a **specialized search engine** (also called a vertical search engine or vortal), which lets you conduct narrower but deeper searches into a particular field. Specialized search engines are databases created by researchers, government agencies, businesses, or other parties with a deep interest in a topic. Examples include Science Tracer Bullets Online, a specialized search engine sponsored by the Library of Congress that contains research guides on science and technology subjects, and Bioethics.gov, a specialized search engine sponsored by the President's Council on Bioethics.

To find a search engine geared specifically to your topic, try Googling your topic term with the keywords *search engine*. For example, a search for *global warming* AND *search engine* will lead you to many dedicated sites, some reputable and others not. Only by carefully evaluating each site will you be able to determine its credibility.

New specialized search engines emerge all the time; here are four well-known (and comparatively broad) ones geared to college students and researchers:

- 24HourScholar.com (contains articles on subjects in the humanities, sciences, and social sciences)
- GoogleScholar.com (lets you search specifically for scholarly literature, including peer-reviewed papers, theses, books, preprints, abstracts, and technical reports from all broad areas of research)
- FindArticles.com (culls articles from leading academic, industry, and general-interest publications).
- Answers.com (a reference search service that provides concise answers drawn from over a hundred authoritative encyclopedias, dictionaries, glossaries, and atlases)

SUBJECT DIRECTORIES

A **subject directory** is a searchable database of Web sites organized by categories (see Figure 10.2). Three of the most comprehensive subject directories on the Web are:

- Open Directory Project or DMOZ (www.dmoz.org)
- Yahoo! Directory (dir.yahoo.com)
- Academic Info (www.academicinfo.net)

Subject directories allow you to progressively narrow your search, or "drill down" your topic, until you find what you are looking for. If your speech is on some aspect of baseball teams, for example, you would follow these links, continuing until you find what you want:

sports ⇒ baseball ⇒ amateur ⇒ leagues ⇒ teams

Figure 10.2 Home Page for the Open Directory Project (DMOZ)

If you attempt to search in a manner other than by subject (e.g., by proper name), the directory will not return results.

Unlike search engines, which rely on automated crawlers to retrieve documents matching your keywords, people create and manage subject directories. (Note that directories do vary in how and to what extent submissions are assessed.) To find a subject directory for a specific topic or field, try using one of the general directories or search engines listed earlier. If your topic is Afghanistan, for example, key in *Afghanistan* AND *directory* or *Web directories*. Among other hits, this search yields the excellent specialized directory Afghana! at www.afghana.com.

CHOOSING BETWEEN SEARCH ENGINES AND SUBJECT DIRECTORIES

Both search engines and subject directories offer valuable help in locating supporting materials for your speech, but each is best used for a somewhat different purpose. Because search engines index so many documents, they often find information that isn't listed in subject directories, making them extremely useful when you want to locate a wide variety of materials. In addition, because they scan the full text of a document rather than just its title, first few pages, or URL address, search engines are the tool of choice when you need to find very defined information (such as specific terms, facts, figures, or quotations) that may be buried within documents.

In contrast, subject directories are more useful in both finding and narrowing a topic (see Chapter 7). When you are looking for information on a general topic such as automobiles, for instance, subject directories offer a far easier and less time-consuming way of surveying information. In this case, you might find links to fifty sites that have been selected by the editors or maintainers of the directory; these selected sites may have a higher probability of being relevant to your search. With a search engine, you would be faced with the task of sifting through countless documents containing the word *automobile*, many of which would not be relevant.

✓ **CHECKLIST**

**Choosing between a Subject Directory
and a Crawler-Based Search Engine**

✓   If you are looking for a list of reputable sites on the same subject, use a subject directory.

✓   If you are looking for a specific page within a site, use a search engine.

✓   If you need to find specific terms, facts, figures, or quotations that may be buried within documents, use a search engine.

✓   If you want to locate a wide variety of materials related to your search, use a subject directory first and then use a search engine.

COMMERCIAL FACTORS AFFECTING SEARCH RESULTS

In addition to authorship and timeliness, when evaluating Internet sources, you will want to consider any commercial influence on your search results — specifically, whether a particular listing appears in your search results merely because an advertiser has paid to put it there.

In the first few years of their existence, search engines ranked their listings solely according to strict algorithms. As noted in a major study by *Consumer Reports* WebWatch, however, "Pure results are now the exception, rather than the rule."[8] Advertising on the Internet is now a billion-dollar industry, and much of the revenue search engines garner from it come from (1) fees that companies pay them for a guaranteed higher ranking within search results (called **paid placement**) and (2) fees that companies pay to be included in a search engine or subject directory's full index of possible results, without a guarantee of ranking (called **paid inclusion**).[9]

When you are looking to purchase something, finding links that advertisers have paid to include is not necessarily a bad thing. But when you need unbiased information of a factual nature, it clearly is a problem. Identifying paid-placement listings is relatively easy: Look for a heading labeled "Sponsored Links" or "Sponsored Results" at the top, side, or bottom of the main page. Be aware that these headings are in an inconspicuous color or small font and may be hard to read.

Identifying paid-inclusion listings is much more difficult because they are mixed in with the main results. Sometimes they may be grouped under headings such as "Web Results" or "Web Pages," but most often there is no way to identify whether or not someone paid to include the listing in the search engine's index (recall that paid inclusion does not guarantee any particular ranking in the listings). Consumer protest has led some search engines to stop the practice, and Google, AOL, and Netscape have never sponsored paid-inclusion programs. However, many other search engines continue to offer paid-inclusion programs, prompting the *Consumer Reports* WebWatch to offer tips on ways to minimize the potential influence of commercial interests on your search (see the accompanying checklist).

 CHECKLIST

Identifying Paid Listings in Search Results

✓ Look for a heading labeled "Sponsored Links" or "Sponsored Results" at the top, side, or bottom of the main page. This indicates a paid-placement listing.

✓ Use multiple search engines and compare the results.

✓ Beware of meta-search engines, which often include many paid-inclusion listings.

✓ Click beyond the first page of your search results to find relevant sites.

✓ Read the fine print on a search engine's disclosure pages to find its policy on paid inclusion.

INFORMATION GATEWAYS

A **gateway** or **information portal** is an electronic entry point into a large collection of research and reference materials that have been selected and reviewed by experts. Gateways thus include large specialized search engines and subject directories whose links have been evaluated by experts. University and public libraries maintain gateways that often are accessible with an assigned PIN number or other form of identification.

In addition to the home pages of actual libraries, a host of **virtual libraries** can be found on the Internet. The Library of Congress (www.loc.gov/rr/index .html) and Internet Public Library (www.ipl.org) sites are excellent gateways offering links to a rich array of resources for the public speaker (see Figure 10.3).

Because information gateways often take you to links that do not readily appear in general search engines and subject directories, they are sometimes considered part of the **invisible Web** — the portion of the Web that general search engines fail to find. Common estimates of the portion of the Web that is invisible range between 60 and 80 percent;[10] it is therefore a mistake to rely on a single large search engine such as Google for your speech sources. A list of virtual libraries appears in Table 10.3.

Figure 10.3 Virtual Research Library from the Library of Congress

---

TABLE 10.3 • Selected Virtual Libraries

- **The Library of Congress:** www.loc.gov/rr/index.html
- **Librarians' Index to the Internet:** lii.org/search
- **Internet Public Library (IPL):** www.ipl.org
- **WWW Virtual Library:** vlib.org
- **Academic Info:** www.academicinfo.net
- **Digital Librarian:** www.digital-librarian.com
- **Infomine:** infomine.ucr.edu

Conduct Smart Searches

To maximize the odds of finding the materials you need, take some time to familiarize yourself with the search commands of the search tools you select. Go to the Help command located near the search window. Here you will find tips for entering your search commands most efficiently. Most search tools provide guidance for conducting both simple and more advanced searches. Advance search functions allow you to further refine your search criteria — by looking for sites in a particular language, limiting the search by date, or searching for specific kinds of files (such as sound or picture files).

USE BASIC SEARCH COMMANDS

Most search tools are programmed to respond to the following basic commands:

- Quotation marks (" ") to find exact phrases (e.g., *"white wine"*). Without the quote marks, search tools will list all relevant sites with the word *white* as well as those with the word *wine.*

- **Boolean operators**, words placed between the keywords in a search that specify how the keywords are related,[11] include AND, OR, and NOT. They act as filters to help you eliminate potential items that are unrelated to your search.

    - AND *narrows* your search to the words you include. For example, *Bill Gates* AND *speeches* AND *Bill and Melinda Gates Foundation* eliminates speeches given by Bill Gates about other topics, such as those about Microsoft.

    - OR *expands* your search by permitting results that contain alternative terms. For example, (*preschool* OR *nursery school*). Note: Include OR searches within parentheses. This search will find documents that contain *preschool, nursery school,* or both.

    - NOT *restricts* your search by excluding specific terms from the results. For example, *"bed and breakfasts"* NOT *motels* will find all documents that contain the exact phrase *bed and breakfast* but that aren't motels.

- Plus (+) and minus (–) signs placed directly in front of keywords indicate whether you want the term included or excluded from the search (e.g., *+publishing –printing*).

USE FIELD SEARCHING TO FURTHER NARROW RESULTS

Field searching goes beyond the basic search commands to narrow results even further. Using this function (also called an advanced search) will take you slightly longer at the start, but it can save considerable time overall by returning closer matches.

Search engines sort results according to several attributes or "fields" common to all pages on the World Wide Web. Most search tools provide advanced search options that enable you to target these more specific search parameters to further narrow search results. To locate the field search option, look for a link on the front page of any given search engine.

A field search option generally includes the following fields:

- *Keywords:* "All," "exact phrase," "at least one," and "without" filter results for keywords in much the same way as the basic search commands. Keyword field searches allow you the option of limiting your search to a Web site's title or URL.

- *Language* includes search results with pages written in the specified language. A search for the exact phrase *"gas prices"* and the language specified as Polish produces results listing sites originating in English and sites originating in Polish.

- *Country* searches result in documents originating in the specified country.
- *File format* returns results with links to particular document formats, such as Microsoft Word (.doc), Adobe Acrobat (.pdf), PowerPoint (.ppt), and Excel (.xls).
- *Domain* searches limit results to sites residing in the specified Internet domain (e.g., .com, .edu, .gov, .org). Both Yahoo! and Google enable more restricted domain searching to specific sites (e.g., harvard.edu; fcc.gov). (See Figure 10.4.)
- *Date* searches focus on a specified range of time. For example, if you search early in the semester on your topic and later want to know if new information has appeared, you could limit your search to the last three months or even the last week.
- *Safe-search,* usually the default setting in the major search engines, filters out most obscene and adult-oriented material and in some instances information that is potentially violent or hate-oriented. Safe-search is an especially important feature when doing image searches or searches on sensitive topics, although it is by no means fail-safe.
- *Page-specific* searches attempt to obtain a very limited set of results by seeking pages that contain the same basic information as a known page does or that link to the known page.

Figure 10.4 Google's Advanced Search Page for Conducting Field Searches

Orally Cite and Record Internet Sources

Your research online may turn up information drawn from company or personal Web sites, library e-resources, electronic publications, email, newsgroups, and so forth. Whatever its origin, always reveal to your audience the source of any direct quotations, paraphrased information, facts, opinions, statistics, or other information contained in your speech that are not your own and are outside the pool of common knowledge (see Chapter 4). For visual guidelines on citing electronic sources and incorporating source material into your speeches, see "From Source to Speech" on citing Internet sources (p. 162).

ESTABLISH THE SOURCE'S CREDIBILITY

Rather than offering a bare-bones citation such as "Hamlin, 2006, claims that . . . ," make sure to establish the source's reliability for listeners, if only briefly. Otherwise, they are unlikely to place much stock in your evidence. For each source, plan on alerting audience members to:

1. The *type of source* (e.g., organization Web site, online interview, email— "The Consumer Reports WebWatch Web site, a project of the nonprofit consumer advocacy publisher Consumer Union")
2. The *author or origin of the source* (e.g., "Jorgen Wouters, author of a report on advertising in search results, published by Consumer Reports Webwatch")
3. The *title or a description of the source, especially if the author name is not given* (e.g., "In an article entitled 'Searching for Disclosure,' published by Consumer Reports WebWatch . . .")
4. The *date of the source,* though this may be approximate for purposes of informing audience of time range of study (e.g., "In a 2004 study of paid advertising in search results . . .")

Refer to Chapters 4, 8, and 9 for additional tips on orally citing both online and written sources.

KEEP TRACK OF INTERNET SOURCES

When using Internet sources, it is especially important for you to keep track of your sources because Internet sites often change. Remember that when you give a speech, you are in the spotlight. Your information may be challenged by an audience member, and you will need to prove that you have based your speech on credible information from reliable sources. If there is any chance that your speech may be published, the publisher will want to include a list of references.

Refer to Chapter 9 for instructions for maintaining a working bibliography.

From Source to Speech

Recording and Citing Web Sources

When using a Web article as a source, record the following elements:

1️⃣ Author of the Work   4️⃣ Date of Publication/Last Update

2️⃣ Title of the Work   5️⃣ Access Information

3️⃣ Title of the Web Site

1 by Anders Cullhed

2 Nobel Prize Authors on Time

Nobel Prize Authors on Time
by Anders Cullhed

What is Time?

Ever since the thinkers of classical Greece tried to understand the swiftness of our seconds, minutes and hours - the impossibility of stepping into the same river twice - the problem of time has haunted our imagination. It is even more than a problem, it is a mystery.

"What is time? It is a secret - lacking in substance and yet almighty." Those are the words of the German Nobel Prize winner in Literature, Thomas Mann, in his great novel *The Magic Mountain* (1924). Mann was a very modern writer, and yet his definition of time was more or less the same as the one provided by the Roman Church Father Saint Augustine in his famous autobiography, *Confessions*, more than fifteen hundred years earlier:

What, then, is time? I know well enough what it is, provided that nobody asks me; but if I am asked what it is and try to explain, I am baffled.

4 May 26, 2005

5 http://nobelprize.org/literature/articles/cullhed/index.html

For guidelines on various citation styles including Chicago, APA, MLA, CBE/CSE, and IEEE see Appendices F–J.

Your Notes

When taking notes, create a separate heading for each idea and record the source. Insert quotation marks around any quoted material, label paraphrased material, and otherwise indicate the source of your ideas.

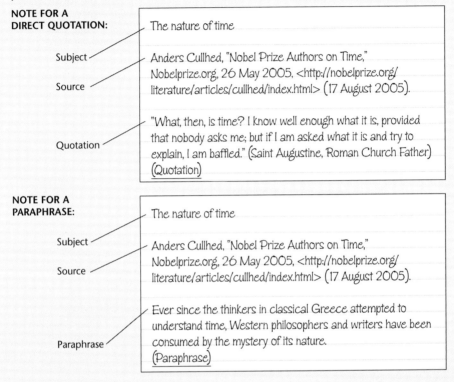

NOTE FOR A DIRECT QUOTATION:

Subject

Source

Quotation

> The nature of time
>
> Anders Cullhed, "Nobel Prize Authors on Time," Nobelprize.org, 26 May 2005, <http://nobelprize.org/ literature/articles/cullhed/index.html> (17 August 2005).
>
> "What, then, is time? I know well enough what it is, provided that nobody asks me; but if I am asked what it is and try to explain, I am baffled." (Saint Augustine, Roman Church Father) (Quotation)

NOTE FOR A PARAPHRASE:

Subject

Source

Paraphrase

> The nature of time
>
> Anders Cullhed, "Nobel Prize Authors on Time," Nobelprize.org, 26 May 2005, <http://nobelprize.org/ literature/articles/cullhed/index.html> (17 August 2005).
>
> Ever since the thinkers in classical Greece attempted to understand time, Western philosophers and writers have been consumed by the mystery of its nature. (Paraphrase)

Your Speech

When orally citing sources in your speech, identify direct quotations and indicate the source of paraphrased material and other ideas not your own:

SPEECH EXCERPT INDICATING A DIRECT QUOTATION:

Many famous thinkers have grappled with the concept of time. For example, Saint Augustine wrote in his autobiography, *Confessions,* "What, then, is time? I know well enough what it is, provided that nobody asks me; but if I am asked what it is and try to explain, I am baffled."

SPEECH EXCERPT INDICATING A PARAPHRASE:

In an article on the nature of time posted on the Web site Nobleprize.org, professor of comparative literature Anders Cullhed notes that beginning with thinkers in ancient Greece, Western philosophers and writers have tried to understand the nature of time.

CHECKLIST

Documenting Internet Sources

As in documentation of print sources, styles of documenting Internet sources for a written bibliography vary according to discipline. Three of the most widely used formats are the American Psychological Association (APA) style, the Modern Language Association (MLA) style, and the *Chicago* style. (See Appendices F through J for specific documentation guidelines.) Each referencing style varies in the precise ordering and formatting of information, but all generally require that you provide as much of the following information as possible:

✓ Name of the author, editor, or site maintainer (if applicable). (Some sources may be identified only by a log-in name.)

✓ Publication information of any print version

✓ Date of electronic publication or last revision (if known)

✓ Title of document, whether it's a scholarly project, database, periodical, or, for a professional or personal site with no title, a description such as a home page

✓ Title of complete work of which it is a part (if relevant)

✓ Other relevant information (volume number, page numbers, etc.)

✓ Retrieval date statement (e.g., "Retrieved on March 16, 2006" or "Accessed on March 16, 2006")

✓ URL

Source: Andrew Harnack and Eugene Kleppinger, *Online! A Reference Guide to Using Internet Sources* (Boston: Bedford/St. Martin's, 2002).

Organizing and Outlining

Organizing and Outlining

Speaker's Reference
Organizing and Outlining

11. Organizing the Speech

Create Main Points That Express Your Key Ideas and Major Claims

- Use the specific purpose and thesis statements as guides. (p. 173)
- Check that each main point flows directly from these statements. (p. 173)

Restrict the Number of Main Points, and Focus on One Idea per Point

- Strive to cover between two and five main points. (p. 174)
- Focus each main point on a single idea. (p. 175)
- Present each main point as a full-sentence statement. (p. 176)
- Reflect the main points back to the purpose statement. (p. 176)

Use Supporting Points to Substantiate or Prove Your Main Points

- Create supporting points with your research materials. (p. 176)
- Ensure that supporting points follow logically from main points. (p. 177)
- Check that supporting points are in fact subordinate in weight to main points. (p. 177)

Create Speech Points That Are Unified, Coherent, and Balanced

- Focus each point, whether main or subordinate, on a single idea. (p. 178)
- Review the logical connections between points. (p. 178)
- Dedicate roughly the same amount of time to each main point. (p. 179)
- Ensure that the introduction and the conclusion are approximately of the same length and that the body is the longest part of the speech. (p. 179)
- State the points of your speech in parallel form. (p. 179)
- Substantiate each main point with at least two supporting points. (p. 179)

Use Transitions to Signal Movement from One Point to Another

- Use clear transitions to move from point to point. (p. 180)
- Use full-sentence transitions to move from one main point to another. (p. 180)

- Use internal previews to help listeners anticipate what's ahead. (p. 182)
- Use internal summaries to help listeners review what's been said. (p. 182)

12. Types of Organizational Arrangements

Be Audience-Centered When Arranging Main Points

- Select a pattern that listeners can easily follow. (p. 184)
- Select a pattern that helps you achieve your speech goals. (p. 184)
- Subpoints need not always follow the pattern selected for main points. (p. 184)

Choose from a Variety of Organizational Patterns

- To stress natural divisions or categories in a topic, consider a *topical pattern*. (p. 184)
- To motivate listeners to adopt a course of action, consider *Monroe's motivated sequence*. (p. 185 and Chapter 26)
- To demonstrate the superiority of one viewpoint or proposal over another, consider the *comparative advantage pattern*. (p. 185 and Chapter 26)
- To disprove an opposing claim to your position, consider the *refutation pattern*. (p. 185 and Chapter 26).
- To describe a series of developments in time or a set of actions occurring sequentially, consider a *chronological pattern*. (p. 186)
- To emphasize physical arrangement, consider a *spatial pattern*. (p. 186)
- To demonstrate a topic in terms of its underlying causes (or its effects), consider a *causal (cause-effect) pattern*. (p. 187)
- To demonstrate a problem and then provide justification for a solution, consider a *problem-solution pattern*. (p. 188)
- To convey speech ideas through a story, consider a *narrative pattern*. (p. 189)
- To demonstrate how each speech idea builds on the previous idea and in turn supports the thesis, consider a *circular pattern*. (p. 190)

13. Outlining the Speech

Plan on Developing Two Outlines before Delivering Your Speech

- Begin by creating a working outline in sentence format. (p. 192)
- Transfer your ideas to a speaking outline in phrase or key-word format. (p. 194)

Become Familiar with Sentence, Phrase, and Key-Word Outlines

- Sentence outlines express speech points in full sentences. (p. 192)
- Phrase outlines use shortened versions of the sentence form. (p. 194)
- Key-word outlines use just a few words associated with the specific point. (p. 194)

Know the Benefits and Drawbacks of the Three Outline Formats

- Sentence outlines offer the most protection against memory lapses but sacrifice eye contact. (p. 194)
- The less you rely on your outline notes, the more eye contact you can have with the audience. (p. 194)
- Key-word outlines promote eye contact and natural delivery, *if* you are well rehearsed. (p. 194)

Plan Your Speech with a Working Outline

- Treat the working outline as a document to be revised and rearranged. (p. 195)
- Include everything you want to say in your working outline. (p. 195)
- Check for correct coordination and subordination of speech points. (p. 195)
- Separate the introduction and conclusion from the body of the speech. (p. 195)
- Create a bibliography. (p. 195)
- Assign the speech a title. (p. 196)

Create a Speaking Outline to Deliver the Speech

- Condense the working outline into a phrase or key-word outline. (p. 200)
- Clearly indicate delivery cues. (p. 200)
- Print large enough for your words to be seen at a glance. (p. 201)

KEY TERMS

Chapter 11

arrangement	indentation	full-sentence transitions
outlining	roman numeral outline	signposts
introduction	unity	restate-forecast form
body	coherence	rhetorical questions
conclusion	coordination and subordination	preview
main points		preview statement
parallel form	balance	internal preview
supporting points	transitions	internal summary

Speaker's Reference

Chapter 12

topical pattern of arrangement	causal (cause-effect) pattern of arrangement	narrative pattern of arrangement
chronological pattern of arrangement	problem-solution pattern of arrangement	circular pattern of arrangement
spatial pattern of arrangement		

Chapter 13

working outline	sentence outline	key-word outline
speaking outline	phrase outline	delivery cues

Organizing the Speech

Audience members quickly note the difference between a well-organized speech and one that has been put together haphazardly, with decidedly negative results when the speech is disorganized. Listeners' understanding of a speech, for example, is directly linked to how well it is organized.[1] Apparently, a little bit of disorganization won't ruin a speech if the speaker is otherwise engaging, but audience attitudes plummet when the speech is very disorganized.[2] Listeners also find speakers whose speeches are well organized more credible than those who present poorly organized ones.[3] Given all this, you won't want to skip the crucial steps of arranging and outlining speech points.

Organizing the speech (also called **arrangement** by classical scholars) is the strategic process of deciding how to order speech points into a coherent and convincing pattern for your topic and audience. **Outlining** is the physical process of plotting those speech points on the page in hierarchical order of importance. An *outline* is an essential tool that lets you check for logical inconsistencies in the placement of speech points and pinpoint weaknesses in the amount and kind of support for them. Rather than making the job of drafting a speech harder, outlining your speech provides a vivid snapshot of its strengths and weaknesses and clearly points to how you can fix the flaws. Although a few famous speakers have managed to deliver successful speeches without first arranging and outlining them, for the vast majority of us, the success or failure of a speech will depend on doing so.

Beyond the Speech: Organization as a Life Skill

As well as being of immense practical value in fashioning better speeches, skill in arranging and outlining information can have far-reaching positive effects on many aspects of your academic and professional life. As noted in Chapter 1, written and verbal skill in communication rank first in employers' "wish list" for employees.[4] Employers seek workers who can communicate ideas logically and convincingly. Nearly all professional-level jobs, for example, require you to prepare well-organized written and oral reports, PowerPoint presentations, and so forth. Similarly, written assignments in the classroom depend upon how convincingly and logically you present your viewpoint. Learning how to arrange ideas into a coherent pattern and gaining proficiency with outlining — a skill that depends on the logical coordination and subordination of ideas (see p. 178) — will serve you well as a public speaker and in these other arenas (see Tables 11.1 and 11.2).

TABLE 11.1 • Principles of Coordination and Subordination

- Assign ideas that are coordinate equal weight.
- Assign ideas that are subordinate relatively less weight.
- Indicate coordinate points by their parallel alignment.
- Indicate subordinate points by their indentation below the more important points.
- Every point must be supported by two points or none at all (consider how to address one "dangling" point in the point above it).

TABLE 11.2 • Sample Outline Format

Extended Outline Format:

I. Main point
  A. Subordinate to main point I
  B. Coordinate with subpoint A
    1. Subordinate to subpoint B
    2. Coordinate with sub-subpoint 1
      a. Subordinate to sub-subpoint 2
      b. Coordinate with sub-subpoint 2
        (1) Subordinate to sub-sub-subpoint b
        (2) Coordinate with sub-sub-sub-subpoint (1)
II. Main point: Coordinate with main point I

A speech structure is quite simple, composed of just three general parts: an introduction, a body, and a conclusion. The **introduction** establishes the purpose of the speech and shows its relevance to the audience. It lets listeners know where the speaker is taking them. The **body** of the speech presents main points that are intended to fulfill the speech purpose. Main points are developed with various kinds of supporting material to fulfill this purpose. The **conclusion** ties the purpose and the main points together. It brings closure to the speech by restating the purpose and reiterating why it is relevant to the audience, and by leaving audience members with something to think about. In essence, the introduction tells listeners where they are going, the body takes them there, and the conclusion lets them know that they have arrived.

Chapters 12 and 13 describe the various patterns you can use to order speech points and illustrate the three types of outline formats — sentence, phrase, and key word. Chapters 14 and 15 focus on how to create effective introductions and conclusions. In this chapter, we explore the body of the speech.

Main Points, Supporting Points, and Transitions

A speech body consists of three elements. The *main points* represent each of the main elements or claims being made in support of the speech topic. *Supporting points* do just as their name suggests: They support the information or arguments put forth in the main points. *Transitions* (discussed in detail later in this chapter) serve as links for audience members, alerting them to the speaker's direction as he or she moves through the speech.

Main Points: Making the Claim

Main points express the key ideas and major themes of the speech. Their function is to represent each of the main elements or claims being made in support of the speech topic. The first step in creating main points is to identify the central ideas and themes of the speech. What are the most important ideas you seek to convey? As you review your research, what important ideas emerge? What ideas can you substantiate with supporting material? Each of these ideas or claims should be expressed as a main point.

USING THE PURPOSE AND THESIS STATEMENTS AS GUIDES

You can use the specific purpose and thesis statements as reference points to help generate main points. As discussed in Chapter 7, the *specific purpose statement* expresses the goal of the speech. Formulating it in your mind allows you to articulate precisely what you want the speech to accomplish (without stating it directly in the speech itself). The *thesis statement* (which is stated in the speech) expresses the speech's theme or central idea. It concisely lays out what the speech is about. The main points should flow directly from these two statements expressing the speech goal and the central idea, as seen in the following examples:

SPECIFIC PURPOSE: (what you want your audience to get from the speech; not stated in speech itself): To show my audience, through a series of easy steps, how to perform meditation.

THESIS: (the central idea of the speech; thesis is expressed in speech): When performed correctly, meditation is an effective and easy way to reduce stress.

Main Points:

I.   The first step of meditation is "positioning."

II. The second step of meditation is "breathing."

III. The third step of meditation is "relaxation."

THESIS STATEMENT: To ensure financial security in retirement, young adults need to set investment goals, invest early, and commit to the long haul.

Main Points:

I.   Setting investment goals is the first step that young adults need to take to ensure financial security in retirement.

II. Young adults should begin investing as early as they can and put away as much as possible.

III. It is important that young adults invest for the long haul.

> ✓ **CHECKLIST**
>
> **Do the Speech Points Illustrate or Prove the Thesis?**
>
> _____ 1. Are the most important ideas in your speech expressed in the main points?
>
> _____ 2. Are any key ideas implied by your thesis not addressed by main points?
>
> _____ 3. Does each supporting point offer sufficient evidence for the corresponding main point?
>
> _____ 4. Do your supporting points reflect a variety of appropriate supporting material, such as examples, narratives, testimony, and facts and statistics?

NUMBER OF MAIN POINTS

Most speakers find that audiences can comfortably take in only between two and five main points. (Although most classroom speeches fit this category, research has shown that in longer speeches listeners can follow up to seven main points.[5]) As a rule, the fewer main points in a speech, the greater are the odds that you will keep your listeners' attention. Listeners have a better recall of the main points made at the beginning and at the end of a speech than of those made in between (unless the ideas made in between are far more striking than the others). Thus, if it is especially important that listeners remember certain ideas, introduce those ideas near the beginning of the speech and reiterate them at the conclusion.

STRATEGIES FOR LIMITING MAIN POINTS

Audiences become overwhelmed when presented with too much information, tending to tune out in response. Therefore, if you find you have too many main points while organizing your speech, consider whether your topic is sufficiently narrow (see Chapter 7). At the same time, check whether you amply support each main point with a variety of sources. This "narrow but deep" approach helps prevent loss of attention and encourages audience members to follow your message.

If the problem does not lie in an overly broad topic, review your main and supporting points for proper subordination. Do any points more properly belong as subpoints to other main points? In a speech draft about interviewing and etiquette training, University of Oklahoma student Amber Pointer found this to be the case when she saw that she had created six main points:

I.   Interviewing is competitive and requires preparation.

II. As in sports, interviewing requires training to compete well against others.

III. When you sell yourself in an interview, you want to make your best impression.

IV. When you take a course on interviewing, you become more competitive.

V. Dressing appropriately is critical to making a good impression.

VI. Proper table manners are key to making a positive impression during a luncheon interview.

Upon examination, Amber realized that main points II and IV are actually subpoints of point I:

I. Interviewing is competitive and requires preparation.

II̶. a. As in sports, interviewing requires training to compete well against others.

IV̶. b. When you take a course on interviewing, you become more competitive.

Similarly, points V and VI are subpoints of point III (which now becomes main point II):

II. When you sell yourself in an interview, you want to make your best impression.

V̶. a. Dressing appropriately is critical to making a good impression.

VI̶. b. Proper table manners are key to making a positive impression during a luncheon interview.

As she examined her outline, Amber realized that she had introduced ideas toward the end of her speech that properly supported the first main point and presented material early on that was actually subordinate to her second main point. Rather than six main points, Amber's speech in fact consists of just two.

FORM OF MAIN POINTS

A main point should not introduce more than one idea. If it does, it should be split into two (or more) main points:

Incorrect:

I. West Texas has its own Grand Canyon, and South Texas has its own desert.

Correct:

I. West Texas boasts its own Grand Canyon.

II. South Texas boasts its own desert.

Whenever possible, main points should also be stated in **parallel form**— that is, in similar grammatical form and style. (See Chapter 16 for a discussion of parallelism.) This helps listeners understand and retain the points and lends power and elegance to your words:

THESIS STATEMENT: The Group of Eight (G8) of the world's leading industrial nations should take stronger steps at its next summit to reduce carbon dioxide emissions linked to global warming.

Incorrect:

I. The U.S. must adopt new stricter policies to reduce carbon dioxide emissions.

II. Canada failed to adopt a sound global-warming policy.

III. Switzerland didn't do anything either.

Correct:

I. The U.S. must adopt stricter policies to reduce carbon dioxide emissions.

II. Canada must readdress the question of carbon dioxide emissions in its next session of parliament.

III. Switzerland must reevaluate its position on carbon dioxide emissions in its next plenary session.

Always create your main points as full sentences, and strive to express them in straightforward statements (e.g., as declarative sentences). Presenting each main point as a declarative statement emphasizes the point and makes it stand out from the others. For instance, if one of your main points is that poor children are suffering because of changes in welfare laws, you should clearly state, "Today, poor children are suffering because of changes in the welfare laws." Main points reflect back to the purpose statement, and this connection between purpose statement and main points keeps the audience on track.

Supporting Points: Substantiating the Claim

Supporting points represent the supporting material you have gathered to fill out or justify the main points and lead the audience to accept the purpose of the speech (see Chapter 8). It is here that you substantiate or prove your thesis with examples, narratives, testimony, and facts and statistics.

Listeners respond most favorably to a variety of supporting materials derived from multiple sources to illustrate each main point.[6] Alternating among different types of supporting material — such as beginning with a short story, followed by examples, statistics, and perhaps credible testimony — sparks interest and builds credibility while simultaneously appealing to listeners' different learning styles. For example, to support the claim that Michael Jordan was the most dominant player in the history of the game, you could relate a story about how he won the final game of the 1998 NBA championship against the Utah Jazz team, quote from journalist David Halberstam's biography of Jordan, and then provide some of Jordan's lifetime stats.

To determine whether they have the right amount and kind of supporting points, some speakers check them against a series of questions used by journalists: *who* (did it), *what* (did they do), *when* (did they do it), *where* (did it occur), *why* (did it happen), and *how* (did it happen)? This formula dictates that every news story should answer these questions, usually in descending order of importance in case the story has to be shortened. While these particular questions may not reflect the most relevant criteria for your selection of supporting materials, the idea is to carefully evaluate whether your subpoints satisfactorily flesh out your main claims and that they do so with a mix that is likely to appeal to listeners.

POSITION OF SUPPORTING POINTS

In an outline, supporting points appear in a subordinate position to main points. This is indicated by **indentation**. As with main points, supporting points should be ordered in a logical fashion — that is, arranged in order of their importance or relevance to the main point. The most common format is the **roman numeral outline** (used thus far in this chapter). Main points are enumerated with uppercase roman numerals (I, II, III . . .), supporting points are enumerated with capital letters (A, B, C . . .), third-level points are enumerated with arabic numerals (1, 2, 3 . . .), and fourth-level points are enumerated with lowercase letters (a, b, c . . .), as seen in the following format (see also Figure 11.1):

I. Main point
    A. Supporting point
        1. Sub-supporting point
            a. Sub-sub-supporting point
            b. Sub-sub-supporting point
        2. Sub-supporting point.
            a. Sub-sub-supporting point
            b. Sub-sub-supporting point
    B. Supporting point
II. Main point

Here is an example from a speech about children's negative attitudes toward school:

I. The increase in study drill sessions in preparation for standardized tests, from one hour to three hours daily, is causing school-age students to experience anxiety about attending school.
    A. Teachers report that students' reactions to the lengthened study drills have been negative.
        1. Teachers report a noticeable rise in acting-out behaviors.
        2. Teachers report a tenfold increase in class-time requests to visit the nurse.

B. During the past two months, 600 parents have lodged complaints with the principal about the extended study drill sessions.
1. The majority (85%) said that their children cried at night about the lengthy study sessions.
2. A minority (15%) reported that their children had to be forced to go to school.

II. The elimination of the art and science classes in favor of longer drill sessions has only increased students' negative feelings toward school.
A. Art classes have long been a favorite of school-age children.
B. Student reaction to the elimination of science classes has been strongly negative.
1. Students staged a sit-down strike in the cafeteria to protest the elimination of science classes.
2. Several students transferred to other schools in order to take science classes.

Note that different levels of points are also distinguished by different levels of indentation. These differences clearly indicate the direction of your speech. They also enhance your recollection of points and make it easy for you to follow the outline as you speak.

Principles of Organizing Main and Supporting Points

Whether you are creating a painting, an essay, a musical composition, or a speech, certain principles of good form apply. A well-organized speech is characterized by unity, coherence, and balance. Try to adhere to these principles as you arrange your speech points.

UNITY

There is a type of skilled speaker — often a preacher — who routinely seems to meander off point, only to surprise the audience at the end by artfully tying each idea to the speech theme. Such speeches retain the quality of unity, if only at the last minute. A speech exhibits **unity** when it contains only those points that are implied by the purpose and thesis statements. Nothing is extraneous or tangential. Each main point supports the thesis, and each supporting point provides evidence for the main points. Each subpoint supports each supporting point. Each point focuses on a single idea.

COHERENCE

Coherence refers to clarity and logical consistency. A coherent speech is one that is organized logically. The speech body should follow logically from the introduction, and the conclusion should follow logically from the body. Within the body of the speech itself, the main points should follow logically from the thesis statement, and the supporting points should follow logically from the main points. Transitions (discussed in the next section) serve as logical bridges that help establish coherence.[7] You can ensure coherence by adhering to the principle of **coordination and subordination** — the logical placement of ideas relative to their importance to one another. Ideas that are *coordinate* are given equal weight. An idea that is *subordinate* to another is given relatively less weight. Outlines are based on the principle of coordination and subordination. Coordinate points are indicated by their parallel alignment, and subordinate points are indicated by their indentation below the more important points:

I.   The electronic media have profoundly altered the form and substance of political campaigns.
   A.   Today's campaigns rely largely on television's fast-paced visual images and sound bites.
      1.   Politicians must manage themselves "telegenically."
      2.   Politicians must compress issues into phrases that can fit into two-minute reports on the evening news and into thirty-second commercials.
   B.   Politicians and their pollsters now use computers, sophisticated telephone linkups, faxes, and online services to take the public's pulse.
II.   The altered form of political campaigns threatens the health of our democracy.
   A.   Politicians use the new technology to constantly take the public's "temperature."
   B.   Politicians now spend more time reacting to minute shifts in public opinion polls than they do in governing.

As you can see, coordinate points are aligned with one another, while subordinate points are indented below the points that they substantiate. Thus main point II is coordinate with main point I, subpoint A is subordinate to main point I, subpoint B is coordinate with subpoint A, and so forth.

BALANCE

One common mistake on the part of many inexperienced public speakers is to give overly lengthy coverage to one point and insufficient attention to others. Another mistake is to give scanty evidence in the body of the speech after presenting an impressive introduction. Yet another error is jumping right into the speech without properly introducing the topic. The principle of **balance** suggests that appropriate emphasis or weight be given to each part of the speech relative to the other parts and to the theme.

The body of a speech should always be the longest part, and the introduction and the conclusion should be roughly the same length. Stating the main points in parallel form is one aspect of balance. *Assigning each main point at least*

✓ **CHECKLIST**

Do the Speech Points Reflect Unity, Coherence, and Balance?

_____ 1. Does each main point refer directly to your specific purpose or thesis statement?

_____ 2. Does each point focus on a single idea?

_____ 3. Do your main points follow logically from your thesis statement?

_____ 4. Do your supporting points follow logically from the main points?

_____ 5. Do you spend roughly the same amount of time on each main point?

_____ 6. Is each main point substantiated by at least two supporting points?

_____ 7. Are the speech points stated in parallel form?

two supporting points is another. Students often forget this and assign a main point only one subpoint. If you have only one subpoint, consider how you might incorporate it into the superior point. Think of a main point as a table-top and supporting points as table legs; without at least two legs, the table cannot stand.

Transitions: Giving Direction to the Speech

Transitions are words, phrases, or sentences that tie the speech ideas together and enable the speaker to move smoothly from one point to the next. Transitions can be considered the "neurosystem" of speeches: They provide consistency of movement from one point to the next and cue the audience that a new point will be made. (See Table 11.1 for a list of common transitions.) As you develop your speech, think about using transitions to move listeners from one main point to the next, from main points to supporting points, and from one supporting point to another supporting point. Transitions are also used to move from the introduction to the body of the speech, and from the body to the conclusion. Transitions can take the form of full sentences, phrases, or single words.

TRANSITIONS AMONG MAIN POINTS

When moving from one main point to another, **full-sentence transitions** are especially effective. For example, to move from main point I in a speech about sales contests ("Top management should sponsor sales contests to halt the decline in sales over the past two years") to main point II ("Sales contests will lead to better sales presentations"), the speaker might use the following transition:

Next, let's look at exactly what sales contests can do for us.

TABLE 11.1 • Transitional Words and Phrases

Function	Example
To show comparisons	similarly, in the same way, likewise, in comparison, just as
To contrast ideas	on the other hand, and yet, at the same time, in spite of, however, in contrast
To illustrate cause and effect	as a result, therefore, hence, because, thus, consequently, so the evidence shows, for this reason
To illustrate sequence of time or events	first, second, third, following this, before, after, later, earlier, at present, in the past, until now, tomorrow, next week, eventually
To indicate explanation	for example, to illustrate, in other words, to simplify, to clarify
To indicate additional examples	not only, in addition to, let's look at
To emphasize significance	most importantly, above all, remember, keep in mind
To summarize	as we have seen, altogether, in summary, finally, in conclusion, let me conclude by saying

In a speech on spyware (see Chapter 13), student John Coulter effectively transitions between his first and second main points:

> But leaving aside the finer distinctions between spyware and other types of computer menaces, what is crystal clear is that spyware represents a growing threat. Consider some of the symptoms and problems associated with spyware.

TRANSITIONS AMONG SUPPORTING POINTS

Transitions among supporting points can be handled with full sentences. For example, the transition from supporting point A ("Sales personnel will be motivated by competition") to supporting point B ("Contests are relatively inexpensive") could be made by the following transition:

> Another way that sales competitions will benefit us is by their relative cost effectiveness.

Likewise, the transition from supporting point B1 ("Contests cost less than losses in sales revenues") to supporting point B2 ("Contests cost less than training new sales staff") could be stated as follows:

> In addition to costing less than a loss in revenues, sales competitions are less expensive than training new people.

Conjunctions or phrases (sometimes called **signposts**) such as the following can be just as effective:

> Next, . . .
>
> First, . . . (second, third, and so forth)
>
> We now turn . . .
>
> Finally, let's consider . . .
>
> If you think that's shocking, . . .
>
> Similarly, . . .

SAMPLE TECHNIQUES FOR POSING TRANSITIONS

Transitions are often posed in **restate-forecast form**. That is, the transition restates the point just covered and previews the point to be covered next:

> Now that we've established a need for sales contests *(restatement)*, let's look at what sales contests can do for us *(forecast)*.

Transitions can also be stated as **rhetorical questions**, or questions that do not invite actual responses. Instead, they make the audience think (see Chapter 14):

> Will contests be too expensive? Well, actually . . .
>
> How do the costs of contests stack up against the expense of training new people?

USING INTERNAL PREVIEWS AND SUMMARIES AS TRANSITIONS

Previews are transitions that tell the audience what to expect next. In a speech introduction, the **preview statement** describes what will be covered in the body of the speech (see Chapter 14). In the body itself, **internal previews** can be used to alert audience members to ensuing main points:

> Victoria Woodhull was a pioneer in many respects. Not only was she the first woman to run her own brokerage firm, but she was also the first to run for the presidency of the United States, though few people know this. Let's see how she accomplished these feats. . . .

Similar to the internal preview, the **internal summary** draws together ideas before proceeding to another speech point. Internal summaries help listeners review and evaluate the thread of the theme thus far:

> It should be clear that the kind of violence we've witnessed in the schools and in our communities has a deeper root cause than the availability of handguns.

✓ **CHECKLIST**

Using Transitions

____ 1. Do you include enough transitions to adequately guide your listeners through your speech?

____ 2. Do you use appropriate transitions when making comparisons, showing cause and effect, illustrating a sequence in time, contrasting ideas, summarizing information, and so forth?

____ 3. Do you include full-sentence transitions that alert listeners to shifts from one main point to the next?

____ 4. Do you make appropriate use of internal previews and summaries? The restate-forecast technique? Rhetorical questions?

____ 5. Do you use a transition to alert listeners to the conclusion of the speech?

Our young children are crying out for a sense of community, of relatedness and meaning, that they just aren't finding in the institutions that are meant to serve them.

(See Chapter 13 for more on how to include transitions in the speech outline.)

12 Types of Organizational Arrangements

Once you select the main points for your speech, you must decide on a type of organizational arrangement or combination of arrangements for them. Public speeches make use of at least a dozen different organizational arrangements. Here we look at seven commonly used patterns for all forms of speeches: topical, chronological, spatial, causal, problem-solution, narrative, and circular. Chapter 26 covers three additional patterns of organization: *Monroe's motivated sequence* and *refutation,* which are designed specifically for persuasive speeches, and *comparative advantage,* which can be applied to both informative and persuasive speeches. (See Table 12.1 and Chapter 26.)

As you review these organizational designs, bear in mind that there are multiple ways to organize a speech. Each method communicates something different, even if the topic is the same. Your goal should be to choose one that listeners can easily follow.

Once you select an organizational arrangement, you can proceed to flesh out the main points with subordinate ideas. *Your subpoints need not always follow the pattern you select for your main points.* For instance, for a speech about the recent history of tattooing in the United States, you might choose a chronological pattern to organize the main points but switch to a cause-effect arrangement for some of your subpoints about why tattooing is on the rise today. (See Table 12.1 for descriptions of patterns.) Organization, whether of main points or subpoints, should be driven by what's most effective for the particular rhetorical situation.

Arranging Speech Points Topically

When each of the main points is a subtopic or category of the speech topic, the **topical pattern of arrangement** (also called the *categorical pattern*) may be most appropriate. Consider preparing an informative speech about choosing Chicago as a place to establish a career. You plan to emphasize three reasons for choosing Chicago: the strong economic climate of the city, its cultural variety, and its accessible public transportation. Of relatively equal importance, these three points can be arranged in any order without affecting each other or the speech purpose negatively. For example:

THESIS: Chicago is an excellent place to establish a career.

    I.   Accessible transportation

    II. Cultural variety

    III. Economic stability

TABLE 12.1 • Types and Functions of Organizational Arrangements

Function	Pattern of Organization
Topical	To stress natural divisions in a topic; allows points to be moved around to emphasize listeners' needs and interests
Chronological	To describe a series of developments in time or a set of actions occurring sequentially
Spatial	To describe or explain the physical arrangement of a place, scene, event, or object
Causal (Cause-Effect)	To explain or demonstrate a topic in terms of its underlying causes or effects
Problem-Solution	To demonstrate the nature and significance of a problem and provide justification for a proposed solution
Narrative	To convey ideas through the medium of a story with characters, settings, and a plot
Circular	To demonstrate how one idea leads to another and then another, all of which leads back to the speech thesis
Monroe's Motivated Sequence	To motivate listeners to adopt a course of action (see Chapter 26)
Refutation	To disprove an opposing claim to your position (see Chapter 26)
Comparative Advantage	To demonstrate the superiority of one viewpoint or proposal over another (see Chapter 26)

This is not to say that when using a topical arrangement you should arrange the main points without careful consideration. If your main points permit it, you may want to arrange them in ascending or descending order according to their relative importance, complexity, or timeliness. Perhaps you have determined that listeners' main concern is the city's economic stability, followed by an interest in its cultural variety and accessible transportation. You may then decide to arrange the points in the order of the audience's most immediate needs and interests:

I.   Economic stability

II. Cultural variety

III. Accessible transportation

Topical arrangements give you the greatest freedom to structure main points according how you wish to present your topic. You can approach a topic by dividing it into two or more categories, for example, or you can lead with your strongest evidence or leave your most compelling points until you near the conclusion. If your topic does not call out for one of the other patterns described in this chapter, be sure to experiment with the topical pattern.

Arranging Speech Points Chronologically

Some speech topics lend themselves well to the arrangement of main points according to their occurrence in time relative to each other. The **chronological pattern of arrangement** (also called the *temporal pattern*) follows the natural sequential order of the main points. To switch points around would make the arrangement appear unnatural and might confuse the audience. Topics that describe a series of events in time (e.g., events leading to the adoption of a peace treaty) or develop in line with a set pattern of actions or tasks (e.g., building a model car, procedures for admitting patients to a hospital) call out to be organized according to a chronological pattern of arrangement. For example, a speech describing the development of the World Wide Web calls for a chronological, or time-ordered, sequence of main points:

THESIS STATEMENT: The Internet evolved from a small network designed for academic scientists into a vast system of networks used by billions of people around the globe.

    I.   The Internet was first conceived in 1962 as the ARPANET to promote the sharing of research among scientists in the U.S.

    II. In the 1980s a team created TCP/IP, a language that could link networks, and the Internet as we know it was born.

    III. At the end of the cold war, the ARPANET was decommissioned and the World Wide Web made up the bulk of Internet traffic.

    IV. The Internet celebrates its twenty-fifth anniversary, with 10 million people connected.[1]

In addition to topics that involve time lines, the chronological arrangement is appropriate for any topic that involves a series of sequential steps. A scientist might describe the steps in a research project on fruit flies, for example, or a cook might explain the steps in a recipe.

Arranging Speech Points Using a Spatial Pattern

When the purpose of your speech is to describe or explain the physical arrangement of a place, a scene, or an object, logic suggests that the main points be arranged in order of their physical proximity or direction relative to each other. This calls for the **spatial pattern of arrangement**. For example, you can select a spatial arrangement when your speech provides the audience with a "tour" of a particular place:

THESIS STATEMENT: El Morro National Monument in New Mexico is captivating for its variety of natural and historical landmarks.

I.   Visitors first encounter an abundant variety of plant life native to the high-country desert.

II.   Soon visitors come upon an age-old watering hole that has receded beneath the 200-foot cliffs.

III.   Beyond are the famous cliff carvings made by hundreds of travelers over several centuries of exploration in the Southwest.

IV.   At the farthest reaches of the magnificent park are the ancient ruins of a pueblo dwelling secured high atop "the Rock."

In a speech describing a computer company's market growth across various regions of the country, a student speaker uses the following spatial arrangement:

THESIS STATEMENT: Sales of Digi-Tel Computers have grown in every region of the country.

I.   Sales are strongest in the Eastern Zone.

II.   Sales are growing at a rate of 10 percent quarterly in the Central Zone.

III.   Sales are up slightly in the Mountain Zone.

IV.   Sales in the Western Zone are lagging behind the other regions.

Arranging Speech Points Using a Causal (Cause-Effect) Pattern

Some speech topics represent cause-effect relationships. Examples might include (1) events leading to higher interest rates, (2) reasons students drop out of college, and (3) causes of spousal abuse. In speeches on topics such as these, the speaker relates something known to be a "cause" to its "effects." The main points in a **causal (cause-effect) pattern of arrangement** usually take the following form:

I.   Cause

II.   Effect

Sometimes a topic can be discussed in terms of multiple causes for a single effect, or a single cause for multiple effects:

Multiple Causes for a Single Effect (Reasons Students Drop Out of College)	**Single Cause for Multiple Effects (Reasons Students Drop Out of College)**
I. Cause 1 (lack of funds)	I. Cause (lack of funds)
II. Cause 2 (unsatisfactory social life)	II. Effect 1 (lowered earnings over lifetime)
III. Cause 3 (unsatisfactory academic performance)	III. Effect 2 (decreased job satisfaction over lifetime)
IV. Effect (drop out of college)	IV. Effect 3 (increased stress level over lifetime)

Some topics are best understood by presenting listeners with the effect(s) first and the cause(s) subsequently. In an informative speech on the 1988 explosion of Pan Am flight 103 over Lockerbie, Scotland, for instance, a student speaker arranges his main points as follows:

THESIS STATEMENT: The explosion of Pan Am flight 103 over Lockerbie, Scotland, killed 270 people and resulted in the longest-running aviation investigation in history.

    I. (Effect) Two hundred and fifty-nine passengers and crew members died; an additional eleven people on the ground perished.

    II. (Effect) To date, it is the longest-running aviation investigation in history.

    III. (Cause) The court found that the cause was a terrorist act; specifically, a bomb planted by Libyan citizen Al Megrahi.

    IV. (Cause) Many people believe that Megrahi did not act alone, if he acted at all.

In this case, the speaker presents the effects of the airplane explosion as the first two main points. He subsequently addresses the causes of the explosion in the ensuing main points.

Arranging Speech Points Using a Problem-Solution Pattern

The **problem-solution pattern of arrangement** organizes main points both to demonstrate the nature and significance of a problem and to provide justification for a proposed solution. This type of arrangement can be as general as two main points:

I. Problem (define what it is)

II. Solution (offer a way to overcome the problem)

However, many problem-solution speeches require more than two points to adequately explain the problem and to substantiate the recommended solution:

I.   The nature of the problem (identify its causes, incidence, etc.)
II. Effects of the problem (explain why it's a problem, for whom, etc.)
III. Unsatisfactory solutions (discuss those that have not worked)
IV. Proposed solution (explain why it's expected to work)

Following is a partial outline of a persuasive speech about teen pregnancy arranged in a problem-solution format (see also Chapter 26):

THESIS STATEMENT: Once you realize the nature and probable causes of the problem of teen pregnancy, it should be clear that current solutions remain unsuccessful and an alternative solution — peer counseling — should be considered.

    I.   Early unwed pregnancies
       A.   Average age of teen mothers
       B.   National and local incidence
    II. Probable causes of teen pregnancy
       A.   Lack of knowledge about contraception
       B.   Lack of motivation to use contraception
       C.   Dysfunctional social relationships
    III. Unsuccessful solutions
       A.   School-based sex education
       B.   Mass-media campaigns encouraging abstinence
    IV. Peer counseling as a possible solution
       A.   How peer counseling works
       B.   Peer counseling coupled with school-based sexuality curriculum

Arranging Speech Points Using a Narrative Pattern

Storytelling is often a natural and effective way to get your message across. In the **narrative pattern of arrangement**, the speech consists of a story or a series of short stories, replete with characters, settings, plot, and vivid imagery. However, most speeches built largely upon a story (or a series of stories) are likely to incorporate elements of other organizational arrangements described in the chapter. For example, you might present the story in a time sequence, thus using a chronological design. Or the story could be organized in an effect-cause design, in which you first reveal why something happened (such as a drunken driving accident) and then describe the events that led up to the accident (the causes).

Whatever the structure, simply telling a story is no guarantee of giving a good speech. Any speech should include a clear thesis, a preview, well-organized main points, and effective transitions. In a speech entitled "Tales of the Grandmothers,"[2] professor of communication Anita Taylor illustrates her thesis — that the U.S economy would not be what it is today without the range of "home work" that women have traditionally performed — by relating an extended story about her female ancestors, beginning in 1826. Although the story dominates the speech, Taylor frequently leaves off and picks up its thread in order to orient her listeners and drive home her theme. In addition to explicitly stating her thesis, Taylor pauses to preview main points:

> My grandmothers illustrate the points I want to make. . . .

Taylor also makes frequent use of transitions, including internal previews, summaries, and simple signposts, to help her listeners stay on track:

> But, let's go on with Luna Puffer Squire Nairn's story.

And here, Taylor signals the conclusion:

> So here we are today. . . . And finally. . . .

Arranging Speech Points Using a Circular Pattern

In the **circular pattern of arrangement**, the speaker develops one idea, which leads to another, which leads to a third, and so forth, until he or she arrives back at the speech thesis.[3] This type of organization can be useful when you want listeners to follow a particular line of reasoning, especially when your main goal is persuasion. In a speech on the role that friendship plays in physical and mental well-being, a student speaker showed how acts of consideration and kindness lead to more friendships, which in turn lead to more social support, which then results in improved mental and physical health. Each main point leads directly into another main point, with the final main point leading back to the thesis.

✓ CHECKLIST

Matching the Organizational Pattern to the Audience

_____ 1. Does the arrangement move the speech along in a logical and convincing fashion?

_____ 2. Do my ideas flow naturally from one point to another, leading to a satisfying conclusion?

_____ 3. Does the organizational pattern lend my speech momentum?

_____ 4. Does the organizational plan convey the information listeners expect or need in a way that they will be able to grasp?

Public Speaking in Cultural Perspective
Arrangement Formats and Audience Diversity

Studies confirm that the way you organize your ideas affects your audience's understanding of them.[1] Another factor that may affect how we organize relationships among ideas is culture.[2] Are certain organizational formats better suited to certain cultures? Consider the chronological arrangement format. It assumes a largely North American and Western European orientation to time because these cultures generally view time as a linear (or chronological) progression in which one event follows another along a continuum, with events strictly segmented. In contrast, some Asian, African, and Latin American cultures view time more fluidly, with events occurring simultaneously or cyclically.[3] Thus, when a speaker follows a chronological arrangement of the typical linear fashion, audience members from cultures with different time orientations may have difficulty making the connections among the main points. For these audiences, an alternative arrangement, such as the narrative or circular pattern, may be a more appropriate form in which to express speech ideas.

1. R. G. Smith, "Effects of Speech Organization upon Attitudes of College Students," *Speech Monographs* 18 (1951): 547–49; E. Thompson, "An Experimental Investigation of the Relative Effectiveness of Organizational Structure in Oral Communication," *Southern Speech Journal* 26 (1960): 59–69.
2. Devorah A. Lieberman, *Public Speaking in the Multicultural Environment*, 2nd ed. (Englewood Cliffs, N.J.: Prentice Hall, 1997).
3. Edward T. Hall, *The Dance of Life: Other Dimensions of Time* (New York: Doubleday, 1983); J. K. Burgoon, D. B. Buller, and W. G. Woodall, *Nonverbal Communication: The Unspoken Dialogue* (New York: Harper & Row, 1989).

⑬ Outlining the Speech

Producing an outline lies at the very heart of creating a speech, being at once a tool for brainstorming and a blueprint for the presentation. By plotting ideas in hierarchical fashion (such that coordinate ideas receive relatively equal weight and subordinate ideas relatively less so), and by using indentation to visually represent this hierarchy, you can't help but examine the underlying logic of the speech and the relationship of ideas to one another.[1] (For a review of the principles of coordination and subordination and the mechanics of outlining, see Chapter 11 and Figure 11.1.)

From Working Outline to Speaking Outline

As you develop a speech, you will actually create two outlines: a working outline and a speaking, or delivery, outline. A **working outline** (also called a *preparation outline*) is an essential tool in composing a speech. Here you refine and finalize the specific purpose and thesis statements, firm up and organize main points, and develop supporting points to substantiate them. It is at this point that you decide what supporting material you want to keep or need to add, and how it can best be incorporated into a coherent train of thought.

Once you complete the working outline, you must transfer its ideas to a **speaking outline** (also called a *delivery outline*) — the one you will use when you are practicing and actually presenting the speech. (See Figure 13.1.) Speaking outlines, which contain your ideas in condensed form, are much briefer than working outlines.

Some instructors may require three distinct outlines — working, formal, and speaking — with a *formal outline* containing the entire speech, worded much as the speaker plans to present it and including a title and bibliography. Alternatively, as shown in this chapter, you can simply refine the working outline until it in essence becomes a formal outline.

TYPES OF OUTLINE FORMATS

Speeches can be outlined in complete sentences, phrases, or key words.

The Sentence Outline Format

Sentence outlines represent the full "script," or text, of the speech. In a **sentence outline** each main and supporting point is stated in sentence form as a declar-

TABLE 13.1 • Steps in Organizing and Outlining the Speech
1. Create the Main Speech Points
2. Note Any Obvious Subpoints
3. Select an Organizational Pattern
4. Create a Working Outline
• Organize Main Points and Subpoints
• Check Main Points and Subpoints for Coordination and Subordination
• Revise Thesis Statement in Light of Final Organization
5. Transfer the Working Outline to a Speaking Outline Using Phrases or Key Words

ative sentence (one that makes a statement or an assertion about a subject). So, too, are the introduction, the conclusion, and the transition statements. Often, these sentences are stated in the way the speaker wants to express the idea during delivery.

Generally, sentence outlines are used for working outlines, although they may be recommended for use in delivery under the following conditions:

1. When the issue is highly controversial or emotion-laden for listeners and precise wording is needed to make the point as clear as possible

2. When the material is highly technical and exact sentence structure is critical to an accurate representation of the material

3. When a good deal of material relies on quotations and facts from another source that must be conveyed precisely as worded.

Note that while one or more of these conditions may suggest the use of a sentence outline, most speaking professionals recommend the actual speaking outline be prepared using phrases or key words. If there are points in your speech where you want to note exact quotations or precisely state complicated facts or figures, you can write those out in full sentences within your key-word or phrase speaking outlines.

In a speech on keeping prescription drugs safe while making them more affordable, Mark B. McClellan, commissioner of the U.S. Food and Drug Administration, discussed three main points, one of which was to "set forth the serious problems facing the safety and security of our drug supply. . . ."[2] In sentence format, this point (along with its subpoints) appears as follows:

I.   The prescription drug supply is under unprecedented attack from a variety of increasingly sophisticated threats.

    A.   Technologies for counterfeiting—ranging from pill molding to dyes—have improved across the board.

    B.   Inadequately regulated Internet sites have become major portals for unsafe and illegal drugs.

The Phrase Outline Format

A **phrase outline** uses a partial construction of the sentence form of each point, instead of using complete sentences that present precise wording for each point. The idea is that the speaker is so familiar with the points of the speech that a glance at a few words associated with each point will serve as a reminder of exactly what to say. A section of McClellan's sentence outline would appear as follows in phrase outline form:

I.   Drug supply under attack
      A.   Counterfeiting technologies more sophisticated
      B.   Unregulated Internet sites

The Key-Word Outline Format

The briefest of the three forms of outlines, the **key-word outline** uses the smallest possible units of understanding associated with a specific point to outline the main and supporting points. A section of McClellan's outline would appear as follows in key-word outline form:

I.   Threats
      A.   Counterfeiting
      B.   Internet

OUTLINE FORMATS AND SPEECH DELIVERY

The type of outline you select will affect how well you deliver the speech. Of the three types of outline formats (sentence, phrase, and key word), sentence outlines permit the least amount of eye contact with listeners. However, eye contact is essential to the successful delivery of a speech. Sentence outlines offer the most protection against memory lapses, but they may prompt you to look at the outline rather than at the audience. The less you rely on your outline notes, the more eye contact you can have with audience members. For this reason, phrase outlines or key-word outlines are recommended over sentence outlines in delivering most speeches, with the key-word outline often being the preferred format.

Key-word outlines permit more eye contact, greater freedom of movement, and better control of your thoughts and actions than any of the other outline formats. They are also less conspicuous to the audience. However, if at any time during the speech you experience stage fright or a lapse in memory, a key-word outline may not be of much help. This is why preparation is essential when using one. You must be confident in knowing the topic and the speech arrangement well enough to deliver the speech extemporaneously. *Extemporaneous speeches* are carefully planned and practiced in advance and are then delivered from a key-word or phrase outline. (See Chapter 17 for a discussion of extemporaneous and other types of speech delivery.)

Preparing the Working Outline

As the name implies, working outlines are works in progress. They are meant to be changed as you work through the mass of information you've collected. At several points in this process, you will probably find it necessary to rearrange the main points or to omit and add different kinds of supporting materials before deciding on the precise arrangement you want to use.

The outline should give you confidence that you've satisfactorily fleshed out your ideas. Instead of worrying about whether you will have enough to say, or whether your speech will be well organized, you'll have a realistic picture of what you'll be able to communicate. Rather than writing out the speech word for word, however, focus on charting a coherent and well-supported course. This will give you the freedom to "think on your feet" during delivery.

SEPARATE THE INTRODUCTION AND CONCLUSION FROM THE BODY

Whether in a working or speaking outline, the introduction and the conclusion are separate from the main points. The introduction is the preface; the conclusion is the epilogue. The actual main points — or body — of the speech come between the preface and the epilogue, or the head and the feet.

In outlines, treatments of the introduction can vary. You can use such labels as *Attention Getter, Thesis,* and *Preview* to indicate how you will gain the audience's attention, introduce the thesis, and preview the speech topic and main points (see Chapter 14 for more on developing the introduction). Alternatively, your instructor may prefer that you assign the introduction its own numbering system or simply write it out in paragraph format.

Similarly, in the conclusion you can indicate where you signal the close of the speech, summarize main points, reiterate the thesis and purpose, and leave the audience with something to think about (or otherwise offer a memorable close) — or, again, assign it its own numbering system or write it out. (See Chapter 15 for more on developing the conclusion.)

LIST YOUR SOURCES

As you work on the outline, clearly mark where speech points require source credit. Directly after the point, either insert a footnote *or* enclose in parentheses enough of the reference to be able to retrieve it in full. Once you complete the outline, order the references consecutively, as they appear in the speech, and place them on a sheet titled "Notes" or "References." (Some instructors may prefer an alphabetically arranged bibliography, "works cited," and/or "works consulted" list. For guidelines on what to include in a source note, see Chapters 9 and 10 (especially the From Source to Speech sections); see Appendices F–H for particular citation styles.

CREATE A TITLE

As the last step, assign the speech a title. Neatly crafted titles communicate the essence of a speech. At times, you might even refer to the title in the introduction, as a means of previewing the topic. Whether mentioned or not, a title should inform any readers of the speech of its subject, and in a way that invites them to read it.

✓ CHECKLIST

Steps in Creating a Working Outline

_____ 1. Write out your topic, general purpose, specific speech purpose, and thesis—to keep them in focus.

_____ 2. Establish your main points (optimally two to five).

_____ 3. Flesh out supporting points.

_____ 4. Check for correct subordination and coordination; follow the numbering system shown in Table 11.2 (p. 172).

_____ 5. Label each speech part (e.g., introduction, body, and conclusion).

_____ 6. Write out each speech point in sentence form (unless directed otherwise).

_____ 7. Label and write out transitions.

_____ 8. Note sources in parentheses.

_____ 9. Prepare a list of sources, and append it to the outline.

_____ 10. Assign the speech a title.

SAMPLE WORKING OUTLINE

The following outline is from a speech delivered by John Coulter at Salt Lake Community College. It uses the sentence format and includes labeled transitions.

Staying Ahead of Spyware

JOHN COULTER
Salt Lake Community College

TOPIC:	Problems and solutions associated with spyware
SPECIFIC PURPOSE:	To inform my audience members of the dangers of spyware so that they may take appropriate steps to prevent infection
THESIS STATEMENT:	Computer users must understand the nature of spyware and how it works in order to take the necessary steps to protect themselves.

Introduction

I. Imagine how you would feel if someone was tracking everything you did on the Internet, including recording your passwords and credit card numbers. *(Attention getter)*

II. A type of software known as spyware can install itself on your computer without your knowledge and harvest this sensitive information.

III. To protect yourself, you need to understand how spyware works. *(Thesis)*

IV. Today, I'll talk about what spyware is, the harm it causes, who it affects, and how to keep your computer from becoming infected. *(Preview)*

TRANSITION: So, what exactly is spyware?

Body

I. Spyware is relatively new and appears in many guises.

    A. Until the year 2000, *spyware* referred to monitoring devices on cameras. (FTC, March 2004 report)

        1. Its first link to a software context apparently was in connection with the introduction of a security program called ZoneAlarm.

        2. Today, the Federal Trade Commission defines spyware as any computer code that installs itself on your computer, gathers data from it, and sends it back to a remote computer without your consent. (FTC, *Consumer Alert*)

            a. Spyware includes software that will advertise on your computer.

            b. It also includes software that collects personal information.

TRANSITION: You may be wondering how spyware gets into your computer and what it does once it gets there.

    B. Spyware installs itself silently, often "piggybacking" onto other downloaded programs such as file sharing applications and games.

        1. Links in pop-up ads and the "unsubscribe" button in spam are known sources.

        2. Some types of spyware track your Web-browsing habits and sell this information to marketers.

        3. A type of spyware called adware loads ads onto the computer but doesn't monitor browsing habits.

        4. The most dangerous (and rarest) type of spyware, keystroke logging, records and transmits keystrokes to steal such personal information as tax returns, Social Security numbers, and passwords.

   C. Distinctions remain fuzzy between spyware and other kinds of programs that install themselves on computers. (FTC, March 2004)

      1. Industry people disagree over whether software that the manufacturer discloses in the licensing, but in print so fine that it isn't likely to be read or understood, should be considered spyware or adware.

      2. Disagreement exists over whether software that the manufacturer "piggybacks" onto free downloads in order to advertise itself, but that doesn't install monitoring code, should be called spyware or adware.

      3. People agree that to qualify as spyware, it must serve the interests of someone other than the user: "Spyware alters the PC's behavior to suit the interests of outside parties rather than the owner or user." (Mossberg, *WSJ*, July 14, 2005)

TRANSITION: There's a lot of confusion regarding the differences between spyware and computer viruses — and even whether there are any.

   D. Spyware is different from a virus in a variety of ways.

      1. Viruses are generally written by individuals in order to brag about causing damage. (CNET.com video)

      2. Spyware is written by teams employed by companies, not all of them shady, to make money.

      3. Viruses have been around for more than two decades; everyone agrees on how to define them; and they are illegal.

      4. Few laws exist governing spyware, though legislation is pending in many states and on the federal level.

TRANSITION: Leaving aside the finer distinctions between spyware and other types computer menaces, what is crystal clear is that spyware represents a growing threat.

II. Users can learn to recognize the symptoms and problems associated with spyware.

   A. One sign of infiltration is a constant stream of pop-up ads. (Vara, *WSJ*, July 18, 2005)[6]

   B. Strange toolbars may appear on the desktop.

   C. Browser settings may be hijacked, forcing users to strange Web pages.

   D. The computer may behave sluggishly or become unstable.

      1. Files may become displaced or disappear.

      2. The computer may crash.

III. Spyware is the leading cause of computer-related problems today.

A. Tanner Nielson of Totally Awesome Computers in Salt Lake City, Utah, reports that the majority of problems brought into the store are spyware related. (Nielson interview)[7]

B. A 2005 *Consumer Reports* national survey finds that spyware is a leading cause of computer malfunction. (*Consumer Reports, 2005*)[8]

1. Within the past two years, one-third of users with home Internet access experienced severe computer problems and/or financial losses.

2. Eighteen percent said that their hard drives were so seriously infected that the contents had to be erased.

TRANSITION: Spyware can do some nasty things to your computer as well as to your wallet.

IV. Prevention is the best way to avoid spyware's harmful and potentially dangerous effects.

A. Keep your browser up-to-date to take advantage of security updates.

B. Invest in one of the three top antispyware programs recommended by *Consumer Reports*: Webroot's Spy Sweeper, Computer Associates' Pest-Patrol, and Spybot's Search & Destroy. (*Consumer Reports, 2005*)[9]

C. Don't install any software without reading the fine print.

D. Download free software only from sites you know and trust.

E. Don't click on links in pop-up windows.

F. Don't reply to or even open spam or any email that isn't from someone you know.

G. Don't hit the "unsubscribe" button in spam because spyware is known to lurk here.

H. Exercise caution when surfing online: Spyware tends to be loaded onto disreputable sites containing pornography and even on sites advertising spyware solutions.

Conclusion

I. The makers of spyware are in it for the money, so the problem is likely to be long lasting. (*Signals close of speech*)

II. Spyware can do serious damage to your computer and your finances, but by taking the right steps you can avoid major problems. (*Summarizes main points*)

A. An increasing number of solutions to spyware exist, including more secure browsers and good antispyware programs.

B. The steps I've laid out should help you protect your computer from becoming infected.

C. One final piece of advice is to keep abreast of developments related to spyware by reading reputable computer publications such as *PC Magazine* and visiting reputable Web sites such as CNET.com. (*Leaves audience with something to think about*)

III. Forewarned is forearmed. Good luck! (*Memorable close*)

Works Cited

Federal Trade Commission, Monitoring Spyware on Your PC: Spyware, Adware, and Other Software. Mar. 2005. 8 Aug. 2005 <http://www .ftc.gov/os/2005/03/050307spywarerpt.pdf>.

Federal Trade Commission, Web Site for the Consumer. "Consumer Alert on Spyware." 8 Aug. 2005 <http://www.ftc.gov/bcp/conline/pubs/alerts/ spywarealrt.htm>.

Mossberg, Walter J. "Despite Others' Claims, Tracking Cookies Fit My Spyware Definition." Wall Street Journal 14 July 2005. 19 July 2005 <http://ptech.wsj.com/archive/ptech-20050714.html>.

"Net Threat Rising." Consumer Reports Sept. 2005: 12–15.

Nielson, Tanner. Personal interview. 12 May 2005.

Vara, Vauhini. "Lurking in the Shadows," Wall Street Journal 18 July 2005. 19 July 2005 <http://online.wsj.com/article/0,,SB112128460774484814, 00-search.html>.

"Virus vs. Spyware." CNET.com, Videos section. 9 aug. 2005 <http://reviews .cnet.com/Virus_vs_spyware/4660-10620_7-6273711.html>.

Preparing the Speaking Outline

Once you complete a full-sentence working outline, it is time to transfer your ideas to a speaking outline, using a key-word or phrase format. While the speaking outline uses the same numbering system (see Table 11.2 on p. 172) and parallel form as the working version, it contains just enough words to jog your memory. Exceptions are made for any quotations, statistics, or other information that you will deliver word for word; these should be written out in full.

CLEARLY INDICATE DELIVERY CUES

Include in the speaking outline any brief reminder notes, or **delivery cues**, that will be part of the speech. As seen in Figure 13.2, common delivery cues include transitions, timing, speaking rate and volume, presentation aids, quotations, statistics, and difficult-to-pronounce names or words. So that they are easily visible at a glance, you might capitalize the cues, place them in parentheses, and/or highlight them.

TABLE 13.2 • Common Delivery Cues

Delivery Cue	Example
Transitions	(TRANSITION)
Timing	(PAUSE)
	(SLOW DOWN)
	(REPEAT)
Speaking rate and volume	(SLOWLY)
	(LOUDER)
	(SOFTLY)
Presentation aids	(SHOW MODEL)
	(SHOW MAP)
	(SLIDE 3)
Sources	(*Atlanta Constitution*, August 2, 2005)
Statistics	(2002, boys to girls = 94,232; U.S. Health Human Services)
Quotations	Eubie Blake, 100: "If I'd known I was gonna live this long, I'd have taken better care of myself."
Difficult-to-pronounce names or words	Eowyn (A-OH-win)

Place the outline on 4 x 6-inch notecards or 8.5 x 11-inch sheets of paper. Some speakers dislike notecards, finding them too small to contain enough material and too easily dropped. Others find notecards small enough to be handled unobtrusively but large enough to accommodate key words (assuming about one main point and supporting points per card). Whichever you use, be sure to print large and bold enough so that your words will be easily seen at a glance.

✓ **CHECKLIST**

Tips on Using Notecards or Sheets of Paper

_____ 1. Leave some blank space at the margins to find your place as you glance at the cards.

_____ 2. Number the notecards or sheets so that you can follow them with ease.

_____ 3. Instead of turning the cards or sheets, slide them under one another.

_____ 4. Do not staple notes or sheets together.

_____ 5. If you use a lectern, place the notes or sheets near eye level.

_____ 6. Do not use the cards or sheets in hand gestures, as they become distracting pointers or flags.

PRACTICE THE SPEECH

The key to the successful delivery of any speech, and particularly one delivered with an outline in key-word format, is practice. The more you rehearse your speech, the more comfortable you will become when you speak from the key-word outline. For additional information on rehearsing the speech, see Chapter 19, "The Body in Delivery."

✓ **CHECKLIST**

Steps in Creating a Speaking Outline

——— 1. Select large notecards or sheets of paper that you can easily handle without distraction.

——— 2. If the outline is prepared on a computer, use a large-size print (at least 14 inches) that can be comfortably read at a glance. If it's handwritten, use easy-to-read ink and large letters.

——— 3. Identify each main and subpoint with a key word or phrase that is likely to jog your memory accurately.

——— 4. Include delivery cues.

——— 5. Write out quotations word for word as well as other information that you need to cite verbatim.

——— 6. Using the speaking outline, practice the speech at least five times.

SAMPLE SPEAKING OUTLINE

Staying Ahead of Spyware

JOHN COULTER
Salt Lake Community College

TOPIC:	Problems and solutions associated with spyware
SPECIFIC PURPOSE:	To inform my audience members of the dangers of spyware so that they may take appropriate steps to prevent their occurrence
THESIS STATEMENT:	Computer users must understand the nature of spyware and how it works in order to take the necessary steps to protect themselves.

Introduction

I.   Imagine, feel? *(Attention Getter)*

II. Can happen; spyware installs, harvests

III. To protect, understand how *(Thesis)*

IV. What, harm, who affects, avoid *(Preview)*

So, what exactly. . . ?)

    [PAUSE]

Body

I.   Relatively new, many guises

    A. Until 2000, monitoring devices on cameras (FTC, March 2004 report)

        1. First link to software content, ZoneAlarm.

        2. FTC defined: installs, gathers data, sends to remote computer, no consent

            a. Install advertising

            b. Collect personal data

(TRANSITION: May be wondering . . .)

    B. Installs silently, "piggybacks"

        1. Known sources — pop-up ads, "unsubscribe" button in spam

        2. Some track browsing habits, sell info

        3. Adware loads ads; no monitoring

        4. Keyloggers steal info [SHOW SLIDE]

    C. Fuzzy distinctions (FTC, March 2004)

        1. Disclosed in licensing agreement, fine print?

        2. Free downloads; no code?

        3. All agree serves others: "Spyware alters the PC's behavior to suit the interests of outside parties rather than the owner or user." (Mossberg, *WSJ*, July 14, 2005)

(TRANSITION: There's a lot of confusion . . .)

    D. Different from virus

        1. Individuals; to brag, damage. (CNET.com video)

        2. Spyware — teams, companies, money

        3. Viruses two decades; all defined; illegal

        4. Few laws

(TRANSITION: Leaving aside distinctions, growing threat . . .)

II. Recognize symptoms, problems

    A. Stream pop-ups (Vara, *WSJ*, July 18, 2005)

  B. Toolbars on desktop. [SHOW SLIDE]

  C. Browser settings hijacked

  D. Computer sluggish, unstable

   1. Files displaced, disappear

   2. Crash

 III. Leading cause computer problems

  A. Nielson; majority of problems (Nielson interview)

  B. *Consumer Reports,* 2005 survey

   1. Past two years; one-third severe problems computer and/or financial

   2. 18% hard drives seriously infected; erase

(TRANSITION: Nasty things to computer, wallet)

 IV. Prevention key

  A. Update browser; security updates.

  B. Antispyware: Webroot's Spy Sweeper, Computer Associates' PestPatrol, Spybot's Search & Destroy. (*Consumer Reports,* 2005) [SHOW BOX]

  C. Don't install w/o fine print

  D. Beware free downloads

  E. Don't click pop-up links

  F. Links in spam

  G. "Unsubscribe" button

  H. Caution! Disreputable sites, even spyware solutions!

[PAUSE]

Conclusion

 I. Money, problem long lasting

 II. Damage computer, finances, right steps

  A. Solutions, browsers, antispyware

  B. Steps laid out

  C. *PC Magazine,* CNET.com.

 III. Forewarned is forearmed. Good luck!

FULL-TEXT SPEECH

Following is the full text of the speech outlined in this chapter. John's assignment was to deliver a four- to five-minute informative speech citing at least three authoritative sources, incorporating at least one presentation aid, and including a list of references in either APA or MLA style.[3]

Spyware

JOHN COULTER
Salt Lake Community College

How would you feel if someone was watching and recording everything you typed on the Internet—your passwords, personal letters, and perhaps even your credit card numbers? Well, it just might be. There are plenty of software programs out there that can install themselves on your computer without your knowledge. Once they're installed, they're able to harvest sensitive information such as this. •

In order to protect yourself, it is necessary to understand how these types of programs, known as spyware, work. •

Today, I'll talk about the danger of spyware and how to avoid it. I'll discuss four main points relating to spyware: what it is, the harm it causes, who it affects, and how to keep your computer from becoming infected by it. •

So, what exactly is spyware? •

To begin, spyware is relatively new. According to a March 2004 report by the Federal Trade Commission (FTC), until the year 2000 the term *spyware* referred to monitoring devices on cameras. Its first link to a software context apparently was in connection with the introduction of a security program called ZoneAlarm. Today, the FTC defines spyware as any computer code that installs itself on your computer, gathers data from it, and sends it back to a remote computer without your consent. • This includes software that will advertise on your computer, collect personal information, and change your computer's configuration.

You may be wondering how spyware gets into your computer and what it does once it gets there. •

Spyware installs itself silently, often "piggybacking" onto other downloaded software programs such as file sharing applications and games. Links in pop-up ads and the "unsubscribe" button in spam are other known sources. Some types of spyware track your Web-browsing habits and sell this information to marketers; other kinds, sometimes called adware, merely load ads on your computer but don't

- John gains listeners' attention by relating the topic to their concerns.
- He introduces the speech thesis.

- He previews the main points.
- John uses a transition to signal the move into the body of the speech.

- John alternates among a mix of credible sources throughout the speech, beginning here with a government report.
- This transition shifts the focus from definitions of spyware to examples of it.

monitor your browsing habits. The most dangerous (and rarest) type of spyware, keystroke logging, or simply keyloggers, records and transmits keystrokes. Keyloggers can steal information as personal as your tax returns, Social Security number, and passwords, sending it along to identity thieves.

Each of these examples represents an instance of spyware. Yet, as noted in the report by the FTC, distinctions remain fuzzy between spyware and other kinds of software programs that install themselves on computers.

Is it spyware, for example, if the manufacturer discloses what the software does in the licensing agreement, but in print so fine that it isn't likely to be read or understood? Some people in the industry say yes; others, no. Is it spyware if the manufacturer "piggybacks" it onto a free download in order to advertise itself on your computer, but otherwise doesn't install monitoring code? • Here again, opinion is divided. People do agree that to qualify as spyware, it must serve the interests of someone other than the user. As computer guru Walter Mossberg of the *Wall Street Journal* put it in his July 14, 2005, column, "Spyware alters the PC's behavior to suit the interests of outside parties rather than the owner or user."

• Repetition of a rhetorical question—"Is it spyware . . . ?" lends rhythm to this section.

You may be wondering about the differences between spyware and computer viruses—or whether there are any. •

• Internal preview alerts the audience to what's ahead.

Spyware is different from a virus in a variety of ways. According to a video tutorial on the Web site CNET.com, viruses are generally written by individuals in order to brag or cause damage. Spyware is written by teams employed by companies, many but not all of them shady, in order to make money. Viruses have been around for more than two decades; everyone agrees on how to define them; and they are illegal. Currently, few laws exist governing spyware, though legislation is pending in many states and on the federal level.

But leaving aside the finer distinctions between spyware and other types of computer menaces, what is crystal clear is that spyware represents a growing threat. Consider some of the symptoms and problems associated with spyware. •

• Restate-forecast transition: Restates the point just covered and previews the upcoming one.

As described by Vauhini Vara in the July 18, 2005, edition of the *Wall Street Journal,* one sign that your computer's been infiltrated with spyware is a constant stream of pop-up ads. Another is the appearance of strange toolbars on your desktop or even a different homepage. The settings on your browser may be changed or "hijacked," forcing you to strange Web pages and ignoring the addresses you type in. Your computer may behave sluggishly or become unstable. The monitor may start to do weird things; files may become displaced or disappear altogether. The worst case scenario? Your computer crashes.

How many people are plagued by problems such as these? •

● Transition stated as a rhetorical question.

In a conversation with Tanner Nielson of Totally Awesome Computers right here in Salt Lake City, Utah, the majority of issues on computers brought into their store are spyware related. Nielsen's observation is borne out by a nationally representative survey conducted in 2005 by *Consumer Reports.* It found that within the past two years one-third of users with home Internet access experienced severe problems with their computer systems and/or financial losses. Eighteen percent said that their hard drives were so seriously infected that the contents had to be erased.

So spyware can do some nasty things to your computer as well as to your wallet. Prevention is the best way to avoid these harmful and potentially dangerous effects. • A recent Federal Trade Commission *Consumer Alert* advises keeping your browser up-to-date so that it can take advantage of security updates. Second, invest in an antispyware program. The three top antispyware programs cited by *Consumer Reports* are Webroot's Spy Sweeper, Computer Associates' PestPatrol, and Spybot's Search & Destroy. Third, don't install any software without reading the fine print, and download free software only from sites you know and trust. Fourth, do *not* click on links in pop-up windows. Don't reply or even open any e-mail that isn't from someone you know. Never reply to spam, and don't hit the "unsubscribe" button. Spyware is known to lurk here.

● Another restate-forecast transition.

Finally, be careful about the Web sites you visit. Spyware tends to be loaded onto disreputable sites containing pornography and even Web sites advertising solutions to spyware. Know the nature of the sites you visit whenever possible. •

Unlike individuals who create computer viruses, the makers of spyware are in it for the money. Thus, the problem is likely to be a long-lasting one. At the same time, much is being done to counteract spyware, including making browsers more secure and developing effective antispyware programs.

Spyware can do serious damage to your computer and to your finances. The steps I've laid out should help you protect your computer from becoming infected. The antispyware programs I've mentioned are easy to install and very helpful. One final piece of advice is to keep abreast of developments related to spyware by reading reputable computer publications such as *PC Magazine* and visiting reputable Web sites such as CNET.com.

Forewarned is forearmed. Good luck! •

• Signal words—
"first," "second,"
"finally"—move
listeners from one
point to another.

• Concluding paragraphs signal the close of the speech, reiterate the theme, offer a summary, and end with a memorable phrase.

Introductions, Conclusions, and Language

Introductions, Conclusions, and Language

Speaker's Reference
Introductions, Conclusions, and Language

14. Developing the Introduction

Use the Introduction to Capture the Audience's Attention

- Lead with a quotation. (p. 215)
- Tell a story. (p. 216)
- Pose questions. (p. 217)
- Say something startling. (p. 218)
- Bring in humor. (p. 218)
- Refer to the occasion. (p. 219)
- Establish common ground. (p. 219)

Alert the Audience to Your Speech Topic and Purpose

- Declare what your speech is about and what you hope to accomplish. (p. 219)

Preview the Main Points

- Help listeners mentally organize the speech by telling them what the main points will be and in what order you will address them. (p. 220)

Demonstrate Why the Audience Should Care about Your Topic

- Consider pointing out the topic's practical implications. (p. 221)
- Consider specifying what the audience stands to gain by listening. (p. 221)

Establish Your Credibility

- Briefly state your qualifications for speaking on the topic. (p. 222)
- Emphasize some experience, knowledge, or perspective you have that is different from or more extensive than that of your audience. (p. 222)

Prepare the Introduction

- Prepare the introduction after you've completed the speech body. (p. 222)
- Keep the introduction brief: It should occupy no more than 10 to 15 percent of the overall speech. (p. 222)

15. Developing the Conclusion

Alert the Audience to the Conclusion of Your Speech

- Use transitional words or phrases. (p. 223)
- Indicate by the manner of your delivery that the speech is coming to an end. (p. 223)
- Once you've signaled the conclusion, finish the speech quickly. (p. 223)

Summarize the Key Speech Points

- Reiterate the main points of speech, but don't do it in a rote way. (p. 224)
- Remind listeners of the topic and purpose of your speech. (p. 224)

Challenge the Audience to Respond to Your Ideas or Appeals

- If the goal is informative, challenge listeners to use what they've learned in a way that benefits them. (p. 224)
- If the goal is persuasive, challenge listeners to act in line with your message. (p. 224)

Employ Vivid Language and Attention-Getting Devices

- Use quotations. (p. 226)
- Tell a story. (p. 227)
- Pose rhetorical questions. (p. 227)

Prepare the Conclusion

- Keep the conclusion brief: It should be only one-sixth the length of the overall speech. (p. 227)
- Carefully consider your use of language. (p. 227)

16. Using Language to Style the Speech

Strive for Simplicity

- Try to say what you mean in short, clear sentences. (p. 229)
- Steer clear of unnecessary jargon. (p. 230)
- Avoid words unlikely to be understood by your audience. (p. 230)

Aim for Conciseness

- Use fewer rather than more words to express your thoughts. (p. 230)
- Experiment with phrases and sentence fragments. (p. 230)
- Use contractions (*it's* instead of *it is*). (p. 230)

Use Repetition and Transitions

- Repeat key words and phrases to emphasize important ideas and to help listeners follow your logic. (p. 232)
- Make liberal use of transitional words and phrases, internal previews, and internal summaries. (p. 232)

Use Personal Pronouns

- Make specific references to yourself and to the audience. (p. 233)
- Foster a sense of inclusion by using the personal pronouns *I, you,* and *we.* (p. 233)

Use Culturally Sensitive and Unbiased Language

- Avoid language that relies on unfounded assumptions, negative descriptions, or stereotypes of a group's characteristics. (p. 234)
- Avoid colloquial expressions the audience may not understand. (p. 234)
- Work towards developing *cultural intelligence.* (p. 235)

Choose Concrete Words

- Use concrete nouns and verbs. (p. 235)
- Avoid abstract language that is open to interpretation — unless that is your intent. (p. 235)

Use Vivid Imagery

- Use colorful language. (p. 237)
- Appeal to listeners' senses: smell, taste, sight, hearing, and touch. (p. 237)
- Use *similes, metaphors, analogies,* and other figures of speech. (p. 237)

Choose Language That Builds Your Credibility

- Use language that is appropriate to the audience, occasion, and subject. (p. 239)
- Use language accurately. (p. 239)
- Choose words that are both denotatively (literally) and connotatively (subjectively) appropriate for the audience. (p. 239)

Choose Words That Express Confidence and Conviction

- Use the active voice. (p. 240)
- Use "I" language. (p. 240)
- Avoid powerless speech, such as hedge and tag questions. (p. 240)

Choose Language That Creates a Lasting Impression

- Repeat key words, phrases, or sentences at various intervals (anaphora). (p. 241)
- Choose words that repeat the same sounds in two or more neighboring words or syllables (alliteration). (p. 242)
- Arrange words, phrases, or sentences in similar form (parallelism). (p. 243)
- Use *antithesis* (juxtaposing two ideas in balanced opposition to each another) or *triads* (grouping concepts into threes). (p. 243)

KEY TERMS

Chapter 14

anecdote
rhetorical questions

previewing
ethical appeal

Chapter 15

call to action

Chapter 16

style
rhetorical device
jargon
contractions
biased language
colloquial expression
sexist pronoun
persons with disabilities (PWD)
cultural intelligence
concrete language
abstract language
figures of speech

simile
metaphor
cliché
mixed metaphor
analogy
personification
understatement
irony
allusion
hyperbole
onomatopoeia
malapropism

denotative meaning
connotative meaning
active voice
hedges
tag questions
repetition
anaphora
alliteration
hackneyed
parallelism
antithesis
triads

Developing the Introduction (14)

Many novice speakers think that if the body of their speech is well developed they can "wing" the introduction and conclusion. Leaving these elements to chance, however, is a formula for failure. Although the introduction and conclusion are not more important than the body of the speech, they are critical to its overall success. Introductions prepare the audience to hear the speech. A good opening previews what's to come in a way that invites listeners to stay the course. An effective conclusion ensures that the audience remembers the speech and reacts in a way that the speaker intends.

This chapter describes the techniques speakers use to lead into their speeches. Chapter 15 addresses the conclusion.

Functions of the Introduction

The choices you make about the introduction can affect the outcome of the entire speech. In the first several minutes (one speaker pegs it at ninety seconds[1]), audience members will decide whether they are interested in the topic of your speech, whether they will believe what you say, and whether they will give you their full attention. A good introduction serves to:

- Arouse the audience's attention and willingness to listen.
- Introduce the topic and purpose of the speech.
- Preview the main points.
- Motivate the audience to accept the speaker's goals.
- Make the topic relevant.

GAIN ATTENTION: THE FIRST STEP

The first challenge faced by any speaker is that of winning the audience's attention. Some of the more time-honored techniques for doing this include using quotations, telling a story, posing questions, saying something startling, using humor, referring to the occasion, and establishing a feeling of common ground with the audience.

Use a Quotation

A good quotation, one that elegantly and succinctly expresses an idea, is a very effective way to draw the audience's attention. Quotations can be culled from literature, poetry, film, or directly from individuals.

Audiences instinctively confer credibility on speakers who adroitly weave statements by people of renown into their remarks. In a sense, the speaker "borrows" the source's status. In the following example from a speech on the importance of history, historian David McCullough uses quotes from Harry Truman, eighteenth-century author Lord Bolingbroke, and historian Daniel Boorstein to capture his audience's attention and introduce a central point of his speech:

> Harry Truman once said the only new thing in the world is the history you don't know. Lord Bolingbroke, who was an 18th century political philosopher, said that history is philosophy taught with example. An old friend, the late Daniel Boorstein, who was a very good historian and Librarian of Congress, said that trying to plan for the future without a sense of the past is like trying to plant cut flowers. We're raising a lot of cut flowers and trying to plant them, and that's much of what I want to talk about tonight.[2]

Quotations need not be restricted to the famous. Clever sayings of any kind, whether spoken by a 3-year-old child or by a wise friend, may express precisely the idea you are looking for.

Tell a Story

Noted speechwriter and language expert William Safire once remarked that stories are "surefire attention getters."[3] Speakers like to use stories (also known as *narratives*) to illustrate points, and audiences like to hear them, because they make ideas concrete and colorful.[4] Stories personalize issues, encouraging identification and making things relevant. Most important, they entertain.

Recall from Chapter 7 that an **anecdote** is a brief story of interesting, humorous, or real-life incidents. As rhetorical scholar Edward Corbett notes, anecdotes are "one of the oldest and most effective gambits for seizing attention."[5] Corbett's assessment is supported by a 1998 study conducted by Dutch researchers, who found that speeches with anecdotal openers both motivate the audience to listen and promote greater understanding and retention of the speaker's message.[6] The key to successfully introducing a speech with an anecdote is choosing one that strikes a chord with the audience. Here, for example, Antoinette Baley uses a humorous anecdote to begin a speech on diversity:

> I'd like to begin by retelling a story. . . . Three businessmen — a Frenchman, a Japanese man, and an American — are lined up before a firing squad. According to ancient custom, each is granted a final wish. The Frenchman says he would die happy if he could sing "La Marseillaise" one more time. He does . . . and he sings this old revolutionary song so well that it brings tears to the eyes of the riflemen. Even so, they take steady aim and shoot the Frenchman dead.
>
> The Japanese businessman is inspired by the patriotic example of the Frenchman. He expresses his desire to give one last speech on *Kaizen*, the

Japanese for encouraging incremental improvements in the production system. However, before he can get started, the American rises and insists that he be the next to go. "I will die happy," says the American, "if I don't have to listen to one more lecture on Japanese management."[7]

Baley uses the anecdote to make the point that her topic, diversity, has become "one of the buzzwords in American businesses and society" and that "anything that buzzes is likely to be a source of annoyance." Having acknowledged the often hackneyed treatment of her topic, Baley proceeds to treat it with insight and originality.

Like a joke, stories should be able to stand on their own. People want to be entertained. They don't want to listen to the speaker's explanation of what the story means. Of course, not all stories have to be real. Hypothetical stories can serve the same purpose as real ones. Just remember that the hypothetical story must be plausible.

Pose Questions

Can you recall a speech that began with a question? Posing questions is an effective opening technique. Doing so draws the audience's attention to what you are about to say. Questions can be real or rhetorical. **Rhetorical questions** (like the one that opens this paragraph) do not invite actual responses. Instead, they make the audience think.

Whenever you use a rhetorical question in an introduction, always let the audience know that your speech will attempt to answer it:

> Are you tired of paying more and more taxes every year? Are you fed up with having no control over how your money is spent? If so, I'm glad you're here. Today I'm going to talk about some concrete steps you can take to lessen your tax burden.

Posing questions that seek an actual response, either in a show of hands or by verbal reply, also sparks interest. Here is an example of how a speech about dieting might be introduced by using real, or "polling," questions:

> How many of you have tried to diet? (*Speaker waits for a show of hands.*) How many of you kept the weight off when you stopped dieting? (*Speaker waits for a show of hands.*) How many of you would like to try a diet that doesn't make you feel starved all the time? (*Speaker waits for a show of hands.*) As you can see by looking around this room, you are not alone. Today I'm going to discuss a way of eating that is both satisfying and healthful.

Polling audience members is an effective way to gain their attention, but there are several potential drawbacks to this approach. It is possible that no one will respond, that the responses will be unexpected, or that the speaker will be called on to answer in unanticipated ways. If you incorporate questions, make sure that you feel comfortable improvising if things don't go according to plan.

Say Something Startling

"Did you know that virtually no one is having babies anymore in parts of Western Europe?" Surprising audience members with startling or unusual information is one of the surest ways to get their attention. Such statements stimulate your listeners' curiosity and make them want to hear more.

Speakers frequently base their startling statements on statistics, a powerful means of illustrating consequences and relationships — how one thing affects another. Statistics can quickly bring things into focus. In the following example, a student addressing the issue of minimum wages uses statistics to drive home the main point:

> Imagine going to work for nine hours a day, five days a week, fifty-two weeks a year, and having only about $8,600 to show for it (before taxes). Now imagine having to support not only yourself but your spouse and kids as well. The next step to imagine is you standing in welfare lines.

Use Humor

Few things build rapport and put people at ease as effectively as humor. Introducing a speech with a short joke or a funny story can set a positive tone for what's to follow. Handled well, humor is also an excellent way to make key points and introduce the theme of a speech. The drier and more difficult the topic, the greater are the odds that a speech will be enlivened by humor.

Yet you should use humor with caution. Simply telling a series of unrelated jokes might initially attract the audience's attention, but unless the jokes make a relevant point they will probably do more harm than good. Moreover, few things turn an audience off more quickly than tasteless or inappropriate humor. Speech humor should always match the audience, topic, purpose, and occasion. It should also match your personal style. Humor or sarcasm that belittles others — whether on the basis of race, sex, ability, or otherwise — should be strictly avoided in any speech.

✓ CHECKLIST

Using Humor Appropriately

_____ 1. Is your humor appropriate to the occasion?

_____ 2. Does your humor help you make a point about your speech topic or the speech occasion?

_____ 3. Have you avoided any potentially offensive targets, such as race or religion?

_____ 4. Is your humor likely to insult or demean anyone?

_____ 5. Will the audience understand your humor?

_____ 6. Have you given your humor a trial run?

_____ 7. Is your humor funny?

Self-deprecating humor often gets a chuckle, and it's usually safe. In the following example, Charlton Heston makes light of his age with a quip:

> My daughter called me with some words of advice for today's talk. She said, "Don't tell them any funny stories about me when I was child, or how tough you had it during the Great Depression."[8]

Refer to the Occasion

Introductions that include references to the speech occasion and to any relevant facts about the audience also tend to capture attention and, crucially, establish goodwill. People appreciate a direct reference to the event, and they are interested in the meaning the speaker assigns to it. In a speech on management, Vance Coffman began in this fashion:

> Let me say, right here at the beginning, that it is an honor—and a great personal pleasure—to be invited to participate in this Executive Forum of Mercer University. I understand that this is the 20th anniversary season of these innovative forums, so let me congratulate you and wish you every good fortune in continuing its success for at least another 20 years.[9]

Establish Common Ground

Just as friendships are formed by showing interest in others, audiences are won over when speakers express interest in them and show that they share similar interests and goals. Establishing a feeling of common ground demonstrates interest and respect, and thereby builds speaker credibility.

When Nelson Mandela, an anti-apartheid leader in South Africa who later became the country's president, was first released from prison after twenty-seven years of incarceration, he addressed a huge crowd of supporters. He began this way:

> Friends, comrades, and fellow South Africans. I greet you all in the name of peace, democracy, and freedom for all. I stand here before you not as a prophet but as a humble servant of you, the people. Your tireless and heroic sacrifices have made it possible for me to be here today. I therefore place the remaining years of my life in your hands.[10]

Although Mandela had just tasted his first hours of freedom after more than two decades in prison, he chose to focus on the members of the audience rather than on himself, expressing respect and establishing common ground. In response, Mandela's listeners could not help but hold him in even higher esteem.

INTRODUCE THE PURPOSE AND TOPIC

The introduction should alert the audience to the speech topic and purpose. In the attention-getting phase of the introduction, you may already have alluded to your topic, sometimes very clearly. If not, however, you now need to declare

Public Speaking in Cultural Perspective
Humor and Culture: When the Jokes Fall Flat

While humor can be a highly effective tool for introducing speeches, it can also be the cause of communication breakdowns. As one scholar notes, "Humor goes beyond language; it takes us into the heart of cultural understanding."[1] Humor assumes shared understanding. When that understanding is absent, the jokes fall flat. Humor breakdowns can occur any time audience members do not share the same cultural assumptions as the speaker. These assumptions may be based on gender, social class, educational background, ethnicity, or nationality.[2] A new employee may not get a joke told by a presenter with a long history in the corporate culture. A non-native speaker may not be familiar with an idiom used to express humor or may not share the underlying belief on which the humor is based. An English-speaking American may find the humor in other English-speaking countries baffling.

How can you avoid using humor that your audience won't understand? The obvious answer is to carefully consider your audience. Be as confident as possible that your material will make sense and be humorous to your listeners. Be particularly alert to nonverbal feedback. If you receive puzzled stares, consider clarifying your meaning. You might even acknowledge the cultural assumptions that your humor tacitly expresses.

1. William Lee, "Communication about Humor as Procedural Competence in Intercultural Encounters," in *Intercultural Communication: A Reader*, 7th ed., Larry A. Samovar and Richard E. Porter (Belmont, Calif.: Wadsworth, 1994), 373.
2. Ibid., 381.

---

what your speech is about and what you hope to accomplish by incorporating your thesis statement (see Chapter 7). Note an exception to this rule: When your goal is to persuade, and the audience is not yet aware that this is your intention, such "forewarning" may predispose listeners in the opposite direction. However, when the audience knows of your persuasive intent, previewing the topic and purpose can enhance understanding.[11]

Topic and purpose are clearly explained in this introduction to a speech by Marvin Runyon, postmaster general of the United States:

> This afternoon, I want to examine the truth of that statement—"Nothing moves people like the mail, and no one moves the mail like the U.S. Postal Service." I want to look at where we are today as a communications industry, and where we intend to be in the days and years ahead.[12]

PREVIEW THE MAIN POINTS

After indicating the topic and purpose, your introduction should preview the main points of the speech. **Previewing** the main points helps audience members mentally organize the speech and helps you, the speaker, keep their attention. Introductory previews are straightforward. You simply tell the audience what the main points will be and in what order you will address them.

In a speech titled "U.S. Roads and Bridges: Highway Funding at a Crossroads," the president of the American Automobile Association, Robert L. Darbelnet, effectively introduces his topic, purpose, and main points:

> Good morning. When I received this invitation, I didn't hesitate to accept. I realized that in this room I would find a powerful coalition: the American Automobile Association; the National Asphalt Pavement Association. Where our two groups come together, no pun intended, is where the rubber meets the road.
>
> Unfortunately, the road needs repair.
>
> My remarks today are intended to give you a sense of AAA's ongoing efforts to improve America's roads. Our hope is that you will join your voices to ours as we call on the federal government to do three things:
>
> Number one: Perhaps the most important, provide adequate funding for highway maintenance and improvements.
>
> Number two: Play a strong, responsible yet flexible role in transportation programs.
>
> And Number three: Invest in highway safety.
>
> Let's see what our strengths are, what the issues are, and what we can do about them.[13]

When previewing your main points, simply mention those points, saving your in-depth discussion of each one for the body of your speech.

MOTIVATE THE AUDIENCE TO ACCEPT YOUR GOALS

A final function of the introduction is to motivate the audience to care about your topic and believe what you have to say about it. In order for this to occur, audience members must believe that (1) the topic is relevant and (2) you are qualified to address it.

✓ CHECKLIST

How Effective Is Your Introduction?

_____ 1. Does the introduction capture the audience's attention?

_____ 2. Does the introduction establish a positive bond with listeners?

_____ 3. Does the introduction alert listeners to the speech purpose and topic?

_____ 4. Does the introduction motivate listeners to accept your speech goals?

MAKE THE TOPIC RELEVANT

A good introduction demonstrates why your listeners should care about your topic. One way to do this is to describe the practical implications the topic has for them. Another is to convince audience members that your speech purpose is consistent with their motives and values. Yet another strategy is to specify what the audience stands to gain by listening to you. A student speech about groundwater shows how this can be accomplished:

> Any time we are thirsty, water is available through a tap or drinking fountain. None of us ever stops to think about where water comes from or how it's processed. It may surprise you to learn that frequently in the United States simple tap water has been found to contain dozens of pollutants and impurities. Fertilizers from irrigation fields, petroleum products from leaking underground storage facilities, and even the motor oil your neighbor dumped in the alley may end up in your drinking water.

ESTABLISH CREDIBILITY AS A SPEAKER

During the introduction, audience members make a decision about whether they are interested not just in your topic but also in you. They want to know why they should believe you, and they will look to you for reasons to do so. Thus **ethical appeals** are particularly important when the audience does not know you well and when it is important to establish your professionalism.[14] To build your credibility, make a simple statement of your qualifications for speaking on the topic at the particular occasion and to the specific audience. Briefly emphasize some experience, knowledge, or perspective you have that is different from or more extensive than that of your audience.

Guidelines for Preparing the Introduction

Although the introduction comes first in a speech, it should be prepared after you've completed the speech body. When you then turn to the introduction, you will know exactly what your speech message is and what you need to preview.

Keep the introduction brief—as a rule, it should occupy no more than 10 to 15 percent of the overall speech. Nothing will turn an audience off more quickly than waiting interminably for you to get to the point. Finally, practice delivering your introduction until you feel confident that you've got it right. Use a tape recorder and seek out friends or colleagues who will give you constructive feedback.

 CHECKLIST

Guidelines for Preparing the Introduction

✓ Prepare your introduction after you've completed the body of the speech.
✓ Review your research for material that you can use in the introduction.
✓ Keep the introduction brief. As a general rule, it should make up no more than 10 to 15 percent of the entire speech.
✓ Time your introduction before delivery.
✓ Revise the introduction freely until you're completely satisfied.

Developing the Conclusion

Just as a well-crafted introduction gets your speech effectively out of the starting gate, a well-constructed conclusion ensures that you go out with a bang and not a whimper. Conclusions give you the opportunity to drive home your purpose, and they offer you a final chance to make the kind of impression that will accomplish the goals of your speech. Conclusions also provide the audience with a sense of logical and emotional closure.

Functions of Conclusions

Like introductions, conclusions consist of several elements that work together to make the end of a speech as memorable as the beginning. Conclusions serve to:

- Signal to the audience that the speech is coming to an end and provide closure.
- Summarize the main points and goals.
- Reiterate the thesis or central idea of the speech.
- Challenge the audience to respond.

SIGNAL THE CLOSE OF A SPEECH AND PROVIDE CLOSURE

People who listen to speeches are taking a journey of sorts, and they want and need the speaker to acknowledge the journey's end. The more emotional the journey, as in speeches designed to touch hearts and minds, the greater is the need for logical and emotional closure.

One way to alert the audience that a speech is about to end is by using a transitional word or phrase to signal closure: *finally, looking back, in conclusion, in summary, as I bring this to a close,* or *let me close by saying* (see Chapter 11). You can also signal closure more subtly by adjusting your manner of delivery; for example, you can vary your tone, pitch, rhythm, and rate of speech to indicate that the speech is winding down (see Chapter 18).

Few things annoy listeners more than hearing a speaker say "in conclusion," and then having to sit through another twenty minutes of the speech. Once you've signaled the end of your speech, conclude in short order (though not abruptly). Although there are no hard-and-fast rules about length, as a general rule about one-sixth of the speech can be spent on the introduction, one-sixth on the conclusion, and the remaining four-sixths on the body of the speech.[1]

SUMMARIZE THE MAIN POINTS AND GOALS

One bit of age-old advice for giving a speech is: "Tell them what you are going to tell them (in the introduction), tell them (in the body), and tell them what you told them (in the conclusion)." The idea is that emphasizing the main points three times will help the audience to remember them.

Summarizing the main points in the conclusion accomplishes the last step of "telling them what you've told them." However, the summary or review should be more than a rote recounting. Consider how Holger Kluge, in a speech titled "Reflections on Diversity," summarizes his main points:

> I have covered a lot of ground here today. But as I draw to a close, I'd like to stress four things.
>
> First, diversity is more than equity. . . .
>
> Second, weaving diversity into the very fabric of your organization takes time. . . .
>
> Third, diversity will deliver bottom line results to your businesses and those results will be substantial, if you make the commitment. . . .
>
> Fourth, and above all, remember this. Diversity means recognizing the uniqueness of another person whether they are a customer, an employee, or ourselves. It means acknowledging their right to be who they are.[2]

As the speaker reiterates each point, audience members are able to mentally check off what they've heard during the speech. Did they get all the main points? A restatement of points like the ones above brings the speech full circle.

REITERATE THE TOPIC AND SPEECH PURPOSE

Another function of the conclusion is to reiterate the topic and speech pur-pose—to imprint it in the audience's memory. In the conclusion to a speech about preventing school violence, William Kirwan reminds his listeners of his central idea:

> What I've tried to convey this afternoon are the kinds of efforts it will take for us to save the next Nick Johnson and all the other tragedies like his that are lurking out there. We can build a network of metal detectors and surveil-lance cameras and hope that we catch a future Nick before he fires. Or, we can build a community that could save him long before he turns down the road toward destruction. Do we want to catch him, or do we want to save him?[3]

CHALLENGE THE AUDIENCE TO RESPOND

A strong conclusion challenges audience members to put to use what the speaker has taught them. This applies to both informative and persuasive speeches. In an *informative speech,* the speaker challenges audience members to use what they've learned in a way that benefits them. In a *persuasive speech,* the challenge usually comes in the form of a **call to action**. Here the speaker chal-lenges listeners to act in response to the speech, see the problem in a new way, change their beliefs about the problem, or change both their actions and their beliefs about the problem.

A concluding challenge is important because it shows audience members that the problem or issue being addressed is real and personally relevant to them. In the introduction, part of the goal is to show audience members how the topic is relevant to them; the call to action is a necessary part of completing that goal in the conclusion.

Note how Hillary Rodham Clinton makes a specific call to action in her conclusion to an address presented to the United Nations Fourth World Conference on Women:

> *Now it is time to act on behalf of women everywhere. If we take bold steps to better the lives of women, we will be taking bold steps to better the lives of children and families too.* . . . As long as discrimination and inequities remain so commonplace around the world — as long as girls and women are valued less, fed less, fed last, overworked, underpaid, not schooled and subjected to violence in and out of their homes — the potential of the human family to create a peaceful, prosperous world will not be realized. Let this conference be our — and the world's — call to action.[4]

In this direct call to action, Rodham Clinton appeals to her audience to act to better the lives of women around the world. Moreover, she specifically calls the conference a "call to action" to highlight the fact that she wants audience members to personally take steps to fulfill this goal.

Make the Conclusion Memorable

Beyond summarizing and providing closure, a key function of the conclusion is to make the speech memorable. A good conclusion increases the odds that the speaker's message will linger after the speech is over. A speech that makes a lasting impression is one that listeners are most likely to remember and act on.

 CHECKLIST

Making the Conclusion Memorable

✓ Use quotations — including poetry, lyrics, and pertinent statements from others.

✓ Pose rhetorical questions to make your audience think about the speech topic and your speech goals.

✓ Tell a story that illustrates or sums up a key speech idea.

✓ Use humor.

✓ Issue a challenge.

✓ Make a startling statement.

✓ Link back to the introduction to give the audience a sense of having come full circle.

Effective conclusions are crafted with vivid language that captures the audience's attention (see Chapter 16). Conclusions rely on (but are not limited to) the same devices for capturing attention as introductions — quotations, stories, questions, startling statements, humor, and references to the audience and the occasion. Here we offer examples of speech conclusions that make use of quotations, stories, and rhetorical questions.

USE QUOTATIONS

As with introductions, using a quotation that captures the essence of the speech can be a very effective way to close a speech. Note how Sue Suter uses a quotation from a character in *Star Trek* to conclude her speech on discrimination and the disabled:

> That brings us to the final lesson from *Star Trek*. I'd like to leave you with two quotations from Captain Picard that define what it means to be human. In *The Next Generation,* Picard confronts discrimination by agreeing that, yes, we may be different in appearance. Then he adds, "But we are both living beings. We are born, we grow, we live, and we die. In all the ways that matter, we are alike."[5]

Quoting from poetry is also a highly effective way to conclude a speech, as seen in this commencement address given by Oprah Winfrey to graduates of Wellesley College:

> I want to leave you with a poem that I say to myself sometimes. . . . Maya Angelou wrote a poem and I don't know a poem more fitting than "Phenomenal Woman" for this crowd, because you are and these words are for you.
> She says, "Pretty women, honey, they wonder just where my secret lies 'cause I'm not cuter, built to suit a fashion model size, but when I start to tell them, they say, Girl, you're telling lies and I said, no, honey, it's in the reach of my arms, it's in the span of my hips, it's in the stride of my stepping, it's

---

✓ CHECKLIST

How Effective Is Your Conclusion?

Does your conclusion . . .

_____ 1. Alert the audience that the speech is ending?

_____ 2. Actually come to an end soon after you say you will finish?

_____ 3. Last no more than about one-sixth of the time spent on the body of the speech?

_____ 4. Reiterate the main points?

_____ 5. Remind listeners of the speech topic and purpose?

_____ 6. Challenge the audience to respond to your ideas or appeals?

_____ 7. Provide a sense of closure and make a lasting impression?

in the curl of my lips, 'cause I'm a woman, honey, phenomenally, phenomenal, phenomenal woman."[6]

TELL A STORY

A short concluding story, or *anecdote,* can bring the entire speech into focus very effectively. It helps the audience to visualize the speech:

> I would conclude with a story that applies to all of us in this industry. In ancient times there was a philosopher who had many disciples. . . .

Another technique is to pick up on a story or an idea that you mentioned in the introduction, bringing the speech full circle:

> Remember the story of Timmy that I told in the beginning, the young hero who gave up everything he ever wanted to help his family? Well, I am happy to tell you that Timmy, or I should say Tim, is today one of the most successful entrepreneurs in the state of Florida.

POSE A RHETORICAL QUESTION

Yet another effective way to make a speech linger is to leave the audience with a *rhetorical question.* Just as such questions focus attention in the introduction, they can drive home the speech theme in the conclusion. A speech on groundwater contamination, for example, might end with a rhetorical question:

> Water has been cheap and plentiful, for most of us, for our entire lives. Easy access to our most necessary resource is now greatly threatened. Given this danger, we need to ask ourselves, "How long can we ignore the dangers of groundwater contamination?"

Guidelines for Preparing the Conclusion

As with the introduction, prepare the conclusion after you've completed the speech body. Keep it brief—as a rule, no more than about one-sixth of the overall speech. And, just as you should outline the introduction in full-sentence and then key-word form, do so for the conclusion (see Chapter 13). Carefully consider your use of language in the conclusion. More than in other parts of the speech, the conclusion can contain words that inspire and motivate (see Chapter 16).

Finally, practice delivering the conclusion until you feel confident that you've got it right. Use a tape recorder or video camera, and seek out friends or colleagues for constructive feedback. While practicing, work on ensuring that audience members will understand the speech is ending through your word choice and vocal intonation (see Chapter 18), and be sure to rehearse how you will leave the podium or speech area (see Chapter 19).

✓ **CHECKLIST**

Guidelines for Preparing the Conclusion

✓   During the research phase, be on the lookout for material that you can use in the conclusion.

✓   Do not leave the conclusion to chance. Prepare both a full-sentence outline and a key-word outline.

✓   Keep the length of the conclusion to about one-sixth of the overall speech.

✓   Practice delivering the conclusion often.

Using Language to Style the Speech

Words are the public speaker's tools of the trade, and the words you choose to style your speech will play a large role in how well it is received. **Style** involves both specific word choices and **rhetorical devices** (techniques of language) that speakers use to express their ideas and achieve their speech purpose.

Used in all its richness, language allows us to visualize an image and even get a sense of sound or smell. Poets and novelists use descriptive language to breathe life into that someone or something and to make their words leap off the page into the reader's mind. In public speaking, you too can use the evocative power of language to captivate your audience. Carefully choosing the right words and images is crucial to connecting with your audience. Doing so will increase the odds that your listeners will understand, believe in, and retain your message.[1]

Write Your Speeches for the Ear

In the book *Reagan: In His Own Hand,* former Secretary of State George P. Shultz recalls how President Ronald Reagan once approved a foreign policy speech that Shultz was about to deliver but then added, "Of course, if I were giving that speech, it would be different." The text, he opined to an abashed Shultz, had been written to be read in the *New York Times,* not to be spoken aloud. Flipping through the manuscript, Reagan penciled in a few changes and marked out the section that contained, or should contain, the "story." Nothing of substance was altered, but, writes Shultz, "I saw that he had changed the tone of my speech completely."[2]

Former President Reagan, a masterful public speaker, was keenly aware that written language and oral language differ in several respects. Whereas readers who fail to understand something can go back and reread a passage until they are satisfied that they understand what the writer means, listeners have only one chance to get the message. If the language in your speech is unclear, listeners will have a tough time getting the meaning you intend to convey.

The next time you listen to a speech or even a classroom lecture, consider how the presenter's language differs from that of this textbook. Here are some things you are likely to note:

- More so than written texts, effective speeches use familiar words, easy-to-follow sentences, and straightforward syntax (subject-verb-object agreement).

- Speeches make more frequent use of repetition and transitions than do most forms of written communication.

- Because you cannot "rewind" a speaker's words, speeches must be more clearly organized than written language. A clear organizational pattern provides listeners with the necessary framework to follow spoken messages.

- Spoken communication is more interactive than written language. When you deliver a speech, you can adjust the content based on audience feedback. If listeners appear not to understand you, for example, you can supply additional examples or otherwise attempt to increase shared meaning.

Keeping these differences between oral and written language in mind, consider how you can use the following tips to write your speeches to be heard rather than read.

STRIVE FOR SIMPLICITY

To make certain that your audience understands you, strive for simplicity of expression in your speeches. When selecting between two synonyms, choose the simpler term. And unless the audience consists of specialized professionals, translate **jargon** — the specialized language of a given profession — into commonly understood terms. As former presidential speechwriter Peggy Noonan notes in her book *Simply Speaking:*

> Good hard simple words with good hard clear meanings are good things to use when you speak. They are like pickets in a fence, slim and unimpressive on their own but sturdy and effective when strung together.[3]

William Safire, another master speechwriter, puts it this way:

> Great speeches steer clear of forty-dollar words. Big words, or terms chosen for their strangeness — I almost said "unfamiliarity" — are a sign of pretension. What do you do when you have a delicious word, one with a little poetry in it, that is just the right word for the meaning — but you know it will sail over the head of your audience? You can use it, just as FDR used "infamy," and thereby stretch the vocabulary of your listeners. But it is best if you subtly define it in passing, as if you were adding emphasis.[4]

AIM FOR CONCISENESS

Concise wording is another feature of an effective speech. As a rule, use fewer rather than more words to express your thoughts. As you work on your speech drafts, edit any unnecessary words and phrases, bearing in mind that, in general, easy-to-pronounce words and shorter sentences are more readily understood. Because they reflect how the English language is actually spoken, use **contractions** — shortened forms of the verb *to be* and other auxiliary verbs in conjunction with pronouns (*I, he, she, you*) and proper nouns (*John, Juanita*). Thus, rather than

I am so happy to be here today. I will first turn . . .

Say,

I'm happy to be here. I'll first turn . . .

Refer to the accompanying ESL Speaker's Notes for a list of common English contractions.

ESL Speaker's Notes
Using Contractions

Learning to use contractions is an excellent way for non-native speakers to sound like experienced speakers of English. Using contractions will make your language sound more natural, thereby helping your audience to feel more at ease with your speech patterns. As you work on your speeches, practice using the contraction forms in this chart.

Auxiliary Verb Form	Contractions with Pronouns	Contractions with Nouns	Contractions with Question Words
am	*I'm* swimming this morning.		*What'm* I supposed to do? (Common only in spoken English.)
is	*She's* going to come. *She's* a teacher. *It's* easy!	*Ahmed's* at home. *Joan's* playing the piano at the moment.	*Who's* on the telephone? *What's* he doing?
are	*You're* a great cook! *They're* playing tennis this afternoon.	The *books're* on their way. (Common only in spoken English.)	*What're* you going to do? (Common only in spoken English.)
has	*He's* been to Cairo twice. *It's* been such a long time! *She's* been painting all day.	*Mary's* gone to the store.	*What's* she been doing? *Who's* been invited?
have	*I've* eaten for the day. *They've* got six dogs.	The *students've* finished their homework. (Common only in spoken English.)	*Where've* you been all day? (Common only in spoken English.)

(Continued)

had	*He'd* been outside all day.		*What'd* you done before that? (Common only in spoken English.)
	We'd better be going.		
will	*I'll* find your book tomorrow.	*Peter'll* catch the train to New York. (Common only in spoken English.)	*What'll* we do?
	We'll be there soon.		*Where'll* you take us? (Common only in spoken English.)
would	*I'd* like some food.	*Jane'd* love to come. (Common only in spoken English.)	*Where'd* you like to go? (Common only in spoken English.)
	They'd like to ask her some questions.		

Source: Adapted from "Using Contractions," About.com section on English as a second language, with Kenneth Beare, http://esl.about.com/library/grammar/blgr_contractions.htm (accessed May 12, 2002).

CONSIDER PHRASES AND SENTENCE FRAGMENTS

Although they are often avoided in written language, phrases and sentence fragments can sometimes help to communicate an oral message concisely. The following example, by a speaker trained as a physician, demonstrates how they can add punch to a speech:

> I'm just a simple bone-and-joint guy. I can set your broken bones. Take away your bunions. Even give you a new hip. But I don't mess around with the stuff between the ears. . . . That's another specialty.[5]

Beware of shortening merely for shortening's sake, however. Your first goal should always be to help the audience see the connection between ideas.[6] Repetition and transitions can often help you to accomplish this.

USE REPETITION AND TRANSITIONS

Good speeches often repeat key words and phrases. Indeed, even very brief speeches make use of this extremely important linguistic device. Repetition adds emphasis to important ideas, helps listeners follow the speaker's logic, and imbues language with rhythm and drama. Similarly, threaded through a typical speech are numerous transitional words, phrases, and sentences, such as *next, first, second, third,* and so forth; and *we now turn to.* Along with more lengthy internal previews and internal summaries, these transitions guide the listener from one main point to the next, from main points to supporting points, and from one supporting point to another (see Chapter 11).

Does Your Speech Incorporate Effective Oral Style?

_____ 1. Can you use fewer rather than more words to clearly express your thoughts?

_____ 2. Is your speech free of unnecessary jargon?

_____ 3. Do you steer clear of terms that are difficult to pronounce (and therefore difficult to decipher)?

_____ 4. Do you avoid any unnecessary "forty-dollar words"?

_____ 5. Do you use frequent transitions, internal previews, and summaries (see Chapter 11)?

_____ 6. Do you judiciously use the personal pronouns *I* and *you* to personalize the occasion and foster a sense of inclusion?

_____ 7. Would interjecting some phrases and sentence fragments in place of full sentences add punch to your speech?

_____ 8. Do you make sufficient use of repetition and transitions?

USE PERSONAL PRONOUNS

Oral language is often more interactive and inclusive of the audience than is written language. The personal pronouns *we, us, I,* and *you* occur more frequently in spoken than in written text. Audience members want to know what the speaker thinks and feels, and to be assured that he or she recognizes them and relates them to the message. Speakers accomplish this by making specific references to themselves and to the audience, as in this excerpt from a speech to a group of people working in public relations:

> My talk today is about you. Each one of you personally. I know you hear many presentations. For the most part, they tend to be directed mostly to others with very little for you. My presentation today is different; the topic and the information will be important to every one of you, especially if you're at all interested in having a happy, successful, and important life. I'm going to show and tell each of you how to become a verbal visionary.[7]

Consult the accompanying checklist for additional tips on personalizing your speech with personal pronouns.

Personalizing Your Speech with Personal Pronouns

✓ "*I* am indebted to the ideas of . . ."

✓ "Those of *us* who have lived during a world war . . ."

✓ "*We* cannot opt out of this problem . . ."

✓ "To *me,* the truly great lessons . . ."

✓ "Some of *you* will recall . . ."

Choose Language That Encourages Shared Meaning

Words have a power that goes beyond mere description. They can encourage shared meaning or serve as obstacles to understanding. They can build trust or engender hostility. Language that encourages shared meaning is culturally sensitive and unbiased, concrete, and vivid.

USE CULTURALLY SENSITIVE AND UNBIASED LANGUAGE

Perhaps more than any other aspect of human society, language defines and creates culture. Through language people are able to communicate with one another—to share meaning. *Language* is the distinctive words, phrases, and colloquial expressions that pass from one generation to the next and that define and perpetuate a unique culture.

As a public speaker, it is critical to be sensitive to cultural variations in language, whether you are addressing people of another nationality or audiences for whom local variations in language are significant. Demonstrating sensitivity to your audience begins with using language that is free of bias. **Biased language** relies on unfounded assumptions, negative descriptions, or stereotypes of a given group's age, class, gender, disability, geographic, ethnic, racial, or religious characteristics. In addition to being unethical, biased language reflects poorly on a speaker's credibility and may lead to the audience's rejecting both the speaker and the message of the speech. (See the Public Speaking in Cultural Perspective box on p. 235.)

As you review your speech draft, consider whether you use **colloquial expressions** (regional variations in expressions) that may confuse listeners. Some members of your audience may understand expressions such as "back the wrong horse," "hit the nail on the head," and "wet behind the ears," but others may not. Since colloquialisms can add color and richness to your speech, rigidly eliminating them may not always be desirable. However, if you do use a colloquial expression, be sure to include simple definitions for it. (See Chapter 3 for more on cultural barriers to understanding, and Chapter 6 for more on adapting to ethnic and cultural backgrounds.)

One common mistake that persists despite ongoing attempts to remedy it is the use of **sexist pronouns**, which unnecessarily restrict the gender of the person or persons in question. Steer clear of the generic pronoun *he* to refer to both women and men, using *she or he* instead. Also avoid stereotyping jobs or social roles by gender. For example, a speaker who continually refers to engineers as "he" and to nurse practitioners as "she" is guilty of using sexist language. Try to use gender-neutral terms when possible, such as *chairperson* instead of *chairman*.

Another mistake many speakers make is failing to recognize the range of physical and mental disabilities that their listeners may experience. Yet about one out of every five people in the United States has some sort of physical or mental disability.[8] Thus another way that you can demonstrate cultural sensitivity is to familiarize yourself with issues that are important to **persons with disabilities (PWD)**, and then ensure that your language accords them dignity, respect, and fairness.

Public Speaking in Cultural Perspective
Adapting Your Language to Diverse Audiences

Using language that is appropriate to each of your listeners is one of the most important challenges facing you as a public speaker. Consider, for example, that many students at your school may be Arab, Jewish, Asian, African, or Hispanic American. Others may have families that come from Europe, Canada, Mexico, and elsewhere.

How do members of the co-cultures in your audience want you to refer to them? Rather than being a monolithic group, Asian Americans and Pacific Islanders in the United States include those of Chinese, Samoan, Pakistani, Bangladeshi, Native Hawaiian, Vietnamese, Korean, Thai, and Japanese descent, and this is merely a partial listing of countries of origin. Some Asian Americans have limited English proficiency (LEP) and live in linguistically isolated households in which all members 14 years and older speak limited English,[1] while others excel at elite universities and in high-powered careers. Rather than treating any individual merely as a member of a broad category, audience members want to be addressed as individuals and to be recognized for their unique characteristics and life circumstances.

Similarly, a common misconception of Arab Americans is that they are a homogeneous group. For example, many people believe that all Arab Americans are practicing Muslims. In fact, the largest portion are Catholics (42 percent); most of the six million Muslims in this country are not Arab Americans. Rather than sharing a religion, Arab Americans belong to many religions, including Islam, Christianity, Druze, Judaism, and others.[2] Using biased language based on these and other misconceptions can only alienate your listeners.

All people look to speakers to use language that is respectful and inclusive of them. As you prepare your speeches, consider whether you include terms that might leave your listeners feeling less than respected. For the long term, make learning about other cultures an ongoing endeavor. In this way, you will truly be able to address the sensitivities of diverse audiences.

1. "The Diverse Face of Asians and Pacific Islanders in California," National Asian Pacific American Legal Consortium (San Francisco: 2005), http://www.napalc.org/?id=61&cid=4&pid=3&oid=1 (accessed April 28, 2005).
2. Arab American Institute, "About Arab Americans," http://www.aaiusa.org/definition.htm (accessed April 28, 2005).

As described in Chapter 1, **cultural intelligence**[9] is the willingness to learn about other cultures and gradually reshape your thinking and behavior in response to what you've learned.[10] As you craft the language in your speech, consider your own cultural intelligence quotient (see the accompanying checklist).

CHOOSE CONCRETE WORDS

Another way to build common ground is by using **concrete language** — language that is specific, tangible, and definite. The flip side of concrete language is **abstract language** — language that is general or nonspecific. Studies show that listeners retain concrete nouns and verbs more easily than they retain

> ✓ **CHECKLIST**
>
> ### Considering Your Cultural Intelligence Quotient
>
> ✓ Have you learned about the background of your audience members?
> ✓ Can you identify cultural values and attitudes that may affect how audience members will receive your speech?
> ✓ Have you considered your use of colloquial expressions?
> ✓ Does your language include any unintentional assumptions about a given group, such as assigning all members a general characteristic?
> ✓ Does your language reflect any disparagement toward a person's or a group's nationality, geographic origin, or religion?

abstractions. In fact, each time listeners hear an abstract word they try to find a concrete reference for it, and if you haven't given it they will search their own experience for it. The meaning they ultimately attach to the word may not match yours and, furthermore, if they are sufficiently puzzled they will be distracted from focusing on the remainder of your message.

Note the following ten words, all of which are some of the most overused abstractions in student speeches:[11]

old	bad	a lot	short	good
thing	big	long	new	late

The following examples illustrate abstract versus concrete language:

ABSTRACT: The big police officer was mean to us.

CONCRETE: The police officer, who must have weighed 350 pounds, screamed obscenities at us.

ABSTRACT: That iPod has a lot of accessories.

CONCRETE: Along with the iPod itself, she purchased a sleek Sportwrap armband and Nike Flight sport headphones.

> ✓ **CHECKLIST**
>
> ### Is Your Speech Language Concrete?
>
> As you construct your speech, consider which words and phrases may be abstract. Consult a dictionary or thesaurus to find more concrete words that would strengthen your message. For example, consider the following levels of concreteness:
>
> | *Abstract* | *Less Abstract* | *Concrete* |
> |---|---|---|
> | summer ────→ | hot weather ────→ | sweltering heat |
> | congestion ────→ | traffic jam ────→ | gridlock |

OFFER VIVID IMAGERY

Vivid images paint a mental picture for listeners, inviting them to use their imaginations and thereby become involved in your message. Paint vivid images with colorful and concrete words that appeal to the senses and with figures of speech, such as similes, metaphors, and analogies.

Select Words That Are Colorful and Concrete

Merely by modifying nouns and verbs with descriptive adjectives and adverbs, you can create many colorful and concrete images. For example, rather than characterizing the sky merely as "blue," you can specify it as "faint blue," "sea blue," "blue with feathers of white," or "blue with pillows of dark gray."

Appeal to the Senses

Use language that appeals to listeners' sense of smell, taste, sight, hearing, or touch. Consult the checklist on concrete language (p. 236), as well as the following discussion of similes and metaphors, for more on translating abstractions into vivid images that appeal to the senses.

Use Figures of Speech

Figures of speech, including similes, metaphors, and analogies, make striking comparisons that help listeners visualize, identify with, and understand the speaker's ideas. A **simile** explicitly compares one thing to another, using *like* or *as* to do so: "He works *like* a dog" and "The old woman's hands were *as* soft as a baby's." A **metaphor** also compares two things, but does so by describing one thing as actually *being* the other. Metaphors do not use *like* or *as*: "Time is a thief," "All the world's a stage," and "Love is a rose." Used properly, metaphors express ideas compactly and cleverly. However, try not to use overused metaphors that are **clichéd**, or predictable and stale (as in the above examples). Similarly, beware of using clichéd similes. In addition, beware of using **mixed metaphors**, or those that juxtapose or compare unlike images or expressions: "Burning the midnight oil at both ends" incorrectly joins the expressions "burning the midnight oil" and "burning a candle at both ends."

An **analogy** is simply an extended metaphor or simile that compares an unfamiliar concept or process to a more familiar one to help listeners understand the unfamiliar one.[12] When Martin Luther King Jr. delivered his now-famous "I Have a Dream" speech on the steps of the Lincoln Memorial in 1963, he began with a financial metaphor of a bad check. As he spoke, he extended the metaphor to include the "bank of justice" and the "vaults of opportunity":

> In a sense we have come to our nation's capital to write a check. When the architects of our republic wrote the magnificent words of the Constitution and the Declaration of Independence, they were signing a promissory note to which every American has fallen heir. This note was a promise that all men would be guaranteed the unalienable rights of life, liberty, and the pursuit of happiness.
>
> It is obvious today that America has defaulted on this promissory note insofar as her citizens of color are concerned. Instead of honoring this sacred

obligation, America has given the Negro a bad check; a check which has come back marked "insufficient funds." But we refuse to believe that the bank of justice is bankrupt. So we refuse to believe that there are insufficient funds in the great vaults of opportunity of this nation.[13]

More recently, African American minister Phil Wilson used metaphoric language in his 2001 sermon to a Los Angeles congregation about the dangers of AIDS:

Our house is on fire! The fire truck arrives, but we won't come out, because we're afraid the folks from next door will see that we're in that burning house. AIDS is a fire raging in our community and it's out of control![14]

See Table 16.1 for other figures of speech that contribute to vivid imagery, including **personification, understatement, irony, allusion, hyperbole,** and **onomatopoeia.**

TABLE 16.1 • Figures of Speech

Figure of Speech	Description	Example
Personification	Endowing abstract ideas or inanimate objects with human qualities.	"Computers have become important members of our family."
Understatement	Drawing attention to an idea by minimizing or lowering its importance.	"Flunking out of college might be a problem."
Irony	Using humor, satire, or sarcasm to suggest a meaning other than the one that is actually being expressed.	"Our football players are great. They may not be big, but they sure are slow."
Allusion	Making vague or indirect reference to people, historical events, or concepts to give deeper meaning to the message.	"His meteoric rise to the top is an example for all of us."
Hyperbole	Using obvious exaggeration to drive home a point.	"Have you seen those students carrying backpacks the size of minivans filled with five-course dinners, cell phones, and an occasional textbook or two?"
Onomatopoeia	The imitation of natural sounds in word form; it adds vividness to the speech.	"The rain dripped a steady *plop plop plop* on the metal roof; the bees *buzzed* through the wood."

Source: Some examples taken from Andrea A. Lunsford, *The St. Martin's Handbook,* 5th ed. (Boston: Bedford/St. Martin's, 2003).

Choose Language That Builds Credibility

As you draft your speeches, consider whether your language builds trust and credibility. When you wield words correctly—that is, by being appropriate, being accurate, and showing confidence in your topic—you demonstrate the competence and trustworthiness that audiences look for in a speaker.

USE APPROPRIATE LANGUAGE

The language you use in a speech should be appropriate to the audience, the occasion, and the subject matter. As a rule, strive to uphold the conventional principles of grammar and usage associated with Standard English. The more diverse the audience and the more formal the occasion, the closer you will want to remain within these bounds. Sometimes, however, especially when the audience is more homogeneous, it may be appropriate to mix casual language, regional dialects, or even slang in your speech. As long as the meaning is clear, interposing such terms into an otherwise more formal speech can simultaneously reveal who you are and add vivid imagery to your speech. Consider the following excerpt:

> On the gulf where I was raised, *el valle del Rio Grande* in South Texas—that triangular piece of land wedged between the river *y el golfo* which serves as the Texas–U.S./Mexican border—is a Mexican *pueblito* called Hargill.[15]

USE LANGUAGE ACCURATELY

Words can evoke powerful responses in listeners. To build trust and credibility, language must be accurate—that is, it must be both correct in usage and truthful in expression. (See also the discussion of slander in Chapter 4 and of fallacies of reasoning in Chapter 25.) One error that speakers sometimes commit is the **malapropism**—the inadvertent use of a word or a phrase in place of one that sounds like it.[16] Malapropisms—"It's a strange *receptacle*" for "It's a strange *spectacle*"—do nothing to enhance the speaker's credibility.

More broadly, speakers sometimes fail to choose words that are both denotatively and connotatively appropriate for the audience. The **denotative meaning** of a word is its literal, or dictionary, definition. Although some concrete words have mainly denotative meanings—*surgery* and *saline,* for example—through long use most words have acquired special associations that go beyond their dictionary definitions. The **connotative meaning** of a word is the special association that different people bring to bear on it. For instance, you may like to be called slender but not skinny, or thrifty but not cheap.

Ask yourself whether the words you have chosen carry connotative meanings to which the audience might react negatively. For example, members of a mainstream church or synagogue may associate the word *cult* with an off-center or even bizarre religious group. But to people who belong to an emerging religious group (which, according to sociologists of religion, is the denotative meaning of *cult*) being described as a cult may be offensive.

CHOOSE WORDS THAT CONVEY CONFIDENCE AND CONVICTION

To inspire trust in your listeners, you must express yourself with confidence and conviction. Three ways to convey these qualities are by using the *active voice,* using *personal pronouns* or "I" language, and *avoiding hedges and tag questions.*

Use the Active Voice

Voice is the feature of verbs that indicates the subject's relationship to the action. A verb is in the **active voice** when the subject performs the action. A verb is in the *passive voice* when the subject is acted upon or is the receiver of the action.[17] As in writing, speaking in the active rather than the passive voice will make your statements clear and assertive instead of indirect and weak:

PASSIVE: A test was announced by Ms. Carlos for Tuesday.
             A president was elected by the voters every four years.

ACTIVE: Ms. Carlos announced a test for Tuesday.
             The voters elect a president every four years.

Use "I" Language

As well as fostering a sense of inclusion, "I" language (as expressed through the personal pronouns *I, me,* and *my*) creates an impression of conviction. Instead of saying "This is a good idea for our university," it would be more convincing for you to say "I personally support this idea." If audience members are expected to accept your ideas and arguments, you must indicate convincingly that you accept them as well. Unless audience members believe you to be an expert on your topic, however, in most cases they will want you to back up your assertions with credible supporting material drawn from other sources (see Chapter 8 for more on supporting your speech).

Avoid Powerless Speech

Despite the great strides made toward gender equality in the United States, research shows that many women, and to a lesser extent men, tend to use weak language that undermines their message. In addition to the passive voice, linguists Robin Lakoff and Deborah Tannen, among others, note that women are particularly prone to using weak language forms such as hedges and tag questions.[18] **Hedges** are unnecessary words and phrases that qualify or introduce doubt into statements that should be straightforward. Hedges make you sound as if you doubt your own words, thereby undermining your authority in the eyes of the audience. Examples of hedges include:

I guess my question is . . .

In my opinion . . .

I may not be right, but . . .

> ✔ **CHECKLIST**
>
> **Does Your Language Build Trust and Credibility?**
>
> _____ 1. Is your language appropriate to the audience, occasion, and sub-ject matter?
>
> _____ 2. Is your speech free of slander?
>
> _____ 3. Are your word choices accurate?
>
> _____ 4. Do any of the words you have chosen carry connotative meanings to which the audience might react negatively?
>
> _____ 5. Do you construct your sentences using the active voice?
>
> _____ 6. When appropriate, do you use the personal pronoun _I_ to express conviction and ownership of your ideas?
>
> _____ 7. When appropriate, do you use the personal pronoun _you_ to foster a sense of recognition and a feeling of inclusion in your listeners?
>
> _____ 8. Is your language free of hedges and tag questions?

Tag questions are unnecessary questions that are appended to statements or commands. Like hedges, tag questions undermine the speaker's authority by turning straightforward statements into questions that are left to the audience to resolve. Examples include:

The project was poorly managed, _or at least I thought so._

The proposal was too expensive, _wasn't it?_

I will next address the issue of economics, _okay?_

Choose Language That Creates a Lasting Impression

Just as certain lyrics and bits of music replay themselves in our minds, oral language that is artfully arranged and infused with rhythm leaves a lasting impression on listeners. You can create the cadenced arrangement of language through rhetorical devices such as repetition, alliteration, and parallelism.

USE REPETITION FOR RHYTHM AND REINFORCEMENT

One of the most effective strategies for creating a lasting impression in a speech is **repetition**. Repeating key words, phrases, or even sentences at various intervals throughout a speech creates a distinctive rhythm and thereby implants important ideas in listeners' minds. This technique captures the audience's attention and brings the speaker closer to his or her listeners. Repetition works extremely well when it is delivered with the appropriate inflections and pauses. Note, for example, President George W. Bush's use of this device in a speech delivered shortly after the 9/11 terrorist attacks:

We will not waver; we will not tire; we will not falter; and we will not fail. Peace and freedom will prevail.[19]

In a form of repetition called **anaphora**, the speaker repeats a word or phrase at the beginning of successive phrases, clauses, or sentences. Bush uses anaphora in the preceding example ("We will not . . ."), as does Martin Luther King Jr. in his famous "I Have a Dream" speech, repeating the phrase "I have a dream" numerous times, each with an upward inflection followed by a pause.

Speakers have made use of anaphora since the earliest times: For example, Jesus preached: "*Blessed are* the poor in spirit. . . . *Blessed are* the meek. . . . *Blessed are* the peacemakers. . . ."[20]

In a speech about becoming an organ donor, Manchester Community and Technical College student Ed Partlow uses anaphora this way:

Today *I'm going to talk about* a subject that can be both personal and emotional.

I'm going to talk about becoming an organ donor.

In addition to capturing the audience's attention and reinforcing key ideas, anaphora and other kinds of repetition can be used to create a thematic focus for your speech. Speakers do this by repeating key phrases that emphasize a central or recurring idea. The theme words generally appear first in the introduction, then the idea is repeated in the body, and the words or phrases are repeated in the conclusion. In the following example from a speech delivered to a conference of teenagers in Atlanta, the Reverend Jesse Jackson repeats the theme that teenagers "are somebody":

This morning I want to speak on the subject "It's Up to You," for it is important for you to get involved and be part of what's happening. You must feel that you count in order to appreciate yourself and develop yourself in relation to other people.

People to my right, I am. [Audience answers] "I am." Now don't sound all scared and timid. I know better. I am. [Audience answers] "I am." Somebody. [Audience answers] "Somebody."[21]

Jackson continues in this vein, repeating the phrase "I am somebody" at various points throughout the speech. He concludes by saying:

My mind is a pearl. I can learn anything in the world. I am somebody. Nobody will save us but us. Right on![22]

USE ALLITERATION FOR A POETIC QUALITY

Alliteration is the repetition of the same sounds, usually initial consonants, in two or more neighboring words or syllables. Political campaign slogans often use alliteration to catch the attention of voters. Phrases such as Jesse Jackson's

"Down with dope, up with hope" and former U.S. vice president Spiro Agnew's disdainful reference to the U.S. press as "nattering nabobs of negativism" are examples of alliteration in speeches.

Alliteration lends speech a poetic, musical rhythm. When used well, it drives home themes and leaves listeners with a lasting impression. When alliteration is poorly crafted or **hackneyed**, it can distract from a message. Use only those alliterative phrases that convey your point more concisely and colorfully than it can otherwise be conveyed.

USE PARALLELISM TO DRIVE YOUR POINTS HOME

Another rhetorical device that is characteristic of memorable speeches is **parallelism**—the arrangement of words, phrases, or sentences in a similar form. Parallel structure can help the speaker emphasize important ideas in the speech. Like repetition, parallelism creates a sense of steady or building rhythm.[23] Orally numbering your points—for example, "first, second, and third"—is one use of parallel language. Another method, which works well when your speech contains chronological material, is to state the relevant years, months, or days when introducing an idea or presenting evidence. A speaker recapping the major events of World War II might begin each main point with a phrase such as "December 1942" or "March 1943," followed by a pause.

Parallelism in speeches often makes use of **antithesis**—setting off two ideas in balanced (parallel) opposition to each other to create a powerful effect:

One small step for man, one giant leap for mankind. —Neal Armstrong on the moon, 1969

To err is human, to forgive divine. —Alexander Pope, 1711

For many are called, but few are chosen. —Matthew 22:14

Speakers often make use of three parallel elements or **triads**. This combination of three elements may be natural to a speech (such as in one describing the three branches of the U.S. government). In other cases, a speech may be manipulated to accommodate the use of triads. In fact, many speeches are carefully confined to three main points in order to take advantage of triads. There is something powerful about grouping concepts or ideas into threes. Consider the following examples:

. . . of the people, by the people, and for the people. —Abraham Lincoln

If 60 million Anglo-Saxons can have a place in the sun,
If 60 million Japanese can have a place in the sun,
If 7 million Belgians can have a place in the sun,
I cannot see why 400 million black people cannot. —Marcus Garvey

As these examples indicate, when parallelism is used appropriately, it creates a powerful, poetic effect for the audience.

Vocal and Nonverbal Delivery

Vocal and Nonverbal Delivery

Speaker's Reference
Vocal and Nonverbal Delivery

17. Methods of Delivery

Strive for Naturalness in Your Delivery

- Think of your speech as a particularly important conversation. (p. 252)
- Rather than behaving theatrically, strive for naturalness. (p. 252)

Show Enthusiasm

- Show enthusiasm for your topic and for the occasion. (p. 253)
- Speak about what excites you. (p. 253)

Project a Sense of Confidence and Composure

- Focus on the ideas you want to convey rather than on yourself. (p. 253)
- Inspire audience members' confidence in you by appearing confident. (p. 253)

Engage Your Audience by Being Direct

- Establish eye contact with your listeners. (p. 253)
- Use a friendly tone of voice. (p. 253)
- Smile whenever it is appropriate. (p. 253)
- Consider positioning yourself close to the audience. (p. 253)

If You Must Read from a Prepared Text, Do So Naturally

- Vary the rhythm of your words. (p. 255)
- Become familiar with the speech so you can establish some eye contact with the audience. (p. 255)
- Consider using compelling presentation aids. (p. 255)

In General, Don't Try to Memorize Entire Speeches

- Consider memorizing parts of your speech, such as quotations. (p. 256)
- Brief remarks, like toasts, can be well served by memorization. (p. 256)
- When delivering material from memory, know it well enough to do so with enthusiasm and directness. (p. 256)

247

When Speaking Impromptu, Maximize Any Preparation Time

- Anticipate situations that may require impromptu speaking. (p. 257)
- Consider what would best serve the audience. (p. 257)
- As you wait your turn to speak, take notes on what others are saying. (p. 257)
- Jot down a few key ideas in key-word form. (p. 257)
- Stay on topic. (p. 257)

In Most Situations, Select the Extemporaneous Method of Delivery

- Prepare and practice your speech in advance of delivery. (p. 257)
- Speak from an outline of key words and phrases. (p. 257)
- Use eye contact and body orientation and movement to maximize delivery. (p. 259)

18. The Voice in Delivery

Adjust Your Speaking Volume

- The bigger the room and the larger the audience, the louder you need to speak. Yet the volume must not be too loud for those in front. (p. 260)
- Be alert to signals from the audience indicating problems in volume. (p. 260)

Beware of Speaking in a Monotone

- Vary your intonation to reflect meaning. (p. 261)
- Use pitch to animate your voice. (p. 261)

Adjust Your Speaking Rate for Comprehension and Expressiveness

- To ensure that your speaking rate is comfortable for your listeners (neither too fast nor too slow), be alert to their reactions. (p. 262)
- Vary your speaking rate to indicate different meanings. (p. 262)

Use Strategic Pauses and Avoid Meaningless Vocal Fillers

- Use pauses to emphasize points, to draw attention to key thoughts, or to allow listeners a moment to contemplate what you've said. (p. 262)
- Eliminate distracting vocal fillers, such as "uh," "hmm," "you know," "I mean," and "it's like." (p. 262)

Vocal Variety

- Use the various vocal elements — volume, pitch, rate, and pauses — to create an effective delivery. (p. 263)
- Use a mix of these elements throughout your speech. (p. 263)

Be Conscious of How You Pronounce and Articulate Words

- Learn to pronounce words correctly. (p. 264)
- If you use a dialect, make sure that your audience understands it. (p. 264)
- Don't mumble or slur your words. (p. 265)

19. The Body in Delivery

Remember the Importance of Your Nonverbal Behavior

- Audiences are attuned to a speaker's vocal delivery (how you say something) and physical actions (facial expressions, gestures, body movement, and physical appearance). (p. 267)
- Audiences notice discrepancies between what you say and how you say it. (p. 269)
- Audiences do not so much listen to a speaker's words as they "read" the speaker who delivers them. (p. 269)

Animate Your Facial Expressions in Appropriate Ways

- Avoid a deadpan expression. (p. 269)
- Establish rapport with your audience with a smile. (p. 269)
- Avoid expressions that are out of character for you. (p. 269)

Maintain Eye Contact with Your Audience

- Establish eye contact to indicate that you recognize and respect listeners. (p. 269)
- Scan the room with your eyes, pausing to gaze at selected listeners. (p. 270)

Use Gestures That Feel Natural to Fill in Gaps in Meaning

- Use gestures to clarify your message. (p. 270)
- Avoid exaggerated gestures, but make them broad enough to be visible. (p. 270)
- Use appropriate gestures that arise from your feelings. (p. 270)

Avoid Standing Stiffly behind the Podium

- As space and time allow, try to get out from behind the podium. (p. 271)
- Move around at a comfortable, natural pace. (p. 271)
- Be aware of your posture. Stand erect, but not ramrod straight. (p. 271)

Pay Attention to Your Clothes and Grooming

- Choices of clothing and grooming will probably be the first thing your listeners notice about you. (p. 271)
- Dress appropriately for the occasion: dark-colored suits convey a sense of authority, while medium-blue or navy suits enhance credibility. (p. 271)
- Keep your hands free of distracting objects, such as pens and notecards. (p. 273)

Practice Your Speech Using a Speaking Outline

- Focus on your speech ideas rather than on yourself. (p. 273)
- After you've practiced several times, record or videotape your delivery. Incorporate changes and record it again. (p. 273)
- Rework unsatisfactory parts of your speech as you practice. (p. 274)
- Practice under realistic conditions. (p. 274)
- Visualize the audience as you speak. (p. 274)
- Practice using your speaking notes unobtrusively. (p. 274)
- Ask at least one other person to serve as a constructive critic. (p. 274)
- Time each portion of your speech (introduction, body, conclusion). (p. 274)
- Evaluate and adjust your rate of speech. (p. 274)
- Don't wait until the last minute to begin practicing. (p. 275)
- For an extemporaneous speech, plan to practice five times. (p. 275)

KEY TERMS

Chapter 17

effective delivery	TelePrompTer	speaking impromptu
elocutionary movement	speaking from memory	speaking
speaking from manuscript	oratory	extemporaneously

Chapter 18

volume	speaking rate	articulation
lavalier microphone	vocal fillers	dialects
handheld or fixed microphone	pauses	mumbling
pitch	vocal variety	lazy speech
intonation	pronunciation	

Chapter 19

aural channel	visual channel	talking head
paralanguage	scanning	

17 Methods of Delivery

I wish you to see that public speaking is a perfectly normal act, which calls for no strange, artificial methods, but only for an extension and development of that most familiar act, conversation.   —James Albert Winans, *Public Speaking*[1]

For most of us, the mechanics of putting together a speech may be challenging, but what often creates the bigger challenge is contemplating or actually getting up in front of an audience and speaking. Added to this uneasiness is the unfounded idea that speech delivery should be formulaic, mechanical, and highly exaggerated—that it is, in a way, unnatural or artificial. But as the late public-speaking scholar James Albert Winans noted, a speech is really just an enlarged conversation, "quite the natural thing."

In some ways, of course, delivering a speech is like giving a performance. Skilled actors artfully combine both verbal and nonverbal behavior to captivate an audience. Similarly, each component of your speech "performance," from the quality of your voice to your facial expressions, gestures, and manner of dress, affects how your listeners respond to you. As audience members listen to your words, they are simultaneously reacting to you on a nonverbal level—how you look, how you sound, and how you respond to them.

The comparison between performance and delivery must be made with care, however. Although as a speaker you want to be in command of expressive behaviors involving both voice and body, naturalness rather than theatricality should be the ultimate goal. As communications scholar James C. McCroskey has noted, effective delivery rests on the same natural foundation as everyday conversation. It doesn't call attention to itself.[2]

Qualities of Effective Delivery

Speakers who deliver well-received speeches or presentations share several characteristics at the podium: They are natural, enthusiastic, confident, and direct. **Effective delivery** is the skillful application of natural conversational behavior in a way that is relaxed, enthusiastic, and direct. As Winans has noted, effective delivery is characterized by "a style at once simple and effective."[3]

STRIVE FOR NATURALNESS

Had you been a student in the early 1900s, during the heyday of the **elocutionary movement**, feeling uneasy about delivery would have been justified. The elocutionists regarded speechmaking as a type of performance, much like acting.[4] Students were given a rigid set of rules on how to use their eyes, faces, gestures, and voices to drive home certain points in the speech and to manipulate audience members' moods. Delivery was emphasized to such an extent that it often assumed more importance than the content of the speech.

Today, the content or message itself, rather than the delivery, is seen as being most important. Nevertheless, delivery remains a critical part of successful speechmaking. Instead of stressing theatrical elements, contemporary delivery emphasizes naturalness.

SHOW ENTHUSIASM

Enthusiasm is contagious. When you talk about something that excites you, you talk more rapidly, use more gestures, look at your listeners more frequently, use more pronounced facial expressions, and probably stand closer to your listeners and perhaps even touch them more. Your enthusiasm spills over to your listeners, drawing them into your message. As their own enthusiasm grows, they listen more attentively because they want to know more about the thing that excites you. In turn, you sense their interest and responsiveness and realize that you are truly connecting with them. The value of enthusiastic delivery is thus accomplished: It focuses your audience's attention on the message.

PROJECT A SENSE OF CONFIDENCE

Speeches delivered with confidence and composure inspire the audience's confidence in you and in your message. Your focus is on the ideas that you want to convey, not on memorized words and sentences. Instead of thinking about how you look and sound, you're thinking about what you're trying to say and how well your listeners are grasping it. Confident delivery directs the audience's attention to the message and away from the speaker's behavior.

BE DIRECT

To truly communicate with an audience, you must build a rapport with your listeners. You need to show that you care about them and their reasons for listening to you. This is generally done in two ways: by making your message relevant to the interests and attitudes of audience members, and by demonstrating your interest and concern for them in your delivery. The best way to do the latter is by being direct: Maintain eye contact; use a friendly tone of voice; animate your facial expressions, especially positive ones such as smiling; and position yourself so that you are physically close to the audience. Of course, you don't want to go overboard by becoming annoying or overly familiar with the audience. But neither do you want to appear distant, aloof, or uncaring. Both extremes draw audience attention away from the message. (Chapters 18 and 19 focus on techniques for using your voice and body, respectively, to achieve a natural, enthusiastic, confident, and direct delivery. In the following section, we consider the major methods of delivery.)

Select a Method of Delivery

As a speaker, you can choose from four basic methods of delivery: speaking from manuscript, speaking from memory, impromptu speaking, and extemporaneous speaking. Each method is distinguished by the expressive voice and body behaviors it uses or restricts, and by the qualities of delivery it promotes or impedes (see Table 17.1).

TABLE 17.1 • Methods of Delivery and Their Probable Uses

Method of Delivery	Description	Probable Uses
Manuscript	Speech is read from fully prepared text.	When precise wording is called for; for instance, when a speaker wants to avoid being misquoted or misconstrued, or when he or she is communicating exact descriptions and directions.
Memory	Speech is delivered entirely from memory.	When a speaker is called on in special occasion circumstances, such as short toasts and introductions; when quotations are used (partial memorization).
Impromptu	Speech is delivered without preparation or practice.	When a speaker is called on or elects to speak without prior planning or preparation; this occurs in many speaking situations.
Extemporaneous	Speech is well practiced and delivered from a key-word or phrase outline.	When the goal is to deliver a speech exhibiting a natural conversational quality of delivery that is nonetheless well prepared and practiced; this is the most widely used form of delivery.

SPEAKING FROM MANUSCRIPT

When **speaking from manuscript,** you read a speech verbatim — that is, from prepared written text (either on paper or on a **TelePrompTer**) that contains the entire speech, word for word.

As a rule, speaking from manuscript restricts eye contact and body movement, and may also limit expressiveness in vocal variety and quality. Watching a speaker read a speech can be monotonous and boring for the audience. Quite obviously, the natural, relaxed, enthusiastic, and direct qualities of delivery are all limited by this method. Commenting on the dangers of reading from a TelePrompTer, for instance, columnist and former speechwriter William Safire notes that it can make the speaker appear "shifty and untrustworthy."[5]

At certain times, however, it is advisable or necessary to read a speech, such as when you must convey a very precise message. As with politicians and busi-

ESL Speaker's Notes
Avoiding the Pitfalls of Manuscript Delivery

Speaking from manuscript may be difficult and perhaps even ill-advised for some ESL speakers. Reading a speech aloud, word for word, is likely to exaggerate existing problems with pronunciation and word stress, or the emphasis given to words in a sentence. These emphasized words or syllables are pronounced more loudly and with a higher pitch. Robbin Crabtree and Robert Weissberg note:

> One of the most characteristic features of spoken English is the tendency of native speakers to take one word in every sentence and give it a stronger push than the others. This feature is called *primary stress*. If you try out a couple of sample sentences, you'll note that the primary stress normally falls at the end, or very close to the end, of the sentence:
> "That was one of the best speeches I've ever heard."
> "Let me know if you have trouble; and I'll be glad to help."[1]

If you have difficulty with word and sentence stress and you find that you need to deliver a speech from manuscript, follow the advice described in these pages. In addition, spend extra practice time reading your speech with the aim of ensuring that your word and sentence stress align with the meaning you intend.

1. Robbin Crabtree and Robert Weissberg, *ESL Students in the Public Speaking Classroom: A Guide for Teachers* (Boston: Bedford/St. Martin's, 2000), 24.

ness leaders, you may know that you will be quoted and must avoid misinterpretation. Or perhaps you have been charged with addressing an emergency and need to convey exact descriptions and directions (see Chapter 28 on crisis communication). In some speech circumstances, such as when an award is being presented, tradition may dictate that your remarks be read from a manuscript.

When you must give a speech from manuscript, practice reading it often until you are satisfied that your delivery is expressive. Use a large font and double- or triple-space the manuscript so that you can read without straining. Vary the rhythm of your words (see Chapter 18), and become familiar enough with the speech text so that you can look at the audience occasionally. Consider using some compelling presentation aids to add interest and movement to your delivery (see Chapter 20).

SPEAKING FROM MEMORY

The formal name for **speaking from memory** is *oratory*. The term is reminiscent of ancient public speakers whose speeches (some of which were extremely long) were fully committed to memory. If you were to use the oratorical style, you would put the entire speech, word for word, into writing and then commit it to memory. In the United States, instances of speaking from memory rarely occur, though this form of delivery is common in other parts of the world.[6] Memorization is not a natural way to present a message. It stifles authentic and sincere enthusiasm, and it poses a considerable threat to maintaining a relaxed delivery. Since you are required to recall exact words from memory, true eye contact with the audience is unlikely (try maintaining eye contact with someone while you recall something from memory; you'll notice a loss of directness if you can manage to maintain eye contact at all). Moreover, memorization invites potential disaster during a speech, because there is always the possibility of a mental lapse or block. When a mental block occurs, you are left optionless and directionless, in silence, having focused practice on nothing else but the exact wording of the speech.

Some kinds of brief speeches, however, such as toasts and introductions, can be well served by memorization. Sometimes it's helpful to memorize a part of the speech, especially when you must present the same information many times in the same words, or when you use direct quotations as a form of support. By and large, though, there will seldom be a need for you to memorize an entire speech of any kind. If you do find an occasion to use the memorization strategy, be sure to learn your speech so completely that in actual delivery you can focus on conveying enthusiasm and directness.

SPEAKING IMPROMPTU

The word *impromptu* means "unpracticed, spontaneous, or improvised." **Speaking impromptu** involves speaking on relatively short notice with little time to prepare. It's not advisable to speak impromptu when you've been given adequate time to prepare and practice a speech (that's called procrastination). However, there are many occasions that require you to make some remarks on the spur of the moment. For example, an instructor may invite you to summarize key points from the weekend reading assignment; a fellow employee who was scheduled to speak on the new marketing plan may be sick, and your boss has

---

✓ **CHECKLIST**

Speaking Off-the-Cuff: Preparing for the Impromptu Speech

To succeed at giving impromptu speeches, follow these steps:

_____ 1. Find a pen and a piece of paper as quickly as possible.

_____ 2. Take a minute to reflect on how you can best address the audience's interests and needs. Take a deep breath, and focus on your expertise on the topic or on what you really want to say.

_____ 3. Jot down in key words or short phrases the ideas you may want to cover.

_____ 4. Stay on the topic. Don't wander off track.

_____ 5. If your speech follows someone else's, acknowledge that person's statements.

_____ 6. State your ideas, and then summarize them.

_____ 7. Use transitions such as *first, second,* and *third,* both to organize your points and to help listeners follow them.

asked you to take his or her place; or during a meeting you might feel compelled to state your opposition to a proposal.

Impromptu speaking rattles many people because they have so little time to gather their thoughts (and, therefore, their composure). To succeed in delivering impromptu remarks:

- *Follow the lead of Academy Award nominees: Be prepared.* Try to anticipate situations that may require you to speak impromptu. If there is any chance that this might occur, prepare some remarks beforehand.

- *Think on your feet—and think first about your listeners.* Consider their likely needs and interests, and try to shape your remarks accordingly. For example, who are the people present, and what are their views on the issue?

- *As you wait your turn to speak, listen to what others around you are saying.* Take notes in a key-word or phrase format and arrange them into ideas or main points from which you can speak. Organizing a few thoughts beforehand will help you make your point and prevent you from talking aimlessly.

- *When you do speak, give a brief statement, if appropriate, summarizing what you've heard from others.* Then state your own position, make your points, and restate your position, referring as needed to your notes.

Taking steps like these will enhance your effectiveness because you will maintain the qualities of natural, enthusiastic, and direct delivery. And having even a hastily prepared plan can give you greater confidence than having no plan at all.

SPEAKING EXTEMPORANEOUSLY

Speaking extemporaneously falls somewhere between impromptu and written or memorized deliveries. In an extemporaneous speech, you prepare well and practice in advance, giving full attention to all facets of the speech—content, arrangement, and delivery alike. Instead of memorizing or writing the speech word for word, you speak from an outline of key words and phrases (see Chapter 13), having concentrated throughout your preparation and practice on the ideas you want to communicate.

Probably more public speeches—from business presentations and special occasion speeches to formal public addresses—are delivered by extemporaneous delivery than by any other method. Because extemporaneous speaking is the technique that is most conducive to achieving a natural, conversational quality of delivery, many speakers consider it to be the preferred method of the four types of delivery. In fact, since special occasion speeches—such as toasts, introductions, tributes, and eulogies—are among the most common types of speeches made beyond the classroom, mastering the extemporaneous method of delivery can be especially beneficial. Knowing your idea well enough to present it without memorization or manuscript gives you greater flexibility in adapting to the specific speaking situation. You can modify wording, rearrange your points, change examples, and omit information in keeping with the audience and the setting. You can have more eye contact, more direct body orientation, greater freedom of movement, and generally better control of your thoughts and actions than with any of the other delivery methods.

However, there are several possible drawbacks to extemporaneous delivery to keep in mind. For one, it is relatively easy to get off track when using this method. Because you aren't speaking from specifically written or memorized text, you may become repetitive and wordy. Fresh examples or points may come to mind that you want to share, so the speech may take longer than you anticipated. Occasionally, even a glance at your speaking notes will fail to jog your memory on a point that you wanted to cover, and you may momentarily find yourself searching for what to say next. The remedy for these potential pitfalls is, of course, *practice.* If you practice delivering your speech using a speaking outline often enough, you will probably have no difficulty staying on target.

Ethically Speaking
A Tool for Good and Evil

The philosopher Plato believed that the art of public speaking—or rhetoric, as the ancients referred to it—was too often corrupt.[1] Plato's cynicism toward public speaking was the result of unethical practices that he witnessed among his peers and other leaders in ancient Greece. From his perspective, rhetoric (at least as practiced) too often distorted the truth. Today, few people condemn public speaking per se as a dishonest form of communication. But many are aware of the power of delivery to corrupt. If history is any guide, these fears are well founded: one has only to think of such modern-day dictators as Mao Tse-tung, Joseph Stalin, Adolf Hitler, and Saddam Hussein, all of whom deliberately used delivery as a means of manipulation. Hitler's forceful delivery—a scorching stare, gestures, and a staccato voice—so mesmerized his listeners that millions accepted the horrific idea that an entire people should be annihilated. Historians note how Hitler spent countless hours practicing his vocal delivery and body language to achieve maximum hypnotic effect. As he did this, he would have himself photographed so that he could hone individual gestures to perfection.[2]

Like any tool, delivery can be used for both ethical and unethical purposes. Countless speakers, from Abraham Lincoln to Martin Luther King Jr., have used their flair for delivery to uplift and inspire people. Yet there will always be those who try to camouflage weak or false arguments with an overpowering delivery. You can ensure that your own delivery is ethical by reminding yourself of the ground rules for ethical speaking described in Chapter 4: trustworthiness, respect, responsibility, and fairness. Always reveal your true purpose to the audience, review your evidence and reasoning for soundness, and grant your audience the power of rational choice.

1. Thomas M. Conley, *Rhetoric in the European Tradition* (New York: Longman, 1990).
2. Ian Kershaw, "The Hitler Myth," *History Today* 35, no. 11 (1985): 23.

✓ CHECKLIST

Ready for the Call: Preparing for the Extemporaneous Speech

Follow these general steps below to prepare effective extemporaneous speeches:

____ 1. Focus your topic as assigned or as appropriate to the audience and occasion.

____ 2. Prepare a thesis statement that will serve as the central point or idea of your speech.

____ 3. Research your topic in a variety of sources to gather support for your thesis and add credibility to your points.

____ 4. Outline main and subordinate points.

____ 5. Practice the speech at least six times.

(See Chapter 2 for more on speech preparation.)

18 The Voice in Delivery

Your voice is a powerful instrument of expression, and one to which audiences are highly sensitive. Used properly in the speaking situation, it should express who you are and convey your message in a way that engages listeners. Your voice is also key in determining whether the audience perceives you to be in control of the situation.[1] Regardless of the quality and importance of your message, if you have inadequate mastery of your voice, you may lose your audience's attention and fail to deliver a successful speech. Fortunately, as you practice your speech, you can learn to control each of the elements of vocal delivery. These include volume, pitch, rate, pauses, vocal variety, and pronunciation and articulation.

Volume

Volume, the relative loudness of a speaker's voice while giving a speech, is usually the most obvious and frequently cited vocal element in speechmaking. If you do not speak loud enough for the entire audience to hear you, your speech is essentially a failure. *The proper volume for delivering a speech is somewhat louder than that of normal conversation.* Just how much louder depends on three factors: (1) the size of the room and the number of people in the audience, (2) whether or not you use a microphone, and (3) the level of background noise.

Speaking at the appropriate volume is critical to how credible your listeners will perceive you to be. Speakers whose volume is too low are viewed less positively than those who project their voices at a pleasing volume. One expert suggests that, as a rule, when you speak too softly, you will initially have to project more than you think is necessary:

> As you breathe from your diaphragm, you will gain the force for vocal projection from your diaphragm — not your vocal cords. So don't strain your vocal cords; instead, start the breath with your diaphragm and let it propel your voice beyond the last row of the audience.[2]

The easiest way to judge whether you are speaking too loudly or too softly is to be alert to audience feedback.

Tips on Using a Microphone

_____ 1. Perform a sound check with the microphone at least several hours before delivering your speech.

_____ 2. When you first speak into the microphone, ask your listeners if they can hear you clearly.

_____ 3. Speak directly into the microphone; if you turn your head or body, you won't be heard.

_____ 4. To avoid broadcasting private statements, beware of "open" mikes.

_____ 5. When wearing a **lavalier microphone** attached to your lapel or collar, speak as if you were addressing a small group. The amplifier will do the rest.

_____ 6. When using a **handheld** or **fixed microphone**, beware of _popping_, which occurs when you use sharp consonants, such as _p, t,_ and _d,_ and the air hits the mike. To prevent popping, move the microphone slightly below your mouth and about six inches away.

Source: Susan Berkley, "Microphone Tips," _Great Speaking_ 4, no. 7 (2002), http://www.antion.com/ezine/v4n7.txt (accessed July 16, 2005).

Pitch

Imagine the variation in sound between the left end and the right end of a piano or a harmonica. This variation represents the instrument's **pitch**, or range of sounds from high to low (or vice versa). Pitch is determined by the number of vibrations per unit of time; the more vibrations per unit (also called _frequency_), the higher the pitch, and vice versa.[3] The classic warm-up singing exercise "_Do re mi fa so la ti do_" is an exercise in pitch. Vocal pitch is important in speechmaking — indeed, in talk of any kind — because it powerfully affects the meaning associated with spoken words. For example, say "Stop." Now, say "_Stop!_" Hear the difference? The rising and falling of voice pitch across phrases and sentences, termed **intonation**,[4] conveys two very distinct meanings. Intonation, or pitch, is what distinguishes a question from a statement:

It's time to study already.

It's time to study al_ready_?

What differences in meaning do you get from these two expressions?

As you speak, pitch conveys your mood, reveals your level of enthusiasm, expresses your concern for the audience, and signals your overall commitment to the occasion. When there is no variety in pitch, speaking becomes monotonous. A monotonous voice is the death knell to any speech. Speakers who are consistently monotonous rapidly lose the audience's attention, along with its goodwill. If you tend to be monotonous, practice and listen to your speeches with a tape recorder. You will readily identify instances that require better inflection.

Rate

The most effective way to hold an audience's attention, as well as to accurately convey the meaning of your speech, is to vary your **speaking rate**, the pace at which you convey speech. A slow rate at the right time indicates thoughtfulness, seriousness, solemnity, and the like. A lively pace indicates excitement, adventure, happiness, and so on.

The normal rate of speech for adults is estimated to be between 120 and 150 words per minute. The typical public speech occurs at a rate slightly below 120 words per minute, but there is no standard, "ideal," or most effective rate. Being alert to the audience's reactions is the best way to know whether your rate of speech is too fast or too slow. An audience will get fidgety, bored, listless, perhaps even sleepy if you speak too slowly. If you speak too rapidly, listeners will appear irritated and confused, as though they can't catch what you're saying. One recent study suggests that speaking too fast will cause listeners to perceive you as tentative about your control of the situation.[5] *To control your rate, count 150 words from your speech, and time yourself as you read it aloud. Do this until you achieve a comfortable speaking rate.*

Pauses

Many novice speakers are uncomfortable with pauses. It's as if there were a social stigma attached to any silence in a speech. We often react the same way in conversation, covering pauses with unnecessary and undesirable **vocal fillers**, such as "uh," "hmm," "you know," "I mean," "it's like," and "anyways." Like pitch, however, pauses are important strategic elements of a speech. **Pauses** enhance meaning by providing a type of punctuation, emphasizing a point, drawing attention to a key thought, or just allowing listeners a moment to contemplate what is being said. In short, they make a speech far more effective than it might otherwise be. Both the speaker and the audience need pauses.

In his well-known "I Have a Dream" speech, Martin Luther King Jr. exhibits masterful use of strategic pauses. In what are now the most memorable segments of the speech, King pauses, just momentarily, to let the audience anticipate the words that are about to be spoken:

> I have a dream [*pause*] that one day on the red hills of Georgia. . . .
>
> I have a dream [*pause*] that one day even the great state of Mississippi. . . .[6]

Imagine how diminished the impact of this speech would have been if King had uttered "uh" or "you know" at each of these pauses!

Vocal Variety

Rather than operating separately, all the vocal elements described so far—volume, pitch, rate, and pauses—work together to create an effective delivery. Indeed, the real key to effective vocal delivery is to vary all these elements, thereby demonstrating **vocal variety**. For example, as King speaks the words "I have a dream," the pauses are immediately preceded by a combination of reduced speech rate and increased volume and pitch—a crescendo, you might say. The impact of this variety leaves an indelible impression on anyone who has heard his speech.

✓ **CHECKLIST**

Practice Check for Vocal Effectiveness

_____ 1. As you practice, does your voice project authority?

_____ 2. Is your voice too loud? Too soft?

_____ 3. Do you avoid speaking in a monotone? Do you vary the stress or emphasis you place on words to clearly express your meaning?

_____ 4. Is your rate of speech comfortable for listeners?

_____ 5. Do you avoid unnecessary vocal fillers, such as "uh," "hmm," "you know," and "I mean"?

_____ 6. Do you use silent pauses for strategic effect?

_____ 7. Does your voice reflect a variety of emotional expressions? Do you convey enthusiasm?

ESL Speaker's Notes
Vocal Variety and the Non-Native Speaker

Learning to deliver a speech with the vocal variety that English-speaking people in the United States expect can be particularly challenging for non-native speakers. In addition to having concerns about pronunciation and articulation, the non-native speaker may also be accustomed to patterns of vocal variety—volume, pitch, rate, and pauses—that are different from those discussed in this chapter.

The pronunciation of English depends on learning how to combine a series of about forty basic sounds (fifteen vowels and twenty-five consonants) that together serve to distinguish English words from one another. Correct pronunciation also requires that the speaker learn proper word stress, rhythm, and intonation or pitch.[1] As you practice your speeches, pay particular attention to these facets of delivery. Seek feedback from others to ensure that your goal of shared meaning will be met whenever you deliver speeches.

1. Maryann Cunningham Florez, "Improving Adult ESL Learners' Pronunciation Skills," National Clearinghouse for ESL Literacy Education, 1998, http://www.cal.org/caela/digests/Pronun.htm (accessed July 16, 2005).

One key to achieving effective vocal variety is enthusiasm. Vocal variety comes quite naturally when you are excited about what you are saying to an audience, when you feel it is important and want to share it with your listeners. If you strive for these kinds of feelings when planning and practicing your speeches, vocal variety should follow naturally. However, be careful not to let your enthusiasm overwhelm your ability to control your vocal behavior. Talking too rapidly can lead to more filled pauses because you forget what you want to say. Overexcitement can also result in a consistently high pitch that becomes monotonous. Hence, it is essential to practice your vocal delivery even when you are already enthusiastic about a speech.

Pronunciation and Articulation

Another important element of vocal delivery involves correctly saying the words you speak. Few things distract an audience more than improper pronunciation or unclear articulation of words. **Pronunciation** is the correct formation of word sounds. **Articulation** is the clarity or forcefulness with which the sounds are made, regardless of whether they are pronounced correctly. In other words, you can be articulating clearly but pronouncing incorrectly. In this way, good articulation may betray poor pronunciation. It is important to pay attention to and work on both areas.

Consider these words that are routinely mispronounced:

- effect (*ee-fect*) is stated as *uh-fect*.
- anyway (*any-way*) is said as *any-ways*.
- mobile (*mo-bel*) is said as *mo-bull* or *mo-bill*.
- leaves (*leevz*) is stated as *leephs*.

Public Speaking in Cultural Perspective
Vocal Delivery and Culture

Every culture has subcultural variations on the preferred pronunciation and articulation of its languages. These variations represent **dialects** of the language. In the United States, for example, there is so-called Standard English, Black English (or, more recently, Ebonics), Tex-Mex (a combination of Spanish and English spoken with a distinct Texas drawl or accent), and such regional variations as those found in the South, New England, and along the border with Canada. In parts of Texas, for example, a common usage is to say "fixin' to" instead of "about to," as in "We're fixin' to go to a movie."

Your own dialect may be a factor in the effectiveness of your delivery when speaking to an audience of people whose dialect is different. At the least, your dialect might call attention to itself and be a distraction to the audience. One strategy that you can use is to determine which words in your usual vocabulary are spoken dialectically and then practice articulating them in Standard English pronunciation.

✓ **CHECKLIST**

Overcoming Articulation Problems

_____ 1. If you mumble, practice speaking more loudly and with emphatic pronunciation.

_____ 2. If you tend toward lazy speech, put more effort into your articulation.

_____ 3. Consciously try to say each word clearly and correctly.

_____ 4. Practice clear and precise enunciation of proper word sounds. Say _articulation_ several times until it seems to roll off your tongue naturally.

_____ 5. Do the same for these words: _want to, going to, Atlanta, chocolate, sophomore, California._

_____ 6. As you practice giving a speech, consider words that might pose articulation and pronunciation problems for you. Practice saying them over and over until doing so feels as natural as saying your name.

Incorrect pronunciations are a matter of habit. Normally you may not know that you are mispronouncing a word because most people you talk with probably say the word much the same way you do. This habit may be associated with a regional accent or dialect. In that case, speaking to an audience of local origin may pose few problems if you pronounce words in regionally customary ways.

But if you are speaking to members of an audience for whom your accent and pronunciation patterns are not the norm, it becomes especially important to have practiced and to use correct pronunciations to the fullest extent possible. In fact, the better your pronunciation all around, the more enhanced will be the audience's perceptions of your competence, and the greater will be the potential impact of your speech. (See Table 18.1 and Appendix D for lists of commonly mispronounced words.)

Articulation problems are also a matter of habit. (Exceptions are problems associated with oral, periodontal, or other conditions that impede articulate speech, such as wearing orthodontics, having a cleft palate or a tongue thrust, or having injuries to the teeth or gums.) A very common pattern of poor articulation is **mumbling** — slurring words together at a very low level of volume and pitch so that they are barely audible. Sometimes the problem is **lazy speech**. Common examples include saying "fer" instead of "far," "wanna" instead of "want to," "gonna" instead of "going to," and "theez' er" instead of "these are." Like any habit, poor articulation can be overcome by unlearning the problem behavior (see the accompanying checklist on overcoming articulation problems).

TABLE 18.1 • Thirteen Commonly Mispronounced Words

Correct Spelling	Wrong Pronunciation	Right Pronunciation
acts	aks	akts
asked	aks	askt
et cetera	ek set er uh	et set er uh
facts	faks	fakts
fifth	fith or fif	fifth
genuine	jen yu wine	jen yu in
hundred	hun dert	hun dred
international	innernashunal	in ter na shuh nal
introduce	innerdoos	in tro dyoos
nuclear	nookyouluhr	nook klee uhr
picture	pi chur	pik chur
products	prah duks	prah dukts
recognized	rekunized	re kug nized

Source: Lillian Wilder, *Seven Steps to Fearless Speaking* (New York: Wiley, 1999), 210–11. Reprinted with permission.

The Body in Delivery 19

Beyond the actual words that are spoken, audiences receive information from a speech through two nonverbal channels of communication: the aural and the visual. The **aural channel** is made up of the vocalizations that form and accompany spoken words. These vocalizations, or paralanguage, include the qualities of volume, pitch, rate, variety, and pronunciation and articulation described in Chapter 18. **Paralanguage** refers to *how* something is said, not to *what* is said.

The **visual channel** includes the speaker's physical actions and appearance — facial expressions, gestures, general body movement, physical appearance, dress, and objects held. These nonverbal elements have been called the *silent language*. Paralanguage and the visual elements of a speech are critical to an audience's full understanding of the message you wish to convey. According to one study, listeners derive only 7 percent of the meaning of any message about feelings and attitudes from the speaker's words, while 38 percent comes from the speaker's voice and 55 percent comes from the speaker's facial expressions and body language.[1]

Functions of Nonverbal Communication in Delivery

Researchers have identified several ways in which nonverbal communication works together with the verbal component of a speech:[2]

- Nonverbal communication clarifies the meaning of verbal messages.
- Nonverbal communication facilitates feedback, creating a loop of communication between speaker and audience.
- Nonverbal communication helps establish a relationship between speaker and audience.
- Nonverbal communication helps establish speaker credibility.

CLARIFY VERBAL MESSAGES

The impact of the verbal component of your speech — what you say — depends largely on what you are doing vocally and bodily while saying it. The same words spoken with different body movements or different vocal emphasis convey different meanings. For instance, consider how saying "I hate you" jokingly to a friend who just got a new car that you want differs in tone and emphasis from screaming "I *hate* you!" to someone who has done you a grave injustice. Similar shifts in meaning occur with gestures. If you said "I hate you" while screwing your face up into a nasty grimace and shaking your fist, you would convey a greater sense of vehemence than would be the case if you said it in a flat tone without this gesture.

FACILITATE FEEDBACK

Listeners use a host of body cues—head shaking (either in agreement or in disagreement), smiles or frowns, arms rigidly folded across the chest, and friendly gazes or facing-away postures—to communicate their pleasure or displeasure with a speech. Being alert to such feedback and responding to it can mean the difference between an alienated audience and one that feels recognized and respected. Coughing and excessive shifting around, for example, may indicate difficulty in hearing and flagging interest. In response, you might try to increase your speaking volume and look in the direction of the affected listeners more frequently and for longer periods. If you receive negative cues such as frowns and head shaking, you might try presenting some additional evidence or interjecting some relevant humor.

ESTABLISH RELATIONSHIPS BETWEEN SPEAKER AND AUDIENCE

Nonverbal behavior, such as how you position yourself vis-à-vis your listeners, allows you to adjust your relationship with them, establishing a level of familiarity and closeness that is suitable to the topic, purpose, and occasion. To stimulate a sense of informality and closeness, for example, you can move out from behind the podium and walk or stand among audience members. Pioneering talk-show host Phil Donahue was a master of this technique, which is now emulated by many of today's television talk-show hosts and news anchors. By taking off his suit coat, loosening his tie, speaking at a moderate rate, and engaging in spontaneous movement, Donahue established a casual speech atmosphere. Conversely, remaining behind the speaker's stand, using a more reserved vocal quality, and speaking at a somewhat slower and consistent rate establish a more formal relationship with listeners.

ESTABLISH SPEAKER CREDIBILITY

Nonverbal communication plays a key part in the audience's perception of your competence, trustworthiness, and character.[3] For example, audiences are more readily persuaded by speakers who emphasize vocal variety, eye contact, nodding at listeners, and standing with an open body position than by those who minimize these nonverbal cues.[4] Audience members also respond more positively to speakers whom they perceive to be well dressed and attractive. They are apt to take them more seriously and are more objective in their responses than they are to speakers whom they do not find attractive.

Pay Attention to Body Language

Audience members are quick to detect discrepancies between what you say and how you say it. As they listen to you, they are simultaneously evaluating the messages sent by your facial expressions, eye behavior, gestures, and general body movements. Audiences do not so much listen to a speaker's words as they "read" the speaker who delivers them.[5]

ANIMATE YOUR FACIAL EXPRESSIONS

From our facial expressions, audiences can gauge whether we are excited about, disenchanted by, or indifferent to our speech — and the people to whom we are presenting it. Facial expressions are an asset to public speakers, but only if they make use of them.

Few behaviors are more effective for building rapport with an audience than *smiling*. A smile is a sign of mutual welcome at the start of a speech, of mutual comfort and interest during the speech, and of mutual goodwill at the close of a speech. In addition, smiling when you feel nervous or otherwise uncomfortable can help you relax and gain heightened composure. Of course, facial expressions need to correspond to the tenor of the speech. Doing what is natural and normal for the occasion should be the rule.

✓ **CHECKLIST**

Tips for Using Effective Facial Expressions

_____ 1. Avoid a deadpan expression.

_____ 2. Use animated expressions that feel natural and express your meaning.

_____ 3. Never use expressions that are out of character for you or inappropriate for the speech occasion.

_____ 4. In practice sessions, loosen your facial features with exercises such as widening the eyes and moving the mouth.

_____ 5. Align your facial expressions with your feelings.

_____ 6. Establish rapport with the audience by smiling naturally when appropriate.

MAINTAIN EYE CONTACT

If smiling is an effective way to build rapport, maintaining eye contact is mandatory in establishing a positive relationship with your listeners. Eye contact with the audience is one of the most, if not *the* most, important physical actions in public speaking. Eye contact maintains the quality of directness in speech delivery. It lets people know they are recognized, indicates acknowledgment and respect, and signals to audience members that the speaker sees them as unique human beings.

With an audience of a hundred to more than a thousand members, it's impossible to look at every listener. But in most speaking situations you are likely to experience, you should be able to look at most people in the audience by using a technique called **scanning**. When you scan an audience, you move your gaze from one listener to another and from one section to another, pausing as you do so to gaze briefly at each individual. One speaking professional suggests following the "rule of three": Pick three audience members to focus on — one in the middle, one on the right, and one on the left of the room; these audience members will be your anchors as you scan the room.[6] Initially, this may be difficult. But with just a little experience you will find yourself doing it naturally.

USE GESTURES THAT FEEL NATURAL

Friend 1 to Friend 2: "How was the fishing trip?"

Friend 2: "Great! The best I've had in years."

Friend 1: "Caught a monster, eh? How big was it?"

Friend 2 [*extending two hands, palms facing each other*]: "About this big!"

Words alone seldom suffice to convey what we want to express. Head, arm, hand, and even leg gestures are often critical in helping to clarify the meanings we try to convey in words. Physical gestures fill in the gaps, as in illustrating the size or shape of an object (e.g., showing the size of a fish by extending two hands, palms facing each other), expressing the depth of an emotion (pounding a fist on a podium), or emphasizing a certain word (using one's index finger to "write" the word in the air while saying it).

To achieve a natural, relaxed quality in delivery, use gestures to fill in gaps in meaning, as you would in everyday conversation. Gestures should arise from genuine emotions and should conform to your personality.[7]

✓ **CHECKLIST**

Tips for Effective Gesturing

_____ 1. Use natural, spontaneous gestures.
_____ 2. Use gestures to generate interest and clarify your message.
_____ 3. Use gestures that are appropriate to the topic and to the occasion.
_____ 4. Avoid exaggerated gestures, but use gestures that are broad enough to be seen by each member of the audience.
_____ 5. In practice sessions, analyze your gestures for effectiveness.
_____ 6. Practice movements that feel natural to you.

BE AWARE OF GENERAL BODY MOVEMENT

General body movement is also important in maintaining audience attention and processing of your message. Audience members soon tire of listening to a **talking head** who remains steadily positioned in one place behind a microphone or a podium. When this position is unavoidable, either because there is a fixed microphone at the podium or because there is too little space to allow unrestricted movement, gestures and facial expressiveness become all the more important. But as space and time allow, try to get out from behind the podium and stand with the audience. As you do, move around at a comfortable, natural pace.

A speaker's posture sends a definite message to the audience. Listeners perceive speakers who slouch as being sloppy, unfocused, and even weak. Strive to stand erect, but not ramrod straight. The goal is to appear authoritative, not rigid.

DRESS APPROPRIATELY

As superficial as it may sound, the first thing an audience is likely to notice as you approach the speaker's position is your clothing. How you dress when delivering a speech is therefore important. The critical criteria in determining appropriate dress for a speech are audience expectations and the nature of the speech occasion. If you are speaking as a representative of your business, for example, you will want to complement your company's image.[8] Many jobs and many speaking occasions permit casual dress; but take care not to confuse casual with sloppy or unkempt.[9] Even casual business attire should be professional in the sense that it conveys a responsible, credible, and confident image. Consider Bono, the celebrity activist and front man of the rock group U2, who regularly delivers speeches to international organizations, political gatherings, and universities about the critical economic and health conditions in Africa and developing nations.[10] When speaking Bono tends to choose an outfit that is sensibly casual but appropriate — a dress jacket over dress shirt, with no necktie and with an open collar — attire that reflects his rock star image while respecting the official nature of each occasion.

✔ **CHECKLIST**

Broad Dress Code Guidelines

_____ 1. Dress well and appropriately for each speech occasion.

_____ 2. For a "power" look, wear a dark-colored suit.

_____ 3. Medium-blue or navy suits, slacks, or skirts paired with white shirts or blouses will enhance your credibility.

_____ 4. When selecting accessories (ties, scarves, kerchiefs, and the like), consider that the color yellow conveys friendliness and the color red focuses attention on you.

_____ 5. Flashy jewelry distracts listeners.

Your attire reveals an attitude about what you are doing and the amount of effort you seem willing to put into it. The more professional you look, the more professional you will feel, and the more positive the attitude you will convey to audience members. If Bono were to stand before his speech audiences looking and acting just as he does for his band's performances, his credibility on the speech topic would be diminished. As noted by fashion expert David Wolfe in the context of job security:

Dressing down could imply that you don't need to be taken seriously, or don't need the job. People are starting to realize that offices aren't the beach, and work is not a casual occasion.[11]

Public Speaking in Cultural Perspective
Nonverbal Communication Patterns in Different Cultures

As a speaker, it's important to remember that, like verbal communication, non-verbal communication is also profoundly influenced by culture. Gestures, for example, have entirely different meanings in different cultures, and many an un-suspecting speaker has inadvertently made a rude gesture in his or her host's culture. In the late 1950s, for instance, then-Vice President Richard Nixon made a goodwill tour of Latin America, where there were feelings of hostility toward the United States. On one of his stops, Nixon stepped off his plane and, smiling, gestured with the A-OK sign to the waiting crowd. The crowd booed. In that culture, Nixon's gesture meant "Screw you." Days of delicate diplomacy were undone by two seconds of nonverbal behavior.[1] This same gesture, incidentally, means "zero" in French and "money" in Japan. Roger Axtell catalogs a variety of gestures in his book *Gestures: The Do's and Taboos of Body Language around the World*. This eye-opening account demonstrates how something in one culture can mean literally the opposite in another (e.g., nodding means "yes" in the United States but can mean "no" in the former Yugoslavia and Iran).

The display of emotions is also guided by the social rules of the culture. The Japanese are conditioned to mask emotion, whereas Americans express emotion more freely. Speakers in different cultures thus use different facial expressions to convey emotions. Eye behavior also takes quite different forms; people in the United States and Canada use eye contact as a form of acknowledgment or po-liteness in greeting, but in other cultures, such as those of Nigeria and Puerto Rico, this is often considered disrespectful. Finally, appearance preferences also change from one culture to another.

No speaker should feel obliged to adopt nonverbal behaviors that are not his or her own. At the same time, a successful speech depends on shared meaning. As such, a thorough audience analysis is key, as is anticipating potential mis-understandings that might occur nonverbally.

1. Roger Axtell, *Gestures: The Do's and Taboos of Body Language around the World* (New York: Wiley, 1991).

Source: Adapted from Dan O'Hair et al., *Competent Communication*, 2nd ed. (Boston: Bedford/St. Martin's, 1997), 146–47.

This advice is no less important for your classroom speeches than it is for speeches given elsewhere. You should dress for your speeches in class just as you would if you were delivering them to a business or professional group that you want to impress. At the very least, it's good practice, and it's likely to benefit your speech by showing your respect for both the occasion and the audience.

An extension of dress is the possession of various objects on or around your person while giving a speech — pencil and pen, a briefcase, a glass of water, or papers with notes on them. Always ask yourself if these objects are really necessary. A sure way to distract an audience from what you're saying is to drag a briefcase or backpack to the speaker's stand and open it while speaking, or to hold a pen or other object. Similarly, fumbling around with a pointer can be distracting unless it's being used to refer to certain visual displays.

Practice the Delivery

Practice is essential to effective delivery. The more you practice, the greater your comfort level will be when you actually deliver the speech. More than anything, it is uncertainty that breeds anxiety. By practicing your speech using a fully developed speaking outline (see Chapter 13), you will know what to expect when you actually stand in front of the audience.

Indeed, public speaking involves a set of motor skills much like playing a sport does. Consider the amount of time an individual golfer spends on the driving range and putting greens to improve skills and raise scores. When preparing to deliver a speech, mentally going through the motions while seated at your desk will provide some benefit, but practicing by actually standing up and talking out loud is necessary to perform successfully. You will be more comfortable with the sound of your own voice and with your gestures and will be confident that you can pronounce difficult words correctly. You will have a good sense of how your vocal quality will vary from one section of the speech to another. In other words, you will know what you are getting into.

FOCUS ON THE MESSAGE

The purpose of your speech is to get a message across, not to display extraordinary delivery skills. Keep this goal foremost in your mind. Psychologically, too, focusing on your message is likely to make your delivery more natural and more confident.

RECORD THE SPEECH

Once you've practiced your speech several times, talk it out into an audio recorder. At a later stage in the practice process, you can place the recorder across the room from you and practice projecting your voice to the back row of the audience. To accurately gauge how you sound, use a good-quality recording device.

Videotaping two practice sessions can provide valuable feedback. As you watch your initial recording, make notes of the things you'd like to change. Before rerecording, practice several more times until you are comfortable with the changes you've incorporated. Note that no one is ever entirely thrilled with his or her videotaped image, so try to avoid unnecessary self-criticism. Videotape your speech a second time, paying close attention to the areas of speech delivery that you want to improve.

BE PREPARED TO REVISE YOUR SPEAKING NOTES

As you practice, be prepared to revise your speech as needed. If your introduction or conclusion isn't as effective as you would like, rework it. Make other adjustments as necessary to improve your speech and make the outline easier to follow.

PRACTICE UNDER REALISTIC CONDITIONS

As closely as possible, try to simulate the actual speech setting as you practice. Keep the seating arrangement in mind as you speak, picturing the audience as you go along. Turn various objects in the room into imaginary audience members, and project your voice in their direction. Practice with a podium of some kind (unless you know that you won't be using one). Stack some boxes to form a makeshift podium if you have to. Practice working with your speaking notes until you are confident that you can refer to them without overly relying on them. Practice placing your notes on a podium and moving around the podium for effective delivery.

At some point, practice your speech in front of at least one other person. Ask your volunteer(s) to identify the purpose and key points of your speech. Question them about what they did or did not understand. Seek detailed feedback about the quality of your delivery.

TIME YOUR SPEECH

As you practice, time each part of the speech (introduction, body, and conclusion) so that if you exceed your time limit you can adjust these sections accordingly. Recall that, as a general rule, the introduction and the conclusion should make up no more than 10 or 15 percent of your entire speech (see Chapters 14 and 15). If the speech is too long, look for extraneous material that can be cut. Consider your rate of speech. If it is too slow, practice speaking more concisely. If the speech is too short, review your evidence and make certain that you adequately support your main points. If your rate of speech is too fast, practice slowing your tempo.

PLAN AHEAD AND PRACTICE OFTEN

If possible, begin practicing your speech at least several days before you are scheduled to deliver it. Many expert speakers recommend practicing your speech about five times in its final form. Given that few speeches are longer than twenty minutes, and most are shorter, this represents a maximum of two hours of practice time — time that is well spent.

✓ **CHECKLIST**

Practicing Your Speech

_____ 1. Practice with your speaking notes.

_____ 2. Revise those parts of your speech that aren't satisfactory, altering your speaking notes as you go.

_____ 3. Focus on your speech ideas rather than on yourself.

_____ 4. Visualize the setting in which you will speak as you practice, projecting your words to different parts of the space to reach audience members.

_____ 5. Practice your speech several times, and then record it with an audio recorder.

_____ 6. Time each part of your speech — introduction, body, and conclusion.

_____ 7. If possible, videotape yourself twice — once after several practice sessions and again after you've incorporated changes into your speech.

_____ 8. Practice the speech under realistic conditions, paying attention to projecting your voice and working with your speaking notes unobtrusively.

_____ 9. Practice in front of at least one volunteer, and seek constructive criticism.

_____ 10. Schedule your practice sessions early in the process so that you have adequate time to prepare.

_____ 11. Practice your speech at least five times.

Presentation Aids

Presentation Aids

Speaker's Reference
Presentation Aids

20. Using Presentation Aids in the Speech

Using Presentation Aids to Increase Understanding and Retention

- Presentation aids can concisely express complex ideas. (p. 283)
- Statistical relationships can be made clear through graphs and charts. (p. 283)
- Well-prepared presentation aids can boost your credibility. (p. 283)
- Beware of losing credibility with sloppily conceived aids. (p. 283)

Consider Using Props and Models

- Inanimate or live *props* can solidify your descriptions. (p. 283)
- In many disciplines, *models* are a central component of presentations. (p. 283)

Consider Illustrating Key Points with Pictures

- Look for visually arresting *photographs*. (p. 284)
- Create a *diagram* to demonstrate how something is constructed or used. (p. 284)
- Use a *map* to pinpoint an area or illustrate proportions. (p. 284)
- Use a *poster* to convey a brief message forcefully. (p. 286)

Use Graphs and Charts to Show Trends and Demonstrate Relationships

- Select a *line graph* to represent trends and other information that changes over time. (p. 286)
- Choose a *bar graph* to compare quantities or magnitudes. (p. 286)
- Use a *pie graph* to show proportions. (p. 286)
- Use a *pictogram* to show comparisons in picture form. (p. 287)
- Use a *flowchart* to diagram a procedure or process. (p. 288)
- Use an *organizational chart* to illustrate hierarchical relationships. (p. 288)
- Use a *table* to summarize large amounts of information. (p. 290)

Think About the Possible Use of Audio and Video to Add Interest

- Choose clips that illustrate ideas or bring humor to the mix. (p. 290)
- Consider incorporating clip into Microsoft's PowerPoint. (p. 291)

Consider Using Multimedia to Enhance Key Speech Points

- Be familiar with presentation software programs that effectively incorporate multimedia. (p. 291)

Consider the Options for Displaying Presentation Aids

- Ensure the smooth display of overhead transparencies. (p. 291)
- Choose the most appropriate graphics and displays for the occasion. (p. 292)
- Write neatly when using a flip chart or chalkboard. (p. 294)
- Time the distribution of handouts. (p. 294)

21. Designing Presentation Aids

Present One Major Idea per Aid

- Limit the amount of information in any single visual. (p. 295)
- Use phrases rather than full sentences. (p. 295)
- Limit words to no more than eight per line. (p. 295)
- Limit lines to no more than eight per aid. (p. 295)
- Use parallel sentence structure. (p. 295)

Apply the Same Design Decisions to Each Aid

- Apply consistent colors, fonts, capitalization, and styling. (p. 296)

Use Type Large Enough to Be Read Comfortably

- For slides, use a sans serif typeface for titles and major headings. (p. 297)
- Experiment with a serif typeface for the body of the text. (p. 298)
- Experiment with 36-point type for major headings, 24-point type for subheadings, and 18-point type for the body of the text. (p. 298)
- Use upper- and lowercase type rather than all capitals. (p. 298)

Use Color Wisely

- Use bold, bright colors (yellow, orange, red) to highlight text or objects. (p. 300)
- Use neutral colors such as blue, green, tan, and white for backgrounds. (p. 300)

- For typeface and graphics, use colors that contrast with the background color. (p. 300)
- Restrict the number of colors to two, three, or four, and use the same colors consistently. (p. 300)

22. Using Presentation Software

Remember That You're Giving a Speech, Not a Slide Show

- Don't overuse aids. (p. 302)
- Don't let technical wizardry distract from the focus on message and audience. (p. 302)
- Avoid hiding behind your electronic presentation. (p. 302)

Refer to Chapter Text for Tips on Using Microsoft PowerPoint

- Become familiar with toolbars and icons on the various PowerPoint screens. (p. 303)
- Use the AutoContent Wizard for the best assistance in developing your aid. (p. 304)

Practice Using Presentation Aids Until They Flow Smoothly with the Speech

KEY TERMS

Chapter 20

presentation aids	bar graph	multimedia
prop	pie graph	overhead transparency
model	pictogram	computer-generated graphics
pictures	chart	LCD panel
diagram	flowchart	LCD projector
map	organizational chart	video projector
poster	table	flip chart
graph	audio clip	chalkboard
line graph	video	handout

Chapter 21

eight-by-eight rule	fonts	sans serif typefaces
typeface	serif typefaces	

Chapter 22

transition effects	Meeting Minder
animation effects	pointer

20 Using Presentation Aids in the Speech

An old cliché states, "A picture is worth a thousand words." To modernize the cliché we should say, "A picture plus sound plus motion and other special effects are worth a thousand words"—that is, of course, when they are used in a context that is appropriate to the topic, the audience, and the occasion (e.g., the rhetorical situation).

Presentation aids include objects, models, pictures, graphs, charts, video, audio, and multimedia. Each of these elements, used alone and in combination, helps listeners to see relationships among concepts and elements, to store and remember material, and to critically examine key ideas. The strength of a presentation aid lies in the context in which it is used. No matter how powerful a photograph or chart or video may be, the audience will be less interested in merely gazing at it than in discovering how you will relate it to a specific point. If even superior-quality aids are poorly related to a speech, listeners will be turned off. Thus presentation aids should be used to *supplement* rather than to serve as the main source of your ideas.

Functions of Presentation Aids

Used judiciously, presentation aids can help listeners process and retain information, spark interest, convey information in a time-saving fashion, and enhance an image of professionalism.

HELP LISTENERS PROCESS AND RETAIN INFORMATION

Most people process and retain information best when they receive it in more than one format. Research findings indicate that we remember only about 20 percent of what we hear, but more than 50 percent of what we see *and* hear.[1] Further, we remember about 70 percent of what we see, hear, and actually do. Messages that are reinforced visually and otherwise are often more believable than those that are simply verbalized. As the saying goes, "Seeing is believing."

PROMOTE INTEREST AND MOTIVATION

Effective presentation aids draw audience members into a speech and provide stimulation that keeps them interested. They allow listeners to engage the right side of their brains—the hemisphere that plays an important role in such nonverbal tasks as visualization, music, and drawing. Literally seeing the facts of an

Tips for Using Props Effectively

_____ 1. Choose props that illustrate and reinforce key points.

_____ 2. Beware of using humorous props, such as wigs or costumes. Unless they match the levity of the topic, such props can easily undermine your credibility.

_____ 3. Make sure the prop is big enough for everyone to see (and read, if applicable).

_____ 4. Show the prop slowly and make sure that every member of the audience can see it.

_____ 5. In most cases, keep the prop hidden until you are ready to use it.

_____ 6. Don't let the prop distract you or the audience. Put it away when you are finished with it.

_____ 7. Practice your speech with the prop.

Source: Selected ideas based on Andrea Nierenberg, "Props Help Bring Content into the Visual Realm," *Presentations* 16 (April 2002): 4, 54.

PICTURES (PHOTOGRAPHS, DRAWINGS, DIAGRAMS, MAPS, AND POSTERS)

Few verbal descriptions can match the powerful impact that a strong visual image creates. Photographs, drawings, paintings, and other illustrations are all forms of **pictures** — two-dimensional representations of people, places, ideas, or objects produced on an opaque backing. Among the types of pictures commonly used by speakers are photographs, line drawings, diagrams, maps, and posters.

A **diagram** (also called a *schematic drawing*) explains how something works or how it is constructed or operated. Diagrams are best suited to simplifying and clarifying complicated procedures, explanations, and operations. They are the aid of choice when you need to explain how to construct or use something. Figure 20.1 is a diagram that shows how to assemble monitor stand cables for a computer.

A **map** is a representation of a whole or a part of an area on a flat surface.[3] Maps help audience members to visualize geographic areas and to illustrate various relationships among them. At the simplest level, maps illustrate the layout of a geographic region. Thus if your speech is about becoming familiar with a company's various offices worldwide, you could incorporate a map depicting the location of the offices into your talk. Maps are also an excellent way to illustrate the proportion of one thing to something else in different areas of a region. You could create a map to illustrate the proportion of manufacturing plants to distribution centers, for example, or of distribution centers to retailers, and so forth. As seen in Figure 20.2, for a speech on finding a suitable Ph.D. program in communications in a certain region of the country, you could create a map illustrating the number of Ph.D.-granting institutions in that region.

Figure 20.1 Diagram or Schematic Drawing of Monitor Stand Cables

Rear Cover

Video Cable

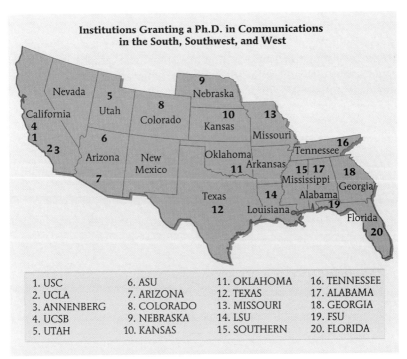

Institutions Granting a Ph.D. in Communications
in the South, Southwest, and West

1. USC	6. ASU	11. OKLAHOMA	16. TENNESSEE
2. UCLA	7. ARIZONA	12. TEXAS	17. ALABAMA
3. ANNENBERG	8. COLORADO	13. MISSOURI	18. GEORGIA
4. UCSB	9. NEBRASKA	14. LSU	19. FSU
5. UTAH	10. KANSAS	15. SOUTHERN	20. FLORIDA

Figure 20.2 Map Illustrating Number of Universities in the South, Southwest, and West Granting a Ph.D. in Communications

A **poster** is a large, bold, two-dimensional design incorporating words, shapes, and, if desired, color, placed on an opaque backing. Posters are used to convey a brief message or point forcefully and attractively. They make a good choice for introducing topics or concepts early in the introductory part of a presentation, as well as later, when simple concepts need to be introduced. Posters are economical and easy to use; they are a good choice for speakers who give the same presentation many times. Easels are useful if you have several posters to show successively, and chalkboard railings can hold posters as well. As described in Chapter 30, posters are featured in one form of presentation called the *poster session*.

GRAPHS AND CHARTS

A **graph** represents numerical data in visual form. Graphs neatly illustrate relationships among components or units and demonstrate trends. Four major types of graphs are line graphs, bar graphs, pie graphs, and pictograms.

A **line graph** displays one measurement, usually plotted on the horizontal axis, and units of measurement or values, which are plotted on the vertical axis. Each value or point is connected with a line. Line graphs are especially useful in representing information that changes over time, such as trends. For example, Figure 20.3 represents fluctuations in fruit production over a five-year period. Line graphs remain a favorite among most presenters and listeners because they simplify complex information and are easier to read than more complicated tables and charts of data.

A **bar graph** uses bars of varying lengths to compare quantities or magnitudes. As seen in Figure 20.4, bars may be arranged either vertically or horizontally. Speakers sometimes use multidimensional bar graphs, or bar graphs distinguished by different colors or markings, when they need to compare two or more different kinds of information or quantities in one chart. A **pie graph** depicts the division of a whole. In this type of graph, the pie, which represents

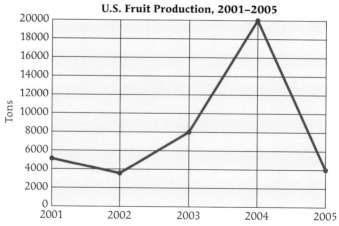

Figure 20.3 Line Graph of U.S. Fruit Production, 2001–2005

100 percent, is divided into portions or segments called slices. Each slice constitutes a percentage of the whole. A **pictogram** shows comparisons in picture form. The pictures represent numerical units and are drawn to relate to the items being compared. Figure 20.5 is a pictogram that demonstrates an increase in the number of college students.

Vertical Bar Graph

Horizontal Bar Graph

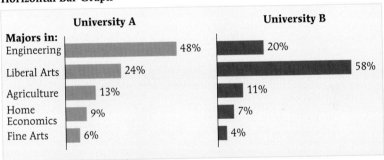

Figure 20.4 Bar Graphs of Quantities and Magnitudes

New College Freshmen

Figure 20.5 Pictogram Showing Increase in College Students

A **chart** visually organizes complex information into compact form. Several different types of charts are helpful for speakers: flowcharts; organizational charts; and tabular charts or tables. A **flowchart** is a diagram that shows step-by-step progression through a procedure, a relationship, or a process. Usually the flow of a procedure or a process is drawn horizontally or vertically and describes how key components fit into a whole. To show the sequence of activities or the directional flow in a process, the flowchart is the visual aid of choice (see Figure 20.6).

An **organizational chart** illustrates the organizational structure or chain of command in an organization. It shows the interrelationship of the different positions, divisions, departments, and personnel. Figure 20.7 shows an organizational chart for a hypothetical organization.

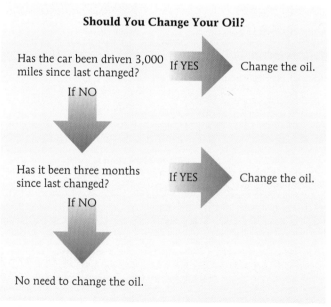

Figure 20.6 Flowchart Showing Oil-Changing Decision Process

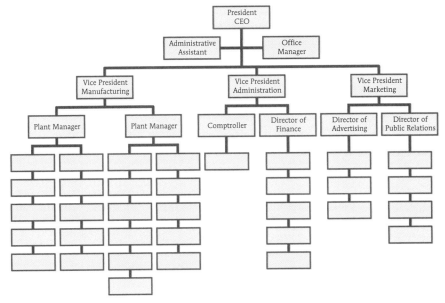

Figure 20.7 Organizational Chart Showing Personnel Hierarchy

✔ **CHECKLIST**

Tips for Creating Effective Line, Bar, and Pie Graphs

_____ 1. Make sure that you label both axes of the line or bar graph appropriately.

_____ 2. Start the numerical axis of the line or bar graph at zero.

_____ 3. Compare only like variables.

_____ 4. Put no more than two lines of data on one graph.

_____ 5. Assign a clear title to the graph.

_____ 6. Clearly label all relevant points of information in the graph.

_____ 7. When creating multidimensional bar graphs, do not compare more than three kinds of information.

_____ 8. When creating a pie graph, restrict the number of pie slices to seven.

_____ 9. When creating a pie graph, make sure that you identify the value or percentage of each pie slice, and make sure that each slice of the pie accurately represents the value or percentage (e.g., use half of the pie to show 50 percent).

_____ 10. When creating a pie graph, consider using color or background markings to distinguish the different slices of the pie.

A tabular chart, or **table**, is a systematic grouping of data or numerical information in column form. Tables are not truly graphics, because they are not really pictures. However, even if they lack visual appeal they often present valuable data that the viewer can examine quickly and make comparisons about easily. Table 20.1, for example, summarizes the best uses of different types of graphs and charts.

TABLE 20.1 • Best Use of Different Types of Graphs and Charts	
Types of Graph or Chart	**Best Use**
Line graph	To represent trends or information that changes over time
Bar and column graph	To compare individual points of information, magnitudes
Pie graph	To show proportions such as sales by region, shares
Pictogram	To show comparisons in picture form
Flowchart	To diagram processes
Organizational chart	To show reporting relationships in a hierarchy
Table	To show large amounts of information in easily viewable form

AUDIO AND VIDEO

An **audio clip** is a short recording of sounds, music, or speech. Introducing sound into a speech can add interest, illustrate ideas, and even bring humor to the mix. **Video**—including movie, television, and other recording segments— can also be a powerful presentation aid that combines sight, sound, and movement to illustrate key speech concepts. Because most facilities that regularly host presentations own audio and video equipment as part of their in-house supplies and because the equipment is relatively simple to operate, both are generally a safe choice as presentation aids. Tapes are reusable, which makes the medium both durable and cost-effective.

✓ **CHECKLIST**

Tips on Incorporating Audio and Video into Your Presentation

_____ 1. If you are using traditional audio or video playback equipment, be sure to cue the audio- or videotape to the appropriate segment before the presentation. Fumbling for the right spot during your speech is a sure way to lose credibility and attention.

_____ 2. Alert audience members to what they will be viewing before you show the tape.

_____ 3. Reiterate the main points of the audio or video clip once it is over.

_____ 4. Always check to see whether the audio or video material you are using is copyrighted, and that you are using it in a manner consistent with copyright laws.

With presentation software programs such as Microsoft's PowerPoint, you can also incorporate audio and video into an electronic presentation. (See Chapter 22 for tips on incorporating sound and video file formats into electronic presentations.)

MULTIMEDIA

Multimedia combines several media (stills, sound, video, text, and data) into a single production. The idea behind multimedia is that the more senses you evoke, the more memorable the event will be. Studies confirm that the visual and auditory reinforcement of multimedia helps people learn and master information more quickly than they would by conventional means. But even though it's an increasingly popular option, multimedia does require more planning than other forms of presentation aids. It is also more time-consuming. To produce multimedia, you need to become familiar with presentation software programs such as Microsoft PowerPoint, Adobe Persuasion, and CorelDraw, to name just a few (see Chapter 22).

Options for Displaying the Presentation Aid

Once you've selected the types of aids that are best suited for communicating your ideas (e.g., chart or graph and so forth), you can select from a variety of options for displaying them during your speech. On the more traditional side, popular devices include overhead transparencies, slide transparencies, flip charts, chalkboards, and handouts. Many presenters create computer-generated graphics, which they then display with computer projection or other display technology such as LCD panels and projectors (see Chapter 22).

OVERHEAD TRANSPARENCIES

An **overhead transparency** (also called an *overhead acetate*) is an image on a transparent background that can be viewed by transmitted light, either directly or through projection onto a screen or a wall. The images may be written or printed directly onto the transparency. If the transparency is handwritten during the presentation, it can be used much like a chalkboard (see p. 294). Parts of the transparency may be covered with opaque paper and revealed progressively during the presentation. Alternatively, transparencies may be overlaid on each other so that successive details can be added. Objects may also be placed on the stage of the projector to project silhouettes.

Because transparencies have several distinct advantages, they are among the most common presentation media, especially in settings such as schools. First, most facilities that host presentations have overhead projectors. Second, transparencies are inexpensive and overhead projectors are portable and simple to operate. Third, overhead projection is flexible. Material may be added to or taken away from the projector during the presentation, making the overhead a

---

✓ **CHECKLIST**

Tips for Successfully Incorporating Presentation Aids into Your Speech

_____ 1. Talk to your audience rather than to the screen—insofar as possible, don't turn your back to the audience.

_____ 2. Concentrate on maintaining eye contact with the audience.

_____ 3. Avoid putting the aid directly behind you. Place it to one side so that the entire audience can see it and you can move away from it and still face the audience.

_____ 4. Display the aid only when you are ready to discuss it.

_____ 5. Incorporate any aids you plan to use into your practice sessions. Continue to practice with the aids until you are confident that you can handle them without causing undue distractions.

_____ 6. If you decide to use a pointer, don't brandish it about. Once you've indicated the point you wish to make with the pointing instrument, put it down.

---

good choice for presentations that require multiple visual aids. Fourth, projection allows you to interact with the audience easily. Unlike writing on a chalkboard or handing out other visual aids, overhead projection allows you to face the audience while using it. In addition, users can keep lights on while using overhead transparencies. The checklist on page 293 offers some pointers on using overhead transparencies.

COMPUTER-GENERATED GRAPHICS AND DISPLAYS

With presentation software programs such as Microsoft PowerPoint, many speakers create slides, transparencies, and other presentation aids on a computer. You can project these **computer-generated graphics** directly from a computer (using computerized projection and display devices such as LCD panels and projectors; see below), or you can transfer the images to overhead transparencies. (See Chapter 22 for a discussion of how to use presentation software.)

LCD stands for _liquid crystal diode_. LCD display technology is now widespread and can be found in laptop computer screens, digital watches, and countless other digitized products. Projection devices that use LCD technology to display information come in two forms. The **LCD panel**, which connects to a computer, is a square, thin box that sits on top of an overhead projector. In the middle of the box is a screen on which images appear. The computer sends what is on its screen to the LCD panel and the image appears on the screen. The overhead projector provides the illumination necessary to project the image onto a wall or a projection screen. The **LCD projector** comes with an illumination or light source, which eliminates the need for an overhead projector. LCD panels are less expensive and more portable than LCD projectors, but the latter are fully self-contained and are becoming smaller and more common. Re-

---

✓ **CHECKLIST**

Tips on Using Overhead Transparencies

_____ 1. Practice using your transparencies before your presentation.

_____ 2. Store your transparencies in a sturdy folder or box. Have blank transparencies available so that you can add information during the presentation.

_____ 3. Ensure that the projector is in good order: Make sure it does not block the audience's view; have a spare projector bulb available; tape the power cord to the floor.

_____ 4. Stand to the side of the projector—to the right if you are right-handed or to the left if you are left-handed.

_____ 5. Face the audience, not the projected image.

_____ 6. When adding transparencies, check that they remain clear and properly placed.

_____ 7. Use a pointer to indicate specific sections of a transparency—point to the transparency, not to the screen. Use objects such as a coin, pen, or arrow to mark the slide.

_____ 8. If creating transparencies by writing or drawing during the presentation, use a water-soluble transparency pen and make sure you write clearly.

_____ 9. Use overlays to show successive layers of detail.

_____ 10. Cover transparencies when you are done using them to avoid distracting your audience. Use heavy paper or cardboard so it will not be moved by the projector's fan.

Source: Adapted from Lenny Laskowski, "Using Overhead Transparencies," http://www.ljlseminars .com/ransp.htm (accessed September 1, 2005); and Media Services, Robert A. L. Mortvedt Library, Pacific Lutheran University, "Using Overhead Projectors," http://www.plu.edu/~libr/workshops/ multimedia/overhead.html (accessed September 1, 2005).

---

member, if you take your presentation on the road, you can never be sure of the quality of the overhead projector that will be provided for you. LCD panels require overhead projectors with a very bright projection light; if the meeting room in which you will be presenting has a poor-quality projector, the projected image may be compromised. LCD projectors are favored when the speaker wants a freestanding device that eliminates the worry of hassling with an overhead projector.

When your presentation requires high resolution, crisp color, and a large projected image, the **video projector** offers an attractive alternative. Used most frequently in large meeting rooms or auditoriums, video projectors, like LCD panels/projectors, connect to a computer and project an image as large as 25 feet long. Video projectors display a sharp, large image through three lenses (red, green, blue). The downsides of video projectors include their expense—two to three times more costly than devices using LCD technology—as well as their size and weight. Video projectors weigh between 80 and 100 pounds, rendering them very limited portable devices. Video projectors usually remain at a fixed site.

FLIP CHARTS

A **flip chart** is simply a large (27–34 inches) pad of paper on which a speaker can illustrate speech points. Many such aids are prepared in advance, although you can also write and draw on the paper as you speak. As you progress through the speech, you simply flip through the pad to the next exhibit. The flip chart is one of the most inexpensive ways of displaying aids. In terms of equipment, a ruler and colored markers are all that are required. To compete with other kinds of aids, however, you do need some artistic skill so that your images aren't sloppy and awkward.

CHALKBOARDS

On the lowest-tech end of the spectrum lies the **chalkboard** — a black (or white or blue or green) board on which you can write with chalk (or a marker if the board is the chalkless type). Chalkboards are useful for impromptu explanations, as when someone asks a question for which you do not have an aid but feel you can clarify with words or drawings. In general, try to reserve the chalkboard for quick explanations, such as presenting simple processes that are done in steps. If you have the time to prepare a speech properly, however, don't rely on a chalkboard. Chalkboards force the speaker to turn his or her back to the audience; they make listeners wait while you write on the board; and they require legible handwriting that will be clear to all viewers.

HANDOUTS

No consideration of presentation aids would be complete without a discussion of the **handout** — page-size items that convey information that is either impractical to give to the audience in another manner or intended to be kept by audience members after the presentation. Handouts can convey large amounts of information to an audience effectively and cost-efficiently because elements may be included that are not covered in depth, or at all, during the actual presentation. Handouts can also be used when it is best to have audience members follow along with you while you go over information.

To avoid distracting your listeners, unless you specifically want them to read the information as you speak, *wait until you are done before you distribute the handout.* If you do want the audience to view a handout during the speech, pass it out only when you are ready to talk about it. Finally, remember that having too many handouts may undercut their effectiveness. Sifting through pages and pages of information may become tiresome for audience members, who may decide that it isn't worth the trouble and lose interest.

Designing Presentation Aids

Once you select the types of presentation aids you will use in your speech and decide on the method of displaying them (see Chapter 20), you can begin design and construction. Whether you fashion the aids with pen and paper or generate them on a computer, certain general principles of design apply.

Simplicity

Presentation aids that try to communicate too many messages will quickly overwhelm the audience. To communicate your points effectively in the brief period of time the audience has to view the aid (for slides, this amounts to an average of about thirty seconds[1]), strive for simplicity. Concentrate on presenting one major idea per aid. If you want to cover and discuss a series of points, use a sequential layout of separate aids.

The purpose of a presentation aid is to reinforce, support, or summarize what you say, not to repeat verbatim what you've already verbalized in your speech. Thus, rather than using full sentences that mirror your speech statements, where possible present your points in short phrases. Also, minimize the number of words you use in each presentation aid. Keep them to a maximum of eight words per line and eight lines per aid. Limiting the number of words in an aid lessens the likelihood that the audience will spend too much time reading the aid rather than listening to you.

Another way to keep your aids simple and uncluttered is to construct your text in active verb form and parallel grammatical structure (see Chapter 16 on language). For example, community college student Courtney Phelps delivered a persuasive speech on the need to spay or neuter pets. She prepared a PowerPoint slide labeled "Excuses for Not Neutering Pets." Note in Figure 21.1 the differences between her first draft and her final slide.

In reviewing Courtney's first-draft slide, note the lack of parallel structure (each phrase is constructed differently); her use of full sentences throughout; the passive construction in points 1 and 4 ("It is believed that . . ." and "It is thought that . . ."); and the switching among different terms for neutering ("fixing," "neutering," and "spaying").

In her final slide, Courtney switched from passive to active construction (deleting "It is believed that" and "It is thought that," leaving only "interferes with nature" and "costs too much"). Two of her four points thus became phrases rather than full sentences. Finding no other way to express the ideas, she kept points 2 and 3 as full sentences. Since neither exceeded the **eight-by-eight**

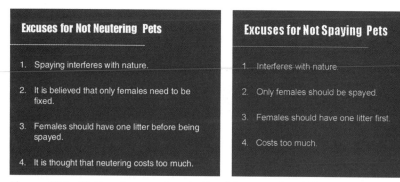

Excuses for Not Neutering Pets	Excuses for Not Spaying Pets
1. Spaying interferes with nature.	1. Interferes with nature.
2. It is believed that only females need to be fixed.	2. Only females should be spayed.
3. Females should have one litter before being spayed.	3. Females should have one litter first.
4. It is thought that neutering costs too much.	4. Costs too much.

Figure 21.1 Cluttered versus Easy-to-Read Presentation Aid

rule — using no more than eight words in a line and eight lines on one slide — her audience members were not likely to be confused by them. Finally, rather than switching among different terms, she used "spaying" consistently. Each of these changes reduced the chances for confusion.

Continuity

The principle of continuity dictates that you apply the same design decisions you make for one aid to all of the aids you display in a speech. Doing so will ensure that viewers don't become distracted (and irritated) by a jumble of unrelated visual elements.

To help maintain continuity, your choice of any key design elements — colors, fonts, upper- and lowercase letters, styling (boldface, underlining, italics) —

 CHECKLIST

Applying the Principles of Simplicity and Continuity

✓ Restrict your coverage to one idea per aid.
✓ Use as few words as possible to get your ideas across clearly.
✓ Where possible, use key phrases rather than full sentences.
✓ Keep text to no more than eight words per line and eight lines per aid.
✓ Create concise titles that tell viewers what to look for in the aid and that reinforce your message.
✓ Maintain design consistency across all aids. Use the same combinations of fonts, upper- and lowercase lettering, styling (use of boldface, underlining, and italics), and spacing.
✓ Use colors consistently across all aids. If an object is red in one slide and you repeat the same object in another slide, render it in the same color.
✓ Apply the same style and typeface to titles throughout all aids.
✓ Carry through any repeating symbols, such as logos or pictograms, across all aids.

should be carried through to each aid. If you select a certain color background for one aid, for instance, repeat the same background for each subsequent aid. Follow the same general page layout throughout, placing repeating elements, such as titles, in the same place and in the same style and typeface. Use the same symbols in every aid, whether they are colors, pictograms, or logos of one sort or another. For example, if in an aid comparing the computer-buying habits of men and women you illustrated the buying habits of men in red and those of women in green, you would continue using these colors in subsequent aids.

Typeface Style and Font Size

A **typeface** is a specific style of lettering, such as Arial, Times Roman, or Courier. Typefaces come in a variety of **fonts**, or sets of sizes (called the point size) and upper- and lowercases.

Designers divide the thousands of typefaces available today into two categories: serif and sans serif. (There are additional categories, such as script typefaces and those that mimic cursive writing, but these aren't recommended for presentation aids because they are difficult to read from a distance.) **Serif typefaces** include small flourishes, or strokes, at the tops and bottoms of each letter. **Sans serif typefaces** are more blocklike and linear; they are designed without these tiny strokes. Studies have shown that when a body of text is being read, serif typefaces are easier on the eye (see Figure 21.2). Small amounts of text, however, such as headings, are best viewed in sans serif type. Depending on how much text you insert into a slide, consider a sans serif typeface for the

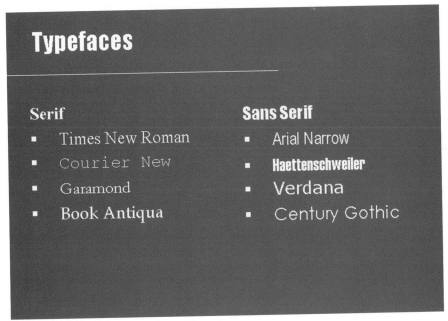

Figure 21.2 Serif and Sans Serif Typefaces

heading and a serif typeface for the body of the text. If you include only a few lines of text, however, consider using sans serif type throughout.

There are thousands of typefaces beyond those found in word processing programs, many of which can be purchased in separate software packages or downloaded from the Internet. Following are a few key points to observe when selecting type styles for presentations:

1. Whether you are using a hand-drawn poster board or a computer-generated graphic, check your lettering for legibility, taking into consideration the audience's distance from the presentation. Most text for on-screen projection should be a minimum of 18 points or larger. Titles or major headings should be 36 points. One guideline is that major headings within the presentation should be displayed in 36-point type, subheadings should use 24-point type, and regular text should be 18-point type (see Figure 21.3).

2. Check that your lettering stands apart from your background. For example, don't put black type on a dark blue background.

3. Use a typeface that is simple and easy to read, not distracting. It should be consistent with the image you are trying to present and match your meaning.

4. Don't overuse **boldface**, underlining, or *italics*. Instead, use them sparingly to call attention to or emphasize the most important points.

5. Use upper- and lowercase type. This combination is easier to read than all capitals.

Figure 21.3 Use Appropriate Font Sizes

✓ **CHECKLIST**

Tips for Using Typefaces, Fonts, and Sizes Effectively

✓ For on-screen projection, don't use anything smaller than 18-point text. For larger rooms, consider 24-point text or larger.

✓ Avoid ornate typefaces—they are difficult to read.

✓ Use a sans serif typeface for titles and major headings.

✓ Experiment with a serif typeface for the body of the text.

✓ Select a style of type that suits your message.

✓ Experiment with 36-point type for major headings, 24-point type for subheads, and 18-point type for text.

✓ As a rule, use no more than two different typefaces in a single visual aid.

✓ Avoid using all capitals. Use upper- and lowercase type.

✓ Don't overuse boldface, underlining, or italics.

Color

As any artist will attest, color has an amazing ability to stimulate the senses. By doing so, it helps listeners to see comparisons, contrasts, and emphases. The skillful use of color can draw attention to key points, set the mood of a presentation, and make things easier to see. However, color that isn't used wisely can easily backfire. Poor color combinations will set the wrong mood, render an image unattractive, or make it just plain unreadable. Table 21.1 describes the effects of several color combinations.

In addition, because colors evoke distinct associations in people, care must be taken as you design the aid not to summon an unintended meaning or mood. Unless you specifically wish to remind viewers of the holidays of Halloween and Christmas, for example, when addressing audiences in the United States steer clear of combining orange with black and red with green.[2] Table 21.2 describes some of the subjective interpretations different audiences attach to four colors.

TABLE 21.1 • Effect of Color Combinations

Color	Effect in Combination
Yellow	Warm on white, harsh on black, fiery on red, soothing on light blue
Blue	Warm on white, hard to see on black
Red	Bright on white, warm or difficult to see on black

Source: Cheryl Currid, *Make Your Point: The Complete Guide to Successful Business Presentations Using Today's Technology* (Rocklin, Calif.: Prima Publishing, 1995), 75.

TABLE 21.2 • Subjective Interpretations of Color by Different Audiences

Color Hue	Financial Managers	Health Care Professionals	Control Engineers
Blue	Corporate, reliable	Dead	Cold, water
Green	Cool, subdued	Infected, bilious	Safe
Yellow	Important	Jaundiced	Caution
Red	Unprofitable	Healthy	Danger

Source: Adapted from Cheryl Currid, *Make Your Point: The Complete Guide to Successful Business Presentations Using Today's Technology* (Rocklin, Calif.: Prima Publishing, 1995), 74.

Following are some tips for using color effectively in your presentation aids:

- Use *bold, bright colors* to emphasize important points. For instance, speakers often use bright yellow to draw attention to important points. Warm colors such as yellow, red, and orange move to the foreground of a field. For this reason, they are good colors to use when you want to highlight something. But be careful: These colors can be difficult to see from a distance.

- Use *softer, lighter* colors to de-emphasize less important areas of a presentation.

- Keep the *background color* of your presentation constant, and avoid dark backgrounds. As a general rule, the best background colors are the lighter, more neutral colors of tan, blue, green, or white.

- For typeface and graphics, use colors that contrast rather than clash with or blend into the background color.

- Limit the number of colors you use in a graphic to two or three (or four at the most). More color choices can be used in complex and detailed aids.

- Be aware that many presentation software packages provide templates with preselected colors.

✓ **CHECKLIST**

Optimizing Your Use of Color

✓ Yellow, orange, and red rank highest in visibility, so use these colors to highlight text or objects within a frame.

✓ To de-emphasize less important areas of a presentation, use softer, lighter colors.

✓ For typeface and graphics, use colors that contrast rather than clash with or blend into the background color.

✓ Use blues, greens, and neutral colors such as tan and white for backgrounds.

✓ Use no more than four colors in a graphic; two or three are even better.

✓ Stay within the same family of hues.

Using Presentation Software

Various presentation software packages offer public speakers powerful tools for creating and displaying professionally polished visual aids. With just the click of a mouse, programs such as Microsoft PowerPoint, Lotus Freelance Graphics, and CorelDraw allow you to transform your ideas into eye-catching graphics. You can project the aids directly from the computer via an LCD panel or projector, or you can convert them into handouts or overhead transparencies, which can then be displayed using traditional devices such as a carousel or an overhead projector. Preloaded templates provide expert guidelines for font, color, and background combinations; users can also design their own arrangements. Presentation software programs also allow you to import video and sound into your presentation as part of a multimedia presentation. A key advantage of presentation software programs over traditionally rendered means of producing aids is that the former gives users the ability to modify and revise the aids until the last minute before the speech is delivered.

This is not to say that creating aids with presentation software is effortless or lacks potential pitfalls. Learning to use any software program takes time, and presentation software is no exception. A more insidious danger is the potential for mishaps during the speech. Speakers who rely on electronic presentations run the risk of performance snafus because of technical errors. These include files that won't open or weren't properly saved to a disk, incompatible versions of the software, incompatibilities between computers and projectors, and entire system failures during the speech. The accompanying checklist on preventive maintenance describes steps you can take to prevent these problems from occurring.

 CHECKLIST

Preventive Maintenance: Minimizing the Odds of Last-Minute Technical Glitches

✓ Check to make sure that the operating system of the computer you will use during your speech (e.g., Windows XP, Mac OS X) is compatible with the operating system used to create the aids.

✓ Make sure that the version of the presentation software used to create the aids matches the one that is loaded onto the computer you will use in the presentation. Incompatibilities between versions can cause distortions in your graphics, sound, and video; in some cases one version may not recognize another.

(Continued on p. 302)

(Continued)

✓ Properly save all the files associated with your presentation (i.e., images, sound files, videos) onto the disk you will use in your presentation.

✓ Save any images or videos within your presentation onto the same disk as the rest of your presentation.

✓ Verify that the format you've saved the files to, whether it's a floppy disk, zip drive, flash drive, or CD-ROM disk, is compatible with (i.e., will be accepted by) the presentation computer.

✓ Before the speech—if only minutes before—familiarize yourself with the layout and functioning of the presentation computer. This will facilitate smooth operation during the presentation.

✓ If you are concerned about losing your computer-generated presentation— due to a system failure, power outage, or connection error—prepare a hard-copy backup of your presentation. In PowerPoint, for example, you would use the slide-sorter tool to print out your slides for use as handouts.

Maintaining the Proper Focus: It's a Speech, Not a Slide Show

Another potential drawback of electronic presentations is the temptation to focus on the aids rather than on the speech itself. Some speakers become so enamored of generating graphics or creating a jazzy multimedia program that they forget their primary mission: to communicate through the spoken word and through their physical being. Other speakers are tempted to hide behind their aids, focusing on them rather than giving their attention to the audience. Presentation aids can help with speech anxiety by taking the focus off the speaker and by jump-starting memory. This is all to the good, as long as your message and the audience remain your primary focus. As public-speaking author Ron Hoff notes, "It's OK to be partially electronic — everybody can use a bit of glitz — but when all votes are counted and all scores are in, the presenter who is most alive will carry the day."[1]

Using Microsoft PowerPoint: A Brief Guide

Among the most popular presentation programs on the market today is Microsoft PowerPoint. It can be used to generate slides containing text, artwork, photos, charts, graphs, tables, clip art, video, and sound. PowerPoint is also used to produce handouts, outlines, and notes based on the slide presentation. It has the capability to download presentations onto the Web, and with additional software, it can even broadcast your presentation in real time. This section offers a brief overview of PowerPoint's features based on PowerPoint 2002. For more guidance on using PowerPoint, consult the "Visual Presentation Tutorial" at bedfordstmartins.com/speakersguide.

BECOMING FAMILIAR WITH THE TOOLBARS

To work with PowerPoint, you'll need to familiarize yourself with the toolbars and icons at the top and bottom of the main screen. The toolbars, which include many typical icons with which you may be familiar from using other Microsoft software, allow quick access to the most frequently used program functions: New, Open, Save, Print, Spell Check, Cut, Copy, and Paste. Other icons in the PowerPoint toolbars include Insert Chart, Insert Clip Art, New Slide, Slide Layout, and Apply Design. (See Figure 22.1.)

BECOMING FAMILIAR WITH THE PRESENTATION OPTIONS

After you launch PowerPoint, the program displays a blank slide with options for creating a new presentation or opening a preexisting one (Figure 22.2). (Older versions of PowerPoint show a separate box with various presentation options.) At the right of this screen are a number of options for creating a new

Figure 22.1 PowerPoint Toolbars

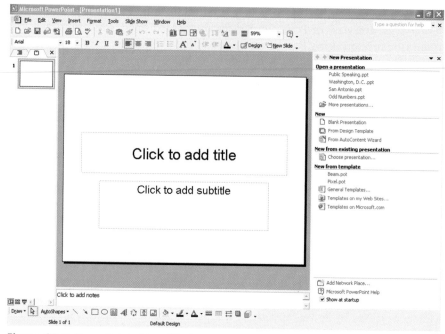

Figure 22.2 PowerPoint: New File Screen in PowerPoint 2002

presentation or revising an existing file. PowerPoint offers three options for creating a new presentation: AutoContent Wizard, Design Template, and Blank Presentation. To revise an existing presentation file, select an option from the Open a Presentation menu.

AutoContent Wizard

If you aren't familiar with PowerPoint, the AutoContent Wizard offers the greatest degree of assistance, including predetermined organization and design strategies to convert your content into a presentation (see Figure 22.3). With AutoContent Wizard, you choose the type of presentation you want from about two dozen options, such as Marketing Plan, Introducing a Speaker, Product/Services Overview, and Presenting a Technical Report. AutoContent Wizard then applies an outline for your presentation. You select the presentation medium (on-screen, Web, overheads) and enter some basic information, such as speaker name and presentation title. The AutoContent Wizard then sets up an index of slides (generally from six to twelve) with preloaded slide titles, points, subpoints, colors, and designs. Clicking on the slide icon in the index allows you to edit the slide and add your own content to customize the presentation.

Design Template Option

For speakers who want more flexibility in designing their graphics, the Design Template option includes approximately forty-eight predesigned templates (see

Figure 22.3 PowerPoint's AutoContent Wizard

Figure 22.4). With the Design Template option, you decide how to organize your points and subpoints; the template you select then applies a consistent layout and color scheme to each slide in the presentation. Each template is designed to convey a certain look or feel.

✓ **CHECKLIST**

Using PowerPoint's AutoContent Wizard Option

_____ 1. Choose File New or press CTRL+N. PowerPoint displays the New Presentation dialog box.

_____ 2. Select the AutoContent Wizard option from the right-hand navigation bar (or from the dialog box), and then choose OK. The AutoContent Wizard dialog box appears.

_____ 3. Read the information in the Step 1 dialog box, and then choose the Next button.

_____ 4. Select the type of presentation you want to give, and then choose the Next button.

_____ 5. Select the type of output you want to use, and then choose the Next button.

_____ 6. Enter the information for creating a title slide, and then choose the Next button.

_____ 7. Choose the Finish button to exit the Wizard and create your presentation.

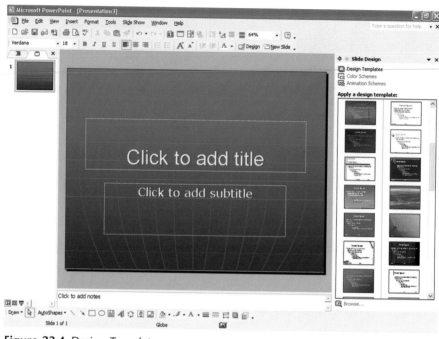

Figure 22.4 Design Template

Blank Presentation Option

In Blank Presentation mode, users customize every aspect of the presentation: layout, color, font type and size, organization of content, and graphics. Of the three options, Blank Presentation allows the greatest degree of creativity and flexibility. The downside is that each slide's design essentially starts from scratch.

To create a new presentation in this mode, select Blank Presentation from the New Presentation menu on the New File screen or from the New File icon on the standard toolbar. Layout templates will then appear on the right side of the screen (see Figure 22.5). Each layout offers a different way of organizing your text and other content on the slide.

Existing Presentation Option

Use this option to open, view, and edit an existing PowerPoint presentation file.

BECOMING FAMILIAR WITH THE VIEW OPTIONS

Newer versions of PowerPoint combine a number of tools in one place to help you create presentations. PowerPoint 2002 and later versions offer three different ways to view the aids you create (as opposed to five in previous versions): normal view, slide-sorter view, and slide-show view. Each may be found via the View menu on the top toolbar or via buttons on the bottom left of the screen.

1. *Normal view* allows you to view (and edit) one entire slide on the screen, alongside an outline of the entire presentation (based on the textual con-

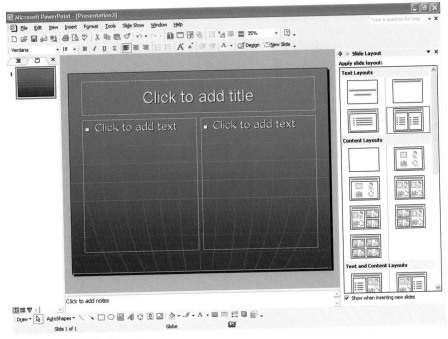

Figure 22.5 Slide Layout

tent of each slide) on the left and options for various slide layouts on the right. Below the slide is an area to add notes. You can use the outline to navigate through a presentation, and you can print out the notes pages for use during presentations.

2. *Slide-sorter view,* providing a graphical representation of all the slides in the presentation, allows you to click and drag slide icons to reorganize the presentation or delete slides (see Figure 22.6).

3. *Slide-show view* is meant to be used during projection to an audience. The slide takes up the entire screen and starts with the first slide.

BECOMING FAMILIAR WITH THE "MASTERS" FOR SLIDES, HANDOUTS, AND NOTES

For every graphic you create, PowerPoint creates a set of "masters." The Slide Master, Handout Master, and Notes Master correspond with the slides, hand-outs, and speaker's notes components of the presentation. Slide Masters contain the elements (text and pictures) that you want to appear on every presentation slide. For example, if you want a logo, image, or line of text to appear on each slide, add that item to the Slide Master and it will automatically appear on each slide.

To display a master, go to the View menu and scroll down to Master; then, from the submenu, choose Slide Master, Handout Master, or Notes Master.

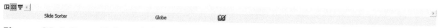

Figure 22.6 PowerPoint: Slide-Sorter View

BECOMING FAMILIAR WITH TEXT TRANSITION AND ANIMATION EFFECTS

As you move from one slide to the next in your presentation or as you move from one point to another within the same slide, you may wish to add transition effects and text animations. **Transition effects** add special motion and sound effects as you move from one slide to another. For example, you can play a sound when the slide appears, or you can make the slides dissolve into black or red as you move from one to another.

To set transition effects for a single slide or for all slides in a presentation:

1. On the Slide Show menu, click Slide Transition.
2. In the resulting Slide Transition menu, click the transition type you want.
3. To apply the transition to all the slides, click Apply All.
4. To apply transitions to a group of slides within a presentation, highlight the slides in the outline by selecting more than one while holding down the Shift key. Open the Slide Transition box and click Apply for the transition type you've selected.

Animation effects — sometimes referred to as *builds* — allow you to decide how you want to reveal text or graphics within a slide during a presentation. You can reveal one letter, word, or paragraph at a time, for example, as you discuss each item. Or you can make text or objects look dimmer or change color when you add another element.

PowerPoint comes with both preset and custom animations. Preset animations determine the options for you—such as whether an object flies in from the top, bottom, left, or right of the slide. Custom animations allow you to select your own options—the order in which animations will occur or whether sound effects will accompany the animations.

To apply an animation scheme:

1. Select the object you want to animate (e.g., a text placeholder or a piece of art).
2. On the Slide Show menu, click Animation Schemes.
3. Click the animation effect you want.
4. To change the preset settings for this object after assigning a preset animation, select Custom Animation from the Slide Show menu.

Note: Some preset animations have a sound associated with the effect. To turn off the sound, first create the preset animation and then go to Custom Animation to remove the sound.

To apply a custom animation:

1. Select the object you want to animate (e.g., a piece of WordArt or just regular text).
2. On the Slide Show menu, click Custom Animation.
3. Choose Add Effect, and then select the animation effect you want.
4. Use the tabs to choose your desired options.

A word of warning about transitions and animations: When used sparingly, transition and animation effects can strengthen your presentation. When overused, however, they can be distracting. Text animations should also be kept consistent from one slide to the next. If you were planning to use the "fly in from left" effect, for example, you would want to apply it on all slides that you build as opposed to using a different effect for each slide. The same guidelines apply to slide transitions. A different transition between every slide set tends to distract the audience. Keep the transitions consistent either throughout the entire slide show or within different sections of your presentation.

ENTERING AND EDITING TEXT

Whenever you choose a slide layout (other than a blank layout), you replace the sample text in a placeholder with your own text. To select a text placeholder, click anywhere within the placeholder. The faint outline is replaced by a wide hashed border. This line indicates that the current placeholder has been selected. The sample text disappears and a flashing, vertical insertion point appears within the placeholder, indicating that you can now insert text. When you finish entering the text, deselect the placeholder by clicking a blank area of the slide. Notice that the object is no longer defined with the faint dotted line.

To add text when you do not have a placeholder, follow these steps:

1. Click the Text Box button in the Drawing toolbar.
2. Position the pointer (now a vertical bar with a small cross-bar) where you want the top left corner of the text box to position.
3. Click and drag the mouse diagonally down and to the right to form a box of the appropriate width.
4. Release the mouse button. The text box will be bordered by wide hashed lines, and a flashing vertical insertion point indicates that you are ready to enter text.

After entering text in a text box, you will probably want to change the content or correct errors. Making changes is as easy as clicking and retyping.

INSERTING OBJECTS INTO SLIDES

PowerPoint allows you to create or import drawings, clip art, tables, worksheets, and graphs in slides.

Clip Art

One way to add visual or auditory interest to a presentation is to insert a clip-art drawing. The PowerPoint ClipArt Gallery contains more than a thousand drawings that cover a wide range of topics; you can also import clip art from other programs. Microsoft's online Clip Gallery (office.microsoft.com/clipart) contains more than 120,000 graphic images and sounds, including clip art, photographs, and Web animations. PowerPoint also has the ability to insert video files.

You can insert clip art into a slide in several ways. If you are using Auto-Layout, you simply double-click on the clip-art placeholder. You can also insert clip art by following these steps:

1. Display the slide into which you want to insert clip art.
2. From the Insert menu, choose Picture and then Clip Art.
3. Search for clip art in the subject fields provided, or select an option from the category list (ClipArt, Pictures, Sounds, or Videos).
4. Select a picture, and then choose OK. PowerPoint closes the ClipArt Gallery dialog box and inserts the picture into your slide.

Charts

To insert a chart into a slide, select Chart from within the pull-down menu under Insert on the main toolbar. You will see a sample chart with data sets (see Figure 22.7). You can select the type of chart you want to create (column, bar,

Figure 22.7 Using Charts to Add Visual Impact

line, pie, and so on) and input the appropriate data. The chart will automatically be inserted into the slide.

Tables and Worksheets

In a slide, a table or a worksheet can convey useful information as long as it is simple and large enough to read. To insert a table in PowerPoint, select Table from the pull-down menu under Insert on the main toolbar. For older Power-Point versions, import tables from Word or Excel. See the accompanying checklist for step-by-step directions on inserting tables and worksheets into older versions of PowerPoint.

Movies and Sounds

Recent versions of PowerPoint allow you to include movie clips or sounds in your presentations. PowerPoint comes with a variety of built-in movie and sound clips, or you can import them from other sources to add interest to your presentation. PowerPoint can also play a track from a compact disc connected to your computer.

MAKING HARD COPIES

In case of technical problems or to help audience members follow along, many instructors urge their students to provide hard copies of their PowerPoint presentations. PowerPoint offers a number of options for formatting hard copies of your presentations. To choose an option, select the File button from the main

---

✓ CHECKLIST

Inserting Tables and Worksheets into PowerPoint

____ 1. To create a table or a worksheet using an older version of Power-Point, choose Insert Microsoft Word Table or Insert Microsoft Excel Worksheet in the standard toolbar. A drop-down grid of cells appears.

____ 2. Click and drag the mouse pointer across the cells in the grid to indicate how many rows or columns you want in your table or worksheet. When you release the mouse button, PowerPoint inserts a special object into your slide. Toolbars for either Word or Excel will replace the PowerPoint toolbars when the special object is selected. In effect, with the special object you are using either Word or Excel inside a PowerPoint window.

____ 3. To create the content of the table or worksheet, use the mouse, the tab key, or the arrow keys to move from cell to cell and type in the text. When you have entered all of the desired content, select Exit to insert the object into the slide. Deselect the object by clicking in a blank area of the slide.

---

menu and then select Print. Under the Print What label are four choices for output format. To see how an option will look, select it and then click the Preview button. The four options are as follows:

1. The *Slides* option displays each slide on a single piece of paper, as it will appear on the screen.

2. The *Handouts* option displays slides either three or six to a page (with three to a page, there are useful lines for note taking adjacent to each slide).

3. The *Notes Pages* option provides each slide on a single piece of paper with space for note taking.

4. The *Outline* option offers the text of the slides organized into outline format.

Remember that providing handouts or hard copies can sometimes be distracting; consider giving them to audience members only after your speech or if you have technical problems with PowerPoint.

RUNNING THE PRESENTATION

There are several ways to run a PowerPoint slide show (see Table 22.1). You can run an on-screen slide show by completing the following steps:

1. Open the presentation for which you want to run a slide show.

2. Choose the Slide Show command under View in the standard toolbar, or click the Slide Show button in the lower-left corner of the screen.

TABLE 22.1 • Commands to Run a PowerPoint Slide Show

Function	Method
Show the next slide	Click the left mouse button or press the space bar, N, right arrow, down arrow, or Page Down
Show the preceding slide	Click the right mouse button or press Backspace, P, left arrow, up arrow, or Page Up
Show a specific slide	Type the number and press Enter
Access Meeting Minder or pointers	Click the right mouse button and select the appropriate option
Toggle the mouse pointer on or off (show or hide)	Type A or the equal sign
Toggle between a black screen and a current screen	Type B or a period
Toggle between a white screen and a current screen	Type W or a comma
End the show	Press ESC, hyphen, or CTRL-Break
Pause and resume an automatic slide show	Type S or the plus sign

3. During your presentation, you can control your slides using the commands listed in Table 22.1 or move the pointer to the lower-left corner of the screen; a small pop-up will appear, and clicking it brings a menu with options.

PowerPoint offers a number of tools that you can use during a presentation. By clicking the right mouse button, you can access navigation tools, the Meeting Minder, and a variety of pointers. The **Meeting Minder** is a note-taking tool that allows you to take notes and give assignments known as "Action Items" in the middle of a presentation. Action Items are placed on the final slide of the presentation. This tool can be especially useful during a group presentation or a business meeting. The **pointer** tool allows you to show parts of a slide during your presentation; pointer options include an arrow and a pen that can be controlled by the mouse.

Downloading Stills, Sound, and Video in PowerPoint

With PowerPoint, you can import still images, clip art, video, or sound directly into your slides, either by downloading the files from the Internet or accessing them from a computer disk. Depending on your speech topic, you may be able to find files on the Internet that meet your needs.

For downloadable *digital images*, try the following Web sites:

Corbis.com (pro.corbis.com): Contains more than two million photographs, prints, and paintings, 35,000 of which you can download for your personal use (for a fee of about $6 per image).

Google (www.google.com) and *Yahoo!* (www.yahoo.com): Popular search engines that have evolved to include image searches.

The following sites contain free *photographs and other still images:*

www.encore.net   www.mcad.edu

www.freefoto.com   www.PictureQuest.com

The following sites offer downloadable *music files:*

www.kazaa.com   www.mp3now.com

www.mp3.com   www.RioPort.com

Try these sites if you're looking for *audio clips:*

www.dailywav.com   www.soundamerica.com

www.4wavfiles.4anything.com   www.wavcentral.com

www.freeaudioclips.com   www.wavsounds.com

The following sites contain useful *video clips:*

CNN Video Select (www.cnn.com/video) and *ABCNews.com Newsclips* (abcnews.go.com/sections/us/video_index/video_index.html): Especially useful for speech topics on current events or timely social issues.

Yahoo! Video Search (video.search.yahoo.com): Offers an advanced search for Creative Commons content to help determine whether a video clip is copyrighted or in the public domain.

 CHECKLIST

Tips for Successfully Incorporating Electronic Presentations into Your Speech

✓   Don't let the technology get in the way of relating to your audience.

✓   As with nonelectronic presentations, talk to your audience rather than to the screen. Maintain eye contact as much as possible.

✓   Have a backup plan in case of technical errors.

✓   If you use a pointer (laser or otherwise), turn it off and put it down as soon as you have made your point.

✓   Never shine a laser pointer into anyone's eyes. It will burn them!

✓   Incorporate the aids into your practice sessions until you are confident that they strengthen, rather than detract from, your core message.

Forms of
Speeches

Forms of Speeches

Speaker's Reference
Forms of Speeches

23. The Informative Speech

Build Awareness and Understanding in Your Informative Speech

- Strive to enlighten (informative intent) rather than to advocate (persuasive intent). (p. 327)
- Choose compelling supporting material. (p. 327)
- Use clear transitions, introductions, and conclusions. (p. 328)
- Control your vocal delivery. (p. 328)
- Use presentation aids where appropriate. (p. 328)

Analyze the Audience's Informational Needs

Consider the Types of Informative Speeches

- Speeches about objects or phenomena (p. 330)
- Speeches about people (p. 330)
- Speeches about events (p. 330)
- Speeches about processes (p. 330)
- Speeches about issues (p. 331)
- Speeches about concepts (p. 331)

Choose Strategies for Conveying Information

- Use *definition* to clarify. (p. 332)
- Provide *descriptions* to paint a picture. (p. 333)
- Provide a *demonstration*. (p. 333)
- Offer an in-depth *explanation*. (p. 334)

Clarify Complex Information

- Build on prior knowledge. (p. 335)
- Use analogies that link concepts to something familiar. (p. 335)
- Use visual aids, including models and drawings. (p. 336)
- Demonstrate underlying causes. (p. 336)
- Check for understanding. (p. 337)

Arrange Speech Points in an Organizational Pattern

319

24. The Persuasive Speech

Select a Persuasive Purpose If Your Goal Is To:

- Influence an audience's attitudes, beliefs, or understanding of an issue. (p. 346)
- Influence an audience's behavior. (p. 346)
- Reinforce existing attitudes, beliefs, or behavior. (p. 346)

Increase the Odds of Achieving Your Persuasive Speech Goal By:

- Conducting a thorough audience analysis. (p. 348)
- Making your message relevant to the audience. (p. 348)
- Showing your listeners how the change you seek benefits them. (p. 348)
- Addressing topics that the audience feels strongly about. (p. 348)
- Seeking minor rather than major changes. (p. 348)
- Establishing credibility with your audience. (p. 349)

When Appealing to Emotion, Use Sound Reasoning

- Avoid deliberately arousing fear or otherwise manipulating listeners' emotions. (p. 352)

To Increase the Odds That Listeners Will Act on Your Message:

- Appeal to their needs. (p. 355)
- Appeal to the reasons they act as they do. (p. 356)
- Stress the message's relevance to listeners. (p. 358)
- Present the information at an appropriate level of understanding. (p. 358)
- Establish your credibility: Emphasize your expertise for speeches that stress facts and analysis; emphasize commonality with the audience for personal speeches. (p. 358)

25. Developing Arguments for the Persuasive Speech

Structure the Claims According to the Issue You Are Addressing

- When addressing whether something is or is not true, or whether something will or will not happen, make a *claim of fact*. (p. 364)
- When addressing an issue that relies on individual judgment of right and wrong for its resolution, make a *claim of value*. (p. 365)

- When proposing a specific outcome or solution to an issue, make a *claim of policy.* (p. 365)

Consider the Kinds of Evidence That Best Support Your Claim

- When audience members are aware of the issue in question, consider using evidence with which they are already familiar, based on adequate audience analysis focusing on their opinions of your topic. (p. 367)
- If your knowledge and credentials are such that the audience will find your opinions credible and convincing, consider using your own expertise as evidence. (p. 367)
- If the audience lacks knowledge of the topic and you are not a known expert on the subject, consider using examples, stories, testimony, facts, and statistics from external sources. (p. 368)

Test Your Evidence

- Is it directly relevant to your claim? (p. 368)
- Is it timely? (p. 368)
- Will the audience find the evidence and its source credible? (p. 368)

Employ Appropriate Lines of Reasoning to Validate Claims

- You can use the needs, desires, emotions, and values of audience members as the basis of their accepting some evidence *(motivational warrants).* (p. 369)
- You can rely on audience members' beliefs about the credibility of a source as the basis of their accepting some evidence *(authoritative warrants).* (p. 370)
- You can use audience members' beliefs about the reliability of factual evidence as the basis of their accepting some evidence *(substantive warrants).* (p. 371)
- Use *warrants by cause* when offering a cause-effect relationship as proof of the claim. (p. 371)
- Use *warrants by sign* when the topic allows you to infer that such a close relationship exists between two variables that the presence or absence of one may be taken as an indication of the presence or absence of the other. (p. 371)
- Use *warrants by analogy* when the topic allows you to compare two similar cases and infer that what is true in one case is true in the other. (p. 372)

Anticipate and Plan on Addressing Counterarguments to Your Position

- If you ignore obvious counterclaims to your position, you may lose credibility. (p. 372)

Beware of Logical Fallacies That Will Weaken Your Arguments

- Avoid *begging the question,* or using circular reasoning to state an argument in such a way that it cannot help but be true. (p. 373)
- Do not rely on popular opinion as evidence that your claim is true (*bandwagoning*). (p. 374)
- Avoid framing your argument as an either-or proposition (*either-or fallacy*). (p. 374)
- Avoid *ad hominem arguments* that attack an opponent instead of attacking the opponent's arguments. (p. 374)
- Avoid relying on irrelevant information to argue your point (*red herring fallacy*). (p. 374)
- Avoid *appeals to tradition.* (p. 375)

26. Organizing the Persuasive Speech

Select an Organizational Pattern Based on Your Argument, Audience, and Speech Goal

- Choose a pattern that works with your particular argument and evidence. (p. 376)
- Choose a pattern that will help you appeal to the target audience. (p. 377)
- Consider the refutation or problem-solution pattern for a hostile or a critical and conflicted audience. (p. 377)
- Consider the narrative pattern for sympathetic listeners. (p. 377)
- For an uninformed, less educated, or apathetic audience, focus on gaining listeners' attention and establishing credibility. Consider arranging points logically in a topical pattern. (p. 377)
- Choose a pattern that will help you elicit the reaction you seek from your audience (your *specific speech purpose*). (p. 378)

Use the Problem-Solution Pattern to Demonstrate the Nature of a Problem and Provide Justification for a Solution

- Define the problem and offer a solution (*problem-solution*). (p. 378)
- Define the problem, cite reasons for the problem, and offer a solution (*problem-cause-solution*). (p. 379)

Consider the Motivated Sequence Pattern When Urging Action

- Step 1: *Attention* — address listeners' core concerns. (p. 380)
- Step 2: *Need* — show listeners they have a need or problem that must be satisfied or solved. (p. 381)

- Step 3: *Satisfaction* — introduce the solution to the problem. (p. 381)
- Step 4: *Visualization* — provide a vision of outcomes associated with the solution. (p. 382)
- Step 5: *Action* — make a direct request of listeners. (p. 383)

If the Audience Is Already Aware of an Issue and Agrees That It Should Be Addressed, Consider the Comparative Advantage Pattern

- Determine alternatives to the problem — both pro and con to your position — that the audience will be aware of. (p. 383)
- Organize points to favorably compare your position to alternatives. (p. 383)
- The summary should include brief but compelling evidence demonstrating the superiority or comparative advantage of your option over competing ones. (p. 383)

If Listeners Disagree with You or Are Conflicted, Consider the Refutation Pattern

- State the opposing claim. (p. 384)
- Explain ramifications of the opposing claim. (p. 384)
- Present your argument and the evidence. (p. 384)
- Show the superiority of your claim through contrast. (p. 384)

27. Special Occasion Speeches

Identify the Primary Purpose of Your Special Occasion Speech

- Is it to *entertain* the audience? (p. 393)
- Is it to *celebrate* or recognize a person, place, or event? (p. 393)
- Is it to *commemorate* a person, place, or event? (p. 394)
- Is it to *inspire* your listeners? (p. 394)
- Is it to establish or reinforce the goals and values of the group sponsoring the event (*setting a social agenda*)? (p. 394)

Focus Your Speech of Introduction on Motivating the Audience to Listen to the Speaker

- Establish the speaker's credibility by describing relevant facts about his or her background and qualifications for speaking. (p. 395)
- Briefly describe the speaker's topic and establish its relevance to the audience. (p. 395)
- Keep your remarks brief. (p. 395)

Focus Your Speech of Acceptance on Expressing Gratitude for the Honor Bestowed on You

- If you know that you are to receive an award or suspect that you may be honored, prepare the speech in advance. (p. 397)
- Let the audience know what the award means to you. (p. 397)
- Express yourself genuinely and with humility. (p. 397)
- Thank each of the individuals or organizations involved in giving you the award. (p. 398)
- Acknowledge others who helped you attain the achievement. (p. 398)

Focus Your Speech of Presentation on Explaining the Award and the Reason It Is Being Bestowed on the Recipient

- Explain what the award represents. (p. 398)
- Explain why the recipient is receiving the award. (p. 399)

Focus Remarks Made at Roasts and Toasts on the Person Being Honored

- For a roast, prepare a humorous tribute to the person. (p. 399)
- For a toast, pay brief tribute to the person or event. (p. 399)
- Prepare your remarks in advance. (p. 399)
- Rehearse any jokes in advance. (p. 400)
- Keep within your time limits. (p. 400)

When Delivering a Eulogy, Pay Tribute to the Life of the Deceased

- Stay in control of your emotions. (p. 400)
- Refer to each family member of the deceased by name. (p. 401)
- Focus on the person's life rather than on the circumstances of death. (p. 401)
- Emphasize the person's positive qualities. (p. 401)

When Delivering an After-Dinner Speech, Balance Insight and Entertainment

- Begin by recognizing the occasion and linking it to your theme. (p. 402)
- Avoid stand-up comedy. Use humor that is consistent with your personality. (p. 402)
- When addressing serious issues and causes, keep an eye on the audience's comfort level. (p. 403)

Focus Your Speech of Inspiration on Uplifting the Audience

- Seek to arouse the audience's better instincts. (p. 403)

- Focus on creating positive speaker ethos (see Chapter 4). (p. 403)
- Appeal to the audience's emotions through vivid descriptions and emotionally charged words. Consider the use of repetition, alliteration, and parallelism (see Chapter 16). (p. 403)
- Consider using real-life stories and examples. (p. 403)
- Strive for a dynamic delivery style. (p. 404)
- Clearly establish your speech goal. (p. 404)
- Consider using an acronym to organize your message. (p. 404)
- Make your conclusion strong. (p. 405)

KEY TERMS

Chapter 23

informative speaking
operational definition
definition by negation

definition by example
definition by synonym

definition by etymology (word origin)
analogies

Chapter 24

persuasion
persuasive speaking
forms of rhetorical proof
logos
syllogism
major premise
minor premise
deductive reasoning

hasty overgeneralization
enthymeme
pathos
demagogue
fear appeal
propaganda
ethos
Maslow's hierarchy of needs

expectancy-outcome values theory
elaboration likelihood model (ELM) of persuasion
central processing
peripheral processing
speaker credibility

Chapter 25

argument
claim
evidence
warrants
claims of fact
speculative claims
claims of value
claims of policy

motivational warrants
authoritative warrants
substantive warrants
warrants by cause
warrants by sign
warrants by analogy
inoculation effect
logical fallacy

begging the question
bandwagoning
either-or fallacy
ad hominem argument
red herring fallacy
appeal to tradition

Chapter 26

claim of policy
claim of value
claim of fact
cause-effect pattern of organization
target audience

hostile audience or one that strongly disagrees
critical and conflicted audience
narrative organizational pattern

sympathetic audience
uninformed, less educated, or apathetic audience
topical pattern of arrangement
specific speech purpose

problem-solution pattern
of arrangement

problem-cause-solution
pattern of arrangement

motivated sequence
pattern of arrangement

comparative advantage
pattern of arrangement

refutation pattern of
organization

Chapter 27

special occasion speech

social agenda–setting

speech of introduction

speech of acceptance

speech of presentation

roast

toast

eulogy

after-dinner speech

canned speeches

sermons

speech of inspiration

The Informative Speech 23

Ever wondered how to prune a tree so that it will flower profusely the following year? Or which careers will be most financially rewarding in the next decade? What are the facts about outsourcing? Exactly where are the jobs going, and which jobs are likely to remain in the United States? What about the difference between a stock and a bond? What is a nebula, and how is one formed?

Informative speaking about these and countless other topics is one of the primary ways in which we share knowledge and keep abreast of ideas and events. In the guise of the classroom lecture, you've been exposed to informative speaking since grade school. Beyond the classroom, managers gather employees to explain new procedures and generate enthusiasm for new projects. Researchers report and explain their findings to their colleagues and to the press, while authorities on everything from team sports to terrorism share their expertise from the podium.

Goals and Strategies of Informative Speaking

To *inform* is to communicate knowledge. The goal of **informative speaking** is to increase the audience's awareness and understanding by imparting knowledge. Informative speeches provide an audience with new information, new insights, or new ways of thinking about a topic. As an informative speaker, you might introduce listeners to new ideas, events, people, places, or processes. You might explain information with which listeners have some familiarity but little real understanding, thereby shaping their perceptions. Your speech might be an in-depth analysis of a complex subject, a simple description of an event, or a physical demonstration of how something works. As long as your audience learns something, the options are nearly limitless.

LOOK FOR WAYS TO INCREASE UNDERSTANDING

People are not simply empty vessels into which you can pour facts and figures and expect them to recognize and remember all that information. Before we can retain information, we must be motivated to listen to it and be able to recognize and comprehend it.[1] Many of the public speaking principles described in previous chapters directly apply to presenting information in a speech. For example, Chapter 8 discusses how to flesh out speech points with compelling supporting materials, such as examples, stories, opinions, and facts. Chapter 16 demonstrates ways you can use language to connect to your audience and help listeners to visualize ideas; it also demonstrates how rhetorical devices such as repetition and parallelism can reinforce information and drive home key themes. Research confirms[2] that our ability to process information delivered in oral form is also aided by:

- *An appropriate organizational pattern.* Audience members' understanding of a speech is directly linked to how well it is organized (see Chapters 11–13 and 26).[3]
- *Clear transitions.* Signal words, phrases, and sentences that tie speech ideas together help listeners follow the speaker's points (see Chapter 11).
- *Introductions and conclusions.* The introduction clearly previews main points and the conclusion concisely summarizes them (see Chapters 14 and 15).
- *Controlled vocal delivery.* Crucial to communicating any oral message is speaking slowly and clearly enough to permit listeners to process the words (see Chapter 18).
- *Presentation aids.* People process and retain information best when it is reinforced visually and otherwise (see Chapters 20–22).[4]

 CHECKLIST

Help Listeners Process and Retain Information

✓ Make ample use of transitions to help guide listeners.
✓ Concisely preview main points in the introduction and summarize them in the conclusion.
✓ Control your vocal delivery.
✓ Reinforce your message visually and otherwise where appropriate.

DIFFERENTIATE BETWEEN INFORMING AND PERSUADING

The goal of an informative speech stands in contrast to that of the persuasive speech, which explicitly attempts to influence people's attitudes, values, beliefs, or behavior about an issue. Whereas a persuasive speech would seek to modify attitudes or ask the audience to adopt a specific position, an informative speech stops short of this. Yet scholars of public speaking point out that there is no such thing as a purely informative or persuasive speech; that is, there are always elements of persuasion in an informative speech, and vice versa. Rarely are we entirely dispassionate about a subject, especially one that tends to elicit strong reactions. Nevertheless, if you keep in mind the general informative speaking goal, you will be able to deliver an informative speech whose primary function is to enlighten rather than to advocate.

GAUGE THE AUDIENCE'S INFORMATIONAL NEEDS

An understanding of audience members and the factors that affect them is critical to delivering an effective informative speech. Listeners must be able to identify with the topic, see its relevance to their lives, and follow it to its logical conclusion. They must see how they can use and benefit from the information you give them. To ensure that this occurs, you will need to gauge what your listeners already know about a topic as well as what they want and need to know about it (see Chapter 6).

DEMONSTRATE THE TOPIC'S RELEVANCE EARLY ON

Whenever possible, early on in your speech (in your preview statement, for example) tell audience members why they should listen to you. Do this by pointing out how what they will learn from your presentation will benefit them. Giving listeners a reason to care can motivate them to pay attention to your message.

PREVIEW MAIN POINTS

Give listeners a sense of the whole before plunging into particulars, and offer them specific signposts they can follow (see Chapter 11). In the introduction, preview your main points and summarize what you want them to gain from the speech:

> I'll begin by defining what the music industry means by "pirating." Next I will discuss the Supreme Court's ruling in *MGM v. Grokster*. . . . By the end of this presentation, I hope that you will. . . .

PRESENT NEW AND INTERESTING INFORMATION

Audiences seek knowledge, which means learning something new. To satisfy this drive, try to uncover information that is fresh and compelling. Seek out unusual sources (but make certain they are credible), novel (but sound) interpretations, startling facts, compelling examples, and moving stories. As professional speaker Vickie K. Sullivan notes:

> The first point that transforms an ordinary speaker into an industry beacon is a new perspective on a major problem. . . . If the speech does not convey provocative information, audience members feel their time has been wasted (and rightfully will feel offended). They expect their thinking to be challenged.[5]

Types of Informative Speeches

Informative speeches are sometimes categorized according to the subject matter they address. Thus an informative speech may be about objects or phenomena, people, events, processes, issues, or concepts. These are not hard-and-fast divisions—a speech can be about both the process of dance and the people who perform it, for example — but they show the range of informative subjects and may point you in the direction of a suitable organizational pattern (see the section on organizing the informative speech on pages 337–338).

SPEECHES ABOUT OBJECTS OR PHENOMENA

Speeches about objects or phenomena explore anything that isn't human; it can be animate, as in the animal kingdom, or inanimate, as in skis or skates. Topics for such speeches run the gamut from ribbons used to raise awareness about diseases such as breast cancer and AIDS to seeing-eye dogs and the musical score for *Spamalot*. Phenomena such as the history of lacrosse as a sport and the evolution of "Texas English" also belong to this broad category.

SPEECHES ABOUT PEOPLE

Speeches about people inform audiences about historically significant individuals and groups, those who have made contributions to society (both positive and negative) or those who for one reason or another we simply find compelling. Who are the Lost Boys of Sudan, and why are they noteworthy? What led Mother Teresa to devote her life to the poor?

Rather than someone's fame, the key to giving an effective speech about a person is sharing stories that resonate with the audience. People are naturally curious about others, but they also need a reason to care. Often this can be accomplished by recounting anecdotes or extended stories that stress the person's achievements and human qualities (see Chapter 8).

SPEECHES ABOUT EVENTS

Speeches about events focus on noteworthy occurrences, past and present. What led up to the 1952 proclamation of Puerto Rico as a commonwealth? What occurred at the battle of Puebla in 1862 that led to victory of the Mexican army over the French and is celebrated today as Cinco de Mayo? Speeches about events can have any number of specific purposes. One speaker may wish to paint a vivid picture or description of what it was like to narrowly escape an avalanche while on a snowmobile. Another speech on the same topic might focus more on the incidences of avalanches in the United States, their major causes, and ways to safeguard against them.

SPEECHES ABOUT PROCESSES

Speeches about processes refer to a series of steps that lead to a finished product or end result. In this type of speech you can talk about how something is done, how it is made, or how it works. Sample speech topics might include how a hybrid car works or finishing furniture.

When discussing a process, you will probably have one of two purposes. One is to explain how something works or develops. How will the male birth-control pill work? How do baby penguins develop? The other is to actually teach audience members to perform the process. Such topics might include how to share an electronic photo album online, make salsa at home, or interview for a job.

When describing how to do something, speakers often perform the actual task during the speech, demonstrating each step as they describe it. When it is not possible to perform the task, visual or audio aids may be used to illustrate the steps involved. Visual aids are also essential in explaining processes. To illustrate how to make a Shaker-style table, for example, you might use drawings or photographs showing the table at various stages of construction.

To see the nearly infinite number of processes that can be used as the basis of a speech of demonstration, visit Wikipedia's "how-to" Web site and Google's eHow.com. Both may be found at www.ehow.com. For ideas about visually showing how things work, see HowStuffWorks.com at www.howstuffworks.com.

SPEECHES ABOUT ISSUES

An *issue* is a problem or a matter in dispute, one that people seek to bring to a conclusion. Informative *speeches about issues* provide an overview or a report of problems in order to increase understanding and awareness. Pornography on the Internet and teaching alternative theories to evolution are examples of topics about issues.

Of the various types of informative speeches, speeches about issues have the greatest potential of "crossing the line" into the persuasive realm. Yet as long as your goal is to inform rather than to advocate, you can legitimately address issues in an informative speech. Thus, in a speech on teenage pregnancy, you might define the nature of the problem and describe the various positions people take with respect to it. Such a speech might also offer explanations of why teenage pregnancy occurs. On the other hand, you would refrain from attributing teenage pregnancy to one cause (such as premarital sex) and advocating one solution to it (such as abstinence).

SPEECHES ABOUT CONCEPTS

Speeches about concepts focus on abstract or complex ideas or theories and attempt to make them concrete and understandable to an audience. What is chaos theory? What is art? Is it a child's drawing, a master's painting, or both? We've heard the term *hate speech,* but we're confused because it seems to encompass everything from racist expressions to racist actions.

Listeners may not be able to see a concept, but a good speaker can deftly evoke its meaning by associating it with certain actions or behaviors. In describing anxiety, for example, the speaker might describe the increased heart rate and distressed facial expressions that accompany the condition. Because they address abstract or complex ideas, speeches about concepts have the potential to confuse audience members. To ensure that this does not occur, follow the guidelines in "Strategies for Reducing Confusion" later in this chapter (p. 335).

Approaches to Conveying Information

Typically, speakers communicate information by defining, describing, demonstrating, and/or explaining. Some informative speeches rely almost exclusively on a single approach (e.g., their main purpose is to demonstrate how something works or to describe what something is). Many speeches, however, employ a combination of strategies in a single presentation. As you prepare your speech, ask yourself, "By which of these means can I best convey my ideas?"

DEFINITION

Informative speaking often involves defining information. When you define information, you identify the essential qualities and meaning of something. What is a fractal? What is cholesterol? What does "equilibrium price" mean in business studies? Many informative speeches focus on questions such as these, addressing the meaning of a new or complex concept. A speaker might choose to define a new software program to a group of colleagues; a corporate spokesperson might define the Americans with Disabilities Act to the heads of various divisions within a company.

You might also select definition when clarifying a complex or controversial idea or issue. For example, many of us are aware that prayer in the public schools has been ruled unconstitutional, but precisely how does the Constitution or its amendments define prayer?

Defining information may sound straightforward, but there are in fact a number of ways to define something, including the following:

- **Operational definition:** Defines something by explaining what it does. For example: "A computer is something that processes information."
- **Definition by negation:** Defines something by describing what it is not. For example: "Courage is not the absence of fear."

 CHECKLIST

Define Your Terms

Clear definitions are especially important in informative speeches. If you are unsure whether audience members will know the meaning of a term, plan to define it in one or more of the following ways:

✓ Define your term by explaining what it does.
✓ Define your term by describing what it is not.
✓ Define your term by providing several concrete examples of it.
✓ Define your term by comparing it with something with which it is synonymous.
✓ Define your term by illustrating the root meaning of the term.

- **Definition by example:** Defines something by providing several concrete examples of it. For example: "Health professionals include doctors, nurses, EMTs, and ambulance drivers."
- **Definition by synonym:** Defines something by comparing it to something with which it is synonymous. For example: "A friend is a comrade or a buddy."
- **Definition by etymology (word origin):** Defines something by illustrating the root meaning of the word in question. For example, "Our word *rival* derives from the French word, which in turn derives from the Latin word *rivalis*. The original meaning of *rivalis* is 'one living near or using the same stream.'"[6]

DESCRIPTION

When you describe information, you provide an array of details that paint a mental picture of your topic. You may be recounting a bullfight in Pamplona, Spain, or describing the physical ravages wrought by drug abuse. Regardless of the specific subject, the point of speeches relying on description is to offer a vivid portrayal of the topic.

While all types of speeches involve description, some speeches focus on this task more centrally than others. For example, the goal of your speech of description might be to offer your audience a "virtual tour" of the top of Mount Everest, the 1937 World's Fair in Paris, or a painting by Pablo Picasso.

DEMONSTRATION

Yet another approach to presenting information is to explain how something works or to actually demonstrate it. The many "how to" shows on television, ranging from cooking to carpentry, rely on demonstration. Speech topics such as "childproofing your home" or "bidding on eBay" may not include an actual physical demonstration, but the speaker will nevertheless verbally demonstrate the steps involved. Speeches that rely on demonstration often work with the actual object, representations or models of it, or visual aids that diagram it. Table 23.1 contains sample topics for a speech of demonstration.

TABLE 23.1 • Sample Topics for a Speech of Demonstration

• Mastering the position of attention for a military drill	• Performing the Heimlich maneuver on infants
• Treating a burn	• Pulling a shot of espresso
• Selling on eBay	• Drawing blood from an animal
• Stippling a wall	• Performing an emergency tracheotomy
• Marbleizing furniture	• Making stained glass
• Raising ducks	• Waxing skis and snowboards
• Giving an insulin shot	• Framing a picture
• Programming a cell phone/DVD player	

EXPLANATION

Explanation goes beyond simple clarification of terms or concepts or a description of them. When you explain something, you provide reasons or causes, demonstrate relationships, and offer interpretation and analysis. The classic example of explaining information is the classroom lecture (see Chapter 30). But many kinds of speeches rely on explanation, from those that address difficult or confusing theories and processes to ideas that challenge conventional

TABLE 23.2 • Types of Informative Speeches, Sample Topics, and Selected Informational Strategies

Subject Matter	Sample Topics	Informational Strategy (*definition, description, demonstration, explanation*)
Speeches about objects or phenomena	• Digital cameras • Texas English • Comparison of weight-loss diets • El Niño wind patterns in the western U.S.	*Define* and *describe* the object or phenomenon in question. Depending on your specific speech purpose, either conclude at that point or continue with an in-depth *explanation* or a *demonstration* of the object or phenomenon.
Speeches about people	• Athletes • Authors • Inventors • Political leaders • Soldiers • War or hurricane refugees	Paint a vivid picture of your subject using *description*. Use *explanation* to address the person's or group's significance.
Speeches about events	• Live Aid and Live 8 concerts • Democratic or Republican national conventions • Battle of Gettysburg • National College Cheerleading Finals	Use *description* to paint a vivid picture. Use *explanation* to analyze the meaning of the event.
Speeches about processes	• Isolating DNA in cells • How lightning forms • How the thyroid regulates metabolism • How to practice Power Yoga • Using visualization in sports	If physically showing a process, rely on *demonstration*. If explaining a process, vary strategies as needed. See the checklist on p. 337 for strategies for explaining complex processes.
Speeches about issues	• Racial profiling • Alternative theories to evolution • Political issues in the Middle East • Outsourcing • Climate change • No Child Left Behind legislation	Focus on *description* and *explanation*.
Speeches about concepts	• Einstein's theory of relativity • Artificial intelligence • Fractals • Nanotechnology • Free speech	Focus on clear *definitions* and *explanations;* the more difficult a concept is, the more ways you will want to define and explain it. Vivid *description* can also be useful.

thinking. What is the relationship between the glycemic index, which measures how quickly a carbohydrate raises blood sugar, and glycemic load? Why do researchers say that sometimes emotion makes us more rather than less logical?

✓ CHECKLIST

Use the Power of Language to Connect with the Audience

_____ 1. Use concrete and colorful nouns and verbs that convey your meaning in a specific and tangible way.

_____ 2. Use repetition to help listeners retain information.

_____ 3. Appeal to listeners' sense of smell, taste, sight, hearing, and touch.

_____ 4. Use *similes*—figures of speech that compare one thing to another (see Chapter 16).

_____ 5. Use *metaphors*—figures of speech that compare two things by describing one thing as being the other (see Chapter 16).

Strategies for Reducing Confusion

New information can be hard to grasp, so if your topic has the potential for confusion, consider why this might be so. Generally, audience members tend to find information daunting for one or more of the following reasons:[7]

1. The information entails *difficult concepts or terms;* for example, concepts such as *equilibrium* in engineering, *liability* in business, or *techtonics* in geology.

2. The information involves a *difficult-to-envision process or structure;* for example, the *process of cloning* in science, *cash flow management* in business, or *structure of DNA.*

3. The information involves a *counterintuitive idea,* one that challenges accepted ways of thinking about things. Many scientific concepts challenge commonsense thinking and are hard to grasp; for example, that seemingly solid materials are made of tiny atoms and mostly empty space or that medical studies indicate that drinking one glass of red wine a day is healthy.

Useful for any informative speech, the following strategies are especially helpful when attempting to clarify complex ideas.

USE ANALOGIES TO BUILD ON PRIOR KNOWLEDGE

It is easier to understand a new concept if we can relate it to something that we already know. Indeed, the process of learning itself is sometimes defined as constructing new knowledge from prior knowledge.[8] Explanations that link the unfamiliar with the familiar often take the form of **analogies** (see Chapter 16). For example, to explain the unpredictable paths that satellites often take when they fall to Earth, one speaker likened its effects to dropping a penny into water: "Sometimes it goes straight down, and sometimes it turns end over end and changes direction. The same thing happens when an object hits the atmosphere."[9]

Speakers will sometimes organize part or even all of a speech around an analogy. When explaining how the thyroid functions, for instance, you could liken it to a conductor directing a symphony (the body).[10] Bear in mind, however, that no analogy can exactly represent another concept; at a certain point, the similarities will end.[11] Therefore, you may need to alert listeners to the limits of the comparison. The statement "The heart is like a pump, *except that the heart actually changes size as it pushes blood out*" demonstrates that, though similar, a heart and a pump are not the same.[12]

Analogies, as well as metaphors and similes (see Chapter 16), can help establish a common ground of understanding. Once this occurs, your listeners will have an easier time venturing into new territory, especially if the information you present is counterintuitive.

In the following excerpt from a speech about nanotechnology, Wolfgang Porod explains the size of a nanometer by comparing it to the diameter of the moon. Note how he attempts to reduce confusion by first defining the root *nano* and then comparing it to the size of the moon:

> What is a nano and what is special about a nano? *Nano* is a prefix derived from the Greek word for dwarf and it means one billionth of something. So a nanosecond is a billionth of a second. A nanometer is a billionth of a meter. Now, just saying that doesn't really tell you that much. So what does it mean to have the length scale of a billionth of a meter? Well, imagine the diameter of the moon. It just happens to be, roughly . . . a billion meters. So take that and shrink it down to the length scale of a meter, which is what it means to go a billion size scales. So a nanometer is a billionth of a meter.[13]

USE VISUALIZATION

As described in Chapter 20, people grasp information best when it is presented in more than one format. Presentation aides — drawings, models, videos, and other graphic illustrations — can help listeners see the "big picture."[14]

DEMONSTRATE UNDERLYING CAUSES

Oftentimes listeners will fail to understand a process because they lack an understanding of its underlying causes. They may believe that something "obviously" works a certain way when in fact it does not. To counter faulty assumptions, first acknowledge common misperceptions and then offer an accurate explanation or causal model.[15]

Dry hands thoroughly with a clean paper towel. To prevent chapping, pat rather than rub hands dry and apply lotion liberally and frequently.

[WALK TO DOOR AND HOLD DOORKNOB] When exiting the restroom, use a paper towel to open the door, as the CDC estimates that only one out of three people washes their hands after using the restroom. Putting a barrier between your hands and the doorknob will prevent the recontamination of your hands.

If there is no soap or water available, there are other alternatives. For example, you can use an antibacterial, waterless hand sanitizer, such as Purel brand Instant Hand Sanitizer. You can use the larger bottle at home or maybe on your desk at work. The small bottles fit very nicely in a purse, pocket, tackle box, or glove compartment.

You can also use moist towelettes that contain an antibacterial agent, such as the Wet Ones brand. These can be conveniently kept in a purse or pocket. You can find these moderately priced hand sanitizers or towelettes in most supermarkets, drugstores, or department stores.

Washing your hands regularly can certainly save a lot of medical bills. • Because it costs less than a penny, you could say that this penny's worth of prevention could save you a fifty-dollar visit to the doctor.

> • The speaker points to another benefit to the audience, offering yet another new insight on a familiar process.

Now that you understand the importance of hand washing and how to properly wash your hands, practice and teach the proper hand-washing techniques to others, especially children, so that they too can form a good habit of hand washing. •

> • The speaker signals the close of the speech.

It's a simple fact. When hand washing is done correctly, it is the number-one means of preventing the spread of infection. • You don't have to take these rubber gloves into the public rest room with you. You just have to follow these simple steps. Doing so will make the world a healthier place for everyone.

> • The speaker concludes by reiterating the importance of handwashing.

Sample Informative Speech

Nonmonetary Uses of Gold

CHRISTA KIM

Santa Rosa Junior College

In this speech about an object or phenomenon (gold), Christa Kim reveals a "treasure trove" of new information about the world's most venerated metal. Christa's speech is organized topically, in which the main points describe gold's various properties and applications.

Conveys enthusiasm during the introduction

King Midas was desperately poor but had a good heart. As a reward for his compassion, the gods granted him a single wish, and King Midas, seeking to alleviate his poverty, immediately wished that everything he touched would turn into solid gold. •

The story illustrates the point that, like King Midas, when we think of gold, we too usually focus only on the monetary value of it, whether it is the gold bricks in Fort Knox or expensive jewelry.

• Kim captures listeners' attention with an interesting story.

What we don't realize is that gold plays a much bigger role in all of our lives. So tonight we are going to explore the nonmonetary uses of gold. To do this, we will first unearth the unique properties of this metal. We will then see how these characteristics have panned out in the medical field to both prevent and alleviate diseases. Finally, we will sift through some applications made by NASA. •

• Kim succinctly states the thesis, previews the main points, and makes skillful use of metaphoric language ("unearth," "pan," and "sift").

Now, the first unique characteristic of gold is its extreme density. •

• Kim uses a full-sentence transition to move into her first main point.

When we usually think of dense elements, we think of lead, which is extremely dense. In fact, lead is so dense that whenever we get an X-ray, we wear a lead apron to protect us from radiation. Well, gold, according to the 1996 Macmillan *Encyclopedia of Earth Sciences*, is one and a half times more dense than lead. •

Reveals visual aid no. 1

Engineers have already taken advantage of this characteristic by using extremely thin films of gold to coat electronic switches and relays. In telephones, for example, there are over thirty-three of these gold-plated contacts, which work within the main component of the phone, the diaphragm, to transform electric signals into sound.

• Kim uses a series of blown-up illustrations to help the audience visualize her points. Placing them face down on an easel, she turns them over to show listeners only when she makes her point. In this way, the images do not distract audience members.

coated with gold to shield and protect the astronaut from harmful radiation. • Gold, therefore, has become a critical element in space travel.

Shows visual aid no. 3

In addition to enabling communication and exploration in space, gold, believe it or not, is also working to preserve a bit of our own culture. Once formed, gold maintains its shape whatever the environmental conditions. It is for this reason that gold was the material selected to press the record *Sounds of Earth*, which, according to Carl Sagan in his book *Cosmos*, was sent aboard the *Voyager* spacecraft in 1977 and is only now exiting our solar system. The record jacket gives instructions in scientific notation for how to play the record, while the record itself contains information about Earth's cultures and civilizations.

Visual aid no. 4 includes two complementary images

Included on this record is information about our genes, our anatomy, and our DNA. The record includes greetings from over sixty different cultures as well as music. We placed the record on *Voyager* with the hope that a bit of our culture would be preserved and perhaps even found by distant beings. And because gold is so durable, this golden record, which tells so much about the planet's journey through space and time, will long outlive all life on Earth.

Offers a warm smile after closing the speech

While gold will continue to play an important role monetarily, it should now be clear that the nonmonetary uses of gold have a huge impact on our daily lives. • On Earth, doctors are able to utilize the characteristics of density, ductility, and noncorrosiveness to treat conditions such as lagophthalmos, rheumatoid arthritis, and potentially even the HIV virus. In space, NASA is able to utilize these very same characteristics to enable satellite communication and exploration and to preserve a bit of our own culture. It should now be apparent that these doctors, researchers, and engineers who are using gold in nonmonetary ways to enrich our everyday lives truly do possess the real Midas touch. •

• A photograph helps visualize Kim's verbal description.

• Kim concludes her speech by summarizing her main points.

• She brings the speech full circle with her reference to the "Midas touch."

24   The Persuasive Speech

Persuasive speaking is a type of public speaking you will practice frequently throughout your professional and personal life. To persuade is to influence, advocate, or ask others to accept your views. Whether you are bargaining for a raise, convincing a fellow town resident of the need for a new school, or giving a formal speech, success or failure rests on how well or how poorly you understand the principles and practices of the art of persuasion.

What Is a Persuasive Speech?

Persuasive speeches are meant to appeal to the audience's attitudes, beliefs, and values about the issue in question and to sway listeners to the speaker's point of view. Derived from the Greek verb meaning "to believe,"[1] **persuasion** is the process of influencing attitudes, beliefs, values, and behavior. **Persuasive speaking** is speech that is intended to influence the attitudes, beliefs, values, and acts of others.

PERSUASIVE SPEECHES ATTEMPT TO INFLUENCE AUDIENCE CHOICES

Chapter 23 describes the general goal of informative speeches as that of increasing understanding and awareness. Persuasive speeches also serve to increase understanding and awareness. They present an audience with new information, new insights, and new ways of thinking about an issue. In fact, persuasive speeches do all the things informative speeches do. But rather than only seeking to increase understanding and awareness, the explicit goal of the persuasive

---

✓ **CHECKLIST**

Conditions for Choosing a Persuasive Purpose

You should select a persuasive purpose if:

_____ 1. Your goal is to influence an audience's beliefs or understanding about something.

_____ 2. Your goal is to influence an audience's behavior.

_____ 3. Your goal is to reinforce audience members' existing attitudes, beliefs, or behavior so they will continue to possess or practice them.

TABLE 24.1 • Characteristics of Persuasive Speeches

- Persuasive speeches attempt to influence the attitudes, beliefs, values, and acts of others.
- Persuasive speeches limit alternatives.
- Persuasive speeches seek a response.
- Persuasive speeches respect audience choices.

speech is to influence audience choices.[2] The persuasive speaker tries to some-how influence the opinions or actions of his or her audience. These choices may range from slight shifts in opinion to wholesale changes in behavior.

PERSUASIVE SPEECHES LIMIT ALTERNATIVES

Any issue that would constitute the topic of a persuasive speech represents at least two viewpoints. For example, there are "pro-choice" advocates and "right-to-life" advocates; supporters of candidate Brezinski and supporters of candidate Morales; those who oppose a new holiday bonus plan and those who advocate it; and those who prefer brand X MP3 player over brand Y. With any such issue, it is the objective of a persuasive speaker to limit the audience's alternatives to the side the speaker represents. This is done not by ignoring the unfavorable alternatives altogether but by contrasting them with the favorable alternative and showing it to be of greater value or usefulness to the audience than the other alternatives.

PERSUASIVE SPEECHES SEEK A RESPONSE

By showing an audience the best of several alternatives, the persuasive speaker asks listeners—sometimes explicitly and sometimes implicitly—to make a choice. If the speech is effective, the audience's choice will be limited; that is, listeners will understand that the alternative presented by the speaker is the "right" choice.

Ethically Speaking
Persuasive Speeches Respect Audience Choices

Even though persuasive speeches present audiences with a choice, the ethical persuasive speaker recognizes that the choice is ultimately the audience members' to make—and he or she respects their right to do so. People take time to consider what they've heard and how it affects them. They make their own choices in light of or despite the best evidence. Your role as a persuasive speaker is not to coerce or force your listeners to accept your viewpoint but to present as convincing a case as possible so that they might do so willingly. For instance, you might want to persuade members of your audience to become vegetarians, but you must also respect their choice not to adopt this path.

The Process of Persuasion

Persuasion is a complex psychological process of reasoning and emotion. When you speak persuasively, you try to guide the audience to adopt a particular attitude, belief, or behavior that you favor. But getting people to change their minds, even a little, is difficult and requires considerable skill. Just because you think something is reasonable or right does not guarantee that someone else will think so, too. Each of us has a unique way of looking at the world based on our own particular blend of attitudes, beliefs, and values.

Discovering your listeners' attitudes, beliefs, and values provides crucial clues to how receptive they will be toward your topic and your position on it. (See Chapter 6 for a review of the definitions of these terms.) As in informative speeches, therefore, *audience analysis* is extremely important in persuasive speeches. To influence your listeners, you must try to understand how their attitudes, beliefs, and values might affect the way they view your position. Once you have this information, you can adapt your appeals in ways that might best reach them. As one scholar of persuasion notes, "Persuasion requires curiosity. It demands a willingness to explore the mind-set of others . . . a Sherlock Holmes mentality."[3]

Be aware, however, that regardless of how thoroughly you have conducted audience analysis or how skillfully you present your point of view, audiences seldom respond immediately or completely to a persuasive appeal. Persuasion does not occur with a single dose. An audience can be immediately "stirred," as the Roman orator Cicero put it, with relative ease. However, producing a lasting impact on listeners' attitudes, beliefs, and behavior is a more difficult matter. Changes tend to be small, even imperceptible, especially at first.

Several key factors increase the odds that your efforts at persuasion will succeed:

- To be most persuasive, your message should be personally relevant to the audience.[4]

- Barring coercion, people are unlikely to change unless they can see how doing so will benefit them.[5]

- People are more likely to act on strong attitudes than on weak ones.[6]

- People who feel highly involved in your message will react differently than those who feel less involved.[7]

- The persuader who seeks only minor changes is usually more successful than the speaker who seeks major ones.

- Audience members' feelings toward you strongly influence how receptive they will be to your message. Attitude change is related to the extent to which the speaker is perceived to be credible.[8]

- People want to feel satisfied and competent. If you can show that an attitude or a behavior might keep them from this state, they are more likely to be receptive to change.

Increasing the Odds of Achieving Your Persuasive Speech Goal

_____ 1. Clearly demonstrate your topic's relevance to the audience.

_____ 2. Clearly demonstrate how any changes you propose will benefit the audience.

_____ 3. Target issues that audience members are likely to feel strongly about. If they don't much care about an issue, it is unlikely that they will pay much attention to it.

_____ 4. Set modest goals. Expect minor rather than major changes in your listeners' attitudes and behaviors.

_____ 5. Establish your credibility with your listeners.

_____ 6. Expect to be more successful when addressing an audience whose position differs only moderately from yours.

_____ 7. Try to convince your listeners that by taking the action you propose they will be rewarded in some way.

- You are more likely to persuade audience members if their position differs only moderately from yours. For example, if you are trying to persuade an audience to support a bill that protects the environment, you are more likely to convince those who in general are favorably disposed toward environmentalism than those who have a consistently strong track record of opposing such legislation.

- In order for change to endure, listeners must be convinced that they will be rewarded in some way. For example, to persuade people to lose weight and keep it off, you must make them believe that they will be healthier if they do so. Persuaders who achieve this are skilled at motivating their listeners to help themselves.[9]

Following is a brief overview of how the ancient scholars of rhetoric, and Aristotle in particular, viewed the process of persuasion. Much of classical theory on persuasion remains relevant today. Next is a review of how contemporary social scientists approach persuasion. Both of these perspectives provide useful tools for creating successful persuasive speeches. Both approaches recognize that all persuasive messages depend on appeals to listeners' reasoning, emotions, and feelings about the speaker.

Classical Persuasive Appeals

In his classical treatise on rhetoric, Aristotle explained that persuasion could be brought about by the speaker's use of three means of persuasion, or **forms of rhetorical proof**. The first concerns the nature of the message in a speech; the second, the nature of the audience's feelings; the third, the qualifications and personality of the speaker. According to Aristotle, and generations of theorists and practitioners who followed him, you can build an effective persuasive speech with any one or a combination of these factors.

LOGOS: APPEALS TO AUDIENCE REASON

Many persuasive speeches focus on issues that require considerable thought. Should universities abolish tenure? Should pregnant teenagers be required to seek their parents' permission in order to have an abortion? Are certain television programs too violent for children? When an audience needs to make an important decision or reach a conclusion regarding a complicated issue, appeals to reason and logic are necessary. Aristotle used the term **logos** to refer to persuasive appeals directed at the audience's reasoning on a topic. Such appeals make considerable use of *arguments* — that is, stated positions, with support for or against an idea or issue.

Aristotle differentiated between two forms of rational appeal and offered the second as especially useful for persuasive speaking. The first is the **syllogism**, a three-part argument consisting of a **major premise**, or general case; a **minor premise**, or specific case; and a conclusion logically following from the first two steps. The classic example is this:

MAJOR PREMISE: All men are mortal.

MINOR PREMISE: Socrates is a man.

CONCLUSION: Therefore Socrates is a mortal.

Syllogisms are a form of **deductive reasoning**, or reasoning from a general condition to a specific instance.[10] Some are positive and constructive, leading to clearer understanding of an issue; others are inappropriate and poorly applied, leading to unfounded conclusions. Here is an example of a contemporary syllogism that has positive implications:

MAJOR PREMISE: Regular exercise enhances your ability to study productively.

MINOR PREMISE: Swimming is good exercise.

CONCLUSION: Swimming regularly will enhance your ability to study productively.

And here is one that has negative implications:

MAJOR PREMISE: Rosslyn gets all A's even though she never attends class.

MINOR PREMISE: Rosslyn is on the college softball team.

CONCLUSION: All college athletes get all A's even though they never attend class.

The preceding example shows how erroneous conclusions can be reached if you begin with a major premise that is unfounded. In this case, the major premise is a **hasty overgeneralization**, or an attempt to support a claim by asserting that a particular piece of evidence (an isolated case) is true for all individuals or conditions concerned. (See the section on fallacies in reasoning in Chapter 25.) Although the minor premise may be true, the conclusion is based on an overgeneralization. In contrast, the first example is an effective syllogism. It reaches a sound conclusion from an accurate major premise applied to a minor premise. Thus appeals to reason using syllogism in a persuasive speech require accurate knowledge of the information that forms your major and minor premises. This is a key consideration as you build your arguments.

A second form of rational appeal in a persuasive speech is the enthymeme. An **enthymeme** is a syllogism presented as a probability rather than as an absolute, and it states either a major or a minor premise but not both. The premise not stated is implied and serves as a mental tool for connecting the speaker and audience.[11] The syllogism about Socrates leads to the absolute conclusion that Socrates is a mortal if both of the stated premises are accurate and true. The syllogism about swimming can be restated as an enthymeme so that the conclusion is probably true but not necessarily always true:

MAJOR PREMISE TO CONCLUSION: Regular exercise enhances your ability to study productively, so swimming regularly should enhance your studying.

Implied in this example is that swimming is a good form of exercise. Implied in the next example is that exercise will enhance your ability to study well:

MINOR PREMISE TO CONCLUSION: Swimming is good exercise and should enhance your studying.

The use of "should" in each case makes the conclusion tentative instead of absolute. Why would you want to offer probable conclusions in a persuasive speech instead of certain conclusions? *Because most arguments are not based on certainty.* It is not absolutely certain, for example, that swimming regularly will enhance your studying because many other factors are involved in studying. The point is, if your argument is to hold sway, the conclusion has to be certain enough for the audience to accept the premise. The key for both syllogisms and enthymemes is that your premises be acceptable according to sound reasoning or logic. (See Chapter 25 for an in-depth discussion of building arguments for the persuasive speech.)

PATHOS: APPEALS TO AUDIENCE EMOTION

Another means of persuasion is appealing to listeners' emotions. The term Aristotle used for this is **pathos**. It requires "creating a certain disposition in the audience."[12] Aristotle taught that successful public speakers identify and appeal to four sets of emotions in their listeners.[13] He presented these sets in opposing

Ethically Speaking
Using Emotions Ethically

The most successful persuaders are those who are able to understand the mind-set of others. With such insight comes the responsibility to use emotional appeals in speeches for ethical purposes only. As history attests only too amply, not all speakers follow an ethical path in this regard. Demagogues, for example, clutter the historical landscape. A **demagogue** relies heavily on irrelevant emotional appeals to short-circuit the listeners' rational decision-making process.[1] Senator Joseph McCarthy, who conducted "witch hunts" against alleged Communists in the 1950s, was one such speaker. Many cult leaders are also masters of manipulating their followers' emotions toward unscrupulous ends. Adolf Hitler played on the fears and dreams of German citizens to urge them toward despicable ends.

Persuasive speakers can manipulate their listeners' emotions by arousing fear and anxiety and by using propaganda.

- *Fear and anxiety.* Some speakers deliberately arouse fear and anxiety in an audience so that listeners will follow their recommendations. Sometimes this is done by offering a graphic description of what will happen if the audience doesn't comply (e.g., people will get hurt, children will starve). Although the **fear appeal** has a legitimate place in persuasion — as in demonstrating to children the harm caused by smoking, or showing a group of drunken drivers graphic pictures of the results of their actions — it must be used carefully and fairly. (Note that for a fear appeal to succeed, it must be delivered by a speaker whom the audience perceives to be highly credible.)[2]

- *Propaganda.* Speakers who employ **propaganda** aim to manipulate an audience's emotions for the purpose of promoting a belief system or dogma. Propagandists tell audiences only what they want their listeners to know, deliberately hiding or distorting opposing viewpoints. They engage in name-calling and stereotyping to arouse their listeners' emotions. (See also the Ethically Speaking box in Chapter 10, "Learn to Distinguish among Information, Propaganda, Misinformation, and Disinformation.")

Unlike the ethical persuader, the propagandist does not respect the audience's right to choose; nor does the speaker who irresponsibly uses fear appeals. Ethically, appeals to emotion in a persuasive speech should always be supported by sound reasoning.

1. Charles U. Larson, *Persuasion: Reception and Responsibility,* 6th ed. (Belmont, Calif.: Wadsworth, 1992), 37.
2. Joseph C. Gardiner, "An Experimental Study of the Effects of Evidence and Fear Appeals on Attitude Change and Source Credibility," research monograph, Department of Communication, Michigan State University, 1969; G. M. Miller and M. A. Hewgill, "Some Recent Research on Fear-Arousing Message Appeals," *Speech Monographs* 33 (1966), 377–91, cited in James C. McCroskey, *An Introduction to Rhetorical Communication,* 8th ed. (Boston: Allyn and Bacon, 2001).

pairs: anger and meekness, love and hatred, fear and boldness, shame and shamelessness. Means of invoking these emotions in a speech include the use of *vivid description* and *emotionally charged words.* Consider the following example of vivid description from Mario Cuomo, former governor of New York, who delivered the keynote speech at the Democratic National Convention on July 16, 1984. The speech praises the values of America's working class and the freedom given these individuals by a democratic government to pursue their work and their dreams. Cuomo uses his father as an example:

> I watched a small man with thick calluses on both hands work fifteen and sixteen hours a day. I saw him once literally bleed from the bottoms of his feet, a man who came here uneducated, alone, unable to speak the language, who taught me all I needed to know about faith and hard work by the simple eloquence of his example. I learned about our kind of democracy from my father. I learned about our obligation to each other from him and from my mother. They asked only for a chance to work and to make the world better for their children and to be protected in those moments when they would not be able to protect themselves. This nation and its government did that for them.[14]

The vivid description of what Cuomo learned from observing his immigrant father evokes emotions of boldness and pride in his democratic heritage, and perhaps anger toward those who would oppose that heritage.

Although emotion is a powerful means of moving an audience, relying solely on naked emotion to persuade will fail most of the time. As Aristotle stressed, *pathos functions as a means to persuasion not by any persuasive power inherent in emotions per se but by the interplay of emotions—or desire—and sound reasoning.* Emotion gets the audience's attention and stimulates a desire to act on the emotion; reason is then presented as justification for the action. Recent persuasion research confirms this effect.[15] For example, a popular television advertisement depicts a grandfatherly man in a series of activities with family members. An announcer makes the logical appeal that people with high blood pressure should maintain their prescribed regimen of medication; this is followed by the emotional appeal "If not for yourself, do it for them." The message invokes the desire to stay healthy as long as possible for the benefit of loved ones. The reasoning is sound enough: Blood pressure is controllable with medication, but one must take the medicine in order for it to work. In this case, as in many, emotion helps communicate the idea.

Appealing to an audience's emotions on the basis of sound reasoning ensures that your speech is ethical. However, as seen in the Ethically Speaking box (p. 352), there are a host of ways in which emotions can be used unethically.

ETHOS: APPEALS TO SPEAKER CHARACTER

No matter how well reasoned a message is or which strong emotions its words target, if audience members have little or no regard for the speaker they will not respond positively to his or her persuasive appeals. Aristotle believed that speechmaking should emphasize the quality and impact of ideas, but he recognized that the nature of the speaker's character and personality also plays an important role in how well the audience listens to and accepts the message. He referred to this effect of the speaker as **ethos**, or moral character.

Displaying Ethos in the Persuasive Speech

- Demonstrate your competence as a speaker by knowing your subject well and by emphasizing your expertise.
- Be straightforward and honest in presenting the facts of your argument as you see them.
- Reveal your personal moral standards vis-à-vis your topic early in the speech.
- Demonstrate a genuine interest in and concern for the welfare of your listeners.

Exactly which elements of a persuasive appeal are based on ethos? Let's briefly consider each element in turn, and how you as the speaker can demonstrate them. The first element is *good sense*. Another term for this element of ethos is *competence*, or the speaker's knowledge of and experience with the subject matter. Ethos-based appeals emphasize the speaker's grasp of the subject matter. Skillfully preparing the speech at all stages, from research to delivery, as well as emphasizing your own expertise, evokes this quality.

The second element of an ethos-based appeal is the speaker's *moral character*. This is reflected in the speaker's straightforward and honest presentation of the message. The speaker's own ethical standards are central to this element. Current research suggests, for example, that a brief disclosure of personal moral standards relevant to the speech or the occasion made in the introduction of a speech will boost audience regard for the speaker.[16] Indeed, you should prepare and present every aspect of your speeches with the utmost integrity so that your audiences will regard you as trustworthy. The fact that you are an honest person will not be the most memorable aspect of your speeches, but the very fact that dishonesty is not expected of you makes it easy to identify in the content or delivery of your message.

The third element of an ethos-based appeal is *goodwill* toward the audience. Everything this text has discussed regarding audience analysis and knowledge of the speech occasion applies to this element. A strong ethos-based appeal demonstrates an interest in and a concern for the welfare of your audience. Speakers who understand the concerns of their listeners and who address their needs and expectations relative to the speech exhibit this aspect of the ethos-based appeal.

Contemporary Persuasive Appeals

The classical modes of persuasion are as useful today as they were more than 2,000 years ago. However, with the application of scientific methods to the study of communication, the approaches taught by Aristotle have been significantly refined and expanded.[17] Contemporary research in persuasion focuses on the factors that cause us to change or maintain our attitudes. These theories suggest that for persuasion to succeed, the message must effectively target (1) audience members' needs, (2) their underlying motivations for feeling and acting as they do, and (3) their likely approach to mentally processing the persuasive message.

PERSUADING LISTENERS BY APPEALING TO THEIR NEEDS

Have you ever wondered why there are so many fast-food commercials during and after the evening news? Advertisers know that by this time of night many viewers are experiencing a strong need—to eat! Appealing to audience needs is one of the strategies most commonly used to motivate people, whether in advertising or in public speaking.

Perhaps the best-known model of human needs is that formulated by Abraham Maslow in the 1950s.[18] Maslow maintained that each person has a set of basic needs ranging from the essential, life-sustaining ones to the less critical, self-improvement ones. This set includes five categories arranged hierarchically (see Figure 24.1). According to Maslow, an individual's needs at the lower, essential levels must be fulfilled before the higher levels become important and motivating. **Maslow's hierarchy of needs** has long been a basis for motivation-oriented persuasive speeches. The principle behind the model is that people are motivated to act on the basis of their needs; thus to best persuade listeners to adopt suggested changes in attitudes, beliefs, or behavior, point to some need they want fulfilled and then give them a way to fulfill it. Critics of this approach suggest that needs may not be organized in a hierarchy and that, in fact, we may be driven as much by wants as by needs.[19] Nevertheless, the theory points to the fact that successful appeals depend on trying to understand what motivates the audience. Table 24.2 describes the five basic needs that Maslow identifies and suggests actions that you as a speaker can take to appeal to them.

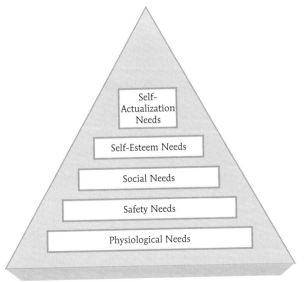

Figure 24.1 Maslow's Hierarchy of Needs

TABLE 24.2 • Using Needs to Motivate Listeners

Need	Speech Action
Physiological needs (the need for basic sustenance, including food, water, and air)	• To ensure that your listeners can give their full attention to your persuasive message, plan for and accommodate the audience's physiological needs in the speech situation (e.g., are they likely to be hot, cold, hungry, or thirsty?).
Safety needs (the need to feel protected and secure)	• Appeal to the safety benefits your listeners will reap by adopting your message (e.g., if you want them to wear seat belts, vote for a bill to stop pollution, or buy a home security system, stress how taking certain steps will protect them from harm).
Social needs (the need to establish and maintain lasting, meaningful relationships with others)	• Appeal to the social benefits your listeners will reap by adopting your message (e.g., if you want an audience of teenagers to quit smoking, stress that if they quit they will appear more physically fit and attractive to their peers; if you want your listeners to oppose a piece of legislation, tell them about other supporters with whom they are likely to positively identify).
Self-esteem needs (the need to feel good about ourselves — that we matter and that we are worthwhile)	• Appeal to the emotional benefits your audience will reap by adopting your position (e.g., when proposing a change in attitudes or behavior, stress that the proposed change will make listeners feel better about themselves).
Self-actualization needs (the need to reach our highest potential; to achieve what we wish to accomplish; to reach the goals that we have set for ourselves)	• Appeal to your listeners' need to fulfill their potential (e.g., stress how adopting your position will help them "be all that they can be").

PERSUADING LISTENERS BY APPEALING TO THE REASONS FOR THEIR BEHAVIOR

The audience is not merely a collection of empty vessels waiting to be filled with whatever wisdom and knowledge you have to offer. Members of an audience are rational, thinking, choice-making individuals. Their day-to-day behavior is directed mainly by their own volition, or will. According to **expectancy-outcome values theory**, which was developed by Icek Ajzen and Martin Fishbein, each of us consciously evaluates the potential costs and benefits (or "value") associated with taking a particular action. As we weigh these costs and benefits, we consider our attitudes about the behavior in question (e.g., "Is this a good or a bad behavior?") as well as what other people who are important to us might think about the behavior (e.g., "My friend would approve of my taking this action"). On the basis of these assessments, we develop expectations about what will happen if we do or do not take a certain action (e.g., "My friend will think more highly of me if I do this"). These expected "outcomes" become our rationale for acting in a certain way. *Thus when you want to persuade listeners to change their behavior, you should try to identify these expected outcomes and use them to appeal to your audience.*[20]

The principles of expectancy-outcome values theory can help you plan a persuasive speech in which the specific purpose is to target behavior. A thorough audience analysis (in the form of a questionnaire) is critical to this approach, however (see the section on surveys in Chapter 6). Putting the theory into practice, as you conduct your audience analysis, you will need to seek out (1) your listeners' attitudes about the behavior you are proposing that they change, as well as (2) their feelings about the consequences associated with that behavior. Consider the case of unsafe sex. If your goal is to persuade audience members to practice safe sex, using a questionnaire you could identify (1) listeners' feelings about the practice and (2) their feelings about the consequences of not practicing safe sex. Assume you find that most audience members consider safe sex to be a good practice and most agree that not practicing safe sex has potentially serious negative risks. Knowing these attitudes, you have a good foundation for presenting your listeners with evidence that will support their attitudes and strengthen your argument that they should practice safe sex.

Third (3), try to determine what audience members believe other significant people in their lives think about the behavior in question, and the audience members' willingness to comply with those beliefs. Continuing with the example of practicing safe sex, you could question audience members about the extent to which they think their partners and close friends care about practicing safe sex and whether the audience members would be more or less willing to comply with these other people's presumed preferences. Assume you find that most audience members believe their partners support practicing safe sex and that most would go along with their partners' preferences. You now have a basis for appealing to your audience's concern for their partners' preferences regarding the practice of safe sex. Figure 24.2 illustrates the steps to take when seeking to persuade an audience to adopt a course of action, based on the principles of expectancy-outcome values theory.

1. Investigate listeners' attitudes toward the specific behavior you are targeting in your speech (e.g., practicing safe sex, taking vitamin supplements, adopting a vegetarian diet, etc.).

↓

2. Identify listeners' beliefs about the consequences of their behavior (e.g., "I believe I will contract a venereal disease if I don't practice safe sex" or "I believe I will remain disease-free even if I don't practice safe sex").

↓

3. Investigate what the audience members believe *significant others in their lives* think about the behavior in question (e.g., my girlfriend is very concerned about health).

↓

4. Demonstrate the positive outcomes of adopting a course of action *favored by audience members' significant others* (e.g., "Practicing safe sex will lead to a great level of trust and intimacy between you and your partner").

Figure 24.2 Steps in Persuading Listeners to Change Their Behavior

PERSUADING LISTENERS BY FOCUSING ON WHAT'S MOST RELEVANT TO THEM

According to Richard Petty and John Cacioppo's **elaboration likelihood model (ELM) of persuasion**, each of us mentally processes persuasive messages by one of two routes, depending on the degree of our involvement in the message.[21] When we are motivated and able to think critically about the content of a message, we engage in **central processing** of the message. That is, we seriously consider what the speaker's message means to us and who are the ones most likely to act on it. We are the listeners who are most likely to experience a relatively enduring change in thinking that is favorable to the speaker's position.

Not everyone listens critically, however. When we lack the motivation (or the ability) to pay close attention to the issues, we engage in **peripheral processing** of information. In this form of mental processing of the speaker's persuasive message, we respond to it as being irrelevant, too complex to follow, or just plain unimportant.

Listeners who process messages peripherally are far more likely to be influenced by such non-content issues as the speaker's appearance or reputation, certain slogans or one-liners, and obvious attempts to manipulate emotions. Even though such listeners may "buy into" the speaker's message, they do so not on the strength of the arguments but on the basis of such factors as the speaker's reputation or personal style. In this case, the listener "goes with whatever the speaker says" because of who the speaker is, not because of the quality or substance of the message. Although this may seem like a positive speech outcome, the problem is that such shallow acceptance of a speaker's message has very limited impact on the listener's enduring thoughts and feelings about the matter. Listeners who use peripheral processing are unlikely to experience any meaningful changes in attitudes or behavior. Central processing produces the more long-lasting changes in audience perspective.

To put the principles of the ELM model of persuasion into practice when planning a persuasive speech, (1) make certain that your message is relevant to your listeners, (2) make certain that you present it at an appropriate level of understanding, and (3) establish your credibility with the audience (Figure 24.3). Establish a common bond with your listeners, and ensure that they see you as trustworthy. These steps will increase the odds that your persuasive appeal will produce lasting, rather than fleeting, changes in their attitudes and behavior.

PERSUADING LISTENERS THROUGH SPEAKER CREDIBILITY

Beyond the qualities of speaker knowledge, moral character, and goodwill toward the audience that ancient scholars such as Aristotle described in terms of ethos, modern behavioral science has identified four other speaker-based factors that affect the outcomes of persuasive messages: expertise, trustworthiness, speaker similarity, and physical attractiveness. Taken as a set, these factors are referred to as **speaker credibility**.

The audience's perceptions of a speaker's expertise and trustworthiness are critical contributors to persuasiveness.[22] Speaker *expertise* contributes to the

Make your message relevant to your specific audience.

("How many times have you wanted to express your opinion about an important issue such as tuition and fees or stem cell research but can't find the right forum?")

↓

Present your message at an appropriate level of understanding.

("An intriguing option for expressing your opinions is to post them on blogs. A blog is an online journal offering a writer's thoughts in chronological order and sometimes including space for replies. Let me give you an example . . .")

↓

Establish your credibility with the audience.

("In this screen capture from my own blog, you will see an entry I posted and the almost forty responses that I received.")

Figure 24.3 Steps in Increasing Acceptance of Your Persuasive Message

persuasive outcomes of a speech under two conditions. First, when audience members are relatively unmotivated or unable to fully grasp a message, their responses to the speech will probably be in the speaker's favor if the speaker is perceived as an expert on the subject. Second, when audience members themselves are well informed about the message and perceive the speaker as someone who has expertise, he or she will be more apt to persuade them. Note that "expert" doesn't mean you're a world authority on the topic or issue of your speech. What it does mean is that you have enough knowledge and experience on the subject to be able to help the audience to better understand and accept it.

If there is one speaker attribute that is more important than others, it is probably *trustworthiness*.[23] It's a matter of the "goodwill" that Aristotle taught—audiences want more than information and arguments; they want what's relevant to them from someone who cares. Indeed, audience members who perceive the speaker to be high in credibility will regard the communication as more truthful than a message delivered by someone who is seen to have low credibility.[24]

Speaker Similarity

Two additional critical elements in the speaker-audience relationship that influence the outcome of a persuasive message are speaker similarity and physical attractiveness. *Speaker similarity* involves listeners' perceptions of how similar the speaker is to themselves, especially in terms of attitudes and moral character. Generally, audience members are more likely to respond favorably to the persuasive appeals of a speaker whom they perceive to be a lot like them. This is not always the case, however. In certain situations we attach more credibility to people who are actually dissimilar to us. For example, we are more likely to be persuaded by a dissimilar speaker, especially one viewed as an "expert," when the topic or issue emphasizes facts and analysis. This is why lawyers seek the expert testimony of psychiatrists or other specialists to provide insight into the

✓ **CHECKLIST**

Tips for Increasing Speaker Credibility

____ 1. Prepare well and demonstrate a thorough grasp of your topic.

____ 2. Enlighten your audience with new and relevant information.

____ 3. Demonstrate your trustworthiness by presenting your topic honestly and in a way that shows concern for your listeners.

____ 4. For speeches that involve a lot of facts and analysis, emphasize your expertise on the topic.

____ 5. For speeches of a more personal nature, emphasize your commonality with the audience.

____ 6. Be well groomed.

personality of a suspect, the features of a crime scene, and the like. On the other hand, an audience is more likely to be persuaded by a similar speaker when the subject is personal or relational. For example, we prefer to watch *The Oprah Winfrey Show* instead of *60 Minutes* when the subject is fathers and daughters, or bosses and secretaries. We tend to perceive Oprah Winfrey as being more similar to us in relational concerns than we do Leslie Stahl. But if the issue involves new details in a political scandal or a foreign agreement, we would probably turn to Ed Bradley as our preferred source. These facts point to an important lesson for the persuasive speaker: *For speeches that involve a lot of facts and analysis, play on whatever amount of expertise you can summon. For speeches that concern matters of a more personal nature, however, it's best to emphasize your commonality with the audience.*

Speaker Attractiveness

Finally, the *physical attractiveness* of the speaker affects persuasive outcomes. A quick look at the physical features of any of a dozen television news anchors and talk-show hosts suggests that physical attractiveness is a significant benefit to speakers. By and large, looking good does pay off for a speaker in terms of persuasive outcomes. In our culture, attractive people are perceived to be competent, in control of themselves, well organized, and confident. We tend to generalize these perceptions to public speakers as well. But there are limitations, even drawbacks, to physical attractiveness as a factor in persuasive speaking. First, highly attractive speakers can be a distraction to an audience, drawing their attention away from the message. Second, physical attractiveness can interfere with persuasive appeals when the speaker's appearance violates expectations for the occasion or the topic. Third, any positive outcomes of a persuasive speech that can be attributed to the speaker's attractiveness will probably be short-term gains at best. Our tendency is to respond positively to attractive speakers because we want to be like them or be associated with them. But responding primarily on that basis leads only to a superficial understanding of the message and fleeting attention to it.

Developing Arguments for the Persuasive Speech 25

The process of reasoning can be defined in different ways depending on the context in which it is applied. One definition of *reasoning* is "the power of comprehending, inferring, or thinking, especially in orderly, rational ways."[1] Reasoning in this sense is the process of critical thinking that we try to engage in throughout our everyday lives and in our roles as public speakers and active listeners. Another definition of *reasoning,* one that applies directly to creating a persuasive speech, is "the process of proving inferences or conclusions from evidence."[2] Reasoning in this sense is synonymous with argument, the topic of this chapter. Reasoning through a persuasive speech is a process of building one or more arguments created to change people's opinions, influence behavior, or justify the arguer's beliefs or actions.[3]

This chapter describes how to use argument as a framework for making appeals in persuasive speeches. Most persuasive speeches consist of several arguments.

What Is an Argument?

An **argument** is a stated position, with support for or against an idea or issue. Persuasive speeches use arguments to present one alternative as superior to other alternatives that are available to an audience. Speakers who present arguments ask listeners to accept a conclusion about some state of affairs by providing evidence and reasons that the evidence logically supports the claim. The core elements of an argument consist of a claim, evidence, and warrants:[4]

1. The claim states the speaker's conclusion, based on evidence, about some state of affairs.
2. The evidence substantiates the claim.
3. The warrants provide reasons that the evidence is valid or supports the claim.

STATING A CLAIM

To state a **claim** (also called a *proposition*) is to declare a state of affairs. Claims are often (but not always) presented as thesis statements. Claims answer the question "What are you trying to prove?"[5] If you want to convince audience members that they need to be more careful consumers of herbal supplements,

361

you might make this claim: "Many herbal supplements contain powerful substances that may interact in harmful ways with over-the-counter (OTC) or prescription drugs." This claim asserts that taking herbal supplements together with certain OTC or prescription drugs potentially poses a health risk. But unless your listeners already agree with the claim, it's unlikely that they'll accept it at face value. To make the claim believable, the speaker must provide proof, or evidence in support of the claim.

PROVIDING EVIDENCE

Every key claim you make in a speech must be supported with **evidence**, or supporting material that provides grounds for belief (see Chapter 8, "Developing Supporting Material"). In a speech about herbal supplements, for example, to support the claim that they can cause harm by interacting with OTC or prescription drugs, you might provide *statistics* showing the number of persons in a given year who were hospitalized as a result of such interactions. You might then couple these data with *testimony* from individuals who experienced health problems because of such drug interactions or from physicians who treated such patients.

The goal in using evidence is to make a claim more acceptable, or believable, to the audience. If the evidence itself is believable, then the claim is more likely to be found acceptable by the audience.

WARRANTS: JUSTIFYING THE LINK BETWEEN THE CLAIM AND EVIDENCE

Warrants, the third component of arguments, help both to support a claim and to substantiate in the audience's mind the link between the claim and the evidence. They show why the link between the claim and evidence is valid, or *warranted*. Other terms for warrants are *reasoning* and *justification*.

Although a piece of evidence may provide strong support for a claim, in order for listeners to accept the argument, the connection between the claim and the evidence must be made clear and justified in their minds. A warrant serves as a bridge between a claim and evidence. For example, the claim that some herbal supplements, in conjunction with other drugs, can cause health problems may not be clear to listeners. Some good warrants can make the link between claim and evidence clearer. The argument can be supported by showing that:

> According to the American Council on Science and Health, serious side effects have occurred in cases where people consumed prescription blood thinners such as warfarin (Coumadin®) with herbal supplements such as St. John's Wort, Kava, and Valerian. Further, drugs that suppress the immune system, such as corticosteroids or cyclosporine, have been shown to have harmful effects when interacting with supplements such as Echinacea, St. John's Wort, and Zinc.[6] [EVIDENCE]

The link between the claim and the evidence can be justified by the following:

> Several leading medical journals and organizations, including the American Council on Science and Health, have reported cases documenting harmful interactions between a variety of supplements and medications. [WARRANT]

This provides a justification for accepting the link between the evidence and the claim. The claim is supported.

Diagramming the argument allows you to visualize how the evidence and warrants can be presented in support of your claim. Figure 25.1 illustrates the three components of the preceding argument about the dangers of drug–supplement interactions. As you consider formulating an argument, try to diagram it in a similar fashion:

1. Write down the claim.
2. List each possible piece of evidence you have in support of the claim.
3. Write down the corresponding warrants, or justifications, that link the evidence to the claim.

In the following excerpt from a 2002 address to the United Nations, President George W. Bush speaks about the threat to peace posed by Iraq under the regime of Saddam Hussein. Bush claims that Iraq's decade-long defiance of U.N. demands to comply with its Security Council resolutions can no longer be

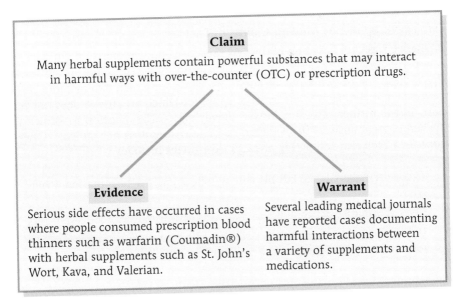

Figure 25.1 Core Components of Argument

tolerated. In the speech, Bush makes several claims and offers evidence and support for each of them. Excerpted here are several claims from the speech:

> In 1991 the U.N. Security Council . . . demanded that Iraq denounce all involvement in terrorism and permit no terrorist organizations to operate in Iraq. Iraq's regime agreed. It broke this promise. [CLAIM]
>
> In violation of Security Council Resolution . . . Iraq continues to shelter and support terrorist organizations that direct violence against Iran, Israel, and Western governments. Iraqi dissidents abroad are targeted for murder. . . . In 1993 Iraq attempted to assassinate the emir of Kuwait and a former American president. [EVIDENCE]
>
> The history, the logic and the facts lead to one conclusion: Saddam Hussein's regime is a grave and gathering danger. [WARRANT][7]

Types of Claims, Evidence, and Warrants

A variety of claims, evidence, and warrants are at your disposal for making an argument. The ones you select will depend on the nature of your topic and the specific purpose of your persuasive speech.

CLAIMS USED IN PERSUASIVE SPEECHES: FACT, VALUE, AND POLICY

Depending on the nature of the issue being addressed, a persuasive speech can consist of three different kinds of claims: of fact, of value, and of policy. Different types of claims require different kinds of supporting evidence.

Persuasive Speeches Making Claims of Fact

Persuasive speeches based on **claims of fact** focus on whether something is or is not true or whether something will or will not happen. Claims of fact usually address one of two kinds of questions: those for which two or more controversial, competing answers exist; or those for which an answer does not yet exist. In the former case, the answer already exists. The question is, Which is the best or right answer? In the latter case, the answer does not yet exist. Questions for which two competing answers exist might include:

- Did actor Robert Blake kill his wife despite a jury's determination otherwise?
- Does affirmative action discriminate against nonminority job applicants?
- Is homosexuality a genetically determined orientation, an outcome of environmental influences, or the result of a combination of factors?

An argument based on any of these questions will need to give evidence in support of one answer as superior to an alternative answer.

The other kind of question of fact addresses questions for which answers are not yet available. Probable answers to such questions are called **speculative claims**. Such questions might include:

- Will a woman president be elected in the United States within the next ten years?
- Will the World Trade Organization (WTO) change its charter in response to criticisms by opponents of globalization?
- Will currency be completely replaced by credit cards within the next ten years?

Persuasive Speeches Making Claims of Value

When relatives or physicians assist a terminally ill patient in planning a suicide, questions arise about the morality of assisted suicide, suicide in general, and the role of medical practitioners in aiding death as they aid life. Situations such as these lie in the realm of claims of value. Persuasive speeches based on **claims of value** address issues of judgment. Is assisted suicide ethical? Should doctors be in the business of helping patients to die as well as to live? When, if ever, is suicide justified? Rather than attempting to prove the truth of something, as in claims of fact, a speaker arguing a claim of value tries to show that something is right or wrong, good or bad, worthy or unworthy.

Like claims of fact, claims of value require evidence. However, the evidence in support of a value claim tends to be more subjective than factual. In defending assisted suicide, for example, a speaker might be able to show that in certain situations compassion requires us to help terminally ill people take their own lives.

Persuasive Speeches Making Claims of Policy

Speakers use **claims of policy** when recommending that a specific course of action be taken, or approved of, by an audience. Legislators regularly construct arguments based on claims of policy: Should we pass a law restricting the use of handguns/abortion/firecrackers? Anyone can argue for a claim of policy as long as he or she advocates for or against a given plan. Such claims might include:

- Full-time students who commute to campus should be granted reduced parking fees.
- Students who earn an A average on all speech assignments should be exempt from the final exam.
- Property taxes should be increased to fund classroom expansions at the city's elementary schools.

Notice that in each claim the word *should* appears. A claim of policy speaks to an "ought" condition, proposing that certain better outcomes would be realized if the proposed condition was met.

To build a strong case for a claim of policy, you must provide the audience with a three-part justification consisting of (1) a need or a problem, (2) a solution, and (3) evidence of the solution's feasibility. (See Chapter 26 for more on the problem-solution pattern of arrangement.)

By nature, claims of policy involve claims of fact and often claims of value as well. Consider the following example:

POLICY CLAIM: The city should provide walking paths in all municipal parks.

FACT: Almost every park in the city is busy several times each day with recreational walkers. This activity is noticeably greater on weekends.

VALUE: Walking on properly maintained paths is healthier both for walkers and for the park landscape.

The fact and value claims become, essentially, pieces of evidence in support of the policy claim. The fact statement provides objective evidence, and the value statement offers a more subjective justification of the policy. This suggests that successful speakers need to be quite familiar with all three kinds of argument (see Table 25.1).

So far, we have seen that persuasive speeches can consist of three different kinds of claims: of fact, of value, and of policy. Regardless of the type of claim you make, if you fail to provide convincing evidence in support of it, the audience will not accept it. The following section reviews the different types of evidence used to support these claims.

TABLE 25.1 • Sample Claims for Speeches of Fact, Value, and Policy

Type of Speech	Claim of fact *(focuses on whether something is or is not true or whether something will or will not happen)*	Claim of value *(addresses issues of judgment)*	Claim of policy *(recommends that a specific course of action be taken, or approved of, by an audience)*
Sample Claim	• Demand for online college courses will be strong in the next decade. • Interactions between herbal supplements and OTC drugs can be harmful. • Breastfeeding is healthier than bottle feeding in the first year.	• The three strikes law is unfair. • The "ideal weight" chart is not ideal. • Title IX hurts male athletes.	• Cigarette prices should be lowered. • Airport security measures should be revamped. • The NBA draft should be changed.

USING EVIDENCE TO SUPPORT YOUR CLAIMS

In addition to the kinds of evidence described in Chapter 8 (examples, narratives, testimony, facts, and statistics), all of which can be considered as external evidence (see p. 368), several other kinds of evidence exist that you can use to persuade audiences to believe your claims.[8] You might, for example, rely on audience members' existing knowledge and opinions—on what listeners already think and believe—as evidence for their claims. Or you might use your own knowledge and expertise as evidence. Finally, you might use the kind of external evidence with which you are already familiar—that of narratives, testimony, facts, and statistics.

Audience Knowledge and Opinions

Research suggests that what your listeners already know or think about your topic ultimately determines their acceptance or rejection of claims you make about it.[9] Nothing is more persuasive to listeners than a reaffirmation of their own attitudes, beliefs, and values, especially when making claims of value and policy. For this reason, the *audience's knowledge and opinions* on the topic can often be the most persuasive evidence. Using the audience's existing knowledge and beliefs as evidence for a claim works something like this:

CLAIM:	Natural life support for human activity on the moon may come sooner than we think.
AUDIENCE KNOWLEDGE AS EVIDENCE:	You've no doubt read in the papers and seen on the news that scientists recently discovered sources of water on the moon.
WARRANT:	Water found on the moon can be used to produce oxygen for human life support.

Here the speaker uses the audience's knowledge of the discovery of water on the moon to support the claim that natural life support will eventually be possible there. The warrant that water on the moon could be converted into oxygen creates a bridge between the evidence and the claim.

The key to using an audience's knowledge and opinions to support your claim is audience analysis. For example, if your topic is privacy on the Internet, you could conduct interviews or distribute surveys that elicit audience members' opinions and gauge what they know about privacy laws or other pertinent information. On the basis of their responses, you could select the evidence with which they are most likely to have some familiarity. Of course, if an audience lacks knowledge on the subject of your claims, you cannot use this kind of evidence. Another kind of evidence is required.

Speaker Knowledge and Opinions

Arguments can sometimes be built on the basis of the *speaker's knowledge and opinions*, or expertise. Doing so, however, will work only if the audience believes the speaker has the authority or credibility to speak on the matter. This credibility may derive from the speaker's personal experience or from his or her original contribution to the topic. As support for a claim, speaker expertise might work like this:

CLAIM:	Natural life support for human activity on the moon may come sooner than we think.
SPEAKER KNOWLEDGE AS EVIDENCE:	My colleagues and I recently found signs of the existence of water on the moon.
WARRANT:	Water found on the moon can be used to produce oxygen for human life support.

In this case, the speaker is one of a group of scientists who discovered that reserves of water exist on the moon. The audience accepts the speaker's professional assertion as evidence.

No matter how credible, the speaker's knowledge and opinion are still "once removed" from the audience. And, as noted, nothing is more persuasive to listeners than a reaffirmation of their own attitudes, beliefs, and values. Nevertheless, if audience members find a speaker credible, they will generally accept his or her knowledge and opinions. Be aware, however, that unless you are truly an expert on a topic, very few speeches can be convincingly built on speaker experience and knowledge alone. Some points in a speech might be substantiated by your own credentials but not most. For that reason, it is important that you do your research.

If the audience lacks sufficient knowledge to use as evidence and you are not a known expert on the subject, you will need to use yet another type of evidence to support your claims. This is the kind of evidence with which you are already familiar (see Chapter 8).

External Evidence

External evidence is any information in support of a claim that originates with sources other than the audience or the speaker. External evidence consists of the kind of supporting material discussed in Chapter 8 — examples, narratives, testimony, facts, and statistics drawn from outside sources. Importantly, unlike evidence based on audience knowledge and beliefs, external evidence is most

---

✓ **CHECKLIST**

Testing the Strength of Your Evidence

As you identify and apply evidence to a claim, keep in mind the three tests of evidence:

_____ 1. Is the evidence directly relevant to the claim?
_____ 2. Is it timely, or recent and up-to-date?
_____ 3. Will audience members find it credible, or from a source they can trust?

powerful when you cite information that the audience has not previously used in forming an opinion.[10] Thus, when using external evidence to prove your claims, seek out information your audience is not likely to know but will find persuasive.

In order to successfully support a claim with external evidence, your audience must believe that your information is credible. Consider a speech based on a speculative claim of future fact. In it, you argue that in five years half of all textbooks will be published only in "e-book" format. That is, they will be available to students in electronic form only.

CLAIM: In five years, half of all the textbooks in the U.S. will be available only in electronic form.

EXTERNAL EVIDENCE: As chair of the committee on the future of the textbook, I have reports from all major publishers on their plans for electronic publication.

WARRANT: Apparently, publishers believe that enough students are online and dislike the price of paper textbooks to commit to this course of action.

In this case, the speaker gets evidence for the claim from her own knowledge and opinions. The strength of the evidence for the audience's acceptance of the claim depends on the level of credibility the audience assigns to the outside source—in this case, her position as chair of the committee on the future of the textbook.

TYPES OF WARRANTS USED TO LINK CLAIMS WITH EVIDENCE

As with claims and evidence, depending on the nature and goal of your persuasive speech, you will want to select different kinds of warrants for your arguments. *Motivational warrants* appeal to the audience's needs and emotions. In Aristotle's terms, the motivational warrant makes use of *pathos. Authoritative warrants* appeal to the credibility the audience assigns to the source of the evidence; again, in classical terms this appeal is based on *ethos. Substantive warrants,* based on *logos,* appeal to the audience's beliefs about the reliability of any factual evidence you offer. (See Chapter 24 for a review of these classical terms.)

Motivational Warrants: Appeals to Emotion

No doubt most readers have seen television and magazine advertisements asking viewers to give just pennies a day to sponsor a starving child in a distant land. The claim may say, "You can easily afford to join this organization dedicated to ending the hunger of thousands of children." The evidence may be stated as "For the price of one soft drink you can feed a child for a week." What's the warrant? "You don't want any child to starve or go without proper medical care." The speaker intends the warrant to motivate listeners by arousing their sympathy for those who lack basic human necessities. **Motivational**

warrants use the needs, desires, emotions, and values of audience members as the basis for accepting some evidence as support for a claim, and thus accepting the claim itself. More often than not, motivational warrants are implied rather than stated outright. In terms of the ad to support a starving child, we don't have to be told that we don't want children to starve; if the value or desire is meaningful to us, we realize it while attending to other parts of the message. Here are some other needs and values that can operate as motivational warrants in arguments:

career success	meaningful	health and wellness
quality leisure time	friendships	quality education
financial security	good taste	fine material
physical attractiveness	wealth	possessions
strong marriages	happy families	

Authoritative Warrants: Appeals to Credibility

Just as one form of evidence relies on the speaker's knowledge and opinions, some warrants rely on an audience's beliefs about the credibility or acceptability of a source of evidence. Such is the case with **authoritative warrants**. For example, in terms of sponsoring a hungry child, the speaker might make the claim that we should contribute financially to an agency that feeds hungry children. The speaker's evidence is that any amount we give, however small, will go far in meeting the agency's objectives. As a warrant, the speaker notes that a certain celebrity or popular politician works with the agency and its recipients; perhaps that individual is even offering the message.

The success or failure of authoritative warrants rests on how highly the audience regards the authority figure. If listeners hold the person in high esteem, they are more likely to find the evidence and the claim acceptable. Thus authoritative warrants make the credibility of sources of evidence all the more important. In other words, it's possible that naming the source of evidence can also provide the authoritative warrant. For example, in support of the claim that "McDonald's Big Mac sandwiches are among the most popular fast-food sandwiches enjoyed by famous people," you could offer the evidence that "Celebrity X has said that Big Macs are his favorite fast food"; this gives both the evidence (a famous person who eats Big Macs) and the warrant (the specific famous person is Celebrity X) in the same sentence.

If you happen to be highly knowledgeable on a subject, an authoritative warrant can be made by reference to yourself. In this case, the warrant provides the speaker's knowledge and opinions as evidence. For example, in a speech on diet plans that work, you might claim that "Diet Plan B is more effective than Plan A or Plan C for many people" and use yourself both as a source of evidence and as a basis for the warrant: "I have used all three plans and have had the most success with Plan B." Your experience offers evidence for the claim, and you, having had the experience, give warrant to the evidence.

Substantive Warrants: Appeals to Reasoning

Substantive warrants operate on the basis of the audience's beliefs about the reliability of factual evidence. If you claim that your fellow college students should concern themselves more with learning from courses than with the grades they receive, you might offer as evidence the point that what is learned in a course is more applicable to future job responsibilities than the grade received in the course, and you might provide as the warrant a statement that "whereas better grades may lead to more job opportunities, better learning leads to better grades." The relationship between the claim and the evidence is that students will increase their chances for job opportunities if they concentrate on learning instead of on grades; for example, better grades follow from better learning.

There are several types of substantive warrants, or ways of factually linking evidence with a claim. Three that occur most commonly in speeches are causation, sign, and analogy.

Warrants by cause (also called *reasoning by cause*) offer a cause-and-effect relationship as proof of the claim. For example, welfare critics often reason by cause when they suggest that providing funds to people without making them work causes them to be lazy. Their opponents also reason by cause when they rebut this argument. Rather than suggesting a cause-to-effect relationship, however, they might suggest an effect-to-cause relationship, as in: "Welfare mothers don't work outside the home [effect] because the welfare system does not help them with day care [cause]." Similarly, a speaker might argue the following:

CLAIM:	Candidate X lost his 2002 bid for the Senate largely because of his age.
EVIDENCE:	Many available media reports refer to the age issue with which Candidate X had to contend.
WARRANT:	Our society attributes less competence to people who are older versus those who are younger.

Older age is assumed to be a cause of Candidate X's loss in the senatorial campaign. The warrant substantiates the relationship of cause (age) to effect (loss of race) on the basis of society's negative stereotypes of older people.

As pointed out in the accompanying checklist, when using warrants by cause, it is essential to make relevant and accurate assertions about cause and effect.

Warrants by sign (also called *reasoning by sign*) infer that such a close relationship exists between two variables that the presence or absence of one may be taken as an indication of the presence or absence of the other.[11] For example, smoke is a sign of fire. Coughing and sneezing are signs of a cold. A claim and evidence are often associated by sign:

CLAIM:	Summer job opportunities for college students will probably decline at resort locations in the southern Rocky Mountains.

✓ **CHECKLIST**

Making Effective Use of Reasoning by Cause

_____ 1. Avoid making hasty assertions of cause or effect on the basis of stereotypes.

_____ 2. Avoid making hasty assertions of cause or effect based on hearsay or tradition.

_____ 3. Be certain that you don't offer a single cause or effect as the only possibility when others are known to exist.

_____ 4. When multiple causes or effects can be given, be sure to note their importance relative to one another.

EVIDENCE:	Throughout the southern Rockies in the late winter and early spring, there was a record number of forest fires that destroyed many resorts.
WARRANT:	Widespread natural disasters curtail employment in the affected areas.

In this example, negative effects on employment are an economic sign of natural disasters. The claim is supported by the evidence if the audience accepts the warrant that employment becomes unstable in the wake of natural disasters.

Finally, **warrants by analogy** (also called _reasoning by analogy_) compare two similar cases and infer that what is true in one case is true in the other. The assumption is that the characteristics of Case A and Case B are similar, if not the same, that what is true for B must also be true for A. Warrant by analogy or comparison occurs frequently in speeches. Consider this example:

CLAIM:	Students will have a better feeling about Mr. Honnacker's speech class if he drops the absence policy.
EVIDENCE:	Student satisfaction increased substantially in Ms. Orlander's math class when she dropped the absence policy.
WARRANT:	Mr. Honnacker's speech class and Ms. Orlander's math class are equivalent with respect to other factors that satisfy students.

Here the speaker compares the speech class with the math class, assuming that both have in common students who are equally satisfied or dissatisfied depending on the nature of the absence policy. The analogy links the evidence from the math class example to the claim about the speech class.

ADDRESSING THE OTHER SIDE OF THE ARGUMENT

There are at least two sides to every argument. Thus all attempts at persuasion are subject to counterpersuasion. Your listeners may be persuaded to accept your claims, but once they are exposed to counterclaims they may change their minds. According to a theory called the **inoculation effect**, by anticipating counterarguments and then addressing or rebutting them, you can "inoculate" your listeners against the "virus" of these other viewpoints. The theory rests on the biological principle of inducing resistance through exposure to small quantities of a harmful substance. Just as you can induce resistance to disease in this manner, the inoculation theory posits that you can induce resistance to counterclaims by acknowledging them.

As noted, if your listeners are unaware of any counterclaims, they may be persuaded by your arguments for a time. However, once they hear other viewpoints, they may change their minds. If listeners are aware of counterclaims and you ignore them, you risk a loss of credibility. As described in the accompanying checklist on addressing competing arguments, however, this does not mean that you need to painstakingly acknowledge and refute all opposing claims.

✔️ **CHECKLIST**

Techniques for Addressing Competing Arguments

____ 1. If the audience knows of claims and evidence that oppose yours, and those claims and evidence can be refuted, raise them in your speech and refute them.

____ 2. If you don't have time to refute counterclaims that are known to your audience, mention the counterclaims and concede them if your evidence can withstand it. In other words, simply note that there are claims to the contrary, specify the claims, reiterate your own claim, and then move on.

____ 3. If there are counterclaims that your audience may be unaware of, ignore them if there is no time to refute them. Otherwise, if time permits state the counterclaims and refute them.

____ 4. From an ethical perspective, you may ignore competing claims only when they do not severely weaken your own claims and when you have no time to address them adequately.

Source: Adapted from James C. McCroskey, *An Introduction to Rhetorical Communication,* 6th ed. (Englewood Cliffs, N.J.: Prentice-Hall, 1993).

Fallacies in Reasoning

A **logical fallacy** is an invalid or deceptive line of reasoning.[12] As a speaker, you need to be aware of fallacies, both in order to avoid making them in your own speeches and to be able to identify them in the speeches of others. Many fallacies of reasoning exist; here, we note only a few.

BEGGING THE QUESTION

Begging the question is a fallacy in which an argument is stated in such a way that it cannot help but be true, even though no evidence has been presented.

"The television special on PBS proved that chlorine causes cancer in humans" is an example of an argument that relies on the kind of circular thinking characteristic of the begging-the-question fallacy. "War kills" is another. In neither statement has the speaker offered any evidence for the conclusion.

BANDWAGONING

Speakers who rely on **bandwagoning** phrase arguments as if they were true because "general opinion" supports them. "Nikes are superior to other brands of shoes because everyone wears Nikes" and "Everyone agrees that Coke is better than Pepsi" are examples of bandwagoning. The critical listener will ask, "Just who is 'everyone'?"

EITHER-OR FALLACY

The **either-or fallacy** poses an argument in terms of two alternatives only, even though there may be many additional arguments to be made. "If you don't send little Susie to private school this year, she will not gain admission to college" is an example of an argument posed as an either-or fallacy. The statement presumes that no alternatives other than the ones stated in the argument exist, even though there may be multiple ways of viewing the issue.

AD HOMINEM ARGUMENT

The **ad hominem argument** targets a person instead of the issue at hand in an attempt to incite an audience's dislike for an opponent. "I'm a better candidate than X because, unlike X, I work for a living" is an example of an ad hominem argument. "My neighbor who works for K-Mart isn't trustworthy; therefore, K-Mart is not a trustworthy company" is another illustration of an ad hominem argument.

RED HERRING

In the **red herring fallacy**, the speaker relies on irrelevant information for his or her argument. In this fallacy, the premises of an argument are irrelevant to the conclusion. "The recent tax hike by Governor Lambert has hurt working families across the state, and therefore you should vote against Mr. Morales for mayor" is an example of the red herring fallacy because there is no connection between Governor Lambert's policy and Mr. Morales's candidacy for mayor. Another example would be if an executive was indicted on sexual harassment charges and when giving a statement to the press claimed that the CEO was misusing company funds. This is an example of the red herring fallacy because the executive's indictment on sexual harassment has nothing to do with the misuse of company funds.

APPEAL TO TRADITION

Speakers who use the **appeal to tradition** phrase arguments to suggest that the audience should agree with the claim because that is the way it has always been done. "A marriage should be between a man and a woman because that is how it has always been" is an example of an appeal to tradition, as is "The president of the United States must be a man because a woman has never been president."

26 Organizing the Persuasive Speech

Once you've developed your speech claims, the next step in drafting a persuasive speech is to structure your speech points using one (or more) of the organizational patterns described in Chapter 12 — topical, chronological, spatial, causal (cause-effect), problem-solution, narrative, and circular — and in this chapter. There is no one "best way" to organize a persuasive speech — or any kind of speech. Instead, individual speeches must be put together strategically in ways that will best achieve the goals you have set for them.

Factors to Consider when Choosing an Organizational Pattern

Three factors are critical to consider when selecting an organizational pattern: (1) the nature of your arguments and evidence, (2) the nature of your target audience, and (3) the nature of your specific speech purpose. These considerations apply equally to your selection of types of evidence and persuasive appeals (see Chapter 25). An additional consideration is that of culture (see the Public Speaking in Cultural Perspective box in Chapter 12, p. 191).

ARGUMENTS AND EVIDENCE

As described in Chapter 12, some speech topics or claims clearly suggest a specific design. A speech that argues for a reduction in the price of cigarettes, for example, implies that high cigarette prices represent a *problem* and that lower prices represent a *solution*. Thus one obvious way to arrange speech points is with the *problem-solution pattern* (see Chapter 12 and p. 378). Many such **claims of policy** (e.g., claims that address an "ought condition" and use the word "should") fit naturally into the problem-solution pattern.

Similarly, consider a speech in which it is argued that young children do best when their mothers stay home with them full-time for at least the first six months of life. This **claim of value** (e.g., claims that address issues of judgment) implies that for at least a limited period, staying home is superior to working. One potentially effective way of ordering this claim is with the *comparative advantage pattern of arrangement* (see p. 383). Here, the speaker arranges main points to demonstrate a series of advantages associated with his or her claim versus an alternative position or positions — in this case, mothers who don't stay home.

Finally, consider the **claim of fact** (i.e., claims addressing whether something is or is not true or will or will not happen) that SUVs hurt the environment by releasing up to 30 percent more carbon monoxide and hydrocarbons and 75 percent more nitrogen oxide than passenger cars.[1] The claim implies that greater emissions of noxious gases (cause) lead to degradation of the environment (effect). Hence one way to arrange speech points for this claim is by using the **cause-effect pattern of organization** (see Chapter 12 for a description and sample outlines of this pattern). Alternatively, you could argue this claim in a *problem-solution* or *problem-cause-solution pattern,* so that the first point establishes the problem (SUVs hurt the environment) and subsequent points explain reasons for the problem (SUVs use too much fuel) and provide a solution (enact tougher fuel economy standards).

TARGET AUDIENCE

The fact that an organizational pattern seems self-evident in light of your arguments and evidence doesn't necessarily mean it is the best choice for a given audience or speech purpose. Another factor to consider when deciding how to arrange your persuasive speech is what your **target audience** knows about the topic and how audience members stand in relation to it (see Chapter 6).

Persuasion scholar Herbert Simon describes four types of potential audiences and suggests a different organizational pattern for each[2] (see Figure 26.1). For example, the *refutation pattern of organization,* in which points are arranged as a series of rebuttals of opposing claims, has been shown to soften the reservations of the **hostile audience or one that strongly disagrees**, as well as the **critical and conflicted audience**. The **narrative organizational pattern**, in which you frame your speech as a story with characters, plot, and setting, is particularly effective in addressing a **sympathetic audience** that is already on your side (see Chapter 8). For the **uninformed, less educated, or apathetic audience**, getting your listeners' attention and establishing speaker credibility are

1. Review topic/argument/evidence for likely pattern.

↓

2. Determine where the audience stands in relation to the message. Are listeners hostile to it? Sympathetic? Critical? Informed or uninformed? Involved or apathetic?

↓

3. Identify the type and degree of change you seek from the audience. Modify attitudes and values? Change behavior? To what degree?

↓

4. Consider the cultural composition of the audience (see Chapter 12, p. 191).

↓

5. Select an organizational pattern.

Figure 26.1 Factors to Consider When Organizing Your Persuasive Speech

TABLE 26.1 • Persuasive Strategies and Audience Type

Audience	Strategies
Hostile Audience or One That Strongly Disagrees	• Stress areas of agreement. • Address opposing views. • Don't expect major change in attitudes. • Consider the refutation pattern. • Wait until the end before asking the audience to act, if at all.
Critical and Conflicted Audience	• Present strong arguments and evidence. • Address opposing views, perhaps by using the refutation pattern.
Sympathetic Audience	• Use motivational stories (the narrative pattern; emotional appeals) to reinforce positive attitudes. • Stress your commonality with listeners. • Clearly tell your listeners what you want them to think or do.
Uninformed, Less Educated, or Apathetic Audience	• Focus on capturing listeners' attention. • Stress personal credibility and "likability." • Arrange points logically, perhaps using a topical pattern.

critical to their acceptance of your message; of secondary importance is how the speech is organized. One strategy that may work well is arranging points logically, using a **topical pattern of arrangement** (see Chapter 12). Table 26.1 offers strategies for various audiences. Table 26.2 (p. 385) summarizes the patterns discussed in this chapter.

SPECIFIC SPEECH PURPOSE

A third consideration in choosing how you will order speech points is your **specific speech purpose** — how you want your audience to react to your message. Persuasive speeches attempt to influence audience attitudes or behavior. Some speeches attempt to modify audience attitudes and values so that they move in the direction of the speaker's stance, while others aim for an explicit response, as when a speaker urges listeners to donate money for a cause or to vote for a candidate. Sometimes a speech will attempt to modify both attitudes and actions. Thus a final consideration in choosing a pattern for speech points is the type and degree of change you seek in your audience. Do you want to modify attitudes and values? If so, to what degree? Do you want to get the audience to act? To do both? Keep in mind that it is far easier to modify attitudes or behavior slightly than it is to do so to a great extent.

Problem-Solution Pattern of Arrangement

One commonly used design for persuasive speeches, especially those based on claims of policy and claims of fact, is the **problem-solution pattern of arrangement** (see Chapter 12). Here you organize speech points to demonstrate the nature and significance of a problem and then to provide justification for a proposed solution:

I.   Problem (define what it is)

II.   Solution (offer a way to overcome the problem)

But many problem-solution speeches require more than two points to adequately explain the problem and to substantiate the recommended solution. Thus a **problem-cause-solution pattern of arrangement** may be in order:

I.   The nature of the problem (identify its causes, incidence, etc.)

II.   Reasons for the problem (explain why it's a problem, for whom, etc.)

III.   Unsatisfactory solutions (discuss those that have not worked) *(optional step)*

IV.   Proposed solution (explain why it's expected to work)

A claim of policy can be organized effectively using the problem-solution or the problem-cause-solution pattern. One way to build a strong claim of policy, for example, is to provide the audience with a four-point justification consisting of (1) a need or a problem, (2) reasons for the problem, (3) a solution to the need or problem, and (4) evidence of the solution's feasibility.

 CHECKLIST

Organizing a Claim of Policy

✓   Describe the need or problem.

✓   Discuss reasons for the problem.

✓   Offer a solution to the need or problem.

✓   Offer evidence of the solution's feasibility.

First comes a *need* or a *problem.* The policy must speak to a real issue that the audience would like to have resolved. This assumes that the audience will benefit if the proposal is adopted. If your claim is that "the NBA draft should be changed so that young athletes aren't tempted to throw away an opportunity to get an education," the need is for a revamping of the NBA draft policy to encourage athletes to complete their college education. Second, the justification for a policy must provide *reasons for the problem.* Some reasons that the NBA draft needs to be fixed might include the statement that its present policies lure young athletes to pursue unrealistic goals of superstardom and that immature players weaken the quality of the game. Next, you must provide a *solution to the problem,* a specific way to address the need. The policy claim that the NBA draft should be changed must then offer an alternative policy, such as "the NBA draft needs to adopt a minimum age of 20." Fourth, the justification for the policy claim should offer *evidence of the solution's feasibility.* In this case, the speaker could provide evidence showing that sports organizations in other countries have successfully adopted a minimum age:

GENERAL PURPOSE:	To persuade
SPECIFIC PURPOSE:	To persuade my audience that the NBA draft should be changed so that young athletes are no longer tempted to throw away their chance to get an education.
THESIS STATED AS NEED OR PROBLEM:	The NBA draft should be changed so that athletes like you aren't tempted to throw away an opportunity to get an education.
MAIN POINTS:	I. The NBA draft should be revamped so that college-age athletes are not tempted to drop out of school. (*Need/problem*)
	II. Its present policies lure young athletes to pursue un-realistic goals of superstardom while weakening the quality of the game with immature players. (*Reasons for the problem*)
	III. The NBA draft needs to adopt a minimum age of 20. (*Solution to the problem*)
	IV. National leagues in countries X and Y have done this successfully. (*Evidence of the solution's feasibility*)

Monroe's Motivated Sequence

The **motivated sequence pattern of arrangement**, developed in the mid-1930s by Alan Monroe,[3] is a five-step process that begins with arousing listeners' attention and ends with calling for action. This time-tested variant of the problem-solution pattern of arrangement is particularly effective when you want the audience to do something — buy a product, donate time or money to a cause, and so forth. Yet it is equally useful when you want listeners to reconsider their present way of thinking about something or continue to believe as they do but with greater commitment.

STEP 1: ATTENTION

The *attention step* addresses listeners' core concerns, making the speech highly relevant to them. Here is an excerpt from a student speech by Ed Partlow on becoming an organ donor:

> Today I'm going to talk about a subject that can be both personal and emotional. I am going to talk about becoming an organ donor. Donating an organ is a simple step you can take that will literally give life to others — to your husband or wife, mother or father, son or daughter — or to a beautiful child whom you've never met.
>
> There is one thing I want to acknowledge from the start. Many of you may be uncomfortable with the idea of becoming an organ donor. I want to establish right off that it's OK if you don't want to become a donor.

Many of us are willing to donate our organs, but because we haven't taken the action to properly become a donor, our organs go unused. As a result, an average of fifteen people die every day because of lack of available organs.

In this first step, the speaker makes the topic relevant to listeners by showing how their actions could help those closest to them. He further involves the audience by acknowledging the sensitive nature of his topic and assuring them that he respects their right to make up their own minds. The statistics he cites underscore the seriousness of his purpose.

STEP 2: NEED

Sometimes called the problem step, the *need step* isolates and describes the issue to be addressed. Referring to it as a "need" reminds us that if you can show the members of an audience that they have an important need that must be satisfied or a problem that must be solved, they will have a reason to listen to your propositions (see Chapter 24). Continuing with the organ donor speech, here the speaker establishes the need for organ donors:

According to the U.S. Department of Health and Human Services, there are approximately 80,000 people on the waiting list for an organ transplant. Over 50,000 are waiting for kidney transplants alone, and the stakes are high: 90 percent of patients who receive a kidney from a living donor live at least ten years after the transplant. One of the people on the waiting list is Aidan Malony, who graduated from this college two years ago. Without a transplant, he will die. It is agonizing for his family and friends to see him in this condition. And it is deeply frustrating to them that more people don't sign and carry organ donor cards. I have always carried my organ donor card with me, but I didn't realize the extreme importance of doing so before talking to Aidan.
Every sixteen minutes another name joins that of Aidan Malony and is added to the National Transplant Waiting List.

STEP 3: SATISFACTION

Once you have gotten your listeners' attention and have established a need or a problem that is personally important to them, you are ready to introduce your proposed solution to the problem. The *satisfaction step* identifies the solution. This step begins the crux of the speech, offering audience members a proposal to reinforce or change their attitudes, beliefs, and values regarding the need at hand. Here is an example from the speech on organ donation:

It takes only two steps to become an organ donor.
First, fill out an organ donor card and carry it with you. You may also choose to have a note added to your driver's license the next time you renew it.
Second and most important, tell your family that you want to become an organ donor and ask them to honor your wishes when the time arrives. Otherwise, they may discourage the use of your organs should something happen

to you. Check with your local hospital to find out about signing a family pledge—a contract where family members share their wishes about organ and tissue donation. This is an absolutely essential step in making sure the necessary individuals will honor your wish to become an organ donor. Despite what you see on *ER* (the television program), often medical personnel do not get access to your license or your card. I've been a firefighter for over twenty years and can verify this.

The satisfaction step continues by providing more detail about the solution. In this case, the speaker goes on to provide support for why organ donation leads to so many lives being saved. In general, support in the satisfaction step includes evidence that illustrates or demonstrates the feasibility of the proposed solution and its superiority to other alternatives and to the status quo.

STEP 4: VISUALIZATION

In the *visualization step,* you provide the audience with a vision of anticipated outcomes associated with the solution. Its purpose is to carry audience members beyond accepting the feasibility of your proposal to seeing how it will actually benefit them:

> There are so many organs and such a variety of tissue that may be transplanted. One organ donor can help up to fifty people. Who can forget the story of 7-year-old American Nicholas Green, the innocent victim of a highway robbery in Italy that cost him his life? Stricken with unfathomable grief, Nicholas's parents, Reg and Maggie Green, nevertheless immediately decided to donate Nicholas's organs. As a direct result of the donation, seven Italians thrive today, grateful recipients of Nicholas's heart, corneas, liver, pancreas cells, and kidneys. Today, organ donations in Italy are twice as high as they were in 1993, the year preceding Nicholas's death. The Italians called this phenomenon "The Nicholas Effect."

 CHECKLIST

Steps in the Motivated Sequence

✓ **Step 1: Attention**   Address listeners' core concerns, making the speech highly relevant to them.

✓ **Step 2: Need**   Show listeners that they have an important need that must be satisfied or a problem that must be solved.

✓ **Step 3: Satisfaction**   Introduce your proposed solution to the problem.

✓ **Step 4: Visualization**   Provide listeners with a vision of anticipated outcomes associated with the solution.

✓ **Step 5: Action**   Make a direct request of listeners that involves reconsidering their present way of thinking about something, continuing to believe as they do but with renewed vigor, or implementing a new set of behaviors or plan of action.

STEP 5: ACTION

The *action step*, the final element in the motivated sequence, involves making a direct request of the audience. Here the speaker asks audience members to act according to their acceptance of the message. This may involve reconsidering their present way of thinking about something, continuing to believe as they do but with greater commitment, or implementing a new set of behaviors or plan of action. The speaker seeks an implicit or explicit response of "I agree with you all the way. I am going to do it." Here, the speaker makes an explicit call to action:

> It takes courage to become an organ donor.
> You have the courage to become an organ donor.
> All you need to do is say yes to organ and tissue donation on your donor card and/or driver's license and discuss your decision with your family.
> Be part of "The Nicholas effect."

The nature of the issue you are addressing will dictate how you implement the motivated sequence. If you're presenting a highly complex problem, you may need to spend much of the speech detailing the characteristics and effects of the problem. If you're talking to an audience that is familiar with the problem, you'll need only to highlight the problem and spend most of the speech on satisfaction and visualization. The extent of the material required for the attention step and the nature of the specific statement of action will depend on your own relationship with your listeners — how well they know you, your experience with the problem, and so on.

Comparative Advantage Pattern of Arrangement

Another way to organize speech points is to show how your viewpoint or proposal is superior to one or more alternative viewpoints or proposals. This design, called the **comparative advantage pattern of arrangement**, is most effective when your audience is already aware of the issue or problem and agrees that a need for a solution (or an alternative view) exists. Because listeners are alert to the issue, you don't have to spend time establishing its existence. Instead, you can proceed directly to favorably comparing your position with the alternatives. With this strategy, you are assuming that your audience is open to various alternative solutions.

In order to maintain your credibility, it is important that you identify alternatives that your audience is familiar with as well as those that are supported by opposing interests. If you omit familiar alternatives, your listeners will wonder if you are fully informed on the topic and become skeptical of your comparative alternative as well as your credibility. The final step in a comparative advantage speech is to drive home the unique advantages of your option relative to competing options with brief but compelling evidence.

Using the comparative advantage pattern, the main points in a speech addressing the best way to control the deer population might look like this:

THESIS:	Rather than hunting, fencing, or contraception alone, the best way to reduce the deer population is by a dual strategy of hunting and contraception.
SPECIFIC SPEECH PURPOSE:	To convince my audience that controlling the deer population through a combination of hunting and contraception is superior to a strategy of fencing, hunting, or contraception alone.
MAIN POINT I:	A combination strategy is superior to hunting alone because many areas are too densely populated by humans to permit hunting; in such cases contraceptive darts and vaccines can address the problem. (*Advantage over alternative No. 1*)
MAIN POINT II:	A combination strategy is superior to relying solely on fencing because fencing is far too expensive for widespread use. (*Advantage over alternative No. 2*)
MAIN POINT III:	A dual strategy is superior to relying only on contraception because only a limited number of deer are candidates for contraceptive darts and vaccines. (*Advantage over alternative No. 3*)

Refutation Pattern of Arrangement

In the **refutation pattern of organization**, each main point addresses and then refutes (disproves) an opposing claim to your position. The aim here is to bolster your own position by disproving the opposing claim. Note that it is important to refute strong rather than weak objections to the claim, since refuting weak objections won't sway the audience.[4] Further, it is probably best to use this pattern when you are confident that the opposing argument is weak and vulnerable to attack. If done well, refutation may influence audience members who either disagree with you or are conflicted about where they stand.

Main points arranged in a refutation pattern follow a format similar to this:

MAIN POINT I:	State the opposing position.
MAIN POINT II:	Describe the implications or ramifications of the opposing claim.
MAIN POINT III:	Offer arguments and evidence for your position.
MAIN POINT IV:	Contrast your position with the opposing claim to drive home the superiority of your position.

Consider the speaker who argues for increased energy conservation versus a policy of drilling for oil in protected land in Alaska:

THESIS:
Rather than drilling for oil in Alaska's Arctic National Wildlife Refuge (ANWR), as the Bush administration proposes, we should focus on energy conservation measures as a way of lessening our dependence on foreign oil.

SPECIFIC PURPOSE:
To convince my audience that rather than drilling for oil in the ANWR, we should maintain the refuge's protected status and focus instead on conserving energy.

MAIN POINT I:
Bush claims that drilling in the Arctic refuge is the only way to increase our energy independence; that it will have little negative impact on the environment; and that if we don't take this step our reliance on foreign energy will only increase. (*Describes opposing claims*)

MAIN POINT II:
By claiming that drilling in the refuge is the only solution to our reliance on foreign energy, Bush sidesteps the need for stricter energy conservation policies, as well as the need to protect one of the last great pristine lands. (*Describes implications and ramifications of opposing claims*)

MAIN POINT III:
The massive construction needed to access the Tundra will disturb the habitat of thousands of species and shift the focus from energy conservation to increased energy consumption, when the focus should be the reverse. (*Offers arguments and evidence for the speaker's position, as developed in subpoints*)

TABLE 26.2 • Organizational Formats

Organizational Format	Description
Problem-Solution	Speech points arranged to demonstrate a problem and then to offer solution.
Problem-Cause-Solution	Speech points arranged in order to demonstrate problem, reasons for problem, and solution to problem.
Monroe's Motivated Sequence	Speech points arranged to motivate listeners to act on something or to shift their attitudes in direction of speaker's.
Cause-Effect	Speech points arranged to demonstrate that a particular set of circumstances leads to a specific result (either desirable or undesirable) or, conversely, that various results (effects) follow from a particular set of circumstances.
Comparative Advantage	Speech points arranged to demonstrate that your viewpoint or proposal contrasts favorably with (is superior to) one or more alternative positions.
Refutation	Speech points arranged to disprove opposing claims.

MAIN POINT IV: Bush's plan would encourage consumption while also en-
dangering the environment; my plan would encourage
stricter energy conservation while protecting one of the
world's few remaining wildernesses. *(Contrasts the speaker's position with the opposition's to drive home the former's
superiority)*

Sample Persuasive Speech

The Need for Disability Awareness

AMY TABER

Manchester Community and Technical College

*The following persuasive speech is by community college stu-
dent Amy Taber. Amy's specific speech purpose is to raise
awareness among her audience members and to convince them
that along with society as a whole, they need to practice disability awareness. Amy organizes her speech along the lines of
Monroe's motivated sequence.*

Imagine being in a bad car crash. One day you're on
the men's or women's basketball team. The next day
you're paralyzed and wheelchair-bound. Will you be
ready to drop all your dreams just like that? •

Until very recently, we lived in a world where
having a disability—either as a result of an accident of birth or of fate—meant the death of your
dreams. At best, you were invisible. You were kept
apart from the mainstream of society. You were
seen as less than a whole person. "Normal" people
assumed you couldn't make decisions for yourself.
You were treated as if you would never amount to
anything. Legally, you had no rights to fight such
discrimination.

Today persons with disabilities (PWD) are no
longer so invisible or powerless. The Civil Rights
Movement of 1964, the Americans with Disabilities
Act of 1990, and the heroic efforts of disability
rights activists have helped to change all this. Many
people with disabilities now attend regular public
schools. They are an active part of the workforce.
They can live independently. And when they meet
discrimination, they have legal recourse to do something about it.

• Amy captures her
classmates' attention
by making her topic
relevant to them—
the first step in the
motivated sequence.

Each of these so-called "now-open doors" represents a milestone for people with disabilities. But the battle is far from over. The disabled have successfully overcome many legal hurdles, but disability awareness in the general population remains low. As a result, we have yet to enact much of what the Americans with Disabilities Act promises us. Today the need is less for legal remedies than for disability awareness. By raising our level of what being disabled entails, we can ensure that it doesn't mean the automatic death of our dreams. •

Let me begin by describing a little about the Americans with Disabilities Act (ADA). The first President George Bush signed the law on July 26, 1990; it protects the civil rights of individuals with disabilities and guarantees them equal opportunity in the workplace, public accommodation (such as access to public parks and buildings), transportation, public services, and telecommunications. The model for this landmark legislation was the 1964 Civil Rights Act, which prohibits discrimination based on race, color, sex, religion, or national origin.

A person is considered to have a *disability* if he or she has, and I quote from the ADA, "a physical or mental impairment that substantially limits one or more major life activities, has a record of such an impairment, or is regarded as having such an impairment." • As you can see, disabilities can be both *visible* and *invisible*. Disabled people may be sight- or hearing-impaired or wheelchair-bound. They may suffer from mental illness or a history of alcoholism from which they are recovering. They may have a physical and/or emotional impairment as the result of a violent crime. They may have been born with a genetic condition, such as Down syndrome or autism, that endows them with special needs.

According to the latest U.S. government figures, some 54 million Americans have some sort of disability. With a total population of some 281 million people, this translates into one out of every five people in the U.S. Any of us can become disabled at any time. No one is exempt from this risk. Not those of us who plan on having children. Not those who, like Christopher Reeve, decide one day to go

• Here Amy offers her thesis: the need for disability awareness. Arguing for such a need can be seen as a claim of policy.

• Amy credits this direct quotation.

horseback riding. Not those who, like the thousands of spinal-cord–injury victims, become injured in the course of their daily lives. We are all vulnerable, and we are all valuable. This is why it is so very important to understand and practice disability awareness. ●

Sheer numbers suggest that we need to practice disability awareness. Spiritually and morally, the call is stronger still to "desegregate" the disabled through widespread disability awareness. Only by doing this can we realize the full potential offered by the Americans with Disabilities Act. The government cannot and should not be expected to enact all of the provisions of the act. This volunteer nation of ours must take that spirit into the realm of disability awareness. ●

What, exactly, is disability awareness? At the broadest level, it means understanding and accepting people with disabilities in our midst — in our communities. Disability awareness means changing our attitudes about people with disabilities. It means recognizing that people with disabilities (PWD) are the largest minority group in the United States and in the world. Practicing disability awareness means being aware of how we use language to talk about disability. Another is courtesy — how we behave toward those with disabilities. It means getting to know people with disabilities. Asking them questions. Thinking before you speak or act.

On a practical level, disability awareness means taking action whenever and wherever we can to bring our society "up to code." As a result of disability awareness in concert with the Americans with Disabilities Act, ramps appear where none existed. Curb cuts let people maneuver their wheelchairs. City playgrounds sprout newly accessible surfaces and paths. Visual alarms notify patrons who are deaf or hard of hearing of an emergency. Untimed standardized tests permit more qualified people to enter schools of law and medicine. Casey Martin, a golfer with a rare disability that limits his ability to walk, can compete in the PGA using a golf cart. And it's wonderful that so many previously locked doors are now open as a result of disability awareness. ●

The Americans with Disabilities Act came about because of disability awareness on the part of dedi-

● Amy moves to step 2 of the motivated sequence, showing listeners that they face a problem (they may be disabled or may become disabled) that must be addressed (they will need access to opportunity).

● Here Amy indicates her proposed solution to the stated need to realize the promise of the Americans with Disabilities Act — the practice of disability awareness. This represents step 3 (the satisfaction step) of the motivated sequence.

● In step 4 (visualization) of the motivated sequence, the speaker provides listeners with a vision of anticipated outcomes associated with the solution.

cated individuals. Today, thirteen years later, it is our responsibility to ensure that we fulfill the promise it represents. • I urge you to take a lesson from the residents of San Antonio, Texas, who made their beautiful 2.5-mile Riverwalk truly wheelchair-friendly. Follow the lead of residents of Simsbury, Connecticut, who erected a "boundless" playground. Like the residents of Fernandina Beach, Florida, work with your local officials to install pool lifts in your public pools. Most important, try to be aware of and sensitive to issues related to disability on a daily basis.

● The final, "action" step of the motivated sequence involves making a direct request of listeners—to reconsider their present way of thinking about something, continue to believe as they do but with renewed vigor, or implement a new set of behaviors or plan of action. Here Amy makes a direct request of her audience to practice disability awareness.

Works Cited

"ADA Regulations and Technical Assistance Materials." Americans with Disabilities Act Homepage. 23 Aug. 2002. 12 Aug. 2003 <http://www.ada.gov/publicat .htm#Anchor-ADA-44867>.

"Americans with Disabilities Act: Questions and Answers." Disabilityinfo.gov. 23 Aug. 2002. 29 Aug. <http://www.usdoj.gov/crt/ada/q&aeng02.htm>.

"Facts about the Americans with Disabilities Act." U.S. Equal Employment Opportunity Commission. 29 Aug. 2002 <http://www.eeoc.gov/facts /fs-ada.html>.

"Inspiration for Boundless Playgrounds." National Center for Boundless Playgrounds. 1 Aug. 2002 <http://www.boundlessplaygrounds.org/aboutus /why_overview.php>.

Sample Persuasive Speech

The Importance of Community Service and Civic Engagement

STEPHANIE POPLIN

University of Oklahoma

In this speech, Stephanie Poplin argues that by volunteering we can enrich our lives (a claim of value). Organizationally, the speech incorporates elements of the comparative advantages pattern, in which Stephanie describes the many positive effects of volunteering and then addresses the alternative of inaction. As a final step, she drives home the advantages of engagement.

Stands at attention before the speech

"Great social forces are the mere accumulation of individual actions." Think about that — "Great social forces are the mere accumulation of individual actions." • That was said by Nancy Gibb in a *Time* magazine article written about the recent tsunami. And it's true, right? Everything from the Red Cross to the Peace Corps to the civil rights movement was made up of individual actions, yet all those actions were history changing.

* Stephanie uses a quotation both as an attention-getter and to introduce her theme.

I'm Stephanie Poplin, and I would like to speak to you today about why it is imperative that you give yourself the opportunity to live a successful and meaningful life. •

* Stephanie introduces herself with a direct statement of persuasive intent.

One way of achieving this seemingly unattainable lifestyle is by contributing — by putting yourself into the community that surrounds you. I'm refer-

Appropriate dress — casual but respectful

ring to community service and civic engagement. Today, I will talk to you about what you can personally gain from your involvement and participation in your community, and I will also address some concerns and reservations you may have about donating your time and your talents. •

* Stephanie clearly states her claim and previews the two main points she will cover.

Now, traditionally, when you hear the word *volunteer,* what do you think of? Someone who wants to do good, someone who wants to improve the lives of those who are less fortunate. And while this remains true, the attitudes of volunteers are beginning to change. Volunteers are beginning to realize that there are some major personal benefits that come along with their involvement in community service. No longer are volunteers getting involved purely for altruistic reasons. In 2001, Student Vol-

Warm smile connects with audience

unteering UK conducted research into the benefits of volunteering. • The study looked at how volunteering can enhance employability, and it emphasized that volunteer participation helps to develop and strengthen new and different skills and to improve job prospects. I think we would

* Stephanie offers a study that students are likely to find credible.

all agree that's a necessity for us, especially in the stages we are in in our lives right now. •

In today's job market, it is becoming evident that college graduates need more than just paper qualifications. We will need to be able to stand out from the crowd, to be resourceful, to be initiators, to be team players, and to possess a get-up-and-go attitude. These are now the desired skills of employers, and volunteering can provide all of this. According to the study's evidence, virtually every paid job can be mirrored by a volunteering opportunity. Taking part in community service is a new and pioneering form of work experience. Not only is it seen as work experience, but employers look at the act of volunteering as taking great initiative and commitment.

The evidence of this study also lists benefits, other than résumé building, that students felt they had gained through their participation in volunteering. These included building confidence and influencing career choices; they were able to experience making a difference, and volunteering opened up new opportunities and challenges. So whether you just want to help, make new friends, improve your job prospects, test a potential career, or build confidence, volunteering can be the answer. •

Effective hand gesture

So now that we have seen some personal benefits you can gain, I would like to address some concerns you may have. • I realize that some of you may have some reservations about volunteering. Namely, can one person really make a difference? You may be thinking, "If I am giving my time, and my talents, and my effort, to one specific cause, can I even make a dent in the desired outcome?" So next, I would like to elaborate on the

Quick pause to check notecard

idea that one person can make a difference. You might be thinking, "What can I possibly do?" But if you have ever spent any time reading or just hanging out with a lonely child, you know that even a small amount of attention and compassion can make a world of difference.

• Stephanie shows topic relevance to audience by drawing a link between community service and job prospects.

• Stephanie directly addresses audience needs and wants.

• Here Stephanie anticipates reservations listeners may have and addresses them.

I have experienced this firsthand through my involvement in Habitat for Humanity. • Habitat for Humanity is an international organization fueled by hundreds of thousands of volunteers who join with future homeowners to build simple and affordable houses. It wasn't until my first experience building a home, here in Norman, that I realized the impact this organization has on its volunteers and the families involved. I have always had a bedroom of my own to escape to, and I have always had a kitchen to make breakfast in the morning, but there are two little boys who will have this for the first time, thanks to the OU chapter of Habitat for Humanity. I have always taken my home for granted, but now I can be a part of giving these little boys a home of their own. • We need to prepare ourselves for the possibility that sometimes big changes follow from small events, such as me sheetrocking an empty space that will eventually become a living room that these little boys and their mom and dad can enjoy together.

In summary, we have seen how you can personally benefit from contributing to your community. • Not only do you gain valuable work experience, as well as the opportunity to develop new skills and improve your job prospects, but people who have spent time volunteering report they get back in personal fulfillment and satisfaction more than they ever expend in inconvenience and effort. I've also talked about the theory that one person can make a difference, and I encourage you to explore every possibility and as many organizations as you can to find the volunteer opportunity that fits your personality — one that you will enjoy and love to do.

Brief pause adds emphasis

Someone once told me, "You don't find yourself; you create yourself." As college students, we have every opportunity in the world to create a life that is successful and meaningful. Use your good fortune, and choose to create a life that is service-oriented. Give back to the community that surrounds you. We all have the power to make an impact one way or another. After all, "Great social forces are the mere accumulation of individual actions." •

Thank you.

• Personal testimony builds credibility and demonstrates how one person's volunteer work can have a major impact.

• Stephanie lends power to her words by twice repeating the phrase "I have always had" (the technique of anaphora; see Chapter 16).

• Stephanie uses the transition "In summary" to signal her conclusion and her summary of points.

• Stephanie repeats the quote from the introduction, reinforcing her points and bringing the speech full circle.

Special Occasion Speeches

Special occasions stand out from the ordinary rhythm of life, marking passages, celebrating life's highlights, and commemorating events. Such occasions often include the observance of important ceremonies and rituals as well as speeches. The ceremonies and rituals symbolically express the event's meaning to the gathered community, while the speaker's words literally give voice to that meaning. When it is delivered well, a special occasion speech forges a bond among audience members and helps them put the significance of the occasion in perspective.

Functions of Special Occasion Speeches

There are many kinds of occasions that call for speeches, some serious and some lighthearted. As is evidenced by its name, a **special occasion speech** is one that is prepared for a specific occasion and for a purpose dictated by that occasion. In the special occasion speech, the occasion gives rise to the speech content, at least in its broad contours. Dedication ceremonies call for speeches that pay tribute. Awards ceremonies call for presentation speeches that acknowledge accomplishments, and acceptance speeches that display gratitude. In each of these instances, audiences have definite expectations of the speaker. More so than in other kinds of speeches, they look to the speaker to fulfill specific functions dictated by the event.

Special occasion speeches can be informative or persuasive or, often, a mix of both. However, neither of these functions is the main goal; the underlying function of a special occasion speech is to entertain, celebrate, commemorate, inspire, or set a social agenda.

ENTERTAINMENT

Many kinds of special occasions call for a speech that entertains. Banquets, awards dinners, and roasts, for example, frequently highlight speakers whose main purpose is to entertain those in attendance. In such cases, listeners expect a lighthearted speech that amuses them. Depending on the event, they may also expect the speaker to offer a certain degree of insight into the topic at hand.

CELEBRATION

Often a special occasion speech will celebrate a person, a place, or an event. Weddings, anniversaries, retirement parties, and awards banquets all call for speeches that recognize the person(s) or event being celebrated. The audience expects the speaker to praise the subject of the celebration and to cast him or her in a positive light. The listeners also expect a certain degree of ceremony in accordance with the norms of the occasion.

COMMEMORATION

Certain special occasion speeches, called *commemorative speeches,* focus on remembrance and tribute. Commemorative speeches mark important anniversaries, such as the fiftieth anniversary of the landing of Allied troops in Normandy or the anniversary of the Columbine High School shootings. Speakers deliver commemorative speeches about events or people of note at memorials dedicated to them or at gatherings otherwise held in their honor.

INSPIRATION

Inaugural addresses, keynote speeches at conventions, and commencement speeches all have inspiration as their main function. With their examples of achievement and heroism, many commemorative speeches also inspire audiences as well as pay homage to the person or event being commemorated.

SOCIAL AGENDA–SETTING

Yet another function of the special occasion speech is **social agenda–setting** — establishing or reinforcing the goals and values of the group sponsoring the event. Occasions that call for agenda-setting speeches include gatherings of issues- or cause-oriented organizations, fund-raisers, campaign banquets, conferences, and conventions. Speakers asked to deliver keynote addresses at conferences or conventions are charged with establishing the theme of the meeting and with offering a plan of action related to that theme. Similarly, politically oriented organizations also routinely hold meetings at which invited speakers perform the function of agenda-setting.

TABLE 27.1 • Functions of Special Occasion Speeches

- Entertainment
- Celebration
- Commemoration
- Inspiration
- Social agenda–setting

Types of Special Occasion Speeches

Special occasion speeches include (but are not limited to) speeches of introduction, speeches of acceptance, award presentations, roasts and toasts, eulogies and other speeches of tribute, after-dinner speeches, and speeches of inspiration.

SPEECHES OF INTRODUCTION

A **speech of introduction** is a short speech with two goals: to prepare or "warm up" the audience for the speaker, and to motivate audience members to listen to what he or she has to say. Many occasions call for speeches of introduction. You might be asked to introduce a guest speaker at a monthly meeting of a social organization to which you belong, to introduce an award presenter at your company's annual banquet, or to introduce an outside expert at a quarterly sales meeting. A good speech of introduction balances four elements: the speaker's background, the subject of the speaker's message, the occasion, and the audience.

Describe the Speaker's Background

A key part of the introducer's task is to tell the audience something about the speaker's background and qualifications for speaking. The object is to heighten audience interest and build the speaker's credibility. If you don't know the speaker personally, be sure to contact him or her days or even weeks before the event. Ask the speaker to describe important achievements, offices held, and other activities that will show audience members what kind of speaker they are about to hear and why they should listen.

Briefly Preview the Speaker's Topic

Part of the introducer's job is to give audience members a sense of why the speaker's subject is of interest to them. Is the subject timely? What significance does it have for the audience? What special connections exist between the subject or the speaker and the occasion? Is he or she an expert on the topic? Why was the speaker invited? Details like these help the audience to understand the speaker's role and build his or her credibility. Keep in mind, however, that it is not the introducer's job to evaluate the speech or otherwise offer critical commentary on it. *The rule is: Get in and out quickly with a few well-chosen remarks.* Introducers who linger on their own thoughts run the risk of stealing the speaker's thunder.

Ask the Audience to Welcome the Speaker

A final part of the introducer's task is to cue the audience to welcome the speaker. This can be done very simply by saying something like "Please welcome Anthony Svetlana." Hearing this, the audience will provide applause, thereby paving the way for the speaker to take his or her place at the podium.

In the following excerpt from a speech by Frank D. Stella, of F. D. Stella Products Company, Stella introduces Richard A. Grasso, former chairman and chief executive officer of the New York Stock Exchange, to the Economic Club of Detroit. Notice how Stella makes use of the date of the occasion—April 15, or income tax day—to engage the audience. Stella also provides a quick overview of who the speaker is and a reference to why he was a good choice for this occasion.

> Happy April 15! This may be only a quirk of history, but do you realize that not only is today Tax Day, it is also the anniversary of the sinking of the *Titanic*! Talk about double jeopardy!

It's interesting, therefore, that we have scheduled today's speaker for April 15: If your company or individual stock did well in 1995 and was listed on the New York Stock Exchange, you can, in part, thank Dick Grasso for keeping the Exchange so strong and competitive; but if your taxes went up because your stocks did so well, you can thank Dick for capital gains, the market up-surge, and profitability.

It is a distinct honor for me to introduce Richard A. Grasso, chairman and chief executive officer of the New York Stock Exchange. He has enjoyed a remarkable 28-year-career at the Exchange. [Mr. Stella goes on to provide a more detailed background on Mr. Grasso.][1]

Respond to Introductions

Speakers who have been introduced should respond to the introduction in some way. Acknowledging and thanking the introducer is the most common method. For example:

- I appreciate those kind words.
- Thank you for making me feel welcome today.
- This is a wonderful event, and I appreciate being a part of it.

If you are comfortable ad-libbing, you might decide to respond to the intro-ducer's remarks. Notice how the following speakers use this strategy:

- Thank you so much, Helen. I have to agree with you that this audience must really be committed to the United Way — or hungry! — to be here on a stormy day like this.
- I am honored to be with you tonight. Something that Brad said in his re-marks earlier really struck me. If we are to truly make a difference, we have to be able to think out of the box. The box I would like for us to think our way out of tonight is . . .

Most of us are not used to being publicly honored, and accepting praise and accolades from a speaker who introduces us can be awkward. One of the ways to show your humility toward a gracious introduction is through humor:

- That introduction was so gracious; you were more than halfway through it before I realized you were talking about me.[2]
- Thank you, Mr. Secretary, for that incredible introduction. If I had known you were going to eulogize me, I would have done the only decent thing and died.[3]
- I'm really not as good as she said, but neither am I as bad as my mother-in-law thinks. So I guess it averages out.[4]

SPEECHES OF ACCEPTANCE

A **speech of acceptance** is made in response to receiving an award of some sort. Its purpose is to express gratitude for the honor bestowed on the speaker. The speech should reflect that gratitude.

Guidelines for Introducing Other Speakers

_____ 1. Clearly demonstrate to the audience why the speaker is relevant to the occasion. Describe his or her achievements, offices held, and other facts that are germane to the occasion.

_____ 2. Identify the speaker correctly. Assign him or her the proper title, such as "vice president for public relations" or "professor emeritus."

_____ 3. Correctly pronounce the speaker's name. Practice difficult-to-pronounce names several times before actually introducing the speaker.

_____ 4. Contact the speaker ahead of time to verify the accuracy of any facts about him or her that you plan to cite.

_____ 5. Mention enough of the speaker's awards and achievements to convince audience members that they should be interested in this person, but not so many that they cause the audience to glaze over.

_____ 6. Consider devices that will capture the audience's attention, such as quotes, short anecdotes, and startling statements (see Chapter 14). Don't burden the speaker with the added task of having to overcome the audience's boredom brought on by your introduction.

_____ 7. Be brief. The introducer should speak just long enough to accomplish the goals of preparation and motivation. One well-known speaker recommends a two-minute maximum.

Source: Roger E. Axtell, _Do's and Taboos of Public Speaking: How to Get Those Butterflies Flying in Formation_ (New York: Wiley, 1992), 150.

Prepare

If you know that you will be given an award, be sure to prepare an acceptance speech. Because the award is not a surprise, the audience will probably expect a fairly sophisticated acceptance speech. If you think it is at all likely that you will receive an award, prepare in advance so that your acceptance will go smoothly and you can avoid using standard responses such as "I really just don't know what to say."

React Genuinely and with Humility

Genuineness and humility are possibly the most important parts of expressing gratitude. Offering a sincere response shows your audience how much the award means to you. If you are surprised to receive the award, show it. If you are not surprised, don't try to feign excitement. Explain why the award is important to you and describe the value you place on it. Tell your listeners how it will affect your future and how it gives meaning to whatever you did in the past that led to its receipt. Express your gratitude with humility, acknowledging your good fortune in having received it.

Guidelines for Delivering Speeches of Acceptance

_____ 1. If you know or even suspect that you are to receive an award, prepare an acceptance speech in advance of the event.

_____ 2. In the speech, explain why the award is important to you and describe the value you place on it.

_____ 3. Express your gratitude to the people who are giving you the award. Be specific in citing each of the organizations or individuals involved in the award.

_____ 4. Thank any significant people who helped you attain the achievement for which you are being honored.

_____ 5. Do not belabor your acknowledgments.

_____ 6. Accept the award gracefully by showing that you value it and the people who gave it to you.

_____ 7. End your speech with an explicit expression of gratitude for the award.

Thank Those Giving the Award

Even though the attention is focused on you, don't forget to express your gratitude to the people who are giving you the award. If the award is given by an organization, specifically thank that organization. If it is given by a combination of organizations, remember to mention all of them. If there is a sponsor of the award, such as a donor that makes the award possible, remember to acknowledge the donor as well.

Thank Others Who Helped You

If the reason for your award represents a team effort, be sure to thank all members. If there are people who gave you the inspiration that helped you achieve the award, thank them.

SPEECHES OF PRESENTATION

The job of presenting an award can be an honor in itself. Whether you are presenting a bowling trophy or a Video Music Award, your goal in the **speech of presentation** is twofold: to communicate the meaning of the award and to explain why the recipient is receiving it.

Convey the Meaning of the Award

It is the presenter's task to explain the meaning of the award to the audience. What is the award for? What kind of achievement does it celebrate? Who or what does the award represent? What is the significance of its special name or title? You might offer a brief history of the award, such as when it was founded and the names of some of its previous recipients. If the award has a unique shape or design, explain the significance of that shape or design. If there is an inscription, read it. Because you are a presenter, it is also your job to identify the sponsors or organizations that made the award possible and to describe the link between the sponsor's goals and values and the award. This is information that the audience will be curious about, and mentioning it establishes the award's credibility and increases the honor for the recipient.

The following excerpt is a common way of communicating to the audience the significance of an award:

> It is an honor and a privilege to be the one making this presentation today. This plaque is only a token of our appreciation for Seamus's achievements, but we hope that this symbol will serve as a daily reminder of our admiration for his great work. Let me read the inscription. "Seamus O'Leary, in apprecia-tion for the outstanding work . . ."

Talk about the Recipient of the Award

The second part of the presenter's task is to explain why the recipient is receiv-ing the award. Tell the audience why the recipient has been singled out for spe-cial recognition. Describe this person's achievements, the kind of work he or she does, and special attributes that qualify him or her as deserving of the award. Explain how the recipient was selected. What kind of selection process was used? What set this individual apart from other nominees or finalists? The following example illustrates how this can be done:

> And, I might add, these were just some of the accomplishments of Carol Bosno. When the selection committee reviewed all the nominees (some eighty-four of them), it became clear that Carol would be our choice. The committee met four times to narrow the list of nominees, and at each meet-ing it was clear who our winner would be. The other nominees were outstand-ing in their own right, but Carol stood apart in many ways.

Consider the Physical Presentation

Plan the actual presentation of the award. Don't set yourself or the recipient up for an awkward presentation. If you are to hand the award to the recipient, make sure that you do so with your left hand so that you can shake hands with your right hand.

ROASTS AND TOASTS

A **roast** is a humorous tribute to a person, one in which a series of speakers jok-ingly poke fun at him or her. A **toast** is a brief tribute to a person or an event being celebrated. Both roasts and toasts call for short speeches whose goal is to celebrate an individual and his or her achievements. Should you be asked to speak at such events, it will be helpful to follow these guidelines.

Prepare

Remember that the audience is looking to you to set the tone and to express the purpose of the gathering. Being caught off guard and stammering for something to say can really let the air out of your speech and make it less than meaningful.

Also, remember that others who speak before you may use material you had planned to use. Don't be alarmed. Make reference to this fact and put a different spin on it.

Before delivering a roast or a toast, many speakers rehearse in front of a trusted friend or friends. This is especially helpful if you are considering telling a joke that you are unsure about. Practicing with friends also allows them to time your speech. People often speak much longer than they realize. Have someone listen to your presentation and time you. In that way you can see if your speech fits into the time limitations set for your presentation.

Highlight Remarkable Traits of the Person Being Honored

Because these speeches are usually short, try to restrict your remarks to one or two of the most unique or recognizable attributes of the person. Convey what sets this person apart—the qualities that have made him or her worthy of celebrating. In other words, what would you want said about you if you were being honored?

Be Positive

Even if the speech pokes fun at someone, as in a roast, keep the tone good-natured and positive. Remember, the overall purpose of your speech is to pay tribute to the honoree. It's great to have fun, but avoid saying anything that might embarrass the person being honored. Doing so could turn what should be a festive atmosphere into an uncomfortable situation.

Be Brief

Usually several speakers are involved in roasts and toasts. Be considerate of the other speakers by refraining from taking up too much time. This is particularly important for toasts, which are expected to be very short. Violating these expectations can make the toast awkward, especially if everyone is holding a glass in anticipation of the toast ending.

EULOGIES AND OTHER TRIBUTES

The word **eulogy** derives from the Greek word meaning "to praise." Those delivering eulogies, usually close friends or family members of the deceased, are charged with celebrating and commemorating the life of someone while consoling those who have been left behind. Given these goals, the eulogy can be one of the most difficult and challenging special occasion speeches to deliver. At the same time, probably more people with little or no experience in public speaking deliver a eulogy at one time or another than all other types of special occasion speeches.

Should you be called upon to give a eulogy, the following guidelines will help to ensure an effective speech.

Balance Delivery and Emotions

Many speakers fight the tendency to become overly emotional in a eulogy. Despite the sense of grief the speaker may be feeling, his or her job is to help others feel better. The audience looks to the speaker for guidance in dealing with the loss, and for a sense of closure. Therefore, it is essential to stay in control. Showing intense grief will probably make the audience feel worse. If you do feel that you are about to break down, pause, take a breath, and focus on your next thought.

Refer to the Family of the Deceased

Families suffer the greatest loss, and a funeral is primarily for their benefit. Make sure your presentation shows respect for the family; mention each family member by name. Make it clear that the deceased was an important part of a family by humanizing that family.

Commemorate Life — Not Death

Make sure that you focus on the life of the person rather than on the circumstances of his or her death. A eulogy should pay tribute to the deceased as an individual and remind the audience that he or she is still alive, in a sense, in our memories. Talk about the contributions the person made and the achievements that he or she accomplished. Focus on demonstrating the kind of character the person had. You might want to tell a story or an anecdote that illustrates the type of person you are eulogizing. Even humorous stories and anecdotes may be appropriate if they effectively humanize the deceased.

Be Positive but Realistic

Emphasize the deceased's positive qualities. This seems obvious, but care must be taken in selecting stories and anecdotes, as well as in planning descriptions of the person, to ensure that none of the speech is interpreted as casting the deceased in a negative light. It is also important, however, to avoid excessive praise. This may ultimately sound insincere and provide a distorted picture of the person.

✓ CHECKLIST

Tips for Delivering Effective Eulogies

_____ 1. Stay in control of your emotions.

_____ 2. Refer to the family of the deceased, mentioning each family member by name.

_____ 3. Rather than focusing on the circumstances of the death, talk about the contributions the deceased person made during his or her lifetime.

_____ 4. Consider telling a story or an anecdote that illustrates the type of person you are eulogizing. Humor that is respectful may be appropriate.

_____ 5. Emphasize the person's positive qualities, but do not be insincere.

In the course of his career, Mark Twain, the nineteenth-century humorist and writer, was said to have given more than 150 after-dinner speeches. Extremely popular at the time, lavish dinner affairs were attended by a host of male notables who spent several hours eating and drinking, after which they spent several more hours listening to humorous toasts and speeches.[5] Twain's speeches were so well received that many of them were reprinted in the next day's newspaper.

Today, after-dinner speaking continues to take place around the time of a meal, although not necessarily at a dinner. The contemporary **after-dinner speech** is just as likely to occur before, during, or after a breakfast or lunch seminar or other type of business, professional, or civic meeting as it is to follow a formal dinner. In general, an after-dinner speech is expected to be lighthearted and entertaining (see the following exceptions). At the same time, listeners expect the speaker to provide insight into the topic at hand. Balancing these two goals can make the after-dinner speech one of the most challenging but enjoyable kinds of speeches you deliver.

Recognize the Occasion

Be sure to connect the speech you are giving with the occasion. Delivering a speech that is unrelated to the event that has given rise to it may leave the impression that the speech is canned — that is, one that the speaker uses again and again in different settings. **Canned speeches** can be an immediate turnoff for many audiences. Further, audience members want to be recognized for who they are and for the event they have come to participate in.

Avoid Stand-Up Comedy

Many speakers are tempted to treat the after-dinner speech as an opportunity to engage in stand-up comedy, stringing together a series of jokes only loosely centered on a theme. There are two problems with this approach. First, the after-dinner speech is still a speech. A comedy routine does not have a recognizable introduction, body, or conclusion. This absence of a structure makes it difficult to deliver the serious point that the after-dinner speaker seeks to make because there will be no place where such points naturally fit. Second, most people are not comedians. Keeping an audience laughing for any length of time requires a great deal of practice and skill, as well as a major investment in speechwriting. For noncomedians, this can be a challenge too difficult to overcome.

The most convincing speakers are the ones who are most naturally believable. Trying to become funnier — or more serious — than you normally are will probably set you up to fail because it will make your job harder. The speech becomes an acting challenge. If you are naturally very funny, use that skill. If you have more of a dry sense of humor, plan jokes that reflect that kind of humor. Do not be fooled into thinking that expressing humor means that you have to become a Chris Rock or a Jerry Seinfeld.

The After-Dinner Speech and Social Agenda–Setting

Rather than entertainment, the purpose of certain after-dinner speeches is **social agenda–setting**. For example, each year the members and supporters of the Sierra Club gather to celebrate the date that the organization was founded. At every dinner event, an individual who is prominent in politics or the environmental movement addresses the group. Clearly, when the purpose of the after-dinner speech is agenda-setting, the speaker must focus more closely on the serious side of the equation than on that of entertainment. Nevertheless, even when charged with this goal, the after-dinner speaker should make an effort to keep his or her remarks low-key enough to accompany the digestion of a meal.

SPEECHES OF INSPIRATION

Many of the types of special occasion speeches discussed so far may well be inspiring. For example, presentation and acceptance speeches might inspire by highlighting the receiver as a model of the values embodied in the award. Certain occasions, however, call for a speech that is meant to inspire as its main goal. Every week, ministers, rabbis, priests, and mullahs deliver inspirational speeches in the form of **sermons**. Commencement addresses, "pep talks" at sales meetings, and nomination speeches at rallies and conventions are all inspirational in nature. In the business world, occasions for inspirational speeches are so frequent that some people earn their living as inspirational speakers. A **speech of inspiration** seeks to uplift the members of the audience and to help them see things in a positive light. Effective speeches of inspiration touch on deep feelings in the audience. Their emotional force is such that our better instincts are aroused. They urge us toward purer motives and harder effort and remind us of a common good.

Thus, as in a persuasive speech, to create an effective inspirational speech you'll need to appeal to the audience's emotions (pathos) and display positive ethos. Two means of evoking emotion, or pathos, are *vivid description* and *emotionally charged words* (see Chapter 24). This and other techniques of language, such as repetition, alliteration, and parallelism, can help transport the audience from the mundane to a loftier level (see Chapter 16).

Use Real-Life Stories

Another way to inspire listeners is through real-life examples and stories. Few things move us as much as the example of the ordinary person who achieves the extraordinary, whose struggles result in triumph over adversity and the realization of a dream. Recognizing this, in their State of the Union addresses several recent U.S. presidents have taken to weaving stories about "ordinary American heroes" into their remarks. Ever cognizant of the power of the televised sound bite, the politicians usually invite these people to attend the speech and then strategically seat them to permit the best camera angles.

✓ **CHECKLIST**

Delivering a Successful Speech of Inspiration

_____ 1. Focus the speech on uplifting the audience.

_____ 2. Seek to arouse the audience's better instincts.

_____ 3. Use emotional appeals.

_____ 4. Concentrate on creating positive speaker ethos (see Chapter 24).

_____ 5. Appeal to the audience's emotions through vivid description and emotionally charged words.

_____ 6. Consider the use of repetition, alliteration, and parallelism (see Chapter 16).

_____ 7. Consider using real-life stories and examples.

_____ 8. Strive for a dynamic style of delivery.

_____ 9. Clearly establish your speech goal.

_____ 10. Consider using an acronym to organize your inspirational message.

_____ 11. Make your conclusion strong.

Be Dynamic

If it fits your personality, use a dynamic speaking style to inspire not only through content but through delivery as well. An energetic style can do a great deal to motivate the audience; when it is combined with a powerful message, this can be one of the most successful strategies for inspirational speaking.

Make Your Goal Clear

Inspirational speeches run the risk of being vague, leaving the audience unsure what the message was. Make sure that the audience cannot mistake your message for something else. Whatever you are trying to motivate your listeners to do, let them know. If you are speaking about a general goal, such as remaining positive in life, let your listeners know that. Make it clear that you are speaking on a general level, and that you are trying to motivate them in a manner that will affect their lives in a broad way. If you are trying to motivate your listeners to perform a specific action, such as donating money to a particular charity, clearly tell them so.

Consider a Distinctive Organizing Device

Many successful inspirational speakers, especially those in the business world, use devices such as _acronyms_ or steps to organize their speeches. This clarifies the organizational pattern of the speech and helps the audience to remember the message. For example, a football coach speaking at a practice session might organize a short inspirational speech around the word _win_. His main points might be Work, Intensity, and No excuses, forming the acronym WIN. This device emphasizes the goal of the constituent elements of the speech. All three are aimed at winning games.

Ethically Speaking
Beware of Violating Audience Expectations

More so than in other kinds of speech, audience expectation that the speaker will fulfill a specific need is quite high in the special occasion speech. People listening to a eulogy, for example, will be very sensitive to what they perceive to be inappropriate use of humor or a lack of respect shown to the deceased. Those attending a dedication ceremony for a war memorial will expect the speaker to offer words of inspiration and will be disappointed if the speaker's attempts fall flat. Participants in a roast will expect humor but may balk at a speaker who crosses the line by making obscene or racist jokes. When a speaker violates audience expectations in situations like these, the reaction is usually pronounced. When giving a special occasion speech, it is therefore critical to plan your speech with audience expectations firmly in mind.

Here is an example of using steps. Giving an inspirational speech titled "Give Your Life a Dream with Design" to a graduating high school class, David Magill organized his presentation around three steps: "1. Design Your Vision," "2. Just Do It," and "3. Dig Deeper." Magill introduced his main points by saying, "My advice is simple, has three steps, and is easy to remember because the operative word in each step begins with the same letter with which *dream* begins — the letter *D*."[6]

Close with a Dramatic Ending

Using a dramatic ending is one of the best means of inspiring your audience to feel or act in the ways suggested by the theme of your speech. Recall from Chapter 15 the various methods of concluding a speech, including with a quotation, story, rhetorical question, or call to action.

Sample Special Occasion Speech

2004 University of Pennsylvania Commencement Address

BONO

In this commencement address delivered to the graduating class of the University of Pennsylvania on May 17, 2004, Bono, activist and lead singer of the rock group U2, nicely incorporates several qualities of an effective special occasion speech. He combines a serious message about the abolition of poverty and AIDS in Africa with a more relaxed, laid-back attitude typically associated with rock stars. This juxtaposition makes it more likely that Bono's student audience will be receptive to his call to action.

My name is Bono and I am a rock star. •

. . . Doctor of Laws, wow! I know it's an honor, and it really is an honor, but are you sure? . . . I never went to college, I've slept in some strange places, but the library wasn't one of them. I studied rock and roll and I grew up in Dublin in the '70s; music was an alarm bell for me, it woke me up to the world. I was 17 when I first saw the Clash, and it just sounded like revolution. The Clash were like, "This is a public service announcement — with guitars." •

Bono addresses the crowd at graduation.

I was the kid in the crowd who took it at face value. Later I learned that a lot of the rebels were in it for the t-shirt. They'd wear the boots but they wouldn't march. They'd smash bottles on their heads but they wouldn't go to something more painful, like a town hall meeting. By the way, I felt like that myself until recently. I didn't expect change to come so slow. So agonizingly slow. I didn't realize that the biggest obstacle to political and social progress wasn't the Free Masons, or the Establishment, or the boot heel of whatever you consider the man to be, it was something much more subtle.

. . . So for better or worse that was my education. I came away with a clear sense of the difference music could make in my own life, in other people's lives if I did my job right, which if you're a singer in a rock band means avoiding the obvious pitfalls, like say a mullet hairdo. If anyone here doesn't know what a mullet is, by the way, your education's certainly not complete. I'd ask for your money back. For a lead singer like me, a mullet is, I would suggest, arguably more dangerous than a drug problem. Yes, I had a mullet in the '80s. •

Bono acknowledges the occasion. His appearance mixes formal robes with casual sunglasses and open collar.

Now this is the point where the faculty start smiling uncomfortably and thinking maybe they should have offered me the honorary bachelor's degree instead of the full blown ("He should have been the bachelor's one; he's talking about mullets and stuff . . ."); and if they're asking what on earth

• Of course he is. Bono's opening remark is a guaranteed crowd-pleaser. His audience knows who he is, but stating it is unexpected and humorous.

• Bono uses personal history to argue that rock music can be revolutionary. He will revisit the theme when he addresses poverty in Africa.

• Self-effacing humor establishes rapport with the listeners and shows Bono to be more personable than they might expect of a celebrity.

I'm doing here, I think it's a fair question: what am I doing here? More to the point: what are you doing here? Because if you don't mind me saying so, this

is a strange ending to an Ivy League education. Four years in these historic halls thinking great thoughts and now you're sitting in a stadium better suited for football listening to an Irish rock star give a speech that is so far mostly about himself. What are you doing here?

Smile underscores humor

. . . For four years you've been buying, trading, and selling, everything you've got in this marketplace of ideas. The intellectual hustle. Your pockets are full, even if your parents' are empty, and now you've got to figure out what to spend it on. Well, the going rate for change is not cheap. Big ideas are expensive. The University has had its share of big ideas. Benjamin Franklin had a few, so did Justice Brennan and in my opinion so does Judith Rodin. What a gorgeous girl. • They all knew that if you're gonna be good at your word, if you're gonna live up to your ideals and your education, it's gonna cost you. So my question, I suppose, is: What's the big idea? What's your big idea? What are you willing to spend your moral capital, your intellectual capital, your cash, your sweat equity in pursuing outside of the walls of the University of Pennsylvania? •

There's a truly great Irish poet; his name is Brendan Kennelly, and he has this epic poem called the *Book of Judas,* and there's a line in that poem that never leaves my mind: "If you want to serve the age, betray it." • What does that mean to betray the age? Well to me betraying the age means exposing its conceits, its foibles, its phony moral certitudes. It means telling the secrets of the age and facing harsher truths. Every age has its massive moral blind spots. We might not see them, but our children will. Slavery was one of them and the people who best served that age were the ones who called it as it was, which was ungodly and inhuman. Ben Franklin called it when he became president of the Pennsylvania Abolition Society. Segregation. There was another one. America sees this now but it took a civil rights movement to betray their age. And 50 years ago the

• References to U Penn history build credibility. Franklin was the founder of the college, Brennan a famous alumnus, and Rodin the president.

• Appropriate for a commencement speech, Bono challenges the graduates to question what they plan to do with their education.

• Bono effectively quotes a poem to support and extend his message.

Pauses for emphasis

U.S. Supreme Court betrayed the age [when on] May 17, 1954, *Brown vs. Board of Education* came down and put the lie to the idea that separate can ever really be equal. Amen to that.

Fast forward 50 years [to] May 17, 2004: what are the ideas right now worth betraying? What are the lies we tell ourselves now? What are the blind spots of our age? What's worth spending your post-Penn lives trying to do or undo? It might be something simple. It might be something as simple as our deep down refusal to believe that every human life has equal worth. Could that be it? Could that be it?

Each of you will probably have your own answer, but for me that is it. And for me the proving ground has been Africa. Africa makes a mockery of what we say, at least what I say, about equality. It questions our pieties and our commitments because there's no way to look at what's happening over there and its effect on all of us and conclude that we actually consider Africans as our equal before God. There is no chance.

An amazing event happened here in Philadelphia in 1985, Live Aid, that whole "We Are the World"

Looks down at notes

phenomenon, the concert that happened here. Well after that concert I went to Ethiopia with my wife, Ali; we were there for a month and an extraordinary thing happened to me. We used to wake up in the morning and the mist would be lifting; we'd see thousands and thousands of people who'd been walking all night to our food station where we were working. One man — I was standing outside talking to the translator — had this beautiful boy and he was saying to me in Amharic, I think it was, I said I can't understand what he's saying; and this nurse who spoke English and Amharic said to me, he's saying will you take his son. He's saying please take his son; he would be a great son for you. I was looking puzzled and he said, "You must take my son because if you don't take my son, my son will surely die. If you take him

In this sequence, Bono effectively uses hand gestures.

he will go back to where he is and get an education." (Probably like the ones we're talking about today.) I had to say no; that was the rules there and I walked away from that man. ●

I've never really walked away from it. But I think about that boy and that man and that's when I started this journey that's brought me here into this stadium. Because at that moment I became the worst scourge on God's green earth, a rock star with a cause. Except it isn't the cause. Seven thousand Africans dying every day of preventable, treatable disease like AIDS? That's not a cause. That's an emergency. And when the disease gets out of control because most of the population lives on less than one dollar a day? That's not a cause. That's an emergency. ●

● A story humanizes Bono's cause and puts a face on suffering in Africa.

● Bono uses repetition for emphasis.

. . . But the scale of the suffering and the scope of the commitment, they often numb us into a kind of indifference. Wishing for the end to AIDS and extreme poverty in Africa is like wishing that gravity didn't make things so damn heavy. We can wish it, but what the hell can we do about it? Well, more than we think. We can't fix every problem — corruption, natural calamities are part of the picture here — but the ones we can, we must. The debt burden, as I say, unfair trade, as I say, sharing our knowledge, the intellectual copyright for lifesaving drugs in a crisis; we can do that. And because we can, we must. Because we can, we must. ● Amen.

. . . The fact is that this generation — yours, my generation — we're the first generation that can look at poverty and disease, look across the ocean to Africa and say with a straight face, we can be the first to end this stupid extreme poverty, where, in a world of plenty, a child can die for lack of food in its belly. . . . We can be that generation that says no to stupid poverty. It's a fact, the economists confirm it. It's an expensive fact but cheaper than say the Marshall Plan that saved Europe from communism and fascism. And cheaper I would argue than fighting

● Again, Bono uses repetition for emphasis.

Bono becomes more animated as the speech becomes more passionate.

wave after wave of terrorism's new recruits. . . . So why aren't we pumping our fists in the air and cheering about it? Probably because when we admit we can do something about it, we've got to do something about it. For the first time in history we have the know-how, we have the cash, we have the lifesaving drugs, but do we have the will? •

Yesterday, here in Philadelphia, at the Liberty Bell, I met a lot of Americans who do have the will. From arch religious conservatives to young secular radicals, I just felt an incredible overpowering sense that this was possible. We're calling it the ONE campaign, to put an end to AIDS and extreme poverty in Africa. They believe we can do it; so do I. I really, really do believe it. •

. . . I know idealism is not playing on the radio right now; you don't see it on TV; irony is on heavy

Bono scans the crowd during his call to action.

rotation, the knowingness, the smirk, the tired joke. I've tried them all out but I'll tell you this, outside this campus, and even inside it, idealism is under siege beset by materialism, narcissism and all the other isms of indifference.

. . . But I don't want to make you cop to idealism, not in front of your parents, or your younger siblings. But what about Americanism? Will you cop to that at least? It's not everywhere in fashion these days. . . . But it all depends on your definition of Americanism. Me, I'm in love with this country called America. I'm a huge fan of America, I'm one of those annoying fans, you know the ones that read the CD notes and follow you into bathrooms and ask you all kinds of annoying questions about why you didn't live up to that. I'm that kind of fan. •

. . . I love America because America is not just a country; it's an idea. You see my country, Ireland, is

• Multiple examples support Bono's claim that his humanitarian goals are reachable.

• A local example extends Bono's message.

• Good use of humor and a nice ironic touch—Bono is used to being on the other side of that kind of fandom.

a great country, but it's not an idea. America is an idea, but it's an idea that brings with it some baggage, like power brings responsibility. It's an idea that brings with it equality, but equality, even though it's the highest calling, is the hardest to reach. The idea that anything is possible, that's one of the reasons why I'm a fan of America. It's like hey, look there's the moon up there, let's take a walk on it, bring back a piece of it. That's the kind of America that I'm a fan of.

. . . So what's the problem that we want to apply all this energy and intellect to? Every era has its defining struggle and the fate of Africa is one of ours. It's not the only one, but in the history books it's easily going to make the top five, what we did or what we did not do. It's a proving ground, as I said earlier, for the idea of equality. But whether it's this or something else, I hope you'll pick a fight and get in it. ● Get your boots dirty; get rough; steel your courage with a final drink there at Smoky Joe's, ● one last primal scream and go. Sing the melody line you hear in your own head; remember, you don't owe anybody any explanations; you don't owe your parents any explanations; you don't owe your professors any explanations.

● Bono makes his call to action, challenging his listeners to pick their fight.

● Mentioning a local bar builds credibility.

. . . The world is more malleable than you think and it's waiting for you to hammer it into shape. Now if I were a folksinger I'd immediately launch

into "If I Had a Hammer" right now, get you all singing and swaying. But as I say I come from punk rock, so I'd rather have the bloody hammer right here in my fist. That's what this degree of yours is, a blunt instrument. So go forth and build something with it. Remember what John Adams said about Ben Franklin, "He does not hesitate at our boldest Measures but rather seems to think us too irresolute." Well this

Bono concludes with emphasis.

is the time for bold measures and this is the country and you are the generation. ●

Thank you.

● Bono's final call to action revisits his opening themes of music and revolution.

Speaking beyond the Speech Classroom

Speaking beyond the Speech Classroom

Speaker's Reference
Speaking beyond the Speech Classroom

28. Communicating in Groups

Keep Your Focus on the Goal(s) of the Group

- Keep in mind that your purpose is to address a specific issue. (p. 421)
- Critically evaluate information in light of the group's goals. (p. 421)
- Create and follow an agenda. (p. 421)

Center Disagreements on Issues Rather than Personalities

- Engage in issues-based conflict, not personal-based conflict. (p. 423)

Don't Accept Information and Ideas Uncritically Merely to Get Along

- Resist groupthink. (p. 423)
- Apply critical thinking skills to solve the problem at hand. (p. 423)
- Engage in devil's advocacy and dialectical inquiry. (p. 423)

As Leader, Set Goals and Identify the Problem

- Set a performance goal. (p. 424)
- Identify the resources necessary to achieving the goal. (p. 424)
- Recognize contingencies that may arise. (p. 424)
- Obtain feedback. (p. 424)

As Leader, Encourage Active Participation among Group Members

- Directly ask members to contribute. (p. 425)
- Redirect the discussion. (p. 425)
- Set a positive tone. (p. 425)

Adopt the Six-Step Framework for Making Decisions and Reaching Goals

- Identify the problem. (p. 425)
- Conduct research and analysis. (p. 425)
- Establish guidelines and criteria. (p. 425)
- Generate solutions. (p. 425)

415

- Select the best solution. (p. 425)
- Evaluate solutions. (p. 425)

For Group Presentations, Decide on Each Person's Responsibilities

- Who will present the introduction? The body? The conclusion? (p. 427)
- Who will coordinate presentation aids? (p. 427)
- Who will manage the question-and-answer session? (p. 427)

Practice as a Group until the Presentation Proceeds Smoothly

29. Business and Professional Presentations

Prepare a *Sales Presentation* to Persuade Potential Buyers to Purchase a Service or Product

- Consider basing the organization of your sales presentation on Monroe's motivated sequence. (p. 432)
    Draw the potential buyer's attention to the product.
    Isolate and clarify the buyer's need for the product.
    Describe how the product will satisfy the buyer's need.
    Invite the buyer to purchase the product.

Prepare a *Proposal* When Promoting an Idea, Product, or Procedure

- Organize lengthy proposals as follows: (p. 433)
    Introduce and state the problem.
    Describe the method of inquiry.
    Describe the facts learned.
    Offer explanations and interpretations of the findings.
    Offer recommendations.
- Organize brief proposals as follows: (p. 433)
    State the recommendations.
    Offer a brief overview of the problem.
    Review the facts on which the recommendations are based.

Prepare a *Staff Report* When Informing Personnel of Developments Affecting Them and When Reporting on the Completion of a Task

- Organize the staff report as follows: (p. 434)
    State the issue.
    Provide a description of procedures and facts used in addressing the issue.
    Discuss facts that are most pertinent to the issue.
    State the conclusions and the recommendations.

Prepare a *Progress Report* to Offer Updates on Developments in an Ongoing Project

- For long-term projects, prepare reports at designated intervals throughout the duration of the project. (p. 435)
- For short-term projects, prepare reports daily or as requested. (p. 435)
- Provide the following information in the progress report: (p. 435)
    Briefly review progress made up to the time of the previous report.
    Describe new developments since the previous report.
    Describe the personnel involved and their activities.
    Detail time spent on tasks.
    Describe supplies used and costs incurred.
    Explain any problems and their resolution.
    Provide an estimate of tasks to be completed for the next reporting period.

Prepare a *Crisis-Response Presentation* When Seeking to Reassure an Organization's Various Audiences and Restore Its Credibility

30. Speaking in Other College Courses

Expect to Prepare Oral Presentations in a Variety of Formats

- You will be asked to prepare both *individual* and *team presentations*. (p. 439)
- You may engage in *debates*. (p. 440)
- You may prepare *poster sessions*. (p. 440)

Expect to Adjust Your Presentations for Various On-the-Job Audiences

- Expert or insider audience (p. 440)
- Colleagues within the field (p. 440)
- Lay audience (p. 440)
- Mixed audience (p. 440)

In Science and Mathematics Courses, Expect to Present the Results of Experiments or Solutions to Problems

- The *research presentation* describes original research you have done, either alone or as part of a team. (p. 441)
- The *methods/procedure presentation* describes and sometimes demonstrates an experimental or mathematical process, including the conditions under which the report can be applied. (p. 442)

- The *research overview presentation* provides context and background for a research question or hypothesis that will form the basis of an impending undertaking. (p. 443)
- The *extended research or field study project* describes an extended field study or research project. (p. 443)

Ground Scientific and Mathematical Presentations in the Scientific Method

- Provide detailed information about the methods used in gathering and analyzing data. (p. 444)
- Be prepared to use observations, proofs, and experiments as support for the presentation. (p. 444)
- Be selective in your choice of details. (p. 444)
- Use presentation aids. (p. 445)
- Use analogies to build on prior knowledge. (p. 445)

In Technical Courses such as Engineering, Computer Science, and Architecture, Expect to Describe Projects

- The *design review* reports on the results of a design project. (p. 446)
- The *request for funding* provides evidence that a project is worth funding. (p. 446)
- Incorporate diagrams, prototypes, and other aids into the technical presentation. (p. 447)

In Social Science Courses, Expect to Focus on Qualitative *and* Quantitative Research

- Be prepared to describe experiments, naturalistic observations, case studies, and surveys. (p. 447)
- Expect to explain social or psychological phenomena by answering *what*, *how*, and *why* questions. (p. 447)

In Social Science Courses, Expect to Review and Evaluate the Research

- The *review of the literature presentation* examines the body of research related to a given topic or issue and offers conclusions about the topic based on this research. (p. 448)
- The *explanatory research presentation* reports on studies that attempt to analyze and explain a phenomenon, such as teen alcohol abuse or infant neglect. (p. 448)
- The *evaluation research presentation* examines the effectiveness of programs developed to address various issues. (p. 448)

- The *policy recommendation report* offers recommendations to solve a problem or address an issue. (p. 448)

In Arts and Humanities Courses, Focus on Interpreting and Analyzing the Topic

- Explain in an informative speech the relevance of a historical or contemporary person or event; a school of philosophical thought; or a piece of literature, music, or art. (p. 449)
- Compare and contrast events, stories, artifacts, or people in order to highlight the similarities or differences between them. (p. 450)
- Engage in debates. (p. 450)
- Research a topic and then lead a classroom discussion on it. (p. 450)

In Education Courses, Expect to Prepare Lectures and to Lead Group Activities and Classroom Discussions

- Pay careful attention to organizing and supporting presentations in education courses. (p. 452)
- Demonstrate how material in the lecture relates to the overall course content. (p. 452)
- Use student-friendly examples as evidence and support. (p. 453)

In Nursing and Allied Health Courses, Expect to Address a Range of Audiences on Health-Care Practices and Techniques

- You may be assigned a *community service learning project,* in which you report on the agency and its client base and your role in the project. (p. 453)
- You may prepare a *case conference,* in which you describe the patient's status, outline steps for treatment, review financial needs, and assess resources. (p. 453)
- You may be assigned a *shift report,* in which you give an oncoming caregiver a concise report of the patient's needs and status. (p. 454)
- You may prepare a *policy recommendation report,* in which you recommend a new or modified health plan or policy. (p. 454)

KEY TERMS

Chapter 28

small group	interpersonal roles	collective mind
virtual group	counterproductive roles	groupthink
presentational speaking	productive conflict	devil's advocacy
agenda	personal-based conflict	dialectical inquiry
task roles	issues-based conflict	participative leader

Chapter 29

presentational speaking
sales presentation
basic sales technique

proposal
staff report
progress report

crisis-response
presentation

Chapter 30

team presentation
debate
poster session
expert or insider
audience
colleagues within the
field audience
lay audience
mixed audience
science-related disciplines
research presentation
methods/procedure
presentation
research overview
presentation
panel discussion

extended research or
field study project
abstract
technical disciplines
design review
prototype
request for funding
presentation
qualitative research
quantitative research
review of the literature
presentation
explanatory research
presentation
evaluation research
presentation

policy recommendation
report
lecture
group activity
presentation
classroom discussion
presentation
community service
learning project
case conference
shift report
policy recommendation
report
evidence-based practice

Communicating in Groups （28）

Many of the experiences you'll have as a speaker and an audience member are likely to be related to your job, and most of those occasions will be in the context of a **small group** (usually between three and twenty people) as opposed to a large public audience. In fact, a substantial portion of your professional life will be spent participating in groups and teams.[1] Many of you will also participate in **virtual groups**, in which members who are geographically dispersed interact and exchange ideas through mediated communication such as e-mail, chat rooms, and video conferencing.[2]

Whether they are virtual or face-to-face, groups that form for work-related purposes frequently must report orally on the results they've achieved. A manager might ask a committee to devise a new system for promoting employees, for example. As part of their assignment, the committee members must present their findings to senior management. Many professionals are called upon to address a small group of peers, colleagues, or customers on a business or a professional issue. Oral reports such as these are a form of **presentational speaking** — reports delivered by individuals or groups within the business or professional environment. (See Chapter 29 for distinctions between public speaking and presentational speaking.)

Becoming an Effective Group Participant

Clear communication is vital to working cooperatively in groups and to getting to the point where you have something worthwhile to report. Unfortunately, not all interactions in groups are effective, efficient, or productive. The quality of a group's product is largely determined by how closely the participants keep sight of the group's goals and avoid behaviors that detract from these goals. The more you use the group's goal as a steadying guide, the less likely you are to be diverted from your real responsibilities as a participant. Setting and following an agenda can help you do this. An **agenda** identifies the items to be accomplished during a group meeting; often it will specify time limits for each item of business.[3] Figure 28.1 offers an example of an agenda.

ASSUMING ROLES WITHIN THE GROUP

Group members generally assume two types of roles within the group: a task role and an interpersonal role. **Task roles** directly relate to the group's

421

AGENDA

Staff meeting, May 25, 2006
New Horizons Group
9 to 11 A.M.
Third Floor Conference Room

Participants: Lisa Gomez, Jonathan Halberstat, Juliann Chen,
Georgianna Walker, Carol Ludlow, Jerry Freely

1. Welcome and call to order
2. Opening remarks
3. Approval of minutes from previous meeting
4. Briefing from product line managers
5. Update on federal regulations
6. Report from consultants on new product line rollouts
7. Report on architecture designs for new assembly plant in Mexico
8. Summary
9. Adjournment

Figure 28.1 Sample Meeting Agenda

Source: Adapted from H. Dan O'Hair, James S. O'Rourke, and Mary John O'Hair, *Business Communication: A Framework for Success* (Cincinnati: South-Western, 2001), 492.

accomplishment of its objectives and missions — these are roles that directly "make things happen." "Recording secretary" and "moderator" are examples of task roles. Other common task roles include "initiator" (helps the group get moving by generating new ideas, offering solutions), "information giver" (offers input), and "information seeker" (seeks clarification and input from the group).[4]

Members also adopt various **interpersonal roles**, or styles of interacting in the group. These "relational" roles facilitate group interaction. For example, one person will act to smooth out tension in the group ("the harmonizer"), another will assume the role of keeping the discussion moving and getting everyone's input ("the gatekeeper"), while a third will express group feelings or mood in an effort to clarify the climate.[5]

Both task roles and interpersonal roles help the group maintain cohesion and achieve its mission. Sometimes, however, group members focus on individual versus group needs. These needs are usually irrelevant to the task at hand and are not oriented toward maintenance of the group as a team. Such individuals can be said to display negative interpersonal roles, or **counterproductive roles**. Examples of counterproductive roles include "hogging the floor" (not allowing others to speak), "blocking" (being overly negative about group ideas or raising issues that have been settled), "distracting" (distracting the group from tasks at hand), and "recognition seeking" (acting to call attention to self rather than to group tasks).

USING PRODUCTIVE CONFLICT TO FOCUS ON THE ISSUES

Whenever people come together to consider an important issue, conflict is inevitable. But conflict doesn't have to be destructive. In fact, the best decisions are usually those that emerge from productive conflict.[6] It is through productive conflict that groups grow, mature, and realize a heightened sense of accomplishment. In **productive conflict**, questions are clarified, ideas are challenged, counterexamples are presented, worst-case scenarios are considered, and proposals are reformulated. After a process like this, the group can be confident that its decision has been put to a good test. Because the group members have had a part in analyzing, synthesizing, and constructing the decision, it will be one that the entire group can support. Group members will have considerable investment in and therefore ownership of the decision that is reached.

Productive conflict is *issues-based* rather than *personal-based*. In **personal-based conflict**, members argue about one another instead of about the issues, subsequently wasting time and impairing motivation. The group's assigned tasks remain incomplete and issues remain unresolved. Whereas personal-based conflict detracts a group from its mission, **issues-based conflict** allows members to test and debate ideas and potential solutions. It requires each member to ask tough questions, press for clarification, and present alternative views.[7]

PURSUING A COLLECTIVE MIND WHILE AVOIDING GROUPTHINK

For groups to be truly effective, group members eventually need to form a **collective mind**.[8] Groups that manifest a collective mind engage in communication that is critical, careful, consistent, and conscientious.[9] Maintaining a collective mind obviously requires the careful management of issue-based and personal-based conflict, but at the same time groups must avoid the tendency to think too much alike. **Groupthink** is the tendency to accept information and ideas without subjecting them to critical analysis.[10] Groupthink results from strong feelings of loyalty and unity within a group. When these feelings are more motivating than the desire to critically analyze ideas and test solutions, the quality of the group's decisions suffers.

Groups prone to groupthink typically exhibit these behaviors:

- Participants reach a consensus and avoid conflict in order not to hurt others' feelings, but they do so without genuinely agreeing.
- Members who do not agree with the majority of the group are pressured to conform.
- Disagreement, tough questions, and counterproposals are discouraged.
- More effort is spent rationalizing or justifying the decision than testing it.

The best way to maintain a collective mind while avoiding groupthink is to engage in productive conflict, as described above, and to make sure that the discussion includes some level of **devil's advocacy** (arguing for the sake of raising issues or concerns about the idea under discussion) or **dialectical inquiry** (devil's advocacy that goes a step further by proposing a countersolution to the idea).[11] Like productive conflict management, these methods of argument are invaluable for finding a more optimal solution and avoiding groupthink during a group process.

Leading a Group

Capable leadership is critical to the success of any group effort. It is the group leader's task to set goals and to encourage active participation among group participants. Four broad styles of leadership are possible within groups: *autocratic* (leaders make decisions and announce them to the group), *consultative* (leaders make decisions after discussing them with the group), *participative* (leaders make decisions with the group), and *delegative* (leaders ask the group to make the decision).[12] Research suggests that of these four types of leaders, the most effective is the **participative leader** — that is, one capable of facilitating a group's activities and interaction in ways that will lead to a desired outcome. Following the steps below will help you become an effective participative leader.

SETTING GOALS

Most negative experiences in groups result from a single underlying problem: lack of a clear goal. Each member of a group should be able to clearly identify the purpose(s) of the group and the goals it is charged with reaching. The group leader should be a catalyst in setting these goals and ensuring that they are reached, either independently or in collaboration with other group members. The latter option is preferable because group members are likely to be more committed and excited about goals that they have helped to create. The accompanying checklist contains guidelines for setting group goals.

✓ **CHECKLIST**

Guidelines for Setting Group Goals

_____ 1. Identify the problem.
_____ 2. Set a performance goal.
_____ 3. Identify the resources necessary to achieving the goal.
_____ 4. Recognize contingencies that may arise.
_____ 5. Obtain feedback.

ENCOURAGING ACTIVE PARTICIPATION

Each group member has something unique to contribute, but perhaps not at all times. Sometimes, however, a group member does not participate even if he or she has something valuable to offer. The following are a few reasons for non-participation:

- *Apprehension:* Members may experience fear or anxiety about expressing themselves in the group.
- *Lack of self-esteem:* Members may doubt the value of their contributions.
- *Dominance:* Other group members may control the floor.
- *Status differences:* Group members lower in the hierarchy of positions may choose not to comment on stances taken by superiors in the group. Some group members may not participate because they are sensitive to differences in class, race, or gender.

Whatever the root cause, problems arise when participation is unbalanced. A study by Hoffman and Maier,[13] for example, found that groups adopt solutions that receive the largest number of favorable comments, whether these comments emanate from one individual or from many. If only one or two members participate, it is their input that sets the agenda, whether or not their solution is optimal. The following checklist offers guidelines for encouraging group participation.

 CHECKLIST

Techniques to Encourage Group Participation

✓ *Directly ask members to contribute.* The leader can influence involvement by taking note of participants who are quiet and asking them to contribute ("Patrice, we haven't heard from you yet" or "Juan, what do you think about this?").

✓ *Redirect the discussion.* Sometimes one person or a few people can dominate the discussion. To encourage others to contribute, the leader can redirect the discussion in their direction.

✓ *Set a positive tone.* Some people are reluctant to express their views because they fear ridicule or attack. A good leader minimizes such fears by setting a positive tone, stressing fairness, and encouraging a climate of politeness and active listening.

✓ *Ensure that some level of devil's advocacy and dialectical inquiry takes place.*

Making Decisions in Groups

Effective groups do not make decisions arbitrarily or haphazardly. Rather, they engage in a deliberate process resulting in decisions that all participants understand and are committed to. Group decision making is best accomplished through a six-step process of reflective thinking based on the work of the educator John Dewey.[14] The steps include: (1) identifying the problem, (2) conducting research and analysis, (3) establishing guidelines and criteria, (4) generating solutions, (5) selecting the best solution, and (6) evaluating solutions. In the words of John Dewey, this sequence of steps encourages group members to

Step 1   Identify the Problem
- What is being decided upon?

Group leader summarizes problem, ensures that all group members understand problem, and gains agreement from all members.

↓

Step 2   Conduct Research and Analysis
- What information is needed to solve the problem?

Conduct research to gather relevant information. Ensure that all members have relevant information.

↓

Step 3   Establish Guidelines and Criteria
- Establish criteria by which proposed solutions will be judged.

Reach criteria through consensus and record criteria.

↓

Step 4   Generate Solutions
- Conduct brainstorming session.

Don't debate ideas; simply gather and record all ideas.

↓

Step 5   Select the Best Solution
- Weigh the relative merits of each idea against criteria.
  Select one alternative that can best fulfill criteria.

If more than one solution survives, select solution that best meets criteria. Consider merging two solutions if both meet criteria. If no solution survives, return to problem identification step.

↓

Step 6   Evaluate Solutions
- Does the solution have any weaknesses or disadvantages?
- Does the solution resemble the criteria that were developed?
- What other criteria would have been helpful in arriving at a better solution?

Figure 28.2 Making Decisions in Groups: John Dewey's Six-Step Process of Reflective Thinking

"think reflectively" about their task. In this way, all the relevant facts and opinions can be discussed and evaluated, thereby ensuring a better decision. See Figure 28.2 for an explanation of each step.

Making Presentations in Groups

Once the group has achieved its goal, members face the task of communicating their results to others in the form of a written report, an oral presentation, or a combination of the two. Group presentations have many of the same characteristics as presentations done individually, but there are differences; while in an individual presentation one person assumes all responsibility for presenting a topic, in a group presentation some or all of the group members share re-sponsibility.

   Group presentations (also called *team presentations*) can be an exciting way to present information and to motivate and persuade an audience to accept your communication goals. In order for this to occur, however, all members must be willing to pull their weight. Successful group presentations require co-operation and planning. The first step is to select a leader.

DESIGNATE A TEAM LEADER

The leader ensures coordination among different members, working with each member to map out a strategy for presenting the information. Thorough audi-ence analysis and examination of topic and purpose are critical to a successful team presentation. Once the strategy is in place, the leader should make certain that each member clearly understands it. Only then should the team move on to assigning roles and tasks.

ASSIGN ROLES AND TASKS

In some group presentations one person may present the introduction, one or more others may deliver the body of the speech, and another may conclude the presentation. Together with the group leader, members must decide who will do what. Assignments are often linked to each member's task roles in the group. The "initiator" of the group might present background information and explain the problem; the "group statistician" might explain how the data was collected; the "elaborator" might present the findings and conclusions; and the "in-formation gatherer" might offer the group's recommendations. Since intro-ductions set the tone for a presentation and conclusions linger in audience members' minds, consider placing members with the strongest presentation skills and speaker credibility at the start and finish lines. A skilled listener might be asked to moderate the question-and-answer session (see Appendix B).

 CHECKLIST

Assigning Roles for the Group Presentation

✓ Choose the person with the strongest presentation style and credibility level for the opening.

✓ Put the weaker presenters in the middle of the presentation.

✓ Select a strong speaker to conclude the presentation.

✓ Assign someone to handle the presentation aids.

✓ Assign someone with good listening skills to manage the question-and-answer session.

Source: L. Kroeger, *The Complete Idiot's Guide to Successful Business Presentations* (New York: Alpha Books, 1997), 113.

ENSURE CONSISTENCY OF DELIVERY

Audiences become distracted by marked disparities in style, such as a captivating speaker followed by an extremely dull one. As in individual presentations, practice is key to achieving a good balance of delivery styles. Together with the other members, each participant should practice his or her portion of the presentation in the same order in which it will be given in the final form, and do so until it proceeds smoothly.

ESTABLISH A CONSISTENT FORMAT

Both the verbal and the visual/audio portions of the presentation should follow a consistent format. Members should be sure to use shared terminology, for example. If more than one person will be showing PowerPoint slides, the slides should be similarly formatted. One person should also be designated to check that these elements are consistent in terms of style and content, and to proof them for spelling, grammar, and formatting.

 CHECKLIST

Team Presentation Tips

✓ Research your audience to find out who will be attending and what audience members expect to hear.

✓ Write out each member's responsibilities regarding content and the use of any presentation aids.

✓ Practice introductions and transitions in order to create the impression of one seamless presentation.

✓ Decide how each presenter will hand the presentation over to the next speaker. Determine how introductions will be made—all at once at the beginning or as each speaker introduces the next speaker.

✓ Establish an agreed-upon set of hand signals that will indicate when a speaker is speaking too loud or soft, or too slow or fast.

✓ Rehearse the presentation several times from start to finish.

ESTABLISH TRANSITIONS BETWEEN SPEAKERS

Work out transitions between speakers ahead of time—for example, whether one team member will introduce every speaker or whether each speaker will introduce the next speaker upon the close of his or her presentation.

REHEARSE THE PRESENTATION

Rehearsal time is critical to a successful team presentation. As with individual presentations, if you have the time, try to hold five practice sessions over several days. The techniques for rehearsal described in Chapter 19, including using a tape recorder or videotaping the presentation, will be helpful.

Public Speaking in Cultural Perspective
A Balancing Act

What happens to the dynamics of a group or team when one or more of its members come from a diverse cultural background other than that of the majority? In the classroom, for example, you might have a group in which some members are native born, while a few are from nations as diverse as Chile, China, India, or Senegal. Or a research team at a U.S.-based pharmaceutical company may have several scientists from a variety of international backgrounds.

On the one hand, a mix of people with diverse backgrounds presents an opportunity to raise the level of creativity of the overall group. At the same time, different group challenges must be anticipated. Research on culturally diverse groups[1] demonstrates that a diverse mix can increase the number of ideas generated in groups and increase the quality of group decision making. The downside is that the distinctive norms and values of group members may lead to an increase in personal-based group conflict.

The key to balancing these competing issues and ensuring that cultural diversity is an asset lies in reinforcing strong group communication skills.[2] Groups must be vigilant in monitoring the participation level of all members; the group leader should elicit comments from everyone. Above all, members must be alert to instances of groupthink in which majority opinions seem to dominate group interaction.

1. Research summarized by Beth B. Haslett and Jenn Ruebush, "What Differences Do Individual Differences in Groups Make?" in *Handbook of Group Communication Theory and Research,* ed. L. R. Frey (Thousand Oaks, Calif.: Sage, 1999).
2. Ibid. See also H. Dan O'Hair, James S. O'Rourke, and Mary John O'Hair, *Business Communication: A Framework for Success* (Cincinnati: South-Western, 2001).

29 Business and Professional Presentations

In many sectors of the workplace, business and professional presentations serve as a primary medium for disseminating vital company information. These presentations cover a wide range of topics, audiences, and speech purposes. Rather than being formal public speeches, business and professional presentations are forms of **presentational speaking** — reports delivered by individuals or groups within the business or professional environment. Presentational speaking includes individual speakers addressing groups of colleagues, managers, clients, or customers, as well as multiple members of work groups addressing similarly composed audiences.

Public versus Presentational Speaking

Business and professional presentations have much in common with formal public speeches. Still, Priscilla Rogers, a professor of business communication, notes that there are some important differences between speeches delivered in public and presentations delivered in a business and professional environment.[1] First, the audience for a presentation can be as small as three people. Second, presentational speaking is less formal than public speaking. Rogers suggests that on a continuum presentational speaking would lie midway between public speaking at one end and conversational speaking at the other.[2] In addition, presentational speaking usually occurs in more limited settings than does public speaking. Public speeches can be delivered just about anywhere an audience can gather — indoors or outdoors, at a large arena or a small park. In contrast, presentations made in a business or a professional context are more likely to be delivered indoors at a business site, notes Frank Dance, a professor of communication and business consultant.[3]

In addition to audience size, level of formality, and setting, Dance suggests several other factors that distinguish presentational from public speaking. These include topic selection, audience composition, audience participation, and speaker expertise.[4]

TOPIC SELECTION

Topics for public speeches can be assigned but are often left to the speaker's discretion. Even when a topic is assigned, public speakers are given some leeway in developing and presenting it. They can even be excused for deviating from a predetermined topic if the topic they prefer to present is relevant to the audience.

In contrast, topics for business presentations are either assigned by the presenter's superiors or clients or assumed as part of one's role in a work group or a project. Presentational speakers often follow a prescribed or traditional approach depending on the kind of presentation being made. Presentational topics are more specific, task-oriented, and management- or client-directed.

AUDIENCE COMPOSITION

Public speaking audiences may be more diverse than presentation speaking audiences. They are more likely to be self-selected or voluntary, and they probably expect to be attending a onetime event. In contrast, listeners who attend a business or a professional presentation are more likely to be part of a "captive" audience. As a group they are also more similar, in that there is an ongoing relationship among the participants; that is, they work closely together over a period of time and are sometimes part of a team.

AUDIENCE PARTICIPATION

In general, the public speaker delivers his or her speech uninterrupted. If there is a question-and-answer period, it almost always takes place at the end of the speech. In business and professional presentations, verbal interaction between speaker and audience is generally the rule rather than the exception. Audience members ask questions and make comments during and after the talk, and it isn't unusual for a presentation to be stopped midway when a discussion ensues or time runs out.

SPEAKER EXPERTISE

Listeners generally assume that a public speaker has more expertise or considerably more firsthand knowledge than they do on a topic. The speaker is frequently the reason many audience members attend a speech, regardless of the topic. Presentational speakers, in contrast, are more properly thought of as "first among equals," in that they may be no more expert on the topic than the members of the audience. It just happens that the presenter has been designated to fulfill this particular task for the moment or for a time. A presentation audience attends more to gain information than to hear the presenter.

Common Types of Business and Professional Presentations

Five of the most common types of business and professional presentations are *sales presentations, proposals, staff reports, progress reports,* and *crisis-response presentations.*[5] Any of these oral reports can be delivered by individuals or by multiple presenters. Keep in mind that many industries and professions have their own preferred styles and requirements. The following discussion provides some basic and common features of these presentations.

SALES PRESENTATIONS

Purpose

A **sales presentation** attempts to lead a potential buyer to purchase a service or a product described by the presenter. The general purpose of sales presentations is to persuade.

Audience

A sales presentation can be directed to an audience of one or many. It depends on who has the authority to make the purchase under consideration. Some sales presentations are invited by the potential buyer. Others are "cold sales" in which the presenter/seller approaches a first-time potential buyer with a product or a service. In some cases the audience might be an intermediary — a community agency's office manager, for example, who then recommends to the agency director whether the purchase would be worthwhile. Sales presentations are most successful when they are clearly audience-directed. That is, the product or service must be presented in such a way as to show how it meets the needs of the potential buyer.

Organization

With its focus on audience needs, the motivated sequence pattern developed by Alan Monroe (see Chapter 26) offers an excellent way to organize sales presentations. Sometimes referred to as the **basic sales technique**, Monroe's sequence involves (1) drawing the potential buyer's attention to the product, (2) isolating and clarifying the buyer's need for the product, (3) describing how the product will satisfy the need and provide other long-term benefits, and (4) inviting the buyer to purchase the product. The extent to which the speaker focuses on each segment depends on the nature of the selling situation. In cold-call sales situations, the seller/presenter may have to spend more time discovering the potential buyer's needs. For invited sales presentations, the buyer's needs will probably be known in advance. In this event, the presenter can spend more time detailing the characteristics of the product and showing how it will satisfy the buyer's needs.

✔ **CHECKLIST**

Using Monroe's Motivated Sequence to Organize a Sales Presentation*

_____ 1. Draw the potential buyer's attention to the product.

_____ 2. Isolate and clarify the buyer's need for the product.

_____ 3. Describe how the product will satisfy the buyer's need.

_____ 4. Invite the buyer to purchase the product.

*See Chapter 26, pp. 380–383.

PROPOSALS

Purpose

Organizations must make decisions constantly on whether to modify or adopt a product, procedure, or policy. Should Armen Construction purchase new drill bits? Should Kmart stores implement a new employee-grievance procedure? Such information is routinely delivered as a **proposal**. For example, the Giant Lollipop Company might be interested in upgrading its telephone system. The facilities manager is given the task of consulting the original system provider to learn about the recommended equipment for making the upgrade. The manager then prepares a presentation that will provide the necessary information to assist the company in making its decision.

Proposals may be strictly informative, as in the example of the facilities manager providing information to his or her superiors. Often, proposals are persuasive in nature, with the presenter arguing in favor of one course of action over another.

Audience

The audience for a proposal can vary from a single individual to a large group; the individual or individuals have primary or sole decision-making responsibility. In the example of the telephone system, the facilities manager will present his or her report to company officers who are authorized to decide, on the basis of the report, whether to upgrade to the newer system. Because many proposals seek to persuade listeners, careful adaptation to the audience is critical to an effective presentation.[6]

✓ CHECKLIST

Preparing a Proposal

Organize lengthy proposals as follows:

_____ 1. Introduce the issue.
_____ 2. State the problem.
_____ 3. Describe the method by which the problem was investigated.
_____ 4. Describe the facts learned.
_____ 5. Offer explanations and an interpretation of the findings.
_____ 6. Offer recommendations.

Organize brief proposals as follows:

_____ 1. State your recommendations.
_____ 2. Offer a brief overview of the problem.
_____ 3. Review the facts on which the recommendation is based.

Organization

Depending on its subject, a proposal can be quite lengthy and formally orga-nized or relatively brief and loosely structured. The organization of a lengthier, more formal report includes a full introduction, a statement of the problem, the method of inquiry, a summary of the facts learned, an explanation, a conclu-sion, and a recommendation. If the facilities manager of the aforementioned telephone system must interview several people and read several sources of in-formation pertaining to the upgrade, the presentation might be suited to the more formal plan. On the other hand, if the information is relatively straight-forward and limited in scope, the presenter can begin with a statement of rec-ommendation, a brief overview of the problem, and a review of the facts on which the recommendation is based.

STAFF REPORTS

Purpose

A **staff report** informs managers and other employees of new developments that affect them and their work. For example, a company's personnel division might implement a new plan for subscribers to the company's health insurance program. To explain the changes, the personnel director will present the plan at a meeting of the sales division. He or she will review the reasons for the new plan, explain how it works, and describe its ramifications. Another function of staff reports is to provide information on the completion of a project or task. For instance, the district manager of a restaurant chain might assign three local restaurant managers the task of devising a plan for expanding the seating ca-pacity at each location. The managers will present their designs at the next dis-trict meeting.

Audience

The audience for a staff report is usually a group, but it can be an individual. The managers of the chain restaurant will make their report in a meeting at-tended only by the district manager, or in a meeting at which managers from

---

✓ **CHECKLIST**

Preparing a Staff Report

_____ 1. State the problem or question under consideration.
_____ 2. Provide a description of procedures and facts used to address the issue.
_____ 3. Discuss the facts that are most pertinent to the issue.
_____ 4. Provide a statement of the conclusions.
_____ 5. Offer recommendations.

the entire district are present. The recipients of a staff report then use the information to implement new policy, to coordinate other plans, or to make other reports to other groups.

Organization

Formal staff reports typically include a statement of the problem or question under consideration (sometimes called a "charge" to a committee or a subcommittee), a description of procedures and facts used in addressing the problem, a discussion of the facts that are most pertinent to the problem, and a statement of conclusions followed by recommendations.

PROGRESS REPORTS

Purpose

A progress report is similar to a staff report, with the exception that the audience can include people *outside* the organization as well as within it. A **progress report** updates clients or principals on developments in an ongoing project. On long-term projects, such reports may be given at designated intervals or at the time of specific task completions throughout the duration of the project. For example, subcontractors on a housing-construction project meet weekly with the project developers. On short-term projects, reports can occur daily. For example, medical personnel in the intensive-care unit of a hospital meet each morning to review the treatment protocol and progress of each patient.

Audience

The audiences for progress reports vary greatly. An audience might be a group of clients or customers, developers and investors, next-line supervisors, company officers, media representatives, or same-level co-workers assigned to the same project. For example, a work team consisting of workers from various departments (engineering, marketing, and cost analysis) may be assigned to the

---

✓ CHECKLIST

Preparing a Progress Report

_____ 1. Briefly review progress made up to the time of the previous report.

_____ 2. Describe new developments since the previous report.

_____ 3. Describe the personnel involved and their activities.

_____ 4. Detail time spent on tasks.

_____ 5. Describe supplies used and costs incurred.

_____ 6. Explain any problems and their resolution.

_____ 7. Provide an estimate of tasks to be completed for the next reporting period.

development of a new product. Once a week, members of the team present the rest of the division with a progress report, especially during the early stages. Once the project is well under way and activity is focused on one particular segment, such as marketing, those representatives may be the only personnel to make progress reports, and the audience may extend to potential buyers, corporate officers, and other staff in the various departments. Progress reports are commonplace in staff and committee meetings where subcommittees report on the development of their designated tasks. Audience questions are common at the end of progress reports. (See Appendix B, "How to Handle Question-and-Answer Sessions.")

Organization

There is no set pattern of organization for a progress report. In many instances the report begins with a brief statement to review progress made up to the time of the previous report, followed by a more thorough statement of new developments since the previous report was made. This statement may include descriptions of personnel involved and their activities, time spent on tasks, supplies used and costs incurred, problems encountered and how they were handled, and an estimate of tasks to be completed for the next reporting period.

CRISIS-RESPONSE PRESENTATIONS

Purpose

The purpose of the **crisis-response presentation** (also called *crisis communication*) is to reassure an organization's various audiences (its "publics") and restore its credibility in the face of potentially reputation-damaging situations such as contaminated products, layoffs, chemical spills, or bankruptcy. For example, in 1982 Tylenol was faced with a potentially disastrous reputation-damaging crisis when seven people were killed as a result of a lethal contamination of the company's extra-strength painkiller. In addition to recalling the product and improving safety packaging, top management held numerous press conferences and otherwise made themselves available to the press and the public. Today, perhaps as a result of an increase in societal violence, the need for crisis communication arises in both the profit and the nonprofit sectors. In 2005, for example, following Hurricane Katrina, local police and local, state, and federal officials briefed the public on the status of the evacuation and rebuilding efforts.

Audience

Crisis-response presentations may target one, several, or multiple audiences, both inside and outside of an organization. A personnel manager may address a group of disgruntled employees who are unhappy about a new vacation policy. Seeking to allay fears of ruin and shore up stockholder confidence, the CEO of an embattled corporation may target anxious employees and shareholders alike.

ESL Speaker's Notes
Steps to Counteract Problems in Being Understood

With the exception of young children, virtually everyone who learns to speak another language will speak that language with an accent. This issue is especially important in business and professional settings, where being understood can have a direct impact on your career. What steps can you take when your accent will make your oral presentation difficult for the audience to understand?

In the long term, interacting with native speakers in everyday life will help enormously. With immersion, non-native speakers can begin to stop translating word for word and start thinking in English. Using a tape recorder and practicing your speech in front of others is also very important.

But what if, although your experience with English is limited, you must nonetheless give an oral presentation? Robert Anholt, a scientist and author, suggests the following:

1. Practice the presentation often, preferably with a friend who is a native English speaker.
2. Learn the presentation almost by heart.
3. Create strong presentation aids that will convey most of the story by themselves, even if your speech is hard to understand.

By practicing often and ensuring that your presentation aids convey the bulk of your meaning, you can be confident that you will get your message across. And with time and effort, be assured that even the most difficult accent can be tamed to the point where speech is clearly understood.

Source: Robert Anholt, *Dazzle 'Em with Style: The Art of Oral Scientific Presentation* (New York: W. H. Freeman, 1994), 156.

Organization

Of all the types of business and professional presentations, the crisis-response presentation is perhaps the most complex to plan and deliver. A variety of strategies exist, ranging from simple denial to "mortification," or admitting responsibility for a crisis and asking forgiveness.[7] Familiarity with a range of *image-restoration strategies* will allow the speaker to select the techniques that best apply to the situation at hand.[8] In essence, however, the crisis-response presentation is based on persuasion and argument. Sound reasoning and evidence are essential to its effectiveness. Depending on the issue and the audience(s) involved, one of the four organizational patterns described in Chapter 26 would be appropriate.

Ethically Speaking
Code of Ethics for Professional Communicators

Because hundreds of thousands of business communicators worldwide engage in activities that affect the lives of millions of people and because this power carries with it significant social responsibilities, the International Association of Business Communicators developed the Code of Ethics for Professional Communicators.

Articles

1. Professional communicators uphold the credibility and dignity of their profession by practicing honest, candid, and timely communication and by fostering the free flow of essential information in accord with the public interest.

2. Professional communicators disseminate accurate information and promptly correct any erroneous communication for which they may be responsible.

3. Professional communicators understand and support the principles of free speech, freedom of assembly, and access to an open marketplace of ideas, and act accordingly.

4. Professional communicators are sensitive to cultural values and beliefs and engage in fair and balanced communication practices that foster and encourage mutual understanding.

5. Professional communicators refrain from taking part in any undertaking that the communicator considers to be unethical.

6. Professional communicators obey laws and public policies governing their professional activities and are sensitive to the spirit of all laws and regulations. Should any law or public policy be violated, for whatever reason, they act promptly to correct the situation.

7. Professional communicators give credit for unique expressions borrowed from others and identify the sources and purposes of all information disseminated to the public.

8. Professional communicators protect confidential information and, at the same time, comply with all legal requirements for the disclosure of information that affects the welfare of others.

9. Professional communicators do not use confidential information gained as a result of professional activities for personal benefit and do not represent conflicting or competing interests without the written consent of those involved.

10. Professional communicators do not accept undisclosed gifts or payments for professional services from anyone other than a client or an employer.

11. Professional communicators do not guarantee results that are beyond the power of the practitioner to deliver.

12. Professional communicators are honest not only with others but also, and most important, with themselves as individuals; for a professional communicator seeks the truth and speaks that truth first to the self.

Source: International Association of Business Communicators (IABC) Web site, http://www.iabc.com/members/joining/code.htm (accessed September 20, 2002).

Speaking in Other College Courses 30

Your opportunities to speak publicly at college won't end once you complete the introductory public speaking course. Whether you're enrolled in an undergraduate course in art history or a graduate seminar in zoology, oral presentations are likely to be a part of your course requirements. One task that is commonly assigned across the curriculum, for example, is the oral *review of academic articles.* A biology instructor might ask you to deliver an oral review of a study on cell regulation published in *Cell Biology,* while a psychology teacher may require that you talk about a study on fetal alcohol syndrome published in the journal *Neuro-Toxicology.* The checklist below details what instructors typically expect from students in a review of an academic article.

Often, you will be called on to prepare course-specific oral presentations in your major or other general-education courses. As an engineering student, for example, you might prepare an oral design review of your major project (see p. 446). A student of history might deliver a presentation linking a historical event with a contemporary issue. Nursing majors might be asked to communicate a treatment plan to a medical team. As part of your grade in chemistry, you may be required to report on an experiment.

In addition to (or in place of) the individual presentation, instructors in your various courses may require that you participate in team presentations or

---

 CHECKLIST

Preparing an Oral Review of an Academic Article

Typically, when you are asked to review an academic article your instructor will expect you to:

✓ Identify the author's thesis.

✓ Explain the methods by which the author arrived at his or her conclusions.

✓ Explain the author's findings.

✓ Identify the author's theoretical perspective, if applicable.

✓ Evaluate the study's validity, if applicable.

✓ Describe the author's sources and evaluate their credibility.

✓ Show how the findings of the study might be applied to other circumstances, and make suggestions for how the study might lead to further research.

Source: With thanks to Michal Dale of Southwest Missouri State University's Department of Communication.

engage in debates. The **team presentation** is an oral presentation prepared and delivered by a group of three or more individuals (see Chapter 28). In a **debate**, two individuals or groups consider or argue an issue from opposing viewpoints (see Appendix A for guidelines on participating in debates). Another format you may encounter is the poster session, especially to convey technical, scientific, and social scientific information. A **poster session** presents information about a study or an issue concisely and visually on a poster (see p. 443).

Preparing to Address Audiences on the Job

At times your professors may require that you tailor your remarks to a mock on-the-job audience, acting as though your classmates represent that audience. Corresponding to the audience types you will likely address once you are employed in your field of training, these audiences include the **expert or insider audience**, the **colleagues within the field audience**, the **lay audience**, and the **mixed audience**. (See Table 30.1 for a description of each type of audience.) Note that individual instructors or people in the work world may not use the same terminology employed here to refer to these audiences.

Speaking in Science and Mathematics Courses

Science-related disciplines include the physical sciences (e.g., chemistry and physics), the natural sciences (e.g., biology and medicine), and the earth sciences (e.g., geology, meteorology, and oceanography). Fields related to mathematics include accounting, statistics, and applied math. Oral presentations in science and mathematics often describe the results of original or replicated re-

TABLE 30.1 • Types of Audiences in the Working World

Type of Audience	Characteristics
Expert or insider audience	People who have intimate knowledge of the topic, issue, product, or idea being discussed—such as researchers on the same project, design team members, technicians working on similar challenges, and clinicians working with similar clients.
Colleagues within the field audience	People who share the speaker's knowledge of the general field under question (e.g., psychology or computer science) but may not be familiar with the specific topic under discussion (e.g., short-term memory or voice-recognition systems, respectively)—such as academic colleagues, managers, project coordinators, and team leaders.
Lay audience	People who have no specialized knowledge of the general field related to the speaker's topic or of the topic itself.
Mixed audience	An audience composed of a combination of people—some with expert knowledge of the field and topic and others with no specialized knowledge. This is perhaps the most difficult audience to satisfy.

CHECKLIST

Tips on Presenting to a Mixed Audience

✓ Find out as much information as you can about the audience.

✓ Prepare both detailed and general content.

✓ Alert the audience to the order of your coverage: "I will first focus on the big picture and on management (marketing/sales) issues. I will then present design specifications and data analysis." In this way, each audience segment will know what to expect and when.

✓ Consider devoting half to two-thirds of your time to an introduction or overview of your subject and saving the highly technical material for the remaining time.[1]

✓ Be clear about the level at which you are speaking: "I am going to present the primary results of this project with minimal detailed information, but I'll be happy to review the statistics or experimental results in more detail following the presentation."

✓ If you notice that your listeners are experiencing discomfort, consider stopping and asking for feedback about what they want. You might then change course and opt for a more in-depth, high-level approach, depending on what they say.[2]

1. Office of Naval Research, "Tips for Preparing and Delivering Scientific Talks and Using Visual Aids," http://www.onr.navy.omil/onr/speak (accessed January 1, 2001).
2. Frederick Gilbert Associates, "Power-Speaking Tips," http://www.powerspeaking.com/powerspeaking/pstips.cfm (accessed August 30, 2000).

search. Instructors want to know the processes by which your experimental results were obtained. For example, your biology instructor might assign an oral report on the extent to which you were able to replicate an experiment on cell mitosis. A mathematics instructor might ask you to apply a mathematical concept to an experiment or issue facing the field. For a geology course, you might be asked to describe the findings of your fieldwork.

THE RESEARCH PRESENTATION

Among the most common types of presentations delivered in the sciences is the research presentation. In it, you describe original research you have done, either alone or as part of a team. The **research presentation** (also called an *oral scientific presentation*) usually follows the model used in scientific investigations (see Figure 30.1) and includes the following elements:

1. *Introduction* describing the research question or issue and the scope and objective of the study
2. *Description of methods* used to investigate the research question including where it took place and the conditions under which it was carried out (lab or field study, for example)

3. *Results* of the study summarizing key findings and highlighting the answers to the questions/hypotheses investigated

4. *Conclusion* (also called *Discussion*), in which the speaker interprets the data or results and discusses their significance

Figure 30.1 Steps in a Scientific Investigation

Formulate a Hypothesis

↓

Select a Research Method

↓

Collect the Data

↓

Analyze the Data

↓

Report the Findings

 CHECKLIST

Evaluating Your Original Research Presentation

✓ Do you state the research question?

✓ Do you clearly state the hypothesis, or hypothetical answer to the research question?

✓ Do you adequately describe and explain the study's research design?

✓ Do you describe the methods used to obtain the results?

✓ Do you explain and evaluate the results of the study?

✓ Do you address the significance of the study?

THE METHODS/PROCEDURE PRESENTATION

Some instructors may require you to describe how an experimental or mathematical process works and under what conditions it can be used. This is generally a ten- to fifteen-minute individual presentation. In a theoretical math class, for example, your assignment might be to describe an approach to solving a problem, such as the Baum Welch algorithm, including examples of how this approach has been used, either inappropriately or appropriately. This type of **methods/procedure presentation** generally does the following:

1. Identifies the conditions under which this particular process should be used

2. Offers a detailed description of the process (at times including an actual demonstration; see Chapter 23)

3. Discusses the benefits and shortcomings of the process

THE RESEARCH OVERVIEW

The **research overview presentation** provides background for a research question that will form the basis of an impending experiment or investigation. Instructors often ask students to organize research overviews into the following sections:

1. Overview of research relevant to the question at hand
2. Discussion of studies central to the question
3. Analysis of the strengths and weaknesses of research in light of the current hypothesis or question

The format for the research overview may be an individual presentation or a **panel discussion**, with several individuals exploring specific lines of research that contribute to a general hypothesis or question. (See Appendix D for a review of panel discussions and symposiums.)

THE EXTENDED RESEARCH OR FIELD STUDY PRESENTATION

You may sometimes be called on to describe an **extended research or field study**. A geology student may be asked to report on a dig, for example. The extended research or field study presentation can be delivered individually, in teams, or in poster session format. A *poster session* presents information about a study or an issue concisely and visually. Presenters display their findings on posters, which are hung on freestanding boards; on hand are copies of the written report, with full details of the study highlighted in the poster session (see the accompanying checklist for more on producing effective poster sessions).

 CHECKLIST

Tips for Producing Effective Poster Sessions

In anticipation of future professional requirements on the job, instructors in scientific, technical, and social scientific disciplines (and, to a lesser extent, the humanities) sometimes direct students to prepare poster sessions.

When you prepare for a poster session, pay particular attention to the following:

✓ Select a concise and informative title for your display.

✓ Include an **abstract** (a brief summary of the study) along with several key points related to a study's research questions/problems, methodologies, results, and conclusions.

✓ Present two to three key points from each section of your paper.

✓ Begin the display by placing, in the upper right-hand corner, a concise introduction that indicates the purpose of the presentation.

✓ Place your conclusions and summary in the lower right-hand corner of the display.

(Continued on p. 444)

(Continued)

✓ Use standard-size poster board of 1.1 m (3'8") by 1.75 m (5'8").

✓ Select a muted color such as gray, beige, light blue, or white.

✓ Make sure your type is large enough to be read comfortably from a distance of at least three feet.

✓ Design figures and diagrams to be viewed from a distance.

✓ Label each figure.

✓ Place concise summaries of each figure in legends beneath the figure.

✓ Be prepared to provide brief descriptions of your poster when asked to do so, remembering to keep your explanations short.

✓ Be prepared to answer questions.

Source: Some points derived from Robert Anholt, *Dazzle 'Em with Style: The Art of Oral Scientific Presentation* (New York: W. H. Freeman, 1994); see also Colorado State University, "Guides about Speeches and Presentations," http://writing.colostate.edu/references/speaking.htm, section on poster sessions, August 28, 2000 (accessed September 2, 2000).

Whatever the format, included in the extended research study are the following details:

1. Overview of the field research
2. Methods used in the research
3. Analysis of the results of the research
4. Time line indicating how the research results will be used in the future

FEATURES OF EFFECTIVE PRESENTATIONS IN SCIENCE AND MATHEMATICS

Science and mathematics instructors will expect your presentations to be grounded in the scientific method and to provide detailed information about methods used in gathering and analyzing data. Credible presentations must clearly illustrate the nature of the research question and the means by which results were achieved. In many kinds of scientific and mathematical presentations, instructors will expect you to do the following:

*   *Use observation, proofs, and experiments as support.* Depending on the nature of the report, instructors may also expect you to recount experiences in the field or to offer observations or experimental findings (e.g., describe what happened to the chemicals in a chemistry experiment or to the physical objects in a physics experiment).

*   *Be selective in your choice of details,* highlighting specific scientific evidence critical to the outcome of the study but not overwhelming listeners with details they can learn about by referring to the written paper and the cited sources.

CHECKLIST

Tips for Preparing Successful Scientific Presentations

✓ Create an informative title that describes the research.
✓ Place your presentation in the context of a major scientific principle.
✓ Focus on a single issue and adjust it to the interests of your audience.
✓ Identify the underlying question you will address, divide it into subquestions, and answer each question.
✓ Follow a logical line of thought.
✓ Explain scientific concepts unambiguously, with a minimum of professional jargon.
✓ Use appropriate analogies and metaphors to associate the unknown with familiar knowledge.
✓ End with a concise, clearly formulated conclusion in the context of your chosen scientific principle.

Source: Based on Robert Anholt, *Dazzle 'Em with Style: The Art of Oral Scientific Presentation* (New York: W. H. Freeman, 1994), 89–90.

- *Use presentation aids* (ranging from slides generated with presentation software programs to equations drawn on a chalkboard) to visually illustrate important processes and concepts. Remember that the more simply you can render complex information (without distorting findings), the more likely it is that audience members will grasp your points.

- *Use analogies to build on prior knowledge and demonstrate underlying causes.* See Chapter 23 for detailed guidelines on explaining difficult concepts.

Speaking in Technical Courses

Technical disciplines include the range of engineering fields (mechanical, electrical, chemical, civil, aerospace, industrial, nuclear), computer-science fields (computer and software engineering), and design-oriented fields (industrial design, architecture, graphic design). Oral presentations in technical courses often relate to a project you are working on—a set of plans for an architecture firm, a prototype robot for a mechanical engineering design team, or an innovative computer-circuit design in electrical engineering. Rather than addressing prior research, as is often the case in oral scientific and social scientific reports, the focus of technical presentations usually rests on the product itself.

Several of the types of presentations you are likely to deliver in a technical course are reviewed in Chapter 29, "Business and Professional Presentations," including proposals and progress reports (see pp. 433–437). Other kinds include (but are not limited to) the design review and the request for funding.

THE DESIGN REVIEW

The **design review** provides information on the results of a design project. Many capstone-engineering courses require that students prepare design reviews, which are generally informative in nature, although their purpose may include convincing the audience that the design decisions are sound. Design reviews often incorporate a prototype demonstration. A **prototype** is a model of the design. Usually, design reviews are delivered as team presentations (of about thirty minutes in length) or in poster-session format. Design reviews typically include the following:

1. Overview of the design
2. Description of the unique specifications or features of the design
3. Discussion of any experimental testing that has been completed on the design
4. Discussion of future plans and unresolved problems
5. Discussion of marketing and economic issues

THE REQUEST FOR FUNDING

In the **request for funding presentation**, a team member or the entire team provides evidence that a project, proposal, or design idea is worth funding. As such, this kind of presentation is persuasive in nature. Requests for funding usually cover the following ground:

1. Overview of customer specifications and needs
2. Analysis of the market and its needs
3. Overview of the design idea or project and how it meets those needs
4. Projected costs for the project
5. Specific reasons why the project or idea should be funded

The request for funding may be delivered as an individual or team presentation. On the job, the audience for the request for funding is made up of people who are concerned with the marketing, economic, and customer aspects of the idea or project (i.e., colleagues within the field; see Table 30.1).

FEATURES OF EFFECTIVE TECHNICAL PRESENTATIONS

Technical presentations sell ideas, provide hard data, rely on visual aids, and are results oriented.[1] As you prepare your technical presentation, pay particular attention to the following:

- *Lead with the results.* Technical disciplines such as engineering are about results — the end product. Therefore, consider telling the audience the most important result first. Then fill in the details.[2]

- *Gear the information to the appropriate level.* Because of the complexity of technical information, it is especially important to convey it at a level appropriate to the audience. Typically, people who attend technical presentations possess a range of technical knowledge — from little or none to an expert understanding of the topic at hand (see Table 30.1). See also the checklist on p. 441 for tips on presenting to a mixed audience.

- *Use ample presentation aids.* Use diagrams, prototypes, and drawings, including design specifications, computer simulations, physical models, and spreadsheets. Construct aids early in the process, and use them continually as you practice your speech.

- *Use a persuasive design — sell your ideas.* The technical presenter must persuade clients, managers, or classmates that a design, idea, or product is a good one. As one instructor notes, "You can never assume that your product or design will just sell — you have to do that."[3]

- *Provide hard data.* Good technical presentations are detailed and specific and use numbers as evidence. Instead of general, sweeping statements, audiences expect hard data and clearly stated experimental results.

Speaking in Social Science Courses

Students in the social sciences (including psychology, sociology, political science, and communication) learn to evaluate and conduct **qualitative research** (in which the emphasis is on observing, describing, and interpreting behavior) as well as **quantitative research** (in which the emphasis is on statistical measurement).[4] Research methods and areas of investigation can range from experiments on the behavior of neuroreceptors to studies of the effects of natural disasters on people's psychological and sociological well-being.

Social scientists often attempt to explain social or psychological phenomena by answering *what, how,* and *why* questions.[5] As a social science student, you might be asked to evaluate a theory or body of research, debate an issue, review the relevant literature, or make policy recommendations. Additionally, as in science and mathematics courses, you might prepare a research, field study, or methods/procedure presentation.

THE DEBATE

Students in the social sciences often must prepare for *debates* on controversial issues (see Appendix A for more on debates). Sometimes an assignment involves advocating a position that you do not support. For example, a sociology instructor may require students who oppose school vouchers to defend the policy. Whichever side of an issue you address, you will need to prepare a well-composed argument with strong supporting evidence.

THE REVIEW OF THE LITERATURE

Reviewing the literature is an important step in shaping research questions. The **review of the literature presentation** reviews the body of research related to a given topic or issue and offers conclusions about the topic based on this research. A psychology student, for example, in a review of the literature on psychological dysfunction in the military family, would describe the available research on the topic, offer conclusions about the risk factors uncovered by the research, and suggest directions for future research. A review of the literature presentation typically includes the following:

1. Description of the available research
2. Evaluation and conclusions about the research
3. Suggested directions for future study

THE EXPLANATORY RESEARCH PRESENTATION

As stated earlier, social scientists often attempt to explain social or psychological phenomena by answering *what, how,* and *why* questions. The **explanatory research presentation** reports on studies that attempt to analyze and explain a phenomenon, such as the sharp rise in cases of autism. Such presentations typically include the following:

1. Description of the phenomenon under discussion (e.g., "*What* is taking place?")
2. Description of *how* the phenomenon occurs
3. Explanation or theory of *why* it occurs

THE EVALUATION RESEARCH PRESENTATION

In addition to explaining phenomena, professionals in the social sciences often measure the effectiveness of programs developed to address these issues. Rather than asking "How?" or "Why?" evaluation research asks "Does it work?"[6] In preparation for on-the-job delivery, instructors may ask you to evaluate a program or a policy. Typically, the **evaluation research presentation** addresses the following considerations:

1. What is the program's mission?
2. What does the program actually accomplish?
3. How well has the program met its stated objectives?

THE POLICY RECOMMENDATION

Psychologists, sociologists, communications specialists, and others are often asked to offer advice and recommendations on a current issue or problem. These professionals gather research and present recommendations to the person or body commissioning the report. The lay audience (see Table 30.1) usually has a vested interest in the problem but is unfamiliar with the intricacies of the field. In preparation for such situations, instructors sometimes direct a team of students to deliver a **policy recommendation report**, which typically includes the following:

1. Definition of the problem
2. Recommendations to solve the problem or address the issue
3. Plan for implementation of the recommendations
4. Discussion of future needs or parameters to fulfill the recommendations

FEATURES OF EFFECTIVE PRESENTATIONS IN THE SOCIAL SCIENCES

Good social scientific presentations clearly explain the research question, refer to current research, and use timely data.

- *State the research question.* Well-organized presentations include clear explanations of the research question and the means by which the results were achieved.
- *Refer to current research.* Credible social scientific presentations build on current research in the field. Your instructor is more likely to accept experimental evidence if it has been replicated and supported by other, recent studies.
- *Use timely data.* Instructors expect student presentations to include recent data and examples. A report on poverty rates for a sociology course must provide up-to-date data because poverty rates change yearly. A review of treatments for the mentally ill, for example, should accurately reflect current treatments.

Speaking in Arts and Humanities Courses

Speaking assignments in arts and humanities courses (including English, philosophy, foreign languages, art history, theater, music, religion, and history) often require that you interpret the meaning of a particular idea, event, person, story, or artifact. An art history professor, for example, might ask you to identify the various artistic and historical influences on a sculpture or painting. An instructor of literature might require you to explain the theme of a novel or a poem. A theater instructor might ask you to offer your interpretation of a new play. Rather than focusing on quantitative research, presentations in the arts and humanities often rely on the speaker's analysis and interpretation of the topic at hand. These interpretations are nonetheless grounded in the conventions of the field and build on the research within the field.

Oral presentation assignments in arts and humanities courses can range from informative speeches of explanation to debates.

THE PRESENTATION USING COMPARISON AND CONTRAST

A common assignment in arts and humanities courses is the oral presentation in which you compare and contrast events, stories, people, or artifacts in order to highlight the similarities or differences between them. For example, you might compare two works of literature from different time periods, or two historical figures or works of art. These assignments may be informative or persuasive in nature. Presentations that compare and contrast include the following:

1. Thesis statement that outlines the connection between the works, people, or stories
2. Main points that highlight the various similarities or differences
3. Concluding evaluative statement about the comparison (e.g., if the presentation is persuasive in nature, why one piece of literature is more effective than another; if informative in nature, a restatement of similarities and differences)

THE DEBATE

Often students will engage in debates on opposing ideas, historical figures, or philosophical positions. (See Appendix A for more on debates.) In a history class, for example, students might argue whether sixteenth-century women in Western Europe experienced a Renaissance. The speaker must present a brief (three-minute) assertion about the topic; the opposing speaker responds with a position. Whatever side of an issue you address, prepare a well-composed argument with strong supporting evidence (see Chapter 25).

THE CLASSROOM DISCUSSION

Many students taking arts and humanities courses must research a question and then lead a classroom discussion on it. For example, an English student leading a discussion on Anton Chekov's *The Cherry Orchard* would be expected to provide a synopsis of the play's plot, theme, and characters, as well as an analysis of the play's meaning.

FEATURES OF EFFECTIVE PRESENTATIONS IN THE ARTS AND HUMANITIES

Good presentations in the arts and humanities are original in some way. They help the audience think of the topic in a new way by providing a unique interpretation. A presentation on slavery in the United States will be more effective if you offer a new way of viewing slavery, for example, rather than reiterating what other people have said or what is already generally accepted knowledge about slavery. A debate on two philosophical ideas will be most effective when you assert issues and arguments that are different from those that the audience has thought of before. Since many speaking events in the arts and humanities call for interpretation, the more original the interpretation (while remaining logical and grounded in sound evidence), the more persuasive and engaging the audience will perceive the presentation to be. As you prepare your presentation, pay particular attention to the following:

- *Clearly state your thesis.* Tell the audience early on what it is you are trying to explain or prove.
- *Link the discussion to the relevant period in history, school of thought, and/or movement in music, art, or literature.* Provide context for your topic by locating it within its relevant framework.
- *Practice using visual aids.* Often, instructors will expect to see representations of the works under discussion, so spend the necessary time to coordinate slides and other aids with relevant speech points (see Chapter 22).
- *Anticipate questions.* Be prepared to address questions and engage in further discussion after you've delivered the presentation.

Speaking in Education Courses

In education courses (including curriculum and instruction, physical education, secondary and elementary education, and educational administration), the most common and practical speaking event is *teaching in a classroom*. Assignments in education courses often focus on some form of instructional task, such as giving a lecture or demonstrating an activity. In a mathematics education course, you might give a mini-lecture on a particular geometric theorem. In a learning-styles course, you might tailor an activity to a variety of different learners. Each of these tasks requires that you deliver an effective informative speech that defines, describes, explains, or demonstrates information (see Chapter 23).

THE LECTURE

A **lecture** is an informational speech directed to an audience of student learners. Standard lectures range from fifty to ninety minutes in length. A mini-lecture, designed to give students an opportunity to synthesize information in a shorter form, generally lasts about fifteen to twenty minutes. Typically, lectures include the following:

1. Overview
2. Preview of the topic/thesis
3. Reference/link to previous topics covered
4. Discussion
5. Preview of the next assigned topic

THE GROUP ACTIVITY

The **group activity presentation** serves as a short introduction to a group activity that follows a lecture. This presentation is intended to be between six and eight minutes in length, with a primary focus on providing students with clear directions on how to complete the activity. Group activity presentations typically include the following:

1. Brief review of the lecture thesis or main idea
2. Directions on how students should engage in the group activity
3. Preview of what students should get out of the activity (and what the discussion following the activity will cover)

THE CLASSROOM DISCUSSION

One informal kind of presentation for which education majors typically prepare is the **classroom discussion presentation**. These presentations take place following a lecture or class activity. While the initial discussion presentation itself is only one to two minutes in length, preparation is necessary. To lead such a discussion:

1. Outline the critical points to be covered.
2. Prepare several general questions to launch the discussion.
3. Prepare relevant questions and examples to use during the discussion. You should create more questions than you think you will need.

FEATURES OF EFFECTIVE PRESENTATIONS IN EDUCATION

Good presentations in education are marked by clear organization, integration of the material into the broader course content, and student-friendly supporting material.

- *Organize material logically.* Presentations in education must be tightly organized so that the audience can easily access information (see Chapters 12 and 26). In educational settings, the simpler the organizational structure, the better. Be sure to make liberal use of organizing devices (such as preview statements and transitions) and to provide clear and logical directions for group activities.

- *Integrate overall course content.* Connections between the content of a given lecture, activity, or discussion and the overall course content should be made clear. To do this, describe how the lecture for the day relates to the previous days' lectures. In a discussion or group activity, make clear the connections between students' comments and other topics that have been or will be raised.

- *Tailor examples and evidence to the audience.* Use familiar examples and evidence that the audience can grasp easily and that will enhance learning; these examples are often closest to students' experiences.

Speaking in Nursing and Allied Health Courses

Speaking assignments in nursing and allied health courses — including those related to nursing, physical therapy, occupational therapy, dental hygiene, radiology, and other forms of health care — range from reviews of research articles in professional journals to reports on community service projects in a clinical setting. Students are assigned a mix of individual and team presentations that instruct clients on health-care practices and techniques, describe plans of care to medical teams, communicate patients' status at shift changes, and make policy recommendations to managers. Visual aids such as PowerPoint slides may be required; certain courses also entail preparation of individual or team poster sessions.

THE COMMUNITY SERVICE LEARNING PROJECT

In a **community service learning project**, students learn about and help address a need or problem in a community agency, such as a daycare center, mental health facility, or burn center. Typically, reports about such projects include the following:

1. Description of the community agency and its client base
2. Overview of the service project and your role in it
3. Description of your accomplishments
4. Report of any problems encountered
5. Relationship of service learning to course content
6. Summary of what you learned

THE TREATMENT PLAN REPORT (CASE CONFERENCE/ SHIFT REPORT)

Either individually or as part of a health-care team, persons in the helping professions often evaluate patients' conditions and outline plans of treatment. These reports can take the form of a case conference or a shift report. Typically, the **case conference** includes the following:

1. Description of patient status
2. Explanation of the disease process
3. Steps in the treatment regimen

4. Goals for the patient and family
5. Plans for the patient's care at home
6. Review of financial needs
7. Assessment of available resources

A **shift report** is a concise report of the patient's status and needs that is delivered to the oncoming caregiver. It includes the following information:

1. Patient's name, location, and reason for care
2. Current physical status
3. Length of stay in setting
4. Pertinent psychosocial data, including plans for discharge and involvement of family
5. Care needs (physical, hygiene, activity, medication, nutritional)

THE POLICY RECOMMENDATION REPORT

In the **policy recommendation report**, the speaker recommends the adoption of a new (or modified) health practice or policy, such as introducing a new treatment regimen at a burn center. This report, sometimes assigned as part of a capstone course, includes the following:

1. Review of the existing policy or practice
2. Description of the proposed policy recommendation
3. Review of the existing scientific literature on the policy recommendation
4. Plan of action for implementing the policy or practice

FEATURES OF EFFECTIVE PRESENTATIONS IN NURSING AND ALLIED HEALTH COURSES

Good presentations in health-related courses accurately communicate medical information while simultaneously assessing practical conditions. Depending on the audience (e.g., patient or staff), the communication will shift in tone from therapeutic/empathetic to more matter-of-fact, and instructors will expect to see these shifts in tone reflected in your presentations. In general, instructors will expect you to demonstrate evidence-based practice for all assignments. **Evidence-based practice** (EBP) is an approach to treatment in which caregivers make decisions based on current research and "best practices."[7] Instructors will want you to support any assertions and recommendations with the relevant scientific literature and other reports containing evidence of effective clinical practice.

Sample
Speeches

Sample Speeches

Sample Speeches

Speeches That Satisfy

JANE W. TULLY

Jane Tully is a speechwriter and the president of Tully Communications in New York City. Here she delivers an informative speech about the speechwriting process to the New York chapter of Women in Communications. Tully uses the metaphor of the speech as a party as her thematic focus, with the speaker as the party's "host" and the speechwriter (if different from the speaker) as the party's "verbal caterer." Tully's use of related food imagery throughout the speech ties each of her points to her theme.

Thank you all for coming this evening. I'd like to begin by saying that this is the 1 first time I've stepped out from behind the computer screen I write on to talk about the speechwriting process. Preparing this presentation for you has taught me a great deal about the work I do for my clients, and I'm delighted to share some of what I've learned with you.

A number of years ago Mary Clifford, the wife of the noted Washington 2 lawyer Clark Clifford, gave a dinner party. Mrs. Clifford was a popular hostess, and for this occasion she planned a particularly elegant menu in honor of a special guest — Mary Garden. Ms. Garden was an aging opera singer and had been quite a glamorous diva earlier in the century. The meal was to be a feast of culinary delights, starting with freshly shucked Cape Breton oysters, flown in especially for the occasion.

When the oysters were served, Ms. Garden politely declined them. That 3 wasn't too alarming. Many people don't like fresh oysters. But when the second course was served she declined that, too. Mrs. Clifford became alarmed when the main course was served and her guest would have none of it. As it turned out, all Ms. Garden wanted for dinner was what she always had — a bowl of chocolate ice cream and a cup of black coffee!

There was scrambling in the kitchen, and they had to send someone on a 4 quick trip to the store because they were out of ice cream. Mrs. Clifford managed to accommodate her guest and save the occasion, but just barely. I tell you this story because it holds an important lesson, not only for people who entertain but for those of us who write and deliver speeches.

You see, I have a theory that giving a speech is a lot like giving a party. You, 5 the audience, are the invited guests. As the speaker, I am the host — at least for

457

the moment. The speech I am delivering to you is like a meal. I want it to be nourishing food for thought — full of substance, with interesting ideas for you to chew on. I want to present it in a way that's appealing, so you'll be eager to take in my ideas. And, like a good meal, I want my speech to be appropriate for this particular occasion.

If you think of a speech that way, then where does the speechwriter fit in? 6 Actually, I like to think of myself as a kind of verbal caterer. You call on professionals like me when you don't have the time or expertise to do the job yourself, or when you have a special occasion and you want that extra something that will really make your speech stand out.

Like caterers, we speechwriters can help you in a number of ways. Maybe 7 all you need is a little consultation on the menu, so you call on us to help you focus your message and figure out what direction to take it. Or maybe you need a few hors d'oeuvres, so you bring us in to draft some talking points or find just the right quote or story that will bring your speech to life. Sometimes you need the whole thing catered, so we serve up your speech on a silver platter — a full draft, formatted for the podium and ready for delivery.

So in my role as caterer, I'd like to take this opportunity to share my basic 8 recipe for a successful presentation. Follow this easy three-step recipe and you can't go wrong:

- Know who's coming to the party,
- Use only the best ingredients, and
- Focus on the main course.

First, know who's coming.   9

If Mrs. Clifford had done some advance research on her guest list, she 10 might have learned about the peculiar dietary quirks of her special guest and been prepared to graciously accommodate her. Not that she would have changed her whole menu — only adapted her plans to take Ms. Garden's eccentricity into account. Likewise, speakers and their writers need to be alert to their audience's special needs and interests. Knowing who's going to be out there helps the writer shape the message so that listeners won't simply reject the speaker's ideas one by one as they are served up.

What do we need to know about audiences? Size, for one thing. This is im- 11 portant, because smaller audiences pay closer attention. When a group is small, the speaker can easily maintain eye contact and hold people's attention. The larger the audience, the easier it is for listeners to feel anonymous and to drift off, so a speaker has to offer more entertainment value. With large convention-sized audiences of hundreds, or even thousands of people, this is essential: Bring in audiovisual support whenever you can; add stories and humor. Keep it moving, and keep it short, or you'll lose them.

To the extent that it's possible, speechwriters also want to know the age 12 range of the audience. Will it be a group of seniors, or young professionals, or students — or a mixed group? This affects the kinds of stories, humor, and other support material we will choose to make the speaker's points. Because so much of humor comes out of life experience, the jokes Grandma enjoys may fall completely flat with your teenage son. If your audience includes a wide range of ages, you need to find humor that has a very broad appeal.

This is also true for any examples from history. A number of years ago, a 13 friend of mine was once asked to speak to a church youth group on the subject of war and whether or not it is ever justified. He started by telling about how he had felt, as a senior in college at the height of the Vietnam War, when his draft notice arrived in the mail. A young man in the group interrupted him to say, "Oh, yeah, Vietnam. We read about that in history last week." My friend was barely 30 at the time, and he said he had never felt so old in all his life! But it was an important lesson for him as a speaker: Never assume that your audience shares your experience or knowledge of history, and be sure to give your illustrations the historical context they need — especially if you are speaking to a younger audience.

Speechwriters also want to know what the gender mix of an audience will 14 be. Will there be more men than women, or vice versa? Again, this information affects the kinds of illustrations we choose. One of my clients, a product sales manager at Citibank, recently gave a speech to pump up a group of brokers who were being asked to meet some new revenue goals. We used a story featuring the retired Notre Dame coach Lou Holtz. The story ends with a great one-liner about a quarterback who runs eighty-five yards to score a winning goal. The speaker delivered it beautifully, and he got a big laugh — the vast majority of his listeners were men. It was perfect for that group, but if the audience had been more mixed, I probably would have used something different.

For the speech I'm delivering to you, I actually had to think twice about my 15 food image. At first I thought the comparison might be a little too domestic for an audience of professional women. But after giving it some thought, I decided that since so many of the world's great chefs are men, and since we all have to eat, this image can work for both male and female audiences. My point is that it was important for me to go through the process of thinking about the gender of this audience and how that could affect the way you receive my ideas.

Speechwriters also try to find out what feelings or prejudices people bring 16 to the subject of a speech. I've done a great deal of writing for executives at the National Geographic Society who travel around the country promoting geography education and working to bring geography back to the classroom. It's very important for them, and for me as their speechwriter, to know that many people feel about geography the way they do about math. They remember their sixth grade teachers making them memorize the fifty states or the capitals of the world. They think of geography as boring and irrelevant. Before you can persuade such people that they have to know geography to help protect the environment, succeed in the global economy, and make sense of foreign affairs, you have to acknowledge how they feel about their sixth grade lessons! Sometimes all it takes is a little humor to let your audience know that you understand where they're coming from. As soon as they get that message, they can relax and really listen to your ideas.

So . . . know who's coming to the party.   17

Second, use only the best ingredients. When I give a dinner party, I like to 18
experiment with recipes that have an exotic twist—like a special ingredient I
can't get down the street, maybe something I'll only find at Balducci's or the
green market. The shopping is fun and interesting, and the new ingredient gives
a special flavor to the whole meal.

The same is true with researching a speech. It's fun because I'm always 19
learning something new. I have learned that it's worth going out of my way to
find a little-known fact or two that can help make the speech memorable. A National Geographic Society executive was once asked to accept an award on behalf of the Society from the Leukemia Society of America. In researching his
remarks, I learned about a small periwinkle that grows in the tropical rain forest. This little flower is the source of the medication that saves the lives of 95
percent of the children who contract childhood leukemia. With that fact, the
speaker was able to relate National Geographic's interest in saving the environment to the lifesaving work of the Leukemia Society. The extra effort it took to
find that little tidbit of information was really worth it.

Once you have the information you need for a speech, spice it up! A 20
speechwriting guide called *American Speaker* points out that "good quotes in a
speech, like good seasoning in a stew, are meant to add zest without detracting
from the essential nature of the dish and its basic ingredients." That's true not
only of quotes but of anecdotes and humor as well. These elements must add
something to the speech, not detract from it. I think most audiences are impa-
tient with speakers who start out with a belly laugh, then take off in an entirely
different direction. Not only is this annoying but what a waste of a good story!
The whole reason for telling stories in your speech is to help people pay closer
attention and remember your ideas. So make sure your illustrations relate to
your message, and make the connection clear for the audience.

Most stories can be used to make any number of points. When you find a 21
good one, feel free to use it whenever and wherever it will do the job, and don't
worry too much if it's been around awhile. I disagree with those who say you
can't use the same story twice. Like a great piece of music that we enjoy hearing again and again, a good story can be told more than once, as long as it's
freshly interpreted. Even if they've heard it before, audiences appreciate the creative connection you make between the story and your message.

Let me give you an example. There's the one about the little girl who was 22
studying first aid in her fifth grade class. One day when she went home there
was a car accident right in front of her house. The next day she ran to school
to tell her teacher all about it.

"There was a man with his arm bleeding, but I knew what to do!" she said. 23
"Oh, good," her teacher said. "Did you use first aid?" 24
"Oh, yes," she said. "I put my head between my legs so I wouldn't faint!" 25
Now that story has all kinds of possibilities. I once used it in a commencement
address for a group of teachers who had finished an extension course, to make
a point about how well prepared they were to return to the classroom. But it
would work just as well in a corporate setting. Use it to support your education
or training message, to talk about applying academic learning in the real world.

It's also a story about communications, so you could use it to illustrate an idea about management communications and how we personalize the information we're given. Or use it to talk about crisis response. How well prepared is your organization to deal with crisis? Or think about using it in a speech about health care. It could illustrate a message about how our changing health care system is responding — or not responding — to real needs. A little creative analogizing can take a story like this a long way.

Your audience will enjoy the story, but more than that they'll enjoy the way 26 you use it to reinforce your message.

So . . . know who's coming to the party, use only the best ingredients, and, 27 third, focus on the main course. Every great meal has a great main course, a pièce de résistance. And every successful speech has a main focus, a central idea that listeners can take home. This is the concept that pulls the whole speech together and helps your audience remember your supporting points. For example, the focus of this presentation is actually a comparison — I'm saying that a speech is like a meal. If you can remember that, it shouldn't be too hard to remember my supporting ideas.

At the beginning of the speechwriting process, many speakers aren't sure 28 how to focus their messages. At this stage, it's important to ask, "If your audience remembered only one thing, what would you want it to be?" The answer is often a range of choices. When I'm searching for the focus for a speech, I look not only for the idea that is the most intellectually compelling but the one that has the most emotional power for the speaker. That's because we remember ideas when they are presented to us with both clarity and feeling.

I once wrote a commencement address for the head of an education foun- 29 dation. He'd been asked to speak to the graduating class of an environmental school in Idaho. He wanted to say that the lessons the graduates had learned in school really do apply in the outside world and they would succeed in their chosen field because they had been so well prepared. This was not a particularly original thought, but one he felt strongly about. The speaker was also an avid trout fisherman. In fact, he was planning to go fishing the very next day. So to give his speech added punch, we compared fishing and school. He talked about how you have to be patient, choose the right place to do your work, and so forth. He told the students that by graduating they had landed a big fish, and that their skills would land them more big fish in the future. It sounds corny as I recall it, but my point is that he delivered it with real feeling because he loved both fishing and education so much. They loved it.

Having a focus not only helps tie the speech together, it helps answer what 30 I consider to be the most important question in speechwriting: "What should I leave out?" Usually the answer is "Much, even most, of the material I've found." If the idea or example doesn't support your main point in some way, drop it, no matter how fascinating it is. Save it for another speech.

This will help you keep the speech to twenty minutes or so. That's impor- 31 tant, because most audiences begin losing concentration after that amount of time. If you're asked to speak for longer than that, find ways to break it up, perhaps with Q&A, slides, a video, or some kind of interactive exercise. Remember, a speech is like a meal. We can only eat so much at one sitting, and we can only hear so much at one sitting. Mark Twain said that few sinners are saved after the first twenty minutes of a sermon. That's true of just about any oral presentation. So keep it short.

Then you can think of the Q&A as a kind of dessert. Leave room for it, 32 and time. You don't want your listeners to feel like that grand old lady who died during dinner. She was the sister of an eighteenth-century French writer named Brillat-Savarin, and she expired at the table one night just before her one-hundredth birthday. Her last words were "Bring on the dessert. I think I'm about to die." I'm going to stop there while you still have room — and we still have time — for dessert. I'll be happy to answer your questions.

Sample Persuasive Speech

Testimony on Child Labor

CRAIG KIELBURGER

Craig Kielburger, disturbed by a newspaper report from Pakistan about the tragic life and death of a young boy who had been sold into slavery to weave carpets, helped form an organization called Free the Children, a children's rights advocacy group. Amazingly, Craig was twelve years old at the time and in the seventh grade. His work as an advocate for Free the Children has offered him the opportunity to deliver thousands of persuasive speeches to enlist the support of individuals, organizations, and governments to protect children from exploitation.

In the following speech, Kielburger faces a formidable challenge as a thirteen-year-old addressing the U.S. House of Representatives Subcommittee on International Relations and Human Rights. He proves his competence and eloquence at the outset, earning his audience's attention while using both his youthful perspective and his expertise to great effect throughout the speech. As you read Kielburger's words, keep in mind what you learned about developing persuasive arguments in Chapters 24 and 25.

Mr. Chairman, Members of the Committee, Ladies and Gentlemen: 1

I am pleased to be here today to represent children — child labor affects chil- 2 dren — children are being exploited and denied their basic rights, children are being abused. I believe that children must be heard when speaking about child labor — I believe that we must be part of the solution.

I recently spent seven and a half weeks traveling through South Asia to 3 meet with working and street children. I wanted to better understand their reality — to ask them what they wanted so that we would not be imposing our Western culture on them.

I can tell you stories of what I saw — stories which would shock you. I met 4 children as young as four years old, working in brick kilns making bricks seven days a week from dawn to dusk, children working fourteen hours a day load-ing dangerous chemicals into firecracker tubes, children working in metal and glass factories, children physically and verbally abused. Some children I'll never forget—like Nagashar, who worked as a bonded laborer in a carpet factory. He had scars all over his body, including his voice box, where he had been branded with red-hot irons for trying to escape. Or the nine-year-old boy with a deep scar that ran across the top of his head where he had been hit with a metal bar for making a mistake on the job. Then there was Munianal, the eight-year-old girl who worked in a recycling plant taking apart used syringes and needles gathered from hospitals and the streets. She wore no shoes and no protective gear. No one had ever told her about AIDS. These are the working children.

Not just facts and statistics but real children.   5

Some of you may say, "Well these children are poor. Don't they have to   6
work to help their families survive?" Studies by UNICEF, the ILO and other nongovernmental organizations have shown that child labor is actually keeping Third World countries poor, because a child at work means an adult out of work. Factory owners prefer to hire children because they are cheaper labor, eas-ily intimidated and won't organize trade unions. Kailash Satyarthi, who last year won the Robert Kennedy International Award for Human Rights, heads 150 nongovernmental organizations working with child laborers in South Asia. He stresses that India has 50 million child workers, but 55 million adults unem-ployed. And because these children are not able to go to school they remain il-literate, and the cycle of poverty continues. Child labor keeps people poor.

As consumers, we bear part of the responsibility. Is it fair for children to be 7
sitting on the ground for twelve hours a day, for pennies a day sewing famous brand name soccer balls—which they will never get to play with—soccer balls shipped to countries like ours for your children, your grandchildren, or for me?

It is simply a question of greed and exploitation—exploitation of the most 8
weak and vulnerable. These greedy people include companies going into the Third World countries contracting out work to the cheapest factories which will produce goods up to standard. This only encourages factory owners to seek out the cheapest labor—underpaid workers and children. Poverty is no excuse for exploitation. Poverty is no excuse for child abuse.

We the children of North America have formed an organization called Free 9
the Children. Free the Children is a youth movement dedicated to the elimina-tion of child labor and the exploitation of children. Most of our members are between 10 and 15 years old. We now have groups in provinces across Canada and chapters quickly spreading throughout the United States—in Washington, San Francisco, Maryland, Idaho, Iowa. Calls are coming in from all over the world—from young people, from children, who want to help. You don't need a lot of committee meetings to understand that exploiting children in child labor is wrong. We may be young, but it is very clear to us that this child abuse must stop.

We believe that children must be removed from factories and jobs given to 10
adult members of the family—adults who can negotiate for better rights and working conditions.

We believe that companies which go into Third World countries for cheap   11
labor must pay their workers a just wage so that children will not have to work
to supplement their parents' income. These same companies should also be
willing to put money back into the country to help in the education and the
protection of children.

We have consumers calling our Free the Children office from all over North   12
America, telling us that they don't want to buy products made from the suffering children.

That is why a labeling system, with independent monitoring, which clearly   13
identifies items not made by child labor is necessary. Another solution is to hold
importers responsible for making sure that the products they are importing into
North America have not been made from the exploitation of children. Consumers have a right to know who made the products they are buying.

In May 1995, UNICEF set an example with a no child labor clause in its   14
buying policy based on the United Nations Convention on the Rights of the
Child.

I have been told that the United States already has a Tariff Act passed in   15
1930. Section 3:07 prohibits products being made from prison or unindentured
labor from coming into the United States. If this is true then why are carpets,
soccer balls, brick work and other items made by children in bonded and slave
labor not banned from coming into the United States under this law?

Child labor should not be used, however, as an excuse to stop trade with a   16
developing country. We are advocating selective buying, not a boycott of all
products which could harm children even more.

I don't know why anyone would oppose laws which protect the children of   17
the world. Maybe companies, sports and TV personalities, maybe consumers,
might have said until recently, that they didn't know about child labor and the
exploitation of workers in Third World countries but now they do. There is no
excuse anymore. We have all been educated. Knowledge implies responsibility.
You and I, all of us, are now responsible to help these children.

Eliminating child labor comes down to a question of political will. Why are   18
countries with a high incidence of child labor spending on average thirty times
more on the military than on primary education? How serious are world leaders about helping these children? Where is the social conscience of multinational corporations?

I have hundreds of pictures of children which I could have shown you   19
today. I have brought only one. When I was in Calcutta, I participated in a rally
with 250 children who marched through the street with banners chanting, "We
want freedom. We want an education." Children should not work in hazardous
industries — Never Again. Today I am here to speak for these children, to be their
voice. You are an influential nation. You have the power in your words, in your
actions and in your policy making to give children hope for a better life. What
will you do to help these children?

Sample Special Occasion Speech

Eulogy of the *Columbia* Space Shuttle Astronauts

GEORGE W. BUSH

Saturday, February 1, 2003, brought another typically bright, sunny winter morning to Central and East Texas. That morning few people noted that the space shuttle Colum-bia, with its seven-member multinational crew, was scheduled to return to Earth after a sixteen-day mission. Only the most avid followers of shuttle missions watched as the Columbia reentered Earth's atmosphere. But in a horrible moment, NASA Flight Control lost all contact with Columbia. Soon NASA announced the worst: Columbia and its crew of seven astronauts were lost. The loss was a national tragedy. And because the crew of the doomed space shuttle included the first astronaut from Israel and the first woman astronaut born in India, it was an international loss as well.

On February 4, at the memorial service held in honor of the "Columbia Seven" at the NASA Johnson Space Center in Houston, Texas, President George W. Bush delivered the following remarks. Loved ones and relatives of all seven astronauts, members of the president's cabinet and of Congress, representatives of the air force, and others associated with the crew and the space program attended the service, which was conducted outdoors on a lawn in front of NASA headquarters.

The president's speech follows the guidelines for a eulogy described in Chapter 27, "Special Occasion Speeches." The president names each crew member in turn and notes something unique and memorable about that person's ambitions, professional achieve-ments, or contributions to the mission. He is positive about each one without appearing insincere, and in several cases he tells brief but informative anecdotes about how the in-dividuals' lives had led them to become astronauts. The president also mentions family members, friends, and colleagues of the deceased, acknowledging their significant grief and courage and thus humanizing his message and intimating that he knows the memorial event is really for them, the survivors. At the beginning of the speech, the president men-tions the tragedy itself, but he does not dwell on it. Rather, he commemorates the kinds of persons the astronauts were and how important their service was to their countries and indeed to the world.

Their mission was almost complete, and we lost them so close to home. The 1 men and women of the *Columbia* had journeyed more than six million miles and were minutes away from arrival and reunion. The loss was sudden and ter-rible, and for their families the grief is heavy.

Our nation shares in your sorrow and in your pride. 2

We remember not only one moment of tragedy, but seven lives of great pur- 3 pose and achievement.

To leave behind Earth and air and gravity is an ancient dream of humanity. 4 For these seven it was a dream fulfilled. Each of these astronauts had the dar-ing and discipline required of their calling.

Each of them knew that great endeavors are inseparable from great risk. And 5 each of them accepted those risks willingly, even joyfully, in the cause of discovery.

Rick Husband was a boy of four when he first thought of being an astro- 6 naut. As a man and having become an astronaut, he found it was even more important to love his family and serve his Lord.

One of Rick's favorite hymns was "How Great Thou Art," which offers   7
these words of praise: "I see the stars. I hear the mighty thunder. Thy power
throughout the universe displayed."

David Brown was first drawn to the stars as a little boy with a telescope in   8
his backyard. He admired astronauts, but as he said: "I thought they were movie
stars. I thought I was kind of a normal kid."

David grew up to be a physician, an aviator who could land on the deck of   9
a carrier in the middle of the night, and a shuttle astronaut.

His brother asked him several weeks ago what would happen if something   10
went wrong on their mission. David replied, "This program will go on."

Michael Anderson always wanted to fly planes and rose to the rank of lieu-   11
tenant colonel in the air force. Along the way, he became a role model, especially for his two daughters and for the many children he spoke to in schools.

He said to them, "Whatever you want to be in life, you're training for it   12
now." He also told his minister, "If this thing doesn't come out right, don't
worry about me, I'm just going on higher."

Laurel Salton Clark was a physician and a flight surgeon who loved adven-   13
ture, loved her work, loved her husband and her son. A friend who heard Laurel speaking to mission control said, "There was a smile in her voice."

Laurel conducted some of the experiments as *Columbia* orbited the Earth   14
and described seeing new life emerge from a tiny cocoon.

"Life," she said, "continues in a lot of places, and life is a magical thing."   15

None of our astronauts traveled a longer path to space than Kalpana   16
Chawla. She left India as a student, but she would see the nation of her birth,
all of it, from hundreds of miles above.

When the sad news reached her hometown, an administrator at her high   17
school recalled, "She always said she wanted to reach the stars." She went there
and beyond.

Kalpana's native country mourns her today and so does her adopted land.   18

Ilan Ramon also flew above his home, the land of Israel. He said, "The quiet   19
that envelops space makes the beauty even more powerful, and I only hope that
the quiet can one day spread to my country."

Ilan was a patriot, the devoted son of a Holocaust survivor, served his coun-   20
try in two wars.

"Ilan," said his wife Rona, "left us at his peak moment, in his favorite place,   21
with people he loved."

The *Columbia*'s pilot was Commander Willy McCool, whom friends knew   22
as the most steady and dependable of men. In Lubbock today, they're thinking
back to the Eagle Scout who became a distinguished naval officer and a fearless
test pilot.

One friend remembers Willy this way: "He was blessed, and we were blessed   23
to know him."

Our whole nation was blessed to have such men and women serving in our   24
space program. Their loss is deeply felt, especially in this place where so many
of you called them friends.

The people in NASA are being tested once again. In your grief, you are re-   25
sponding as your friends would have wished, with focus, professionalism and
unbroken faith in the mission of this agency.

Captain Brown was correct: America's space program will go on.   26

This course of exploration and discovery is not an option we choose. It is a   27
desire written in the human heart. We are that part of creation which seeks to
understand all creation. We find the best among us, send them forth into un-
mapped darkness, and pray they will return.

They go in peace for all mankind, and all mankind is in their debt.   28

Yet, some explorers do not return, and the law settles unfairly on a few.   29

The families here today shared in the courage of those they loved, but now   30
they must face life and grief without them. The sorrow is lonely, but you are
not alone.

In time, you will find comfort and the grace to see you through. And in   31
God's own time, we can pray that the day of your reunion will come.

And to the children who miss your mom or dad so much today, you need   32
to know, they love you, and that love will always be with you.

They were proud of you, and you can be proud of them for the rest of   33
your life.

The final days of their own lives were spent looking down upon this Earth,   34
and now, on every continent, in every land they can see, the names of these astronauts are known and remembered.

They will always have an honored place in the memory of this country, and   35
today, I offer the respect and gratitude of the people of the United States.

May God bless you all.   36

Reference
and Research
Appendices

Reference and Research Appendices

Guidelines for Debates

Debates offer a unique perspective to the challenge of public speaking, calling upon skills in persuasion (especially the reasoned use of evidence), in delivery, and in the ability to think quickly and critically. Much like a political debate, in an academic debate two individuals or groups consider or argue an issue from opposing viewpoints. Generally there will be a winner and a loser, lending this form of speaking a competitive edge.

Take a Side

Opposing sides in a debate are taken by speakers in one of two formats. In the **individual debate format**, one person takes a side against another person. In the **team debate format**, multiple people (usually two) take sides against another team, with each person on the team assuming a speaking role.

The *pro* side (also called *affirmative*) in the debate supports the topic with a *resolution* — a statement asking for change or consideration of a controversial issue. "Resolved, that the United States government should severely punish flag burners" is a resolution that the affirmative side must support and defend. The pro side tries to convince the audience (or judges) that the topic under consideration should be addressed, supported, or agreed with. The *con* side (also called *negative*) in the debate attempts to defeat the resolution by dissuading the audience from accepting the pro side's arguments.

Advance Strong Arguments

Whether you take the affirmative or negative side, your primary responsibility is to advance strong arguments in support of your position. Arguments usually consist of the following three parts (see also Chapter 25):[1]

- A *claim* makes an assertion or declaration about an issue. "Females are discriminated against in the workplace." Depending on your debate topic, your claim may be one of fact, value, or policy (see Chapter 25).
- *Evidence* is the support offered for the claim. "According to a recent report by the U.S. Department of Labor, women make 28 percent less than men in comparable jobs and are promoted 34 percent less frequently."
- *Reasoning* (also called *warrant*) is a logical explanation of the claim. "Females make less money and get promoted less frequently than males."

Debates are characterized by *refutation,* in which each side attacks the arguments of the other. Refutation can be made against an opponent's claim, reasoning, evidence, or some combination of these elements. In the previous argument, an opponent might refute the evidence by arguing, "The report used by my opponent is three years old, and a new study indicates that we are making substantial progress in equalizing the pay among males and females; thus we are reducing discrimination in the workplace."

Refutation also involves rebuilding arguments that have been refuted or attacked by the opponent. This is done by adding new evidence or attacking the opponent's reasoning or evidence.

"Flow" the Debate

In formal debates (in which judges take notes and keep track of arguments), debaters must attack and defend each argument. "Dropping" or ignoring an argument can seriously compromise the credibility of the debater and her or his side. To ensure that you respond to each of your opponent's arguments, try using a simple technique adopted by formal debaters called "flowing the debate" (see Table A.1). Write down each of your opponent's arguments, and then draw a line or arrow to indicate that you (or another team member) have refuted it.

TABLE A.1 • Flowchart of the Arguments for the Resolution "Resolved That Nonviolent Prisoners Should Be Paroled More Often"

Affirmative → Negative		Affirmative → Negative		Affirmative → Negative	
Nonviolent prisoners should be paroled more often.	Nonviolent prisoners can become violent when they are paroled.	Studies show nonviolent prisoners commit fewer crimes upon their release.	Those studies are outdated and involve only a few states.	My studies are recent and include big states like New York and California.	The studies from New York and California were flawed due to poor statistics.

Tips for Winning Debates

Keep these tactics in mind when participating in debates:

- Present the most credible and convincing evidence you can find.
- Before you begin, describe your position and tell listeners what they must decide.
- If you feel that your side is not popular among audience members, ask them to suspend their own personal opinion and judge the debate on the merits of the argument.

- Don't be timid. Ask audience members to specifically decide in your favor, and be explicit about your desire for their approval.
- Point out the strong points from your arguments. Remind the audience that the opponent's arguments were weak or irrelevant.
- Be prepared to think on your feet (see Chapter 17 for more on impromptu speaking).
- Don't hide your passion for your position. Debate audiences appreciate enthusiasm and zeal.

How to Handle Question-and-Answer Sessions

Many of the speeches and presentations that you will deliver will probably be followed by a question-and-answer session; typically, these sessions last about fifteen minutes, though they often take less time. Just as your key points and your conclusion will linger in listeners' minds, so too will your answers to their post-speech questions. Deftly fielding questions is therefore a final critical component of making a speech or a presentation.

Preparing for Questions

As the last step in preparing your speech, take some time to anticipate and prepare for questions the audience is likely to pose to you:

1. Review your speech with an eye to the probable questions it will elicit from listeners. Consider audience members' reasons for listening to the speech as you brainstorm. What is likely to be of greatest concern to them? Write these questions down, and practice answering them.
2. Focus on the most difficult question that you think is likely to arise, and spend time answering it. The confidence you will gain from adeptly handling a difficult question should spill over to other questions you will face.[1]

Getting Started

If at the beginning of the session you ask for questions and none are forthcoming, don't panic. Many speakers find themselves in this situation, not because their speech bored listeners, but because people are often hesitant to be the first to speak. To ease the tension, try posing the first question yourself (e.g., "When I described the difficulty in finding good-quality daycare, I noticed that many of you nodded your heads"). Chances are, once you've got the ball rolling, the audience will be more forthcoming. You can also give a stab at humor to break the ice (e.g., "I knew this topic would be difficult, but I had hoped it wouldn't put you to sleep").

Protocol during the Session

1. As a matter of courtesy, try to call on audience members in the order in which they raise their hands.

2. Generally, it's a good idea to repeat or paraphrase the question before answering it ("The question is, 'Did the mayor really vote against . . .'"). This will ensure that you've heard it correctly, and that others in the audience know precisely what you are responding to. Repeating the question also gives you time to reflect on and formulate an answer.

   Note that there are a few exceptions to repeating the question. The primary one is doing so when the question is hostile (see the next section). One expert suggests that you should always repeat the question when speaking to a large group; when you're in a small group or a training seminar, however, doing so isn't necessary.[2]

3. When responding to a question, initially make eye contact with the questioner, then move your gaze to other audience members. This makes all audience members feel as though you are responding not only to the questioner but to them as well.

4. Remember your listening skills. Give questioners your full attention and don't interrupt them.

5. Don't be afraid to take pauses while you formulate an answer. Many speakers feel they must feed the audience instantaneous responses; this belief sometimes makes them say things they later regret. This is especially the case in media interviews (see Appendix C). Pauses that seem long to you may not in fact appear lengthy to your listeners.

6. Don't feel that you must answer every question, especially if you don't have enough information or if it is confidential. Trying to wing an answer or, worse, downright faking it, will cost you an instant loss of credibility.[3] If you are in a panel discussion (see Appendix D) and someone poses a question that you don't know, for example, you might say:

   - "Sarah, perhaps you want to take a stab at this?"
   - "Anyone in the audience have a handle on this?"

   You can respond to questions that you aren't at liberty to discuss with statements like these:

   - "I'd love to discuss that with you, but at this stage the information is confidential."
   - "I don't have information on that with me now, but I'd be happy to report back to you."

7. Keep your answers concise. As tempting as it may be, the question-and-answer session isn't the time to launch into a lengthy treatise on your favorite aspect of a topic. Although you want to supply the information the questioner is seeking, you don't want to subject him or her to a second speech.

8. If an audience member is having trouble articulating a question, or piles too many questions on top of one another, respectfully try to help him or her out. Consider statements such as, "Do you mean . . ." or "Perhaps I can tackle the first part of your question for now."

Handling Hostile and Otherwise Troubling Questions

The first rule of thumb in handling hostile questions is not to get defensive. Doing so will damage your credibility and only egg the person on. Similarly, never give the impression that you think a question is stupid or irrelevant, even if it clearly is. Maintain an attitude of respect, and stay cool and in control. Here are some pointers:

1. Never repeat or paraphrase a hostile question. Doing so only lends the question more credibility than it is worth. Instead, try to rephrase it more positively[4] (e.g., in response to the question "Didn't your department botch the handling of product X?" you might respond, "The question was, 'Why did product X experience a difficult market entry?' To that I would say that . . .").

2. Attempt to defuse the hostile questioner with respect and goodwill. Losing your cool will only make the audience lose respect for you.

3. If someone asks you a seemingly stupid question, try not to point it out. Respond graciously.

4. Respond to irrelevant but obviously provocative questions with good humor. You can make a straightforward statement, such as "I don't think that is the point," but don't get testy.[5]

Ending the Session

Never end a question-and-answer session abruptly. As time runs out, alert the audience that you will take one or two more questions and then must end. The session represents one final opportunity to reinforce your message, so take the opportunity to do so. As you summarize your message, thank your listeners for their time. Leave an air of goodwill behind you.

Preparing for Mediated Communication C

Public speaking today often involves communicating through an electronic medium such as television, radio, or the videoconference. The underlying principles described throughout this guidebook will stand you in good stead as you prepare for these circumstances. These speaking engagements do present some unique challenges, however.

Speaking on Television

With the proliferation of cable television and thousands of public-access cable stations, Andy Warhol's famous prophesy that everyone will enjoy their fifteen minutes of fame has never been more true. Content-hungry producers need people to fill air time, and media-savvy organizations and individuals are only too happy to comply. Whether in the role of business executive, professional expert, political advocate, or citizen on the street, chances are strong that you will appear on television.

SPEAKING IN SOUND BITES

In live speaking situations, you control the flow of information. On television, however, you are at the mercy of reporters and producers, who will edit your remarks to fit within their time frame. Depending on the nature of your televised appearance, it may be critical that you learn to convey your message in sound bite form (this is particularly true of interviews). *Sound bites* are succinct statements that summarize your key points in twenty seconds or less. When preparing remarks for a televised appearance, keep the following points in mind:

- To increase the odds that your message won't be distorted or deleted, use simple, jargon-free language and try to reduce your key points to their essentials.
- Find out whether the show will be live or taped. If it's live, will there be an audience?
- Find out who the members of the viewing audience are and what their expectations are likely to be.
- Find out how long you will be on camera.
- All media appreciate a good story. Use anecdotes and humor whenever it's appropriate to do so.[1]

The question of where to direct your gaze is critical during televised appearances. Following are some guidelines:

*   As a rule, don't play to the camera. In a one-on-one interview situation, keep your focus on the interviewer, allowing him or her to maintain eye contact with the camera. Do not look up or down or tilt your head sideways; these movements give the impression that you are uncertain or evasive.[2]

*   If there is both an audience and a camera, treat the camera as just another member of the audience, glancing at it only as often as you would at any other individual as you scan the entire audience during your remarks.

*   If there is only you and the camera, direct your gaze at it as you speak. By doing so, you are in effect looking directly into the eyes of your unseen viewers.

*   Be sure that your posture is erect.

*   Exaggerate your gestures slightly more than you normally would so that every move is captured on camera.

*   Pay particular attention to projecting your voice. Consciously try to be more forceful. If you will be sitting, keep your back straight so that you draw more air into your lungs.

*   Beware of speaking in a monotone.

DRESS AND MAKEUP

To compensate for the glare of studio lights and distortions caused by the camera, give careful consideration to dress and grooming:

*   Choose dark- rather than light-colored clothing. Dark colors such as blue, grey, green, and brown photograph better than lighter shades.

*   Avoid stark white, since it produces an unpleasant glare.

*   Avoid plaids, dots, and other busy patterns, as they tend to jump around on the screen.

*   Avoid glittering jewelry, including tie bars.

*   Bright studio lights tend to make you look washed out, so plan to wear a little more makeup than usual. In addition to putting color back on your face and evening out skin tone, makeup will cut the glare of natural skin oils and lighten shadows under the eyes or around cheekbones.

Speaking on Radio: The Media Interview

If you speak on radio, it will probably be in the context of an interview. Following are some guidelines for preparing for media interviews. These same guidelines can also be applied to the television interview.

- Know the radio audience and the focus of the program. What subjects does the broadcast cover? How long will the interview be? Will it be taped or live?

- Brush up on background information, and have your facts ready. Assume that the audience knows little or nothing about the subject matter.

- For a taped interview, remember that it may be edited. Make your key points in short sentences, and repeat them using different words.[3] Think in terms of sound bites.

- Use the interviewer's name during the interview.

- Anticipate questions that might arise during the interview, and decide how you will answer them.

- Arrive early for on-air interviews so that you can become familiar with your surroundings prior to the interview.

- Prepare a speaking outline for the interview, and put it on notecards. Remember that the microphone will pick up the sound of papers being shuffled.

- Use transition points to acknowledge the interviewer's questions and to bridge your key message points (e.g., "I am not familiar with that, but what I can tell you is . . ."; "You raise an interesting question, but I think the more important matter is . . .").[4]

Speaking in the Videoconference

Videoconferencing is the live connection of two or more people via satellite or the Internet. Videoconferences typically take place in conference rooms, in which participants assemble before cameras — one group in Alabama, for example, and another group in New York. Rather than being transmitted via satellite, desktop videoconferencing systems fit onto personal computers and can be transmitted via the Internet.

As with television, chances are strong that you will find yourself speaking on this medium. Companies use videoconferences in place of face-to-face meetings, thus saving both time and money. Schools also make use of the technology to conduct distance learning.

In general, the long-distance speaker must prepare as he or she would for on-site presentations but must particularly work hard at good diction, delivery, and dynamic body language. Consider these guidelines, suggested by speech instructor Diane Howard, when preparing for a videoconference:[5]

- Rehearse the presentation with the participants. Decide who will speak first. Make sure it is clear what information each participant will address, and in what order.

- Learn names at the long-distance site and use them.

- Realize that the room in which you are presenting is a "set," and make certain that the background behind you is not busy.
- Look into the camera, speaking directly to the long-distance audience.
- Adjust speech and movement to take the time lag between sites into consideration.
- Pause as you speak in order to accommodate time delays.
- Don't make any sudden, abrupt, or sweeping movements.
- Speak and move a little more slowly and deliberately than normal.
- Check with long-distance audience members to determine whether they understand you.
- Enunciate carefully, emphasizing your consonants to ensure good diction.
- Use vocal variety.

Public Discussions: Panels and Symposiums

Symposiums and panel discussions are common formats in which academicians, scientists, students, and experts of every stripe share information in a public setting. Topics range from discussions on electronic privacy to symposiums on breast cancer; in truth, subjects run the gamut from *A* to *Z*, and in virtually every field. Sometimes these public discussions are scheduled to examine or decide upon the findings of a group (see Chapter 28). At other times they are convened to focus on an area of emerging interest or pressing concern.

The Panel Discussion

In a **panel discussion**, a group of people (at least three, and generally not more than nine) discusses a topic in the presence of an audience. Usually the participants are arranged in a semicircle or behind a table placed in front of the audience; participants address their remarks to each other. The purpose of a panel discussion can be either to inform or to persuade audience members on the issue being addressed. Rather than making speeches, participants in a panel discussion speak extemporaneously.

Panels require the presence of a skilled chairperson or moderator to direct the discussion. During the presentation phase, the moderator describes the purpose and topic, or agenda, of the presentation and introduces the panel members. He or she begins the discussion by directing a question to one or more of the participants. At the conclusion of the panel, the moderator summarizes the discussion and directs questions from the audience (see Appendix B).

The Symposium

A **symposium** is a formal meeting at which several speakers (usually three to five) deliver short speeches on the same topic. Symposiums are organized to inform audiences about different aspects of a topic. Unlike panel discussions, speakers in a symposium do not interact with each other, addressing their remarks instead solely to the audience. Participants either address different aspects of a topic or offer contrasting viewpoints. Sometimes the symposium concludes with a question-and-answer period; at other times, it is followed by a panel discussion among members of the symposium.

Requirements for the Public Speaker

When preparing to participate in a symposium, approach the task as you would an individual speaking event. Know in advance what aspects of the topic the other participants will address, and pay particular attention to planning your speech around the time limits.

In the case of a panel discussion, examine the following issues in advance of preparing your remarks:

- What is the agenda for the discussion? (Generally, the moderator will deliver one to you.)
- What are the ground rules? (Generally, the moderator will prepare a list and distribute it to each participant.)
- What are your time constraints?
- What aspects of the topic are the other participants likely to address?
- Will questions be permitted during the discussion or deferred until the panel has ended?

Commonly Mispronounced Words

The following lists of errors in pronunciation are from *Basic Public Speaking,* Third Edition, by Paul L. Soper (Oxford University Press, 1968), with gratitude. The correct pronunciation or proper spelling is given in parentheses.

Misplacing the Accent

admir'able (ad'mirable)

applic'able (ap'plicable)

ce'ment (cement')

compar'able (com'parable)

exemplar'y (exemp'lary)

exig'ency (ex'igency)

finan'cier (financier')

formid'able (for'midable)

hor'izon (hori'zon)

i'dea (ide'a)

impi'ous (im'pious)

impot'ent (im'potent)

incompar'able (incom'parable)

incongru'ous (incon'gruous)

infam'ous (in'famous)

in'terest'ed (in'terested)

irrepar'able (irrep'arable)

municip'al (munic'ipal)

prefer'able (pref'erable)

proj'ectile (projec'tile)

reg'ime (regime')

respite' (res'pite)

superflu'ous (super'fluous)

u'nited (unit'ed)

vehe'ment (ve'hement)

vehi'cle (ve'hicle)

Addition of Sounds

attack-ted (attacked)

athaletics (athletics)

barbarious (barbarous)

colyum (column)

corpse (corps)

drawr (draw)

drownded (drowned)

elum (elm)

enterance (entrance)

ekscape (escape)

filum (film)

grievious (grievous)

height-th (height)

hinderance (hindrance)

idear (idea)

lightening (lightning)

mischievious (mischievous)

of-ten (of[t]en)

rememberance (remembrance)

sing-ger (singer)

stastistics (statistics)

sub-tle (su[b]tle)

sufferage (suffrage)

umberella (umbrella)

warsh (wash)

Omission of Sounds

accerate (accurate)

actully (actually)

assessory (accessory)

blong (belong)

canidate (candidate)

defnite (definite)

guarntee (guarantee)

jography (geography)

ineffecshal (ineffectual)

nuclus (nucleus)

particlar (particular)

pome (poem)

plice (police)

quite (quiet)

reconize (recognize)

resume (résumé)

sedimentry (sedimentary)

simlar (similar)

superntenent (superintendent)

sussinct (succinct)

temperture (temperature)

vilent (violent)

uzhal (usual)

Sound Substitutions

agin (again)

blaytant (blatant)

boquet (bouquet)

brochr (brochure)

calvary (cavalry)

capsl (capsule)

tshasm (chasm)

click (clique)

conscious (conscience)

crooks (crux)

cullinary (culinary)

dictionury (dictionary)

diptheria (diphtheria)

dipthong (diphthong)

dis-hevel (dishevel)

fewtyle (futile)

gesture (g is soft)

genuwine (genuine)

gigantic (first g is soft)

hiccough (hiccup)

homidge (homage)

ullusion (illusion)

interduce (introduce)

irrevelent (irrelevant)

jist (just)

larnyx (larynx)

lenth (length)

loose (lose)

longgevity (longevity)

memor (memoir)

miradge (mirage)

preelude (prelude)

preform (perform)

prespiration (perspiration)

prestidge (prestige)

rench (rinse)

saloon (salon)

strenth (strength)

statue (stature)

substantuate (substantiate)

theayter (theater)

tedjius (tedious)

Chicago Documentation

Two widely used systems of documentation are outlined in *The Chicago Manual of Style*, Fifteenth Edition (2003). The first, typically used by public speakers, provides for bibliographic citations in endnotes or footnotes. This method, which is also frequently used by journalists and scholars in the humanities, is illustrated in this appendix. The second system, often used by writers in the physical and natural sciences, employs an author-date system: sources are cited in the text with full bibliographic information given in a concluding list of references. For information about the author-date system — and more information generally about Chicago-style documentation — consult the *Chicago Manual*, Chapters 16 and 17.

1. Book by a Single Author   Give the author's full name followed by a comma. Then italicize the book's title. In parentheses, give the city of publication followed by a colon, the publisher's name followed by a comma, and the publication date. Place a comma after the parentheses, and then give the page numbers from which your paraphrase or quotation is taken.

1. Eric Alterman, *What Liberal Media? The Truth about Bias and the News* (New York: Basic Books, 2003), 180–85.

2. Book by Multiple Authors   Give all the authors' full names, the book's title in italics, the publication information in parentheses, and the pages from which your paraphrase or quotation is taken.

2. Bill Kovach and Tom Rosenstiel, *The Elements of Journalism: What Newspeople Should Know and the Public Should Expect* (New York: Three Rivers Press, 2001), 57–58.

3. Edited Work without an Author   Give the editor's full name followed by a comma and "ed." for *editor*, then another comma. Then give the title in italics, publication information in parentheses, and the pages you're citing.

3. Joseph B. Atkins, ed., *The Mission: Journalism, Ethics, and the World* (Ames: Iowa State University Press, 2002), 150–57.

4. Encyclopedia or Dictionary   Give the title of the work in italics followed by a comma, the edition (if any), the letters "s.v." (from the Latin *sub verbo*, "under the word"), and then the term you looked up in quotation marks followed by a period.

> 4. *Routledge Encyclopedia of Philosophy,* s.v. "Ethics of journalism."

5. Article in a Magazine   Include the author's full name, the title of the article in quotation marks, the title of the magazine in italics, the publication date, and the pages cited.

> 5. John Leo, "With Bias toward All," *U.S. News & World Report,* March 18, 2002, 8–9.

6. Article in a Journal   Give the author's full name, the title of the article in quotation marks, the title of the journal in italics, the volume and issue numbers, the year of publication in parentheses followed by a colon, and the pages used.

> 6. Tom Goldstein, "Wanted: More Outspoken Views: Coverage of the Press Is Up, but Criticism Is Down," *Columbia Journalism Review* 40 (2001): 144–45.

7. Article in a Newspaper   Include the author's full name, the title of the article in quotation marks, the title of the newspaper in italics, the date of publication, the edition (such as *national edition*) if relevant, and the section of the paper in which the article appeared.

> 7. Felicity Barringer, "Sports Reporting: Rules on Rumors," *New York Times,* February 18, 2002, sec. C.

8. Web Site   Give the name of the author (if available), the title of the page in quotation marks followed by a comma, the title of the Web site, and the site's address. The date you accessed the site is optional; if you include it, add it in parentheses at the end.

> 8. "Challenging Hate Radio: A Guide for Activists," *Fairness and Accuracy in Reporting (FAIR),* http://www.fair.org/activism/hate-radio.html (accessed February 5, 2005).

9. E-Mail Message   Treat e-mail messages like personal communications. Give the sender's full name, the phrase "e-mail message to author," and the date of the message.

> 9. Grace Talusan, e-mail message to author, March 20, 2005.

10. E-Mail Discussion List Message   Give the author's full name, the phrase "e-mail to" followed by the name of the discussion list, the date of the posting, and the URL of the list. Your date of access is optional.

10. Ola Seifert, e-mail to Society of Professional Journalists mailing list, August 23, 2002, http://f05n16.cac.psu.edu (accessed September 14, 2005).

11. Newsgroup Message   Include the author's full name, the phrase "message to" followed by the name of the newsgroup, the date of the posting, and the URL of the newsgroup. Your date of access is optional.

11. Jai Maharaj, message to alt. journalism.newspapers newsgroup, November 11, 2002, http://groups.google.com (accessed December 19, 2005).

12. Electronic Database   Give the author's full name, the title of the article, the title of the periodical, publication information for the periodical, the pages you are citing, and the URL of the database. Your date of access is optional.

12. Mark J. Miller, "Tough Calls: Deciding When a Suicide Is Newsworthy and What Details to Include Are among Journalism's More Sensitive Decisions," *American Journalism Review* 24, no. 10 (2002): 43, http://infotrac.galegroup .com (accessed March 1, 2005).

13. Government Document   Use the governmental body or office as the author. Give the governmental body's name ("U.S. Congress," "U.S. House," "Senate Committee on Foreign Relations"), the title of the article or publication, the usual publication information, and the page numbers you are citing.

13. U.S. Congress, *The Electronic Freedom of Information Improvement Act: Hearing before the Subcommittee on Technology and the Law of the Committee on the Judiciary, 1992* (Washington, D.C.: GPO, 1993), 201.

14. Personal Communication   Give the author's name, the type of communication (e.g., "letter to author," "conversation with author," "telephone conversation with author"), and the date.

14. Soo Jin Oh, letter to author, August 13, 2000.

15. Interview   Give the name of the interviewee, the interviewer, the name of the program or forum, the publication or network, and the date. Interviews that have not been published or broadcast should be cited with a description of the type of interview (e.g., "tape recording") and the place the interview was conducted.

15. Walter Cronkite, Interview by Daniel Schorr, *Frontline,* PBS, April 2, 1996.

16. Video Recording   Give the title of the film or other work, the medium (VHS, DVD), the director, the place and name of the film distribution company, and the date of release.

16. *All the President's Men,* VHS, directed by Alan J. Pakula (Burbank, Calif.: Warner Brothers, 1976).

17. Sound Recording   List the composer or writer, the title of the work, the performer or conductor, the recording company or publisher, and the recording number or date of release.

17. Noam Chomsky, *Case Studies in Hypocrisy,* read by Noam Chomsky (AK Press, 2000).

17. Antonio Vivaldi, *The Four Seasons,* conducted by Seiji Ozawa, Telarc 80070.

APA Documentation (G)

Most disciplines in the social sciences — psychology, anthropology, sociology, political science, education, and economics — use the author-date system of documentation established by the American Psychological Association (APA). This citation style highlights dates of publication because the currency of published material is of primary importance in these fields. For more information about APA format, see the *Publication Manual of the American Psychological Association*, Fifth Edition (2001).

The numbered entries that follow introduce and explain some conventions of this citation style using examples relating to the topic of stress management. Note that in the titles of books and articles only the first word of the title and subtitle and proper nouns are capitalized.

1. Book by a Single Author Begin with the author's last name and initials followed by the date of publication in parentheses. Next, italicize the book's title and end with the place of publication and the publisher.

> Rabin, B. S. (1999). *Stress, immune function, and health: The connection.* New York: Wiley-Liss.

2. Book by Multiple Authors or Editors Begin with the authors' last names and initials followed by the date of publication in parentheses. Next, italicize the book's title and end with the place of publication and the publisher. Invert all authors' names and use an ampersand before the last name.

> Williams, S., & Cooper, L. (2002). *Managing workplace stress: A best practice blueprint.* New York: Wiley.

3. Article in a Reference Work List the author of the article, the publication date, and the article title. This information is followed by the word *In* and the italicized title of the reference work. Include the volume number and inclusive page numbers of the article in parentheses, followed by the place of publication and the publisher.

> Kazdin, A. E. (2000). Stress. In *Encyclopedia of psychology* (Vol. 7, pp. 479–489). New York: Oxford University Press.

4. Government Document Use the office or governmental department as the author followed by the publication date. Italicize the title of the document and end with the place of publication and the publisher (usually Washington, D.C., and the U.S. Government Printing Office). This example refers to a book; for other formats, refer to Appendix D in the APA *Publication Manual.*

> U.S. Department of Health and Human Services. (1997). *Violence in the*
>
> *workplace: Guidelines for understanding and response.* Washington,
>
> D.C.: U.S. Government Printing Office.

5. Journal Article Begin with the author's last name and initials followed by the date of publication in parentheses. Next, list the title of the article and italicize the title of the journal in which it is printed. Then give the volume number, italicized, and the issue number in parentheses if the journal is paginated by issue. End with the inclusive page numbers of the article.

> Dollard, M. F., & Metzer, J. C. (1999). Psychological research, practice, and
>
> production: The occupational stress problem. *International Journal of*
>
> *Stress Management, 6*(4), 241–253.

6. Magazine Article Begin with the author's last name and initials followed by the date of publication, including the month or the month and day, in parentheses. Next, list the title of the article and the title of the magazine, italicized. Give the volume number, italicized, followed by the inclusive page numbers of the article.

> Cobb, K. (2002, July 20). Sleepy heads: Low fuel may drive brain's need to
>
> sleep. *Science News, 162,* 38.

7. Newspaper Article Begin with the author's last name and initials followed by the date of publication, including the month and day, in parentheses. Next, list the title of the article and, in italics, the newspaper in which it is printed. End with the section and page or pages on which the article appears. Note that the abbreviation *p.* or *pp.* is used for newspaper page numbers.

> Goode, E. (2002, December 17). The heavy cost of chronic stress. *The*
>
> *New York Times,* p. D1.

8. Unsigned Newspaper Article If a newspaper article does not list an author, give the title, the publication date in parentheses, the name of the newspaper in italics, and the page on which the article appears.

> Stress less: It's time to wrap it up. (2002, December 18). *Houston Chronicle,*
>
> p. A1.

9. Document from a Web Site List the author or, if no author is given, the name of the site or sponsoring organization, the date of publication, the title of the document, italicized, the date on which you accessed the site, and the URL. No punctuation is needed at the end of the URL.

Centers for Disease Control. (1999, January 7). *Stress . . . at work.* Retrieved

January 6, 2005, from http://www.cdc.gov/niosh/stresswk.html

10. Personal Web Site   To cite a personal Web site, it's usually sufficient to simply note it in your speech. For example,

Dr. Wesley Sime's stress management page is an excellent resource

(http://www.unl.edu/stress/mgmt/).

The APA manual states that personal Web sites should not be included in a bibliography; check with your instructor to see what his or her expectations are for your APA bibliography.

11. E-Mail Discussion List Message   Cite the author's name, the posting date in parentheses, the subject line, the name of the list, and the list's address.

Roseman, J. (1997, September 2). OEM: Stress, health impact, and

social work. Message posted to http://list.mc.duke.edu/cgi-bin/

wa?A2=ind9709&L=occ-env-med-l&F=&S=&P=2391

12. Newsgroup Message   Cite the author's name, the posting date, the subject line, and the URL of the newsgroup.

Dimitrakov, J. (2001, February 21). Immune effects of psychological

stress. Message posted to http://groups.google.com/

groups?q=stress&start=40&hl=en&lr=&ie=UTF-8&selm=

3A9ABDE4%40MailAndNews.com&rnum=44

13. E-Mail Message   To cite personal e-mail correspondence, it's sufficient to simply note it in your speech. For example,

An e-mail message from the staff of AltaVista clarifies this point

(D. Emanuel, personal communication, May 12, 2005).

The APA manual states that e-mail correspondence, like other personal communications, should not be included in a bibliography; check with your instructor to see what his or her expectations are for your APA bibliography.

14. Material from a CD-ROM or Online Database   Begin with the author's last name and initials, followed by the date of publication in parentheses. Next, list the title of the document (followed by the word "Abstract" in brackets if you are citing an abstract rather than the full text of a document). Cite the title of the journal in italics, the volume number, the issue number if the journal is paginated by issue, and the page numbers. Then indicate the database from which you retrieved the information. End with a document number or accession number, if the database provides one.

Waring, T. (2002). Stress management: A balanced life is good for business [Abstract]. *Law Society Journal, 40,* 66–68. Retrieved from Family & Society Studies Worldwide database.

15. Abstract from an Information Service or Online Database   Begin with the author's last name and initials, followed by the date of publication in parentheses. Next, list the title of the document and the name of the journal, the volume number, the issue number if the journal is paginated by issue, and the page numbers. Indicate "Abstract retrieved," followed by your access date and the name of the database.

Viswesvaran, C., Sanchez, J., & Fisher, J. (1999). The role of social support in the process of work stress: A meta-analysis. *Journal of Vocational Behavior, 54,* 314–334. Abstract retrieved January 3, 2005, from ERIC database.

16. Personal Interview   To cite a personal, unpublished interview, it's usually sufficient to simply note it in your speech. For example,

During her interview, Senator Cole revealed her enthusiasm for the new state-funded stress management center (M. Cole, personal communication, October 7, 2005).

The APA manual states that personal interviews, like other personal communications, should not be included in a bibliography; check with your instructor to see what his or her expectations are for your APA bibliography.

MLA Documentation H

Created by the Modern Language Association, MLA documentation style is fully outlined in the *MLA Handbook for Writers of Research Papers* (Sixth Edition, 2003). Disciplines that use MLA style include English literature, the humanities, and various foreign languages. The seventeen sample citations below all relate to a single topic: film appreciation and criticism.

1. Book by a Single Author   Citations for most books are arranged as follows: (1) the author's name, last name first; (2) the title and subtitle, underlined; and (3) the city of publication, an abbreviated form of the publisher's name, and the date. Each of these three pieces of information is followed by a period and one space.

> Berg, Charles Ramírez. Latino Images in Film: Stereotypes, Subversion, and
>
> Resistance. Austin: U of Texas P, 2002.

2. Book by Multiple Authors or Editors   Give the first author's name, last name first, then list the name(s) of the other author(s) in regular order with a comma between authors and the word *and* before the last one. The final name in a list of editors is followed by a comma and "ed." or "eds."

> Hill, John, and Pamela Church Gibson, eds. The Oxford Guide to Film
>
> Studies. New York: Oxford UP, 1998.

3. Article in a Reference Work   Begin with the author of the article; if none is provided, begin with the title of the article. Cite the name of the reference work, followed by the edition (if provided) and the date of publication. If the work is arranged alphabetically, no volume or page numbers are required.

> Katz, Ephraim. "Film Noir." The Film Encyclopedia. 4th ed. 2001.

4. Government Document   In most cases, use the name of the governmental body or office followed by the agency and any subdivision as the author, using standard abbreviations. Underline the title of the document. Congressional documents should include the congressional number, session, house, and type of document (report, resolution, etc.) in abbreviated form, and the number of the material. End with the publication information (the publisher is often the Government Printing Office [GPO]).

United States. Cong. House. Committee on the Judiciary. <u>National Film</u>
<u>Preservation Act of 1996</u>. 104th Cong., 2nd sess., H. Rept. 104-558.
Washington: GPO, 1996.

5. Magazine Article   Along with the author's name, the title of the article, and the title of the magazine, include the full date of publication and inclusive page numbers of the article. The date of publication should be listed with the day first, followed by the month and the year with no commas between them. If no date is provided, list the month and year only. Use three-letter abbreviations for all months except May, June, and July.

Ansen, David. "Lights! Action! Cannes!" <u>Newsweek</u> 19 May 1997:
76-79.

6. Journal Article   Follow the format for magazine articles, but include the journal's volume number and, if the journal is paginated by issue, the issue number, with a period between them. Give the year in parentheses followed by a colon and the page numbers.

Kingsley-Smith, Jane E. "Shakespearean Authorship in Popular British
Cinema." <u>Literature-Film Quarterly</u> 30 (2002): 159–61.

7. Newspaper Article   Documenting a newspaper article is similar to documenting a magazine article. In citing the name of the newspaper, do not include any initial *A, An,* or *The.* Add the city in brackets after the name if it is not well known or is not part of the newspaper's title. Give the date, the edition (if any), a colon, a space, the section number or letter (if any), and the page number(s). If the article appears on discontinuous pages, give the first page followed by a plus sign (+) to indicate that the article continues on other pages.

Sebastian, Pamela. "Film Reviews Have a Delayed Effect on Box-Office
Receipts, Researchers Say." <u>Wall Street Journal</u> 13 Nov. 1997: A1+.

8. Newspaper Editorial   Document it as a standard newspaper article, but add the word "Editorial" after the title. If the editorial is signed, list the author's name first; otherwise, begin with the title.

"The Edgy Legacy of Stanley Kubrick." Editorial. <u>New York Times</u> 10 Mar.
1999: A18.

9. Single-Issue CD-ROM, Diskette, or Magnetic Tape   Cite these electronic sources as you would books. Add the medium and the number of the electronic edition, release, or version (if applicable).

"Pulp Fiction." <u>Blockbuster Movie Trivia</u>. 3rd ed. CD-ROM. New York:
Random, 1998.

10. Online Scholarly Project or Reference Database   Begin with the author if one is listed. Then give the title of the work you are citing, in quotation marks, followed by the title of the site, underlined. If the site has an editor, give the abbreviation "Ed." followed by the editor's name. Then cite the date of electronic publication or of the latest update, the name of the sponsoring organization, the date on which you accessed the site, and the URL in angle brackets.

> "Origins of American Animation." <u>American Memory</u>. 31 Mar. 1999.
>
> > Library of Congress. 26 June 2003 <http://memory.loc.gov/ammem/
> >
> > oahtml/oahome.html>.

11. Commercial Web Site   Include the creator of the Web site if known, the title of the work you are citing, the site's title, the name of any sponsoring institution or organization, your date of access, and the URL in angle brackets.

> "American Beauty." <u>Crazy for Cinema</u>. 24 Oct. 2003 <http://
>
> > crazy4cinema.com/Review/FilmsA/f_american_beauty.html>.

12. Personal Web Site   The guidelines for citing a personal Web site are similar to those for a commercial site. If no title exists, include a description such as "Home page." Note that personal sites do not have sponsors (see Chapter 10 for a discussion of the distinctions among Web sites).

> <u>Jamie's James Bond Site</u>. 8 May 2002 <http://osiris.sund.ac.uk/~ca6jde/
>
> > jamie.htm>.

13. Article in an Online Periodical

> Taylor, Charles. "The Pianist." <u>Salon</u> 27 Dec. 2002. 1 Jan. 2005
>
> > <http://www.salon.com/ent/movies/review/2002/12/27/pianist/
> >
> > index_np.html>.

14. Posting to a Discussion Group   Begin with the author's name; the title of the document in quotation marks; the phrase "Online posting"; and the date of posting. For a posting to an e-mail discussion list, give the name of the list; the number of the posting (if any), the date of access, and the URL of the list or the e-mail address of its moderator. For a newsgroup posting, give the date of access and the URL of the newsgroup in angle brackets.

> Granger, Susan. "Review of <u>The Cider House Rules</u>." Online posting.
>
> > 30 Mar. 2000. Rotten Tomatoes. 2 Oct. 2000 <http://
> >
> > www.rottentomatoes.com/click/source-381/
> >
> > reviews.php?cats=&letter=c&sortby=movie&page=68&rid=775926>.

15. E-Mail Message   Give the writer's name, then the subject of the message in quotation marks, and then the recipient of the message (if the message was addressed to the author of the work in which the message is being cited, write "E-mail to the author"). Include the date of the message.

    Boothe, Jeanna. "Re: Top 100 Movies." E-mail to the author. 16 Feb. 2005.

16. Work of Art or Photograph   Include the artist, the work's title, the museum or other location, and the city.

    Christenberry, William. Grave III. Hunter Museum of Art, Chattanooga.

17. Interview   Begin with the name of the person interviewed. Then specify the type of interview (personal, telephone, or Internet interview) and the date on which it was conducted.

    Sanderson, Andrew. Telephone interview. 12 June 2002.

CBE/CSE Documentation

The CSE (Council of Science Editors, formerly the Council of Biology Editors) style is most frequently used in the fields of biology and environmental science. The current CBE/CSE style guide is *Scientific Style and Format: The CBE Manual for Authors, Editors, and Publishers,* Sixth Edition (1994), and a seventh edition is forthcoming. Publishers and instructors who require the CBE/CSE style do so in two possible formats: a citation-sequence superscript format and a name-year format.

- If you use the citation-sequence superscript format, number and list the references in the sequence in which they are first cited in the speech.
- If you use the name-year format, list the references, unnumbered, in alphabetical order.

In the following examples, all of which refer to environmental issues, you will see that the citation-sequence format calls for listing the date after the publisher's name in references for books and after the name of the periodical in references for articles. The name-year format calls for listing the date immediately after the author's name in any kind of reference. Notice also the absence of a comma after the author's last name, the absence of a period after an initial, and the absence of underlining in titles of books or journals.

1. Book by One Author Be sure to list the total number of pages in the book.

CITATION-SEQUENCE

> 1. Leggett JK. The carbon war: global warming and the end of the oil era. New York: Routledge; 2001. 341 p.

NAME-YEAR

> Leggett JK. 2001. The carbon war: global warming and the end of the oil era. New York: Routledge. 341 p.

2. Book by Two or More Authors

CITATION-SEQUENCE

> 2. Goldstein IF, Goldstein M. How much risk? a guide to understanding environmental health hazards. New York: Oxford Univ Pr; 2002. 304 p.

NAME-YEAR

Goldstein IF, Goldstein M. 2002. How much risk? a guide to understanding environmental health hazards. New York: Oxford Univ Pr. 304 p.

3. Journal Article   CBE/CSE style uses standard scientific abbreviations for titles of journals (Am Sci for *American Scientist*, J Am Med Assoc for *Journal of the American Medical Association*, for instance). One-word titles are never abbreviated.

CITATION-SEQUENCE

3. Stolzenberg, W. Flocking together: Texas and Mexico team up to conserve a hidden sanctuary. Nature 2001;51:20-21.

NAME-YEAR

Stolzenberg, W. 2001. Flocking together: Texas and Mexico team up to conserve a hidden sanctuary. Nature 51:20-21.

4. Magazine Article

CITATION-SEQUENCE

4. Wilcott B. Art for Earth's sake. Mother Jones 2000 Jun:16.

NAME-YEAR

Wilcott B. 2000 Jun. Art for Earth's sake. Mother Jones: 16.

5. Newspaper Article

CITATION-SEQUENCE

5. Parson EA. Moving beyond the Kyoto impasse. New York Times 2001 Jul 1;Sect A:23(col 1).

NAME-YEAR

Parson EA. 2001 Jul 1. Moving beyond the Kyoto impasse. New York Times;Sect A:23(col 1).

6. Web Site   For electronic sources, CBE/CSE recommends the guidelines in the *National Library of Medicine Recommended Formats for Bibliographic Citation Supplement: Internet Formats* (2001). The National Library of Medicine does not give a format for the name-year system; simply follow the citation-sequence format but omit the citation number.

6. Tennessee Department of Environment and Conservation [homepage on the Internet]. Nashville: The Department; [cited 2002 Jun 26]. Available from: http://www.state.tn/us/environment/.

7.   E-Mail Message

7. McGee E. Toxins in the Arkansas River [electronic mail on the Internet]. Message to: Maura O'Brien. 2001 Sep 26, 2:12 pm [cited 2001 Oct 3]. [about 3 screens].

8.   E-Mail Discussion List Message or Newsgroup Message

8. Affleck-Asch W. Three hundred pesticides to be withdrawn in Europe [discussion list on the Internet]. 2002 Dec 2, 6:37 pm [cited 2003 Jan 2]. [about 8 paragraphs]. Available from: http://www.mail-archive.com/ecofem%40csf.colorado.edu

IEEE Documentation

The Institute of Electrical and Electronics Engineers (IEEE) style requires that references appear at the end of the text, not in alphabetical order but in the order in which the sources are cited in the text. A bracketed reference number beginning with B precedes each entry. For speakers, this means creating a bibliography of sources listed in the order in which they are cited in the speech (this is done in bibliographies for speeches in any format). For more information on IEEE documentation, check the *IEEE Standards Style Manual* online at http://standards.ieee.org/guides/style/index.html.

1. Book List the author by last name and first initial followed by a comma. Then list the book's title in italics and the edition (if applicable). Finally, list the place of publication, the publisher, the date of publication, and the pages cited.

> [B1] Vorpérian, V., *Fast Analytical Techniques for Electrical and Electronic Circuits.* New York: Cambridge University Press, 2002, p. 462.

2. Periodical List the author, the title of the article in quotation marks, the title of the periodical in italics, the volume number, the issue number, the pages cited, and the date. Only the first word of the article title and proper nouns are capitalized.

> [B2] Brittain, J. C., "Charles F. Scott: A pioneer in electrical power engineering," *IEEE Industry Applications Magazine,* vol. 287, no. 6, pp. 6–8, Nov./Dec. 2000.

3. Web Page List the author, the title of the Web page, the medium (enclosed in brackets), volume and issue number (for an online journal), page number (if relevant or given), and the year and the month of publication in parentheses. Then provide the full URL or the name of the online service provider prefaced by "Available at:".

> [B3] Harnack, A., and Kleppinger, E., "Beyond the MLA Handbook: Documenting Electronic Sources on the Internet" [On-line style sheet] (June 1996), Available at: http://english.ttu.edu.kairos/1.2/

Glossary Ⓚ

abstract   A brief summary of a study.

abstract language   Language that is general or nonspecific. See also *concrete language*.

active listening   A multistep, focused, and purposeful process of gathering and evaluating information.

active voice   The feature of a verb indicating that the subject performs the action. Effective speeches make ample use of the active voice. See also *passive voice*.

ad hominem argument   A form of fallacious argument that targets people instead of issues and attempts to incite an audience's dislike for an opponent.

after-dinner speech   A speech that is likely to occur before, after, or during a formal dinner, a breakfast or lunch seminar, or other type of business, professional, or civic meeting.

agenda   A document identifying the items to be accomplished during a meeting.

alliteration   The repetition of the same sounds, usually initial consonants, in two or more neighboring words or syllables.

allusion   A figure of speech in which the speaker makes vague or indirect reference to people, historical events, or concepts to give deeper meaning to the message.

almanac   A reference work that contains facts and statistics in many categories, including those that are related to historical, social, political, and religious subjects.

analogy   An extended metaphor or simile that compares an unfamiliar concept or process with a more familiar one in order to help the listener understand the one that is unfamiliar.

anaphora   A rhetorical device in which the speaker repeats a word or phrase at the beginning of successive phrases, clauses, or sentences.

anecdote   A brief story of an interesting, humorous, or real-life incident that links back to the speaker's theme.

animation effects   Sometimes referred to as "builds," animation effects allow you to decide how you want to reveal text or graphics within a slide during a presentation. You can reveal one letter, word, or paragraph at a time, for example, as you discuss each item. Or you can make text or objects look dimmer or change color when you add another element.

antithesis   Setting off two ideas in balanced (parallel) opposition to each other to create a powerful effect.

appeal to tradition   A fallacy of reasoning in which the speaker argues for the truth of a claim based solely on common practices in the past.

argument   A stated position, with support, for or against an idea or issue; contains the core elements of claim, evidence, and warrants.

arrangement   The strategic process of deciding how to order speech points into a coherent and convincing pattern for your topic and audience; also refers to one of the five parts of the classical canons of rhetoric.

articulation The clarity or forcefulness with which sounds are made, regardless of whether they are pronounced correctly.

atlas A collection of maps, text, and accompanying charts and tables.

attitudes A predisposition to respond to people, ideas, objects, or events in evaluative ways.

audience analysis The process of gathering and analyzing demographic and psychological information about audience members with the explicit aim of adapting your message to the information you uncover.

audience centered An approach to speech preparation in which in each phase of the speech preparation process—from selection and treatment of the speech topic to making decisions about organization, language, and method of delivery—is geared toward communicating a meaningful message to the audience.

audience perspective A stance taken by the speaker in which he or she adapts the speech to the needs, attitudes, and values of an audience.

audio clip A short recording of sounds, music, or speech. Introducing sound into a speech can add interest, illustrate ideas, and even bring humor to the mix.

aural channel A nonverbal channel of communication made up of the vocalizations that form and accompany spoken words. These vocalizations, also called *paralanguage,* include the qualities of volume, pitch, rate, variety, and articulation and pronunciation.

authoritative warrant A warrant that appeals to the credibility the audience assigns to the source of the evidence; also called an *ethos-based appeal.*

average A summary of a set of data according to its typical or average characteristics; may refer to the *mean, median,* or *mode.*

balance A principle that suggests that appropriate emphasis or weight be given to each part of the speech relative to the other parts and to the theme.

bandwagoning A fallacious argument that presents itself as true because "general opinion" supports it.

bar graph A type of graph used to compare quantities or magnitudes with the use of bars of varying lengths.

basic sales technique A synonym for *Monroe's motivated sequence,* a five-part process of persuasion. See also *motivated sequence pattern of arrangement.*

begging the question A fallacious argument presented in such a way that it is necessarily true, even though no evidence has been presented.

beliefs The ways in which people perceive reality or determine the very existence or validity of something.

biased language Any language that relies on unfounded assumptions, negative descriptions, or stereotypes of a given group's age, class, gender, disability, and geographic, ethnic, racial, or religious characteristics.

body (of speech) The part of the speech in which the speaker develops the main points intended to fulfill the speech purpose.

Boolean operators Words placed between the keywords in an Internet search that specify how the key words are related; examples include AND, OR, and NOT.

brainstorming A problem-solving technique, useful for developing speech topics, that involves the spontaneous generation of ideas. Among other techniques, you can brainstorm by making lists, using word association, and mapping a topic.

brief example A single illustration of a point.

call to action A challenge to audience members to act in response to a speech, see the problem in a new way, change their beliefs about the problem, or change both their actions and their beliefs with respect to the problem; placed at the conclusion of a speech.

canned speech A speech used repeatedly and without sufficient adaptation to the rhetorical speech situation.

canons of rhetoric A classical approach to speechmaking in which the speaker divides a speech into five parts: invention, arrangement, style, memory, and delivery.

captive audience An audience in attendance not because they necessarily freely choose to listen to a speech but because they must.

card or online catalog A searchable system for books that is organized by author, title, and subject, and usually according to the Library of Congress call number system or a Dewey decimal number system. The card catalog is an older, manual system; the online catalog is computerized.

case conference An oral report prepared by health-care professionals evaluating a patient's condition and outlining a treatment plan.

causal (cause-effect) pattern of arrangement A pattern of organizing speech points in order, first of causes and then of effects or vice versa; it is used when the cause-effect relationship is well established.

central processing A mode of processing a persuasive message that involves thinking critically about the contents of the message and the strength and quality of the speaker's arguments. People who seriously consider what the speaker's message means to them are most likely to experience a relatively enduring change in thinking.

chalkboard A surface used as a visual aid by speakers to illustrate speech points.

channel The medium through which the speaker sends a message (e.g., sound waves, air waves, electronic transmission, and so forth).

chart A method of visually organizing complex information into compact form. Several different types of charts are helpful for speakers: flowcharts, organization charts, and tabular charts or tables.

cherry-picking To selectively present only those facts and statistics that buttress your point of view while ignoring competing data.

chronological pattern of arrangement (also called *temporal pattern*) A pattern of organizing speech points in a natural sequential order; it is used when describing a series of events in time or when the topic develops in line with a set pattern of actions or tasks.

circular pattern of arrangement A pattern of organizing speech points so that one idea leads to another, which leads to a third, and so forth until the speaker arrives back at the speech thesis.

claim The declaration of a state of affairs, often stated as a thesis statement, in which a speaker attempts to prove something.

claim of fact An argument that focuses on whether something is or is not true or whether something will or will not happen.

claim of policy A claim that recommends that a specific course of action be taken, or approved, by an audience.

claim of value A claim that addresses issues of judgment.

classroom discussion presentation A type of oral presentation in which the speaker presents a brief overview of the topic under discussion and introduces a series of questions to guide students through the topic.

cliché An expression that is predictable and stale.

closed-ended question A question designed to elicit a small range of specific answers supplied by the interviewer.

co-culture A community of people whose perceptions and beliefs differ significantly from those of other groups within the larger culture.

coherence Clarity and logical consistency within a speech or an argument

colleagues within the field audience An audience of individuals who share a speaker's knowledge of the general field under question but who may not be familiar with the specific topic under discussion.

collective mind A state of mind adopted by group members in which they determine that the group communication will be careful, consistent, and conscientious.

collectivist culture A culture that tends to emphasize the needs and desires of the larger group rather than those of the individual.

colloquial expression An informal expression characterized by regional variations of speech.

common knowledge Information that is likely to be known by many people and is therefore in the public domain; the source of such information need not be cited in a speech.

community service learning project report Oral report in which the speaker describes a community agency and its client base, his or her role and accomplishments in working with the agency, any problems encountered, and what was learned.

comparative advantage pattern of arrangement A pattern of organizing speech points so that the speaker's viewpoint or proposal is shown to be superior to one or more alternative viewpoints or proposals.

computer-generated graphics Graphics created using a software program such as Microsoft's PowerPoint.

conclusion (of speech) The part of the speech in which the speaker reiterates the speech purpose, summarizes main points, and leaves the audience with something to think about or act upon.

concrete language Specific, tangible, and definite language (nouns or verbs). See also *abstract language.*

connotative meaning The individual associations that different people bring to bear on a word.

contractions Shortened forms of the verb *to be* and other auxiliary verbs in conjunction with pronouns; the use of contractions makes the speaker's language more concise.

coordinate points The alignment of points in a speech outline according to their equal importance to the topic and purpose.

coordination and subordination The logical placement of ideas relative to their importance to one another. Ideas that are coordinate are given equal weight. An idea that is subordinate to another is given relatively less weight.

copyright A legal protection afforded original creators of literary or artistic works, including works classified as literary, musical, dramatic, choreographic, pictorial, graphic, sculptural, audiovisual, sound recording, or architectural.

counterproductive roles Negative interpersonal roles or group members who focus on individual versus group needs. These needs are usually irrelevant to the task at hand and are not oriented toward maintenance of the group as a team.

crisis-response presentation Oral presentation in which the speaker seeks to reassure an organization's various audiences ("publics") and restore its credibility in the face of potentially reputation-damaging situations.

critical and conflicted audience Audience members whose attitudes are critical or conflicted with respect to the speaker's topic.

critical thinking The ability to evaluate claims on the basis of well-supported reasons.

cultural intelligence   The willingness to learn about other cultures and gradually reshape your thinking and behavior in response to what you've learned.

culturally sensitive speaker   A public speaker who assumes differences among various members of an audience and addresses audience members with interest and respect.

database   A searchable place, or "base," in which information is stored and from which it can be retrieved.

debate   An oral presentation in which two individuals or groups consider or argue an issue from opposing viewpoints.

decoding   The process of interpreting a message.

deductive reasoning   Reasoning from a general condition to a specific instance. See also *syllogism*.

defamatory statement   A statement that potentially harms an individual's reputation at work or in the community.

defensive listening   A poor listening behavior in which the listener reacts defensively to a speaker's message.

definition by etymology (word origin)   Defining something by providing an account of a word's history.

definition by example   Defining something by providing an example of it.

definition by negation   Defining something by explaining what it is not.

definition by synonym   Defining something by comparing it with another term that has an equivalent meaning. For example: A friend is a comrade or a buddy.

delivery   The vocal and nonverbal behavior that a speaker uses in a public speech; one of the five canons of rhetoric.

delivery cues   Brief reminder notes or prompts placed in the speaking outline; can refer to transitions, timing, speaking rate and volume, presentation aids, quotations, statistics, and difficult-to-pronounce or remember names or words.

demagogue   An unethical speaker who relies heavily on irrelevant emotional appeals to short-circuit listeners' rational decision-making process.

demographics   Statistical characteristics of a given population. Characteristics typically considered in the analysis of audience members include age, gender, ethnic or cultural background, socioeconomic status (including income, occupation, and education), and religious and political affiliation.

denotative meaning   The literal or dictionary definition of a word.

design review presentation   An oral presentation that provides information on the results of a design project; frequently delivered in technical fields such as engineering, computer science, and architecture.

devil's advocacy   Arguing for the sake of raising issues or concerns about the idea under discussion.

Dewey decimal number   An identifying number that allows the user to retrieve books and other works that have been classified according to the Dewey decimal system.

diagram   A schematic drawing that explains how something works or how it is constructed or operated; used to simplify and clarify complicated procedures, explanations, and operations.

dialect   Subcultural variations of the mainstream pronunciation and articulation of a language.

dialectical inquiry   Devil's advocacy (see above) that goes a step further by proposing a countersolution to an idea.

dignity   The feeling that one is worthy, honored, or respected as a person.

direct quotation   A statement quoted verbatim, or word for word, from a source. Direct quotations should always be acknowledged in a speech. See also *paraphrase*.

disinformation   The deliberate falsification of information.

domain   The suffix at the end of a Web address that tells you the nature of the Web site: educational (.edu), government (.gov), military (.mil), nonprofit organization (.org), business/commercial (.com), or network (.net). A tilde (~) in the address usually indicates that it is a personal page rather than part of an institutional Web site. Understanding the domain can help you assess the credibility of a site.

dyadic communication   Communication between two people, as in a conversation.

effective delivery   The skillful application of natural conversational behavior to a speech in a way that is relaxed, enthusiastic, and direct.

eight-by-eight rule   Rule of design according to which the speaker does not include more than eight words on a line or eight lines on one PowerPoint slide or other kind of visual aid.

either-or fallacy   A fallacious argument that is stated in terms of two alternatives only, even though there may be multiple ways of viewing the issue.

elaboration likelihood model (ELM) of persuasion   A model of persuasion that states that people process persuasive messages by one of two routes—either central processing or peripheral processing—depending on their degree of involvement in the message.

elocutionary movement   An approach to public speaking in which speechmaking is regarded as a type of performance, much like acting.

encoding   The process of organizing a message, choosing words and sentence structure, and verbalizing the message.

encyclopedia   A reference work that summarizes knowledge found in original form elsewhere and provides an overview of subjects.

enthymeme   A syllogism stated as a probability rather than as an absolute. Because it states either a major or a minor premise, but not both, the premise not stated remains implied.

ethical appeal   An attempt to persuade audience members by appealing to speaker credibility.

ethics   The rules or standards of moral conduct, or how people should act toward one another. In terms of public speaking, *ethics* refers to the responsibilities speakers have toward both their audience and themselves. It also encompasses the responsibilities that listeners have toward speakers.

ethnocentrism   The belief that the ways of one's own culture are superior to those of other cultures. Ethnocentric speakers act as though everyone shares their point of view and points of reference, whether or not this is in fact the case.

ethos   The Greek word for "character." According to the ancient Greek rhetorician Aristotle, audiences listen to and trust speakers if they exhibit competence (as demonstrated by the speaker's grasp of the subject matter) and good moral character.

eulogy   A speech whose purpose is to celebrate and commemorate the life of someone while consoling those who are left behind; typically delivered by close friends and family members.

evaluation research presentation   An oral presentation reporting on the effectiveness of programs developed to address various issues; frequently delivered in social scientific fields.

evidence   Supporting material that provides grounds for belief.

evidence-based practice   An approach to medical treatment in which caregivers make decisions based on current research and "best practices."

example   An illustration whose purpose is to aid understanding by making ideas, items, or events more concrete and by clarifying and amplifying meaning.

expectancy-outcome values theory   A theory of persuasion developed by Icek Aizen and Martin Fishbein positing that audience members act according to the perceived costs and benefits ("value") associated with a particular action; useful when developing a persuasive speech targeting behavior.

expert or insider audience   An audience composed of individuals who have an intimate knowledge of the topic, issue, product, or idea being discussed.

expert testimony   Any findings, eyewitness accounts, or opinions by professionals who are trained to evaluate or report on a given topic; a form of supporting material.

explanatory research presentation   An oral presentation focusing on studies that attempt to analyze and explain a phenomenon; frequently delivered in social scientific fields.

extended example   Multifaceted illustrations of the idea, item, or event being described, thereby getting the point across and reiterating it effectively.

extended research or field study project   An oral presentation, typically delivered in the context of science-related disciplines, in which the speaker provides (1) an overview of field research, (2) the methods used in the research, (3) an analysis of research results, and (4) a time line indicating how the research results will be used to go forward.

external listening distraction   Anything in the environment that distracts listeners from receiving the speaker's message.

fabrication   The making up of information, such as falsifying data or experiments or claiming a source where none exists.

fact book   A reference work that includes key information on a given topic (e.g., facts about the geography, government, economy, and transportation of a given country).

facts   Documented occurrences, including actual events, dates, times, places, and people involved.

fair use doctrine   Legal guidelines permitting the limited use of copyrighted works without permission for the purposes of scholarship, criticism, comment, news reporting, teaching, and research.

fear appeal   A persuasive appeal to audience members that deliberately arouses their fear and anxiety.

feedback   Audience response to a message, which can be conveyed both verbally and nonverbally through gestures. Feedback from the audience often indicates whether a speaker's message has been understood.

feedback loop   The continual flow or feedback between speaker and listener. A situation in which successful speakers adjust their message based on their listeners' reactions, and vice versa (also known as *circular response*).

field searching (often called **advanced search**)   A search tool in most Internet search engines that targets specific search parameters to narrow search results.

fighting words   A speech that uses language that provokes people to violence.

figures of speech   Expressions, such as metaphors, similes, analogies, and hyperbole, in which words are used in a nonliteral fashion.

First Amendment The amendment to the U.S. Constitution that guarantees freedom of speech ("Congress shall make no law . . . abridging the freedom of speech . . .").

fixed alternative question A closed-ended question that contains a limited choice of answers, such as "Yes," "No," or "Sometimes."

flip chart A large (27–34 inches) pad of paper on which a speaker can illustrate speech points.

flowchart A diagram that shows step-by-step progression through a procedure, relationship, or process. Usually the flow of a procedure or process is drawn horizontally or vertically and describes how key components fit into a whole.

font A set of type of one size and face.

forms of rhetorical proof Modes of persuasion that concern the nature of the message in a speech, the nature of the audience's feelings, and the qualifications and personality of the speaker.

free speech The right to be free from unreasonable constraints on expression.

frequency A count of the number of times something occurs or appears.

full-sentence transition A signal to listeners, in the form of a declarative sentence, that the speaker is turning to another topic.

full-text database A database in which at least some of the records contain the full text of articles.

gateway (informational portal) A human directory that contains at least one hundred sites that have been reviewed by an expert.

gender Our social and psychological sense of ourselves as males or females.

gender stereotypes Oversimplified and often severely distorted ideas about the innate nature of men or women.

general encyclopedia A reference work that attempts to cover all important subject areas of knowledge.

general speech purpose A declarative statement that answers the question "Why am I speaking on this topic for this particular audience and occasion?" Usually the general speech goal is to inform, to persuade, or to mark a special occasion. See also *specific speech purpose*.

generational identity The collective cultural identity of a generation or a cohort.

graph A graphical representation of numerical data. Graphs neatly illustrate relationships among components or units and demonstrate trends. Four major types of graphs are line graphs, bar graphs, pie graphs, and pictograms.

group activity presentation An oral presentation that introduces students to an activity and provides them with clear directions for its completion.

groupthink The tendency of a group to accept information and ideas without subjecting them to critical analysis. Groupthink results from strong feelings of loyalty and unity within a group and can lead to a decline in the quality of the group's decisions.

hackneyed Language that is poorly crafted and lacking in freshness.

handheld or fixed microphone A microphone that is attached by a cord to an electrical power source.

handout Page-size items that convey information that is either impractical to give to the audience in another manner or is intended to be kept by audience members after a presentation.

hasty overgeneralization A fallacy of reasoning in which the speaker attempts to support a claim by asserting that a particular piece of evidence (an isolated case) is true for all individuals or conditions concerned.

hate speech   Any offensive communication—verbal or nonverbal—directed against people's racial, ethnic, religious, gender, or other characteristics. Racist, sexist, or ageist slurs, gay bashing, and cross burnings are all forms of hate speech.

hedges   Unnecessary words and phrases that qualify or introduce doubt into statements that should be straightforward.

high-uncertainty avoidance culture   One of five "value dimensions," or major cultural patterns, that are significant across all cultures to varying degrees; identified by Geert Hofstede.

hostile audience or those that strongly disagree   One of four potential types of audiences the persuasive speaker may encounter.

hyperbole   A figure of speech in which the speaker uses obvious exaggeration to drive home a point.

hyperlinks   Connections that link individual pieces of information or entire Web sites to other pieces of information or sites.

hypothetical example   An illustration of something that could happen in the future if certain things occurred.

indentation   In an outline, the plotting of speech points to indicate their weight relative to one another; subordinate points are placed underneath and to the right of higher-order points.

identification   A feeling of commonality with another; when appropriate, effective speakers attempt to foster a sense of identification between themselves and audience members.

individual debate format   A debate in which one person takes a side against another person.

individualistic culture   A culture that tends to emphasize personal identity and the needs of the individual rather than those of the group, upholding such values as individual achievement and decision making.

individual search engine   A search engine that compiles its own database of Web pages, such as Google or AltaVista. See also *meta-search engine.*

information   Data set in a context for relevance.

informative speaking   Public speaking that is intended to increase an audience's understanding and awareness by imparting knowledge. Informative speeches provide an audience with new information, new insights, or new ways of thinking about a topic.

inoculation effect   A theory of persuasive speaking in which a speaker anticipates and addresses counterarguments. The theory rests on the biological principle of inducing resistance through exposure to small quantities of a harmful substance.

integrity   The quality of being incorruptible, or able to avoid compromise for the sake of personal expediency.

intellectual property   The ownership of an individual's creative expression.

internal listening distraction   Thoughts and feelings, both positive and negative, that intrude on our attention as we attempt to listen to a speaker.

internal preview   An extended transition used within the body of a speech that alerts audience members to ensuing speech content.

internal summary   An extended transition that draws together important ideas before proceeding to another speech point.

interpersonal roles   Types of roles or styles of interacting in a group that facilitate group interaction.

interview   A type of face-to-face communication conducted for the purpose of gathering information. Interviews can be conducted one-on-one or in a group.

intonation The rising and falling of voice pitch across phrases and sentences. Intonation is what distinguishes a question from a statement.

introduction (of speech) The first part of a speech in which the speaker establishes the speech purpose and its relevance to the audience and previews the topic and the main points.

invention The classical term for the process of selecting information to illustrate or prove speech points.

invisible Web The portion of the Web that includes pass-protected sites, documents behind firewalls, and the contents of proprietary databases.

irony A figure of speech in which the speaker uses humor, satire, or sarcasm to suggest a meaning other than the one that is actually being expressed.

issues-based conflict Conflict that allows group members to test and debate ideas and potential solutions. It requires each member to ask tough questions, press for clarification, and present alternative views.

jargon Specialized terminology developed within a given endeavor or field of study.

key-word outline The briefest of the three forms of outlines, the key-word outline uses the smallest possible units of understanding associated with a specific point to outline the main and supporting points. See also *phrase outline* and *sentence outline*.

lavalier microphone A microphone that attaches to a lapel or a collar.

lay audience An audience of individuals who have no specialized knowledge of the general field related to a speaker's topic or of the topic itself.

lay testimony Testimony by a nonexpert; a form of supporting material.

lazy speech A poor speech habit in which the speaker fails to properly articulate words.

LCD panel A device connected to a computer that is used to project slides stored in the computer; LCD is an acronym for liquid crystal diode.

LCD projector A projector designed for computer images that is equipped with an illumination, or light source, in its own case, thereby eliminating the need for an overhead projector.

lecture An informative speech prepared for an audience of student learners.

library gateway An entry point into a large collection of research and reference information that has been selected and reviewed by librarians.

Library of Congress call number An identifying number that allows the user to retrieve books and other works that have been classified according to the Library of Congress classification system.

line graph A type of graph used to represent trends and other information that changes over time. A line graph displays one measurement on the horizontal axis and other units of measurement or values on the vertical axis. Each value or point is connected with a line.

listening The conscious act of recognizing, understanding, and accurately interpreting the messages communicated by others.

listening distraction Anything that competes for a listener's attention; the source of the distraction may be internal or external.

logical fallacy A statement that is based on an invalid or deceptive line of reasoning.

logos An appeal to the audience's reason and logic.

low-uncertainty avoidance culture One of five "value dimensions" or major cultural patterns that are significant across all cultures to varying degrees; identified by Geert Hofstede.

main points   The key ideas or primary points intended to fulfill the speech purpose. Their function is to make claims in support of the thesis. See also *subordinate points*.

major premise   A general case; used in syllogisms and enthymemes. See also *minor premise*.

malapropism   The inadvertent use of a word or phrase in place of one that sounds like it.

map   A representation of a whole area or part of an area on a flat surface.

Maslow's hierarchy of needs   A model of human action based on the principle that people are motivated to act on the basis of their needs.

mass communication   Communication that occurs between a speaker and a large audience of unknown people. In mass communication the receivers of the message are not present with the speaker, or they are part of such an immense crowd that there can be little or no interaction between speaker and listeners. Communication that occurs via a television or radio news broadcast or a mass rally is an example of mass communication.

mean   The sum of the scores divided by the number of scores; the arithmetic (or computed) average.

median   A type of average that represents the center-most score in a distribution, the point above and below which 50 percent of the scores fall.

Meeting Minder   A note-taking tool embedded in Microsoft's PowerPoint that allows users to take notes and give assignments (known as Action Items) in the middle of a presentation.

memory   One of five parts of the classical canons of rhetoric; refers to the practice of the speech until it can be artfully delivered.

message   The content of the communication process — thoughts and ideas put into meaningful expressions. A message can be expressed both verbally (through the sentences and points of a speech) and nonverbally (through eye contact and gestures).

metaphor   A figure of speech used to make an implicit comparison without the use of *like* or *as* (e.g., "Love is a rose"). See also *simile*.

meta-search engine   A search engine that searches several search engines simultaneously. Examples include MetaCrawler and Dogpile. See also *individual search engine*.

methods/procedure presentation   An oral presentation describing and sometimes demonstrating an experimental or mathematical process, including the conditions under which that process can be applied; frequently delivered in scientific and mathematical fields.

minor premise   A specific case; used in syllogisms and enthymemes. See also *major premise*.

misinformation   Information that is false.

mixed audience   An audience composed of a combination of individuals, some of whom have expert knowledge of the field and topic while others have no specialized knowledge.

mixed metaphor   A metaphor that juxtaposes or compares unlike images or expressions ("Before plunging into the pool, let's walk through these steps").

mode   A type of average that represents the most frequently occurring score in a distribution.

model   A three-dimensional, scale-size representation of an object such as a building.

Monroe's motivated sequence   See *motivated sequence pattern of arrangement.*

motivated sequence pattern of arrangement   A five-step process of persuasion developed by Alan Monroe.

motivational warrant   A warrant that uses the needs, desires, emotions, and values of audience members as the basis for accepting evidence in support of a claim.

multimedia   A single production that combines several types of media (stills, sound, video, text, and data).

mumbling   Slurring words together at a very low level of volume and pitch so that they are barely audible.

narrative   A story; it can be based on personal experiences or imaginary incidents.

narrative pattern of arrangement   A pattern of organizing speech points so that the speech unfolds as a story, with characters, plot, setting, and vivid imagery. In practice, this pattern often is combined with other organizational patterns.

neutral question   A question that doesn't lead the interviewee to a desired response.

noise   Anything that interferes with the communication process between a speaker and an audience, so that the message cannot be understood; noise can derive from external sources in the environment or from internal psychological factors.

nonverbal delivery   The speaker's use of facial expressions, gestures, general body movements, and overall physical appearance when presenting the speech.

onomatopoeia   A figure of speech in which the speaker imitates natural sounds in word form in order to add vividness to a speech (e.g., "The rain dripped a steady plop, plop, plop").

open-ended question   A question designed to allow respondents to elaborate as much as possible. Open-ended questions are particularly useful for probing beliefs and opinions. They elicit more individual or personal information about audience members' thoughts and feelings.

operational definition   Defining something by describing what it does (e.g., "A computer is something that processes information").

oratory   In classical terms, the art of public speaking.

organizational chart   A chart that illustrates the structure or chain of command in an organization, plotting the interrelationships among different positions, divisions, departments, and personnel.

outlining   The physical process of plotting speech points on the page in hierarchical order of importance.

overgeneralization   An attempt to support a claim by asserting that a particular piece of evidence is true for everyone concerned.

overhead transparency   An image on a transparent background that can be viewed by transmitted light, either directly or through projection onto a screen or wall. The images may be written or printed directly onto the transparency or handwritten during the presentation.

paid inclusion   The practice of paying a fee to a search engine company for inclusion in its index of possible results, without a guarantee of ranking.

paid placement   The practice of paying a fee to a search engine company for inclusion in its search results and a guaranteed higher ranking within those results.

pandering   To identify with values that are not your own in order to win approval from an audience.

panel discussion   An oral presentation in which a group of three to nine people discuss a topic in the presence of an audience and under the direction of a moderator.

paralanguage   The vocal effects that accompany speech.

parallel form   The statement of equivalent speech points in similar grammatical form and style.

parallelism   The arrangement of words, phrases, or sentences in similar grammatical and stylistic form. Parallel structure can help speakers emphasize important ideas in a speech.

paraphrase   A restatement of someone else's statements or written work that alters the form or phrasing but not the substance of that person's ideas. See also *direct quotation.*

participative leader   A leader who facilitates a group's activities and interactions in ways that will lead to a desired outcome.

passive voice   The feature of a verb indicating that the subject is acted upon or is the receiver of the action. See also *active voice.*

patchwrite plagiarism   A form of plagiarism in which you copy material from a source and then change and rearrange occasional words and sentence structures to make it appear as if the material were your own.

pathos   The appeal to an audience's emotions.

pauses   Strategic elements of a speech used to enhance meaning by providing a type of punctuation, emphasizing a point, drawing attention to a key thought, or allowing listeners a moment to contemplate.

percentage   The quantified portion of a whole, or 100 percent.

performance anxiety   A form of *public speaking anxiety (PSA)* that occurs the moment a speaker begins to deliver a speech. See also *preparation anxiety.*

periodical   A regularly published magazine or journal.

peripheral processing   A mode of processing a persuasive message that does not consider the quality of the speaker's message but is influenced by such non-content issues as the speaker's appearance or reputation, certain slogans or one-liners, or obvious attempts to manipulate emotions. Peripheral processing of messages occurs when people lack the motivation or the ability to pay close attention to the issues.

personal-based conflict   Conflict in which group members personalize disagreements over issues, thereby wasting time, distracting the group from its mission, and impairing motivation.

personification   A figure of speech in which the speaker endows an abstract idea or inanimate object with human qualities (e.g., "Computers have become important members of our family").

persons with disabilities (PWD)   A person whose physical or mental impairment substantially limits his or her major life activities.

perspective-taking   The identification of audience members' attitudes, values, beliefs, needs, and wants and the integration of this information into the speech context.

persuasion   The process of influencing others' attitudes, beliefs, values, and behavior.

persuasive speech   A speech whose general purpose is to effect some degree of change in the audience's beliefs, attitudes, values, or behavior.

phrase outline   A delivery outline that uses a partial construction of the sentence form of each point instead of using complete sentences that present precise wording for each point. See also *key-word outline* and *sentence outline.*

pictogram A type of graph that illustrates comparisons in picture form. The pictures represent numerical units and are drawn to relate to the items being compared.

picture A two-dimensional representation of people, places, ideas, or objects produced on an opaque backing; types of pictures commonly used by speakers include photographs, line drawings, diagrams, maps, and posters.

pie graph A type of graph used to depict the division of a whole. The pie, which represents 100 percent, is divided into portions or segments called "slices." Each slice constitutes a percentage of the whole.

pitch The range of sounds from high to low (or vice versa). Pitch is determined by the number of vibrations per unit of time; the more vibrations per unit (also called *frequency*), the higher the pitch, and vice versa.

plagiarism The act of using other people's ideas or words without acknowledging the source. See also *patchwrite plagiarism* and *wholesale plagiarism*.

pointer A Microsoft PowerPoint tool that allows the user to show parts of a slide during a presentation.

policy recommendation report An oral presentation that offers recommendations for solving a problem or addressing an issue.

poster A large, bold, two-dimensional design incorporating words, shapes, and (if desired) color, placed on an opaque backing; used to convey a brief message or point forcefully and attractively.

poster session A format for the visual presentation of posters, arranged on free-standing boards, that contains the concise display of a study or an issue for viewing by participants at professional conferences. The speaker prepares brief remarks and remains on hand to answer questions as needed.

power distance As developed by Geert Hofstede, a measure of the extent to which a culture values social equality versus tradition and authority.

preparation anxiety A form of *public speaking anxiety (PSA)* that arises when the speaker begins to prepare for a speech, at which point he or she might feel overwhelmed at the amount of time and planning required. See also *performance anxiety*.

pre-performance anxiety A form of *public speaking anxiety (PSA)* that occurs when the speaker begins to rehearse a speech.

pre-preparation anxiety A form of *public speaking anxiety (PSA)* that occurs the moment speakers learn they must give a speech.

presentation aids Objects, models, pictures, graphs, charts, video, audio, and multimedia, used alone or in combination within the context of a speech; such aids help listeners see relationships among concepts and elements, store and remember material, and critically examine key ideas.

presentational speaking Reports delivered by individuals or groups within a business or professional environment.

preview statement A statement included in the introduction of a speech in which the speaker identifies the main speech points that will be covered in the body of the speech.

primary research Original or firsthand research, such as interviews and surveys conducted by the speaker. See also *secondary research*.

problem-cause-solution pattern of arrangement A pattern of organizing speech points so that they demonstrate (1) the nature of the problem, (2) reasons for the problem, (3) unsatisfactory solutions, and (4) proposed solutions.

problem-solution pattern of arrangement   A pattern of organizing speech points so that they demonstrate the nature and significance of a problem first, and then provide justification for a proposed solution.

productive conflict   A form of group conflict in which questions are clarified, ideas are challenged, counterexamples are presented, worst-case scenarios are considered, and proposals are reformulated.

progress report   A report that updates clients or principals on developments in an ongoing project.

pronunciation   The formation of word sounds.

prop   Any live or inanimate object used by a speaker as a presentation aid.

propaganda   Information represented in such a way as to provoke a desired response.

proposal   A type of business or professional presentation in which the speaker provides information needed for decisions related to modifying or adopting a product, procedure, or policy.

prototype   A physical model of a design.

public domain   Bodies of work, including publications and processes, available for public use without permission; not protected by *copyright* or patent.

public performance   A performance, including a speech, of copyrighted material delivered in a public forum other than a classroom. When you incorporate copyrighted material into a speech, you are legally bound to obtain performance rights to do so from the copyright owner or his or her representative.

public speaking   A type of communication in which the speaker delivers a message with a specific purpose to an audience of people who are physically present during the delivery of the speech. Public speaking always includes a speaker who has a reason for speaking, an audience that gives the speaker its attention, and a message that is meant to accomplish a purpose.

public speaking anxiety (PSA)   Fear or anxiety associated with a speaker's actual or anticipated communication to an audience.

qualitative research   Research with an emphasis on statistical measurement.

quantitative research   Research with an emphasis on observing, describing, and interpreting behavior.

questionnaire   A written survey designed to gather information from a large pool of respondents. Questionnaires consist of a mix of *open-* and *closed-ended questions* designed to elicit information.

receiver   The recipient (an individual or a group) of a source's message.

reckless disregard for the truth   A quality of defamatory speech that is legally liable. See also *defamatory statement.*

red herring fallacy   A fallacy of reasoning in which the speaker relies on irrelevant information to support an argument.

reference librarian   A librarian trained to help library users locate information resources.

refutation pattern of organization   A pattern of organizing speech points in which each main point addresses and then refutes (disproves) an opposing claim to the speaker's position.

request for funding presentation   An oral presentation that provides evidence that a project, proposal, or design idea is worth funding; it is frequently delivered in such technical fields as engineering, computer science, and architecture.

research overview presentation   A type of oral presentation in which the speaker provides the context and the background for a research question or hypothesis that will form the basis of an impending undertaking; it is typically delivered within the context of scientific and mathematical disciplines.

research presentation   An oral presentation describing original research undertaken by the speaker, either alone or as part of a team; it is frequently delivered in scientific and social scientific fields.

respect   To feel or show deferential regard. For the ethical speaker, respect ranges from addressing audience members as unique human beings to refraining from rudeness and other forms of personal attack.

responsibility   A charge, trust, or duty for which one is accountable.

restate-forecast form   A type of transition in which the speaker restates the point just covered and previews the point to be covered next.

review of the literature presentation   An oral presentation in which the speaker reviews the body of research related to a given topic or issue and offers conclusions about the topic based on this research; it is frequently delivered in social scientific fields.

rhetoric   The practice of oratory, or public speaking.

rhetorical device   A technique of language to achieve a desired effect.

rhetorical proof   In classical terms, a means of persuasion *(ethos, pathos, logos)*.

rhetorical question   A question that does not invite an actual response but is used to make the audience think.

rhetorical situation   Consideration of the audience, occasion, and overall speech situation when planning a speech.

roast   A humorous tribute to a person, one in which a series of speakers jokingly poke fun at the individual being honored.

roman numeral outline   An outline format in which main points are enumerated with roman numerals (I, II, III), supporting points with capital letters (A, B, C), third-level points with arabic numerals (1, 2, 3), and fourth-level points with lowercase letters (a, b, c).

sales presentation   A presentation that attempts to persuade a potential buyer to purchase a service or product described by the presenter.

sans serif typeface   Typefaces that are blocklike and linear and are designed without tiny strokes or flourishes at the top or bottom of each letter. See also *serif typeface.*

scale question   A *closed-ended question* (also called "attitude scales") that measures the respondent's level of agreement or disagreement with specific issues.

scanning   A technique for creating eye contact with large audiences; speakers move their gaze across the audience from one listener to another and from one section to another, pausing as they do to gaze briefly at individual listeners.

science-related disciplines   Disciplines that include the physical, natural, and earth sciences.

search engine   Using powerful software programs, a search engine scans millions of Web documents that contain the keywords and phrases you command it to search. A program then creates a huge index from the Web pages that have been read, compares it with your search request, and returns matching results to you, usually in order of relevance.

secondary research   The vast world of information gathered by others; can include published facts and statistics, texts, documents, and any other information not originally collected and generated by the researcher. See also *primary research.*

selective perception   A psychological principle that posits that listeners pay attention selectively to certain messages and ignore others.

sentence outline   An outline in which each main and supporting point is stated in sentence form and in precisely the way the speaker wants to express the idea. Generally, sentence outlines are used for working outlines. See also *key-word outline* and *phrase outline.*

serif typeface   Typefaces that include small flourishes, or strokes, at the top and bottom of each letter. See also *sans serif typeface.*

sermon   A speech of inspiration given in a religious context.

sexist language   Language that oversimplifies or distorts ideas about the innate nature of what it means to be male or female. For example the generic use of the pronoun *he* or *she.*

sexist pronoun   A pronoun that is used restrictively to refer to one or the other gender when the antecedent may in fact be either male or female.

shared meaning   The mutual understanding of a message between speaker and audience. Shared meaning occurs in varying degrees. The lowest level of shared meaning exists when the speaker has merely caught the audience's attention. As the message develops, depending on the encoding choices by the source, a higher degree of shared meaning is possible.

shift report   An oral report prepared by health-care workers that concisely relays patient status and needs to incoming caregivers.

signposts   Conjunctions or phrases (such as "Next," "First," "Second," and so forth) that indicate *transitions* between supporting points.

simile   A figure of speech used to compare one thing with another by using the word *like* or *as* (e.g., "He works *like* a dog"). See also *metaphor.*

slander   Defamatory speech.

small group   A group that consists of between three and twenty people as opposed to a large public audience.

small group communication   Communication involving a small number of people who can see and speak directly with one another, as in a business meeting.

social agenda–setting   In a special occasion speech, a type of speech purpose whose goal is to focus on a social/political issue and reinforce a message that relates to it.

source   The source, or sender, is the person who creates a message. The speaker transforms ideas and thoughts into messages and sends them to a receiver, or an audience.

spatial pattern of arrangement   A pattern of organizing main points in order of their physical proximity or direction relative to each other; it is used when the purpose of a speech is to describe or explain the physical arrangement of a place, a scene, or an object.

speaker credibility   The quality that reveals that a speaker has a good grasp of the subject, displays sound reasoning skills, is honest and nonmanipulative, and is genuinely interested in the welfare of audience members; a modern version of *ethos.*

speaking extemporaneously   A type of delivery that falls somewhere between impromptu and written or memorized deliveries. Speakers delivering an extemporaneous speech prepare well and practice in advance, giving full attention to all facets of the speech—content, arrangement, and delivery. Instead of memorizing or writing the speech word for word, they speak from a *key-word outline* or *phrase outline.*

speaking from manuscript   A style of delivery in which the speaker reads the speech verbatim—that is, from a prepared written text (either on paper or on a *TelePrompTer*) containing the entire speech.

speaking from memory   A type of delivery in which the speaker puts the entire speech, word for word, into writing and then commits it to memory.

speaking impromptu   A type of delivery that is unpracticed, spontaneous, or improvised.

speaking outline   A delivery outline to be used when practicing and actually presenting a speech.

speaking rate   The pace at which a speech is delivered. The typical public speech occurs at a rate slightly below 120 words per minute.

specialized encyclopedia   A reference work that delves deeply into one subject area, such as religion, science, art, sports, or engineering.

specialized search engine   A search engine that searches for information only on specific topics.

special occasion speech   A speech whose general purpose is to entertain, celebrate, commemorate, inspire, or set a social agenda.

specific purpose   See *specific speech purpose.*

specific speech purpose   A refined statement of purpose that zeroes in more closely than the general purpose on the goal of the speech. See also *general speech purpose.*

speculative claim   A type of *claim of fact* that addresses questions for which answers are not yet available.

speech of acceptance   A speech made in response to receiving an award. Its purpose is to express gratitude for the honor bestowed on the speaker.

speech of inspiration   A speech whose purpose is to inspire or motivate the audience to positively consider, reflect on, and sometimes even act on the speaker's words.

speech of introduction   A short speech defined by two goals: to prepare or "warm up" audience members for the main speaker and to motivate them to listen to what that speaker has to say.

speech of presentation   A speech whose purpose is twofold: to communicate the meaning of the award and to explain why the recipient is receiving it.

speech purpose   See *general speech purpose* and *specific speech purpose.*

staff report   A report that informs managers and other employees of new developments relating to personnel that affect them and their work.

statistic   Quantified evidence; data that measures the size or magnitude of something, demonstrates trends, or shows relationships with the purpose of summarizing information, demonstrating proof, and making points memorable.

stereotype   A generalization about an apparent characteristic of a group, culture, or ethnicity that falsely claims to define all of its members.

style   The speaker's choice of words and sentence structure.

subject directory   A searchable database of Web sites organized by categories (e.g., Yahoo! Directory).

subordinate points   The alignment of points within a speech outline that have somewhat lesser weight than main points; they provide support for or extend the more central ideas of *main points.*

substantive warrant   A warrant that relies on factual evidence to link a claim to evidence. See also *warrant by analogy, warrant by cause,* and *warrant by sign.*

supporting material   Information (examples, narratives, testimony, and facts and statistics) that clarifies, elaborates, and verifies the speaker's assertions.

syllogism   A form of rational appeal defined as a three-part argument consisting of a major premise or general case, a minor premise or specific case, and a conclusion. See also *deductive reasoning.*

sympathetic audience   An audience that already shares much agreement with the speaker; one of four types of potential audiences that persuasive speakers may encounter.

symposium   A formal meeting at which several speakers deliver short speeches on the same topic.

table   A systematic grouping of data or numerical information in column format.

tag questions   Unnecessary questions appended to statements or commands; the use of such weak language undermines a speaker's authority.

talking head   A speaker who remains static, standing stiffly behind a podium, and so resembles a televised shot of a speaker's head and shoulders.

target audience   Those individuals within the broader audience who are most likely to be influenced in the direction the speaker seeks.

task roles   Types of roles that directly relate to the accomplishment of the objectives and missions of a group. Recording secretary and moderator are examples of task roles.

team debate format   A debate in which multiple people take sides against another team, with each person on the team assuming a speaking role.

team presentation   An oral presentation prepared and delivered by a group of three or more people.

technical disciplines   These include the range of engineering fields (mechanical, electrical, chemical, civil, aerospace, industrial, nuclear), computer-science-oriented fields (computer science, computer engineering, software engineering), and design-oriented fields (industrial design, architecture, graphic design).

TelePrompTer   A device that contains a magnified script of a speech; it is commonly used when a speaker's remarks are televised.

testimony   Firsthand findings, eyewitness accounts, and opinions by people, both lay (nonexpert) and expert.

thesis statement   The theme, or central idea, of a speech that serves to connect all the parts of the speech. The main points, the supporting material, and the conclusion all relate to the thesis.

tilde (~)   A symbol that appears in the domain of a Web address; it usually indicates a personal page rather than an institutional Web site.

toast   A brief tribute to a person or an event being celebrated.

topic   What the speech is about; a topic may be assigned to the speaker, or the speaker may have to choose one based on personal interests, experience, and knowledge.

topical pattern of arrangement (categorical pattern)   A pattern of organizing main points as subtopics or categories of the speech topic; of all organizational patterns, this one offers the most freedom to structure speech points as desired.

topic map   A brainstorming technique in which you lay out the words in diagram form to show categorical relationships among them; it is useful for selecting and narrowing a speech topic.

transition effects   Microsoft PowerPoint tools that add motion and sound effects when moving from one slide to the next in a presentation.

transitions   Words, phrases, or sentences that tie speech ideas together and enable a speaker to move smoothly from one point to the next.

triad   A rhetorical device that makes use of three parallel elements.

trustworthiness   The quality of displaying both honesty and dependability.

typeface   A specific style of lettering, such as Arial, Times Roman, or Courier. Typefaces come in a variety of fonts, or sets of sizes (called the "point size"), and upper- and lowercase.

uncertainty avoidance   The extent to which people feel threatened by ambiguity.

understatement   A figure of speech in which a speaker draws attention to an idea by minimizing its importance (e.g., "Flunking out of college might be a problem").

uninformed, less educated, or apathetic audience   An audience that knows or cares little about a specific topic.

unity   The quality of a speech in which only those points that are implied by the purpose and thesis statements are included. Nothing is extraneous or tangential. Each main point supports the thesis, and each supporting point provides evidence for the main points.

U.S. Government Printing Office (GPO)   Responsible for publishing and distributing all information collected and produced by federal agencies, from the Census Bureau to the Department of Education and the Environmental Protection Agency. GPO publications also include all congressional reports and hearings.

valid generalization   A generalization that is supported by different types of evidence from different sources and that does not make claims beyond a reasonable point.

values   Our most enduring judgments or standards of what's important to us (e.g., equal opportunity, democracy, change and progress, or perseverance).

video   Presentation aids (including movies, television programs, and other recording segments) that combine sight, sound, and movement to illustrate key speech concepts.

video projector   A projector that connects to a computer and displays video.

virtual group   A group in which members who are physically dispersed interact and exchange ideas through mediated communication such as e-mail and videoconferencing.

virtual library   A collection of library holdings available online.

visual channel   A nonverbal channel of communication that includes the speaker's physical actions and appearance—facial expressions, gestures, general body movement, physical appearance, dress, and objects held.

visualization   An exercise for building confidence in which the speaker closes his or her eyes and envisions a series of positive feelings and reactions that will occur on the day of the speech.

vocal delivery   The speaker's use of speech volume, rate, pitch, variety, pronunciation, and articulation to deliver a speech.

vocal fillers   Unnecessary and undesirable phrases or utterances that are used to cover pauses, such as "uh," "hmm," "you know," "I mean," and "it's like."

vocal variety   The variation of volume, pitch, rate, and pauses to create an effective delivery.

volume   The relative loudness of a speaker's voice while giving a speech.

warrant   A core component of an argument that serves to justify the link made between the claim and the evidence.

warrant by analogy   A statement, based on the comparison of two similar cases, that infers that what is true in one case is true in the other. The assumption is that the characteristics of case A and case B are so similar, if not the same, that what is true for B must also be true for A.

warrant by cause   The provision of a cause-effect relationship as proof of a claim.

warrant by sign   A statement based on an inference that such a close relationship exists between two variables that the presence or absence of one may be taken as an indication of the presence or absence of the other (e.g., smoke is a sign of fire).

wholesale plagiarism   A form of plagiarism in which you "cut and paste" material from print or online sources into your speech and represent that material as your own. See also *plagiarism.*

word association   A *brainstorming* technique in which you write down ideas as they occur to you, beginning with a single word, in order to generate and narrow speech topics.

working outline   A preparation or rough outline that refines and finalizes the *specific speech purpose,* firms up and organizes *main points,* and develops *supporting material.*

World Wide Web   The most frequently used portion of the Internet, the Web is a graphics-rich environment of electronic pages or documents that contain text, graphics, sound, video, and — its most distinguishing feature — hyperlinks. See also *hyperlinks.*

Notes

Chapter 1

1. D. Uchida, M. J. Cetron, and F. McKenzie, "What Students Must Know to Succeed in the Twenty-first Century" (special report by the World Future Society based on "Preparing Students for the Twenty-first Century," a report on a project by the American Association of School Administrators, 1996).
2. *Compton's Online Encyclopedia*, s.v. "public speaking," http://www.comptons.com/encyclopedia (accessed June 10, 2000).
3. The scholarly basis for this model is an integration of rhetorical theory (Aristotle), information theory (Shannon and Weaver), semantics (Ogden and Richards), and systems theory (Bertalonffy). Taken together, these important concepts allow us to view communication as a highly interactive yet holistic process.
4. Robert Perrin, "The Speaking-Writing Connection: Enhancing the Symbiotic Relationship," *Contemporary Education* 65 (1994): 62–64.
5. Ibid., 62.
6. David C. Thomas and Kerr Inkson, *Cultural Intelligence: People Skills for a Global Business* (San Francisco: Berrett-Koehler Publishers, 2004), 14.
7. Ibid., 14.
8. Patricia Bizzell and Bruce Herzberg, *The Rhetorical Tradition: Readings from Classical Times to the Present,* 2nd ed. (New York: Bedford/St.Martin's, 2001), 7.

Chapter 3

1. M. Burley-Allen, *Listening: The Forgotten Skill: A Self-Teaching Guide* (New York: Wiley, 1995); M. G. Eskaros, "Fine-Tune Your Listening Skills," *Hydrocarbon Processing* 83 (2004).
2. H. E. Chambers, *Effective Communication Skills for Scientific and Technical Professionals* (Cambridge: Perseus Publishing, 2001).
3. See, for example, J. Fuimano, "Sharp Listening Skills Point Staff in the Right Direction," *Nursing Management* 35 (2004): 12; and Andrew D. Wolvin and C. G. Coakley, "A Survey of the Status of Listening Training in Some Fortune 500 Corporations," *Communication Education* 40, no. 2 (1991): 152–64.
4. Andrew Wolvin and C. Coakley, *Listening,* 4th ed. (Dubuque, Iowa: Brown, 1992).
5. S. Golen, "A Factor Analysis of Barriers to Effective Listening," *Journal of Business Communication* 27 (1990): 25–36.
6. Thomas E. Anastasi Jr., *Listen! Techniques for Improving Communication Skills* (Boston: CBI Publishing, 1982).
7. Ibid.
8. Carole Wade and Carol Tavris, *Psychology,* 4th ed. (New York: HarperCollins, 1996), 31–35.
9. Ron Hoff, *I Can See You Naked,* rev. ed. (Kansas City, Mo.: Andrews McMeel, 1992), 300–301.

Chapter 4

1. Michael Josephson, interview by author, May 10, 1996.
2. *The Compact Edition of the Oxford English Dictionary,* 1971 ed., 2514.

3. Cited in Edward P. J. Corbett, *Classical Rhetoric for the Modern Student* (New York: Oxford University Press, 1990).

4. Dominic A. Infante, Andrew S. Rancer, and Deanna F. Womack, *Building Communication Theory*, 3rd ed. (Prospect Heights, Ill.: Waveland Press, 1997).

5. For an excellent discussion of the tension between these two rights, see Douglas M. Fraleigh and Joseph S. Tuman, *Freedom of Speech in the Marketplace of Ideas* (New York: Bedford/St. Martins, 1997).

6. Steven E. Gillen, "Rights Clearance and Permissions Guidelines" (paper prepared by the law firm Greenebaum, Doll, and McDonald, Cincinnati, 2002).

7. E. D. Steele and W. C. Redding, "The American Value System: Premises for Persuasion," *Western Speech* 26 (1962): 83–91; Robin M. Williams Jr., *American Society: A Sociological Interpretation*, 3rd ed. (New York: Alfred A. Knopf, 1970).

8. Inter-University Consortium for Political and Social Research, "World Values Survey, 1981–1984 and 1990–1993" (Irvine: Social Science Data Archives, University Libraries, University of California, 1997).

9. W. Gudykunst, S. Ting-Toomey, S. Suweeks, and L. Stewart, *Building Bridges: Interpersonal Skills for a Changing World* (Boston: Houghton Mifflin, 1995), 92.

10. Ibid.

11. Josephson, interview.

12. Louis A. Day, *Ethics in Media Communications: Cases and Controversies*, 2nd ed. (Belmont, Calif.: Wadsworth, 1997).

13. Josephson, interview.

14. "President Tobin to Step Down," Hamilton College Web site, October 2, 2002, http://www.hamilton.edu/news (accessed February 10, 2005).

15. Rebecca Moore Howard, "A Plagiarism Pentimento," *Journal of Teaching Writing* 11 (1993): 233.

16. "How to Recognize Plagiarism," Indiana University Bloomington School of Education Web site, http://www.indiana.edu (accessed June 16, 2002).

17. Skyscraper Museum Web site, http://www.skyscraper.org (accessed June 26, 2002).

18. Judy Hunter, "Lecture on Academic Honesty" (presented to entering students at Grinnell College, Grinnell, Iowa), http://ac.grin.edu/~hunterj/achon/lecture97.html (accessed December 10, 1996).

19. U.S. Copyright Office Web site, at www.copyright.gov (accessed January 11, 2006).

20. Gillen, "Rights Clearance."

21. U.S. Copyright Office Web site, section on fair use, http://www.copyright.gov/fls/fl102.html (accessed February 19, 2005).

22. Gillen, "Rights Clearance."

Chapter 5

1. James C. McCroskey, "Classroom Consequences of Communication Anxiety," *Communication Education* 26 (1977): 27–33; James C. McCroskey, "Oral Communication Apprehension: A Reconceptualization," in *Communication Yearbook 6*, ed. M. Burgoon (Beverly Hills: Sage, 1982), 136–170; Virginia P. Richmond and James C. McCroskey, *Communication Apprehension, Avoidance, and Effectiveness*, 5th ed. (Boston: Allyn and Bacon, 1998).

2. Roger E. Axtell, *Do's and Taboos of Public Speaking* (New York: Wiley, 1992), 10.

3. See, for example, M. J. Beatty, "Situational and Predispositional Correlates of Public Speaking Anxiety," *Communication Education* 37 (1988): 28–39.

4. Adapted from James C. McCroskey, "Oral Communication Apprehension: A Summary of Recent Theory and Research," *Human Communication Research* 4 (1977): 79–96.

5. K. Weisul, "Does Giving a Speech Spook Women More?" *Business Week*, April 8, 2002.

6. R. Behnke and C. R. Sawyer, "Anticipatory Anxiety Patterns for Male and Female Public Speakers," *Communication Education* 49 (2000): 187–95.

7. Adapted from S. Tobia, "Anxiety and Cognitive Processes of Instruction," in *Self-Related Cognitions in Anxiety and Motivation*, ed. Ralf Schwarzer (Hillsdale, N.J.: Lawrence Erlbaum, 1986): 35–54.
8. R. Behnke, C. R. Sawyer, and R. Chris, "Milestones of Anticipatory Public Speaking Anxiety," *Communication Education* 48 (April 1999): 165–72.
9. Ibid.
10. David-Paul Pertaub, Mel Slater, and Chris Barker, "An Experiment on Public Speaking Anxiety in Response to Three Different Types of Virtual Audience," *Presence: Teleoperators and Virtual Environments* 11 (2002): 670–78.
11. Joe Ayres, "Coping with Speech Anxiety: The Power of Positive Thinking," *Communication Education* 37 (1988): 289–96; Joe Ayres, "An Examination of the Impact of Anticipated Communication and Communication Apprehension on Negative Thinking, Task-Relevant Thinking, and Recall," *Communication Research Reports* 9 (1992): 3–11.
12. Pamela J. Feldman, Sheldon Cohen, Natalie Hamrick, and Stephen J. Lepore, "Psychological Stress, Appraisal, Emotion, and Cardiovascular Response in a Public Speaking Task," *Psychology and Health* 19 (2004): 353–68; S. Hus, S. Romans-Kroll, and Joung-Min, "Effects of Positive Attitude toward Giving a Speech on Cardiovascular and Subjective Fear Responses During Speech on Anxious Subjects," *Perceptual and Motor Skills* 81 (1995): 609–10.
13. M. T. Motley, "Public Speaking Anxiety qua Performance Anxiety: A Revised Model and Alternative Therapy," *Journal of Social Behavior and Personality* 5 (1990): 85–104.
14. Joe Ayres, C. S. Hsu, and Tim Hopf, "Does Exposure to Visualization Alter Speech Preparation Processes?" *Communication Research Reports* 17 (2000): 366–74.
15. Joe Ayres and Tim Hopf, "Visualization: Is It More Than Extra Attention?" *Communication Education* 38 (1989): 1–5; Joe Ayers and Tim Hopf, *Coping with Speech Anxiety* (Norwood, N.J.: Ablex, 1993).
16. Ayres and Hopf, "Visualization," 2–3.
17. Laurie Schloff and Marcia Yudkin, *Smart Speaking* (New York: Plume, 1991).
18. Lars-Gunnar Lundh, Britta Berg, Helena Johansson, Linda Kjellén Nilsson, Jenny Sandberg, and Anna Segerstedt, "Social Anxiety Is Associated with a Negatively Distorted Perception of One's Own Voice," *Cognitive Behavior Therapy* 31 (2002): 25–30.

Chapter 6

1. James C. McCroskey, Virginia P. Richmond, and Robert A. Stewart, *One-on-One: The Foundations of Interpersonal Communication* (Englewood Cliffs, N.J.: Prentice-Hall, 1986).
2. Daniel O'Keefe notes that while attitudes and behavior are "generally consistent," there are "a large number of possible moderating variables," including the relative demands of the behavior, whether there is a vested position, and others. Daniel J. O'Keefe, *Persuasion: Theory and Research*, 2nd ed. (Thousand Oaks, Calif.: Sage, 2002), 17.
3. McCroskey, Richmond, and Stewart, *One-on-One*.
4. Kenneth Burke, *A Rhetoric of Motives* (Berkeley: University of California Press, 1969).
5. Hillary Rodham Clinton, "Abortion Is a Tragedy," *Vital Speeches of the Day* 71, no. 9 (2005): 266–70.
6. Ann Neville Miller, "An Exploration of Kenyan Public Speaking Patterns with Implications for the American Introductory Public Speaking Course," *Communication Education*, 51, no. 2 (2002): 168–82.
7. American Association of Community Colleges Web site, "Fast Facts," http://www.aacc.nche.edu (accessed March 10, 2005).
8. Geert Hofstede, *Culture's Consequences: International Differences in Work-Related Values* (Beverly Hills: Sage, 1980). Adapted from a discussion in Larry A. Samovar, Richard E. Porter, and Lisa A. Stefani, *Communication between Cultures* (Belmont, Calif.: Wadsworth, 1998).
9. Geert Hofstede, "Business Cultures," *UNESCO Courier* 47, no. 4 (1994): 12.

10. Samovar, Porter, and Stefani, *Communication*.

11. J. G. Melton, *Encyclopedia of American Religions*, 7th ed. (Detroit: Gale Research, 1999).

12. Daniel Canary and K. Dindia, eds., *Sex Differences and Similarities in Communication* (Mahwah, N.J.: Lawrence Erlbaum, 1998).

13. Louis Harris and Associates, "Harris 1989 *BusinessWeek* Survey Study No. 891201," Howard W. Odum Institute for Research in the Social Sciences Web site, http://www.irss.unc.edu/data_archive/pollsearch.html (accessed March 30, 2000).

Chapter 8

1. Rodney Reynolds and Michael Burgoon, "Evidence," in *The Persuasion Handbook: Developments in Theory and Practice*, ed. J. P. Dillard and M. Pfau (Thousand Oaks, Calif.: Sage, 2002), 427–44.

2. Barrington D. Parker, "International Exodus: Visa Delays and Denials," *Vital Speeches of the Day* 70, no. 19 (2004): 583–87.

3. Risa Lavizzo-Mourey, "Childhood Obesity: The Killer Threat Within," *Vital Speeches of the Day* 70, no. 13 (2004): 396–400.

4. Quoted in K. Q. Seelye, "Congressman Offers Bill to Ban Cloning of Humans," *New York Times*, March 6, 1997, sec. A.

5. Mark Turner, *The Literary Mind* (New York: Oxford University Press, 1996).

6. Ibid.

7. Helen Zia, speech delivered to the annual convention of the Asian American Journalists Association, reprinted in *Voices of Multicultural America: Notable Speeches Delivered by African, Asian, Hispanic, and Native Americans, 1790–1995*, ed. Deborah Straub (New York: Gale Research, 1996).

8. Brock Evans, "A Gift for All of America," address delivered to the biennial session of the Wyoming Conservations Congress, Casper, Wyo., July 10, 1999, http://www.votd.com/evans.htm (accessed May 1, 2000).

9. The idea for these questions was prompted by O. M. Walter and R. L. Scott, *Thinking and Speaking: A Guide to Intelligent Oral Communication*, 3rd ed. (New York: Macmillan, 1973), 52.

10. Testimony of Derek P. Ellerman to Subcommittee on Human Rights and Wellness, Committee on Government Reform, U.S. House of Representatives, July 8, 2004, Polaris Project, http://www.polarisproject.org/polarisproject/news_p3/DPETestimony_p3.htm (accessed March 15, 2005).

11. J. C. Reinard, *Foundations of Argument* (Dubuque, Iowa: William C. Brown, 1991).

12. U.S. Census Bureau American Factfinder, Profile of General Demographic Characteristics 2000, Geographic Area Colorado, http://factfinder.census.gov/servlet/QTTable?_bm=n&_lang=en&qr_name=DEC_2000_SF1_U_DP1&ds_name=DEC_2000_SF1_U&geo_id=04000US08.

13. Sara Kehaulani Goo, "Airbus Hopes Big Plane Will Take Off, Beat Boeing," *Washington Post*, December 19, 2004, http://www.washingtonpost.com/wp-dyn/articles/A9900-2004Dec18.html (accessed May 13, 2005).

14. Centers for Disease Control and Prevention, "Births to Youngest Teens at Lowest Levels in Almost 60 Years," http://www.cdc.gov/od/oc/media/pressrel/r041115.htm (accessed May 13, 2005).

15. Bureau of Transportation Statistics, "Airline On-Time Statistics and Delay Causes, On-Time Arrival Performance National," March 2005, http://www.transtats.bts.gov/OT_Delay/OT_DelayCause1.asp (accessed May 16, 2005).

16. Center on Budget and Policy Priorities Web site, "Behind the Numbers: An Examination of the Tax Foundation's Tax Day Report," April 14, 1997, http://www.cbpp.org/taxday.htm (accessed June 7, 2005).

17. "Older Americans 2004: Key Indicators of Well-Being," http://www.agingstats.gov (accessed April 12, 2005).

18. Data from Centers for Disease Control and Prevention, "Youth Risk Behavior Surveillance — United States, 2003," *Morbidity and Mortality Weekly Report,* May 21, 2004, 1–96, http://www.cdc.gov/mmwr/preview/mmwrhtml/ss5302a1.htm (accessed February 3, 2005).
19. Roger Pielke Jr., "The Cherry Pick," *Ogmius: Newsletter for the Center for Science and Technology Research* 8 (May 2004) http://sciencepolicy.colorado.edu/ogmius/archives/issue_8/index.html (accessed May 24, 2005).
20. Ibid.

Chapter 9

1. James C. McCrosky, in *An Introduction to Rhetorical Communication,* 8th ed. (Boston: Allyn and Bacon, 2001), makes this point throughout his text, and particularly on pages 188–89.
2. Jennifer Keohane, reference librarian, Simsbury Public Library, conversation with author, Simsbury, Conn., June 23, 2002.
3. Robert Von Dassanowski, ed., *Gale Encyclopedia of Multicultural America,* 2nd ed. (Detroit, Mich.: Gale Publications, 2000).
4. Robert G. Torricelli, *Quotations for Public Speakers: A Historical, Literary, and Political Anthology* (New Brunswick, N.J.: Rutgers University Press, 2002).
5. Robert J. Morgan, *Nelson's Complete Book of Stories, Illustrations, and Quotes: The Ultimate Contemporary Resource for Speakers* (Nashville, Tenn.: Thomas Nelson, 2000).
6. "The Art of Asking Questions," Poynteronline, http://www.poynter.org/content (accessed January 11, 2006).
7. H. Dan O'Hair, Gustave W. Friedrich, and Linda D. Dixon, *Strategic Communication in Business and the Professions,* 4th ed. (Boston: Houghton Mifflin, 2002), 216.
8. Quoted in ibid.

Chapter 10

1. Susan Gilroy, "The Web in Context: Virtual Library or Virtual Chaos?" Lamont Library of the Harvard College Library Web site, http://hcl.harvard.edu/lamont/resources/guides (accessed May 5, 2005).
2. Ibid.
3. Ibid.
4. Sandra Kerka, "Myths and Realities: Information Management," 1997, ERIC, http://www.eric.ed.gov:80/ERICWebPortal/Home.portal?_nfpb=true&_pageLabel=Home_page (accessed May 16, 2005).
5. "Bare Bones 101: Lesson 5: Evaluating Web Pages," January 5, 2000, University of South Carolina Beaufort Library, http://www.sc.edu/beaufort/library/lesson5.html (accessed April 2, 2000).
6. Jorgen J. Wouters, "Searching for Disclosure: How Search Engines Alert Consumers to the Presence of Advertising in Search Results," *Consumer Reports WebWatch,* November 8, 2004, http://www.consumerwebwatch.org/dynamic/search-report-disclosure-abstract.cfm (accessed May 7, 2005).
7. See, for instance, recommendations made by librarians at UC Berkeley–Teaching Library Internet Workshops, http://www.lib.berkeley.edu/TeachingLib/Guides/Internet/MetaSearch.html (accessed May 10, 2005).
8. Wouters, "Searching for Disclosure."
9. Ibid., 5.
10. "Bare Bones 101: Lesson 4: Gateways and Subject-Specific Databases," September 27, 2004, University of South Carolina Beaufort Library, http://www.sc.edu/beaufort/library/pages/bones/lesson4.shtml (accessed May 12, 2005).
11. Andrew Harnack and Eugene Kleppinger, *Online! A Reference Guide to Using Internet Sources* (Boston: Bedford/St.Martin's, 2002).

Chapter 11

1. E. Thompson, "An Experimental Investigation of the Relative Effectiveness of Organization Structure in Oral Communication," *Southern Speech Journal* 26 (1960): 59–69.
2. R. G. Smith, "Effects of Speech Organization upon Attitudes of College Students," *Speech Monographs* 18 (1951): 292–301.
3. H. Sharp Jr. and T. McClung, "Effects of Organization on the Speaker's Ethos," *Speech Monographs* 33 (1966): 182ff.
4. "Communication Skills, Honesty/Integrity Top Employers' Wish List for Job Candidates," *Job Outlook 2005 Survey,* January 20, 2005, National Association of Colleges and Employers, http://www.naceweb.org/products/jo2005report.htm (accessed June 12, 2005).
5. G. H. Bower, "Organizational Factors in Memory," *Cognitive Psychology* 1 (1970): 18–46.
6. Rodney Reynolds and Michael Burgoon, "Evidence," in *The Persuasion Handbook: Developments in Theory and Practice,* ed. J. P. Dillard and M. Pfau (Thousand Oaks, Calif.: Sage, 2002), 427–44.
7. Leonard J. Rosen and Laurence Behren, *The Allyn & Bacon Handbook* (Needham, Mass.: Allyn & Bacon, 1992), 103.

Chapter 12

1. PBS, "Life on the Internet Timeline," http://www.pbs.org/internet/timeline/index.html (accessed April 3, 2000).
2. Anita Taylor, "Tales of the Grandmothers: Women and Work," *Vital Speeches of the Day* 71, no. 7 (2005): 209–12.
3. Sonja K. Foss and Karen A. Foss, *Inviting Transformation: Presentational Speaking for a Changing World* (Prospect Heights, Ill.: Waveland Press, 1994).

Chapter 13

1. For an enlightening review of the history of outlining from Cicero to electronic software, see Jonathan Price, "STOP: Light on the History of Outlining," *Journal of Computer Documentation* 23.3 (August 1999): 69–78.
2. Mark B. McClellan, speech presented at the fifth annual David A. Winston lecture, Washington, DC, October 20, 2003, http://www.fda.gov/oc/speeches/2003/winston1020.html (accessed August 14, 2005).
3. Gratitude goes to Carolyn Clark, Ph.D., of Salt Lake Community College, for sharing this assignment with us.

Chapter 14

1. Ron Hoff, *I Can See You Naked,* rev. ed. (Kansas City, Mo.: Andrews McMeel, 1992), 41.
2. "Openings," *Executive Speaker,* 26, no. 5 (2005): 1.
3. William Safire, *Lend Me Your Ears: Great Speeches in History* (New York: Norton, 1992), 676.
4. For a rich discussion of the role of stories and narratives in communication, see Walter Fisher, "Narration as a Human Communication Paradigm: The Case of Public Moral Argument," *Communication Monographs* 51, no. 1 (1984): 1–22.
5. Edward P. J. Corbett, *Classical Rhetoric for the Modern Student,* 3rd ed. (New York: Oxford University Press, 1990).
6. Bas Andeweg and Jap de Jong, "May I Have Your Attention? Exordial Techniques in Informative Oral Presentations," *Technical Communication Quarterly* 7, no. 3 (1998): 271–84.
7. Antoinette M. Bailey, "Thoughts on Building a House for Diversity," *Vital Speeches of the Day* 66, no. 13 (2000): 400–402.
8. Quoted at http://www.executive-speaker.com/spkopxxx.html (accessed July 3, 2005).

9. Vance Coffman, "Help Wanted: 'Busineers,'" *Vital Speeches of the Day* 66, no. 16 (2000): 488–92.

10. Nelson Mandela, "Our March to Freedom Is Irreversible," in *The Penguin Book of Twentieth-Century Speeches,* ed. B. MacArthur (New York: Penguin, 1992).

11. C. A. Kiesler and S. B. Kiesler, "Role of Forewarning in Persuasive Communication," *Journal of Abnormal and Social Psychology* 68 (1964): 547–69, cited in James C. Mc-Crosky, *An Introduction to Rhetorical Communication,* 8th ed. (Boston, Mass.: Allyn & Bacon, 2001), 253.

12. Marvin Runyon, "No One Moves the Mail like the U.S. Postal Service," *Vital Speeches of the Day* 61, no. 2 (1994): 52–55.

13. Robert L. Darbelnet, "U.S. Roads and Bridges: Highway Funding at a Crossroads," *Vital Speeches of the Day* 63, no. 12 (1997): 379.

14. Andeweg and de Jong, "May I Have Your Attention."

Chapter 15

1. R. O. Skovgard, interview by author, June 10, 1995.

2. Holger Kluge, "Reflections on Diversity," *Vital Speeches of the Day* 63, no. 6 (1997): 171–72.

3. William E. Kirwan, speech delivered to the SUNY Stony Brook Student–Community Wellness Leadership Symposium, Stony Brook, N.Y., February 15, 2000.

4. Hillary Rodham Clinton, "Women's Rights Are Human Rights" (speech delivered to the United Nations Fourth World Conference on Women, Beijing, China, September 5, 1995).

5. Sue Sutter, "Adapting to Change, while Holding on to Values: *Star Trek*'s Lessons for the Disability Community" (speech delivered to the Annual Conference of the Association for the Severely Handicapped, Springfield, Ill., September 22, 1999).

6. Oprah Winfrey, speech delivered at Wellesley College commencement, Wellesley, Mass., May 30, 1997, http://www.wellesley.edu/PublicAffairs/Commencement/1997/winfrey.html (accessed April 2, 2000).

Chapter 16

1. Robert Harris, "A Handbook of Rhetorical Devices," July 26, 2002, *Virtual Salt* http://www.virtualsalt.com/rhetoric.htm (accessed August 5, 2002).

2. Michael J. Lewis, "When Presidents Speak," *Commentary* 111, no. 6 (2001): 48–51.

3. Peggy Noonan, *Simply Speaking: How to Communicate Your Ideas with Style, Substance, and Clarity* (New York: Regan Books, 1998), 51.

4. William Safire, *Lend Me Your Ears: Great Speeches in History* (New York: Norton, 1992), 26.

5. Dan Hooley, "The Lessons of the Ring," *Vital Speeches of the Day* 70, no. 20 (2004): 660–63.

6. Katherine E. Rowan, "A New Pedagogy for Explanatory Public Speaking: Why Arrangement Should Not Substitute for Invention," *Communication Research* 44 (1995): 245.

7. James E. Lukaszewski, "You Can Become a Verbal Visionary" (speech delivered to the Public Relations Society of America, Cleveland, Ohio, April 8, 1997), Executive Speaker Library, http://www.executive-speaker.com/lib_moti.html.

8. "Information for Decision Makers. Population Estimates of Disability and Long-Term Care. February 1995," *ASPE Research Notes,* DisabilityInfo.gov, http://www.disabilityinfo.gov (accessed April 24, 2005).

9. David C. Thomas and Kerr Inkson, *Cultural Intelligence: People Skills for a Global Business* (San Francisco, Calif.: Berrett-Koehler Publishers, 2004), 14.

10. Ibid.

11. Catherine H. Zizik, "Powerspeak: Avoiding Ambiguous Language," *Speech Communication Teacher* (Summer 1995): 8–9.

12. Andrea Lunsford and Robert Connors, *The St. Martin's Handbook,* 3rd ed. (New York: St. Martin's Press, 1995), 101.

13. Safire, *Lend Me Your Ears,* 496–97.
14. L. Clemetson and J. Gordon-Thomas, "Our House Is on Fire," *Newsweek,* June 11, 2001, 50.
15. Gloria Anzaldúa, "Entering into the Serpent," in *The St. Martin's Handbook,* ed. Andrea Lunsford and Robert Connors, 3rd ed. (New York: St. Martin's Press, 1995), 25.
16. P. H. Matthews, *The Concise Oxford Dictionary of Linguistics* (New York: Oxford University Press, 1997).
17. Howard K. Battles and Charles Packard, *Words and Sentences,* bk. 6 (Lexington, Mass.: Ginn & Company, 1984), 110.
18. Robin Lakoff, *Language and Woman's Place* (New York: Harper & Row, 1975); Deborah Tannen, *You Just Don't Understand: Women and Men in Conversation* (New York: William Morrow, 1990); Deborah Tannen, *Talking from 9 to 5* (New York: William Morrow, 1994); Anthony Mulac, "The Gender-Linked Language Effect: Do Language Differences Really Make a Difference?" in D. Canary and K. Dindia, (eds.), *Sex Differences and Similarities in Communication* (Mahwah, N.J.: Lawrence Erlbaum, 1998); Phyllis Mindell, *A Woman's Guide to the Language of Success: Communicating with Confidence and Power* (Englewood Cliffs, N.J.: Prentice Hall, 1995).
19. George W. Bush, presidential address to the nation, October 7, 2001, http://www.whitehouse.gov/news/releases/2001/10/20011007-8.html (accessed January 11, 2006).
20. Cited in Safire, *Lend Me Your Ears,* 22.
21. Jesse Jackson, in *Voices of Multicultural America: Notable Speeches Delivered by African, Asian, Hispanic, and Native Americans, 1790-1995,* ed. Deborah Straub (New York: Gale Research, 1996), 594–99.
22. Ibid.
23. Lunsford and Connors, *The St. Martin's Handbook,* 345.

Chapter 17

1. James A. Winans, *Public Speaking* (New York: Century, 1925). Professor Winans was among the first Americans to contribute significantly to the study of rhetoric. His explanation of delivery is considered by many to be the best coverage of the topic in the English language. His perspective infuses this chapter.
2. James C. McCroskey, *An Introduction to Rhetorical Communication,* 8th ed. (Englewood Cliffs, N.J.: Prentice-Hall, 2001), 273.
3. Winans, *Public Speaking,* 17.
4. Thomas M. Conley, *Rhetoric in the European Tradition* (New York: Longman, 1990).
5. William Safire, PBS *NewsHour,* August 15, 1996, http://www.pbs.org/newshour/gergen/july-dec96/safire_8-15.html (accessed July 15, 2005).
6. Robbin Crabtree and Robert Weissberg, *ESL Students in the Public Speaking Classroom: A Guide for Teachers* (Boston: Bedford/St. Martin's, 2000), 24.

Chapter 18

1. Kyle James Tusing and James Price Dillard, "The Sounds of Dominance: Vocal Precursors of Perceived Dominance during Interpersonal Influence," *Human Communication Research* 26 (2000): 148–71.
2. Caryl Raye Krannich, *101 Secrets of Highly Effective Speakers* (Manassas Park, Va.: Impact Publications, 1998), 121–22.
3. Kenneth C. Crannell, *Voice and Articulation,* 4th ed. (Belmont, Calif.: Wadsworth, 2000), 41.
4. MaryAnn Cunningham Florez, *Improving Adult ESL Learners' Pronunciation Skills,* National Clearinghouse for ESL Literacy Education, 1998, http://www.cal.org/caela/digests/Pronun.htm (accessed July 16, 2005).
5. Tusing and Dillard, "Sounds of Dominance."
6. The digitized audio of King's "I Have a Dream" speech can be accessed at http://www.americanrhetoric.com/speeches/Ihaveadream.htm.

Chapter 19

1. Robert Rivlin and Karen Gravelle, *Deciphering the Senses: The Expanding World of Human Perception* (New York: Simon & Schuster, 1998), 98; see also A. Warfield, "Do You Speak Body Language?" *Training & Development* 55, no. 4 (2001): 60.
2. Judee K. Burgoon, David B. Buller, and W. Gill Woddall, *Nonverbal Communication,* 2nd ed. (New York: McGraw-Hill, 1996).
3. Ibid.
4. Ibid.
5. Reid Buckley, *Strictly Speaking: Reid Buckely's Indispensable Handbook on Public Speaking* (New York: McGraw-Hill, 1999), 204.
6. Laurie Schloff and Marcia Yudkin, *Smart Speaking* (New York: Plume, 1991), 108.
7. Buckley, *Strictly Speaking,* 209.
8. J. P. Davidson, "Shaping an Image That Boosts Your Career," *Marketing Communications* 13 (1988): 55–56.
9. See speaking consultant Rick Segel's witty comments on the problems of dressing down in the workplace at http://www.ricksegel.com/reprints8.html (accessed July 18, 2005).
10. Along with speeches at the White House, economic conferences, and elsewhere, Bono delivered the 2001 commencement address at Harvard University, http://www.commencement.harvard.edu/2001/bono_address.html (accessed August 1, 2005), and the 2004 commencement address at the University of Pennsylvania, http://www.dailypennsylvanian.com/vnews/display.v/ART/4057faca6b12a (accessed August 1, 2005).
11. David Wolfe, *Women's Wear Daily,* as quoted by image consultant Lisa Duncan at http://www.lisaduncan.com/tipstrends.html (accessed July 18, 2005).

Chapter 20

1. Robert Heinich, Michael Molenda, and James D. Russell, *Instructional Media and the New Technologies of Instruction,* 4th ed. (New York: Macmillan, 1993), 66.
2. Cheryl Currid, *Make Your Point: The Complete Guide to Successful Business Presentations Using Today's Technology* (Rocklin, Calif.: Prima Publishing, 1995), 117.
3. *Merriam-Webster's Collegiate Dictionary,* 10th ed. (Springfield, Mass.: Merriam-Webster, 1993).

Chapter 21

1. David M. Orchard, Barry D. Perow, Kenneth Frankes, and Torin Reed, *Figuratively Speaking in the Computer Age: Techniques for Preparing and Delivering Presentations* (n.p.: American Association of Petroleum Geologists, 2000), 83–86.
2. Cheryl Currid, *Make Your Point: The Complete Guide to Successful Business Presentations Using Today's Technology* (Rocklin, Calif.: Prima Publishing, 1995).

Chapter 22

1. Ron Hoff, *I Can See You Naked,* rev. ed. (Kansas City, Mo.: Andrews McMeel, 1992), 143.

Chapter 23

1. Tina Blythe et al., *The Teaching for Understanding Guide* (Hoboken, N.J.: Jossey-Bass, 1997); Kenneth D. Frandsen and Donald A. Clement, "The Functions of Human Communication in Informing: Communicating and Processing Information," in *Handbook of Rhetorical and Communication Theory,* ed. Carroll C. Arnold and John Waite Bowers (Needham, Mass.: Allyn & Bacon, 1984), 334.
2. Katherine E. Rowan, "A New Pedagogy for Explanatory Public Speaking: Why Arrangement Should Not Substitute for Invention," *Communication Education* 44 (1995): 236–50.
3. E. Thompson, "An Experimental Investigation of the Relative Effectiveness of Organization Structure in Oral Communication," *Southern Speech Journal* 26 (1966): 59–69.

4. Rowan, "A New Pedagogy."
5. Vickie K. Sullivan, "Public Speaking: The Secret Weapon in Career Development," *USA Today,* May 2005, 24.
6. Howard K. Battles and Charles Packard, *Words and Sentences,* bk. 6 (Lexington, Mass.: Ginn & Company, 1984), 459.
7. Rowan, "A New Pedagogy."
8. S. Kujawa and L. Huske, *The Strategic Teaching and Reading Project Guidebook,* rev. ed. (Oak Brook, Ill.: North Central Regional Educational Laboratory, 1995).
9. Shawn M. Glynn et al., "Teaching Science with Analogies: A Resource for Teachers and Textbook Authors," National Reading Research Center, Instructional Resource No. 7, Fall 1994.
10. Altoona List of Medical Analogies, "How to Use Analogies," Altoona Family Physicians Residency Web site, http://www.altoonafp.org/analogies.htm (accessed June 13, 2005).
11. Glynn et al., "Teaching Science," 19.
12. Altoona List of Medical Analogies.
13. Wolfgang Porod, "Nanotechnology," *Vital Speeches of the Day* 71, no. 4 (2004): 125–28.
14. Rowan, "A New Pedagogy," p. 245,
15. Tina A. Grotzer, "How Conceptual Leaps in Understanding the Nature of Causality Can Limit Learning: An Example from Electrical Circuits" (paper presented at the annual conference of the American Educational Research Association, New Orleans, April 2000), http://pzweb.harvard.edu/Research/UnderCon.htm (accessed June 17, 2005).

Chapter 24

1. Edward P. J. Corbett, *Classical Rhetoric for the Modern Student,* 3rd ed. (New York: Oxford University Press, 1990).
2. Communications scholars Winston Brembeck and William Howell define the goal in this way: "Persuasion is communication intended to influence choice." See Winston L. Brembeck and William S. Howell, *Persuasion: A Means of Social Influence,* 2nd ed. (Englewood Cliffs, N.J.: Prentice-Hall, 1976).
3. Kathleen K. Reardon, *Persuasion in Practice* (Newbury Park, Calif.: Sage Publications, 1991), 210.
4. Richard E. Petty and John T. Cacioppo, *Communication and Persuasion: Central and Peripheral Routes to Attitude Change* (New York: Springer-Verlag, 1986).
5. Reardon, *Persuasion in Practice,* 210.
6. Russel H. Fazio, "How Do Attitudes Guide Behavior?" in *The Handbook of Motivation and Cognition: Foundations of Social Behavior,* ed. Richard M. Sorrentino and E. Tory Higgins (New York: Guilford, 1986).
7. Sarah Trenholm, *Persuasion and Social Influence* (Englewood Cliffs, N.J.: Prentice Hall, 1989).
8. Joseph R. Priester and Richard E. Petty, "Source Attributions and Persuasion: Perceived Honesty as a Determinant of Message Scrutiny," *Personality and Social Psychology Bulletin* 21 (1995): 637–54. See also Kenneth G. DeBono and Richard J. Harnish, "Source Expertise, Source Attractiveness, and the Processing of Persuasive Information: A Functional Approach," *Journal of Personality and Social Psychology* 55 (1987): 541.
9. Priester and Petty, *Personality,* 11.
10. Eveline Feteris, "A Pragma-Dialectical Approach of the Analysis and Evaluation of Pragmatic Argumentation in a Legal Context," *Argumentation* 16 (2002): 349–67.
11. Nathan Crick, "Conquering Our Imagination: Thought Experiments and Enthymemes in Scientific Argument," *Philosophy and Rhetoric* 37 (2004): 21–41.
12. Edward Corbett, *Classical Rhetoric for the Modern Student,* 1356a, 1377b.
13. Ibid.
14. Reprinted from Gregory R. Suriano, *Great American Speeches* (New York: Gramercy Books, 1993), 298–303.
15. Kim Witte and Mike Allen, "A Meta-Analysis of Fear Appeals: Implications for Effective Public Health Campaigns," *Health Education and Behavior* 27 (2000): 591–615.

16. Robert A. Stewart, "Perceptions of a Speaker's Initial Credibility as a Function of Religious Involvement and Religious Disclosiveness," *Communication Research Reports* 11 (1994): 169–76.
17. For an extensive review of the history of the field of communication from the classical period to the present era, see Dominic A. Infante, Andrew S. Rancer, and Deanna F. Womack, *Building Communication Theory*, 4th ed. (Prospect Heights, Ill.: Waveland Press, 2003).
18. Abraham Maslow, *Motivation and Personality* (New York: Harper & Row, 1954).
19. B. Soper, G. E. Milford, and G. T. Rosenthal, "Belief When Evidence Does Not Support the Theory," *Psychology and Marketing* 12 (1995): 415–22, cited in Stephen M. Kosslyn and Robin S. Rosenberg, *Psychology: The Brain, the Person, the World* (Boston: Allyn & Bacon, 2004), 330.
20. Icek Ajzen and Martin Fishbein, *Understanding Attitudes and Predicting Social Behavior* (Englewood Cliffs, N.J.: Prentice-Hall, 1980).
21. Richard Petty and John T. Cacioppo, "The Elaboration Likelihood Model of Persuasion," in *Advances in Experimental Social Psychology* 19, ed. L. Berkowitz (San Diego, Calif.: Academic Press, 1986), 123–205; Richard Petty and Duane T. Wegener, "Matching versus Mismatching Attitude Functions: Implications for Scrutiny of Persuasive Messages," *Personality and Social Psychology Bulletin* 24 (1998): 227–40.
22. For good reviews of the literature on source credibility in general, see Richard M. Perloff, *The Dynamics of Persuasion* (Hillsdale, N.J.: Lawrence Erlbaum, 1993), and Infante, Rancer, and Womack, *Building Communication Theory*.
23. K. K. Sereno and G. I. Hawkins, "The Effects of Variations in Speakers' Nonfluency upon Audience Ratings of Attitude toward the Speech Topic and Speakers' Credibility," *Speech Monographs* 34 (1967): 58–64.
24. Priester and Petty, "Source Attributions and Persuasion."

Chapter 25

1. *Merriam-Webster's Collegiate Dictionary*, 10th ed. (Springfield, Mass.: Merriam-Webster, 1993).
2. Austin J. Freeley, *Argumentation and Debate*, 8th ed. (Belmont, Calif.: Wadsworth, 1993), 158.
3. Thomas A. Hollihan and Kevin T. Baaske, *Arguments and Arguing* (New York: St. Martin's Press, 1994), 27.
4. The model of argument presented here follows Steven Toulmin, *The Uses of Argument* (New York: Cambridge University Press, 1958), as described in James C. McCroskey, *An Introduction to Rhetorical Communication*, 6th ed. (Englewood Cliffs, N.J.: Prentice-Hall, 1993).
5. Annette Rottenberg, *Elements of Argument*, 4th ed. (Boston: Bedford/St. Martin's, 1994), 10.
6. American Council on Science and Health, "What's the Story? Drug-Supplement Interaction," November 2000, http://www.acsh.org/publications/story/index.html (accessed August 27, 2002).
7. Transcript of President George W. Bush's address to the United Nations, September 13, 2002, *New York Times*, September 13, 2002, A10.
8. Based on James C. McCroskey, *An Introduction to Rhetorical Communication*, 8th ed. (Englewood Cliffs, N.J.: Prentice-Hall, 1993), 119–23.
9. See the discussion of the relationship between attitudes and behavior in Daniel J. O'Keefe, *Persuasion: Theory and Research*, 2nd ed. (Thousand Oaks, Calif.: Sage, 2002), 16–17.
10. Dennis S. Gouran, "Attitude Change and Listeners' Understanding of a Persuasive Communication," *Speech Teacher* 15 (1966): 289–94; J. P. Dillard, "Persuasion Past and Present: Attitudes Aren't What They Used to Be," *Communication Monographs* 60 (1966): 94.
11. Freeley, *Argumentation and Debate*, 175.

12. Edward P. J. Corbett, *Classical Rhetoric for the Modern Student,* 3rd ed. (New York: Oxford University Press, 1990).

Chapter 26

1. *Motor Vehicle Facts and Figures* (American Automobile Manufacturers Association, 1997), 84.
2. Herbert Simon, *Persuasion in Society* (Thousand Oaks, Calif.: Sage, 2001), 385–87.
3. A. H. Monroe, *Principles and Types of Speeches* (Chicago, Ill.: Scott, Foresman, 1935).
4. James R. DiSanza and Nancy J. Legge, *Business and Professional Communication: Plans, Processes, and Performance,* 2nd ed. (Boston: Allyn & Bacon, 2002), 236.

Chapter 27

1. Frank D. Stella, "Introductory Remarks Delivered to the Economic Club of Detroit, Detroit, Michigan," *Executive Speaker* 17 (15 April 1996): 3.
2. G. Parret, *I Love My Boss and 969 Other Business Jokes* (New York: Sterling Publishing, 1993).
3. H. H. Shelton, "Victory, Honor, Sacrifice," *Vital Speeches of the Day* 66, no. 20 (2000): 627.
4. Ibid.
5. Paul Fatout, ed., *Mark Twain Speaks for Himself* (West Lafayette, Ind.: Purdue University Press, 1978).
6. David Magill, "Give Your Life a Dream with Design," *Vital Speeches of the Day* 62, no. 21 (1996): 671–72.

Chapter 28

1. H. Dan O'Hair, James S. O'Rourke, and Mary John O'Hair, *Business Communication: A Framework for Success* (Cincinnati: South-Western, 2001).
2. W. L. Tullar and P. R. Kaiser, "The Effect of Process Training on Process and Outcomes in Virtual Groups," *Journal of Business Communication* 37 (2000): 408–27.
3. H. Dan O'Hair, Gustav Friedrich, and Linda Dixon, *Strategic Communication in Business and the Professions,* 4th ed. (Boston: Houghton Mifflin, 2002).
4. K. D. Benne and P. Sheats, "Functional Roles of Group Members," *Journal of Social Issues* 4 (1948): 41–49.
5. Ibid.
6. M. Afzalur Rahim, *Managing Conflict in Organizations,* 3rd ed. (Westport, Conn.: Greenwood Publishing Group, 2001).
7. H. Dan O'Hair, Gustave Friedrich, John Wiemann, and Mary Wiemann, *Competent Communication,* 2nd ed. (New York: Bedford/St. Martin's, 1997).
8. Karl E. Weick and K. Roberts, "Collective Minds in Organizations: Heedful Interrelating on Flight Decks," *Administrative Science Quarterly* 38 (1993): 357–81.
9. Geoffrey A. Cross, "Collective Form: An Exploration of Large-Group Writing," *Journal of Business Communication* 37 (2000): 77–100.
10. Irving Lester Janis, *Groupthink: Psychological Studies of Policy Decisions and Fiascoes* (Berkeley: University of California Press, 1982).
11. O'Hair, Friedrich, and Dixon, *Strategic Communication.*
12. Victor H. Vroom and Philip Yetton, *Leadership and Decision Making* (Pittsburgh: University of Pittsburgh Press, 1973); C. Pavitt, "Theorizing about the Group Communication-Leadership Relationship: Input-Process-Output and Functional Models," in *Handbook of Group Communication Theory and Research,* ed. Lawrence R. Frey, Dennis Gouran, and Marshall Scott Poole (Thousand Oaks, Calif.: Sage, 1999), 313–34.
13. L. Richard Hoffman and Norman R. F. Maier, "Valence in the Adoption of Solutions by Problem-Solving Groups: Concept, Method, and Results," *Journal of Abnormal and Social Psychology* 69 (1964): 264–71.
14. John Dewey, *How We Think* (Boston: D. C. Heath Co., 1950).

Chapter 29

1. For a review, see Pricilla S. Rogers, "Distinguishing Public and Presentational Speaking," *Management Communication Quarterly* 2 (1988): 102–15.
2. Ibid.
3. Frank E. X. Dance, "What Do You Mean Presentational Speaking?" *Management Communication Quarterly* 1 (1987): 260–71.
4. Ibid.
5. Part of this classification of business presentations is adapted from Raymond V. Lesikar, John D. Pettit Jr., and Marie E. Flatley, *Basic Business Communication,* 8th ed. (New York: McGraw Hill, 1999).
6. H. Dan O'Hair, James S. O'Rourke, and Mary John O'Hair, *Business Communication: A Framework for Success* (Cincinnati: South-Western, 2001).
7. William L. Benoit, *Accounts, Excuses, and Apologies: A Theory of Image Restoration Strategies* (Albany: State University of New York Press, 1995).
8. Ibid.

Chapter 30

1. Deanna P. Daniels, "Communicating across the Curriculum and in the Disciplines: Speaking in Engineering," *Communication Education* 51 (July 2002): 3.
2. Ibid., 261.
3. Ibid.
4. James M. Henslin, *Sociology: A Down-to-Earth Approach,* 4th ed. (Boston: Allyn & Bacon, 1999), 134.
5. William E. Thompson and James V. Hickey, *Society in Focus: An Introduction to Sociology,* 2nd ed. (New York: HarperCollins, 1996), 39.
6. Ibid.

Appendix A

1. Edward S. Inch and Barbara Warnick, *Critical Thinking and Communication: The Use of Reason in Argument,* 3rd ed. (Boston: Allyn & Bacon, 1998).

Appendix B

1. Patricia Nelson, "Handling Questions and Answers," November 3, 1999, Toastmasters International, Edmonton and Area, http://www.ecn.ab.ca/toast/qa.html (accessed September 1, 2000).
2. Diane DiResta, *Knockout Presentations: How to Deliver Your Message with Power, Punch, and Pizzazz* (Worcester, Mass.: Chandler House Press, 1998), 236.
3. Ibid., 239.
4. Ibid., 237.
5. Lillian Wilder, *Talk Your Way to Success* (New York: Eastside Publishing, 1986), 279.

Appendix C

1. Oklahoma Society of CPAs, "Tips for Successful Media Interviewing," http://www.oscpa.com/resources/interviewtips.htm (accessed August 20, 2000).
2. Lillian Wilder, *Talk Your Way to Success* (New York: Eastside Publishing, 1986), 281.
3. D. R. Bowman, *Presentations: Proven Techniques for Creating Presentations That Get Results* (Holbrook, Mass.: Adams Media), 177.
4. Oklahoma Society of CPAs, "Tips for Successful Media Interviewing."
5. Adapted from Diane Howard, "Guidelines for Videoconference Presentations, Performances, and Teaching," http://www.dianehoward.com (accessed August 25, 2000).

Acknowledgments

Thomas E. Anastasi, Jr. Checklist from p. 35 in *Listen! Techniques for Improving Communication* by Thomas E. Anastasi, Jr. CBI Publishing, 1982. Courtesy of Process Associates of America.

Audubon Society. Website home page. www.audubon.org. Reprinted with permission of the Audubon Society.

Bono images (13). Copyright © Creative Video Souvenir Productions. Reprinted with permission.

Cheryl Currid. 2 tables, 21.1, 21.2. Adapted from *Make Your Point: The Complete Guide to Successful Business Presentations Using Today's Technology* by Cheryl Currid. p. 74. Copyright © 1995 by Cheryl Currid. Reprinted with permission.

T. S. Eliot. "Gerontion" (1 verse) and "Four Quartets" (1 line) from *Poems* by T. S. Eliot. Published by Alfred A. Knopf (1920).

Edward Jay Epstein. "Title Page." From *The Big Picture* by Edward Jay Epstein. Copyright © 2005 by Random House, Inc. Used by permission of Random House, Inc.

Lauren Fleishman. 2 photos with "Jamie Oliver Serves Up Lunch." From *Newsweek*, August 8, 2005, p. 50. Copyright © Lauren Fleishman, 2005. Reprinted with permission of the photographer.

Google Advance Search webpage. www.google.com. Reprinted with permission of Google Inc.

Elizabeth Kirk. Adaptation from "Information and Its Counterfeits: Propaganda, Misinformation and Disinformation" from The Sheridan Libraries of the Johns Hopkins University website. www.library.jhu.edu. Copyright © 2001 by Elizabeth E. Kirk. Reprinted with permission of the author.

Julian Makey. Photo of Jamie Oliver, from *Newsweek*, August 8, 2005, p. 50. Reprinted with permission from REX USA.

The Nobel Foundation. Material from Nobelprize.org. Published with permission from the Nobel Foundation. © The Nobel Foundation 2005. www.nobel.se.

Octavio Paz. Verse from "Piedra de sol." Translated by Eliot Weinberger, from *Sunstone*. Copyright © 1957, 1987 by Octavio Paz, 1987 by Eliot Weinberger. Reprinted by permission of New Directions Publishing Corp.

Paul L. Soper. "Table of Errors in Pronunciation." From *Basic Public Speaking* 3e by Paul L. Soper. Copyright © 1968 by Oxford University Press, Inc. Used by permission of Oxford University Press, Inc.

Jane Tully. "Speeches that Satisfy." Copyright © 1998 The Executive Speaker™ Company. Delivered to the NY Chapter of Women in Communication. Reprinted with permission of Tully Communications.

Lilyan Wilder. Excerpt from *7 Steps to Fearless Speaking* by Lilyan Wilder. Copyright © 1999 by Lilyan Wilder. Reprinted with permission of John Wiley & Sons, Inc.

W. B. Yeats. "And Then Did All the Muses Sing" (1 verse) from *Collected Poems of W. B. Yeats Volume 1: The Poems,* revised, edited by Richard J. Finneran. Copyright © 1928 by The Macmillan Company. Copyright © renewed 1956 by Georgie Yeats. Reprinted with the permission of Scribner, an imprint of Simon & Schuster Adult Publishing Group, and A. P. Watt Ltd.

Part Opener Photos
p. 1 (Oprah), Corbis; p. 31 (Roman theater), Corbis; p. 73 (Leno), Getty; p. 107 (girl in library), Corbis; p. 165 (girl on grass), Getty; p. 209 (Dave Matthews), Corbis; p. 245 (McCain), Corbis; p. 277 (businessman), Corbis; p. 315 (high school speaker), Corbis; p. 413 (doctor), Corbis; p. 455 (Kielburger), AP.

Index